AMNESTY INTERNATIONAL

Amnesty International is a global movement of more than 7 million people who campaign for a world where human rights are enjoyed by all. Our vision is for every person to enjoy all the rights enshrined in the Universal Declaration of Human Rights and other international human rights standards. We are independent of any government, political ideology, economic interest or religion and are funded mainly by our membership and public donations.

First published in 2017 by
Amnesty International Ltd

Peter Benenson House,
1, Easton Street,
London WC1X 0DW
United Kingdom

© Amnesty International 2017

Index: POL 10/4800/2017

ISBN: 978-0-86210-496-2

A catalogue record for this book is available from the British Library.

Original language: English

This report documents Amnesty International's work and concerns through 2016.

The absence of an entry in this report on a particular country or territory does not imply that no human rights violations of concern to Amnesty International have taken place there during the year. Nor is the length of a country entry any basis for a comparison of the extent and depth of Amnesty International's concerns in a country.

AMNESTY

INTERNATIONAL

REPORT 2016/17

THE STATE OF THE WORLD'S HUMAN RIGHTS

WITHDRAWN

CONTENTS
ANNUAL REPORT 2016/17

Abbreviations 7
Preface 9
Foreword 12
Africa Regional Overview 16
Americas Regional Overview 24
Asia-Pacific Regional Overview 32
Europe and Central Asia Regional
Overview 40
Middle East and North Africa
Regional Overview 48
Afghanistan 58
Albania 62
Algeria 63
Angola 65
Argentina 68
Armenia 70
Australia 72
Austria 73
Azerbaijan 74
Bahamas 76
Bahrain 77
Bangladesh 80
Belarus 82
Belgium 84
Benin 85
Bolivia 86
Bosnia and Herzegovina 87
Botswana 89
Brazil 91
Brunei Darussalam 95
Bulgaria 96
Burkina Faso 98
Burundi 100
Cambodia 104
Cameroon 106
Canada 109
Central African Republic 111
Chad 114
Chile 116
China 118
Colombia 123
Congo (Republic of the) 128
Côte d'Ivoire 129
Croatia 131

Cuba 133
Cyprus 134
Czech Republic 136
Democratic Republic of the
Congo 137
Denmark 141
Dominican Republic 142
Ecuador 144
Egypt 145
El Salvador 150
Equatorial Guinea 152
Eritrea 153
Estonia 155
Ethiopia 156
Fiji 157
Finland 158
France 160
Gambia 162
Georgia 164
Germany 166
Ghana 168
Greece 170
Guatemala 173
Guinea 174
Guinea-Bissau 176
Haiti 177
Honduras 179
Hungary 181
India 183
Indonesia 187
Iran 191
Iraq 196
Ireland 200
Israel and the Occupied
Palestinian Territories 201
Italy 206
Jamaica 208
Japan 209
Jordan 211
Kazakhstan 213
Kenya 216
Korea (Democratic People's
Republic of) 219
Korea (Republic of) 221

Kuwait 223
Kyrgyzstan 226
Laos 227
Latvia 228
Lebanon 229
Lesotho 231
Libya 233
Lithuania 237
Macedonia 238
Madagascar 239
Malawi 240
Malaysia 241
Maldives 243
Mali 245
Malta 246
Mauritania 248
Mexico 250
Moldova 254
Mongolia 256
Montenegro 257
Morocco/Western Sahara 258
Mozambique 261
Myanmar 263
Namibia 267
Nauru 268
Nepal 269
Netherlands 271
New Zealand 272
Nicaragua 273
Niger 275
Nigeria 276
Norway 281
Oman 282
Pakistan 283
Palestine (State of) 287
Papua New Guinea 290
Paraguay 291
Peru 293
Philippines 295
Poland 297
Portugal 299
Puerto Rico 300
Qatar 301
Romania 303
Russian Federation 305
Rwanda 309
Saudi Arabia 312
Senegal 316
Serbia 317
Sierra Leone 320

Singapore 322
Slovakia 323
Slovenia 324
Somalia 326
South Africa 329
South Sudan 333
Spain 336
Sri Lanka 339
Sudan 342
Swaziland 345
Sweden 347
Switzerland 348
Syria 349
Taiwan 354
Tajikistan 355
Tanzania 357
Thailand 358
Timor-Leste 361
Togo 362
Tunisia 364
Turkey 367
Turkmenistan 371
Uganda 373
Ukraine 375
United Arab Emirates 379
United Kingdom 381
United States of America 385
Uruguay 390
Uzbekistan 391
Venezuela 393
Viet Nam 398
Yemen 400
Zambia 403
Zimbabwe 405

ABBREVIATIONS

ASEAN
Association of Southeast Asian Nations

AU
African Union

CEDAW
UN Convention on the Elimination of All
Forms of Discrimination against Women

CEDAW Committee
UN Committee on the Elimination of
Discrimination against Women

CERD
International Convention on the Elimination of
All Forms of Racial Discrimination

CERD Committee
UN Committee on the Elimination of Racial
Discrimination

CIA
US Central Intelligence Agency

ECOWAS
Economic Community of West African States

EU
European Union

**European Committee for the Prevention of
Torture**
European Committee for the Prevention of
Torture and Inhuman or Degrading Treatment
or Punishment

European Convention on Human Rights
(European) Convention for the Protection of
Human Rights and Fundamental Freedoms

ICC
International Criminal Court

ICCPR
International Covenant on Civil and Political
Rights

ICESCR
International Covenant on Economic, Social
and Cultural Rights

ICRC
International Committee of the Red Cross

ILO
International Labour Organization

**International Convention against Enforced
Disappearance**
International Convention for the Protection of
All Persons from Enforced Disappearance

LGBTI
Lesbian, gay, bisexual, transgender and
intersex

NATO
North Atlantic Treaty Organization

NGO
Non-governmental organization

OAS
Organization of American States

OSCE
Organization for Security and Co-operation in
Europe

UK
United Kingdom

UN
United Nations

UN Convention against Torture
Convention against Torture and Other Cruel,
Inhuman or Degrading Treatment or
Punishment

UN Refugee Convention
Convention relating to the Status of Refugees

UN Special Rapporteur on freedom of expression
UN Special Rapporteur on the promotion and protection of the right to freedom of opinion and expression

UN Special Rapporteur on racism
Special Rapporteur on contemporary forms of racism, racial discrimination, xenophobia and related intolerance

UN Special Rapporteur on torture
Special Rapporteur on torture and other cruel, inhuman or degrading treatment or punishment

UN Special Rapporteur on violence against women
Special rapporteur on violence against women, its causes and consequences

UNHCR, the UN refugee agency
Office of the United Nations High Commissioner for Refugees

UNICEF
United Nations Children's Fund

UPR
UN Universal Periodic Review

USA
United States of America

WHO
World Health Organization

PREFACE

The *Amnesty International Report 2016/17* documents the state of the world's human rights during 2016.

The foreword, five regional overviews and a survey of 159 countries and territories bear witness to the suffering endured by many, whether it be through conflict, displacement, discrimination or repression. The Report also shows that, in some areas, progress has been made in the safeguarding and securing of human rights.

While every attempt is made to ensure accuracy, information may be subject to change without notice.

AMNESTY INTERNATIONAL REPORT 2016/17

PART 1: FOREWORD AND REGIONAL OVERVIEWS

FOREWORD

"2016 saw the idea of human dignity and equality, the very notion of a human family, coming under vigorous and relentless assault from powerful narratives of blame, fear and scapegoating, propagated by those who sought to take or cling on to power at almost any cost."

SALIL SHETTY, SECRETARY GENERAL

For millions, 2016 was a year of unrelenting misery and fear, as governments and armed groups abused human rights in a multitude of ways. Large parts of Syria's most populous city, Aleppo, were pounded to dust by air strikes and street battles, while the cruel onslaught against civilians in Yemen continued. From the worsening plight of the Rohingya people in Myanmar to mass unlawful killings in South Sudan, from the vicious crackdowns on dissenting voices in Turkey and Bahrain to the rise of hate speech across large parts of Europe and the USA, the world in 2016 became a darker and more unstable place.

Meanwhile, the gap between imperative and action, and between rhetoric and reality, was stark and at times staggering. Nowhere was this better illustrated than in the failure of states attending September's UN summit for refugees and migrants to agree any adequate response to the global refugee crisis which assumed still greater magnitude and urgency during the year. While world leaders failed to rise to the challenge, 75,000 refugees remained trapped in a desert no man's land between Syria and Jordan. 2016 was also the African Union's Year of Human Rights; yet three African Union member states announced that they were pulling out of the International Criminal Court, undermining the prospect of accountability for crimes under international law. Meanwhile, Sudan's President Omar al-Bashir roamed the continent freely and with impunity while his government dropped chemical weapons on its own people in Darfur.

On the political stage, perhaps the most prominent of many seismic events was the election of Donald Trump as President of the USA. His election followed a campaign during which he frequently made deeply divisive statements marked by misogyny and xenophobia, and pledged to roll back established civil liberties and introduce policies which would be profoundly inimical to human rights.

Donald Trump's poisonous campaign rhetoric exemplifies a global trend towards angrier and more divisive politics. Across the world, leaders and politicians wagered their future power on narratives of fear and disunity, pinning blame on the "other" for the real or manufactured grievances of the electorate.

His predecessor, President Barack Obama, leaves a legacy that includes many grievous failures to uphold human rights, not least the expansion of the CIA's secretive campaign of drone strikes and the development of a gargantuan mass surveillance machine as revealed by whistleblower Edward Snowden. Yet the early indications from President-Elect Trump suggest a foreign policy that will significantly undermine multilateral co-operation and usher in a new era of greater instability and mutual suspicion.

Any overarching narrative seeking to explain the turbulent events of the past year is likely to be found wanting. But the reality is that we begin 2017 in a deeply unstable world full of trepidation and uncertainty about the future.

Against this background, the surety of the values articulated in the 1948 Universal Declaration of Human Rights is in danger of dissolution. The Declaration, penned in the wake of one of the bloodiest periods in human history, opens with these words:

"Whereas recognition of the inherent dignity and of the equal and inalienable rights of all members of the human family is the foundation of freedom, justice and peace in the world."

Yet despite the lessons of the past, 2016 saw the idea of human dignity and equality, the very notion of a human family, coming under vigorous and relentless assault from powerful narratives of blame, fear and scapegoating, propagated by those who sought to take or cling on to power at almost any cost.

The contempt for these ideals was on plentiful display in a year when the deliberate bombing of hospitals became a routine occurrence in Syria and Yemen; when refugees were pushed back into conflict zones; when the world's near-total inaction in Aleppo called to mind similar failures in Rwanda and Srebrenica in 1994 and 1995; and when governments across almost all regions of the world carried out massive crackdowns to silence dissent.

In the face of this, it has become alarmingly easy to paint a dystopian picture of the world and its future. The urgent and increasingly difficult task ahead is to rekindle global commitment to these core values on which humankind depends.

Among the most troubling developments of 2016 were the fruits of a new bargain offered by governments to their people – one which promises security and economic betterment in exchange for surrendering participatory rights and civil freedoms.

No part of the world was untouched by sweeping crackdowns on dissent – some overt and violent, others subtler and veiled in respectability. The quest to silence critical voices surged in its scale and intensity across large parts of the world.

The killing of Indigenous leader Berta Cáceres in Honduras on 2 March epitomized the dangers faced by individuals who bravely stand up to powerful state and corporate interests. These courageous human rights defenders, in the Americas and elsewhere, are often cast by governments as a threat to economic development because of their efforts to highlight the human and environmental consequences of resource exploitation and infrastructure projects. Berta Cáceres' work to defend local communities and their land, most recently against a proposed dam, had earned her global acclaim. The armed men who killed her in her home sent a chilling message to other activists, particularly those who do not enjoy the same level of international attention.

The security justification for crackdowns was widely deployed across the world. In Ethiopia, in response to largely peaceful protests against unjust dispossession of land in the Oromia region, security forces killed several hundred protesters and the authorities arbitrarily arrested thousands of people. The Ethiopian government used its Anti-Terrorism Proclamation to carry out a sweeping crackdown on human rights activists, journalists and members of the political opposition.

In the wake of a coup attempt in July, Turkey escalated its crackdown on dissenting voices during a state of emergency. More than 90,000 public sector employees were dismissed on grounds of alleged "links to a terrorist organization or threat to national security", while some 118 journalists were held in pre-trial detention and 184 media outlets were arbitrarily and permanently closed down.

Across the Middle East and North Africa, repression of dissent was endemic. In Egypt, security forces arbitrarily arrested, forcibly disappeared and tortured alleged supporters of the banned Muslim Brotherhood organization, as well as other critics and opponents of the government. Bahraini authorities ruthlessly prosecuted critics on a range of national security charges. In Iran, the authorities imprisoned critics, censored all media and adopted a new law that made virtually any criticism of the government and its policies liable to criminal prosecution.

In North Korea, the government furthered its already extreme repression by tightening its stranglehold on communications technology.

Often the stern measures were simply an attempt to mask government failures, such as in Venezuela, where the government sought to silence critics rather than address a spiralling humanitarian crisis.

In addition to the direct threats and attacks, there was an insidious chipping away at established civil and political freedoms in the name of security. For example the UK adopted a new law, the Investigatory Powers Act, which significantly increased the authorities' powers to intercept, access, retain or otherwise hack digital communications and data without any requirement of reasonable suspicion against an individual. By introducing one of the broadest regimes for mass surveillance of any country in the world, the UK took a significant step towards a reality where the right to privacy is simply not recognized.

However, the erosion of human rights values was perhaps most pernicious when officials blamed a specific "other" for real or perceived social problems in order to justify their repressive actions. Hateful, divisive and dehumanizing rhetoric unleashed the darkest instincts of human nature. By casting collective responsibility for social and economic ills onto particular groups, often ethnic or religious minorities, those in power gave free rein to discrimination and hate crimes, particularly in Europe and the USA.

One variant of this was demonstrated by the escalation, with enormous loss of life, of President Rodrigo Duterte's "war on drugs" in the Philippines. State-sanctioned violence and mass killings by vigilantes claimed more than 6,000 lives following repeated public endorsements by the President for those allegedly involved in drug-related crimes to be killed.

When self-styled "anti-establishment" figures blamed so-called elites, international institutions and the "other" for social or economic grievances, they chose the wrong prescription. The sense of insecurity and disenfranchisement – arising from factors such as unemployment, job insecurity, growing inequality and the loss of public services – demanded commitment, resources and policy shifts from governments, not easy scapegoats to blame.

It was clear that many disillusioned people around the world did not seek answers in human rights. However, the inequality and neglect underlying popular anger and frustration arose at least in part from the failure of states to fulfil people's economic, social and cultural rights.

The story of 2016 was in some ways a story of people's courage, resilience, creativity and determination in the face of immense challenges and threats.

Every region of the world saw evidence that where formal structures of power are used to repress, people will find ways of rising up and being heard. In China, despite systematic harassment and intimidation, activists found subversive ways to commemorate online the anniversary of the 1989 Tiananmen Square crackdown. At the Rio Olympic Games, Ethiopian marathon runner Feyisa Lilesa made global headlines with a gesture to draw attention to the government's persecution of Oromo people as he crossed the finishing line to win a silver medal. And on Europe's Mediterranean coasts, volunteers responded to the inertia and failure of governments to protect refugees by physically dragging drowning people out of the water themselves. People's popular movements across Africa – some unthinkable only a year earlier – galvanized and channelled popular demands for rights and justice.

Ultimately, the charge that human rights is a project of the elite rings hollow. People's instincts for freedom and justice do not simply wither away. During a year of division and dehumanization, the actions of some people to affirm humanity and the fundamental dignity of every person shone more brightly than ever. This compassionate response was embodied by 24-year-old Anas al-Basha, the so-called "clown of Aleppo", who chose to remain in the city to bring comfort and joy to children even after government forces unleashed their horrific bombardment. After his death in an air strike on 29 November, his brother paid tribute to him for making children happy in "the darkest, most dangerous place".

As we begin 2017, the world feels unstable and fear for the future proliferates. Yet it is in these times that courageous voices are needed, ordinary heroes who will stand up against injustice and repression. Nobody can take on the whole world, but everyone can change their own world. Everyone can take a stand against dehumanization, acting locally to recognize the dignity and the equal and inalienable rights of all, and thus lay the foundations of freedom and justice in the world. 2017 needs human rights heroes.

AFRICA REGIONAL OVERVIEW

Mass protests, movements, and mobilization – often articulated and organized through social media – swept the continent in 2016. Protesters and human rights defenders repeatedly found inspiring ways to stand up against repression and campaigns such as the #oromoprotests and #amaharaprotests in Ethiopia, #EnforcedDisappearancesKE in Kenya, #ThisFlag in Zimbabwe, and #FeesMustFall in South Africa formed iconic images from the year.

Given the scale and long history of repression, some of the protests – as in Ethiopia and Gambia – would have been unthinkable only a year previously. Demands for change, inclusion and freedom were often spontaneous, viral and driven by ordinary citizens, in particular young people who bear the triple burden of unemployment, poverty and inequality. Although originally largely peaceful, some of the campaigns eventually had violent elements, frequently in reaction to heavy-handed suppression by the authorities and lack of space for people to express their views and organize.

This trend of gathering resilience and the withering of the politics of fear offered cause for hope. People went out to the streets in large numbers, ignoring threats and bans on protest, refusing to back down in the face of brutal clampdowns, and instead expressing opinions and reclaiming their rights through acts of solidarity, boycotts and extensive, creative use of social media.

Despite stories of courage and resilience, repression of peaceful protests reached new highs and there appeared to be little or no progress in addressing the underlying factors behind the mass public discontent.

Dissent was brutally repressed, as evidenced in widespread patterns of attacks on peaceful protests and the right to freedom of expression. Human rights defenders, journalists and political opponents continued to face persecution and assault. Civilians continued to bear the brunt of armed conflicts, which were marked by persistent and large-scale violations of international law. Impunity for crimes under international law and serious human rights violations remained largely unaddressed. And there was much to be done to address the discrimination and marginalization of the most vulnerable – including women, children and lesbian, gay, bisexual, transgender and intersex (LGBTI) people.

CRACKDOWN ON PEACEFUL PROTESTS

The year saw widespread patterns of violent and arbitrary crackdowns on gatherings and protests – hallmarked by protest bans, arbitrary arrests, detentions and beatings as well as killings – in a long list of countries including Angola, Benin, Burundi, Cameroon, Chad, Côte d'Ivoire, Democratic Republic of the Congo (DRC), Equatorial Guinea, Ethiopia, Gambia, Guinea, Mali, Nigeria, Sierra Leone, South Africa, Sudan, Togo and Zimbabwe.

Ethiopian security forces, for example, systematically used excessive force to disperse largely peaceful protests that began in Oromia in November 2015, which escalated and spread into other parts of the country including Amhara region. The protests were brutally suppressed by security forces, including using live ammunition, which resulted in several hundred being killed and the arbitrary arrest of thousands of people. Following the declaration of a state of emergency, the government banned all forms of protest, and blockage of access to internet and social media, which started during the protests, continued.

In Nigeria, military and other security forces embarked on a campaign of violence against peaceful pro-Biafra protesters – resulting in the deaths of at least 100 protesters during the year. There was evidence that the military fired live ammunition with little or no warning to disperse crowds, and of mass extrajudicial executions – including at least 60 people shot dead in the space of two days in connection with protest events to mark Biafra

Remembrance Day on 30 May. This was similar in pattern to the attacks and excessive use of force in December 2015 on gatherings in which the military slaughtered hundreds of men, women and children in Zaria in Kaduna state during a confrontation with members of the Islamic Movement of Nigeria.

In South Africa, student protests resumed in August at universities across the country under the banner of #FeesMustFall. The protests regularly ended in violence. While there may have been some violence on the students' side, Amnesty International documented many reports of police using excessive force, including firing rubber bullets at short range at students and supporters generally. One student leader was shot in the back 13 times with rubber bullets on 20 October in Johannesburg.

In Zimbabwe, police continued to clamp down on protest and strike action in Harare using excessive force. Hundreds of people were arrested for participating in peaceful protests in different parts of the country, including Pastor Evan Mawarire, leader of the #ThisFlag campaign, who was briefly arrested in an attempt to suppress growing dissent, and who eventually fled the country when he feared for his life.

In many of these protests and more, including in Chad, Republic of the Congo (Congo), DRC, Ethiopia, Gabon, Gambia, Lesotho and Uganda, there was an increasing crackdown on social media and patterns of arbitrary restriction or shutting down of access to the internet.

ATTACKS ON HUMAN RIGHTS DEFENDERS AND JOURNALISTS

Human rights defenders and journalists were frequently in the front line of human rights violations, with the right to freedom of expression suffering both steady erosions and new waves of threats. Attempts to crush dissent and tighten the noose around freedom of expression manifested themselves across the continent, including in Botswana, Burundi, Cameroon, Chad, Côte d'Ivoire, Gambia, Kenya, Mauritania, Nigeria, Somalia,

South Sudan, Sudan, Tanzania, Togo and Zambia.

Some had to pay the ultimate price. A prominent human rights lawyer, his client and their taxi driver were subjected to forced disappearance and extrajudicial killing by police in Kenya. They were among more than 177 cases of individuals extrajudicially executed at the hands of security agencies during the year. In Sudan, the murder of 18-year-old Sudanese university student Abubakar Hassan Mohamed Taha and 20-year-old Mohamad Al Sadiq Yoyo by intelligence agents came against a backdrop of intensified repression of student dissent. Two journalists were killed in Somalia by unidentified assailants, in a climate in which journalists and media workers were harassed, intimidated and attacked.

Many others faced arbitrary arrests and continued to face prosecution and detention for their work. Despite some positive steps in Angola – including the acquittal of human rights defenders and release of prisoners of conscience – politically motivated trials, criminal defamation charges and national security laws continued to be used to suppress human rights defenders, dissent and other critical voices. In DRC, youth movements were classified as insurrectional groups. Elsewhere, the whereabouts of politicians and journalists arbitrarily arrested and forcibly disappeared in Eritrea since 2001 remained unknown, despite the government's announcement that they were still alive.

In Mauritania, although the Supreme Court ordered the release of 12 anti-slavery activists, three remained in detention and anti-slavery organizations and activists continued to face persecution by the authorities.

Beyond imprisonment, human rights defenders and journalists also faced physical assaults, intimidation and harassment in many countries including in Chad, Gambia, Kenya, Somalia and South Sudan.

On 18 April, Zimbabwe's Independence Day, state security agents brutally assaulted the brother of disappeared journalist and pro-democracy activist Itai Dzamara, after he held up a placard at an event attended by President Robert Mugabe in Harare. In Uganda, there was a series of attacks on the offices of NGOs and human rights defenders. Continuing lack of accountability for these crimes sent the message that the authorities condoned and tolerated these actions. In one attack, intruders beat a security guard to death.

Media houses, journalists and social media users faced increasing challenges in many countries. Zambia's authorities shut down the independent newspaper *The Post* in a ploy to silence critical media ahead of the election, also arresting senior staff and their family members.

Burundi's already-decimated civil society and independent media came under increasing attack: journalists, members of social media groups and even schoolchildren were arrested simply for speaking out. In Cameroon, Fomusoh Ivo Feh was sentenced to 10 years in prison for forwarding a sarcastic text message about Boko Haram.

In some countries, emerging laws were cause for concern. A draft law under parliamentary consideration in Mauritania restricted the right to freedom of peaceful assembly and association. In Congo, a law increasing government control over civil society organizations was passed. In Angola, the National Assembly approved five draft bills that will impermissibly restrict the right to freedom of expression. Elsewhere, existing laws such as terrorism and state of emergency laws were used to criminalize peaceful dissent. The Ethiopian government – increasingly intolerant of opposing voices – escalated its crackdown on journalists, human rights defenders and other dissenters by using the Anti-Terrorism Proclamation.

On the positive side, there were some hopeful signs of judicial activism and courage – even in extremely repressive countries – which challenged governments' use of the law and judiciary to stifle dissent. In DRC, four pro-democracy activists were released, a rare positive step in a very difficult year for freedom of expression in the country. A landmark court ruling against repressive laws in Swaziland in September was also another victory for human rights. Zimbabwe's High Court overturned a ban on protests. Although another High Court ruling subsequently made this void, the courageous decision – made after President Mugabe threatened the judiciary – represented a victory in defence of human rights and sent a clear message that the right to protest cannot be stripped away on a whim. In Gambia, more than 40 prisoners of conscience, some of whom had been detained for as long as eight months, were released on bail pending appeal immediately following the elections.

POLITICAL REPRESSION

2016 witnessed several contested elections across Africa, characterized by increased repression. In several countries, including in Burundi, Chad, Congo, Côte d'Ivoire, DRC, Gabon, Gambia, Somalia and Uganda, opposition leaders and voices came under severe attack.

In one of the most unexpected developments, tens of thousands of Gambians took part in peaceful gatherings ahead of the Presidential elections, although at the end of the year the election results remained contested.

The months leading up to the elections were marred by serious violations of citizens' rights to express themselves freely. Dozens of opposition members were arrested, and two died in custody after being arrested for participating in peaceful protests. Thirty protesters were sentenced to three years in prison for their involvement in peaceful protests, with 14 others awaiting trial. All were released on bail immediately following the elections on 1 December.

Despite initially conceding defeat to the opposition leader Adama Barrow, President Yahya Jammeh subsequently challenged the results and remained defiant to domestic and international pressure to hand over power.

The Ugandan government undermined the opposition party's ability to legally challenge the results of February's elections. Security forces repeatedly arrested the aggrieved presidential candidate Dr Kizza Besigye and some of his party colleagues and supporters, also besieging his home and raiding the party's office in Kampala.

In DRC, there was a systematic crackdown on opponents of President Joseph Kabila's attempt to stay in power beyond the constitutionally mandated second term – which ended in December – and those criticizing election delays. Security agents arrested and harassed those taking an explicit stand on the constitutional debate or denouncing human rights violations, accusing them of betraying their country.

In Somalia, an acute humanitarian crisis was compounded by a political crisis over electoral colleges for parliamentary and presidential elections, with the armed group al-Shabaab rejecting all forms of elections and calling on its followers to attack polling venues to kill clan elders, government officials and MPs taking part in elections.

Authorities in Congo continued to detain Paulin Makaya, President of "Unis pour le Congo" (UPC), simply for peacefully exercising his right to freedom of expression. After the opposition rejected the results of the March presidential election, the authorities arrested leading opposition figures and suppressed peaceful protest.

The authorities in Côte d'Ivoire targeted opposition members and unfairly restricted their rights to freedom of expression and peaceful assembly, before a referendum on constitutional changes in October. This included the arbitrary arrest and detention of dozens of opposition members at a peaceful protest. Some of them were dropped in several places in the economic capital, Abidjan, others around 100km away from their homes and forced to walk back in a practice known as "mobile detention". In October, during a peaceful protest against the referendum, police fired tear gas, clubbed the leaders and arrested at least 50 people.

ARMED CONFLICT

Civilians in Africa's armed conflicts – including in Cameroon, Central African Republic (CAR), Chad, DRC, Mali, Niger, Nigeria, Somalia, South Sudan and Sudan – faced serious abuses and violations. Gender-based and sexual violence was widespread, and children were recruited as child soldiers.

In west, central and eastern Africa, armed groups such as al-Shabaab and Boko Haram continued to perpetrate relentless violence and abuses, with hundreds of civilians killed and abducted and millions forced to live in fear and insecurity, both within and outside their countries. In Cameroon, over 170,000 people – mostly women and children – were internally displaced across the Far North region as a result of Boko Haram's abuses. In Niger, over 300,000 people needed humanitarian aid during the state of emergency in the Diffa region, where most attacks were carried out by Boko Haram.

Many governments responded to these threats with disregard for international humanitarian and human rights law, including through arbitrary arrests, incommunicado detention, torture, enforced disappearances and extrajudicial killings.

In Nigeria, 29 children under the age of six – including babies – were among more than 240 people who died in horrendous conditions during the year in the notorious Giwa barracks detention centre in Maiduguri. Thousands rounded up during mass arrests in the northeast, often with no evidence against them, continued to be detained in overcrowded and unsanitary conditions, without trial or access to the outside world. Similarly in Cameroon, more than 1,000 people – many arrested arbitrarily – were held in horrific conditions and dozens died from torture, or disease and malnutrition. In cases where detainees suspected of supporting Boko Haram were brought to trial, they faced unfair trials in military courts in which the death penalty was by far the most likely outcome.

Elsewhere, the security and humanitarian situation in Sudan's Darfur, Blue Nile and South Kordofan states remained dire. Evidence of the use of chemical weapons by government forces in the Jabel Marra region of Darfur demonstrated that the regime will continue attacking its civilian population without fear of accountability for its violations of international law.

Despite the signing of the peace deal in South Sudan between government and rival forces, fighting continued in different parts of the country throughout the year, and escalated in the southern Equatoria region after heavy fighting broke out in the capital, Juba, in July. During the fighting, armed forces, particularly government soldiers, committed human rights violations including targeted killings and attacks including against humanitarian personnel. The UN mission in South Sudan (UNMISS) was criticized for its failure to protect civilians during the fighting. A UN Security Council resolution to establish a regional protection force was not implemented. The UN Special Advisor on the prevention of Genocide and the UN Commission on Human Rights in South Sudan raised the alarm that the stage was being set for a genocide.

In CAR, despite peaceful elections in December 2015 and February 2016, the security situation deteriorated later in the year, threatening to plunge the country into more deadly violence. Armed groups launched numerous attacks: on 12 October, ex-Séléka fighters from at least two different factions killed at least 37 civilians, injured 60, and set fire to a camp for internally displaced persons (IDPs), in the city of Kaga Bandoro.

Yet despite such bloodshed and suffering, the world's attention arguably shifted even further away from Africa's conflicts. Certainly, the international community's response to conflict in the continent was woefully inadequate, as evidenced by the UN Security Council's failure on sanctions on South Sudan, and the insufficient capacity of peacekeeping operations to protect civilians in CAR, South Sudan and Sudan. There were hardly any measures, including from the UN Security Council and the African Union (AU) Peace and Security Council, to put pressure on the government of Sudan to allow humanitarian access and to investigate allegations of grave violations and abuses. The AU's response to crimes under international law and other serious human rights violations and abuses committed in the context of conflict and crisis remained mostly slow, inconsistent and reactive rather than forming part of a comprehensive and consistent strategy.

PEOPLE ON THE MOVE

Africa's conflicts – including in Cameroon, CAR, Chad, Mali, Niger, Nigeria, Somalia, South Sudan and Sudan – remained major drivers of the global refugee crisis, and the internal displacement of people within borders. Millions of women, children and men were still unable to return home, or were forced by new threats to flee into unknown dangers and uncertain futures.

People from sub-Saharan Africa formed the majority of the hundreds of thousands of refugees and migrants travelling to Libya fleeing war, persecution or extreme poverty, often in the hope of transiting through the country to settle in Europe. Amnesty International's research revealed horrifying abuses including sexual violence, killings, torture, and religious persecution along the smuggling routes to and through Libya.

In northern Nigeria, at least two million people remained internally displaced – living in host communities and some in overcrowded camps with inadequate food, water and sanitation. Tens of thousands of IDPs were held in camps under armed guard by the military and Civilian Joint Task Force, which were accused of sexually exploiting women.

Thousands of people have died in these camps due to severe malnutrition.

Hundreds of thousands of refugees from CAR, Libya, Nigeria and Sudan continued to live in poor conditions in refugee camps in Chad. According to the UN, more than 300,000 people fled Burundi, most of them to refugee camps in neighbouring Rwanda and Tanzania. More than 1.1 million Somalis remained internally displaced, with another 1.1 million Somali refugees remaining in neighbouring countries and elsewhere.

In the three years since the start of the conflict in South Sudan, the number of refugees in neighbouring countries reached 1 million, while a total of 1.7 million people continued to be displaced within the country, and 4.8 million people were food insecure.

Kenya's government announced its intention to close Dadaab refugee camp, home to 280,000 refugees. Some 260,000 of these people were from Somalia or of Somali descent, who – as a result of other changes to Kenya's refugee policy – were at risk of being forcibly returned, in violation of international law.

IMPUNITY AND FAILURES TO ENSURE JUSTICE

Impunity remained a common denominator in all of Africa's major conflicts, with those suspected of crimes under international law and gross human rights violations rarely held to account.

Despite having a clear mandate, the AU had yet to take concrete steps towards setting up a hybrid court for South Sudan, as required by the country's peace accord. Such a court would represent the most viable option for ensuring accountability for crimes such as war crimes and crimes against humanity committed during the conflict, and for deterring further abuses.

Some progress was made towards setting up the Special Criminal Court in CAR, but the vast majority of suspected perpetrators of serious crimes and gross violations of human rights remained at large, free of any arrest or investigations. In addition to the serious weakness of the UN's CAR peacekeeping mission, impunity remained one of the key drivers of the conflict and civilians faced deadly violence and instability.

In Nigeria there was compelling evidence of widespread and systematic violations of international humanitarian and human rights law by the military, leading to more than 7,000 mainly young Nigerian men and boys dying in military detention and more than 1,200 people killed in extrajudicial executions. However, the government did not take any steps towards investigating such allegations. No one was brought to justice and the violations continued.

The International Criminal Court (ICC) declared the charges against Kenya's Deputy President William Ruto and radio presenter Joshua Arap Sang dismissed, and thus all cases before the ICC in relation to Kenya's post-election violence in 2007-2008 collapsed. This decision was seen as a major setback by thousands of victims who had yet to see justice.

In a betrayal of millions of victims of international crimes across the world, three states in Africa – Burundi, Gambia and South Africa – signalled their intention to withdraw from the Rome Statute.

The AU also continued to call on states to disregard their international obligations to arrest Sudanese President Omar Al-Bashir despite his being wanted by the ICC on charges of genocide. In May, Uganda failed to arrest visiting President Al-Bashir and hand him over to the ICC, failing hundreds of thousands of people killed or displaced in the Darfur conflict.

There were, however, some heartening and historic moments for international justice and accountability.

Many African member states of the ICC affirmed their support for and intention to remain within the Rome Statute's system during the 15th Session of the Assembly of State parties in November. This commitment was previously reflected at July's AU Summit in Kigali where many countries – including Botswana, Côte d'Ivoire, Nigeria, Senegal and Tunisia – opposed a call for a mass withdrawal from the Rome Statute. In December, Gambia's President-elect announced his intention to rescind the government's decision to withdraw from the Rome Statute.

Positive developments included the conviction of Chad's former President Hissène Habré in May for crimes against humanity, war crimes and torture committed between 1982 and 1990. The Extraordinary African Chambers in Dakar sentenced him to life imprisonment, and set a new benchmark for efforts to end impunity in Africa. The case was the continent's first universal jurisdiction case and Habré the first former African leader to be prosecuted before a court in another country for crimes under international law.

In March, the ICC convicted Jean-Pierre Bemba, former Vice-President of DRC, for war crimes and crimes against humanity committed in CAR. The ICC's sentence of 19 years followed its first conviction for rape as a war crime and its first conviction based on command responsibility. The guilty verdict was a key moment in the battle for justice for victims of sexual violence in CAR and around the world.

The ICC also began the trial of Côte d'Ivoire's former President Laurent Gbagbo and his Youth Minister, Charles Blé Goudé, on charges of crimes against humanity. The ICC also convicted Ahmad Al-Faqi Al-Mahdi – an alleged senior member of the Ansar Eddine armed group – for attacks on mosques and mausoleums in Timbuktu, Mali, in 2012, a crime under international law.

Elsewhere, South Africa's Supreme Court rebuked the government for its failure to abide by its domestic and international obligations when it failed to arrest Al-Bashir during a visit to the country in 2015. This affirmed the international norm of rejection of immunity of perpetrators for international crimes, irrespective of official capacity.

DISCRIMINATION AND MARGINALIZATION

Women and girls were frequently subjected to discrimination, marginalization and abuse often because of cultural traditions and norms, and discrimination institutionalized by unjust laws. Women and girls were also subjected to sexual violence and rape in conflicts and countries hosting large numbers of displaced people and refugees.

High levels of gender-based violence against women and girls were reported in many countries such as Madagascar, Namibia and Sierra Leone.

In Sierra Leone, the government continued to ban pregnant girls from going to mainstream schools and taking exams. The President also refused to sign a bill legalizing abortion in certain situations despite it having been adopted by Parliament twice and despite Sierra Leone's high maternal mortality rate. The country rejected UN recommendations to prohibit female genital mutilation by law.

Early and forced marriage in Burkina Faso had robbed thousands of girls as young as 13 of their childhood, while the cost of contraception, along with other barriers prevented them from choosing if and when to have children. But following an intense civil society campaign, the government announced that it would revise the law to increase the legal marriage age to 18.

LGBTI people, or those perceived to be so, continued to face abuse or discrimination in countries including Botswana, Cameroon, Kenya, Nigeria, Senegal, Tanzania, Togo and Uganda. In Kenya, two men petitioned the High Court in Mombasa to declare the anal examination, HIV and hepatitis B tests they were forced to undergo in 2015 were unconstitutional. However, the court upheld the legality of anal examinations on men suspected of engaging in sexual activity with other men. Forced anal examinations violate the right to privacy and the prohibition of torture and other ill-treatment under international law.

In Malawi, an unprecedented wave of violent attacks against people with albinism exposed a systemic failure of policing. Individuals and criminal gangs perpetrated abductions, killings and grave robberies as they sought body parts that they believed contain magical powers. Women and children were particularly vulnerable to killings, sometimes targeted by their own relatives.

In Sudan, freedom of religion was undermined by a legal system under which conversion from Islam to another religion was punishable by death.

Lack of accountability for corporations was also another factor for gross violation of the rights of children. Artisanal miners – including thousands of children – mine cobalt in hazardous conditions in the DRC. This cobalt is used to power devices including mobile phones and laptop computers, and major electronics brands – including Apple, Samsung and Sony – are failing to carry out basic checks to ensure that cobalt mined by child labourers is not used in their products.

LOOKING AHEAD

The AU called 2016 its Year of Human Rights, but many member states failed to convert rhetoric on human rights into action. If there was anything to be celebrated about the year, it was the story of people's resilience and courage as they articulated a clear message that repression and the politics of fear can no longer silence them.

Almost certainly, escalating crises in countries such as Burundi, Ethiopia, Gambia and Zimbabwe could have been averted or minimized had there been the political will and courage to open up space for people to freely express their views.

Despite progress in some areas, the AU's responses to violations of human rights – as the structural causes of conflicts, or emerging out of conflicts – remained largely slow, inconsistent and reactive. Indeed, even when it showed concern, the AU generally lacked the determination and political will to confront such violations head-on. There also appeared to be co-ordination gaps between the peace and security organs and mechanisms – such as the AU's Peace and Security Council and its Continental Early Warning System – and the regional human rights institutions, which limited a comprehensive response to human rights violations leading to or emerging out of conflicts.

The AU has less than four years to realize its aspiration to "silence all guns" on the continent by 2020. It is time to translate this commitment into action, by ensuring an effective response to the underlying structural causes of conflicts, including persistent human rights violations.

More effective measures are also needed to tackle the cycle of impunity – including moving away from politically motivated attacks on the ICC and working towards ensuring justice and accountability for serious crimes and gross human rights violations being committed in countries like South Sudan and elsewhere.

The AU has embarked on designing a 10 Year Action and Implementation Plan on Human Rights in Africa, providing yet another opportunity to address its key challenges. The starting point should be recognition that Africans are rising and claiming their rights, despite repression and exclusion.

AMERICAS REGIONAL OVERVIEW

Despite public discourse about democracy and economic progress as well as hopes of an end at last to its remaining armed conflict in Colombia, the Americas remained one of the world's most violent and unequal regions.

Across the region, the year was marked by a trend of anti-rights, racial and discriminatory rhetoric in political campaigns and by state officials, which was accepted and normalized by mainstream media. In the USA, Donald Trump was elected President in November – following an election campaign in which he provoked consternation through discriminatory, misogynist and xenophobic rhetoric, and caused serious concerns about future US commitments to human rights domestically and globally.

The region's human rights crisis was accelerated by a trend of increased obstacles and restrictions to justice and fundamental freedoms. Waves of repression became more visible and violent, with states frequently misusing their justice and security apparatus to ruthlessly respond to and crush dissent, and increasing public discontent.

Discrimination, insecurity, poverty and environmental damage were rampant throughout the region. Failure to uphold international human rights standards was also laid bare by a wide gulf of inequality – in wealth, social wellbeing and access to justice – which was underpinned by corruption and lack of accountability.

Widespread and entrenched obstacles to accessing justice and a weakening rule of law were common to many countries in the region. Impunity for human rights abuses was high, and in some cases a lack of independent and impartial judicial systems further protected political and economic interests.

This backdrop enabled the perpetuation of human rights violations. Torture and other ill-treatment, in particular, remained prevalent, despite the existence of anti-torture laws in countries including Brazil, Mexico and Venezuela.

Failures of justice systems – together with states' failure to implement public security policies that protect human rights – contributed to high levels of violence. Countries such as Brazil, El Salvador, Honduras, Jamaica, Mexico and Venezuela had the highest homicide rates on the planet.

Endemic violence and insecurity were often linked to, and compounded by, the proliferation of illicit small arms and the growth of organized crime, which in some cases had taken control of whole territories, sometimes with the complicity or acquiescence of the police and military.

Central America's "Northern Triangle" of El Salvador, Guatemala and Honduras was one of the world's most violent places, with more people killed there than in most conflict zones globally. El Salvador's homicide rate of 108 per 100,000 inhabitants was one of the highest in the world. For many, daily life was overshadowed by criminal gangs.

Widespread gender-based violence remained one of the most appalling of states' failures in the Americas. In October, the Economic Commission for Latin America and the Caribbean revealed that 12 women and girls were murdered every day in the region because of their gender (a crime classified as "feminicide"), with most of those crimes going unpunished. According to the US State Department, one in five women in the USA was sexually assaulted during her college years, although just one in 10 incidents was reported to the authorities.

Lesbian, gay, bisexual, transgender and intersex (LBGTI) individuals across the region faced higher rates of violence and discrimination, and more obstacles in getting access to justice. The shooting rampage at a nightclub in Orlando, Florida, demonstrated that LBGTI people were the most likely target of hate crimes in the USA. Brazil, meanwhile, remained the most deadly country in the world for transgender people.

In February, the World Health Organization (WHO) declared Zika a public health emergency after detecting an "explosive" spread of the virus in the region. Fears that mother-to-child transmission of the virus may be linked to microcephaly in newborns – as well as the possible sexual transmission of the virus – highlighted barriers for the effective realization of sexual and reproductive health and rights in the region.

State failures left power vacuums that were occupied by increasingly influential transnational corporations, especially in the extractive and other industries related to the appropriation of territory and natural resources – mostly in land claimed by and belonging to Indigenous Peoples, other ethnic minorities and peasant farmers, without due respect of their right to free, prior and informed consent. Often, these groups suffered harm to their health, environment, livelihoods and culture, and were forcibly displaced, leading to the disappearance of their communities.

Political repression, discrimination, violence and poverty drove another deepening but largely forgotten humanitarian crisis. Hundreds of thousands of refugees – largely from Central America – were forced to flee from their homes to seek protection, frequently placing themselves at risk of further human rights abuses and risking their lives.

Many governments displayed a deepening intolerance to criticism, as they stifled dissent and muzzled freedom of speech.

In Mexico, the authorities' unwillingness to accept criticism was so severe that it retreated into a state of denial about the country's human rights crisis. Despite the fact that almost 30,000 people were reported missing, that thousands had lost their lives due to security operations to combat drug trafficking and organized crime, and that thousands were forcibly displaced from their homes as a result of widespread violence, the authorities ignored criticism from Mexican civil society and international organizations, including the UN.

Denial was also a hallmark of a deteriorating human rights situation in Venezuela, with the government putting at risk the lives and human rights of millions by refuting the existence of a major humanitarian and economic crisis, and refusing to request international aid. Despite severe food and medicine shortages, rapidly rising crime rates and continuous human rights violations – including high levels of police violence – the government silenced its critics instead of responding to people's desperate calls for help.

Notable events during 2016 included US President Barack Obama's historic state visit to Cuba, which put the two countries' human rights challenges – including the ill-treatment of migrants in the USA, the impact of the US embargo on Cuba's human rights situation, and the lack of freedom of expression and the repression of activists in Cuba – in the international spotlight.

The ratification by the Colombian Congress of the peace agreement with the Revolutionary Armed Forces of Colombia (FARC) after more than four years of negotiations finally ended the country's 50-year-long armed conflict with the FARC that devastated millions of lives. A peace process with Colombia's second largest guerrilla group – the National Liberation Army (ELN) – was announced but had yet to start by the end of the year, largely due to the group's failure to release one of its high-profile hostages.

In Haiti, a deadly hurricane caused a major humanitarian crisis, compounding existing damage from natural disasters. Deeply entrenched and structural problems such as a lack of funding and political will had already left Haiti unable to provide adequate housing for 60,000 people living in displacement camps in appalling conditions following the 2010 earthquake. Presidential and legislative elections were postponed twice over allegations of fraud amid protests, against which the police reportedly used excessive force. In November, Jovenel Moïse was elected President.

HUMAN RIGHTS DEFENDERS AT RISK

In many countries in the Americas region, defending human rights remained extremely dangerous. Journalists, lawyers, judges, political opponents and witnesses were particularly targeted with threats, attacks, torture and enforced disappearances; some were even killed by state and non-state actors as a way to silence them. Human rights activists also faced smear campaigns and vilification. Yet there was little progress in investigating these attacks or bringing perpetrators to justice.

Human rights defenders and social movements opposing large-scale development projects and transnational corporations were at particular risk of reprisals. Women human rights defenders as well as those from communities historically excluded were also targeted with violence.

Human rights defenders faced increased attacks, threats and killings in Brazil. In Nicaragua, the government turned a blind eye to human rights violations and persecuted activists. The plight of prisoners of conscience in Venezuela – and the government's willingness to suppress dissent – was highlighted when severely ill opposition leader Rosmit Mantilla was denied surgery and placed in a punishment cell instead; after intense national and international pressure, he received the urgent medical care he needed, and was later released in November.

Honduras and Guatemala were the most dangerous countries in the world for those defending land, territory and the environment, with a wave of threats, trumped-up charges, smear campaigns, attacks and killings targeting environmental and land activists. In March, the murder of prominent Honduran Indigenous leader Berta Cáceres – who was shot in her home by armed men – highlighted the generalization of violence against those working to protect land, territory and the environment in the country.

In Guatemala the criminalization – through baseless criminal procedures and the misuse of the criminal justice system – of human rights defenders opposing projects to exploit natural resources and their identification as "the enemy within" was common. In Colombia, human rights defenders, especially community leaders and environmental activists, continued to be threatened and killed in alarming numbers.

In Argentina, social leader Milagro Sala was arrested and charged with protesting peacefully in Jujuy. Despite her release being ordered, further criminal proceedings were initiated against her to keep her in detention. In October, the UN Working Group on Arbitrary Detention concluded that her detention was arbitrary and recommended her immediate release.

In northern Peru, Máxima Acuña – a peasant farmer caught in a legal battle with Yanacocha, one of the biggest gold and copper mines in the region, over ownership of the land where she lived – won the 2016 Goldman Prize, a highly respected environmental award. Despite a campaign of harassment and intimidation in which security personnel were alleged to have physically attacked her and her family, she stood firm and refused to end her struggle to protect local lakes and remain on her land.

In Ecuador, the rights to freedom of expression and association were severely curtailed by restrictive legislation and silencing tactics. The criminalization of dissent continued, particularly against those who opposed extractive projects on Indigenous Peoples' land.

Despite claims of political openness in Cuba and the re-establishment of relations with the USA the previous year, civil society and opposition groups reported increased harassment of government critics. Human rights defenders and political activists were publicly described as "subversive" and "anti-Cuban mercenaries". Some were subjected to short-term arbitrary detention before being released without charge, often several times a month.

THREATS TO THE INTER-AMERICAN HUMAN RIGHTS SYSTEM

Despite the extent of the region's human rights challenges, the Inter-American Commission on Human Rights (IACHR) – critical to defend and promote human rights as well as ensure access to justice for victims who were unable to do so in their own countries – was affected by a financial crisis for most of the year. This was caused by an insufficient allocation of resources by member states of the Organization of American States (OAS) – a striking demonstration of states' lack of political will to promote and protect human rights both within and beyond their territories.

In May, the IACHR said it faced the worst financial crisis in its history. There was a real danger that progress made by the IACHR in confronting gross human rights violations and structural discrimination would be weakened – precisely when the IACHR needed to play a more vigorous role in ensuring states uphold their obligations under international human rights law.

With an annual budget of US$8 million, the inter-American human rights system remained the world's poorest human rights system, with fewer resources than its corresponding entities in Africa (US$13 million) and Europe (about US$104.5 million).

Although additional funding was eventually received to complement the IACHR income, there were concerns that the political crisis would continue unless states allocated adequate funding to the institution and co-operated with it, regardless of how critical it was of countries' human rights record.

There were more specific failures to support the IACHR too. Mexico's government sought to obstruct its work on the Ayotzinapa case – in which 43 students were forcibly disappeared after being arrested by police in 2014. Despite the authorities' claim that the students were kidnapped by a criminal gang, and their remains burned and thrown in a dumpster, a group of IACHR-appointed experts concluded that it was scientifically impossible for that many bodies to have been burned in the conditions claimed. In November, the IACHR launched a special mechanism to follow up on the experts' recommendations, but appropriate support from the authorities was difficult to guarantee.

REFUGEES, MIGRANTS AND STATELESS PEOPLE

Central America was the source of a rapidly worsening refugee crisis. Relentless violence in this often forgotten part of the world continued to cause a surge in asylum applications from Central American citizens in Mexico, the USA and other countries, reaching levels not seen since most of the region's armed conflicts ended decades ago.

Hundreds of thousands of people travelled through Mexico either to seek asylum there, or to continue to the USA. Many were detained in harsh conditions, killed, abducted or faced extortion by criminal gangs who often operated in collusion with the authorities. Large numbers of unaccompanied children and adolescents were particularly affected by human rights abuses; women and girls were at serious risk of sexual violence and human trafficking.

Despite overwhelming evidence that many asylum-seekers were at risk of extreme violence should they not be granted asylum, deportations from Mexico and the USA remained steady. Many people were forcibly returned back to the life-threatening situations they were fleeing in the first place; some were allegedly killed by gangs after being deported.

Honduras, Guatemala and El Salvador fuelled this deepening crisis by failing to protect people from violence and to set up a comprehensive protection plan for people who were deported from countries such as Mexico and the USA.

Yet, rather than taking responsibility for their role in the crisis, the governments concerned focused only on the human rights abuses that people suffered while travelling through Mexico to the USA. They also falsely argued that most people were fleeing out of economic need rather than soaring violence and homicides, not to mention the daily threats, extortion and intimidation that most of the population faced under struggles for territorial control from gangs.

In the USA, tens of thousands of unaccompanied children, as well as people travelling with their families, were apprehended when attempting to cross the southern border during the year. Families were detained for months, many without proper access to medical care and legal counsel.

Throughout the year, the IACHR expressed concern about the situation of Cuban and Haitian migrants attempting to reach the USA.

Elsewhere, migrants and their families faced pervasive discrimination, exclusion and ill-treatment. In the Bahamas, there was widespread ill-treatment of undocumented migrants from countries including Haiti and Cuba. The Dominican Republic deported thousands of people of Haitian descent – including Dominican-born people who were effectively rendered stateless – while often failing to respect international law and standards on deportations. Upon arrival to Haiti, many people who had been deported settled in makeshift camps, where they lived in appalling conditions.

Despite a commitment from newly elected authorities in the Dominican Republic to address the situation of stateless individuals, tens of thousands of people remained stateless following a 2013 Constitutional Court ruling which retroactively and arbitrarily deprived them of their nationality. In February, the IACHR described a "situation of statelessness… of a magnitude never before seen in the Americas".

More than 30,000 Syrian refugees were resettled in Canada, with a further 12,000 resettled in the USA.

PUBLIC SECURITY AND HUMAN RIGHTS

Non-state actors – including corporations and criminal networks – wielded growing influence and were responsible for increasing levels of violence and human rights abuses.

Overall, however, states mostly failed to respond to the situation in a way that complied with international standards, with significant human rights violations resulting from a tendency to militarize public security.

Some states responded to social unrest – and particularly peaceful protests – with an increased use of the army to undertake public security operations, and adopted military techniques, training and equipment for use by the police and other law enforcement agencies. Although tackling organized crime was frequently used as justification for militarized responses, in reality they enabled states to further violate human rights rather than address the root causes of violence. In countries such as Venezuela, for example, military action in response to protests was often followed by torture and other ill-treatment of protesters.

Protests across the USA – which followed the deadly shooting by police in July of Philando Castile in Minnesota and Alton Sterling in Louisiana – saw police use heavy-duty riot gear and military-grade weapons in response, raising concerns about demonstrators' right to peaceful assembly. There were also concerns about the degree of force police used against largely peaceful protests opposing the proposed Dakota Access Pipeline near the Standing Rock Sioux Reservation in North Dakota. Meanwhile, the US authorities again failed to track the exact number of people killed by law enforcement officials; media reports put the numbers at almost 1,000 in 2016, and at least 21 people died after police used electric-shock weapons on them.

The Olympic Games hosted by Brazil in August were marred by human rights violations by security forces, with the authorities and the event's organizers failing to implement effective measures to prevent abuses. Police killings in Rio de Janeiro increased as the city prepared to host the Games. Violent police operations took place throughout the event with severe repression of protests, including through unnecessary and excessive use of force. Throughout the year, the country's counter-narcotic operations and heavily armed approach to security operations fuelled human rights violations and placed police officers at risk.

Police and other security forces also used excessive and unnecessary force in countries including the Bahamas, Chile, the Dominican Republic, Ecuador, El Salvador, Jamaica, Mexico, Peru and Venezuela.

Unlawful killings in Jamaica were part of a pattern of police operations that had remained largely unchanged for two decades, while many killings by security forces in the Dominican Republic were reported to have been unlawful. In both countries, security forces were exempt of reforms and were rarely held accountable.

ACCESS TO JUSTICE AND THE FIGHT TO END IMPUNITY

Rampant impunity allowed human rights abusers to operate without fear of the consequences, weakened the rule of law, and denied truth and redress to millions.

Impunity was sustained by justice and security systems that remained under-resourced, weak and often corrupt, compounded by a lack of political will to ensure their impartiality and independence.

The resulting failure to bring the perpetrators of human rights violations to justice allowed organized crime and abusive law enforcement practices to take root and prosper.

Denial of meaningful access to justice also left huge numbers of people – including in Brazil, Colombia, Guatemala, Mexico, Honduras, Jamaica, Paraguay, Peru and Venezuela – unable to claim their rights.

In Jamaica, impunity prevailed for the decades-long pattern of alleged unlawful killings and extrajudicial executions by law enforcement officials. While more than 3,000 people have been killed by law enforcement officials since 2000, only a handful of officials have been held accountable to date. In June, the Commission of Enquiry into alleged human rights violations during the 2010 state of emergency made recommendations for police reform; by the end of the year Jamaica

had yet to outline how it would implement the reforms.

In Chile, the crimes of members of the security forces who beat, ill-treated and sometimes even killed peaceful demonstrators and others went largely unpunished. Military courts – which dealt with cases of human rights violations committed by members of the security forces – regularly failed to adequately investigate and prosecute officers suspected of having committed a crime, with trials usually failing to meet the most basic levels of independence and impartiality.

In July, a court in Paraguay sentenced a group of peasant farmers to up to 30 years' imprisonment for the murder of six police officers and other related crimes, in the context of a 2012 land dispute in the Curuguaty district. No investigation was opened into the deaths of 11 peasant farmers in the same incident, however. The General Prosecutor failed to provide a credible explanation for the lack of investigation into these deaths, or to respond to allegations that the crime scene had been tampered with and that peasant farmers had been tortured while in police custody.

By the end of the year – and two years after a US Senate report on the issue – no one had been brought to justice in the USA for human rights violations committed in the secret CIA detention and interrogation programme after the attacks of 11 September 2001.

The prosecution in Mexico of five marines – who were accused of the enforced disappearance of a man who was found dead weeks after his arrest in 2013 – was a positive step that offered hope of a new approach to tackling the country's wave of disappearances. Across the country, the fate and whereabouts of tens of thousands of people remained unknown.

In countries including Argentina, Bolivia, Chile and Peru, ongoing impunity and lack of political will to investigate human rights violations and crimes under international law – including thousands of extrajudicial executions and enforced disappearances –

that were perpetrated in the context of military dictatorships in previous decades continued to deny victims and their families truth, justice and reparation.

However, in Argentina former de facto President Reynaldo Bignone was sentenced to 20 years in prison for his role in hundreds of enforced disappearances during a region-wide intelligence operation; 14 other military officers were also sentenced to prison terms. The rulings were a positive step for justice that, it was hoped, might open the door to further investigations.

Although progress to address impunity in Guatemala was slow, in a landmark decision two former military officials were found guilty of crimes against humanity for the sexual and domestic slavery and sexual violence they inflicted on Indigenous Maya Q'eqchi' women.

In July, El Salvador's Supreme Court declared the Amnesty Law unconstitutional. This marked an important step forward for justice for crimes under international law and other human rights violations committed during the 1980-1992 armed conflict.

In Haiti, no progress was made in the investigation into alleged crimes against humanity committed by former President Jean-Claude Duvalier and his former collaborators.

RIGHTS OF WOMEN AND GIRLS

States made little headway in tackling violence against women and girls. This included failing to protect them from rape and killings as well as failing to hold perpetrators accountable. Reports of gender-based violence came from Brazil, Canada, the Dominican Republic, El Salvador, Jamaica, Nicaragua, the USA and Venezuela, among other countries.

Numerous violations of sexual and reproductive rights had a significant impact on the health of women and girls. The Americas had the highest number of countries with a total ban on abortion. In some countries, women were thrown in prison simply for being suspected of having

had an abortion, sometimes after suffering miscarriages.

Women living in poverty across Nicaragua continued to be the main victims of maternal mortality, and the country had one of the highest teenage pregnancy rates in the region. Women there were also subjected to some of the world's harshest abortion laws; abortion remained banned in all circumstances, even when vital to save a woman's life. In the Dominican Republic, a reform to the Criminal Code that would decriminalize abortion in certain cases was again delayed. Legislative reform proposed to decriminalize abortion in Chile continued to be discussed.

There were, however, small signs of hope. In El Salvador, a court decision to release María Teresa Rivera – who had served four years of a 40-year prison sentence after miscarrying her pregnancy – was a step towards justice in a country where women were treated appallingly. In another human rights victory, a woman sentenced to eight years in prison in Argentina after having a miscarriage was released from detention after a Supreme Court ruling that there were insufficient reasons to keep her detained.

INDIGENOUS PEOPLES' RIGHTS

In June, the American Declaration on the Rights of Indigenous Peoples was adopted by the OAS, after 17 years of negotiations.

In spite of this, Indigenous Peoples across the Americas continued to be victims of violence as well as killings and excessive use of force by the police, with their rights over their land, territory, natural resources and culture often abused. The daily reality for thousands was a life overshadowed by exclusion, poverty, inequality and systemic discrimination – including in Argentina, Brazil, Chile, Colombia, Ecuador, Mexico, Peru and Paraguay.

State and non-state actors – including landowners and businesses – were responsible for forcibly displacing Indigenous Peoples from their own land, in the pursuit of their own economic profit.

Development projects – including by the extractive industry – threatened Indigenous Peoples' culture, sometimes leading to the forced displacement of entire communities. Yet Indigenous Peoples were frequently denied meaningful consultation and free, prior and informed consent. Indigenous and peasant women across the Americas demanded greater attention to the impact on women of natural resource extraction projects and enhanced participation in decision-making processes about development projects impacting their land and territories.

In May, leaders of the Indigenous and Afro-descendant Rama-Kriol communities said that an agreement for the construction of the Grand Interoceanic Canal had been signed without an effective consultation process. There was a surge in violence in Nicaragua's North Atlantic Autonomous Region, where Indigenous Miskitu Peoples were threatened, attacked, subjected to sexual violence, killed and forcibly displaced by non-Indigenous settlers.

Positive developments included the Canadian government announcing the launch of a national inquiry into missing and murdered Indigenous women and girls.

RIGHTS OF LESBIAN, GAY, BISEXUAL, TRANSGENDER AND INTERSEX PEOPLE

Legislative and institutional progress in some countries – such as the legal recognition of same-sex marriage – did not necessarily translate into better protection against violence and discrimination for LGBTI people.

Across the Americas, high levels of hate crime, advocacy of hatred and discrimination, as well as murders and persecution of LGBTI activists persisted in countries including Argentina, the Bahamas, the Dominican Republic, El Salvador, Haiti, Honduras, Jamaica, the USA and Venezuela.

However, in the Dominican Republic the electoral process during the year saw several openly LGBTI candidates run for seats to increase their political visibility and participation.

ASIA-PACIFIC REGIONAL OVERVIEW

While many governments in the Asia Pacific region – home to 60% of the world's population – increasingly repressed people's human rights, there were also signs of positive change in some countries and contexts.

There were loud and insistent demands for freedom of expression and justice, and activism and protests against violations grew. Young people were increasingly determined to speak out for their and others' rights. Online technologies and social media offered expanded opportunities to share information, expose injustices, to organize and advocate. Repeatedly, human rights defenders – often working in the most difficult circumstances and with limited resources – stood firm against heavy-handed state oppression, taking inspirational and courageous action.

Yet the price was often high. Many governments displayed an appalling disregard for freedom, justice and dignity. They strove to muzzle opposing voices and suppress protest and activism, including online dissent, through crackdowns, by force or cynical deployment of old and new laws.

In East Asia, governmental transparency diminished and the perception of a growing gap between governments and their citizens increased. This was compounded by entrenched repression in countries such as China and the Democratic People's Republic of Korea (North Korea). A pattern of deepening intolerance towards criticism and open debate unfolded in South Asia, with bloggers murdered in Bangladesh, media workers assailed in Pakistan and space for civil society in countries such as India shrinking. In Southeast Asia, key rights – freedoms of thought, conscience, religion, opinion, expression, association and assembly – came under extensive assault, with crackdowns by Thailand's military regime and attempts to mute political voices in Malaysia.

As the space for civil society shrank in many countries, discrimination – particularly against racial and ethnic minorities, and women and girls – expanded in a range of countries and contexts.

In many states – including China, Malaysia, Maldives, Nepal, North Korea, the Philippines, Singapore, Thailand, Timor-Leste and Viet Nam – torture and other ill-treatment was among the tools used to target human rights defenders, marginalized groups and others.

Such violations were often sustained by a failure to ensure accountability for torturers and other perpetrators of human rights violations. Impunity was pernicious, frequently chronic, and common to many states. Victims were denied justice, truth and other forms of redress. There was some progress on this front, however. They included slow steps towards delivering accountability for alleged crimes under international law that had plagued Sri Lanka for decades, although widespread impunity persisted; and the bilateral agreement between Japan and the Republic of Korea (South Korea) on the military sexual slavery system before and during World War II which was nonetheless criticized for excluding survivors from its negotiations. In a historic ruling, a court in the Philippines convicted a police officer of torture for the first time under the 2009 Anti-Torture Act. The Office of the Prosecutor of the International Criminal Court indicated that it might soon open an investigation in Afghanistan, which could cover allegations of crimes by the Taliban, the Afghan government and US forces.

In Myanmar, intensification of the conflict in Kachin State, and an eruption of violence in northern Rakhine State – where a security operation forced members of the Rohingya and Rakhine communities to flee their homes – aggravated an already serious human rights and humanitarian situation in which tens of thousands of people had been displaced by violence in recent years. Government restrictions prevented access to humanitarian aid in both states. Afghanistan's armed conflict continued due to a resurgent Taliban, inflicting a devastating toll on civilians.

Armed groups fuelled insecurity and suffering in several countries committing abuses such as abductions and unlawful killings in central and northeastern India and in Jammu and Kashmir state. Bombings and shootings in Indonesia by the armed group calling itself Islamic State (IS) illustrated an utter disregard for the right to life. In Afghanistan armed groups carried out horrific attacks in the capital, Kabul, including on aid agency CARE International, which targeted civilians in an act that constituted a war crime.

The regional backdrop of repression, conflict and insecurity fuelled the global refugee crisis. Across the region, millions became refugees and asylum-seekers, forced from their homes often into appalling and life-threatening conditions. Many were stranded in precarious situations, vulnerable to myriad further abuses. In countries such as Australia and Thailand, governments exacerbated suffering by sending people back to countries where they risked human rights violations. Many others were displaced in their own countries.

Corporations were frequently active or complicit in abuses. The South Korean government allowed private companies to hinder lawful trade union activity, only belatedly addressing ill-health and even deaths caused by exposure to harmful products. In India, the US-based Dow Chemical Company and its subsidiary Union Carbide Corporation failed again to appear before a Bhopal court on criminal charges related to the 1984 gas leak disaster.

The region was frequently at odds with the global trend towards abolition of the death penalty. China remained the world's most prolific executioner, even though the actual figures remained a state secret. In Pakistan, the number of people executed – since 2014 when it lifted a moratorium on executions – rose to more than 400. In contravention of international standards, some of those executed were juveniles at the time of the offence, some had a mental disability, and others had been sentenced after unfair trials. In Japan, executions were shrouded in secrecy. In Maldives, officials threatened to resume executions after a 60-year moratorium. In the Philippines, draft legislation to reintroduce the death penalty was put before Congress. More positively, Nauru became the 103rd country to repeal the death penalty for all crimes.

Major developments included Myanmar's new quasi-civilian government to which Aung San Suu Kyi was appointed de facto leader, a role especially created for her after the National League for Democracy party's election victory in 2015. The new government took steps to improve human rights but faced daunting challenges bequeathed by half a century of repressive military rule. Its power was constrained by the military's enduring influence, including its control of key ministries and retention of a quarter of parliamentary seats. There was little improvement in Myanmar's ongoing conflicts, the Rohingya's plight, humanitarian assistance for displaced communities, impunity for human rights violators and reformation of repressive laws.

In the Philippines, state-sanctioned violence, typically in the form of unlawful killings, occurred on a massive scale under Rodrigo Duterte's presidency. The brutal crackdown on those suspected of involvement in drug crimes led to over 6,000 people killed in the so-called "war on drugs".

In February, the devastating impact of Cyclone Winston on Fiji highlighted the country's inadequate infrastructure when 62,000 people were displaced after their homes were destroyed; discrimination against some groups in aid distribution and a shortage of building materials failed those most in need.

In May, Sri Lanka ratified the International Convention against Enforced Disappearance. It remains to be seen whether Sri Lanka will make enforced disappearance a specific crime in its domestic law. Fiji ratified the UN Convention against Torture with reservations although accountability for torture and other

MURDOCK LEARNING RESOURCE CENTER

ill-treatment was hindered by constitutional immunities and a lack of political will.

EAST ASIA
HUMAN RIGHTS DEFENDERS

In East Asia, human rights defenders came under concerted attacks, with a narrowing space for civil society to raise issues deemed contentious by the authorities.

In China's continuing crackdown under Xi Jinping's rule, human rights defenders, lawyers, journalists and activists faced increasing and systematic intimidation and harassment, including arbitrary arrest and torture and other ill-treatment. Family members of those detained were also subject to police surveillance, harassment and restriction of their freedom of movement. The authorities increased the use of "residential surveillance at a designated location" which allowed police to hold individuals for up to six months outside the formal detention system, without access to legal counsel of their choice or their families. There was also an increase in detainees being forced to make televised "confessions". The authorities continued to block thousands of websites. In Guangdong province, China cracked down on workers and labour rights activists, frequently denying detainees access to lawyers on "national security" pretexts.

The Chinese government also drafted or enacted laws and regulations under the pretext of enhancing national security, but which could be used to silence dissent and suppress human rights defenders under broadly defined offences such as "inciting subversion" and "leaking state secrets". There were fears that the new Foreign Non-Governmental Organizations Management Law could be used to intimidate and prosecute human rights defenders and NGOs, and the new Cyber Security Law could undermine freedom of expression and privacy.

Yet activists dared to be innovative. Four human rights defenders were arrested for commemorating the 27th anniversary of the 4 June 1989 Tiananmen Square crackdown.

They posted an online advertisement for a popular alcohol with a label reading "Remember, Eight Liquor Six Four" – a play on words in Chinese echoing the date of the notorious event, accompanied by "tank man's" picture. The action was covered widely on social media before being censored.

In October, Ilham Tohti – a well-known Uyghur intellectual who fostered dialogue between Uyghurs and Han Chinese – received the 2016 Martin Ennals Award for Human Rights Defenders awarded for deep commitment in the face of great risk. He is currently serving a life sentence on "separatism" charges.

In Hong Kong, students Joshua Wong, Alex Chow and Nathan Law were convicted of "taking part in an unlawful assembly" in connection with their roles in the 2014 events that triggered the pro-democracy Umbrella Movement.

North Korea exercised extreme repression, violating almost the full spectrum of human rights. There were severe restrictions on freedom of expression and no domestic independent media or civil society organizations. Up to 120,000 individuals continued to be held in prison camps where torture and other ill-treatment, including forced labour, was widespread and routine. State control, oppression and intimidation intensified since Kim Jung-un came to power in 2011. The persistent stranglehold on use of communication technology – designed in part to isolate citizens and obscure the appalling human rights situation – continued. People caught using mobile phones to contact loved ones abroad faced incarceration in political prison camps or detention facilities.

In neighbouring South Korea, regressive human rights trends included restrictions on freedoms of peaceful assembly and expression which took new forms such as civil lawsuits. The authorities undercut press freedom through heavier interference with news reporting and the restriction on the exercise of the right to freedom of peaceful assembly, often under the pretext of protecting public order.

The South Korean National Assembly passed an anti-terrorism law substantially expanding powers of surveillance of communications and the collection of personal information of people suspected of terrorist links.

In Mongolia, civil society organizations working for human rights protection faced regular intimidation, harassment and threats mainly by private actors.

In a positive development in Taiwan, the new government dropped charges against more than 100 protesters who participated in the 2014 student-led protests against the Cross Straits Services Trade Agreement between Taiwan and China, known as the "Sunflower Movement". The new Prime Minister, Lin Chuan, stated that the previous government's decision to charge the protesters was a "political reaction" rather than a "legal case".

PEOPLE ON THE MOVE

Japan continued to reject most asylum applications. The South Korean immigration service held more than 100 asylum-seekers for months at Incheon International Airport, including 28 men from Syria whom a court eventually ruled should be released and allowed to apply for asylum. Dozens of asylum-seekers from other countries such as Egypt remained detained at the airport in inhumane conditions.

DISCRIMINATION

Japan's parliament passed its first national law against the advocacy of hatred or hate speech against residents of overseas origin and their descendants, following an increase in pro-discrimination demonstrations. Critics said the law was too narrow and did not contain penalties. Discrimination against sexual or ethnic minorities remained severe.

In China, freedom of religion was systematically violated. Draft amendments to legislation contained provisions to increase state power to control and sanction some religious practices, again in the name of national security to curb "infiltration and extremism". If passed it could be used to further supress in particular the rights to freedom of religion and of belief of Christian communities unrecognized by the state, Tibetan Buddhists and Uighur Muslims. In the Xinjiang Uighur Autonomous Region, the government detained ethnic Uighur writers and Uighur language website editors.

Ethnic Tibetans faced ongoing discrimination and restrictions on their rights to freedom of thought, conscience and religion, expression, association and peaceful assembly. Tibetan blogger Druklo was sentenced to three years' imprisonment for "inciting separatism", including for his online posts on religious freedom and the Dalai Lama. In the Xinjiang Uighur Autonomous Region, the government continued to violate the right to freedom of religion, and cracked down on unauthorized religious gatherings.

SOUTH ASIA
HUMAN RIGHTS DEFENDERS

Human rights defenders were targeted for violations throughout South Asia in several ways. Governments used draconian legislation and new laws aimed at censoring online expression.

India used repressive laws to curb freedom of expression and silence critics. The Foreign Contribution (Regulation) Act was used to restrict civil society organizations receiving foreign funding, and to harass NGOs. The sedition law – used by the British to curb free expression during India's independence struggle – was deployed to harass critics. Human rights defenders also faced intimidation and attacks. Journalist Karun Mishra was killed by gunmen in Uttar Pradesh state, apparently for reporting on illegal soil mining. Rajdeo Ranjan, a journalist who had faced threats from political leaders for his writing, was also shot dead.

In Jammu and Kashmir, security forces used unnecessary or excessive force against demonstrators. The Jammu and Kashmir government also imposed a curfew for over two months. A suspension on private landline, mobile and internet service providers undermined a range of rights and residents said it left them unable to reach urgent medical assistance.

Pakistani media workers faced occupational hazards like abduction, arbitrary arrest and detention, intimidation, killings and harassment by state and non-state actors. A grenade attack on ARY TV's offices in the capital, Islamabad, was one of many strikes against media workers, and freedom of expression generally. Pamphlets left at the scene claimed that an armed group allied to IS was responsible.

In Sri Lanka, Sandhya Eknaligoda – wife of disappeared dissident cartoonist Prageeth Eknaligoda – faced repeated threats and other intimidation after the police identified seven suspects, members of army intelligence, in connection with his enforced disappearance. This intimidation included protests outside the court hearing her husband's habeas corpus case, and a poster campaign accusing her of supporting the Liberation Tigers of Tamil Eelam (LTTE).

Freedom of expression continued to be under attack in Bangladesh where the authorities grew increasingly intolerant of independent media and critical voices. Amid the severely deteriorating human rights situation, a string of journalists were arrested and arbitrarily detained; peaceful dissent was suppressed under draconian laws invoked to hound critics on social media. Student activist Dilip Roy was detained for criticizing the Prime Minister on Facebook, and faced a possible 14-year prison sentence under the vaguely worded Information and Communications Technology Act, used by the authorities to threaten and punish people who peacefully expressed views they disliked.

In Maldives, where human rights had been under increased attack in recent years, the government intensified assaults on freedoms of expression and assembly by imposing arbitrary restrictions to prevent protest. Authorities also silenced political opponents, human rights defenders, and journalists, using legislation criminalizing "defamatory" speech, remarks and other actions.

PEOPLE ON THE MOVE

Due to its ongoing conflict, Afghanistan was the world's second-largest refugee-producing country. The crisis affected huge numbers of people with over two million in Pakistan and Iran alone and large numbers trying to reach the EU. An EU-Afghanistan deal required Afghanistan to re-admit any Afghan citizen who had not been granted asylum in the EU. However, continuing instability made it impossible for many refugees and asylum-seekers to return home voluntarily in safety.

Although Afghans risking their lives on dangerous journeys to Europe made headlines, the vast majority lacked the resources to leave. The number of people forced to flee their homes and becoming internally displaced reached an estimated 1.4 million in 2016, more than twice that of the three previous years. In the same three-year period, international aid to Afghanistan halved as donors' attention shifted following the withdrawal of international troops. The plight of those suffering in appalling conditions and struggling to survive in overcrowded camps with inadequate shelter, food, water and health care was at risk of being forgotten.

For Afghan refugees in Pakistan, the situation was bleak as the Pakistani government planned one of the largest forcible returns of refugees in modern history putting about 1.4 million people, whose registration was expected to expire at the end of the year, at risk. The authorities imposed several unfeasible deadlines, which they then reluctantly extended, for the return of refugees to Afghanistan. The move triggered waves of harassment from police and officials and the refugees were left trapped in the uncertain limbo of their camps.

In other instances, Pakistan breached the principle of *non-refoulement* and placed Afghan refugees at risk of serious abuses. For example, the decision to deport Sharbat Gula back to a country she had not seen in a generation and which her children had never known was emblematic of Pakistan's cruel treatment of Afghan refugees. She was the iconic "Afghan girl" featured on the cover of a 1985 *National Geographic* magazine, and was for decades the world's most famous refugee, a symbol of Pakistan's status as a generous host.

DISCRIMINATION

Thousands protested against discrimination and violence faced by Dalit communities. Marginalized communities continued to be frequently overlooked in the government's push for faster economic growth. Millions demonstrated against changes to labour laws. Black people faced racist harassment, discrimination and violence in various cities. Reports of violent crimes as well as sexual violence against women and girls rose while perpetrators enjoyed impunity, and women from marginalized communities faced systemic discrimination. Indian law criminalized soliciting in public places, leaving sex workers vulnerable to a range of abuses.

Section 377 of India's Penal Code continued to criminalize consensual same-sex relations, despite legal challenges before the Supreme Court. India's cabinet approved a flawed bill on transgender people's rights, which was criticized by activists for its problematic definition of transgender people and inadequate anti-discrimination provisions.

There was a spree of apparently militant-inspired killings and other attacks in Bangladesh, where the authorities arrested nearly 15,000 people in a delayed response to a spate of attacks against bloggers, atheists, foreign nationals and lesbian, gay, bisexual, transgender and intersex (LGBTI) people. The government frequently compromised its obligation to pursue those responsible using measures such as arbitrary and secret detention. Lack of protection for peaceful activists was further underscored by attacks for which no one was held accountable, such as the brutal killing of Xulhaz Mannan, editor of an LGBTI magazine, and his friend Tanay Mojumdar. Human rights activists under similar threat said that the police offered insufficient protection, while others were reluctant to approach the police fearing they would be charged or harassed.

In Sri Lanka, LGBTI people faced harassment, discrimination and violence. High levels of impunity persisted for perpetrators of violence against women and girls, including rape by military personnel, and inadequate efforts were made to address domestic violence. Tamils complained of ethnic profiling, surveillance and harassment by police suspecting them of LTTE links; the UN Committee on the Elimination of Racial Discrimination found that the Sri Lanka Prevention of Terrorism Act was used disproportionately against Tamils. Christians and Muslims were reportedly harassed, threatened and attacked including by supporters of hardline Sinhala Buddhist political groups, with police failing to act or blaming religious minorities for inciting opponents to violence.

SOUTHEAST ASIA AND THE PACIFIC

HUMAN RIGHTS DEFENDERS

Human rights defenders were under threat in Cambodia, Malaysia, Thailand, Viet Nam and other countries including through increased use of new or existing laws which criminalized peaceful expression.

In Thailand, ongoing suppression of peaceful dissent since the 2014 military coup created an environment in which few dared to criticize the authorities publicly. Human rights defenders faced charges of criminal defamation for speaking out about violations or for supporting vulnerable individuals and communities. The government moved to shut down debate ahead of a referendum on a draft Constitution; in one example, around a dozen people commenting on the proposed Constitution on Facebook were detained or charged, and faced up to 10 years' imprisonment under a draconian new government order.

Crackdowns on freedoms of expression, association and peaceful assembly intensified ahead of Cambodia's elections planned for 2017/2018, and the authorities increasingly abused the criminal justice system. The security forces harassed and punished civil society in attempts to silence critics; human rights defenders were threatened, arrested and detained for their peaceful work; and the political opposition was targeted, with activists and officials imprisoned after unfair trials. The authorities continued to hinder peaceful protest.

In Malaysia, attempts to choke peaceful dissent and freedom of speech included the widespread use of national security legislation and other restrictive laws. Rafizi Ramli – a whistle-blowing parliamentarian who exposed information about major corruption – was sentenced to 18 months in prison. Journalists at news site Malaysiakini faced intimidation and threats from vigilantes.

In Viet Nam, human rights defenders faced threats and attacks. Prisoners of conscience were held in prisons and detention centres, and subjected to enforced disappearance, torture and other ill-treatment, including torture with electricity, severe beatings, prolonged solitary confinement sometimes in total darkness and silence, and denial of medical treatment.

The Vietnamese authorities also oversaw suppression of peaceful protesters. As the country hosted a visit by US President Barack Obama in May, the authorities arrested, intimidated and harassed peaceful activists.

Myanmar's new National League for Democracy-led government took steps to amend long-standing repressive laws targeting activists and media workers. Yet cases like the detention of two media workers in November, on suspicion of "online defamation" over an article on allegations of government corruption, showed that much more needed to be done.

Security forces in Timor-Leste were accused of unlawful killings, torture and other ill-treatment, arbitrary arrests, and the arbitrary restriction of freedom of expression and peaceful assembly. Fiji's media was affected by arbitrary restrictions curtailing freedom of expression. Bloggers and dissidents in Singapore were harassed and prosecuted.

Human rights defenders and journalists in the Philippines were targeted and killed by unidentified gunmen and armed militia.

PEOPLE ON THE MOVE

Australia maintained its abusive offshore immigration processing regime on Nauru and Manus Island in Papua New Guinea. Australia's transfer agreement with Nauru contravened international law and effectively trapped refugees and asylum-seekers in an open-air prison. Although not technically detained, these people could not leave and were isolated on the remote Pacific island of Nauru, even when officially recognized as refugees.

The Australian government's policy of "processing" refugees and asylum-seekers on Nauru involved a deliberate and systematic regime of neglect and cruelty, designed to inflict suffering: the system amounted to torture under international law. It minimized protection and maximized harm and was constructed to prevent some of the world's most vulnerable people from seeking safety in Australia.

Mental illness and self-harm among refugees and asylum-seekers in Nauru were commonplace. Omid Masoumali, an Iranian refugee, died after setting himself on fire. Others, including children, suffered inadequate health care, persistent verbal and physical attacks, pervasive hostility, and arbitrary arrests and detentions, with systematic impunity for these types of abuses.

Australia refused to close its centres on Nauru and Manus Island and even planned to introduce a law permanently banning those trapped there from getting an Australian visa, piling injustice onto injustice in violation of international law.

New Zealand publicly reiterated an agreement made with Australia in 2013 to annually resettle 150 refugees from Nauru and Manus Island, although Australia since refused to carry out the deal.

Conditions in Malaysia's overcrowded immigration detention centres were harsh. One thousand people, including over 400 Rohingya – who had been stranded off Malaysia's coastline until the authorities agreed to accept them in May 2015 – endured prolonged detention for over a year in harsh conditions. In June, the majority of the Rohingya were released and some were resettled.

Thailand's lack of legal framework, processes or procedures for hosting refugees and asylum-seekers left many vulnerable to arbitrary detention and other violations of their rights. In the absence of a recognized legal status under Thai law, refugees and asylum-seekers, including children, continued to be treated as irregular migrants and under the Immigration Act could be detained indefinitely in immigration detention centres, which might not meet international standards of detention.

Scores of Rohingya from Myanmar were among those detained in immigration centres, having been held since their arrival by boat in 2015.

The Indonesian authorities engaged in crude intimidation tactics in Aceh, including by endangering the lives of a group of over 40 Sri Lankan Tamil asylum-seekers – among them were a heavily pregnant woman and nine children – by firing warning shots and threatening to push them back out to sea, in violation of international law.

DISCRIMINATION

Tens of thousands of people from Myanmar's Rohingya minority fled northern Rakhine State, where security forces mounted reprisal attacks in response to an assault on three border outposts which killed nine police officers in October. The security forces, led by the military, randomly fired at villagers, torched hundreds of homes, carried out arbitrary arrests, and raped women and girls. Villagers were placed under night curfews and humanitarian agencies were barred from the area. The response amounted to collective punishment of the entire Rohingya community in northern Rakhine State and may have amounted to crimes against humanity. Many Rohingya refugees and asylum-seekers who made it to Bangladesh in desperate need of humanitarian assistance were pushed back into Myanmar.

The crisis arose in a context of unrelenting and severe discrimination against the Rohingya community, in which a number of rights including freedom of movement remained restricted. There was also continuing religious intolerance – exacerbated in recent years by the previous government's failure to effectively investigate violent incidents – often fuelled by hardline Buddhist nationalist groups and directed particularly against Muslims.

The Indonesian authorities often appeared to be more concerned about hardline religious groups than respecting and protecting human rights. For example, the Governor of Jakarta, the capital, a Christian and the first member of Indonesia's ethnic Chinese community to be elected to that position, underwent a criminal investigation on suspicion of "blasphemy". Discrimination against LGBTI people increased after officials made inflammatory, grossly inaccurate and misleading statements.

In Papua New Guinea violence against women was widespread and sex workers were beaten, raped, arbitrarily detained and killed without recourse to justice. They were not adequately protected largely because of laws criminalizing sex work, the stigmatization of sex work and social and cultural norms.

The UN Human Rights Committee and the UN Committee on the Rights of the Child criticized New Zealand's high rates of incarceration, child poverty and domestic violence of Indigenous Māori. Sexual and other physical violence against women and girls also remained widespread despite wide recognition of the problem and efforts to address it.

EUROPE AND CENTRAL ASIA REGIONAL OVERVIEW

On 30 November 2016, "Ahmed H", a Syrian man living in Cyprus, stood trial on terrorism charges in Szeged, in Hungary. He was accused of orchestrating clashes between police and refugees following the sudden closure of Hungary's border with Serbia in September 2015. His prosecution played to the government's conflation of Muslim asylum-seekers with terrorist threats. In reality, Ahmed H was only there because he was helping his elderly Syrian parents flee their war-torn country. Caught in the melee, he admitted to throwing stones at the police, but, for the most part, as numerous witnesses testified, he had been trying to calm the crowd. Nevertheless, he was convicted, becoming a tragic, chilling symbol of a continent turning its back on human rights.

In 2016 populist movements and messages burst into the mainstream. Politicians across the region tapped into widespread feelings of alienation and insecurity. Their targets were many: political elites, the EU, immigration, liberal media, Muslims, foreign nationals, globalization, gender equality and the ever-present threat of terrorism. In power, in countries like Poland and Hungary, they achieved most, but also further west, they forced anxious establishment parties to borrow many of their clothes and usher in many of their policies. The result was a pervasive weakening of the rule of law and an erosion in the protection of human rights, particularly for refugees and terrorism suspects, but ultimately for everyone.

Further east, long-established strongmen strengthened their grip on power. In Tajikistan, Azerbaijan and Turkmenistan, constitutional amendments extending presidential terms were ushered in. In Russia, President Vladimir Putin continued to surf the wave of popularity generated by Russia's excursions in Ukraine and its resurgent influence internationally, while undermining civil society at home. Across the former Soviet Union, the repression of dissent and political opposition remained surgical and constant.

The region's most tumultuous developments took place in Turkey, which was shaken by ongoing clashes in the southeast, a series of bombings and shootings and a violent coup attempt in July. The government's backsliding on human rights accelerated dramatically in its wake. Having identified one-time ally turned bitter foe Fethullah Gulen as responsible, the Turkish authorities moved with speed to crush the extensive movement he had created. Around 90,000 civil servants, most of them presumed Gulenists, were dismissed by executive decree. At least 40,000 people were remanded in custody, amid widespread allegations of torture and other ill-treatment. Hundreds of media outlets and NGOs were closed down and journalists, academics and MPs were arrested as the crackdown progressively moved beyond the nexus of the coup and weaved in other dissenters and pro-Kurdish voices.

PEOPLE ON THE MOVE

Following the arrival by sea of just over a million refugees and migrants in 2015, EU member states were determined to dramatically reduce their number in 2016. In this they succeeded, but only at the considerable, and quite deliberate, expense of their rights and welfare.

At the end of December, around 358,000 refugees and migrants had made the crossing into Europe. There was a modest increase in numbers taking the central Mediterranean route (up to around 170,000), but a sharp decline in numbers arriving on the Greek islands (down from 854,000 to 173,000), owing almost entirely to the migration control deal between EU and Turkey agreed in March. The International

Organization for Migration estimated that a record 5,000 people died at sea compared to around 3,700 last year.

The EU-Turkey deal was the EU's signature response to the so-called "refugee crisis". Turkey was offered €6 billion to police its coastline and accept the return of asylum-seekers who made it across to the Greek islands. The deal was premised on the untrue assertion that Turkey offered asylum-seekers all the protections they would be entitled to in the EU. With a barely functioning asylum system in place, and nearly three million Syrian refugees already struggling to get by, the claim stood testimony to the EU's willingness to ignore the rights and livelihoods of refugees to suit its political purposes.

Even though the numbers of new arrivals slowed to a few thousand a month on average, the reception capacity on the Greek islands was still severely stretched. By the end of the year, some 12,000 refugees and asylum-seekers were stranded there in increasingly overcrowded, insanitary and dangerous conditions in makeshift centres. The poor conditions periodically sparked riots within the camps, while some were attacked by locals accused of links to far right groups. Conditions for the around 50,000 refugees and migrants on the Greek mainland were only marginally better. By the end of the year, most had found shelter in official reception facilities. However, these mostly consisted of tents and abandoned warehouses and were unsuitable for accommodation for more than a few days.

As the year drew to a close, the EU-Turkey deal remained in place, but looked increasingly fragile. By then it was clear, however, that it was only a first line of defence. The second initiative to stop people arriving in Europe was the closure of the Balkan route above Greece in March. Macedonia and successive Balkan countries were prevailed upon to close their borders and assisted in the task by border guards from different European countries. The move was initially championed by Hungarian Prime Minister Viktor Orbán, then taken up by Austria. For many EU leaders, the misery of

refugees trapped in Greece was clearly a price worth paying to discourage more from coming.

The lack of solidarity with refugees and fellow EU member states was typical of the migration policies of most EU countries, which united in their plans to restrict entry and expedite return. This became apparent in the failure of the EU's flagship relocation scheme. Adopted by EU heads of state in September, with a view to distributing the responsibility for receiving the large number of refugees arriving in a small number of countries, the plan foresaw the relocation of 120,000 people from Italy, Greece and Hungary across the EU within two years. After Hungary rejected the scheme, figuring it would be better off simply closing its borders altogether, its quota was reallocated to Greece and Italy. By the end of the year, only around 6,000 people had been relocated from Greece and just under 2,000 from Italy.

The relocation scheme was coupled with another EU initiative from 2015: the "hotspot approach". This EU Commission-inspired plan foresaw large processing centres in Italy and Greece to identify and fingerprint new arrivals, swiftly assess their protection needs and either process their asylum applications, relocate them to other EU countries or return them to their country of origin (or for those arriving in Greece, to Turkey). With the relocation component of the plan effectively falling away, Italy and Greece were left facing enormous pressure to fingerprint, process and return as many migrants as possible. There were incidents of ill-treatment being used to secure fingerprints, arbitrary detention of migrants and collective expulsions. In August, a group of 40 people, many from Darfur, were returned to Sudan shortly after a Memorandum of Understanding was signed by Italian and Sudanese police. Upon arrival in Sudan, the migrants were interrogated by the Sudanese National Intelligence and Security Service, an agency implicated in serious human rights violations.

The drive to return as many migrants as possible increasingly became a key feature of

EU and member state foreign policy. In October the EU and Afghanistan signed the co-operation agreement "Joint Way Forward". Signed on the back of a donor conference, the agreement obliged Afghanistan to collaborate in the return of failed Afghan asylum-seekers (asylum recognition rates for Afghans fell in most countries despite growing insecurity in the country), including unaccompanied minors.

The central place of migration management in EU foreign policy was explicitly laid out in another document, the "Partnership Framework", endorsed by the European Council in June. The plan proposed using aid, trade and other funds to pressure countries to reduce the number of migrants reaching EU shores, while negotiating border control co-operation and re-admission agreements including with serial human rights abusing countries.

The drive to externalize Europe's migration management went hand in glove with measures to restrict access to asylum and related benefits nationally. The trend was particularly observable in previously generous Nordic countries: Finland, Sweden, Denmark and Norway all introduced regressive amendments to their asylum legislation, the last with the intention to ensure that Norway had "the strictest refugee policy in Europe". Finland, Sweden and Denmark, as well as Germany, all restricted or delayed access to family reunification for refugees.

States closest to the EU main external borders adopted the strictest measures. In January, the Austrian government announced a cap of 37,500 asylum applications for the year. In April, an amendment to the Asylum Act granted the government the power to declare an emergency in the event of the arrival of large numbers of asylum-seekers, triggering the accelerated processing of applications at the border and the immediate return, without reasoned motivation, of those rejected.

The deterioration of Europe's asylum system hit its lowest point in Hungary. After constructing a fence along the majority of its border with Serbia in September 2015 and amending its asylum legislation, in 2016 the Hungarian government ushered in a set of measures which resulted in violent push-backs at the border with Serbia; unlawful detentions inside the country and poor living conditions for those waiting at the border. While the Hungarian government spent millions of euros on a xenophobic advertising campaign in support of its ultimately failed referendum to reject the EU relocation scheme, refugees were left to languish. Infringement proceedings initiated by the European Commission for the multiple breaches of EU and international asylum law remained open at the end of the year.

At the opposite end of Europe, in France, the build-up of asylum-seekers and migrants at the "Jungle" camp in Calais and its dismantling in October became as much a symbol of Europe's failed migration policies as the bursting camps on the Greek islands Lesvos and Chios and the makeshift shelters in front of Hungary's razor wire fences.

Germany's impressive efforts to shelter and process the asylum applications of the almost one million people who arrived in Germany the year before was perhaps the only positive government response to the "refugee crisis" in Europe. Overall, it was left to ordinary citizens to show the solidarity their leaders were lacking. In countless reception centres across Europe, tens of thousands of people showed again and again that there was another side to the increasingly toxic migration debate by welcoming and supporting refugees and migrants.

COUNTER-TERROR AND SECURITY

Over a hundred people were killed and many more injured in violent attacks in France, Belgium and Germany. They were shot by armed men, blown up by suicide bombers and deliberately run over as they walked in the street. Protecting the right to life and enabling people to live, to move and to think freely became an increasingly pressing concern for governments across Europe. However, many responded to the challenge of upholding these essential freedoms by rushing through counter-terrorism measures that undermined human rights and the very values that had come under attack.

2016 witnessed a profound paradigm shift: a move from the view that it is the role of governments to provide security so that people can enjoy their rights, to the view that governments must restrict people's rights in order to provide security. The result has been a dangerous redrawing of the boundaries between the powers of the state and the rights of individuals.

One of the most alarming developments was the effort by states to make it easier to invoke and prolong a "state of emergency". Hungary led the way with the adoption of legislation providing for sweeping executive powers in the event of a declared emergency, including the banning of public assemblies, severe restrictions on the freedom of movement and the freezing of assets with no judicial controls. The Bulgarian Parliament passed a similar set of measures at first vote in July. In December, France extended for the fifth time the state of emergency imposed following the November 2015 attacks. The emergency powers were significantly expanded in the July extension, which reintroduced house searches without prior judicial approval (a power dropped from an earlier extension) and new powers to prohibit public events on public security grounds, which were variously used to ban protests. Figures released by the government in December 2016 indicated that since November 2015, 4,292 house searches had been conducted and 612 people had been assigned to forced residency, raising concern that the emergency powers were being used disproportionately.

Measures once viewed as exceptional were embedded in ordinary criminal law in several European states. These included extensions in the period of pre-charge detention for terrorism-related suspects in Slovakia and Poland and a proposal to do the same for all charges in Belgium. In the Netherlands and Bulgaria, proposals were put before Parliament to introduce administrative control measures to restrict people's freedom of movement without prior judicial authorization.

Pioneered in the UK and France, such controls, in some cases amounting to house arrest, were imposed on the basis of secret security files leaving those affected unable to effectively challenge measures with harmful effects on their lives and families.

Hundreds of people were prosecuted, in violation of the right to freedom of expression, for offences of apologizing for or glorifying terrorism, especially in France, often for comments posted on social media, and less frequently in Spain. A proposed EU Directive on Combating Terrorism, which was still pending adoption at the end of the year, would lead to the proliferation of such laws. A proposal to prohibit the vague "promoting terrorism" was put forward in Germany, while bills setting out similar offences were put before Parliament in Belgium and the Netherlands.

Across Europe, states significantly enhanced their surveillance powers, in defiance of repeated rulings by the Court of Justice of the European Union and the European Court of Human Rights that covert surveillance and the interception and retention of communications data would violate the right to privacy unless based on a reasonable suspicion of serious criminal activity and to the extent strictly necessary for making an effective contribution to combating such activity. Both courts have repeatedly stated that national legislation on surveillance must provide sufficient guarantees against misuse, including prior authorization by a court or other independent authority. The UK introduced perhaps the most wide-ranging bulk and targeted surveillance powers with the adoption of the Investigatory Powers Act in November. Commonly referred to as the "snooper's charter", it permitted a broad range of vaguely defined interception, interference and data retention practices, and imposed new requirements on private companies to store communications data. All powers under the new law – both targeted and mass – could be authorized by a government minister after review, in most but not all cases, by a quasi-judicial body composed of members appointed by the Prime Minister. In December, the Court of Justice of the EU ruled that the UK surveillance legislation violated the right to privacy.

In addition to the UK, Austria, Switzerland, Belgium, Germany, Russia and Poland adopted new surveillance-related legislation during the year, all introducing, with minor variations, extensive powers to collect and store electronic data and conduct targeted surveillance activities on loosely defined target groups or suspected individuals with little to no judicial or other oversight. The Netherlands and Finland both had legislative proposals pending at the end of the year.

DISCRIMINATION

Across Europe, Muslims and migrants were vulnerable to racial profiling and discrimination by police, both in connection with anti-terrorism powers and during regular law enforcement operations, including identity checks.

Initiatives to combat violent extremism, often including reporting obligations on public institutions, risked alienating Muslim communities and curbing freedom of expression. Draft legislation banning full-face veils was still pending before the Dutch Parliament by the end of the year, while a similar proposal was put forward in Germany. In France several coastal municipalities sought to ban the wearing of "burkinis" on the beach. The discriminatory provisions were struck down by the Council of State, but a number of municipalities persevered regardless.

Several European countries saw an increase in hate crimes targeting asylum-seekers, Muslims and foreign nationals. In Germany there was a sharp increase in attacks on shelters for asylum-seekers, and in the UK hate crimes surged by 14% in the three months after the referendum on the UK's withdrawal from the EU (Brexit) in June compared to the same period the previous year.

Roma continued to face widespread discrimination across Europe in access to housing, education, health and employment.

Roma remained vulnerable to forced evictions across Central Europe, but also in France and Italy. There was a growing trend of courts finding in favour of evicted communities, but their decisions rarely led to improvements for the affected residents. There were positive developments in the Czech Republic; under the impulse of EU infringement proceedings, a series of reforms to reduce the over-representation of Roma in special schools came into effect with the start of the school year in September.

There was progress, albeit uneven, in the rights of lesbians, gays, bisexual, transgender and intersex (LGBTI) people. France adopted a new law scrapping medical requirements for legal gender recognition and Norway granted the right on the basis of self-identification. Similar moves were under way in Greece and Denmark. A number of countries moved to respect the rights of same-sex couples and second-parent adoptions. Italy and Slovenia adopted legislation recognizing same-sex partnerships. An LGBTI Pride March on 12 June in Kyiv, capital of Ukraine, supported by the authorities and heavily protected by police, passed without incident. With about 2,000 participants, it became the biggest-ever event of its kind in Ukraine.

At the opposite end of the spectrum, consensual same-sex acts remained criminal offences in Uzbekistan and Turkmenistan. In Kyrgyzstan, draft legislation to criminalize "fostering a positive attitude" towards "non-traditional sexual relations" was still under discussion in Parliament, and a constitutional amendment banning same-sex marriage was approved in a referendum in December. There was also push-back from increasingly organized, sometimes state-supported, conservative groups. Proposals for referendums to change constitutional definitions of marriage and family to explicitly exclude same-sex couples were blocked by the President in Georgia, but allowed to be put to Parliament by the Constitutional Court in Romania. A proposal to amend the Lithuanian Constitution to this effect passed the first of two required votes in Parliament in

June, just days after 3,000 people joined a "March for Equality" to celebrate the 2016 Baltic Pride in the capital, Vilnius.

Progress on women's rights was also fitful. Violence against women remained pervasive, despite increasingly strong legislative protections. Bulgaria, the Czech Republic and Latvia signed the Council of Europe Convention on preventing and combating violence against women (Istanbul Convention). It was ratified in Romania and Belgium. In a sharply regressive move, however, the Polish government announced its intention to withdraw from the Convention, only one year after its ratification, and despite an estimated up to one million women victims per year in the country. The ruling party also restricted sexual and reproductive rights. Following a general women's strike on 3 October, the Polish Parliament rejected a bill proposing a near total ban on abortion and criminalization of women and girls who obtained an abortion and anyone assisting or encouraging them to have an abortion. In Ireland, calls to overhaul highly restrictive abortion legislation gained increasing momentum, while the UN Committee on the Rights of the Child called on Ireland to decriminalize abortion. Abortion remained criminalized in all circumstances in Malta.

FREEDOMS OF EXPRESSION, ASSOCIATION AND PEACEFUL ASSEMBLY

The repression of dissent, critical opinion and political opposition remained the norm across the former Soviet Union. It remained particularly acute, but not noticeably worse than in previous years, in Uzbekistan, Turkmenistan and Belarus. There was a marked deterioration in Tajikistan and Kazakhstan, while Russia and Azerbaijan saw the deepening of a long-standing downward trend. Pro-Russian media came under ever greater attack in Ukraine, while pro-Ukrainian and Tatar voices were severely repressed in Crimea and within Russia. Freedom of expression was aggressively restricted in Turkey in the aftermath of the failed coup attempt. The Balkans remained a dangerous

place for investigative journalists, dozens of whom faced prosecution and beatings for exposing abuses, while within the EU, Poland, Hungary and Croatia muzzled public broadcasters.

Russia continued to tighten the noose on NGOs, using defamatory media campaigns and the "Foreign Agents Law" to target the most critical. Dozens of independent NGOs receiving foreign funding were added to the list of "foreign agents" bringing the total number to 146, of which 35 had closed down permanently. Prosecutors also brought the first criminal case for "systematic evasion of duties imposed by the law" against Valentina Cherevatenko, the founder and Chair of the Women of the Don Union. The freedom of peaceful assembly also continued to be tightly controlled.

Kazakhstan also used criminal law provisions targeting NGO leaders for the first time. Dozens of "organizers" and hundreds of participants in protests in April and May against the new land code were detained. There was an increase in prosecutions for posts on social media in violation of the right to freedom of expression, while several prominent journalists were convicted on charges of "knowingly disseminating false information" and embezzlement. In January, changes to the Law on Communications came into force requiring internet users to install a "national security certificate" which allowed authorities to scan communications and to block access to content which the authorities judged to be illegal.

Tajikistan saw a significant crackdown in the wake of the targeting of the banned opposition Islamic Renaissance Party of Tajikistan, 14 of whose leading members were sentenced to long prison terms on terrorism charges in secret trials. In August, the government issued a five-year decree giving it the right to "regulate and control" the content of all television and radio networks through the State Broadcasting Committee. Human rights defenders came under tight surveillance, while independent media outlets and journalists faced intimidation and harassment by police and the security services. The authorities continued to order internet service providers to block access to certain news or social media sites, while a new decree required internet providers and telecommunications operators to channel their services through a new single communications centre under the state-owned company Tajiktelecom.

Azerbaijan continued to repress opposition activists, human rights NGOs and independent media. Twelve prisoners of conscience were released, but 14 remained in jail at the end of the year, including Ilgar Mammadov, whose sentence was upheld by the Supreme Court in November despite the European Court of Human Rights ruling requiring his release. Amnesty International was denied entry to the country, bringing Azerbaijan in line with Uzbekistan and Turkmenistan. Public protests remained severely restricted; the few that took place were dispersed by police with excessive force and political activists were arrested for organizing them.

The media in Ukraine remained generally free, but a number of media outlets perceived as supporting pro-Russian or pro-separatist views and those particularly critical of the authorities faced harassment. Independent journalists were unable to work in Crimea, where the occupying Russian authorities continued to severely restrict the rights to freedom of expression, of association and of peaceful assembly. Crimean Tatars faced particular repression.

The respect for freedom of expression deteriorated sharply in Turkey, especially after the declaration of a state of emergency in the wake of the failed coup attempt in July. There were 118 journalists remanded in pre-trial detention and 184 media outlets were arbitrarily and permanently closed down under executive decrees. Internet censorship increased and 375 NGOs, including women's rights groups, lawyers associations and humanitarian organizations were shut by executive decree in November.

IMPUNITY AND ACCOUNTABILITY

Torture and other ill-treatment was widespread throughout the former Soviet Union; nominal improvements in law continued to be made in a few countries, but impunity remained the norm. The prospect of accountability for the large-scale abuses by law enforcement officials during the Euromaydan protests in 2013-14, the Gezi park protests in 2013 and the ethnic clashes in southern Kyrgyzstan in 2010 receded in Ukraine, remained remote in Turkey and dwindled to vanishing in Kyrgyzstan.

In the EU, accountability for complicity in the US-led rendition programme remained distant, despite ongoing proceedings before the European Court of Human Rights. By the end of the year, not a single person had been found criminally liable for their involvement in the unlawful detention and torture and other ill-treatment of terrorism suspects in Poland, Lithuania or Romania.

Having made notable progress in the eradication of torture in places of detention over the last decade, there was an alarming spike in the number of reported cases in the wake of the failed coup attempt in Turkey. With thousands of people detained in official and unofficial police detention, reports of severe beatings, sexual assault, threats of rape and rape were consistently but implausibly denied by the Turkish authorities.

DEATH PENALTY

Towards the end of the year, Turkey's President Recip Tayyip Erdoğan promised to put the reintroduction of the death penalty before Parliament, in defiance of widespread international condemnation and Turkey's obligations as a Council of Europe member state. Belarus, Europe's last remaining executing state, executed four people in the course of the year, despite the government making – not for the first time – some encouraging noises about its imminent abolition. In Kazakhstan, one man was sentenced to death on terrorism-related charges.

CONFLICT AND ARMED VIOLENCE

In November, the International Criminal Court in its preliminary examination of the fighting in eastern Ukraine concluded that it amounted to an international armed conflict. Sporadic clashes continued, but the overall situation remained militarily and politically deadlocked. The Russian-backed authorities in Donbas retained near total autonomy. By the end of the year, the UN Human Rights Monitoring Mission in Ukraine estimated the number of casualties at almost 10,000, including at least 2,000 civilians. Both the Ukrainian authorities and separatist forces in eastern Ukraine engaged in unlawful detentions of civilians they suspected of sympathizing with the other side, as currency for "prisoner exchanges". All of those known to be secretly detained by Ukrainian forces had been released by the end of the year.

A brief flurry of fighting broke out between Azerbaijan and Armenia in the Armenian-backed breakaway Nagorno-Karabakh region in April. The fighting lasted four days, resulting in small numbers of military and civilian casualties, mutual recrimination and small territorial gains by Azerbaijan.

The Turkish authorities continued to conduct heavily militarized operations in numerous urban areas across southeast Turkey, in response to the digging of trenches and erecting of barricades by the Kurdistan Workers' Party (PKK) affiliated groups towards the end of 2015. These operations were largely over by June, by which time round-the-clock curfews and the use of excessive force, including heavy weaponry, had resulted in hundreds of civilian casualties, large-scale destruction of residential areas and the forced displacement of up to half a million people.

Clashes between the PKK and Turkish forces outside urban areas, and sporadic PKK attacks on government buildings were ongoing at the end of the year as the peace process that broke down in 2015 showed no sign of resuming. The prospect of renewed talks was undermined by a severe crackdown on Kurdish media, civil society and political opposition, including through the use of emergency powers adopted in the wake of the July failed coup.

MIDDLE EAST AND NORTH AFRICA REGIONAL OVERVIEW

During 2016, millions of people across the Middle East and North Africa saw their lives thrown into turmoil, torment and tragedy, and their homes and livelihoods destroyed, by unrelenting state repression and continuing armed conflicts that were marked on all sides by appalling crimes and abuses. So intense was the political and human rights crisis that tens of thousands risked their lives in perilous attempts to cross the Mediterranean Sea rather than remain in the region. In Syria, more than five years of fighting had resulted in the biggest human-made humanitarian crisis of our time, and the armed conflicts in Iraq, Libya and Yemen also took a heavy toll on civilians. Armed conflict and repression exploited and exacerbated long-standing fault lines and increased political and religious polarization, further undermining respect for human rights.

ARMED CONFLICT

The human consequences of more than five years of conflict in Syria were, frankly, incalculable. There was no clear or evident formula sufficient to assess the true scale and dimensions of the suffering caused to Syria's population – the deaths and injuries, the devastation and dislocation of families and livelihoods, or the destruction of homes, property, historical sites and religious and cultural icons. Only raw statistics on the numbers killed or displaced and images of the destruction in cities such as Aleppo gave some indication of the enormous scale and intensity of the crisis. By the end of the year, the conflict had caused the deaths of more than 300,000 people and the forcible displacement of more than 11 million others, including 6.6 million who remained internally displaced and 4.8 million who had fled to

other countries to seek refuge. All the forces engaged in the conflict continued to commit war crimes and other violations of international humanitarian law, flagrantly disregarding the obligation of all parties to protect civilians.

Syrian government forces repeatedly conducted indiscriminate attacks, dropping barrel bombs and other explosives and firing imprecise artillery shells into civilian residential areas controlled by opposition fighters. They also continued to besiege such areas, causing further civilian deaths from lack of adequate food and medicine. Government forces also carried out direct attacks on civilians and civilian objects, relentlessly bombing hospitals and other medical facilities and, on at least one occasion, apparently attacking a UN humanitarian relief convoy. Russian forces allied with the Syrian government continued to carry out air strikes on opposition-held areas, causing thousands of civilian deaths and injuries and destroying civilian homes and infrastructure. As the year closed, the conflict appeared to have reached a decisive phase after government and allied forces wrested control of Aleppo city from opposition forces. In December, a ceasefire agreement between government and some opposition forces, reached under Russian and Turkish auspices, appeared to open the way for new peace talks and the UN Security Council unanimously reiterated its call for all parties to the conflict to allow the "rapid, safe and unhindered" delivery of humanitarian aid across Syria.

In areas that the Syrian government controlled or recaptured, security forces continued to suppress all opposition, detaining thousands, many in conditions of enforced disappearance that denied their families any information on their whereabouts, conditions or fate. Torture and other ill-treatment of detainees continued to be widespread; many died as a result.

Armed groups fighting the Syrian government and each other also committed war crimes and other serious violations of international law. The armed group calling itself Islamic State (IS) carried out direct attacks against civilians in government-held areas of the capital, Damascus, using suicide bombers, and mounted attacks using suspected chemical agents, conducted sieges, and committed unlawful killings in areas it controlled. Other armed groups indiscriminately shelled areas controlled by Syrian government or Kurdish forces, killing and injuring civilians.

Yemen, the poorest country in the Middle East, remained mired in armed conflict between an array of Yemeni and foreign military forces which continued to exhibit a wanton disregard for the lives of civilians, carrying out indiscriminate attacks using bombs, artillery shells and other imprecise weapons, and directly attacking civilians and civilian structures or imperilling civilians by firing weapons from residential areas.

The Huthi armed group and allied army units loyal to Yemen's former President Ali Abdullah Saleh indiscriminately shelled areas of Ta'iz city, killing and injuring civilians, and blocked the entry of food and vital medical supplies, causing a humanitarian emergency. The Huthis also engaged in indiscriminate cross-border shelling of civilian areas in Saudi Arabia. Meanwhile, a Saudi Arabia-led military coalition of Arab state forces dedicated to restoring Yemen's internationally recognized government conducted a relentless campaign of air strikes on areas controlled or contested by the Huthis and their allies, killing and injuring thousands of civilians. Many of the attacks were indiscriminate or disproportionate; others appeared to directly target civilians and civilian objects, such as schools and market places. Aerial bombing repeatedly struck hospitals. Some coalition attacks amounted to war crimes. The UN reported that more than 2 million children in Yemen were acutely malnourished, and 18.8 million people were in need of humanitarian assistance or protection at the end of the year.

Meanwhile, hundreds of thousands of civilians remained caught in the midst of armed conflict in Iraq. Iraqi government forces, mostly comprising Shi'a paramilitary militias and Sunni tribal fighters, and Kurdish Regional Government forces, backed by air strikes and other military support from a US-led international coalition, recaptured Falluja and other cities formerly controlled by IS. At the end of the year, the parties were engaged in an offensive aimed at driving IS forces from Mosul, Iraq's second largest city. All sides committed atrocities. Government forces and allied paramilitary militias committed war crimes and other violations of international humanitarian law and human rights law, mostly against members of the Sunni Arab community, including extrajudicial executions and other unlawful killings, torture and deliberate destruction of civilian homes. They subjected hundreds of men and boys to enforced disappearance and took no steps to clarify the fate and whereabouts of thousands who remained disappeared after being seized by government forces and allied militias in previous years.

In areas it controlled, IS continued to carry out execution-style killings of local people who opposed them or whom they suspected of collaborating with government forces. IS fighters punished individuals they accused of failing to comply with their codes of dress and behaviour, carried out abductions, used torture and inflicted floggings and other cruel punishments, subjected Yazidi women and girls to sexual violence, including sexual slavery, and indoctrinated and recruited boys, including Yazidi captives, and used them in fighting. As government forces advanced, IS forces prevented civilians from fleeing conflict areas, using them as human shields and shooting those who sought to escape and punishing their families. In other areas, including the capital, Baghdad, IS carried out suicide bombings and other deadly attacks that were indiscriminate or deliberately targeted civilians in crowded markets, Shi'a religious shrines and other public spaces, killing and injuring hundreds.

Elsewhere, Libya remained torn and divided by armed conflict, five years after the fall of former leader Colonel Mu'ammar al-Gaddafi. The Presidential Council of the

Government of National Accord (GNA), which emerged from UN-backed talks, failed to consolidate power on the ground. Its legitimacy remained contested by Libya's recognized Parliament and forces supporting rival former governments based in Tripoli, on the one hand, and Tobruk and al-Bayda, on the other. IS lost its stronghold in the city of Sirte to pro-GNA forces after months of fighting which caused another wave of displacement. The conflict continued to be marked on all sides by serious violations of international humanitarian law, including war crimes. Various forces attacked hospitals and carried out indiscriminate air strikes and artillery attacks that killed and injured civilians; in June, the World Health Organization reported that 60% of public hospitals in areas of conflict had ceased to function or were inaccessible.

Armed groups and militias in Libya also carried out abductions, holding victims as hostages for prisoner exchange or ransom, and detained civilians on account of their origin, opinions or perceived political or tribal affiliations. IS forces summarily killed captured opposition fighters and civilians in areas they controlled or contested. Other forces, including those affiliated with the GNA, also committed unlawful killings in Tripoli, Benghazi and elsewhere.

Years of internecine strife in Libya, just as in other countries engulfed in armed conflict, had a devastating impact on the enjoyment of economic, social and cultural rights, as access to food, electricity, health care, education and other services was severely curtailed.

INTERNATIONAL INVOLVEMENT

The armed conflicts in Syria, Yemen, Iraq and Libya were all exacerbated to some extent by foreign involvement. Europeans and other nationals travelled to the region to fight for IS, while Russian, US, Turkish, Saudi Arabian and other armed forces from the region and elsewhere left their deadly mark.

In Syria, government forces recaptured significant territory from opposing armed groups in 2016, aided by Shi'a militia fighters from Lebanon, Iraq and Iran and an intensive Russian bombing campaign that killed and injured thousands of civilians in opposition-held areas. A US-led military coalition also conducted air strikes against IS and other armed groups in Syria and Iraq, killing and injuring civilians, and US forces carried out strikes in Libya and Yemen. The Saudi Arabia-led military coalition in Yemen used internationally banned cluster munitions and other weapons obtained from the USA, the UK and other states in indiscriminate attacks on areas controlled by the Huthis and their allies, in which civilians were killed.

Meanwhile the UN Security Council, critically hamstrung by divisions between its permanent member states, continued to fail to do its job of addressing threats to international peace and security and protecting civilians. UN efforts to promote peace negotiations made little or no progress while UN agencies struggled to address the humanitarian needs that the conflicts generated among the tens of thousands of civilians forced to living under siege, and the millions internally displaced or seeking safety as refugees.

FREEDOMS OF EXPRESSION, ASSOCIATION AND ASSEMBLY

All across the region, state authorities unduly restricted and impeded exercise of the rights to freedom of expression, association and peaceful assembly. Most governments maintained and enforced laws that criminalized peaceful speech, writing or other expression, including social media and other online comment, that they deemed critical, offensive or insulting to public authorities, symbols or religion, or that disclosed information they wished to withhold. In Bahrain, the authorities prosecuted and imprisoned human rights defenders on charges that included "inciting hatred against the regime" and for criticizing Saudi Arabian bombing raids in Yemen, and barred media outlets from employing journalists deemed to have "insulted" Bahrain or other Gulf states.

In Iran, the authorities prosecuted and imprisoned scores of peaceful critics on vague and spurious national security charges. Those targeted included human rights defenders, journalists, lawyers, trade unionists, filmmakers, musicians, women's rights activists, ethnic and religious minority rights activists, and anti-death penalty campaigners. In Kuwait, a new cybercrime law penalized peaceful online criticism of the government and judiciary with up to 10 years' imprisonment and another law barred anyone convicted of insulting the Emir, God or the prophets from standing as a parliamentary candidate. Government critics and journalists were also imprisoned in Oman, where the authorities closed down a newspaper that had published reports alleging official corruption, and in Saudi Arabia, where the courts handed down lengthy prison sentences on overly broad charges such as "breaking allegiance to the ruler". In Jordan, a gunman killed a journalist whom the authorities had accused of posting a cartoon they deemed "offensive" to Islam; the gunman was later charged with murder.

The right to freedom of association was widely curtailed in the region. States including Iran, Kuwait, Qatar and Saudi Arabia did not permit independent political parties. Human rights groups, including those campaigning for women's rights, were targeted by the authorities in a number of countries. In Egypt, the authorities ordered the closure of a centre renowned for its treatment of survivors of torture and victims of political violence, froze the assets of other human rights groups, and published new draft legislation that threatened to make it impossible for independent NGOs to continue to operate. In Algeria, the government sought to undermine local human rights groups, including Amnesty International Algeria, by continuing to block their legal registration. The Moroccan authorities similarly continued to block the legal registration of several human rights groups. In Bahrain, the authorities suspended the main opposition association in June, having imprisoned its leader in 2014, seized its assets, and in July obtained a court order for its dissolution. In Iran, the Association of Iranian Journalists appealed unsuccessfully to the President to honour his 2013 election pledge to lift its suspension, and the authorities refused to renew the licence of the Iranian Teachers' Trade Association, instead imprisoning some of its members on account of their alleged "membership of an illegal group". The Iranian Revolutionary Guards also harassed women's human rights defenders.

In Algeria the authorities maintained their 15-year ban on all demonstrations in the capital, Algiers, forcibly dispersed other protests, and imprisoned peaceful protesters. In Bahrain, the government continued to ban all demonstrations in the capital, Manama, and the security forces used excessive force to disperse protests in predominantly Shi'a villages.

Armed groups also restricted freedoms of expression and association in areas they controlled, including in Iraq, Libya, Syria and Yemen. In Iraq, self-declared IS "courts" ordered stoning for "adultery" and floggings and other corporal punishments against inhabitants for smoking, failing to adhere to the IS-imposed dress code, or other IS rules. In Libya, armed groups harassed, abducted, tortured and killed human rights defenders and journalists.

JUSTICE SYSTEM

Security forces throughout the region arbitrarily arrested and detained actual and suspected government critics and opponents, often using vague and broadly drawn laws. In Syria, many detainees were forcibly disappeared after they were seized by government forces. In Egypt and the United Arab Emirates (UAE), detainees were frequently subjected to enforced disappearance: cut off from the outside world, deprived of legal protection and tortured to force "confessions" that courts used to convict them at trial. Detention without trial was widely used: Israeli authorities held hundreds of Palestinians under indefinitely renewable administrative detention orders, while Jordanian authorities continued to hold thousands under a 1954 law allowing detention without charge or trial for up to one year.

Torture and other ill-treatment of detainees remained rife, particularly in Bahrain, Egypt, Iran, Iraq, Israel and the Occupied Palestinian Territories, Libya, Saudi Arabia, Syria and the UAE. Common torture methods included beatings, electric shocks, sleep deprivation, stress positions, prolonged suspension by the wrists or ankles and threats against detainees and their loved ones. There were new reports of torture in Tunisia although a new Code of Criminal Procedures improved safeguards for detainees (other than terrorism suspects) and a national preventive body created in 2013 slowly began to take shape.

A continuing lack of judicial independence together with the "confession culture" that permeated so many national justice systems saw courts often act as mere tools of government repression rather than independent arbiters of justice upholding international fair trial standards. Courts in Egypt, Iran, Iraq, Saudi Arabia, Syria and the UAE repeatedly failed to conduct fair trials, particularly in cases where defendants faced national security or terrorism-related charges, including in death penalty cases. In Bahrain, the authorities used the courts to obtain orders revoking the nationality of a critical religious cleric and of scores of defendants convicted of terrorism charges, leading to the expulsion of some and rendering many stateless.

Courts in Saudi Arabia continued to impose cruel punishments that included floggings of hundreds of lashes, and courts in Iran sentenced defendants to flogging, amputation of their fingers and toes and blinding.

REFUGEES, INTERNALLY DISPLACED PEOPLE AND MIGRANTS

Across the region, millions of people were on the move seeking to escape armed conflicts or other violence, political repression or economic degradation. They included refugees and asylum-seekers, people displaced within their own country, and migrants from the region and beyond. Many were children; some were unaccompanied and especially vulnerable to human trafficking and sexual and other exploitation and abuse.

The Syrian and other armed conflicts continued to severely impact other states in the region and beyond. Lebanon hosted more than 1 million refugees from Syria and Jordan hosted more than 650,000, according to UNHCR, the UN refugee agency. These main host countries struggled to meet the additional economic, social and other needs that the arrival of so many refugees presented, amid faltering international humanitarian aid and deeply inadequate refugee resettlement provision by European and other states. The principal host states imposed tighter border controls to prevent new arrivals, consigning thousands of people who sought to flee the conflict to precarious conditions on the Syrian side of the border. Lebanese authorities forcibly returned some asylum-seekers to Syria and Turkish authorities carried out mass forced returns and unlawful push-backs of people seeking refuge. Despite international expressions of concern, countries in the Gulf Cooperation Council accepted few refugees from the region's armed conflicts; some provided financial support for international humanitarian assistance.

In host countries, refugees and asylum-seekers frequently lived in insecure and impoverished conditions, were denied employment and faced arrest for not possessing valid documents. In Libya, foreign nationals who entered or remained in the country irregularly, including asylum-seekers and refugees, as well as migrants mostly from sub-Saharan Africa, faced severe repression. Thousands were seized at checkpoints and in raids and incarcerated indefinitely in abusive conditions in both government-run and militia-controlled detention facilities. Others faced abduction for ransom, exploitation and sexual violence by human traffickers and smugglers. These and other "push" factors led tens of thousands to seek refuge elsewhere, often by paying criminal people-smugglers to risk their lives in flimsy, overcrowded craft that set out from Turkish, Libyan and other shores in often vain attempts to cross the Mediterranean Sea. Thousands reached Europe, where they faced uncertain futures; thousands of others, including children, drowned.

Elsewhere in the region, migrant workers, many from Asia, continued to experience exploitation and abuses. In Kuwait, Qatar and the UAE, where migrant workers formed a majority of the population and their labour underpinned the national economies, restrictive sponsorship policies continued to tie workers to employers, increasing migrant workers' vulnerability. In Saudi Arabia, many migrants were left destitute after the government cut spending on construction and other projects. Migrant domestic workers, predominantly women, remained especially vulnerable to abuse by employers – including sexual and other physical and psychological abuse and forced labour – due to the continuing failure of state authorities to extend basic labour law safeguards to the domestic employment sector. In Jordan, some 80,000 women migrants employed as domestic workers were excluded from the protection of labour laws, placing them at risk of violence and exploitation, according to a local workers' rights group.

WOMEN'S RIGHTS

Throughout the region, women and girls were denied equal status with men in law and in practice and were subject to gender-based violence, including sexual violence and killings perpetrated in the name of "honour". Male "guardianship" rules restricted women's freedom of movement and access to higher education and employment in Saudi Arabia, where the authorities also continued to prohibit women from driving motor vehicles.

Family laws discriminating against women in relation to marriage, divorce, child custody and inheritance remained prevalent, and in many countries laws failed to protect from, and even facilitated, sexual violence against women – for example, by failing to criminalize early and forced marriage and marital rape

and by allowing rapists to escape prosecution by marrying their victim. Authorities in Bahrain and Jordan took action during the year to remove or reduce this provision for rapists from their penal codes, and in other positive developments draft laws on combating violence against women appeared to be advancing towards enactment in Morocco and Tunisia. In other states, however, laws continued to prescribe lesser punishment for crimes of violence against women, including murder, if the perpetrators committed them in the name of "family honour", or made women liable to criminal prosecution for reporting rape; these laws perpetuated conditions that both facilitate and obscure potentially high levels of domestic violence against women and girls.

Women's rights activists faced arrest, imprisonment and harassment by Ministry of Intelligence and Revolutionary Guards officials in Iran, and the authorities used "morality police" to enforce compulsory "veiling" laws on women, who regularly suffered harassment, violence, arbitrary arrest and detention on account of their dress. Meanwhile, draft laws that heeded the Supreme Leader's call for greater compliance with women's "traditional" roles as home makers and child bearers threatened to reduce women's access to sexual and reproductive health.

Conditions for women and girls were especially perilous in areas of armed conflict, where they endured siege, aerial bombing and other forms of attack by both government and opposition forces. Many were rendered more vulnerable to abuses such as human trafficking by the death or disappearance of spouses and other male relatives. In areas of Iraq and Syria that they controlled, IS forces continued to hold thousands of Yazidi women and girls captive, subjecting them to sexual violence, enslavement, including sexual slavery, and forced conversion.

MINORITY RIGHTS

Members of ethnic, religious and other minorities continued to face repression in a number of countries, exacerbated by the increased political polarization that both fuelled and flowed from the armed conflicts that dominated the region. In Saudi Arabia, the authorities continued to clamp down on the Shi'a minority, detaining and imprisoning Shi'a activists and executing a leading Shi'a cleric. In Iran, the authorities imprisoned scores of peaceful activists belonging to ethnic minorities, and maintained a raft of discriminatory restrictions that denied members of religious minorities equitable access to employment, education, political office and exercise of their economic, social and cultural rights. In Egypt, Coptic Christians, Shi'a Muslims and Baha'is faced continuing discrimination in law and practice and a new law restricted the building and repair of churches. In Kuwait, the authorities continued to withhold citizenship from more than 100,000 Bidun long-term residents, who remained stateless and unable to access a range of state services.

RIGHTS OF LESBIAN, GAY, BISEXUAL, TRANSGENDER AND INTERSEX PEOPLE

LGBTI people faced arrest and imprisonment on charges of "debauchery" or "indecency", and persecution under laws criminalizing consensual same-sex sexual relations in Bahrain, Egypt, Iran, Morocco and Tunisia.

IMPUNITY

A heavy shroud of impunity prevailed, under which parties to armed conflicts perpetrated war crimes, other grave violations of international law and gross human rights abuses. Elsewhere, state authorities committed unlawful killings, torture and other human rights violations without accountability.

In some cases, impunity continued for crimes committed decades ago. In Algeria, the authorities continued to protect state forces responsible for serious crimes in the 1990s by criminalizing calls for justice, thus turning the law on its head. In Morocco, 10 years after the landmark Truth and Equity Commission reported on decades of grave violations, state policy still firmly shielded

from justice those responsible. Israel's government agreed to pay compensation to the families of Turkish nationals killed by Israeli soldiers in 2010 but failed to ensure accountability either for the extensive war crimes and other grave violations of international law that Israeli forces committed during recent armed conflicts in Gaza and Lebanon or for unlawful killings, torture and other violations that Israeli soldiers and security officials continued to commit against Palestinians in the West Bank and Gaza. The government of Palestine ratified Rome Statute amendments giving the International Criminal Court jurisdiction over the "crime of aggression". Neither the Palestinian government nor the Hamas de facto administration in Gaza took steps to ensure accountability for crimes committed by Palestinian armed groups in previous conflicts, including indiscriminate rocket and mortar attacks on Israel and summary killings of alleged "collaborators".

In Egypt, the security forces continued to commit serious violations with impunity, targeting alleged supporters of the banned Muslim Brotherhood and other critics and opponents for arbitrary detention, enforced disappearance and torture. An amendment to the Police Authority Law prohibited security forces from "ill-treating citizens". But the authorities took no serious steps to hold members of the security forces accountable for unlawful killings and other serious violations committed during years of turmoil since the popular uprising in 2011.

In Bahrain, the international condemnation sparked in 2011 by the authorities' heavily abusive response to popular protests led the government to create, and thereafter to vaunt, official mechanisms mandated to investigate alleged human rights violations by the security forces and ensure accountability. These continued to function in 2016, albeit not in a sufficiently adequate and effective manner, and a small number of low-ranking members of the security forces faced prosecution as a result of investigations. However, by the end of the year, no senior officers or officials responsible for torture, unlawful killings and other excessive use of force in 2011 had been held to account.

Tunisia stood out as the only state in the region undertaking a serious transitional justice process, with its Truth and Dignity Commission reporting that it had received tens of thousands of complaints concerning human rights violations committed between 1955 and late 2013 and undertaking televised, public sessions. Yet a government-proposed law that would offer former officials and business executives immunity if they repaid their proceeds from corruption in former years threatened to undermine the Commission's work.

The UN General Assembly also provided a glimmer of hope in December by establishing an independent international mechanism to ensure accountability for war crimes and crimes against humanity committed in Syria since March 2011. In December too, the UN Security Council demonstrated rare unity when it reaffirmed that Israel's establishment of settlements in Palestinian territory it has occupied since 1967 have no legal validity and constitute a flagrant violation of international law and an obstacle to peace and security. Rather than exercise its veto, the USA abstained while the Council's 14 other member states supported the resolution. Despite these developments, however, the future as regards justice and accountability remained bleak at an international level, with four of the UN Security Council's five permanent member states – France, Russia, the UK and the USA – actively supporting forces that continued to commit war crimes and other grave violations of international law in Syria, Iraq, Yemen and Libya, and themselves implicated in serious violations.

DEATH PENALTY

All countries in the region retained the death penalty but there were wide disparities in the range of offences penalized by it and in its application. No new death sentences were handed down in Bahrain, Oman or in Israel, which has abolished the death penalty for ordinary crimes only. Although courts continued to hand down death sentences in Algeria, Morocco and Tunisia, the authorities there maintained long-standing policies of refraining from executing people. By contrast, the governments of Iran, Saudi Arabia and Iraq remained among the world's foremost executioners: their victims were often sentenced after grossly unfair trials. Some – in Iran, the majority – were sent to their deaths after being convicted of non-violent drugs offences; some were sentenced for crimes committed when they were children. On 2 January the Saudi Arabian authorities executed 47 prisoners at 12 separate locations; on 21 August, the Iraqi authorities executed 36 men sentenced after a perfunctory trial that failed to address their allegations of torture. Executions were also carried out in Egypt, where unfair military and other courts have handed down hundreds of death sentences since 2013.

STANDING UP FOR HUMANITY

While 2016 saw some of the worst forms of human behaviour, it was also a year in which the very best of human conduct shone through. Countless individuals stood up in defence of human rights and victims of oppression, often putting their own lives or freedom in jeopardy to do so. They included medical workers, lawyers, citizen journalists, media workers, women's and minority rights campaigners, social activists and many others – far too many to name or to list. It is their courage and determination in the face of dire abuses and threats that offer hope for a better future for the people of the Middle East and North Africa region.

AMNESTY INTERNATIONAL REPORT 2016/17

PART 2: A-Z COUNTRY ENTRIES

AFGHANISTAN

Islamic Republic of Afghanistan
Head of state and government: **Mohammad Ashraf Ghani**

The intensifying conflict resulted in widespread human rights violations and abuses. Thousands of civilians were killed, injured or displaced in the violence, while ongoing insecurity restricted access to education, health and other services. While armed insurgent groups were responsible for the majority of civilian casualties, pro-government forces also killed and injured civilians. Anti- and pro-government forces continued to use children as fighters. The number of people internally displaced stood at 1.4 million – more than double the number in 2013 – while approximately 2.6 million Afghan refugees lived outside the country, many in deplorable conditions. Violence against women and girls persisted, and there was a reported increase in armed groups publicly punishing women including through executions and lashings. State and non-state actors continued to threaten human rights defenders and impede them from carrying out their work and journalists encountered violence and censorship. The government continued to carry out executions, often after unfair trials.

BACKGROUND

In January, officials from Afghanistan, Pakistan, China and the USA held talks on a roadmap for peace with the Taliban. However, at a conference in January in Doha, attended by 55 senior participants from a diverse international range of backgrounds, including the Taliban, a delegation of the Taliban's political commission based in Doha reiterated that a formal peace process could start only after foreign troops had left the country. They also set out other preconditions including the removal of Taliban leaders' names from the UN sanctions list.

In February, President Ghani appointed Mohammad Farid Hamidi, a prominent human rights lawyer, as Attorney General, and General Taj Mohammad Jahid as Minister of Interior Affairs. President Ghani opened a fund to support women survivors of gender-based violence, to which cabinet members contributed 15% of their February salary.

In March, the UN Security Council renewed the mandate of the UN Assistance Mission in Afghanistan (UNAMA) for another year; the UN Secretary-General appointed Tadamichi Yamamoto as Special Representative of UNAMA.

After years of peace negotiations between the government and the country's second largest insurgent group Hezb-i-Islami, led by Gulbuddin Hekmatyar, on 29 September, President Ghani and Gulbuddin Hekmatyar signed a peace agreement granting Gulbuddin Hekmatyar and his fighters amnesty for alleged crimes under international law and permitting the release of certain Hezb-i-Islami prisoners.

Political instability increased amid growing rifts in the Government of National Unity between supporters of President Ghani and Chief Executive Abdullah Abdullah. In October, an international aid donor conference was held by the EU to pledge aid to Afghanistan over the next four years. The international community pledged around US $15.2 billion to assist Afghanistan in areas including security and sustainable development. Shortly before the conference, the EU and Afghanistan signed a deal permitting the deportation of an unlimited number of failed Afghan asylum-seekers, despite the worsening security situation.

There were serious concerns about a mounting financial crisis as the international presence within the country was diminished and unemployment rose.

There was a rapid increase in September and October of Taliban attacks and attempts to capture large provinces and cities. In October, the Taliban captured Kunduz, during which the city power supply and water was cut; hospitals ran out of medication and civilian casualty numbers rose. The UN Office for the Coordination of Humanitarian

Affairs (UNOCHA) reported some 25,000 Afghans internally displaced during one week from Kunduz to the capital, Kabul, and neighbouring countries.

ARMED CONFLICT

In the first nine months of 2016, UNAMA documented 8,397 conflict-related civilian casualties (2,562 deaths and 5,835 injured). Pro-government forces – including Afghan national security forces, the Afghan local police, pro-government armed groups, and international military forces – were responsible for almost 23%, according to UNAMA.

UNAMA documented at least 15 incidents in the first half of 2016 in which pro-government forces conducted search operations in hospitals and clinics, delayed or impeded the provision of medical supplies, or used health facilities for military purposes. This was a sharp increase on the previous year.

Men dressed in Afghan National Army uniforms entered a health clinic in the Taliban-controlled village of Tangi Saidan, Wardak province, on 18 February. The Swedish aid group that ran the clinic said the men beat staff members and killed two patients and a 15-year-old carer. NATO launched an investigation into the incident; no updates were made public by the end of the year.

No criminal charges were brought against those responsible for an air strike by US forces in October 2015 against a Médecins Sans Frontières hospital in Kunduz which killed and injured at least 42 staff and patients, although approximately 12 US military personnel faced disciplinary sanctions. In March, the new commander of US and NATO forces in Afghanistan issued an apology to the families of the victims.

ABUSES BY ARMED GROUPS

The Taliban and other armed insurgent groups were responsible for the majority of civilian casualties, approximately 60%, according to UNAMA.

On 3 February, the Taliban shot dead a 10-year-old boy on his way to school in Tirin Kot, southern Uruzgan. It was believed that the boy was shot because he had fought the Taliban on earlier occasions alongside his uncle, a former Taliban commander who switched allegiance and became a local police commander.

On 19 April, Taliban militants attacked a security team responsible for protecting high-level government officials in Kabul, killing at least 64 people and wounding 347. It was the biggest Taliban attack on an urban area since 2001.

On 31 May, Taliban militants posing as government officials kidnapped around 220 civilians at a fake checkpoint along the Kunduz-Takhar highway near Arzaq Angor Bagh in Kunduz province. They killed 17 of the civilians and the rest were eventually rescued or released. At least 40 more people were kidnapped and others killed in the same area on 8 June.

On 23 July, a suicide attack claimed by the armed group Islamic State (IS) killed at least 80 people and wounded more than 230 during a peaceful demonstration by members of the Hazara minority in Kabul.

In August, three armed men attacked the American University in Kabul, killing 12 people and injuring nearly 40, mostly students and teachers. No one claimed responsibility for the attack.

On 11 October, IS conducted a co-ordinated attack against a large group of mourners in a Shi'a mosque in Kabul. The attackers used explosive materials and stormed the mosque, reportedly taking hostage hundreds of mourners. At least 18 people were shot dead and over 40 injured, including women and children.

VIOLENCE AGAINST WOMEN AND GIRLS

The Afghan judiciary said that it had registered more than 3,700 cases of violence against women and girls in the first eight months of 2016. The Afghanistan Independent Human Rights Commission also reported thousands of cases in the first six months of the year, including beatings, killings and acid attacks.

In January, a man cut off the nose of his 22-year-old wife in Faryab. The incident was condemned across Afghanistan, including by a Taliban spokesperson.

In July, a 14-year-old pregnant girl was set on fire by her husband and her parents-in-law to punish her father for eloping with a cousin of the girl's husband. She died five days later in hospital in Kabul.

Armed groups targeted women working in public life, including women police officers. Armed groups also restricted the freedom of movement of women and girls, including their access to education and health care, in areas under their control.

UNAMA reported an increase in the number of women punished in public under Shari'a law by the Taliban and other armed groups. Between 1 January and 30 June, UNAMA documented six parallel justice punishments by armed groups of women accused of so-called "moral crimes", including the executions of two women and the lashing of four others.

REFUGEES AND INTERNALLY DISPLACED PEOPLE

According to UNHCR, the UN refugee agency, approximately 2.6 million Afghan refugees were living in more than 70 countries, making them the second largest refugee population worldwide. Around 95% lived in just two countries, Iran and Pakistan, where they faced discrimination, racial attacks, lack of basic amenities and the risk of mass deportation.

Approximately 1.4 million refugees in Pakistan risked mass deportation with their registration tentatively expiring at the end of the year. UNHCR estimated that a further one million undocumented refugees were in Pakistan. According to UNHCR, more than 500,000 Afghan refugees (documented and undocumented) were repatriated from Pakistan during the year. This was the highest number since 2002. Officials reported up to 5,000 returnees during each of the first four days of October. The situation

was intensified with the deal signed between the Afghan government and the EU on 5 October 2016, agreeing to the unlimited return of Afghan refugees from EU member states.

Internally displaced people

By September 2016, the number of people internally displaced reached an estimated 1.4 million. Many continued to live in squalid conditions without access to adequate housing, food, water, health care, education or employment opportunities.

According to UNOCHA, from 1 January to 11 December, 530,000 individuals became internally displaced mainly due to conflict.

The situation facing internally displaced people (IDPs) has worsened in recent years. A national IDP policy launched in 2014 was hindered by corruption, lack of capacity in the government and fading international interest.

IDPs, along with other groups, faced significant challenges in accessing health care. Public facilities remained severely overstretched, and IDP camps and settlements often lacked dedicated clinics. Medicines and private clinics were unaffordable for most IDPs and the lack of adequate maternal and reproductive health care was a particular area of concern.

IDPs also faced repeated threats of forced evictions by both government and private actors.

HUMAN RIGHTS DEFENDERS

Armed groups continued to target and threaten human rights defenders. Women human rights defenders in particular faced death threats against themselves and their families.

In early 2016, a prominent human rights defender received a death threat via Facebook from the Taliban against himself and nine others. After the 10 activists approached the authorities about the threat, the intelligence agency National Directorate of Security arrested two people with reported links to the Taliban, but no subsequent information was provided to the human rights defenders. Threats continued against the activists, who self-censored their human rights work as a result.

In August, the brother of a local women's rights activist in a southern province was kidnapped, tortured and subsequently killed by unidentified individuals. The perpetrators used the man's phone to intimidate the activist and her family, threatening her with fatal repercussions if she did not cease her human rights work. No one had been arrested for the kidnapping and killing by the end of the year.

FREEDOMS OF EXPRESSION AND ASSEMBLY

Freedom of expression, which strengthened after the fall of the Taliban in 2001, has steadily eroded following a string of violent attacks, intimidation and killings of journalists.

Nai, a media freedom watchdog, reported more than 100 cases of attacks against journalists, media workers and media offices between January and November. These included killings, beatings, detention, arson, threats and other forms of violence by both state and non-state actors.

On 20 January, a suicide attack on a shuttle bus carrying staff working for Moby Group, the owner of the country's largest private TV station Tolo TV, killed seven media workers and injured 27 people. The Taliban, which had previously threatened Tolo TV, claimed responsibility.

On 29 January, Zubair Khaksar, a well-known journalist working for Afghan national TV in Nangarhar province, was killed by unidentified armed men while travelling from Jalalabad city to Surkhrood district.

On 19 April, police in Kabul beat two staff media workers of Ariana TV while they were carrying out their reporting duties.

Activists in several provinces outside Kabul said they were increasingly reluctant to stage demonstrations, fearing reprisals from government officials.

TORTURE AND OTHER ILL-TREATMENT

Armed groups including the Taliban continued to carry out killings, torture and other human rights abuses as punishment for perceived crimes or offences. Parallel justice structures were illegal.

Between 1 January and 30 June, UNAMA documented 26 cases including summary killings, lashings, beatings and illegal detention. The punishments were imposed for alleged violations of Shari'a law, spying or connections with the security forces. Most occurred in the western region, particularly in Farah and Badghis provinces.

On 14 February, Afghanistan Local Police in Khak-e-Safid district, Farah province, allegedly detained, tortured and killed a shepherd for his alleged involvement in planting a remote-controlled IED (improvised explosive device) that killed two police officers. UNAMA reported that, although it was aware of the incident, the Afghan National Police prosecution office did not initiate any investigation or arrest any suspects.

DEATH PENALTY

On 8 May, six death row prisoners were executed by hanging in Pol-e Charkhi prison in Kabul. The executions followed a speech by President Ghani on 25 April, soon after the large-scale Taliban attack of 19 April, in which he vowed to implement tough justice, including capital punishment.

It was feared that more executions could follow. Approximately 600 prisoners remained on death row, many convicted of crimes such as murder. Many of their trials did not abide by fair trial standards. Around 100 individuals were sentenced to death during the year for crimes including murder, rape and murder, and terrorism resulting in mass killings.

ALBANIA

Republic of Albania
Head of state: **Bujar Nishani**
Head of government: **Edi Rama**

Roma and Egyptian communities continued to live in poor housing conditions and were at risk of forced evictions. Over 20,000 Albanians sought asylum in the EU.

ENFORCED DISAPPEARANCES

The authorities made no progress in bringing to justice those responsible for the enforced disappearance in 1995 of Remzi Hoxha, an ethnic Albanian from Macedonia. His fate and whereabouts remained unknown.

The government started to co-operate with the International Commission on Missing Persons to locate and identify the remains of Albanians forcibly disappeared under the communist governments between 1944 and 1991; however, by the end of 2016, new exhumations were yet to be carried out. An estimated 6,000 persons remained disappeared.

HOUSING RIGHTS – FORCED EVICTIONS

In June, the local authorities in Tirana threatened to forcibly evict over 80 families – mainly Roma and Egyptian – living in the area of Bregu i Lumit, an area at risk of being flooded by the Tirana River. The authorities failed to provide adequate notice, genuine consultation and alternative housing. Following the intervention by housing activists and the Albanian Ombudsperson, evictions were temporarily suspended at the end of September. As part of an "intervention plan", proposed by the Mayor of Tirana, the families were given options on their eviction and resettlement. By the end of the year, it remained unclear if all families would be able to access resettlement and if the offered alternatives were adequate and sustainable.

JUSTICE SYSTEM

In June, a judge suspended the chief of the national police for abuse of power and participation in planting wiretapping devices in police stations. In response, the Prime Minister and the Minister of Internal Affairs accused the judge of serving the opposition and undermining the independence of the judiciary. The national police chief remained in pre-trial detention at the end of the year.

In July, a justice reform was passed in Parliament. The reform amended dozens of articles of the Constitution and introduced new legislation to ensure the independence and impartiality of the judiciary and to prevent political intervention and corruption.

REFUGEES AND ASYLUM-SEEKERS

Over 1,000 asylum applications were submitted to the authorities as border closures in Greece and Macedonia prompted people to seek protection in Albania. Some refugees and migrants arriving from Greece were summarily returned.

An estimated 20,000 Albanians applied for asylum in EU countries, the majority of them in Germany, but most of them were rejected. In July, the European Parliament proposed an EU common list of "safe countries of origin" to process asylum applications. The list included Albania. This raised concerns about fair and individualized asylum processes for Albanians.

TORTURE AND OTHER ILL-TREATMENT
Prisons

In March, the European Committee for the Prevention of Torture (CPT) expressed concerns over detention conditions in Albania. The CPT documented numerous reports by detainees – including juveniles – of ill-treatment by police officers, in some cases amounting to torture. It also noted that detention conditions remained poor in several locations across the country, and that progress was lacking in health care, activities and specialized care provided to prisoners.

Children's rights

In May, the torture or other ill-treatment of children, including sexual abuse of girls, in an orphanage in the town of Shkodra, caused a national scandal after the district prosecutor revealed the scale of the abuse. Five persons, including the former director of the orphanage, were arrested.

ALGERIA

People's Democratic Republic of Algeria
Head of state: **Abdelaziz Bouteflika**
Head of government: **Abdelmalek Sellal**

The authorities continued to restrict the rights to freedom of expression, association, assembly and religion, and prosecuted peaceful critics, including human rights defenders, in unfair trials. Refugees and migrants were arbitrarily expelled. Impunity for past serious abuses continued to prevail. Courts handed down death sentences; no executions were carried out.

BACKGROUND

In January, the government dissolved the Department for Information and Security (DRS), the main security agency previously associated with torture and other ill-treatment of detainees. It was replaced with a Security Services Directorate that reports directly to the President.

Also in January, changes to the Code of Criminal Procedure came into effect, including new witness protection measures, limits to the right to appeal in minor offence cases and amendments allowing suspects to contact lawyers immediately when they are taken into police custody. The changes did not give suspects the right to have their lawyer present during interrogation.

Constitutional amendments adopted in February included the creation of a National Human Rights Council to replace the National Consultative Commission for Promotion and Protection of Human Rights. Other amendments included making Tamazight a national language, thus enhancing the cultural rights of the Amazigh population.[1]

The authorities continued to block access to Algeria by UN human rights mechanisms, including those with mandates on torture and

other ill-treatment, counter-terrorism, enforced disappearance and freedoms of association and peaceful assembly. The authorities also continued to prevent international organizations, including Amnesty International, from conducting human rights fact-finding visits.

FREEDOMS OF ASSOCIATION AND ASSEMBLY

The authorities continued to leave many civil society associations, including Amnesty International Algeria, in legal limbo by failing to acknowledge their registration applications. Such applications were required under Law 12-06 on associations, which imposed wide-ranging arbitrary restrictions on associations and exposed members of unrecognized associations to up to six months' imprisonment and fines.

The authorities tightly restricted freedom of assembly, maintaining a ban on all demonstrations in the capital, Algiers, under a decree from 2001, and arresting and prosecuting peaceful protesters.

In January a court in Tamanrasset imposed fines and one-year prison sentences on seven peaceful protesters convicted of "unarmed gathering" and "offending public institutions" for protesting in December 2015 about a local land dispute. Six of the seven protesters were released in July under a presidential pardon. The seventh, activist Dahmane Kerami, remained in prison serving a one-year sentence in a separate case. He was convicted of participating in "unarmed gatherings" and "obstructing traffic" during peaceful protests in Tamanrasset in 2015 against shale gas fracking and in support of workers laid off by a local gold mining company. He was released on 31 December after serving his sentence.[2]

In March, a court sentenced activist Abdelali Ghellam to one year in prison and a fine after convicting him of inciting others to participate in an "unarmed gathering" and "obstruct traffic". The charges related to comments about the protest in Tamanrasset that he published on Facebook. He was released in April.

FREEDOM OF EXPRESSION

The authorities prosecuted peaceful critics and forced the closure of media outlets.

In March, a court in Tlemcen convicted and fined Zoulikha Belarbi, a member of the Algerian League for the Defence of Human Rights (LADDH), for defamation and for "offending" the President and a public body. The charges related to her publishing a satirical collage on Facebook depicting President Bouteflika and senior officials. A six-month prison term was added to her sentence on appeal in December.

In June, the authorities arrested the director and the producer of the private Khabar Broadcasting Corporation and a Ministry of Communication official in connection with two popular satirical current affairs programmes. The three were detained for several weeks before a court sentenced them to suspended prison terms of between six months and one year for licensing irregularities. Gendarmes sealed the recording studios in July, forcing both shows off the air.[3]

In July, a court sentenced freelance journalist Mohamed Tamalt to two years' imprisonment after convicting him of "offending" the President and public institutions in comments he published on Facebook and in his blog about corruption and nepotism among leading officials. An appeal court confirmed his sentence in August, following a hearing at which he accused prison guards of beating him. He began a protest hunger strike at the time of his arrest in June, became comatose in August, and died in hospital in December. The authorities failed to adequately investigate his alleged beating in detention, his treatment in prison and his death.[4]

In November, a court in El Bayadh sentenced Hassan Bouras, a journalist and human rights activist, to one year in prison on charges of complicity in offending public officials and a public body after a private television station broadcast film of him interviewing three people alleging police and judicial corruption.[5]

FREEDOM OF RELIGION AND BELIEF

From June onwards, the authorities targeted members of the Ahmadi Muslim community, arresting more than 50 in Blida and Skikda provinces and other parts of the country on account of their faith, according to media reports and civil society groups. Soon after the June arrests in Blida, the Minister of Religious Affairs publicly accused Ahmadis of "extremism" and of serving foreign interests. In November, a court in Skikda sentenced 20 Ahmadis to fines and prison terms ranging from one month to one year; at the end of the year they remained at liberty pending appeal.

In August, a court sentenced Christian convert Slimane Bouhafs from Setif to five years in prison for "denigrating" Islam and "insulting" the Prophet Muhammad in comments he posted on Facebook. An appeal court reduced the sentence to three years' imprisonment.[6]

HUMAN RIGHTS DEFENDERS

The authorities harassed and prosecuted human rights defenders. In March, a court in Ghardaia charged lawyer Noureddine Ahmine with "insulting a public institution" and falsely reporting an offence, in relation to a complaint of torture that he had filed, apparently on behalf of a client, in 2014. Noureddine Ahmine had defended many protesters and journalists facing charges arising from their peaceful exercise of their human rights.

In June, an investigative judge in Ghardaia issued an arrest warrant against lawyer Salah Dabouz, a member of LADDH, in relation to comments he made about unrest in Ghardaia and for allegedly taking a computer and camera into a prison.

JUSTICE SYSTEM

Dozens of people arrested in connection with communal violence in 2015 in the Mzab region remained in pre-trial detention throughout 2016 as the authorities investigated them on charges of terrorism and inciting hatred. They included political activist Kameleddine Fekhar and other supporters of regional autonomy.

In March the UN Human Rights Committee found that Algeria had violated Articles 2, 7 and 9 of the ICCPR. Its findings related to the failure to investigate allegations by businessman Mejdoub Chani that DRS officers had detained him incommunicado and tortured him during interrogation following his arrest for corruption and money laundering in 2009. He remained in prison at the end of the year awaiting the outcome of appeals to the Supreme Court.

WOMEN'S RIGHTS

The Family Code continued to discriminate against women in matters of marriage, divorce, child custody and guardianship, and inheritance. Women and girls remained inadequately protected against gender-based violence in the absence of a comprehensive law. The Penal Code continued to prohibit rape without defining it or explicitly recognizing marital rape as a crime, and allowed men who rape girls under the age of 18 to escape trial by marrying their victim. The Penal Code also continued to criminalize abortions.

REFUGEES' AND MIGRANTS' RIGHTS

The government again failed to enact legislation protecting the right to asylum.

Clashes between local residents and migrants from sub-Saharan Africa occurred in Bechar and Ouargla in March, in Tamanrasset in July, and in Algiers in November.

In December, security forces arrested an estimated 1,500 sub-Saharan African migrants and refugees in Algiers, and arbitrarily expelled hundreds of them to neighbouring Niger within days. Those not expelled were released in the southern city of Tamanrasset and reported being barred from public transport to prevent them returning to Algiers.

COUNTER-TERROR AND SECURITY

Security forces and armed opposition groups clashed in several areas. The authorities said the security forces killed 125 alleged members of armed groups but disclosed few details, raising concern that some may have been extrajudicially executed.

In March, the armed group calling itself al-Qa'ida in the Islamic Maghreb claimed responsibility for a rocket attack on a gas production site in Khrechba. No casualties were reported.

IMPUNITY

The government continued to allow impunity for serious human rights abuses committed during the 1990s, by failing to investigate past abuses and hold those responsible to account. The unlawful killings, enforced disappearances, rape and other torture committed by the security forces, as well as some abuses committed by armed groups, may amount to crimes against humanity.[7]

DEATH PENALTY

Courts continued to impose death sentences. No executions have been carried out since 1993.

1. Algeria: Constitution needs stronger human rights safeguards (MDE 28/3366/2016)

2. Algeria: Further information: Six protesters released, one remains imprisoned (MDE 28/4437/2016)

3. Algeria: End media restrictions (MDE 28/4369/2016)

4. Algeria: Further information: Health concern for British-Algerian journalist: Mohamed Tamalt (MDE 28/4738/2016)

5. Algeria: One year in prison for denouncing corruption: Hassan Bouras (MDE 28/5299/2016)

6. Algeria: Further information: Prisoner of conscience remains in detention: Slimane Bouhafs (MDE 28/4783/2016)

7. Algeria: Time to end impunity for past and present abuses (MDE 28/3521/2016)

ANGOLA

Republic of Angola
Head of state and government: **José Eduardo dos Santos**

The worsening economic crisis triggered price rises for food, health care, fuel, recreation and culture. This led to

continued demonstrations expressing discontent and restrictions on the rights to freedom of expression, association and peaceful assembly. The government misused the justice system and other state institutions to silence dissent. Housing rights and the right to health were violated.

BACKGROUND

The drop in the price of oil put Angola's oil-dependent economy under severe pressure, prompting the government to cut the budget by 20% and seek support from the International Monetary Fund (IMF). In July, the UN Committee on Economic, Social and Cultural Rights (CESCR) expressed concern at regressive austerity measures by the state, including insufficient allocation of resources to the health sector.

On 2 June, President José Eduardo dos Santos appointed his daughter Isabel dos Santos as head of the state oil company Sonangol, the biggest source of state revenue and central to an extensive system of patronage.

In August, the ruling People's Movement for the Liberation of Angola (MPLA) re-elected José Eduardo dos Santos as its leader for a further five years, even though in March he had announced his intention to step down from politics in 2018. He has been President since 1979.

JUSTICE SYSTEM

Politically motivated trials, criminal defamation charges and national security laws continued to be used to suppress human rights defenders, dissent and other critical voices. The acquittal of human rights defenders and release of prisoners of conscience were positive steps, but the gains remained fragile without structural legislative reform and full commitment to international human rights law and standards.

Prisoners of conscience

On 28 March, 17 youth activists known as the Angola 17 were convicted of "preparatory acts of rebellion" and "criminal conspiracy". They were sentenced to prison terms ranging from two years and three months to eight and a half years, fined 50,000 kwanzas (US$300) for court costs and jailed. The security forces had arrested and detained 15 of the activists between 20 and 24 June 2015 in the capital, Luanda, after they attended a meeting to discuss political issues and governance concerns in the country. The two others, both women, were also charged, but only detained after sentencing. Immediately after the convictions, the activists' lawyers lodged two appeals – one before the Supreme Tribunal and the other before the Constitutional Court. They also lodged a writ for habeas corpus, which was heard by the Supreme Tribunal on 29 June: the Tribunal ordered the conditional release of the 17 activists pending a final decision on their case.

On 20 July, the National Assembly approved an amnesty law relating to crimes committed up to 11 November 2015, including the Angola 17 case. Some of the 17 stated that as they had committed no crime they did not want to be granted amnesty. The 17 were prisoners of conscience, imprisoned and convicted solely for the peaceful exercise of their rights.

Two youth activists were punished for criticizing proceedings during the trial. On 8 March, Manuel Chivonde Nito Alves, one of the Angola 17, said out loud in court, "This trial is a farce". He was found guilty of contempt of court, sentenced to six months in prison and fined 50,000 kwanzas.[1] On 5 July, the Constitutional Court ruled on appeal that the trial had violated some of his constitutional rights and ordered his release. The same words were said in court on 28 March by another young activist, Francisco Mapanda (also known as Dago Nível Intelecto). He too was found guilty of contempt of court and sentenced to eight months in prison. He was released on 21 November, seven days earlier than scheduled.[2]

Human rights defenders

Human rights defender and former prisoner of conscience José Marcos Mavungo was released on 20 May following an appeal before the Supreme Tribunal. The Tribunal found that there was insufficient evidence to convict him. José Marcos Mavungo had been sentenced to six years in prison on 14 September 2015 for "rebellion", a state security offence. He had been in detention since 14 March 2015 for involvement in organizing a peaceful demonstration.

On 12 July, Cabinda Provincial Tribunal dismissed the charges against human rights defender and former prisoner of conscience Arão Bula Tempo. He had been arrested on 14 March 2015 and conditionally released two months later. He was charged with "rebellion" and "attempted collaboration with foreigners to constrain the Angolan state", both categorized as state security offences. The charges were based on allegations that Arão Bula Tempo had invited foreign journalists to cover the 14 March protest being planned by José Marcos Mavungo.

FREEDOM OF ASSOCIATION

Civil society organizations working on human rights issues, such as OMUNGA and SOS-Habitat, faced undue restrictions on accessing their own funds, including from international sources. Banks prevented the organizations from accessing their accounts. This not only hampered their legitimate work but also undermined the right of associations to seek and secure resources, and had a broader impact on human rights in general. Despite their complaints to government institutions in charge of overseeing banking activities, no response had been received by the end of the year.

FREEDOM OF ASSEMBLY

The authorities frequently refused to allow peaceful demonstrations to take place, even though they do not require prior authorization in Angola. When demonstrations did take place, police often arbitrarily arrested and detained peaceful protesters.

On 30 July, more than 30 peaceful activists were arbitrarily arrested and detained for up to seven hours in the city of Benguela. They were planning to take part in a peaceful demonstration organized by the

Benguela Revolutionary Movement to demand effective measures against inflation. All were released without charge. A few days later, four of the activists were rearrested, again without a warrant. They were released on bail. They had not been formally charged by the end of the year, but the Public Prosecutor told them that they were suspected of aggravated robbery, drug-trafficking and violence against MPLA supporters.[3] No one was held to account for the arbitrary arrests and detentions.[4]

FREEDOM OF EXPRESSION

On 18 November, the National Assembly approved five draft bills (Press Law, Journalist's Statute, Radio Broadcasting Law, Television Law and Social Communications Regulatory Body Law) that will further restrict freedom of expression. Opposition parties, the Union of Angolan Journalists and other civil society actors criticized the bills for enabling tighter government control over television, radio, the press, social media and the internet.

Among the changes proposed was the creation of a social communications regulatory body with wide regulatory and oversight competences, including determining whether or not a given communication meets good journalistic practices. Such a provision would amount to prior censorship and would hinder the free flow of ideas and opinions. The majority of the regulatory body's members were to be nominated by the ruling party and the party with the most seats in the National Assembly (MPLA in both cases), raising concerns that the body would be a political institution that silences critical voices and dissent.

RIGHT TO HEALTH – YELLOW FEVER OUTBREAK

An outbreak of yellow fever, first reported in Luanda in the last quarter of 2015, continued into the second half of 2016 and included suspected cases in all of the country's 18 provinces. Of the 3,625 cases reported in this period, 357 resulted in death. The outbreak was made worse by a vaccine shortage at the major public hospital in Luanda where cases were first diagnosed. The UN CESCR recommended that Angola increase resources to the health sector, particularly to improve infrastructure and expand health care facilities especially in rural areas.

HOUSING RIGHTS – FORCED EVICTION

In its 2016 review of Angola, the UN CESCR expressed concern at the persistence of forced evictions, including from informal settlements and during development projects, without the necessary procedural guarantees or the provision of alternative housing or adequate compensation to the affected individuals and groups.

Communities were resettled in makeshift homes without adequate access to basic services such as water, electricity, sanitation, health care and education.

On 6 August, a military officer shot dead 14-year-old Rufino Antônio, who was standing in front of his home in an attempt to prevent its demolition. The military police had been deployed there that day to deal with a demonstration against the demolition of houses in Zango II, Viana Municipality in Luanda, in the context of a development project. Those suspected of the killing had not been brought to justice by the end of the year.

1. Urgent Action: Angolan activist convicted after unfair trial: Manuel Chivonde Nito Alves (AFR 12/3464/2016)

2. Urgent Action: Further information: Angolan activist released a week early: Francisco Mapanda (AFR 12/5205/2016)

3. Urgent Action: Angola: Four youth activists detained without charge (AFR 12/4631/2016)

4. Amnesty International, OMUNGA and Organização Humanitária Internacional (OHI) urge Angolan authorities to respect the rights to freedom of expression and peaceful assembly (AFR 12/4590/2016)

ARGENTINA

Argentine Republic
Head of state and government: **Mauricio Macri**

Women and girls faced obstacles in accessing legal abortions; the criminalization of sexual and reproductive rights intensified. Discrimination against Indigenous Peoples continued.

BACKGROUND

The National Congress passed the Law on Access to Public Information (Law 27.275). The National Council of Women presented the National Action Plan for the Prevention, Assistance and Eradication of Violence against Women.

In June and October, mass protests took place under the slogan "Not One Less" over pervasive violence against women, femicide and the lack of public policies to address the situation.

Argentina was subject to the scrutiny of the UN Human Rights Committee, the UN Committee on the Elimination of Discrimination against Women (CEDAW Committee), and the UN Committee on the Elimination of Racial Discrimination.

SEXUAL AND REPRODUCTIVE RIGHTS

In April, a woman from the Tucumán province was found guilty of "murder" and sentenced to eight years in prison after suffering a miscarriage in a hospital, according to her clinical record. She was reported to the police by hospital staff for purportedly inducing an abortion and held in pre-trial detention for over two years. She was first charged with undergoing an illegal abortion and then with aggravated murder for the premeditated killing of a close relative (a crime that carries prison sentences of up to 25 years). In August, the UN Human Rights Committee expressed concern regarding this case, recommending that the government consider decriminalizing abortion and calling for her prompt release. The Committee further called on Argentina to liberalize its laws on abortion, to ensure that all women and girls have access to reproductive health services, and "that women are not obliged, as a consequence of legal obstacles, the exercise of conscientious objection of health workers or the lack of medical protocols, to resort to clandestine abortions that put their lives and health at risk". The Tucumán

Supreme Court ultimately ordered the woman's release that month but had to issue a final ruling on the eight-year sentence imposed on her by the lower court.

In July, a 12-year-old girl from the Wichí Indigenous community was raped by a group of non-Indigenous men. The rape resulted in a pregnancy which she was forced to continue, despite the fact that her parents had reported the rape. At 31 weeks, the girl was allowed to have a caesarean section only because the pregnancy was unsustainable.

In November, the CEDAW Committee urged Argentina to ensure that all provinces approve protocols to facilitate access to legal abortion; ensure that women have access to safe legal abortion and post-abortion services and take definitive steps to prevent "the blanket use of conscientious objection by doctors refusing to perform abortions, considering in particular the situation of early pregnancies as a result of rape and incest that may amount to torture"; and "accelerate the adoption of the draft law for the voluntary interruption of pregnancy increasing legal access to abortion".

INDIGENOUS PEOPLES' RIGHTS

Although the Constitution recognizes the rights of Indigenous Peoples to their ancestral lands and to participate in the management of natural resources, the majority of Indigenous communities remained without legal acknowledgment of their land rights.

Indigenous Peoples reported over 200 cases of violations of their human rights to land, participation and consultation, equality and non-discrimination and access to justice, among other rights.

2016 marked seven years of impunity in the case of Javier Chocobar, leader of the Chuschagasta Indigenous community, who was killed for peacefully defending his land in the Northern Province of Tucumán.

REFUGEES' AND MIGRANTS' RIGHTS

In August, the National Migration Directorate and the Ministry of Security announced the establishment of a detention centre for migrants. This did not comply with the rights to liberty, freedom of movement and the protection from arbitrary detention.

During the Leaders' Summit on Refugees in New York, USA, in September, Argentina pledged to receive 3,000 Syrian refugees, prioritizing families with children. At the end of the year, details of the resettlement programme remained unspecified.

IMPUNITY

Public trials were held for crimes against humanity during the military regime between 1976 and 1983. Between 2006 and December 2016, 173 rulings had been issued, bringing the total number of those convicted to 733.

In May, a historic sentence was passed on the "Plan Cóndor" case, a co-ordinated intelligence plan launched in the 1970s by the de facto governing military regimes in Argentina, Brazil, Bolivia, Chile, Paraguay and Uruguay. Reynaldo Bignone, the last de facto President of Argentina at the time, was sentenced to 20 years' imprisonment. A further 14 military leaders were sentenced to imprisonment. In August, the sentence on the "La Perla" historical trial – which included clandestine centres in Córdoba Province – was rendered, sentencing 28 perpetrators to life imprisonment. Nine sentences were passed for between two and 14 years' imprisonment and six acquittals.

By December, the Bicameral Commission to identify economic and financial interests that had colluded with the military dictatorship, created by Law 27.217 in 2015, had not been established.

The public hearing continued of the cover-up of the investigation into the 1994 attack on the Jewish Mutual Association of Argentina (AMIA) building, in which 85 people were killed. Among those accused were former President Carlos Menem, a former judge and other former officials. The main case relating to the attack had been stalled since 2006. In August, the AMIA Prosecutorial Investigation Unit identified Augusto Daniel Jesús as the final victim who still had to be identified.

FREEDOMS OF EXPRESSION AND ASSEMBLY

Reports of unnecessary and excessive use of force by security forces in the context of public protests continued.

On 16 January, the social leader Milagro Sala was arrested and charged for protesting peacefully in Jujuy in December 2015. Despite her release being ordered in this case, further criminal proceedings were then initiated against her in order to keep her in detention. In October the UN Working Group on Arbitrary Detention concluded that her detention was arbitrary and asked for her immediate release.

On 17 February, the "Protocol on State Security Force Conduct during Public Protests" was published, issued by the National Ministry of Security, stating that forces should repress and the justice system criminally prosecute those exercising their right to peaceful assembly.

On 31 March, the Buenos Aires Public Prosecutor's Office issued judgment FG N 25/2016, which led to serious risks of undue restriction on the right to peaceful assembly.

HUMAN RIGHTS DEFENDERS

The human rights defender Rubén Ortiz was threatened and intimidated over his support for the rights of peasant farmer (*campesino*) communities in the Province of Misiones. An investigation process was ongoing at the end of the year.

TORTURE AND OTHER ILL-TREATMENT

The National Committee for the Prevention of Torture had not been established by the end of the year, despite government regulation of the National System for the Prevention of Torture, comprising legislators, government authorities and representatives of civil society organizations. The duties of the Committee included visits to detention centres, prevention of prison overpopulation and regulations on transfers.

ARMENIA

Republic of Armenia
Head of state: **Serzh Sargsyan**
Head of government: **Karen Karapetyan (replaced Hovik Abrahamyan in September)**

Police used excessive force to suppress largely peaceful demonstrations in the capital, Yerevan, in July. Hundreds of individuals were arbitrarily arrested. Many reported being injured, beaten or otherwise ill-treated during the arrest and while in detention.

BACKGROUND

The year was marked by economic and political volatility, and growing security concerns linked to the outbreak of large-scale military confrontation in April in Nagorno-Karabakh, the breakaway region of Azerbaijan supported by Armenia. On 8 September, Prime Minister Abrahamyan resigned, citing his government's failure to address economic and political challenges. On 13 September, President Sargsyan appointed former Yerevan Mayor Karen Karapetyan as the new Prime Minister.

EXCESSIVE USE OF FORCE

On 17 July a group of armed men stormed a police compound in the Erebuni district of Yerevan, killing one police officer, injuring two and taking several as hostages.

Following the seizure of the compound, hundreds gathered at the Liberty Square to show solidarity with the gunmen and join their calls for the release of the imprisoned opposition activist Jirair Sefilian – who had been charged with illegal arms possession – and to call for the resignation of the President. A two-week-long standoff with police sparked widespread anti-government protests in Yerevan, resulting in several clashes with the police. The protests took place daily and dwindled after the hostage-takers surrendered on 30 July. While police allowed peaceful gatherings in most instances, they regularly detained protesters and others. On several occasions, protests in Yerevan were dispersed with excessive force.

On 20 July, clashes ensued after police refused to allow protesters to pass food to the armed group inside the compound. Some protesters started pushing police officers and throwing stones and water bottles. Police responded by using stun grenades and tear gas indiscriminately and injured many peaceful protesters and bystanders. Police then started dispersing the rally and arresting participants. Several eyewitnesses said that police officers chased and beat fleeing demonstrators before arresting them; 136 people were reported detained, dozens injured.

On 29 July police used excessive force against peaceful demonstrators in Sari-Tagh, near the seized compound. The police warned the crowd to disperse; shortly afterwards they fired tear gas and threw stun grenades indiscriminately, wounding dozens of demonstrators and some journalists. A group of men armed with wooden batons then moved into the crowd from behind the police line and ambushed and beat demonstrators and journalists. Meanwhile, the police blocked the street to prevent the crowd from fleeing and proceeded to arrest all demonstrators. At least 14 journalists reported being deliberately targeted by stun grenades and beaten to prevent them from live reporting. At least 60 people were reported injured and hospitalized, including with severe burns from exploding grenades. During the following weeks, five police officers were suspended for using excessive force; the head of Yerevan police was dismissed and 13 police officers, including some of high rank, were formally reprimanded for "failing to prevent violent attacks on protesters and journalists". Investigations into both incidents were ongoing at the end of the year.

ARBITRARY ARRESTS AND DETENTIONS

Following the events of 17 July, police summoned political activists for questioning. According to media reports, around 200 individuals, mostly opposition supporters and activists, were brought to police stations, without being formally arrested. Activists reported that police visited their family homes, threatened their family members with arrests and conducted illegal searches. Activists were questioned and held in police stations, some for more than 12 hours, and released without charge. They were not allowed to notify their families or relatives of their whereabouts and were denied access to their lawyers.

TORTURE AND OTHER ILL-TREATMENT

Torture and other ill-treatment by police and in detention facilities continued to be widely reported.

In February, the Nubarashen prison administration forced imprisoned activist Vardges Gaspari to undergo a psychiatric examination after he alleged that the administration had ordered his cellmates to beat, threaten and pour cold water on him.

During the July events, a number of activists reported being denied access to water, medicine and necessary medical aid after being detained by the police for participating in protests; in some cases they were held for more than 12 hours without charge. Several individuals reported being severely beaten or otherwise ill-treated at the time of arrest and in detention, and prevented from notifying their relatives and lawyers of their whereabouts.

SEXUAL AND REPRODUCTIVE RIGHTS

In July, the government changed the law on abortion to ban sex-selective abortion between the 12th and 22nd weeks of pregnancy. The new law introduced a mandatory three-day waiting period and counselling for women after they had made the initial appointment for an abortion. Some women's groups raised concerns that the waiting period might be used to discourage women from having abortions and result in increased corruption, unsafe abortions and, consequently, an increase in maternal mortality. According to reports by the United Nations Population Fund (UNFPA) sex-selective abortions were "prevalent" in Armenia.

AUSTRALIA

Australia
Head of state: **Queen Elizabeth II, represented by Peter Cosgrove**
Head of government: **Malcolm Turnbull**

The justice system continued to fail Indigenous people, particularly children, with high rates of incarceration, reports of abuse and deaths in custody. Australia maintained its hardline policies of confining people seeking asylum in offshore processing centres in Papua New Guinea and Nauru, and turning back those attempting to reach Australia by boat. Counter-terror measures violated basic human rights.

INDIGENOUS PEOPLES' RIGHTS

Indigenous children were 24 times more likely to be detained than non-Indigenous children. Despite the recommendation by the UN Committee on the Rights of the Child that the international minimum age of criminal responsibility should be 12, the age was 10 throughout Australia. Children aged 10 or 11 were detained in every state except Tasmania. Nearly three quarters of them were Indigenous children.

Contrary to Article 37(c) of the UN Convention on the Rights of the Child, 17-year-olds were tried as, and jailed with, adults in the state of Queensland. The Queensland government passed legislation to change this in November. In December, the Court of Appeal in Victoria found the detention of children in an adult prison to be unlawful and ordered their transfer to a youth justice facility. Instead, the Victorian government officially renamed part of the adult prison a youth facility.

Leaked footage exposed abuse and other ill-treatment of children in detention in the Northern Territory. Similar abuses were reported in Queensland.[1] This led to the announcement of a Royal Commission into youth detention in the Northern Territory and an independent review in Queensland.

Indigenous adults were 15 times more likely to be jailed than non-Indigenous adults. At least five Indigenous people died in custody in various states and territories throughout the year.

REFUGEES AND ASYLUM-SEEKERS

In April, the Papua New Guinea Supreme Court ruled that the detention of around 900 men held in the Australian-run facilities on Papua New Guinea's Manus Island was unlawful and ordered that they be closed immediately. No timeframe had been made public for the closure of the centres by either the Australian or Papua New Guinean governments by the end of the year (see Papua New Guinea entry).

As of 30 November, there were 383 people, of whom 44 were children, 49 women and 290 men, in an offshore processing centre on Nauru, where they continued to suffer neglect, ill-treatment and other abuse in a deliberate policy to deter asylum-seekers from trying to reach Australia by boat (see Nauru entry).[2]

Around 320 people taken to Australia for medical treatment remained at risk of being returned to either Nauru or Manus Island.

In November, the Australian government announced that some of the refugees detained on Nauru and Papua New Guinea's Manus Island, would be resettled in the US.

During the year, at least three boats carrying asylum-seekers were returned directly to Sri Lanka. In June a boat was returned to Viet Nam before the passengers' claims for asylum had been adequately assessed. An unspecified number of boats were turned back to Indonesia.

Australia continued its policy of mandatory indefinite detention of asylum-seekers. As of 30 November, 1,414 people were held in onshore detention.

More than a year after Australia announced it would resettle an additional 12,000 Syrian and Iraqi refugees, nearly 8,400 refugees had arrived by December.

RIGHTS OF LESBIAN, GAY, BISEXUAL, TRANSGENDER AND INTERSEX PEOPLE

Despite overwhelming support from the public, there was still no legislation on marriage equality. Under the current law, marriage is permissible only between a man and a woman.

COUNTER-TERROR AND SECURITY

New counter-terror laws were proposed and passed. Among those proposed was a continuing detention order allowing for detention beyond expiry of sentence. Legislative changes allowed for children as young as 14 years old to be put under control orders, reduced from 16 years. Citizenship laws with the potential to make people stateless came into effect.

---

1. Australia: Reforms to justice system essential to protect the rights of Indigenous youth (NWS 11/4730/2016)
2. Australia: Appalling abuse, neglect of refugees on Nauru (NWS 11/4586/2016)

AUSTRIA

Republic of Austria
Head of state: **Heinz Fischer (until 8 July 2016), then jointly (ad interim) Doris Bures, Karlheinz Kopf, Norbert Hofer**
Head of government: **Christian Kern (replaced Werner Fayman in May)**

The number of asylum claims registered dropped by half compared to the previous year. However, in April Parliament gave the power to the government to rely on an emergency procedure to curtail the number of asylum-seekers in the country. A new law granted far-reaching surveillance and investigative powers to the intelligence agency.

REFUGEES' AND MIGRANTS' RIGHTS

In January, the government announced a cap on the number of asylum applications for 2016 at 37,500. Between January and November, approximately 39,600 people requested asylum in Austria. Almost 32,300 applications were deemed admissible. In the same period in 2015, approximately 81,000 people had requested asylum.

In April, Parliament passed an amendment to the Asylum Act granting the government the power to declare a threat to public order and security when high numbers of asylum-seekers were entering the country. This decree would trigger a fast-track asylum procedure in which border police would determine the admissibility of applications for international protection. Police would also forcibly return asylum-seekers who had crossed the border to neighbouring countries of transit without being required to provide a reasoned justification. Asylum-seekers would only be able to appeal from abroad as the appeals would be non-suspensive. The implementation of the amendment could result in the violation of the principle of *non-refoulement* and the right to have access to a fair and efficient asylum procedure. At the end of the year, the government had not triggered the procedure.

The amendment also severely limits the possibilities for refugees and beneficiaries of subsidiary protection to obtain family reunification.

While conditions in some reception centres improved, asylum procedures continued to be inadequate in identifying and assisting persons with specific needs, such as victims of torture, human trafficking, or gender-based violence. Support services, including health care for persons in need of special care, including unaccompanied minors, remained insufficient.

DISCRIMINATION

In June, the authorities expressed concern regarding racially motivated attacks on asylum shelters. In the same month, an asylum shelter was set alight before its official opening in the town of Altenfelden. In the first six months of the year, the Ministry of Interior reported almost as many criminal offences against asylum shelters (24) as for the whole of 2015 (25).

In June, an intersex person filed a complaint following the refusal by the civil registry office in Steyr to register their gender as neutral (neither male nor female). The case was pending before the Administrative Court of Upper Austria at the end of the year.

In August, several authorities, including the Federal Chancellor, expressed support for the right of same-sex couples to marry. However, no legislative amendments were tabled to this effect.

COUNTER-TERROR AND SECURITY

In July, the Police State Protection Act entered into force. The new legislation grants far-reaching surveillance and investigative powers to the domestic intelligence agency, the Federal Office for the Protection of the Constitution and the Fight against Terrorism. In particular, the Office can collect and store personal data from a wide variety of sources and launch investigations without informing the affected individuals. The lack of judicial oversight and the discretion with which the Office can exercise its powers raised concerns regarding the respect of the rights to privacy and to an effective remedy, among others.

AZERBAIJAN

Republic of Azerbaijan
Head of state: Ilham Aliyev
Head of government: Artur Rasizade

Some prisoners of conscience were released, but at least 14 remained in prison. Most human rights organizations forced to suspend their activities in previous years were unable to resume their work. Reprisals against independent journalists and activists persisted. International human rights monitors were denied access to Azerbaijan. Torture and other ill-treatment was widely reported, as well as arbitrary arrests of government critics.

BACKGROUND

Azerbaijan's oil-dependent economy was deeply affected by falling oil prices and the decline of its currency, the manat, by half of its value. Food prices rose without an equivalent rise in wages. From early January, spontaneous, and in most cases peaceful, protests against the devaluation of the manat and consequent price hikes spread across the country. The protests were clamped down on by police and security forces. On 18 January, President Aliyev signed a decree increasing the minimum pension and salaries of state employees by 10%. The measure remained insufficient to address the decline in living standards.

In April, hostilities escalated between Azerbaijan and the Armenia-backed break-away Nagorno-Karabakh region. The fighting lasted four days and resulted in civilian and military casualties on both sides and small territorial gains by Azerbaijani forces.

In September, a referendum approved proposed amendments to the Constitution, giving further powers to the President. The amendments extended the presidential term and granted the President the authority to declare early Presidential elections and to dissolve Parliament.

In November, the EU Council approved a new mandate for the negotiation of a "comprehensive" agreement with Azerbaijan to replace the 1996 Partnership and Co-operation Agreement (PCA) which governed EU-Azerbaijan bilateral relations. The political dialogue under the PCA had been halted in recent years as Azerbaijan's human rights record continued to deteriorate.

PRISONERS OF CONSCIENCE

Government critics continued to be incarcerated. In the early part of the year, several high-profile prisoners convicted following politically motivated trials were released, among them at least 12 prisoners of conscience. None of those released were cleared of criminal charges. Following its visit to Azerbaijan in May, the UN Working Group on Arbitrary Detention noted that "human rights defenders, journalists, political and religious leaders continue to be arbitrarily detained".

Some released prisoners of conscience, including journalist Khadija Ismayilova and human rights lawyer Intigam Aliyev, were banned from travelling abroad; most were effectively barred from continuing their work.

The criminal cases opened in 2014 and 2015 against a group of prominent NGOs, which were used as a pretext to arrest several prisoners of conscience for tax evasion and fraud, remained open at the end of the year.

On 10 May, youth activists Giyas Ibrahimov and Bayram Mammadov were detained on trumped-up drug-related charges after they painted political graffiti on a statue of Azerbaijan's former President Heydar Aliyev. They were sentenced to 10 years' imprisonment on 25 October and 8 December respectively.

On 18 November, the Supreme Court rejected the appeal by prisoner of conscience Ilgar Mammadov, upholding his seven-year prison sentence. The sentence was upheld despite a European Court of Human Rights ruling that found Ilgar Mammadov had been arrested without any evidence, and repeated calls by the Committee of Ministers of the Council of Europe for his release.

At the end of the year, at least 14 prisoners of conscience remained in prison. Local human rights activists estimated that more than 100 people remained imprisoned on politically motivated charges.

FREEDOM OF EXPRESSION

All mainstream media remained under government control; independent outlets continued to come under pressure from the authorities. Independent journalists faced intimidation, harassment and physical violence in connection with reporting that criticized the authorities.

On 20 April, the authorities launched a criminal investigation into Meydan TV, an internet-based, independent Azeri-language media outlet, alleging illegal entrepreneurship, large-scale tax evasion and abuse of power. Fifteen Meydan TV

journalists, some reporting from abroad, were also under investigation. Those working in Azerbaijan received travel restrictions prohibiting them from leaving the country. The criminal investigations against them were ongoing at the end of the year.

In November, Afgan Sadykhov and Teymur Kerimov, two journalists reporting on social issues, were detained and charged with assault after they were attacked by unidentified persons.

Zamin Gadji, a journalist with the opposition newspaper Yeni Musavat, was summoned and threatened by police at Baku police station on 28 November over a Facebook post criticizing the government's failure to investigate high-profile murder cases.

On 29 November, Parliament approved amendments to the Criminal Code criminalizing online insults against the honour and dignity of the President. The new law provided for fines and imprisonment for up to three years.

FREEDOM OF ASSOCIATION

Most of the leading Azerbaijani human rights NGOs were unable to resume their work following the freezing of their assets and ongoing harassment of their members, including criminal prosecution. Several NGO leaders convicted of trumped-up charges remained in prison; others were forced into exile for fear of persecution.

Early in the year, the government unfroze the bank accounts of eight NGOs involved in the Extractive Industries Transparency Initiative (EITI), an international group promoting open and accountable management of extractive resources. The decision came after the EITI downgraded Azerbaijan's membership to a Candidate country in 2015 due to the government crackdown on civil society.

FREEDOM OF ASSEMBLY

Police continued to suppress and disperse peaceful protests using excessive force.

During nationwide demonstrations in January, in at least two instances police used excessive force to disperse a peaceful crowd and arrested scores of peaceful demonstrators. Across the country, the authorities also summoned for questioning and arrested a number of political activists, accusing them of organizing the protests.

The Constitutional amendments introduced following the September referendum granted the government even more power to restrict the right to freedom of peaceful assembly. The amendments limited property rights and allowed the restriction of freedom of assembly if it breached "public morals".

TORTURE AND OTHER ILL-TREATMENT

Law enforcement officials continued to commit torture and other ill-treatment with impunity.

Human rights defenders reported torture and other ill-treatment of members of the Muslim Unity movement who had been arrested during clashes with government security forces in the village of Nardaran in 2015. Muslim Unity activists were accused of trying to forcibly change the constitutional system and to create an organized armed group.

The youth activists Bayram Mammadov and Giyas Ibrahimov reported that they were tortured and otherwise ill-treated in detention. Injuries consistent with their allegations were confirmed by the UN Working Group on Arbitrary Detention after visiting the activists in detention. Their findings were ignored by judges during remand and case hearings. Another youth activist, Elgiz Gahraman, told his lawyer he had been subject to torture following his arrest on 12 August. He was held incommunicado for 48 hours and forced to "confess" to charges of drug possession. At the end of the year he remained in detention with his trial pending.

ARMED CONFLICT

Four days of armed clashes between government forces and the forces of the self-declared Republic of Nagorno-Karabakh took place in April. Azerbaijan reported the deaths of six civilians and 31 military personnel; the

Armenian Ministry of Defence reported 93 persons killed on its side, including four civilians. The two parties accused each other of under-reporting military casualties and over-reporting civilian casualties. Both sides reportedly targeted civilian properties, including schools.

BAHAMAS

Commonwealth of the Bahamas
Head of state: Queen Elizabeth II, represented by Marguerite Pindling
Head of government: Perry Gladstone Christie

Widespread ill-treatment and other abuses against irregular migrants from countries including Haiti and Cuba continued. Bahamians voted "no" in a constitutional referendum on gender equality in citizenship matters in June. Discrimination against lesbian, gay, bisexual, transgender and intersex people continued.

LEGAL, CONSTITUTIONAL OR INSTITUTIONAL DEVELOPMENTS

On 7 June, Bahamians voted "no" in a referendum on gender equality in citizenship matters under Bahamian law. The proposed amendments – backed by the government – would have strengthened anti-discrimination protections based on sex.

The result maintained inequality in Bahamian laws so that women and men pass on citizenship to their children and spouses in different ways. The result put at risk the citizenship rights of families, in particular the risk of separation of families with diverse nationalities or children born outside of the Bahamas to Bahamian parents.

RIGHTS OF LESBIAN, GAY, BISEXUAL, TRANSGENDER AND INTERSEX PEOPLE

Stigma and discrimination against lesbian, gay, bisexual, transgender and intersex (LGBTI) people continued.

In April, activists founded the group Bahamas Transgender Intersex United. After its first press conference, members of the group reported receiving threats from members of the public. In May, an MP suggested that transgender people be exiled to another island.

RIGHT TO PRIVACY

Local human rights groups expressed fear regarding government surveillance online. In August, the Supreme Court ruled that the Minister of Education had breached the constitutional rights to privacy and to freedom of expression of members of an environmental group when he obtained and read their private email correspondence in Parliament. Ministers had alleged that the group was seeking to destabilize the government, and argued that parliamentary privilege allowed them to read out the confidential emails. The Court held that parliamentary privilege was subject to the supremacy of the Constitution, and ordered the destruction of the correspondence. At the end of the year, it remained unclear how the government had obtained the emails.

In November, the Inter-American Commission on Human Rights granted precautionary measures to members of the environmental group who allegedly received threats against their lives and personal integrity because of their work as human rights defenders. The government, in response, said the allegations were misrepresented.

BAHRAIN

Kingdom of Bahrain
Head of state: **King Hamad bin Issa al-Khalifa**
Head of government: **Shaikh Khalifa bin Salman al-Khalifa**

The authorities tightened restrictions on the rights to freedom of expression and association and continued to curtail the right to peaceful assembly. They detained and charged several human rights defenders and banned others from travelling abroad, dissolved the main opposition group and stripped more than 80 people of their Bahraini citizenship, forcibly expelling four. Opposition leaders continued to be imprisoned as prisoners of conscience. There were new reports of torture and other ill-treatment and unfair trials. Women continued to be discriminated against in law and practice. Migrant workers and lesbian, gay, bisexual, transgender and intersex people faced discrimination. There were no new death sentences or executions.

BACKGROUND

In March, Bahrain became a state party to the UN Convention on Certain Conventional Weapons.

In May, Bahrain's National Institution for Human Rights (NIHR) received a "B" status from the International Coordinating Committee of National Institutions as it was not fully compliant with the Paris Principles. One of the reasons given by the Committee was that the NIHR decision-making board included government representatives, undermining its independence.

Also in May, the government signed a trade and economic agreement with Switzerland containing two non-legally binding memorandums on the treatment of prisoners and on women's rights in Bahrain. In September the government of the USA blocked sales of fighter jets and related equipment to Bahrain pending human rights improvements.

Bahrain remained part of the Saudi Arabia-led coalition engaged in armed conflict in Yemen (see Yemen entry).

The government did not allow access to representatives from international human rights organizations, including Amnesty International, throughout the year.

FREEDOM OF EXPRESSION

The authorities continued to severely restrict freedom of expression, arresting and prosecuting human rights defenders and religious activists for using public gatherings or social media to criticize the government, the Saudi Arabian authorities and air strikes by the Saudi Arabian-led coalition in Yemen. Opposition leaders sentenced in previous years for their peaceful opposition remained held as prisoners of conscience.

In February a court sentenced Ebrahim Sharif, former Secretary General of the National Democratic Action Society (Waad), to a one-year prison term after convicting him of "incitement to hatred and contempt of the regime". He was released in July after completing his sentence; his one-year prison term was upheld in November. Also in November the authorities charged him with "inciting hatred against the regime" for comments he made in a media interview about the visit to Bahrain of Prince Charles from the UK. The charges were dropped the same month.

In March, the authorities detained activist Zainab al-Khawaja to serve sentences totalling 37 months following her conviction on various charges, including tearing pictures of the King. Her imprisonment was widely condemned. The authorities released her in May on "humanitarian grounds"; she subsequently left Bahrain.

In April a criminal court imposed a one-year prison term on activist Dr Sa'eed Mothaher Habib al-Samahiji for criticizing the Saudi Arabian authorities on Twitter.

In May an appeals court increased the 2015 prison sentence of Sheikh Ali Salman, leader of the main opposition group al-Wefaq National Islamic Society, from four to nine years. The court had overturned his acquittal of the charge of inciting change of the political system "by force, threats and other illegal means". In October the Court of Cassation rejected this decision and returned the case to the appeals court, which upheld its initial nine-year prison sentence in December.

In June, human rights defender Nabeel Rajab was arrested and charged with "spreading false information and rumours with the aim of discrediting the state" during televised interviews. In July, his trial opened in relation to his Twitter posts in 2015 alleging torture in Jaw Prison and criticizing Saudi-led aerial bombing in Yemen. In December, the court ordered his release on bail while his trial was ongoing but he was immediately re-arrested for investigation into the initial charge for which he had been arrested in June. He also faced separate prosecutions for comments he made in a *New York Times* article entitled "Letter from a Bahraini Jail" and in a letter published in *Le Monde* newspaper.

The authorities continued to restrict the media. In February the Minister of Information prohibited media outlets from employing journalists deemed to "insult" Bahrain or other Gulf or Arab states.

FREEDOM OF ASSOCIATION

The authorities tightened restrictions on freedom of association, continuing to imprison some leaders of al-Wefaq and other opposition parties and harassing others by summoning them several times for interrogation.

The authorities suspended al-Wefaq, seized its assets in June and obtained a court order for its dissolution in July for alleged breaches of the Law on Political Associations.

FREEDOM OF ASSEMBLY

The authorities maintained their ban on all public gatherings in the capital, Manama. Frequent protests, including some which turned violent, continued in Shi'a villages, particularly following the enforced dissolution of al-Wefaq. The security forces used excessive force to disperse some protests, firing shotgun pellets and tear gas, and arresting scores of religious activists and other protesters, including children. At least one police officer and one member of the public died in protest-related violence.

In January, the security forces forcibly dispersed people protesting against the execution of Sheikh Nimr al-Nimr in Saudi Arabia. Police used tear gas and shotgun pellets and arrested protesters.

In June, security forces blocked access into Duraz village for all but village residents after protesters gathered and began a sit-in protest outside the home of Shi'a Sheikh Issa Qassem after the authorities revoked his Bahraini citizenship. As the sit-in continued, the authorities arrested or summoned scores of protesters for questioning, including at least 70 Shi'a clerics and several human rights defenders, charging some with "illegal gathering". Courts sentenced 11 Shi'a clerics to one- or two-year prison terms on the same charge.

FREEDOM OF MOVEMENT

The authorities imposed administrative bans that prevented at least 30 human rights defenders and other critics from travelling abroad, including to attend meetings of the UN Human Rights Council in Geneva, Switzerland. At least 12 of them were later charged, including with "illegal gathering".

Deprivation of nationality and forced expulsions

The authorities obtained court orders that stripped at least 80 people convicted of terrorism-related offences of their Bahraini nationality, rendering many of them stateless. In June the Ministry of the Interior also revoked the nationality of Sheikh Issa Qassem, al-Wefaq's spiritual leader; he had not been convicted of any offence. The authorities forcibly expelled four of those whose citizenship they had withdrawn, including human rights lawyer Taimoor Karimi. An appeal court ruled in March that prisoner of conscience Ibrahim Karimi should be forcibly expelled from Bahrain when he completes his 25-month prison sentence in 2018.

TORTURE AND OTHER ILL-TREATMENT

Torture and other ill-treatment continued to be reported, particularly of people suspected of terrorism and other offences under interrogation by the police Criminal Investigations Directorate. Unfair trials continued; courts continued to rely on allegedly coerced "confessions" to convict defendants on terrorism-related charges.

Prisoners held at Dry Dock Prison and Jaw Prison complained of ill-treatment, including solitary confinement and inadequate medical care.

IMPUNITY

Impunity continued largely to prevail although the Ombudsman of the Ministry of the Interior and Special Investigations Unit (SIU) within the Public Prosecution Office continued to investigate alleged human rights violations by the security forces. Several low-ranking members of the security forces were prosecuted, but no senior officers.

The SIU said it received at least 225 complaints and referred 11 members of the security forces for trial on assault charges during the year. At least four members of the security forces were convicted and at least 12 acquitted during the year. In January the Court of Appeal increased from two to seven years the prison sentences imposed on two police officers for causing the death in custody of Ali Issa Ibrahim al-Saqer in 2011. In March the Court sentenced a police officer to three years' imprisonment for the unlawful killing of Fadhel Abbas Muslim Marhoon in 2014, overturning his earlier acquittal.

In February the Court of Appeal confirmed the acquittal of a police officer whose shooting of a peaceful protester at close range in January 2015 was captured on film, ruling that there was no evidence confirming the victim's presence or any injuries found, despite the video footage. In March the Court overturned the convictions of three police officers sentenced in 2015 for causing the death in custody of Hassan Majeed al-Shaikh in November 2014, and reduced the sentences of three other officers from five to two years.

RIGHTS OF LESBIAN, GAY, BISEXUAL, TRANSGENDER AND INTERSEX PEOPLE

The authorities continued to prosecute and imprison people for same-sex sexual conduct under "debauchery" and "obscenity" provisions of the Penal Code.

In January and February, the courts rejected applications by three Bahrainis who had undergone sex-change operations abroad to change their gender in official documents.

In September a court sentenced 28 men to prison terms of between six months and two years after convicting them on "debauchery" and "obscenity" charges for attending a private party at which some wore female clothes. In November, an appeal court reduced their sentences to between one and three months.

WOMEN'S RIGHTS

Women faced discrimination in law and practice. In May, Parliament agreed to abolish Article 353 of the Penal Code, which had allowed rapists to avoid a prison sentence if their victim consented to marry them.

MIGRANT WORKERS' RIGHTS

Migrant workers continued to face exploitation and abuse by employers. In July, more than 2,000 migrant workers participated in a peaceful march to protest against non-payment of their salaries by employers.

DEATH PENALTY

The death penalty remained in force. The courts did not hand down new death sentences but the Court of Cassation confirmed two and overturned four death sentences passed in previous years, three of which were later re-imposed by the court of appeal. There were no executions.

BANGLADESH

People's Republic of Bangladesh
Head of state: **Abdul Hamid**
Head of government: **Sheikh Hasina**

Armed groups claiming to act in the name of Islam killed dozens of people in targeted attacks, including foreign nationals, secular activists and lesbian, gay, bisexual, transgender and intersex (LGBTI) people. The government's response was marked by human rights violations, including arbitrary arrests, enforced disappearances, unlawful killings, torture and other ill-treatment. The

right to freedom of expression was further restricted as the government applied repressive laws and pressed criminal charges against critics.

FREEDOM OF EXPRESSION

Independent media outlets and journalists came under severe pressure by the government. Several journalists faced arbitrary criminal charges, often for publishing criticism of Prime Minister Sheikh Hasina, her family or the Awami League Government. Journalists reported increased threats from government officials or security agencies.

In February, more than 80 sedition and defamation cases were brought against Mahfuz Anam, editor of the newspaper *Daily Star*. The charges related to his admission that he had, under pressure from military intelligence, published unsubstantiated corruption allegations against Sheikh Hasina when she was out of government during the military rule of the 1990s. All charges were stayed by the High Court but the prosecution could reactivate them in the future. In April, 82-year-old journalist and opposition supporter Shafik Rehman was arrested on suspicion of involvement in an alleged plot to "kill and kidnap" the Prime Minister's son, Joy Wazed. After being held for more than four months without charge, including several weeks in solitary confinement, he was released on bail in August.

The government continued to use a range of repressive laws to restrict the right to freedom of expression extensively. It increasingly used the Information and Communications Technology Act which arbitrarily restricted online expression. The human rights organization Odhikar reported at least 35 arrests under the Act, compared to 33 in 2015 and 14 in 2014. Journalists, activists and others were targeted. Dilip Roy, a student activist, was one of those arrested, in September, for criticizing the Prime Minister on Facebook. He was released on bail on 17 November.

In October, parliament adopted the Foreign Donations (Voluntary Activities)

Regulation Act which significantly increased government control over the work of NGOs and threatened them with deregistration for making "inimical" or "derogatory" remarks against the Constitution or constitutional bodies. Several other bills that threatened freedom of expression were proposed in parliament, including the Digital Security Act and the Liberation War Denial Crimes Act.

ENFORCED DISAPPEARANCES

Enforced disappearances continued at an alarming rate, often of supporters of opposition parties Bangladesh National Party and Jamaat-e-Islami. Odhikar reported at least 90 people arrested by security forces and not heard from again. In August, three sons of prominent opposition politicians – Abdullahil Amaan Azmi, Mir Ahmed Bin Quasem and Hummam Qader Chowdhury – were arrested by men in plain clothes, some of whom identified themselves as police officers. The authorities continued to deny responsibility and the victims' families were not informed of their whereabouts.

ABUSES BY ARMED GROUPS

Armed groups killed at least 32 people in targeted attacks in 2016, including secular activists, LGBTI people and religious minorities. Jamaat-ul-Mujahideen Bangladesh (JMB) and Ansar al-Islam, which respectively claimed allegiance to the armed groups Islamic State (IS) and al-Qa'ida, claimed the attacks. In April, Nazimuddin Samad became the sixth secular activist to be hacked to death in a targeted killing in less than two years. The editor of *Roopbaan*, Bangladesh's only LGBTI magazine, and prominent LGBTI rights activist Xulhaz Mannan and his friend Tanay Mojumdar, were also killed by unidentified men. A range of human rights activists received threats from similar groups and said that the police did not offer enough protection, while others were reluctant to approach the police fearing they would be charged or harassed.

In July, JMB gunmen stormed a restaurant in the capital, Dhaka, and killed at least 22 people, including 18 foreign nationals. Police responded with a heavy-handed "anti-terror" crackdown. At least 15,000 people were arrested, and human rights groups raised concerns that several thousand were politically motivated arrests of opposition supporters. Police said at least 45 suspected "terrorists" were killed in shoot-outs in the months following the July attack. Two of the surviving hostages from the attack were detained by police and held incommunicado for several weeks before being presented to court on 4 August. One of them, Hasnat Karim, was still held without charge at the end of the year.

DEATH PENALTY

Scores of people were sentenced to death and several were executed.

In October, one alleged militant convicted of killing a judge in 2005 was executed. The government afterwards said that it would fast track the trials of people accused of crimes under the Anti-Terrorism Act which could lead to the death penalty, and that at least 64 people convicted under this Act since 1992 were on death row.

The International Crimes Tribunal (ICT), a Bangladeshi court established to investigate the events of the 1971 independence war, sentenced at least six people to death. The proceedings were marked by severe irregularities and violations of fair trial rights, such as the arbitrary restriction of the number of defence witnesses allowed. Two people convicted of war crimes and crimes against humanity by the ICT were executed, both senior members of Jamaat-e-Islami – Motiur Rahman Nizami in May and Mir Quasem Ali in September. On 23 August a group of UN human rights experts expressed concern about the fairness of ICT trials, and urged the government to annul Mir Quasem Ali's death sentence and grant him a retrial, stating that proceedings were "marred" by "irregularities".

TORTURE AND OTHER ILL-TREATMENT

Torture and other ill-treatment in custody was widespread; however, complaints were rarely investigated. The 2013 Torture and Custodial

Death (Prevention) Act was poorly enforced due to a lack of political will and awareness among law enforcement agencies. Human rights groups accused several security force branches – including police and the Rapid Action Battalion – of torture and other ill-treatment. Torture was carried out to extract "confessions", for extortion or to punish political opponents of the government.

CHITTAGONG HILL TRACTS

Police in September asked a court to close the investigation into the disappearance of Kalpana Chakma, an Indigenous Peoples' rights campaigner, from the Chittagong Hill Tracts – an area in southeastern Bangladesh – citing a lack of evidence. She was abducted in 1996. Government restrictions on access to the Chittagong Hill Tracts and on communication with "tribal" people there remained in place, arbitrarily restricting the right to freedom of expression of journalists and human rights organizations. Women and girls in the region faced multiple forms of discrimination and violence including rape and murder due to their gender, Indigenous identity and socio-economic status. Victims of gender-based violence continued to be denied justice because of pressure to settle out of court, non-availability of judges or other bureaucratic delays.

VIOLENCE AGAINST WOMEN AND GIRLS

Human rights groups said that rape conviction rates continued to be extremely low, mainly because investigations were not timely or effective. Many women and girls were reluctant to report rape to the authorities, for fear of being stigmatized and subjected to police harassment. Human rights organization Ain o Salish Kendra confirmed that at least 671 rape cases were reported by media, with the actual number of cases likely to be much higher. The rape and murder of 19-year-old Tonu in March sparked outrage and large-scale street protests. Activists claimed the police deliberately delayed the investigation and pressured the survivor's family into making false statements.

BELARUS

Republic of Belarus
Head of state: **Alyaksandr Lukashenka**
Head of government: **Andrey Kabyakou**

Severe restrictions on the rights to freedom of expression, of association and of peaceful assembly remained in place. The government continued to refuse co-operation with the UN Special Rapporteur on human rights in Belarus. At least four people were executed and four people were sentenced to death.

BACKGROUND

On 28 February, the EU lifted all its sanctions against persons and entities in Belarus except those against four former officials suspected of involvement in enforced disappearances committed in 1999-2000.

On 1 July, the government redenominated the value of the Belarusian ruble slashing four zeros, among other measures. This was a response to the continuing economic downfall partially prompted by the downturn in Russia, its principal trading partner.

Also in July, the mandate of the UN Special Rapporteur on human rights in Belarus – established by the UN Human Rights Council in 2012 – was extended for a further year.

In September, the new Parliament was elected against the backdrop of severe restrictions on independent media and the political opposition. Only two parliamentarians regarded as representing political opposition were elected.

On 24 October, the first national Human Rights Strategy was adopted. It outlined legislative reforms, none of which addressed the death penalty, but promised "to consider" Belarus' interest in joining the European Convention on Human Rights and the creation of a national human rights institution.

DEATH PENALTY

On 18 April, Siarhei Ivanou was executed despite the pending review of his case at the UN Human Rights Committee. This was the first execution since November 2014.[1] Around 5 November, Siarhei Khmialeuski, Ivan Kulesh and Hyanadz Yakavitski were executed. Death sentences in Belarus are typically carried out in secrecy and without notifying the family. The Supreme Court rejected the appeal of Siarhei Vostrykau on 4 October.[2] Siarhei Vostrykau was awaiting the outcome of his plea for clemency from the President at the end the year; clemency had been granted only once in over 400 pleas since 1994.

FREEDOM OF EXPRESSION

The Law on Mass Media continued to severely restrict the right to freedom of expression and effectively subjected all media companies to government control. Local journalists working for foreign media were still required to obtain official accreditation, which was routinely delayed or refused arbitrarily.

In January, political blogger Eduard Palchys, known for his critical posts of the Belarusian and Russian authorities and who was residing in Ukraine, was arrested during a visit to Bryansk, Russia. He was remanded in custody by the Russian authorities until his extradition to Belarus on 7 June where he was placed in detention. On 28 October, he was found guilty of "inciting racial, national or religious hatred" and of the "distribution of pornography". He was given a non-custodial sentence on account of having been on remand since January, and was released in court. The hearings of his case were closed, but the courtroom was opened to the public when the sentence was announced.

SURVEILLANCE

The legal framework governing secret surveillance allowed the authorities to undertake wide-ranging surveillance with little or no justification. The System of Operative-Investigative Measures (SORM), a system of lawful interception of all electronic communications, allowed the authorities direct access to telephone and internet communications and associated data. The possible surveillance restricted human rights defenders, other civil society and political activists as well as journalists in exercising their human rights, including the rights to freedom of association, of peaceful assembly and of expression.[3]

FREEDOM OF ASSOCIATION

NGOs and political parties continued to face undue restrictions, including compulsory registration. Registration applications were frequently arbitrarily rejected for minute infractions or on other unexplained grounds. Under Article 193.1 of the Criminal Code, the founding of, or participation in the activities of, an unregistered organization remained a crime punishable by up to two years' imprisonment.

The restrictions imposed on former prisoners of conscience Mikalai Statkevich, Yury Rubtsou and four other activists, as a condition for their early release in 2015, remained in place.

FREEDOM OF ASSEMBLY

The Law on Mass Events, which prohibits any assembly or public protest unless authorized by the authorities, remained in place.

Civil society activist Pavel Vinahradau was placed under "preventive supervision" from 7 June to 13 September after he participated in four "unauthorized" peaceful street protests.[4]

LEGAL, CONSTITUTIONAL OR INSTITUTIONAL DEVELOPMENTS

In October, the tax authorities reported that they had sent notices to over 72,900 individuals who, under the 2015 presidential decree "On preventing social dependency", were required to pay a special tax for being out of work for over 183 days in a given tax year. Failure to comply incurred fines or "administrative arrest" and compulsory community service which could amount to a form of forced labour.

1. Belarus: Amnesty International deplores the execution of Siarhei Ivanou (EUR 49/4014/2016)

2. Further information: Belarus' last prisoner on death row at risk: Siarhei Vostrykau (EUR 49/5274/2016) Belarus: Further information: Gennadii Yakovitskii's death sentence upheld (EUR 49/3890/2016)

3. It's enough for people to feel it exists: Civil society, secrecy and surveillance in Belarus (EUR 49/4306/2016)

4. Belarus: Activist arbitrarily convicted for peaceful protest (EUR 49/4317/2016)

BELGIUM

Kingdom of Belgium
Head of state: **King Philippe**
Head of government: **Charles Michel**

The authorities adopted a wide range of new laws and policies in the aftermath of the attacks in the capital, Brussels, in March. Civil society organizations continued to receive reports of ethnic profiling by police. Prison conditions remained poor; the European Court of Human Rights criticized Belgium for its treatment of mentally ill offenders.

COUNTER-TERROR AND SECURITY

On 22 March, three suicide bombers killed 32 people and injured hundreds in two co-ordinated attacks in Brussels. In the aftermath of the attacks, the authorities intensified the implementation of the wide range of security measures announced after the attacks in Paris, France, in 2015.

The authorities further broadened the scope of the provisions on terrorism-related offences, loosened procedural safeguards and adopted new policies to address "radicalization". Some measures caused concern regarding the principle of legality, including legal clarity, and the respect of the freedoms of association and expression.

In February, the federal government announced the new policy framework "Plan Canal" to address radicalization in several municipalities in the Brussels area. It included the deployment of increased police and tighter administrative controls on associations.

In April, the federal government agreed to establish a database to facilitate the sharing of information between government agencies concerning individuals suspected of having travelled abroad to commit terrorism-related offences. In July, the government announced a similar database for "hate preachers". In December, Parliament adopted a bill aimed at broadening police surveillance powers.

Also in July, the federal Parliament extended the provision on incitement to commit a terrorism-related offence and eased restrictions on the use of pre-trial detention for those suspected of terrorism-related offences. In December, Parliament passed legislation criminalizing preparatory acts to commit a terrorism-related offence and legislation on retention of Passenger Name Records.

Despite the government's commitment at the UPR in May to ensure that measures to counter terrorism respect human rights, little effort was made to assess the human rights impact of new measures.

PRISON CONDITIONS

Conditions of detention remained poor due to overcrowding, dilapidated facilities and insufficient access to basic services, including to health care. In April, a three-month strike by prison staff further worsened prison conditions and access to health care for prisoners.

Despite the entry into force of positive legislative amendments in October, many mentally ill offenders remained detained in regular prisons with insufficient care and treatment. In September the European Court of Human Rights found in *W.D. v Belgium* that the detention of mentally ill offenders without access to adequate care remained a structural problem. The Court ordered the government to adopt structural reforms within two years.

DISCRIMINATION

In April, Belgium's equality body Unia reported a rise in discrimination against persons of Muslim faith in the aftermath of the Brussels attacks, especially in the area of employment. Several individuals and civil society organizations reported ethnic profiling by police against ethnic and religious minorities.

On 9 December, the government agreed on a draft bill amending the law on legal gender recognition. If passed, the draft law would allow transgender people to obtain legal recognition of their gender on the basis of their informed consent and without fulfilling any medical requirements.

ARMS TRADE

Regional governments continued to grant licences to sell arms to parties involved in the conflict in Yemen, in particular to Saudi Arabia. In 2014 and 2015, Saudi Arabia reportedly accounted for by far the highest value of arms export licences from the Wallonia region.

VIOLENCE AGAINST WOMEN AND GIRLS

In March, Belgium ratified the Council of Europe Convention on preventing and combating violence against women and domestic violence (Istanbul Convention). In June, the authorities adopted a new binding policy framework which identified tackling gender-based and domestic violence as a priority for police and prosecutorial authorities.

In May, the National Institute of Criminalistics and Criminology said that 70% of reported domestic violence incidents did not lead to a prosecution and that the current prosecution policy has not been effective in reducing the numbers of recidivists of domestic violence.

BENIN

Republic of Benin
Head of state and government: **Patrice Athanase Guillaume Talon (replaced Thomas Boni Yayi in March)**

The authorities continued to restrict the rights to peaceful assembly and expression. Excessive force was used against peaceful demonstrators, causing at least one death. Prisons remained overcrowded.

BACKGROUND

Patrice Talon was elected President in March. Benin became the eighth AU member state to allow NGOs and individuals direct access to the African Court on Human and Peoples' Rights.

FREEDOMS OF ASSEMBLY AND EXPRESSION

The authorities continued to arbitrarily restrict the right to freedom of peaceful assembly, including by banning several opposition group demonstrations, taking retaliatory measures against organizers of peaceful demonstrations, and using excessive and arbitrary force against protesters.

In the context of the presidential elections, in January and February the authorities banned at least three peaceful demonstrations by opposition groups. Supporters of the ruling party were able to hold demonstrations.

In February, the authorities banned a demonstration by human rights groups to protest against the unlawful killing of a member of the military.

In March, security forces shot and killed one man and injured nine other people, including two children, at a demonstration in Bantè (Collines department). According to eyewitnesses, the demonstration was largely peaceful until the security forces started firing at the crowd with tear gas and live ammunition.

In July, the security forces used tear gas and batons to disperse a peaceful demonstration by students in Cotonou, injuring at least 20 people. At least nine students were arrested following the demonstrations and detained for several weeks before being released. Twenty-one students presumed to have participated were banned from registering at the university for five years. In August, the university decided to invalidate the academic year for all the students in the faculty where most demonstrators were studying. In October, the

Council of Ministers banned all activities by student associations on campuses.

In November, the High Authority of Audiovisual Communication made the arbitrary decision to close seven private media outlets.

UNLAWFUL KILLINGS

In January, Corporal Mohamed Dangou was shot dead by a member of the security services in a military camp in Cotonou. According to an eyewitness he was unarmed. Mohamed Dangou was due to be arrested as part of an investigation into a protest held with other military personnel serving in Côte d'Ivoire calling for the payment of allowances. In July, the Constitutional Court ruled that the armed forces had violated Mohamed Dangou's right to life.

PRISON CONDITIONS

The UN Subcommittee on Prevention of Torture made an unannounced visit to Benin in January. It concluded that detention centres were "overcrowded and lacked adequate staffing and other resources". As of September, Cotonou prison held 1,137 detainees, despite a maximum capacity of 500.

In June, the National Assembly adopted a law on community service which could be used to reduce prison overcrowding by replacing detention with non-custodial sentences.

CHILDREN'S RIGHTS

In February, the UN Committee on the Rights of the Child issued its concluding observations on Benin, expressing concerns about the infanticide of children born with disabilities and the persistence of harmful practices, including the rise of female genital mutilation and early and forced marriage. The Committee highlighted the high rates of girls dying from illegal abortion and urged that girls' rights to education, information and access to quality contraceptive products be guaranteed.

DEATH PENALTY

In January, the Constitutional Court abolished the death penalty in a ruling stating that "no one can now be sentenced to capital punishment". The government had yet to adopt laws removing the death penalty from national legislation.

BOLIVIA

Plurinational State of Bolivia
Head of state and government: Evo Morales Ayma

The creation of a truth, justice and reconciliation commission for human rights violations and crimes under international law committed during the military regimes (1964-1982) remained pending. There were allegations of a failure to seek the free, prior and informed consent of Indigenous Peoples on oil exploration projects in the Amazon. There was some progress in protecting the rights of lesbian, gay, bisexual, transgender and intersex (LGBTI) people and sexual and reproductive rights. Concerns remained about conditions in the penitentiary system.

BACKGROUND

In August, Deputy Minister of the Interior Rodolfo Illanes was killed during miners' protests. Protesters were opposing the enactment of an amendment to the Cooperatives Act, which grants the right to unionization.

IMPUNITY

Bolivia still had not created the truth, justice and reconciliation commission on crimes committed during the military governments promised at a March 2015 public hearing before the Inter-American Commission on Human Rights.

RIGHTS OF PEOPLE WITH DISABILITIES

In September, the UN Committee on the Rights of Persons with Disabilities released its report on Bolivia. Among its recommendations, the Committee urged Bolivia to improve and adapt mechanisms and proceedings to ensure access to justice for people with disabilities and to abolish the practice of sterilizing people with disabilities without their free, prior and informed consent.

FREEDOM OF ASSEMBLY

In June, peaceful protests by people with disabilities demanding a monthly disability allowance were suppressed by police using tear gas. In August, allegations of excessive use of force to repress the protests were reported to the UN Committee on the Rights of Persons with Disabilities, which urged the Bolivian authorities to carry out a thorough and impartial investigation into the incident.

INDIGENOUS PEOPLES' RIGHTS

In March, leaders of Amazonian Indigenous Peoples and the Centre for Documentation and Information of Bolivia (CEDIB) denounced the failure to ensure prior, free and informed consent for oil exploration projects taking place on Indigenous territories.

RIGHTS OF LESBIAN, GAY, BISEXUAL, TRANSGENDER AND INTERSEX PEOPLE

In May, the lower house of the Congress passed the Gender Identity Law, which established administrative procedures for transgender people over 18 to legally change their name, sex and image data on official documents.

In September, the Ombudsman endorsed a bill that would allow same-sex civil marriage and enable LGBTI people to enjoy the same health care and social security rights and guarantees as other couples. The bill was due to be submitted to the Plurinational Legislative Assembly later in the year.

SEXUAL AND REPRODUCTIVE RIGHTS

In August, the Ministry of Health and the University of San Andrés launched the first Observatory of Maternal and Neonatal Mortality to monitor and reduce the high rates of maternal and infant mortality in the country. The Ministry of Health also announced the development of a bill to guarantee timely access to family planning.

FREEDOM OF ASSOCIATION

In July, a petition that two articles of the Law Granting Legal Personality and its regulations were unconstitutional was rejected by the Constitutional Court. The petition had been presented by the Ombudsman on the grounds that the law could violate the right to freedom of association to establish NGOs or foundations. In October, four NGOs filed a petition with the Inter-American Commission on Human Rights regarding the law.

PRISON CONDITIONS

In June, the Ombudsman published a report highlighting the serious problem of overcrowding and corruption in the penitentiary system and persistent human rights violations against those deprived of their liberty.

BOSNIA AND HERZEGOVINA

Bosnia and Herzegovina
Head of state: **Rotating presidency – Bakir Izetbegović, Dragan Čović, Mladen Ivanić**
Head of government: **Denis Zvizdić**

Despite the adoption of progressive new anti-discrimination legislation, vulnerable minorities faced widespread discrimination. Threats and attacks against journalists and media freedom continued. The International Criminal Tribunal for the former Yugoslavia (ICTY) issued verdicts in relation to crimes committed during the 1992-1995 conflict; at the domestic level, access to justice and reparations for civilian victims of war remained limited.

BACKGROUND

In February, Bosnia and Herzegovina (BiH) submitted an application for membership to the EU, which was accepted by the EU in September.

The authorities of Republika Srpska (RS) – one of the two entities of BiH – refused to implement a decision of the BiH Constitutional Court, which had found the RS Law on Holidays (making 9 January the Day of Republika Srpska) unconstitutional and discriminatory against non-Serbs living in the entity.

Nationwide municipal elections held in October were marked by growing nationalist rhetoric. The results of the first post-war census conducted in 2013 were released in June, although RS challenged the collection methodology and the census results.

DISCRIMINATION

The Council of Ministers adopted its first Action Plan on Prevention of Discrimination in April and, in June, the Parliamentary Assembly of BiH adopted amendments to the Law on Prevention of Discrimination. Widely welcomed by civil society, the amended law listed specific grounds for discrimination, including sexual orientation, and significantly broadened the prohibited grounds of inciting discrimination beyond the original racial, religious and nationality grounds.

The Parliament of the Federation of Bosnia and Herzegovina – the other entity of BiH – adopted amendments to the entity criminal code to include hate crimes as a criminal offence. The definition of hate crime included a wide array of prohibited grounds, although the penalties prescribed for the offence of incitement to hatred, hate speech and violence remained limited to national, ethnic and religious grounds and excluded hate speech directed against other marginalized groups.

Social exclusion and discrimination, in particular of Roma and lesbian, gay, bisexual, transgender and intersex (LGBTI) people, remained widespread. Although the number of Roma without identity documents reduced and their access to housing slightly improved, Roma continued to face systemic barriers to education, health services and employment. The National Strategy on Roma Integration and the accompanying Action Plan ended in 2016, without meeting many of its targets. The Council of Ministers re-purposed a portion of the funds originally designated to support the Plan's implementation.

LGBTI people faced ongoing discrimination and intimidation. Civil society groups documented cases of verbal and physical attacks and discrimination, the majority of which were not thoroughly investigated. In March, a group of young men entered a café and cinema popular with the LGBTI community in the capital, Sarajevo, and attacked and threatened the customers. Several people suffered physical injuries, but the police classified the incident as a minor offence. Similarly, the perpetrators of the 2014 attack against the organizers of the Merlinka Queer Film Festival were never criminally charged. The 2016 festival took place under heavy police protection.

The 2009 judgment of the European Court of Human Rights in *Sejdić-Finci v BiH*, which found the power-sharing arrangements set out in the Constitution to be discriminatory, remained unimplemented. Under the arrangements, citizens who would not declare themselves as belonging to one of the three constituent peoples of the country (Bosniaks, Croats and Serbs) were excluded from running for legislative and executive office.

FREEDOM OF EXPRESSION

A pattern of threats, political pressure and attacks against journalists continued in 2016. The Association of Journalists documented repeated attacks against journalists, attacks on freedom of expression and on the integrity of media outlets.

CRIMES UNDER INTERNATIONAL LAW

The ICTY issued first-instance verdicts in cases of former high-ranking officials in relation to crimes committed during the 1992-1995 conflict. In March, the ICTY found Radovan Karadžić, the wartime President of RS, guilty of genocide, war crimes and crimes against humanity and sentenced him to 40 years' imprisonment. Also in March, the ICTY found Vojislav Seselj, the Serb Radical Party leader, not guilty on any counts of crimes against humanity and war crimes.

Lack of capacity and resources, along with ineffective case management and persistent political obstruction, continued to slow down the progress of prosecution and access to redress before domestic courts. In July, an independent analysis commissioned by the OSCE showed that the National War Crimes Strategy had failed to meet its targets, with a backlog of over 350 complex cases still pending before the State Court and Prosecutor's Office.

Despite earlier commitments by the authorities, no progress was made on the adoption of the Law on Protection of Victims of Torture and the harmonization of entity laws regulating the rights of civilian victims of war to enable their effective access to services, free legal aid and effective reparation.

In October, a local court in Doboj city granted financial compensation to a victim of wartime rape and sentenced the perpetrator to five years' imprisonment. This was the second case of financial reparations for war crimes awarded within a criminal proceeding. However, many victims continued to be forced to pursue compensation claims in civil proceedings, where they had to reveal their identity and incurred additional costs. In April, the Constitutional Court declared that the statute of limitations applied to reparation claims for non-material damage and that claims could be directed only against the perpetrators, not the state, further limiting the ability of victims to claim and obtain compensation.

Although more than 75% of the missing persons from the war had been exhumed and identified, there were still 8,000 people missing in connection with the conflict. The process of exhumations encountered significant challenges, including reduced funding for the Missing Persons Institute and limited expertise domestically. The Law on Missing Persons remained unimplemented, with the Fund for the families of missing persons still awaiting establishment.

BOTSWANA

Republic of Botswana
Head of state and government: **Seretse Khama Ian Khama**

The rights to freedom of expression and of assembly were restricted. The rights of refugees were violated. Lesbian, gay, bisexual, transgender and intersex (LGBTI) people continued to have their rights infringed. One prisoner under sentence of death was executed.

FREEDOM OF EXPRESSION

The right to freedom of expression was restricted. In March, police arrested freelance journalist Sonny Serite after a whistleblower gave him documents that related to a corruption case he was covering. Sonny Serite was charged with receiving stolen property; the charges were withdrawn in June. The Whistle Blower Act, which provided no protection to whistleblowers who contacted the media, came into effect on 16 December.

In August, Lobatse High Court ruled that Outsa Mokone, editor of the *Sunday Standard* newspaper, could be charged with sedition. His lawyers had argued that sections of the Penal Code covering sedition infringed his right to freedom of expression and breached the Constitution. Outsa Mokone was arrested in 2014 after an article in the *Sunday Standard* alleged the involvement of Botswana's President in a road accident. The article's author, Edgar Tsimane, fled to South Africa fearing for his life and was granted asylum.

FREEDOM OF ASSEMBLY

The right to freedom of peaceful assembly was curtailed. The Public Order Act required a police permit to protest, but applications are sometimes rejected. In June, youth activist Tlamelo Tsurupe was arrested and held briefly after protesting against youth unemployment in front of parliament and refusing to move. He subsequently launched #UnemploymentMovement. In July, the movement applied for a permit to protest but this was rejected. Despite this, on 8 August the group protested outside parliament. They were beaten by police and four were arrested and held overnight at Central Police Station on charges of "common nuisance". Two of the four needed medical assistance. The police also arrested three journalists covering the protest and forced them to hand over video footage of the protest. The police subsequently granted a permit for a demonstration, which took place on 13 August.

RIGHTS OF LESBIAN, GAY, BISEXUAL, TRANSGENDER AND INTERSEX PEOPLE

Same-sex sexual relationships remained illegal. In August, a man charged under Section 164 of the Penal Code with "having carnal knowledge with another man against the order of nature" was sentenced to three and a half years in prison by Gaborone Magistrates Court. The Botswana Network on Ethics, Law and HIV/AIDS (BONELA), which submitted an appeal, argued that Section 164 discriminates on the basis of sexual orientation and gender identity. The appeal had not been heard by the end of 2016.

In March, in a landmark case, the Lesbians, Gays and Bisexuals of Botswana (LEGABIBO) won its appeal in the High Court to register as an independent organization. The LEGABIBO had been denied registration by the Home Affairs Ministry since 2012. The High Court ruled that the refusal to register LEGABIBO violated the applicants' rights to freedom of expression, association and assembly.

WOMEN'S RIGHTS

Sexual abuse of women and girls was reported. A councillor of the city of Sebina was accused of molesting and impregnating a 16-year-old girl. A case of defilement could not be brought against him because the Penal Code defines defilement as a sexual act with a child aged under 16. No disciplinary action was known to have been taken by the councillor's political party, the Botswana Democratic Party.

RIGHT TO HEALTH – MINEWORKERS

On 7 October, the government closed without warning or consultation the BCL and Tati Nickel mines. The sudden closures threatened anti-retroviral therapy treatment and counselling services for mineworkers living with HIV/AIDS as the government failed to make alternative health care provisions. It also left over 4,700 mineworkers uncertain about their retrenchment benefits.

REFUGEES AND ASYLUM-SEEKERS

The encampment policy, which restricts refugees to the Dukwe camp 547km from the capital, Gaborone, continued to limit refugees' freedom of movement.

The government announced that it had revoked the refugee status of Namibians from 31 December 2015, even though Namibians who had fled conflict in the Caprivi region of Namibia in 1998 still faced persecution there. Refugees who returned to Namibia in late 2015 were convicted of charges ranging from high treason to illegally exiting Namibia. Later in January 2016, the Botswana High Court ruled that Namibian refugees should not be repatriated until a legal case brought against the revocation order had been decided. The High Court judgment was upheld on appeal in March.

DEATH PENALTY

In May, Patrick Gabaakanye was executed for a murder committed in 2014. This brought to 49 the total number of people executed since independence in 1966. Executions were conducted in secret. Families were given no notice and were denied access to the burial site.

BRAZIL

Federative Republic of Brazil
Head of state and government: **Michel Temer (replaced Dilma Rousseff in August)**

Police continued to use unnecessary and excessive force, particularly in the context of protests. Young people and black men, mainly those living in *favelas* and other marginalized communities, were disproportionately targeted with violence by law enforcement officials. Human rights defenders, especially those defending land and environmental rights, faced increased threats and attacks. Violence against women and girls remained widespread. Human rights violations and discrimination against refugees, asylum-seekers and migrants intensified.

BACKGROUND

On 31 August, President Dilma Rousseff was impeached after a long process in Congress, after which Vice-President Michel Temer took office. The new government announced several measures and proposals with the potential to impact human rights, including a constitutional amendment (PEC 241/55) capping government expenses over the next 20 years that could negatively affect investments in education, health and other areas. The amendment was approved in the House of Representatives and the Senate and was heavily criticized by the UN Special Rapporteur on extreme poverty and human rights.

In Congress, several proposals that would impinge on the rights of women, Indigenous Peoples, children, and lesbian, gay, bisexual, transgender and intersex (LGBTI) individuals were pending discussion. In September a special commission in the House of Representatives approved changes to family law to define family as the union between a man and a woman.

Brazil had not yet ratified the Arms Trade Treaty nor signed the Convention on Cluster Munitions. Brazil played a significant role in ongoing negotiations for a treaty that would ban nuclear weapons, to be finalized in 2017.

In December, the Inter-American Court of Human Rights convicted the Brazilian state for tolerating slave labour and trafficking of people, based on conditions of farm workers in the northern state of Pará.

PUBLIC SECURITY

Homicides and gun violence remained high throughout the country, with estimates putting the number of victims of homicides in 2015 at over 58,000. The authorities failed to propose a plan to address the situation.

On 29 January, 10 people were killed and 15 wounded by gunmen in the city of Londrina, Paraná state. Six of the seven people detained during the investigation into the incident were military police officers.

In March, following her visit to Brazil, the UN Special Rapporteur on minority issues presented to the Human Rights Council her recommendations that both the military police and the automatic classification of killings by the police as "resistance followed by death" – which presumes that the police acted in self-defence and does not lead to any investigation – be abolished.

In September the federal government authorized the deployment of armed forces in the state of Rio Grande do Norte to support the police after several days of attacks by criminal gangs on buses and public buildings. At least 85 people were detained for allegedly participating in the attacks.

On 18 November, seven men were shot dead in Imperatriz, Maranhão, after an off-duty military police officer had been targeted for attempted robbery and physical assault.

2016 Olympic Games

The authorities and organizers of the 2016 Olympic Games failed to implement necessary measures to prevent human rights violations by security forces before and during the sporting event.[1] This led to a repetition of violations witnessed during other major sporting events hosted in the city of Rio de Janeiro, namely the Pan American Games in 2007 and the FIFA World Cup in 2014.

Tens of thousands of military and security officers were deployed around Rio de Janeiro. The number of people killed by the police in the city of Rio de Janeiro in the immediate run-up to the games between April and June increased by 103% compared to the same period in 2015.

During the Olympic Games (5-21 August), police operations intensified in specific areas of Rio de Janeiro, including the *favelas* of Acari, Cidade de Deus, Borel, Manguinhos, Alemão, Maré, Del Castilho and Cantagalo. Residents reported hours of intensive shootings and human rights abuses including unlawful searches of homes, threats and physical assaults. The police admitted to killing at least 12 people during the Games in the city of Rio de Janeiro and to engaging in 217 shootings during police operations in the state of Rio de Janeiro.[2]

During the Olympic torch relay throughout the country, peaceful protests in Angra dos Reis and Duque de Caxias – both in Rio de Janeiro state – were met with unnecessary and excessive use of force by the police. Rubber bullets, stun grenades and tear gas were used indiscriminately against peaceful protesters and passers-by, including children.

On 10 May, the so-called "General Law of the Olympics" (13.284/2016) was signed by President Rousseff, amid concerns that it might impose undue restrictions to freedoms of expression and peaceful assembly, contrary to international human rights standards. Under the provisions of the new law, dozens of people were expelled from sports facilities for wearing T-shirts with slogans, carrying flags, or other signs of protest during the first days of the Games. On 8 August, a federal court ruled against the prohibition of peaceful protests inside the Olympic facilities.

On 5 August, the day of the opening ceremony, a peaceful protest over the negative impacts of the Games took place near Maracanã stadium, Rio de Janeiro, and was repressed with unnecessary force by the police, who used tear gas to disperse

protesters in a square where children were playing. Most police officers policing the protest were not properly identified as such.

On 12 August, also near Maracanã stadium, a protest led mainly by students was severely repressed by the military police, who used unnecessary and excessive force. Around 50 protesters, mostly under the age of 18, were detained and one was injured. At the end of the year some of the detainees were being investigated under the Fan Defence Statute, which makes it a crime to disturb order or provoke violence within a 5km radius of a sports facility.

UNLAWFUL KILLINGS

Killings by the police remained high and increased in some states. In the state of Rio de Janeiro, 811 people were killed by the police between January and November. There were reports of several police operations which resulted in killings, most of them in *favelas*. A few measures were adopted to curb police violence in Rio de Janeiro but had yet to produce an impact. Following a resolution from the National Council of Public Prosecution, on 5 January the Public Prosecution Office of Rio de Janeiro state created a working group to oversee police activities and the investigation of killings committed by the police. The Civil Police announced that the investigations of all cases of killings by the police would be progressively transferred to the specialized homicide division.

Most cases of killings by the police remained unpunished. Twenty years after the unlawful killing of a two-year-old during a military police operation in 1996 in the *favela* of Acari, Rio de Janeiro city, no one had been held to account. On 15 April the statute of limitations for the crime expired. In October the first public hearing with regard to the killings of 26 people during police operations in the *favela* Nova Brasília, Rio de Janeiro city, in October 1994 and May 1995 was held before the Inter-American Court of Human Rights. The killings had yet to be investigated and nobody had been brought to justice.

In July the Attorney General requested that the investigation into the killing of 12 people by the police in February 2015 in Cabula, Bahia state, be transferred to a federal authority.

On 6 November, five men, who had disappeared on 21 October after being approached by law enforcement officials, were found dead in Mogi das Cruzes, São Paulo. The bodies showed signs of executions and initial investigations by authorities indicated the involvement of municipal guards.

On 17 November, four young men were shot dead by the military police unit ROTA in Jabaquara, São Paulo.

ENFORCED DISAPPEARANCES

On 1 February, 12 military police officers were found guilty and sentenced for the crimes of torture followed by death, procedural fraud and "occultation' of a corpse" in the case of the enforced disappearance of Amarildo de Souza in Rio de Janeiro.

In April, police investigations named 23 military police officers as suspects in the enforced disappearance of 16-year-old Davi Fiuza in the city of Salvador, Bahia state, in October 2014. However, the case failed to reach the Public Prosecutor's Office and none of the accused had faced trial by the end of 2016.

PRISON CONDITIONS

Prisons remained severely overcrowded, with reports of torture and other ill-treatment. According to the Ministry of Justice, by the end of 2015 the prison system had a population of more than 620,000, although the overall capacity was around 370,000 people.

Prison riots took place throughout the country. In October, 10 men were beheaded or burned alive in a prison in Roraima state and eight men died of asphyxiation in a cell during a prison fire in Rondônia state.

On 8 March the UN Special Rapporteur on torture reported, among other things, poor living conditions and the regular occurrence of torture and other ill-treatment of inmates by police and prison guards in Brazil.

In September a court of appeals declared null a trial and sentences against 74 police officers for a massacre in Carandiru prison in 1992; 111 men had been killed by the police in the massacre.

FREEDOM OF ASSEMBLY

The year was marked by a number of largely peaceful protests throughout the country on issues such as the impeachment process, education reform, violence against women, negative impacts of the 2016 Olympic Games and reduction of public spending in health care and education. The police response was frequently violent, leading to excessive and unnecessary use of force.

Students peacefully occupied up to 1,000 public schools in the country to question the education reform and investment cuts proposed by the government. In June, police in the city of Rio de Janeiro used unnecessary and excessive force to break up a peaceful protest by students in the Secretary of Education headquarters.

The police used unnecessary force in several states to disperse demonstrations against the new government and the proposed constitutional amendment (PEC 241/55) that would restrict public spending. In São Paulo, a student lost the vision in her left eye after the police launched a stun grenade that exploded near her.

In January, Rafael Braga Vieira, a man who had been detained after a protest in Rio de Janeiro in 2013, was again detained on trumped-up charges of drug trafficking.

On 10 August a state court failed to acknowledge the state's responsibility for the loss of vision in one eye of Sergio Silva after he was hit by a device shot by police during a 2013 protest in São Paulo. The court considered that, by being at the protest, he had implicitly accepted the risk of being injured by the police.

In March the Anti-terrorism Law (13.260/2016) was approved in Congress and sanctioned by the President. The law was widely criticized for its vague language and for leaving a margin for its arbitrary application in social protests.

HUMAN RIGHTS DEFENDERS

Attacks, threats and killings targeting human rights defenders increased compared to 2015. At least 47 defenders were killed between January and September – including small-scale farmers, peasants, rural workers, Indigenous Peoples including *quilombola* communities, fisherfolk, riverside dwellers and lawyers – in their fight for access to land and natural resources. Killings, threats and attacks against human rights defenders were rarely investigated and remained largely unpunished.

Despite the existence of a national policy and a programme for the protection of human rights defenders, shortcomings in the programme's implementation and a lack of resources meant that human rights defenders continued to be killed or threatened. In June the suspension of several agreements between governments at federal and state levels to implement the programme as well as spending cuts further undermined its effectiveness.

April marked the 20th anniversary of the Eldorado dos Carajás massacre, when 19 landless farm workers were killed and 69 wounded during a brutal operation involving more than 150 police officers in the southeast of Pará state. Only two commanders of the operation were convicted of murder and assault. No police officers or other authorities were held responsible. Since the massacre, more than 271 rural workers and leaders were killed in Pará alone.

INDIGENOUS PEOPLES' RIGHTS

The demarcation and titling processes of Indigenous Peoples' land continued to make extremely slow progress, despite the expiry 23 years ago of the constitutional deadline for doing so. A constitutional amendment (PEC 215) that would allow legislators to block land demarcations – thus effectively vetoing Indigenous Peoples' rights under the Constitution and international law – was under discussion in Congress. Demarcation of land was in some cases blocked by large-scale landowners using the land for export-led commodities production.

The survival of the Guarani Kaiowá community of Apika'y in the state of Mato Grosso do Sul was at serious risk. In July, the Apika'y community was forcibly evicted from its ancestral lands. Although the community had been notified of the eviction, it was neither consulted nor provided with any relocation options. Apika'y families were left living on the margins of a highway, with restricted access to water and food.

In October, an inquiry by the Federal Prosecution Office concluded that the murder of Terena Oziel Gabriel, an Indigenous man, was caused by a bullet shot by the federal police in a 2013 operation at the Buriti farm, in the state of Mato Grosso do Sul.

During a visit in March, the UN Special Rapporteur on the rights of Indigenous Peoples denounced Brazil's failure to demarcate Indigenous land and the undermining of state institutions charged with protecting Indigenous Peoples' rights.

REFUGEES, ASYLUM-SEEKERS AND MIGRANTS

There were approximately 1.2 million asylum-seekers, refugees and migrants living in the country as of October. The government failed to dedicate adequate resources and efforts to meet asylum-seekers' needs, such as processing their requests for asylum. The average request for asylum took at least two years to process – leaving asylum-seekers in legal limbo during that time.

In December the House of Representatives approved a new migration law safeguarding the rights of asylum-seekers, migrants and stateless persons; the law was under evaluation in the Senate at the end of the year.

Asylum-seekers and migrants reported having routinely suffered discrimination when trying to access public services such as health care and education.

During the year, in Roraima state, 455 Venezuelan nationals – including many children – were deported, many without access to due process of law.

VIOLENCE AGAINST WOMEN AND GIRLS

In May the interim federal government dissolved the Ministry of Women's Affairs, Racial Equality and Human Rights and reduced it to a department within the Ministry of Justice, causing a significant reduction of resources and programmes dedicated to safeguarding women's and girls' rights.

A number of studies during the year showed that lethal violence against women had increased by 24% over the previous decade and confirmed that Brazil was one of the worst Latin American countries in which to be a girl – especially due to extremely high levels of gender-based violence and teenage pregnancy, and low completion rates of secondary education.

The gang rapes of a girl on 21 May and a woman on 17 October in Rio de Janeiro state, drew nationwide attention, further confirming the state's failure to respect, protect and fulfil women's and girls' human rights. Between January and November, there were 4,298 cases of rape reported in the state of Rio de Janeiro, 1,389 of those in the capital.

The year also marked one decade since legislation against domestic violence came into force. The government failed to rigorously implement the law, however, with domestic violence and impunity for it remaining widespread.

CHILDREN'S RIGHTS

In August, one adolescent died and another six were seriously wounded in a fire in a juvenile detention centre in the city of Rio de Janeiro. In September, one adolescent who had been hospitalized after the incident died as a result of injuries. The number of detainees in juvenile detention centres in Rio de Janeiro increased by 48% during the year, aggravating an already critical situation of overcrowding, poor living conditions, as well as torture and other ill-treatment.

A proposed constitutional amendment to reduce the age at which children can be tried as adults from 18 to 16 was still under consideration in the Senate, despite being approved by the House of Representatives in 2015.

1. Brazil: Violence has no place in these games! Risk of human rights violations at the Rio 2016 Olympic Games (AMR 19/4088/2016)

2. Brazil: A legacy of violence: Killings by police and repression of protest at the Rio 2016 Olympics (AMR 19/4780/2016)

BRUNEI DARUSSALAM

Brunei Darussalam
Head of state and government: **Sultan Hassanal Bolkiah**

Lack of transparency made independent monitoring of the human rights situation difficult. The phased implementation of the amended Penal Code continued. The Code, which seeks to impose Shari'a law, provides for the death penalty as well as corporal punishment that amount to torture and other ill-treatment for a range of offences. It also contains provisions which discriminate against women. The Shari'a legislation completed its first phase of implementation. Offences that are punishable with whipping or death sentence such as false claims (Article 206), deriding verses of the Qur'an or Hadith by non-Muslims (Article 111), and abetting or attempt to abet, had not been enforced. In February, the UN Committee on the Rights of the Child urged the government to repeal Penal Code amendments which would impose the death penalty and corporal punishment on children; and to raise the minimum age for marriage.

DEATH PENALTY

Although abolitionist in practice, death by hanging was maintained as punishment for a number of offences including murder, terrorism and drug-related crimes. The amended Penal Code provided for punishment of death by stoning for both Muslims and religious minorities for crimes including "adultery", "sodomy", rape, blasphemy and murder.

TORTURE AND OTHER ILL-TREATMENT

The staged implementation of the amended Penal Code, which began in 2014, provides for whipping or amputation for crimes such as robbery and theft. Caning was regularly used as a punishment for offences including those related to immigration.

FREEDOM OF EXPRESSION

A lack of free and independent media continued. In November, *The Brunei Times* was shut down after it published a politically sensitive article. The act of "printing, disseminating, importing, broadcasting, and distributing publications contrary to Sharia law" constituted a crime for both Muslims and non-Muslims.

FREEDOM OF RELIGION

Muslims as well as religious minorities continued to face restrictions on their right to freedom of thought, conscience and religion. Crimes including blasphemy, insulting the Hadith and any verses of the Qur'an, declaring oneself a prophet or an apostate (for Muslims) were punishable by death under the law.

RIGHTS OF LESBIAN, GAY, BISEXUAL, TRANSGENDER AND INTERSEX PEOPLE

Consensual same-sex sexual activity was a criminal offence with "intercourse against the order of nature" punishable by up to 10 years' imprisonment. The amended Penal Code would make punishment of stoning to death for "sodomy" mandatory. Article 198 cites "Man posing as woman or vice versa" as a crime. In August, a man was arrested for "cross-dressing and improper conduct". Punishment on conviction included a fine of BN$1,000 (approx. US$730) or three months' imprisonment, or both.

COUNTER-TERROR AND SECURITY

Individuals continued to be arrested under the Internal Security Act which allows authorities to detain suspects without trial for indefinitely renewable two-year periods.

BULGARIA

Republic of Bulgaria
Head of State: **Rosen Plevneliev**
Head of Government: **Boyko Borisov**

Bulgaria failed to provide all required services and access to proper procedures for the rising number of migrants and refugees arriving in the country and failed to address the allegations of summary pushbacks and abuse at the border. A climate of xenophobia and intolerance sharply intensified. Roma continued to be at risk of pervasive discrimination. The parliament adopted in first reading a new counter-terrorism law.

REFUGEES' AND MIGRANTS' RIGHTS

In response to Serbia and Hungary increasing their border control measures, the Bulgarian authorities adopted an approach aimed at limiting the number of migrants and refugees entering the country as an alternative route into the EU. Human rights organizations documented frequent allegations of pushbacks, physical abuse and theft by border police. While not openly condoning pushbacks, Prime Minister Borisov conceded that the government had adopted what he termed a "pragmatic approach" to the refugee crisis. He said that over 25,000 people were returned to Turkey and Greece in the period up to August.

There was continued impunity for reported abuses at the border. In July, Burgas District Prosecutor's Office closed criminal proceedings in connection to the October 2015 death of an unarmed Afghan man who was shot by border police.

The majority of migrants and refugees continued to be routinely subject to administrative detention, often for months longer than the legally prescribed period. Two attempts to irregularly cross the border, whether to enter or leave the country, amounted to a criminal offence. Consequently, migrants and refugees apprehended while trying to leave the country irregularly were prosecuted and jailed, some for longer than a year.

Children
The practice of the unlawful detention of unaccompanied children persisted. To circumvent the prohibition of detention of unaccompanied minors, migration authorities arbitrarily assigned unaccompanied children to adults who were not related to them.

Reception centres had inadequate provisions for unaccompanied children. The authorities routinely failed to provide adequate access to legal representation, translation, health services and education, psychosocial support and a safe and secure environment. Due to the lack of specially designated facilities for children, many unaccompanied children were held with adults and without adequate professional supervision, making them vulnerable to sexual abuse, drug use and trafficking.

DISCRIMINATION
Xenophobia
Human rights organizations highlighted concerns over high levels of xenophobia and intolerance directed at groups including refugees, asylum-seekers and migrants, who remained particularly vulnerable to violence and harassment. The government failed to challenge the climate of intolerance and some public officials frequently engaged in discriminatory or xenophobic speech.

In April, local and international media aired footage of so-called "voluntary border patrol" groups rounding up and holding captive Iraqi and Afghan migrants attempting to cross the border from Turkey before handing them over to the police. These illegal "citizens' arrests" were initially widely praised by the authorities and certain sectors of the public. After formal complaints by the Bulgarian Helsinki Committee, local police arrested some of the perpetrators and the Ministry of Interior issued statements asking citizens to refrain from apprehending refugees, asylum-seekers and migrants.

Roma
Social exclusion and widespread discrimination against Roma continued. The UN Committee on the Rights of the Child expressed concern about the continued limited access of Roma children to education, health and adequate housing. Roma remained grossly overrepresented in "special" schools, mental health institutions and juvenile detention centres. The authorities continued to carry out forced evictions without the provision of adequate alternative housing, leaving many families homeless.

Muslim women
In September, the National Assembly approved a national law that prohibited wearing full-face veils in public places. The law was a part of the package of bills proposed by the Patriotic Front, a member of the ruling coalition, allegedly aimed at preventing what was characterized as radicalization. Other bills, still under consideration at the end of the year, proposed far-reaching measures, including the prohibition of "radical Islam", a complete ban on foreign funding for all religious denominations and a mandatory use of the Bulgarian language during all religious services. Earlier in the year, several regional centres, such as Pazardzhik, imposed bans on wearing full-face veils in public. Only a few women in Bulgaria wear full-face veils or burkas, but the national ban could impact unfairly on women belonging to the ethnic Turkish and Muslim Roma minorities.

COUNTER-TERROR AND SECURITY
In July, the National Assembly quickly passed a new counter-terrorism bill that defined a "terrorist act" vaguely and in excessively broad terms.[1] The bill gives the President powers to declare – with approval of the

National Assembly – a "state of emergency" in the aftermath of an act of terrorism against the territory. In such a state of emergency, the authorities could impose blanket bans on public rallies, meetings and demonstrations without any effective and independent oversight. The bill additionally provided a list of administrative control measures, including travel bans and controls of individuals' freedom of movement and association, that could be applied to anyone suspected of "preparing or planning a terrorist act".

Non-refoulement

Bulgaria violated the international legal principle of *non-refoulement* in August. The police apprehended Abdullah Buyuk, a Turkish national who had been residing in Bulgaria since late 2015, and secretly handed him over to Turkish authorities. The authorities acted on the basis of an Interpol warrant, issued at the request of the Turkish government seeking Abdullah Buyuk's extradition on charges of money laundering and terrorism in association with the Gulenist movement. Abdullah Buyuk's lawyer said that he had not been given an opportunity to contact legal counsel or his family, or otherwise challenge the transfer. His request for asylum in Bulgaria had been rejected only days before the handover, which took place despite two earlier court rulings blocking his extradition. In March 2016, Sofia City Court and the Bulgarian Court of Appeal had ruled that Abdullah Buyuk should not be extradited stating that the charges appeared to be politically motivated and that Turkey could not guarantee him a fair trial. The Ombudsman's Office stated publicly that Abdullah Buyuk's return to Turkey had contravened the Bulgarian Constitution, domestic law and Bulgaria's international legal obligations.

---

1. Bulgaria: Proposed counter-terrorism bill would be a serious step back for human rights (EUR 15/4545/2016)

BURKINA FASO

Burkina Faso
Head of state: **Roch Marc Christian Kaboré**
Head of government: **Paul Kaba Thiéba (replaced Yacouba Isaac Zida in January)**

The political turmoil of the previous two years largely receded. Armed groups committed abuses. The rates of maternal mortality as well as early and forced marriage remained high, although the government began to address the issues.

BACKGROUND

In September the government established a commission to draft a new Constitution to usher in the "Fifth Republic".

MILITARY TRIBUNAL

In June, the military tribunal indicted 14 people, including former President Blaise Compaoré, suspected of involvement in the assassination of President Thomas Sankara in 1987. Seven people, including Colonel Alidou Guebré and Caporal Wampasba Nacouma, were arrested in October and charged. In May, Burkina Faso issued an international arrest warrant for the former President and another of those indicted who were living in exile.

Between July and October, 38 of 85 people charged with threatening state security, crimes against humanity and murder following a coup attempt in September 2015 were provisionally released, including journalists Caroline Yoda and Adama Ouédraogo. Former Minister of Foreign Affairs Djibril Bassolé and General Gilbert Diendéré remained in custody awaiting trial by the military tribunal. In April, the authorities lifted the international arrest warrant for Guillaume Soro, President of the National Assembly of Côte d'Ivoire, who had been investigated for alleged involvement in the attempted coup.

ABUSES BY ARMED GROUPS

Throughout the year, armed groups attacked civilians and members of the security forces, in the capital, Ouagadougou, and in the north near the Malian border.

In January, an armed group deliberately and indiscriminately killed and injured civilians in an attack in Ouagadougou. Al-Mourabitoune, a group affiliated to Al-Qa'ida in the Islamic Maghreb, claimed responsibility. At least 30 people were killed, including a photographer and a driver working on behalf of Amnesty International.

In May, June, October and December, the authorities announced that armed groups had attacked police stations near the Malian border, killing 21 people in total and wounding others.

Self-defence militia called "Kogleweogo", mainly comprising farmers and cattle breeders, committed abuses, including beatings and abductions. Civil society organizations criticized the authorities for doing too little to prevent and remedy such abuses. The Minister of Justice pledged to end the militias' activities. In October, a decree was adopted to regulate their activities.

In September, four Kogleweogo members charged in relation to an armed gathering were sentenced to six months in prison, while 26 others were given suspended sentences of between 10 and 12 months.

IMPUNITY

In July, the UN Human Rights Committee stressed that the government should redouble its efforts to fully and impartially investigate all human rights violations committed by armed forces, including the Presidential Guard (RSP), sanction those found guilty and provide remedy to the victims.

The Commission of Inquiry established in 2015 to investigate the killing of at least 10 people and the wounding of hundreds by security forces in October 2014 submitted its report to the Prime Minister. The Commission's conclusions were not made public.

WOMEN'S RIGHTS

The UN Committee on Economic, Social and Cultural Rights stated that women in rural areas were particularly disadvantaged regarding economic, social and cultural rights. The Committee recommended that Burkina Faso revise its legislation on the prevention and punishment of violence against women and girls, and provide more support to survivors. It also recommended that all acts of rape by spouses be punished and that the reporting of such offences be encouraged.

In July, the UN Human Rights Committee noted that more women should have positions in public office.

Sexual and reproductive rights

Only 16% of women in Burkina Faso were using a modern method of contraception and nearly 30% of girls and young women aged 15-19 in rural areas were pregnant or already had a child. Some women and girls reported that they did not know that sexual intercourse could lead to pregnancy. Many said the cost of contraceptives prevented their use or meant they did not use them consistently. These factors resulted in high-risk and unwanted pregnancies that sometimes led to dangerous, clandestine abortions. [1]

At least 2,800 women die in childbirth annually in Burkina Faso. In March, the authorities removed some key financial barriers facing pregnant women, including costs relating to caesarean sections and delivery.

Early and forced marriage

Burkina Faso had one of the world's highest rates of early and forced marriage. Women and girls reported that they were forced to marry as a result of violence, coercion and the pressure linked to the money and goods offered to their families as part of the marriage. In the Sahel region, more than half of girls aged 15-17 were married.

The authorities adopted a national strategy to end child marriage by 2025. The plan defines a child as someone under the age of 18, and considers "marriage" to include all forms of union between a man and woman, whether celebrated by a public officer or a traditional or religious leader. However, serious concerns remained about the legal framework and weaknesses in enforcement of the law.

1. Coerced and denied: Forced marriages and barriers to contraception in Burkina Faso (AFR 60/3851/2016)

BURUNDI

Republic of Burundi
Head of state and government: **Pierre Nkurunziza**

The political crisis became less overtly violent, although serious human rights violations continued, including unlawful killings, enforced disappearances, torture and other ill-treatment and arbitrary arrests. Violence against women and girls increased. The rights to freedom of expression and association were stifled. With increased repression and unchallenged impunity, a climate of fear took hold in the capital and elsewhere. Around 3 million people needed humanitarian assistance by the end of the year due to the political crisis, the collapsing economy and a series of natural disasters.

BACKGROUND

The political crisis sparked by President Nkurunziza's decision in 2015 to stand for a third term became increasingly entrenched and was accompanied by a deepening socio-economic crisis.

Mediation efforts under the auspices of the East African Community stalled, despite the appointment in March of former Tanzanian President, Benjamin Mkapa, as facilitator. The National Commission for Inter-Burundian Dialogue reported that most participants had called for constitutional amendments,

including the removal of term limits. With many Burundians in exile or afraid to express dissent, the Commission's findings risked being one-sided.

The AU stepped back from the protection force proposed in December 2015 and decided instead to send a delegation of five African heads of state and government to Burundi in February. In July, the UN Security Council authorized the deployment of up to 228 police officers, a move rejected by the government.

On appeal in May, the Supreme Court sentenced 21 army and police officers to life imprisonment for their involvement in the failed coup attempt in May 2015. Five others received two-year sentences and two were acquitted. The sentences were heavier than those handed down in January.

On 20 August, General Evariste Ndayishimiye was elected Secretary General of the ruling National Council for the Defense of Democracy-Forces of Defense of Democracy (CNDD-FDD).

After several months of consultations, the EU decided in March to suspend direct financial support to the government, pending regular reviews. In October the EU judged that commitments proposed by the government to address its concerns were insufficient to restart support. The EU renewed sanctions against four men "deemed to be undermining democracy or obstructing the search for a political solution to the crisis in Burundi" by inciting acts of repression against peaceful demonstrations or participating in the failed coup. Similarly, the USA issued sanctions against a further three people, bringing the total under US sanctions to 11.

Access to basic services was hampered by the insecurity and deteriorating economy. Cuts to external financial assistance led to massive budget cuts. Natural disasters, including floods, landslides and storms, exacerbated the situation. Humanitarian organizations estimated that 3 million people needed assistance in October, up from 1.1 million in February. A cholera epidemic was declared in August and cases of malaria were almost double those seen in 2015.

UNLAWFUL KILLINGS

Hundreds of people were unlawfully killed in targeted and indiscriminate killings related to the crisis. NGOs continued to report the discovery of mass graves. Amnesty International's analysis of satellite images and video footage from a site in Buringa near the capital, Bujumbura, supported witness accounts that people killed by security forces in December 2015 were later buried in mass graves.[1] In February, the Mayor of Bujumbura showed the media a grave in the Mutakura neighbourhood of the capital that he alleged was dug by members of the opposition. The government did not take up offers from the Office of the UN High Commissioner for Human Rights and the UN Independent Investigation on Burundi (UNIIB) to help document alleged mass graves.

In early 2016, there were regular grenade explosions in Bujumbura followed by targeted killings. On 22 March, Lieutenant Colonel Darius Ikurakure, an army officer implicated in numerous human rights violations, was shot dead inside the army's headquarters. On 25 April, gunmen fired on the car of General Athanase Kararuza, killing him, his wife Consolate Gahiro and his assistant Gérard Vyimana and fatally wounding his daughter Daniella Mpundu. The previous day Human Rights Minister Martin Nivyabandi and Diane Murindababisha were injured in an attack. On 13 July, unidentified gunmen killed Hafsa Mossi, a former minister and member of the East African Legislative Assembly. A senior presidential adviser, Willy Nyamitwe, was injured in an assassination attempt on 28 November.

ENFORCED DISAPPEARANCES

Reports of enforced disappearances, often implicating the National Intelligence Services (SNR), continued and numerous cases from 2015 remained unsolved.

Jean Bigirimana, a journalist with the independent media outlet Iwacu, was last seen on 22 July.[2] His colleague received a phone call saying he had been taken by people believed to be members of the SNR. Two bodies in an advanced state of decomposition were later found in a river; neither could be identified.

TORTURE AND OTHER ILL-TREATMENT

Torture and other ill-treatment continued to be perpetrated at an alarming rate and with impunity by the SNR, the police and the Imbonerakure, the youth wing of the ruling party. Methods documented included: beating with branches, iron bars and batons; electric shocks; stamping on victims; denial of medical care; verbal abuse; and death threats.[3] People who refused to join the Imbonerakure said they were beaten during arrest and in detention, apparently as a punishment. Others were beaten as they tried to flee the country.

VIOLENCE AGAINST WOMEN AND GIRLS

In November, the UN Committee on the Elimination of Discrimination against Women expressed concern about an increase in serious sexual and gender-based violence against women and girls by the police, military and Imbonerakure.

ARBITRARY ARRESTS AND DETENTIONS

There were regular police searches and arrests in neighbourhoods of Bujumbura where the 2015 protests had been concentrated. In these neighbourhoods and other parts of Burundi, police regularly checked household notebooks in which residents should be registered.

On 28 May, the police arrested several hundred people in the Bwiza neighbourhood of Bujumbura. A police spokesperson was reported as saying that it was normal to arrest people near a grenade attack as the perpetrators might be found among them.

On 25 August, the police presented to the media 93 people who had been arrested and accused of begging as part of the "clean city" operation.

FREEDOM OF EXPRESSION

Freedom of expression was stifled at all levels of society.

Hundreds of secondary school students were suspended for doodling on a photo of the President in their textbooks. In June dozens of students were arrested and accused of insulting the President, including in Muramvya, Cankuzo and Rumonge provinces. Two were charged with participating in an insurrectionary movement and mobilizing students to demonstrate. The rest were released by mid-August.

Burundian and international journalists faced persecution, despite the reopening of two private radio stations in February. Phil Moore and Jean-Philippe Rémy, who were working for the French newspaper *Le Monde*, were arrested in January. Julia Steers, an American journalist; Gildas Yihundimpundu, a Burundian journalist; and their Burundian driver were arrested on 23 October. Julia Steers was taken to the US Embassy the same day, but Gildas Yihundimpundu and the driver were held overnight at the SNR. Léon Masengo, a journalist with Isanganiro FM, was briefly detained on 11 November after he went to cover the interrogation of a police officer accused of many human rights violations.

FREEDOM OF ASSOCIATION

Members of opposition political parties faced repression.

In March, at least 16 members of National Liberation Forces (FNL) party were arrested at a bar in Kirundo province. The police said they were holding an unauthorized political meeting. Local opposition party leaders who opposed President Nkurunziza's re-election were beaten and threatened by the Imbonerakure. Throughout the country, the Imbonerakure put pressure on people to join it or the ruling CNDD-FDD, and carried out campaigns of intimidation against those who refused.

In December, the national assembly adopted two laws on national and foreign NGOs which will impose stricter controls on their work.

HUMAN RIGHTS DEFENDERS

Human rights work became increasingly dangerous and difficult. The SNR increased surveillance of human rights defenders and other perceived government critics. Victims and witnesses of violations were afraid to speak out.

In October, the Minister of Interior banned five leading human rights organizations that had been suspended in 2015. The Minister suspended five others the following week, one of which, Lique Iteka (the Burundian Human Rights League) was permanently closed in December, following the publication of a controversial report.

Following the review of Burundi by the UN Committee against Torture in July, a Burundian prosecutor called on the Bar Association to strike off four lawyers who contributed to the civil society report submitted to the Committee. Pamela Capizzi of Switzerland-based TRIAL International, an NGO, was asked to leave the country on 6 October despite having a visa.

LACK OF ACCOUNTABILITY

Victims of human rights violations continued to face serious challenges in accessing justice. Journalist Esdras Ndikumana was tortured in August 2015 and filed a complaint at the Supreme Court in October 2015. No progress was made in the case in 2016.

Judicial investigations continued to lack credibility. In March, the Prosecutor General announced the findings of a commission of inquiry into alleged extrajudicial executions committed on 11 December 2015 and the subsequent discovery of suspected mass graves. According to the report, all but one person found dead in the Bujumbura neighbourhoods of Musaga, Ngagara and Nyakabiga had participated in the fighting. While an exchange of fire did take place on 11 December, this was followed by cordon-and-search operations in which many people were killed by a bullet to the head and at least one body was found tied up.

The operational phase of the Truth and Reconciliation Commission, which covers 1962 to 2008, was launched in March and began collecting testimonies in September. It does not have judicial authority and the special tribunal that was initially envisaged was not established.

REFUGEES AND INTERNALLY DISPLACED PEOPLE

Approximately 100,000 people fled Burundi in 2016, bringing the total number of Burundian refugees who had fled the ongoing crisis to over 327,000. The Office for the Coordination of Humanitarian Affairs (OCHA) estimated that 139,000 people were internally displaced due to the crisis and natural disasters.

People trying to flee were abused and robbed. Members of the Imbonerakure were largely responsible, although refugees also accused people in police and military uniforms.

WOMEN'S RIGHTS

The Committee on the Elimination of Discrimination against Women expressed concern about: the high secondary school drop-out rate for girls; women's limited access to basic health care and sexual and reproductive health services; the continued criminalization of abortion; and the fact that 45% of incarcerated women were serving sentences for abortion and infanticide. The Committee highlighted the concentration of women working in the informal sector in unskilled and low-paid jobs without social protection. It also noted the lack of protection of domestic workers from exploitation and sexual abuse, and the failure to ban child labour.

INTERNATIONAL SCRUTINY

The situation in Burundi came under intense scrutiny by international and regional bodies, and the government became increasingly hostile in its responses to such initiatives.

In February, the government agreed to an increase in the number of AU human rights observers and military experts to 200. By the end of the year, only a third of these had been deployed and a memorandum of understanding was yet to be signed.

In April, the African Commission on Human and Peoples' Rights presented to the AU's Peace and Security Council the report of its December 2015 fact-finding mission to Burundi. Its recommendations included the establishment of a joint regional and international investigative mechanism.

The UN Committee against Torture requested a special report from Burundi, which was reviewed in July. The government delegation only attended half of the review and did not respond to questions. However, it did submit further feedback in October.

The UNIIB presented its report to the Human Rights Council (HRC) in September.[4] It found that gross, systematic and patterned human rights violations were taking place and that impunity was pervasive. To follow up, the HRC established a commission of inquiry on Burundi. Burundi rejected this move and, in October, banned the three UNIIB experts from Burundi and suspended co-operation with the UN High Commissioner for Human Rights pending renegotiation.

In April, the Office of the Prosecutor of the International Criminal Court (ICC) opened a preliminary examination into the situation in Burundi. On 8 October, both the National Assembly and the Senate voted to leave the ICC.[5] The UN Secretary-General received official notification of Burundi's withdrawal from the Rome Statute of the ICC on 27 October, which will come into effect after a year.

---

1. Burundi: Suspected mass graves of victims of 11 December violence (AFR 16/3337/2016)

2. Burundi: Whereabouts of Burundian journalist unknown – Jean Bigirimana (AFR 16/4832/2016)

3. Burundi: Submission to the United Nations Committee against Torture, 25 July-12 August 2016 (AFR 16/4377/2016)

4. Burundi: Written Statement to the 33rd session of the UN Human Rights Council (AFR 16/4737/2016)

5. Burundi: ICC withdrawal must not block justice for crisis abuses (News story, 12 October)

CAMBODIA

Kingdom of Cambodia
Head of state: King Norodom Sihamoni
Head of government: Hun Sen

Crackdown on the rights to freedom of expression, association and peaceful assembly intensified ahead of elections in 2017/2018. The authorities' misuse of the justice system increased; the security forces continued to harass and punish civil society and silence critics. Human rights defenders were arrested and held in pre-trial detention; several were tried and sentenced, including for previous alleged offences, and others were given suspended sentences or had charges pending against them. Political opposition was targeted, with activists serving long sentences handed down in previous years and new legal action taken against opposition party leaders and others. A prominent political commentator was shot dead and impunity continued for past unlawful killings.

BACKGROUND

Tensions between the ruling Cambodian People's Party (CPP) and the main opposition Cambodian National Rescue Party (CNRP) remained high. The prospect of commune and national elections in 2017 and 2018 respectively created an unstable political environment threatening human rights. From May, CNRP MPs intermittently boycotted the National Assembly in protest at legal action taken against CNRP deputy leader Kem Sokha for failing to appear as a witness in a court case. CNRP leader Sam Rainsy remained in self-imposed exile in France; in October the government formally announced that he was banned from returning to Cambodia. He was targeted with a series of criminal charges against him during the year.

In September, 39 states issued a statement at the 33rd UN Human Rights Council meeting expressing concern about the political situation in Cambodia and calling for a "safe and enabling environment for human rights defenders and civil society".

FREEDOMS OF EXPRESSION AND ASSOCIATION

Legal action against the political opposition escalated in an apparent attempt to hamper activities ahead of commune elections in 2017. At least 16 activists and officials from the opposition remained in prison after unfair trials. They included 14 CNRP members who were convicted of leading and/or participating in an "insurrection" related to a demonstration in July 2014. At least two opposition party members were held in pre-trial detention and at least 13 had charges pending against them.

In December, Sam Rainsy and two assistants were sentenced to five years' imprisonment on charges of being "accomplices" in a 2015 forgery case against opposition party senator Hong Sok Hour, who was convicted in November 2016 on charges of fraud and incitement and given a seven-year prison sentence. Rainsy and the two assistants are in exile in France.

In September, Kem Sokha was sentenced in his absence to five months' imprisonment for refusing to appear as a witness in the prosecution of two CNRP MPs who were charged with "procurement of prostitution". He was pardoned by the King in December at the Prime Minister's request.

In October, CNRP MP Um Sam An was sentenced to two and a half years' imprisonment for incitement related to the CNRP campaign alleging encroachment by Viet Nam into Cambodian territory.

HUMAN RIGHTS DEFENDERS

Human rights defenders were threatened and arrested for peacefully carrying out their work. Intimidation, threats and heavy surveillance caused several to leave the country in fear for their safety.

In May, a landmark case was brought against Ny Sokha, Yi Soksan, Nay Vanda and Lem Mony, staff members from the Cambodian Human Rights and Development Association (ADHOC) who were arrested on

28 April and charged with bribing a witness. Ny Chakrya, a former ADHOC staff member and deputy secretary-general of the National Election Committee (NEC), was also charged as an accomplice. The case was related to advice and material support provided by ADHOC to a woman alleged to have had an extra-marital relationship with Kem Sokha. In October, the investigating judge extended their pre-trial detention to one year. In December, Minister of Interior Sar Kheng announced that the five would be released but no action was taken. The alleged affair led to three separate criminal cases involving eight political and civil society actors, as well as one against the woman. The CPP filed a criminal defamation complaint against political commentator Ou Virak for commenting that the cases were politically motivated. Seang Chet, an opposition commune councillor, was convicted on charges of bribery in one of these cases in December. He received a five-year sentence but was pardoned and released two days later.

In a separate case, Ny Chakrya was sentenced to six months' imprisonment for defamation, malicious denunciation and publication of commentaries intended to unlawfully coerce judicial authorities after criticizing a court in Siem Reap for its handling of a land dispute case in May 2015. In April, NEC member and former union leader Rong Chhun was informed that he would be tried on criminal charges in relation to a 2014 demonstration at which a number of protesting factory workers were shot dead by security forces. Ny Chakrya and Rong Chhun both worked for the NEC and their cases were viewed as targeted attempts to exclude them from their appointed positions.

Try Sovikea, Sun Mala and Sim Samnang, environmental activists from the NGO Mother Nature who had been arrested in August 2015, were sentenced in June to 18 months' imprisonment for threatening to destroy property. They were released after the balance of their sentence after time served was suspended.

FREEDOM OF ASSEMBLY

Peaceful protests continued to be hampered by the authorities. In May, civil society launched a peaceful "Black Monday" campaign to call for the release of four ADHOC staff and one former NEC staff member (see above). Protesters wearing black took part in weekly gatherings and vigils, and posted images on social media. The authorities attempted to ban the protests and threatened, arrested and detained participants who were generally released only after signing undertakings not to protest again. Housing rights activists from the capital, Phnom Penh, were among those routinely targeted.

Tep Vanny and Bov Sophea from Boeung Kak community were arrested on 15 August at a "Black Monday" vigil. They were tried on 22 August and sentenced to six days' imprisonment each for insulting a public official. Bov Sophea was released after time served, and Tep Vanny was held in prison for investigation on a revived charge relating to a 2013 protest. In another revived case, on 19 September, Tep Vanny, Bo Chhorvy, Heng Mom and Kong Chantha, also from the Boeung Kak community, were sentenced to six months' imprisonment for insulting and obstructing public officials in relation to a 2011 protest. Tep Vanny remained imprisoned and the three other women remained free pending an appeal against conviction at the end of the year.

UNLAWFUL KILLINGS

Political commentator Kem Ley was shot dead on the morning of 10 July at a service station where he regularly went to meet people. He was frequently interviewed on radio and news media for his views on political events in Cambodia, including criticism of the government. Oeuth Ang, a former soldier, was arrested shortly afterwards, but the authorities failed to conduct an independent and effective investigation or to inform the public adequately of any investigations into the killing. Prime Minister Hun Sen filed a defamation suit against Sam Rainsy after the latter had posted on Facebook that the government may have been behind the killing. Opposition senator Thak Lany was convicted in her absence of defamation and incitement for allegedly accusing Hun Sen of ordering the killing.

No progress was made in holding anyone to account for the killings of at least six people and the enforced disappearance of Khem Saphath during a violent crackdown by security forces on freedom of peaceful assembly in 2013 and 2014. A renewed investigation ordered in 2013 into the fatal shooting of trade union leader Chea Vichea by unidentified perpetrators in January 2004 also appeared to be making no progress.

RIGHT TO ADEQUATE STANDARD OF LIVING

Land grabbing, Economic Land Concessions granted to private stakeholders, and major development projects continued to impact the right to adequate housing for communities around the country. Work on the proposed Lower Sesan II hydropower dam in the northeast province of Stung Treng progressed, with estimates that around 5,000 members of Indigenous minorities faced relocation due to inundation. The UN Special Rapporteur on Cambodia called for adequate consultation, better understanding of cultural practices and consideration of alternatives proposed by the communities.

REFUGEES AND ASYLUM-SEEKERS

In January the Ministry of Interior confirmed that more than 170 Montagnard asylum-seekers who had fled Viet Nam would have their claims assessed for refugee status, after initially refusing to do so. Thirteen who had earlier been granted refugee status were transferred to the Philippines pending resettlement to a third country. During the year, around 29 returned to Viet Nam voluntarily with assistance from UNHCR, the UN refugee agency.

CAMEROON

Republic of Cameroon
Head of state: **Paul Biya**
Head of government: **Philémon Yang**

The armed group Boko Haram continued to commit serious human rights abuses and violations of international humanitarian law in the Far North region, including killing and abducting hundreds of civilians. In response, the authorities and security forces committed human rights violations, including arbitrary arrests, incommunicado detentions, torture and enforced disappearances. As a result of the conflict, more than 170,000 people had fled their homes since 2014. Freedoms of expression, association and peaceful assembly continued to be restricted. Demonstrations in Anglophone regions from late October were violently repressed by the security forces. Journalists, students, human rights defenders and members of opposition parties were arrested and some faced trial before military courts. Lesbian, gay, bisexual, transgender and intersex (LGBTI) people faced discrimination, intimidation and harassment, although the number of arrests and prosecutions continued to fall.

ABUSES BY ARMED GROUPS – BOKO HARAM

Boko Haram committed crimes under international law and human rights abuses, including suicide bombings in civilian areas, summary executions, torture, hostage-taking, abductions, recruitment of child soldiers, looting and destruction of public, private and religious property. During the year, the group carried out at least 150 attacks, including 22 suicide bombings, killing at least 260 civilians. The crimes were part of a systematic attack on the civilian population across the Lake Chad basin.

Boko Haram deliberately targeted civilians in attacks on markets, mosques, churches, schools and bus stations. In January alone, at least nine suicide attacks killed more than 60 civilians. On 10 February in the town of Nguéchéwé, 60km from Maroua, two women suicide bombers attacked a funeral, killing at least nine civilians, including a child, and injuring more than 40 people. On 19 February, two women suicide bombers killed at least 24 civilians and injured 112 others in a crowded market in the village of Mémé, near Mora. Suicide bombings on 21 August and 25 December killed a total of five people and wounded at least 34 at markets in Mora.

ARBITRARY ARRESTS AND DETENTIONS

Security forces continued to arbitrarily arrest individuals accused of supporting Boko Haram, often with little or no evidence, and detained them in inhumane, often life-threatening conditions. Hundreds of suspects were held in unofficial detention centres, such as military bases or premises belonging to the national intelligence agencies, without access to a lawyer or their families.

The security forces continued to use "cordon and search" operations, leading to mass arrests.

TORTURE, DEATHS IN CUSTODY AND ENFORCED DISAPPEARANCES

Dozens of men, women and children accused of supporting Boko Haram were tortured by members of the Rapid Intervention Battalion (BIR), an elite army unit, at the military base known as Salak, near Maroua, and by officers of the General Directorate of External Research (DGRE), an intelligence service, in premises in the capital, Yaoundé. Some of them died as a result of torture; others disappeared.[1]

FREEDOMS OF EXPRESSION, ASSOCIATION AND ASSEMBLY

Human rights defenders, including civil society activists and journalists, continued to be intimidated, harassed and threatened. In response to curtailed freedoms of expression, association and peaceful assembly, journalists reported that they self-censored to avoid repercussions for criticizing the government, especially on security matters.

Kah Walla, President of the Cameroon People's Party, was victim of several arbitrary arrests. On 8 April, she was detained along with 11 members of her party at the Judicial Police station located at the Elig-Essono neighbourhood in Yaoundé on charges of "insurrection and rebellion against the State", for peacefully protesting against the government. On 20 May, she was detained along with 14 members of her party at the Directorate for the Surveillance of the National Territory in Yaoundé charged with "rebellion, inciting insurrection and inciting revolt"; they were all released the same day without any explanation. On 28 October Kah Walla was arrested at her party headquarters in Yaoundé and detained at the Yaoundé 1 Central Police Station alongside 50 of her supporters as they gathered for a prayer for the victims of the Eseka train crash. The arrest was carried out without any warrant. They were detained for more than seven hours without charge. No reason was given for their arrest.

In late October, lawyers, students and teachers from the Anglophone regions of Cameroon went on strike, in opposition to what they viewed as the marginalization of the Anglophone minority. Protesting erupted in several cities in the southwest and northwest of the country, including Bamenda, Kumba and Buea. Cameroon's security forces arbitrarily arrested protesters and used excessive force to disperse them. In one example, on 8 December, the use of live bullets by security forces led to the deaths of between two and four people during a protest in the northwestern city of Bamenda.

UNFAIR TRIALS

People continued to face unfair trials before military courts.

The trial of Radio France Internationale correspondent Ahmed Abba, who was arrested in Maroua in July 2015, began at Yaoundé Military Court on 29 February. It was marred by irregularities, including witnesses not being called to testify, and documents not being shared with defence lawyers. Charged with complicity with and non-denunciation of terrorist acts, he was tortured while held incommunicado for three months.

The trial of three journalists – Rodrigue Tongué, Felix Ebole Bola and Baba Wamé – continued at Yaoundé Military Court. They were charged in October 2014 with non-denunciation of information and sources. If convicted, they could face up to five years' imprisonment. Trial proceedings were marred by substantive and procedural irregularities, including the refusal by the judges to allow witnesses to testify. Aboubakar Siddiki, leader of the political party Mouvement patriotique du salut camerounais, and Abdoulaye Harissou, a well-known notary, faced trial alongside the three journalists. Arrested in August 2014, they were both held incommunicado at the DGRE for more than 40 days before being transferred to Prison Principale in Yaoundé. They faced charges of illegal possession and use of weapons of war, murder, revolution, insulting the head of state and hostility against the state.

Fomusoh Ivo Feh, arrested in December 2014 in Limbe for forwarding a sarcastic text message about Boko Haram, was sentenced to 10 years in prison by Yaoundé Military Court on 2 November for "non-denunciation of a terrorist act". Convicted on the basis of limited and unverifiable evidence, his trial was marred by irregularities, including the lack of an interpreter.

IMPUNITY

On 11 July, the State Secretary to the Minister of Defence in charge of the national gendarmerie said that a commission of inquiry to investigate crimes committed by the security forces engaged in operations against Boko Haram would be set up. No further information was provided.

In August, the trial of gendarmerie Colonel Zé Onguéné Charles, charged with negligence and breach of custody law, started before Yaoundé Military Court. The Colonel was in charge of the region where, on 27-28 December 2014, at least 25 men accused of supporting Boko Haram died while detained in a gendarmerie building.

PRISON CONDITIONS

Prison conditions remained poor, marked by chronic overcrowding, inadequate food, limited medical care, and deplorable hygiene and sanitation. Maroua prison housed around 1,400 detainees, more than three times its intended capacity. The population of the central prison in Yaoundé was approximately 4,000, despite a maximum capacity of 2,000. In Prison Principale in Yaoundé, the majority of suspected Boko Haram detainees were permanently chained until August.

The main factors contributing to overcrowding included the mass arrests of people accused of supporting Boko Haram, the large number of detainees held without charge, and the ineffective judicial system. The government promised to build new prisons and began constructing 12 new cells for the prison in Maroua. The measures were considered insufficient to resolve the crisis.

REFUGEES' AND MIGRANTS' RIGHTS

At least 276,000 refugees from the Central African Republic lived in harsh conditions in crowded camps or with host families along border areas of southeastern Cameroon. Some 59,000 refugees from Nigeria lived in the UN-run Minawao camp in the Far North region, but around 27,000 others struggled to cope outside the camp, facing food insecurity, lack of access to basic services and harassment by the security forces. The insecurity created by both Boko Haram and the military also led to the internal displacement of around 199,000 people in the Far North region. Agreements between Cameroon, Nigeria, Central African Republic and UNHCR, the UN refugee agency, to facilitate voluntary return of refugees were being finalized at the end of the year.

RIGHTS OF LESBIAN, GAY, BISEXUAL, TRANSGENDER AND INTERSEX PEOPLE

LGBTI people continued to face discrimination, intimidation, harassment and violence. The criminalization of same-sex sexual relations was retained when the Criminal Code was revised in June.

On 2 August, three young men were arrested in Yaoundé and taken to a gendarmerie station where they were beaten, insulted and had their hair partially shaved off. The gendarmes poured cold water on the men, forced them to clean the gendarmerie building, and demanded they "confess" their sexuality. They were released 24 hours later on payment of a bribe.

RIGHT TO AN ADEQUATE STANDARD OF LIVING

The Boko Haram violence exacerbated the hardships of communities in the Far North region, limiting their access to basic social services, and disrupting trade, farming and pastoralism. Some 1.4 million people in the region, most of them children, faced crisis or emergency levels of food insecurity, and 144 schools and 21 health centres were forced to shut down due to insecurity.

An amended version of the Penal Code, passed in July, provided that tenants owing more than two months' rent could be sentenced to up to three years in prison. About a third of households lived in rented accommodation and almost half of the country's population lived below the poverty line.

DEATH PENALTY

People accused of supporting Boko Haram continued to be sentenced to death following unfair trials in military courts; none were executed during the year. The vast majority of cases were prosecuted under a deeply flawed anti-terrorism law passed in December 2014.

---

1. Right cause, wrong means: Human rights violated and justice denied in Cameroon's fight against Boko Haram (AFR 17/4260/2016)

CANADA

Canada
Head of state: **Queen Elizabeth II, represented by Governor General David Johnston**
Head of government: **Justin Trudeau**

Some 38,000 Syrian refugees were resettled. A national inquiry into violence against Indigenous women and girls was launched. Concerns persisted about the failure to uphold the rights of Indigenous Peoples in the face of economic development projects.

INDIGENOUS PEOPLES' RIGHTS

In January, the Canadian Human Rights Tribunal ruled that systemic underfunding of First Nation child protection services constituted discrimination. The government accepted the ruling but failed to bring an end to the discrimination.

In May, the government announced unconditional support for the UN Declaration on the Rights of Indigenous Peoples; by the end of the year it remained unclear how it would collaborate with Indigenous Peoples to implement that commitment.

In May, a provincially funded report confirmed that mercury contamination continued for the Grassy Narrows First Nation in the Province of Ontario.

In July, the government issued permits allowing construction of the Site C dam in the Province of British Columbia to proceed, despite unresolved court cases concerning obligations under a historic treaty with affected First Nations.

In October, the government of the Province of Newfoundland and Labrador agreed to measures to reduce risks to Inuit health and culture from the Muskrat Falls dam, following hunger strikes and other protests.

In November, the British Columbia government acknowledged the need to address the impact of the resource sector on the safety of Indigenous women and girls.

WOMEN'S RIGHTS

In March, the government committed to promoting the sexual and reproductive health and rights of women and girls through its international development programme.

In September, the National Inquiry into Missing and Murdered Indigenous Women and Girls was launched. Its mandate did not explicitly include police actions or measures to address past failures to properly investigate cases. In November, the UN CEDAW Committee called on Canada to ensure that the National Inquiry would investigate the role of policing.

In November, prosecutors in the Province of Quebec laid charges in only two of 37 complaints brought mostly by Indigenous women alleging abuse by police. The Independent Observer appointed to oversee the cases raised concerns about systemic racism. In December the Quebec government announced a public inquiry into the treatment of Indigenous Peoples by provincial bodies.

COUNTER-TERROR AND SECURITY

In February, legislation was introduced to reverse 2014 Citizenship Act reforms allowing for dual nationals convicted of terrorism and other offences to be stripped of Canadian citizenship.

In February, the government withdrew an appeal against the 2015 bail decision releasing Omar Khadr – a Canadian citizen held at the US detention centre in Guantánamo Bay, Cuba, for 10 years beginning when he was 15 years old and transferred to a Canadian prison in 2012.

In November, the Federal Court ruled that the Canadian Security and Intelligence Service practice of indefinitely retaining metadata from phone and email logs was unlawful.

Mediation broke off in the cases of Abdullah Almalki, Ahmad Abou-Elmaati and Muayyed Nureddin who were seeking redress on the basis of a 2008 judicial inquiry report documenting the role of Canadian officials in their overseas arrest, imprisonment and torture.

JUSTICE SYSTEM

Concerns mounted about extensive use of solitary confinement after the case of Adam Capay, an Indigenous man held in pre-trial solitary confinement in Ontario for over four years, became public in October.

In November, the Quebec government launched a public inquiry into surveillance of journalists by police.

REFUGEES AND ASYLUM-SEEKERS

Throughout the year, 38,700 Syrian refugees were resettled to Canada through government and private sponsorship.

In April, the Interim Federal Health Program for refugees and refugee claimants was fully restored, reversing cuts imposed in 2012.

In August, the Minister of Public Safety announced increased funding for immigration detention facilities.

CORPORATE ACCOUNTABILITY

In June, the British Columbia government allowed full operations to resume at the Mount Polley mine, despite an ongoing criminal investigation into the 2014 collapse of the mine's tailings pond and the fact that approval of the company's long-term water treatment plan was pending. In November, a private prosecution was launched against the provincial government and the Mount Polley Mining Corporation for violations of the Fisheries Act.

In May, the fifth annual report assessing the human rights impact of the Canada-Colombia Free Trade Agreement was released. It again failed to evaluate human rights concerns linked to extractive projects' effects on Indigenous Peoples and others.

The government failed to adopt measures to fulfil a 2015 election promise to establish a human rights Ombudsperson for the extractive sector. Canada was urged to take that step by the UN Committee on Economic, Social and Cultural Rights (CESCR) in March and by the CEDAW Committee in November.

Three Canadian companies faced civil lawsuits over alleged human rights abuses associated with overseas projects. A case dealing with HudBay Minerals' Guatemalan mine was proceeding in Ontario. In October, a British Columbia court ruled that a case involving Nevsun Resources' Eritrean mine could proceed. In November, an appeal was heard in British Columbia as to whether a case involving Tahoe Resources' Guatemalan mine could go ahead.

LEGAL, CONSTITUTIONAL OR INSTITUTIONAL DEVELOPMENTS

In February, a 2007 policy limiting government efforts to seek clemency on behalf of Canadians sentenced to death in foreign countries was reversed.

In March, the UN CESCR called on Canada to recognize that economic, social and cultural rights are fully justiciable.

In April, the government approved a Can $15 billion sale of light armoured vehicles to Saudi Arabia despite human rights concerns. A 2015 commitment to accede to the UN Arms Trade Treaty was not met.

In May, the government announced plans to accede to the Optional Protocol to the UN Convention against Torture and launched consultations with provincial and territorial governments.

Also in May, the government introduced legislation to add gender identity and expression as a prohibited ground of discrimination in Canada's Human Rights Act and Criminal Code hate crime laws.

CENTRAL AFRICAN REPUBLIC

Central African Republic
Head of state: **Faustin-Archange Touadéra (replaced Catherine Samba-Panza in March)**
Head of government: **Simplice Sarandji (replaced Mahamat Kamoun in April)**

Conflict between and within armed groups and militias, as well as between international peacekeepers and these groups, continued and involved serious human rights abuses, including crimes under international law. Impunity persisted for those suspected of abuses and crimes under international law. More than 434,000 people were internally displaced and living in harsh conditions, and at least 2.3 million people depended on humanitarian assistance. Allegations of sexual abuse by international peacekeepers continued to be reported.

BACKGROUND

From June onwards, after a period of relative calm, conflict between armed groups and attacks on civilians increased. The conflict, which began in 2013 with the ousting of President François Bozizé, claimed thousands of lives. Armed groups, particularly ex-Seleka and Anti-balaka forces, continued to control large swathes of the country, facilitated by mass circulation of small arms.

Elections were held to replace the transitional government and on 11 April a new government was formed.

Some 12,870 uniformed personnel were deployed as part of the UN Multidimensional Integrated Stabilization Mission in the Central African Republic (MINUSCA), whose mandate was renewed until 15 November 2017. Following criticism of MINUSCA's capacity to respond to attacks, its forces were strengthened.[1] However, it continued to have limited ability to protect civilians, given the vast size of the Central African Republic (CAR) and the significant presence of armed groups and militias. French forces, deployed under Operation Sangaris, were almost completely withdrawn in October.

In October, the CAR acceded without reservation to the UN Convention against Torture and its Optional Protocol; the International Convention for the Protection of All Persons from Enforced Disappearance; the Optional Protocol to CEDAW; and the Optional Protocol to the ICESCR. However, the CAR authorities did not recognize the competence of the relevant treaty bodies.

A major CAR donors' conference was held in Brussels on 17 November. The CAR National Recovery and Peacebuilding Plan 2017-2021 was presented to donors and requested $105 million over five years to support measures to both strengthen the domestic justice system and operationalize the Special Criminal Court (SCC).

ABUSES BY ARMED GROUPS AND CRIMES UNDER INTERNATIONAL LAW

Armed groups and militias committed human rights abuses, including unlawful killings, torture and other ill-treatment, abductions, sexual assaults, looting and destruction of property, and attacks on humanitarian workers and premises. Some of these amounted to crimes under international law. According to the UN, more than 300 security incidents targeting relief agencies were reported and at least five humanitarian workers were killed. More than 500 civilians were also killed in the violence according to international NGOs.

The risk of attack by Anti-balaka forces and their affiliates continued to restrict freedom of movement for Muslims living in enclaves across the country.

On 3 September, two civilians were killed as ex-Seleka fighters clashed with the local population and Anti-balaka forces near Dekoa town, Kemo district. The ex-Seleka fighters had escaped MINUSCA three weeks earlier after the peacekeeping force arrested 11 ex-Seleka members who were part of a convoy of prominent armed leaders, including Abdoulaye Hissène and Haroun Gaye, who also escaped.

On 10 September, 19 civilians were killed during fighting between Anti-balaka and ex-Seleka forces near the southern town of Kouango, Ouaka district. An estimated 3,500 people were displaced and 13 villages burned.

On 16 September, ex-Seleka fighters killed six civilians in the village of Ndomete, near the northern town of Kaga-Bandoro, Nana-Grébizi district, as a result of tensions between the group and Anti-balaka militia.

Between 4 and 8 October, at least 11 civilians were killed and 14 injured in the capital, Bangui, in reprisal attacks triggered by the assassination of a former army colonel by members of a militia based in the Muslim enclave of the capital known as PK5.

On 12 October, at least 37 civilians were killed, 60 injured and over 20,000 displaced when ex-Seleka fighters attacked and burned a camp for internally displaced people in Kaga-Bandoro in reprisal for the killing of an ex-Seleka member.

On 15 October in Ngakobo, Ouaka district, suspected ex-Seleka fighters attacked a camp for displaced people, leaving 11 civilians dead.

On 24 October in Bangui, a protest against MINUSCA led by civilians infiltrated by armed elements left four civilians dead and nine wounded.

On 27 October, 15 people were killed in clashes between ex-Seleka and Anti-balaka in the villages of Mbriki and Belima, near Bambari, Ouaka district.

In late November fighting between rival ex-Seleka factions in Bria left at least 14 civilians dead and 75 wounded.

The southeast of the CAR was also affected by violence, including by the armed group Lord's Resistance Army (LRA). International NGOs reported 103 attacks by the LRA leading to at least 18 civilian casualties and 497 kidnappings since the beginning of the year.

VIOLATIONS BY PEACEKEEPING FORCES

Civilians continued to report sexual abuse by international forces. Following the report of an independent panel in December 2015, and a visit in April by the Special Coordinator on improving the United Nations' response to sexual exploitation and abuse, MINUSCA introduced measures to strengthen monitoring, reporting and accountability in relation to such cases.

Countries contributing peacekeeping troops to the CAR whose soldiers were accused of sexual abuse took some steps to ensure accountability, but prosecutions remained rare. In April, three Congolese peacekeepers accused of sexual abuse in the CAR appeared before a military court in the Democratic Republic of the Congo (DRC).

REFUGEES AND INTERNALLY DISPLACED PEOPLE

More than 434,000 people remained internally displaced. They lived in harsh conditions in makeshift camps, and lacked access to food, water, basic health services and adequate sanitation. The spontaneous return of a small number of internally displaced people caused intercommunal tensions in some areas, especially in the southwest. The returns significantly decreased following the renewed violence from June onward.

IMPUNITY

Members of armed groups, militias and security forces suspected of human rights abuses and crimes under international law did not face effective investigations or trial. Some suspects appeared to be linked to ongoing armed violence, human rights abuses and crimes under international law, and a few held positions of authority. Among them were prominent ex-Seleka leader Haroun Gaye, the subject of an international arrest warrant and UN sanctions, who had admitted orchestrating the kidnapping of six policemen in Bangui on 16 June; and Alfred Yekatom ("Colonel Rambo"), a feared Anti-balaka commander also on the UN sanctions list, who began sitting as an elected member of CAR's National Assembly in early 2016.

MINUSCA arrested 194 individuals under its Urgent Temporary Measures, including prominent ex-Seleka leader Hahmed Tidjani on 13 August.

A weak national justice system undermined efforts to ensure accountability. The presence and functioning of judicial institutions remained limited, especially outside Bangui. In areas controlled by armed groups, such as Ndélé town, the capital of Bamingui-Bangoran, armed groups and/or traditional chiefs administered justice.

Judicial authorities lacked the capacity to investigate and prosecute people suspected of crimes, including serious human rights abuses. In the few cases involving human rights abuses that went to court, defendants were acquitted or convicted of minor offences and immediately released for time spent in prison, and fear of reprisals prevented witnesses and victims testifying.

INTERNATIONAL JUSTICE

Limited progress was made in operationalizing the Special Criminal Court, which would bring together national and international judges to try individuals suspected of serious human rights violations and crimes under international law committed since 2003.

The International Criminal Court (ICC) investigations on the CAR II situation, based on crimes under international law committed from 2012 onward, continued. Two separate teams worked respectively on crimes committed by ex-Seleka and by Anti-balaka and its affiliates. On 20 June, ICC investigations on the CAR I situation, which focused on crimes against humanity and war crimes since 1 July 2002, resulted in the conviction of a Congolese national, Jean-Pierre Bemba Gombo, as a military commander. He was sentenced to 18 years in prison for war crimes and crimes against humanity, including murder, rape and pillaging committed by his militia.

PRISON CONDITIONS

Prison conditions remained poor and security was weak. Of 38 official detention facilities across the country, only eight were functional.

In September, guards severely beat 21 inmates in Ngaragba prison in Bangui. This triggered an attempted prison break, which was foiled by guards using tear gas. An investigation into the events was opened soon afterwards by national authorities.

NATURAL RESOURCES

The Kimberley Process, a global initiative to stop "blood diamonds" from being sold internationally, banned the CAR from exporting diamonds in May 2013. However, the CAR diamond trade continued and armed groups involved in abuses profited from it. In July 2015, the Kimberley Process allowed the resumption of diamond exports from "compliant zones". During 2016, Berberati, Boda, Carnot and Nola, all in the southwest, were deemed to be "compliant zones".

RIGHT TO AN ADEQUATE STANDARD OF LIVING

According to the UN, 2.3 million of the population of 4.8 million needed humanitarian assistance and 2.5 million people remained food insecure. As a result of the conflict, household incomes fell and food prices rose. Basic health services and medicines were provided almost entirely by humanitarian organizations following the collapse of the health system. Less than half of the population had access to effective health care, and virtually no psychosocial support was available. According to the UN, only about a third of the population had access to safe drinking water and adequate sanitation facilities.

---

1. Mandated to protect, equipped to succeed? Strengthening peacekeeping in Central African Republic (AFR 19/3263/2016)

CHAD

Republic of Chad
Head of state: **Idriss Déby Itno**
Head of government: **Albert Pahimi Padacké (replaced Kalzeubet Pahimi Deubet in February)**

The armed group Boko Haram continued to commit abuses around Lake Chad, killing people and looting and destroying property. The violence and the government's response displaced tens of thousands of people, who then faced dire living conditions, including little access to water and sanitation. Presidential elections in April took place against a backdrop of restrictions on freedom of expression, excessive or unnecessary use of force against peaceful demonstrators, and enforced disappearances. More than 389,000 refugees continued to live in harsh conditions in crowded camps. Former President Hissène Habré was sentenced to life imprisonment by the Extraordinary African Chambers (EAC) in Senegal for crimes against humanity, war crimes and torture committed in Chad between 1982 and 1990.

ABUSES BY ARMED GROUPS

Boko Haram carried out attacks on civilians and security forces, killing people and looting and destroying private property and public facilities.

On 31 January, at least three people, including a member of a vigilante group, were killed in two suicide attacks by Boko Haram in the villages of Guié and Miterine, Lake Chad region, and more than 56 people were injured.

FREEDOMS OF EXPRESSION AND ASSEMBLY

The rights to freedom of expression and of association were violated. Human rights defenders continued to be threatened and intimidated, and access to social media was regularly restricted. On 19 March, the government banned all demonstrations that were not part of the election campaign.

On 6 February, 17 peaceful protesters were arrested in the capital, N'Djamena. They were held for two days at the judicial police headquarters, where they were beaten and had tear gas thrown into their cell. At least two of them needed intensive care treatment in hospital.

Between 21 and 23 March, four activists were arrested and charged with "disturbing public order" and "disobeying a lawful order" for planning to organize a peaceful demonstration. They were detained in Amsinene Prison in N'Djamena from 24 March to 14 April. On 14 April they received a four-month suspended sentence and were prohibited from "engaging in subversive activities". On 4 April, activist Dr Albissaty Salhe Alazam was charged with "incitement to take part in an unarmed gathering", "disturbing public order" and "disobeying a lawful order" for organizing a peaceful demonstration on 5 April to demand the release of the four activists. He received a four-month suspended prison sentence.

In mid-April, two human rights activists fled the country after receiving death threats via SMS and anonymous phone calls following their involvement in pre-election protests against the re-election of President Déby.

On 17 November, 11 opposition activists were arrested during an unauthorized protest against the economic crisis and charged with taking part in an "unarmed gathering". They were released on 7 December and the charges were dropped.

EXCESSIVE USE OF FORCE

Security forces used excessive or unnecessary force with impunity to disperse demonstrations in N'Djamena and other towns.

In February and March, security forces violently dispersed several peaceful demonstrations across the country demanding justice for Zouhoura Ibrahim, a 16-year-old student raped on 8 February, allegedly by five young men with links to the authorities and security forces. On 15 February, police killed a 17-year-old student during a peaceful demonstration in N'Djamena, and on 22 February security forces shot dead a 15-year-old student and injured at least five others in the city of Faya Largeau.

On 7 August, police used firearms to disperse a peaceful demonstration in N'Djamena against President Idriss Déby's re-election, killing one young man and seriously injuring another.

ARBITRARY ARRESTS AND DETENTIONS – JOURNALISTS

Journalists continued to be intimidated and routinely subjected to arbitrary arrests and short-term detention for exercising their right to freedom of expression.

On 28 May, a presenter on a national radio station was interrogated by agents of the Directorate of General Information after accidentally referring to the President as Hissène Habré instead of Idriss Déby while on air. He was released seven hours later and suspended from the show.

On 30 August, Stéphane Mbaïrabé Ouaye, Director of Publication of *Haut Parleur* newspaper, was arrested, questioned by agents of the Directorate of General Information and charged with "attempted fraud and blackmail" following an interview with the Director of the Mother and Child Hospital in N'Djamena about allegations of corruption. He was tried and acquitted, and released on 22 September.

On 9 September, Bemadjiel Saturnin, a reporter.at Radio FM Liberté, was arrested while covering a protest, despite having his professional ID. He was questioned at the central police station and released four hours later.

ENFORCED DISAPPEARANCES

On 9 April, at least 64 soldiers were victims of enforced disappearance after refusing to vote for the incumbent President. Witnesses described how security forces identified soldiers who supported opposition candidates, ill-treated them at polling stations, abducted them, and tortured them at both recognized and unrecognized detention centres. Forty-nine of the soldiers were released, but the fate of the other 15 was still unclarified at the end of 2016. Following international pressure, the Public Prosecutor opened an investigation into the case of five of the soldiers, but the case was closed after their release. No investigation was undertaken into the allegations of torture and the other cases of disappearance.

REFUGEES AND INTERNALLY DISPLACED PEOPLE

More than 389,000 refugees from the Central African Republic, Nigeria and Sudan continued to live in poor conditions in refugee camps.

As a result of attacks and threats by Boko Haram, and security operations by the Chadian military, 105,000 people were internally displaced and 12,000 returned from Nigeria and Niger to the Lake Chad

Basin. The deteriorating security situation in the border areas of the Lake Chad region from late July onward affected humanitarian access and the protection of vulnerable populations. Internally displaced people in the Lake Chad Basin lived in dire conditions with extremely limited access to water and sanitation, especially in the Baga-Sola sites of Bol, Liwa and Ngouboua.

RIGHT TO AN ADEQUATE STANDARD OF LIVING, EDUCATION AND JUSTICE

People continued to flee the escalating violence in the Lake Chad area, disrupting agriculture, trade and fishing with dire economic and social consequences. The volatile security situation exacerbated food insecurity. In September, the UN estimated that 3.8 million people were food insecure, including 1 million people at crisis or emergency level.

Delays in salary payments led to regular public sector strikes, restricting access to education and justice.

In August, the government adopted 16 emergency reform measures to tackle the economic crisis linked to the drop in the price of oil, including cancelling scholarships for university students in the countryside. In response, students organized both peaceful and violent demonstrations in the main cities, including N'Djamena, Sarh, Pala and Bongor.

SEXUAL AND REPRODUCTIVE RIGHTS

Despite national law providing for the right of couples and individuals to decide freely the number, spacing and timing of their children, to manage their reproductive health, and to have access to the information and means to do so, many people had no access to reproductive information or care, particularly in rural areas. The UN Population Fund (UNFPA) estimated that only 3% of women used any form of contraception. According to 2014 figures from the National Institute of Statistics, only 5% of married women used modern contraceptive methods.

In December the National Assembly adopted a reform of the penal code raising the legal age of marriage for girls from 16 to 18 years.

INTERNATIONAL JUSTICE

On 30 May, former President Habré was sentenced to life imprisonment by the EAC in Senegal, a court established under an agreement between the African Union and Senegal. He was found guilty of crimes against humanity, war crimes and torture committed in Chad between 1982 and 1990. His lawyers lodged an appeal.

On 29 July, the EAC awarded the victims of rape and sexual violence in the case 20 million CFA (US$33,880) each; the victims of arbitrary detention and torture, as well as prisoners of war and survivors, 15 million CFA (US$25,410) each; and the indirect victims, 10 million CFA (US$16,935) each.

CHILE

Republic of Chile
Head of state and government: **Michelle Bachelet Jeria**

Impunity for past and continuing human rights violations remained a concern. Legal proceedings relating to allegations of past crimes under international law and other human rights violations continued; in a few cases, those involved were imprisoned. For much of the year, cases of unnecessary and excessive use of force by the police continued to be dealt with by the military courts. However, a law passed in November excludes civilians from military jurisdiction. Abortion remained criminalized in all circumstances, although some steps were taken to decriminalize it in limited circumstances.

BACKGROUND

Between April and August, the government carried out a consultation process open to all citizens as the first step towards the adoption of a new Constitution. The current Constitution, adopted during the military government under General Pinochet, contains several provisions that are not in line with international human rights law.

In January, a law entered into force establishing a new Undersecretariat on Human Rights under the Ministry of Justice. The first Undersecretary was appointed in September.

In April, the government announced that plans to reform the law on migration were postponed indefinitely. In December it was announced that the bill would be filed in January 2017.

POLICE AND SECURITY FORCES

Allegations of unnecessary or excessive use of force by the police, especially in the context of public protests, continued to be reported. Children, women, journalists and employees of the National Human Rights Institute acting as observers were among the victims.

Human rights violations involving members of the security forces continued to be dealt with by military courts. However, a new law entered into force in November that expressly stated that civilians, whether accused or the victims of crime, were excluded from military jurisdiction.

In January, the National Human Rights Institute filed a lawsuit to push for further investigation by the ordinary courts into the enforced disappearance of 16-year-old José Huenante; he was last seen being detained by policemen in September 2005. Following the lawsuit, a military court also reopened an investigation. However, at the end of the year, José Huenante's fate and whereabouts remained unclarified and neither investigation had established the facts of the case or identified those responsible.

IMPUNITY

During the year, several convictions for past crimes under international law and other human rights violations committed during the military regime were confirmed. In September, the Supreme Court confirmed the four-year sentences of two former military officials for the torture of General Alberto Bachelet in 1973.

Victims, their relatives and civil society organizations opposed several attempts to obtain the early release on parole of people convicted of human rights violations during the military government under Augusto Pinochet. At the end of the year, a bill was before Congress to deny the possibility of parole for those convicted of crimes against humanity.

A law establishing the crime of torture in Chilean law came into force in November. In September, Chile was one of the countries listed by the UN Subcommittee on Prevention of Torture as having delayed complying with the Optional Protocol to the UN Convention against Torture, because of the absence of a national mechanism for the prevention of torture.

INDIGENOUS PEOPLES' RIGHTS

In January, Congress established a commission to investigate violence in Araucanía, the region most affected by land conflicts involving the Mapuche. The commission focused on crimes allegedly committed by the Mapuche as a form of protest. However, continued allegations of excessive use of force and arbitrary detentions during police operations against Mapuche communities were not investigated as they did not fall within the commission's mandate. The Chamber of Deputies approved the commission's conclusions in September.

In May, the Inter-American Commission on Human Rights extended the precautionary measures ordered in October 2015 in favour of Mapuche leader Juana Calfunao. These measures sought to protect additional members of her family living in the community of Juan Paillalef in the south of Chile from threats to their life and integrity related to a land dispute.

In August, photographer Felipe Durán and Mapuche community member Cristián Levinao were found not guilty of all charges. The two men had been accused of illegal possession of weapons and drug offences and held in preventive detention for over 300 days.

The Machi (Mapuche traditional spiritual authority) Francisca Linconao was detained in March and held pending trial. On four occasions a judge allowed her transfer to house arrest to address serious health concerns. On each occasion this was overturned on appeal and she was returned to prison shortly afterwards. In November she was transferred to hospital. In December she began a hunger strike, demanding to be held in her own home pre-trial, and her defence team filed a writ of *amparo* calling for the same measure. She remained on hunger strike at the end of the year.

SEXUAL AND REPRODUCTIVE RIGHTS

Abortion remained a criminal offence in all circumstances. Several women seeking medical care for complications following unsafe abortions risked criminal charges after being reported to the authorities by health professionals.

In March, the Chamber of Deputies approved a bill decriminalizing abortion when the pregnancy poses a risk to a woman's life, when it is the result of rape and in cases of serious foetal impairment. However, provisions prohibiting health professionals from reporting women were removed from the bill following their rejection by the Chamber of Deputies. The amended bill was pending before the Senate by the end of the year.

RIGHTS OF LESBIAN, GAY, BISEXUAL, TRANSGENDER AND INTERSEX PEOPLE

In September, the Senate Human Rights Commission approved the Gender Identity Bill, the first step towards its approval after three years of debate. Approval by the Senate and the Chamber of Deputies remained pending at the end of the year. The Bill proposed establishing the right of individuals over 18 to have their gender identity legally recognized by changing their name and gender on official documents through an administrative process and without the existing requirements of gender reassignment surgery or medical certification.

In July, Chile reached a friendly settlement before the Inter-American Commission on Human Rights on a complaint on behalf of three gay couples who were denied the right to marry. The settlement included the adoption of a series of measures and policies to promote the rights of LGBTI people. In August, as part of the settlement, the government announced a participatory process with civil society aimed at drafting a bill to establish marriage equality.

CHINA

People's Republic of China
Head of state: **Xi Jinping**
Head of government: **Li Keqiang**

The government continued to draft and enact a series of new national security laws that presented serious threats to the protection of human rights. The nationwide crackdown on human rights lawyers and activists continued throughout the year. Activists and human rights defenders continued to be systematically subjected to monitoring, harassment, intimidation, arrest and detention. Police detained increasing numbers of human rights defenders outside of formal detention facilities, sometimes without access to a lawyer for long periods, exposing the detainees to the risk of torture and other ill-treatment. Booksellers, publishers, activists and a journalist who went missing in neighbouring countries in 2015 and 2016 turned up in detention in China, causing concerns about China's law enforcement agencies acting outside their jurisdiction. Controls on the internet, mass media and academia were significantly strengthened. Repression of religious activities outside of direct state control increased. Religious repression conducted under "anti-separatism" or "counter-terrorism" campaigns remained particularly severe in Xinjiang Uighur Autonomous Region and in Tibetan-populated areas.

LEGAL, CONSTITUTIONAL OR INSTITUTIONAL DEVELOPMENTS

Sweeping national security laws and regulations continued to be drafted and enacted, giving greater powers to the authorities to silence dissent, restrict or censor information and harass and prosecute human rights defenders.

The Foreign NGO Management Law was due to come into force on 1 January 2017, creating additional barriers to the already limited rights to freedom of association, peaceful assembly and expression. Although the law was ostensibly designed to regulate and even protect the activities of foreign NGOs, it transferred to the Ministry of Public Security – the state policing agency – the responsibility to oversee the registration of these NGOs, as well as supervise their operations and pre-approve their activities. The wide discretion given to police to oversee and manage the work of foreign NGOs raised the risk of the law being misused to intimidate and prosecute human rights defenders and NGO staff.

On 7 November, the National People's Congress (NPC) passed the Cyber Security Law, which purported to protect internet users' personal data from hacking and theft, but made it obligatory for internet companies operating in China to censor content, store users' data domestically, and enforce a real-name registration system in a way that runs counter to national and international obligations to safeguard the rights to freedom of expression and privacy. The law prohibited individuals or groups from using the internet to "harm national security", "upset social order", or "harm national interests." – terms that were vague and imprecise under existing Chinese law and could be used to further restrict freedom of expression. The law enshrined the concept of "internet sovereignty", which justified broad censorship and extensive surveillance powers in the name of protecting national security.

Also on 7 November, the NPC passed the Film Industry Promotion Law which prohibited the production of films that include content endangering national security, inciting ethnic hatred and violating religious policies.

JUSTICE SYSTEM

Shortcomings in domestic law and systemic problems in the criminal justice system resulted in widespread torture and other ill-treatment and unfair trials.

The authorities increasingly used "residential surveillance in a designated location", a form of secret incommunicado detention that allowed the police to hold individuals for up to six months outside the formal detention system, without access to legal counsel of their choice, their families or anybody else from the outside world, and placed suspects at risk of torture and other ill-treatment. This form of detention was used to curb the activities of human rights defenders, including lawyers, activists and religious practitioners.

HUMAN RIGHTS DEFENDERS

At the end of the year, five people remained in detention awaiting trial on charges of "subverting state power" or "inciting subversion of state power", and four on charges of "picking quarrels and provoking trouble" or "making arrangements for another person to illegally cross the national border". Their detention followed the unprecedented government crackdown on human rights lawyers and other activists which started in mid-2015, in which at least 248 lawyers and activists were questioned or detained by state security agents. At least 12 of the individuals detained in the crackdown, including prominent human rights lawyers Zhou Shifeng, Sui Muqing, Li Heping and Wang Quanzhang, had been held in "residential surveillance in a designated location" on suspicion of involvement in state security crimes. Family members of those detained were also subject to police surveillance, harassment and restriction of their freedom of movement. Legal assistant Zhao Wei and lawyer Wang Yu were released on bail in early July and early August respectively, although they remained subject to restrictions on their rights to freedom of movement, expression and association for one year and remained at risk of prosecution.

On 2 August, activist Zhai Yanmin was convicted of "subverting state power" and sentenced to three years' imprisonment, suspended for four years. Hu Shigen and lawyer Zhou Shifeng were convicted of the same charge and sentenced to seven and a half years' imprisonment and seven years' imprisonment respectively on 3 and 4 August.

Lawyer Jiang Tianyong went missing on 21 November. His family was notified on 23 December that he had been placed under "residential surveillance in a designated location" under suspicion of "inciting subversion of state power". Liu Feiyue and Huang Qi, both human rights defenders and website founders, were detained in November, accused respectively of "inciting subversion" and "leaking state secrets".

The authorities in Guangdong province, where labour disputes and strikes were on the rise, continued their crackdown on workers and labour rights activists which began in December 2015. At least 33 individuals were targeted; 31 were later released. Labour activist Zeng Feiyang was denied access to lawyers and sentenced to three years' imprisonment, suspended for four years, in early October. Labour activist Meng Han was sentenced to one year and nine months' imprisonment on 3 November. In many cases the detention centres initially denied access to lawyers on the grounds that the cases involved "endangering national security".

Six of the more than 100 people in mainland China detained for supporting the Hong Kong pro-democracy protests in late 2014 were sentenced to prison terms. They included Xie Wenfei and Wang Mo, leaders of the Southern Street Movement, who were sentenced to four and a half years' imprisonment on charges of "inciting subversion". Two others, women's rights activist Su Changlan and Chen Qitang, remained in detention with no dates set for their trials. Zhang Shengyu, who was among those detained for supporting the Hong Kong protests, reported that he was beaten and Su Changlan reported she was denied adequate medical treatment in detention.

The number of carefully choreographed televised "confessions" increased during the year. They included interviews with detained human rights defenders conducted by Chinese state media and, in two cases, by pro-Beijing media outlets in Hong Kong. Although such "confessions" had no legal validity, they undermined the right to a fair trial. Those shown "confessing" on television included lawyers Zhou Shifeng and Wang Yu, activist Zhai Yanmin, Hong Kong bookseller Gui Minhai and Swedish NGO worker Peter Dahlin, who was detained and later deported. Zhao Wei and her lawyer, Ren Quanniu, posted confessions on their social media after they were reportedly released on bail.

Several journalists and activists who went missing outside mainland China were detained or feared to be detained in China. Journalist Li Xin, who revealed in media interviews that Chinese state security officials had put him under intense pressure to act as an informant against his colleagues and friends before he fled China in 2015, went missing in Thailand in January 2016. He telephoned his partner in February and said he had voluntarily returned to China to assist with an investigation. He was not heard from again and his whereabouts were undisclosed at the end of the year. Tang Zhishun and Xing Qingxian went missing in Myanmar in 2015 while helping the son of two detained Chinese lawyers. Without providing any explanation for the time lag, the authorities charged them with "making arrangements for another person to illegally cross the national border" in notices dated May 2016.

In May, pro-democracy activists Jiang Yefei and Dong Guangping were confirmed to have been detained on suspicion of "subverting state power" and "making arrangements for another person to illegally cross the national border". They had been granted refugee status by UNHCR, the UN refugee agency, but were repatriated from Thailand to China in 2015. Neither had access to family or lawyers of their choice for at least the first six months after their return and Dong Guangping still had no access by the end of the year.

Miao Deshun, a labour activist arrested after participating in the pro-democracy Tiananmen Square protests in 1989, was reportedly released in October after 27 years' imprisonment. Activists who commemorated the Tiananmen crackdown continued to be detained, including Sichuan activists Fu Hailu and Luo Fuyu.[1]

FREEDOM OF EXPRESSION

In March, police reportedly detained at least 20 people in connection with the publication of an open letter criticizing President Xi and calling for his resignation. The open letter blamed President Xi for trying to build a "personality cult" and abandoning collective leadership. Those detained included 16 people working for Wujie News, the website which published the letter on 4 March.

On 4 April the government issued guidelines to increase law enforcement of cultural matters in a bid to "safeguard the 'national cultural and ideological security'". The guidelines would increase regulation of many "illegal" and unauthorized activities, including: publishing, film and TV distribution, foreign satellite TV broadcasting, artistic performances, and imports and exports of cultural products.

China made further efforts to reinforce its already oppressive internet censorship architecture. Thousands of websites and social media services remain blocked, including Facebook, Instagram and Twitter, and internet service and content providers were required to maintain extensive censorship on their platforms.

Six journalists from Sichuan-based website "64 Tianwang" were detained for covering protests in relation to the G20 Summit in Hangzhou in September. One, Qin Chao, remained in detention.

FREEDOM OF RELIGION AND BELIEF

Proposed amendments to the Regulations on Religious Affairs issued on 7 September would extend power to various authorities to monitor, control and sanction some religious practice. The amendments, which emphasized national security with a goal of curbing "infiltration and extremism", could be used to further suppress the rights to freedom of religion and belief, especially for Tibetan Buddhists, Uighur Muslims and unrecognized churches.

The campaign to demolish churches and remove Christian crosses from buildings in Zhejiang province, launched in 2013, intensified into 2016. According to international media, more than 1,700 crosses had been removed by the end of 2016, prompting a series of protests.

Zhang Kai, a lawyer who offered legal assistance to the affected churches, appeared on state television on 25 February, looking thin and exhausted, to give a videotaped "confession". He was initially detained in 2015 on suspicion of state security crimes and "disturbing public order" and was later placed under "residential surveillance in a designated location". He was released without explanation and returned to his hometown in Inner Mongolia on 23 March.

On 26 February, Bao Guohua and his wife Xing Wenxiang, pastors from Jinghua city in Zhejiang province, were sentenced to 14 years' and 12 years' imprisonment respectively for embezzling money from their congregation and "gathering a crowd to disturb social order". Bao Guohua had been vocal in opposing the removal of crosses from churches.

Falun Gong practitioners continued to be subjected to persecution, arbitrary detention, unfair trials and torture and other ill-treatment. Falun Gong practitioner Chen Huixia was detained in June and, according to her daughter, tortured in detention because of her beliefs.[2]

DEATH PENALTY

A white paper issued by the government in September claimed that China "[strictly controlled] the death penalty and employ[ed] it with prudence to ensure that it applies only to a very small number of extremely serious criminal offenders". Statistics related to the death penalty continued to be classified as state secrets, making it impossible to verify the number of death sentences handed down and executions carried out.

In December the Supreme People's Court overturned the murder and rape conviction against Nie Shubin, who was executed in 1995. The Supreme People's Court ordered the retrial and agreed with a lower court finding that there was a lack of clear evidence to prove that Nie Shubin was guilty.

TIBET AUTONOMOUS REGION AND TIBETAN-POPULATED AREAS IN OTHER PROVINCES

Ethnic Tibetans continued to face discrimination and restrictions on their rights to freedom of religion and belief, expression, association and peaceful assembly. In August, media reported that Lobsang Drakpa, a Tibetan monk who was detained by police in 2015 while staging a solo protest – an increasingly common form of protest in the Tibetan-populated areas – was sentenced to three years' imprisonment in a closed trial.[3]

At least three people set themselves on fire in Tibetan-populated areas during the year in protest against repressive policies by the authorities. The number of known self-immolations since February 2009 rose to 146.

A Tibetan blogger known as Druklo was sentenced to three years' imprisonment in February for "inciting separatism" for his online posts on religious freedom, the Dalai Lama and other Tibetan issues and his possession of the banned book *Sky Burial*.[4]

Tashi Wangchuk was detained in January and charged with "inciting separatism" for advocating Tibetan language education and giving an interview to the *New York Times*. He remained in detention at the end of the year.[5]

Housing rights – forced evictions

In July, the government began demolishing a large part of Larung Gar, reportedly the largest Tibetan Buddhist institute in the world, located in Seda (Serta) County, in the Ganzi (Kardze) Tibetan Autonomous Prefecture, Sichuan province. Local Chinese authorities ordered the population of Larung Gar to be reduced by more than half to 5,000 in order to carry out "correction and rectification". Thousands of monks, nuns and lay people were at risk of forced evictions.

XINJIANG UIGHUR AUTONOMOUS REGION

In March the Xinjiang Uighur Autonomous Region's (XUAR) Party Secretary, Zhang Chunxian, announced that progress had been made in maintaining social stability in the region, and that cases of "violent terrorism" had decreased. Nonetheless, the government said that it would continue to maintain indefinitely its "strike hard" stance against "violent terrorism".

The government continued to detain ethnic Uighur writers and Uighur language website editors. Human rights defender Zhang Haitao, an ethnic Han, was sentenced to 19 years' imprisonment on charges of "inciting subversion" and "providing intelligence overseas". His lawyers believed that the severity of his sentence was in part due to his commentary on ethnic issues.

The government continued to violate the right to freedom of religion, and crack down on all unauthorized religious gatherings. Abudulrekep Tumniyaz, deputy director of the Xinjiang Islamic Association, said in March that all underground preaching sites in the XUAR had been shut down.

In October, media reported that several localities within the XUAR had announced that they will require all residents to hand in their passports to the police. Thereafter, all XUAR residents would be required to present biometric data – such as DNA samples and body scan images – before being permitted to travel abroad. The measure came amid a security crackdown and greater travel restrictions targeting ethnic minorities in the XUAR.

Cultural rights

In August, the provincial government announced a large-scale plan to send 1,900

Uighur teachers to schools throughout mainland China to accompany Uighur students living in boarding schools in Han-majority areas. The government pledged to increase the number of such dispatched teachers to 7,200 by 2020.

The move is billed as a way to "resist terrorism, violent extremism and separatism and promote ethnic solidarity", but Uighur groups overseas have criticized the plan as a means to dilute Uighur cultural identity.

HONG KONG SPECIAL ADMINISTRATIVE REGION

Five booksellers who went missing in Thailand, mainland China and Hong Kong in late 2015 reappeared on television in mainland China in January and February of 2016. Gui Minhai, Lui Por, Cheung Chi-ping, Lee Po and Lam Wing-kee worked for Mighty Current Media, a Hong Kong company known for its books on Chinese leaders and political scandals. Lam Wing-kee returned to Hong Kong in June and held a press conference in which he said he was arbitrarily detained, ill-treated in detention and forced to "confess".[6]

Students Joshua Wong, Alex Chow and Nathan Law were tried for their part in events outside government headquarters in September 2014 that triggered the pro-democracy Umbrella Movement. In July 2016, Joshua Wong and Alex Chow were found guilty of "taking part in an unlawful assembly" and Nathan Law was found guilty of "inciting others to take part in an unlawful assembly", vague provisions in Hong Kong's Public Order Ordinance. Appeals from both parties were pending at the end of the year.

In November the Standing Committee of the NPC issued an interpretation of Article 104 of the Hong Kong Basic Law concerning oath-taking by two pro-independence legislators. This happened before the Hong Kong High Court could rule on a parallel case raised by the Hong Kong government seeking to disqualify the legislators.

1. China: Two more activists detained for "June 4 baijiu" (ASA 17/4298/2016)
2. China: Falun Gong practitioner said to have been tortured in detention: Chen Huixia (ASA 17/4869/2016)
3. China: Tibetan monk imprisoned after protest (ASA 17/4802/2016)
4. China: Tibetan imprisoned for "inciting separatism" (ASA 17/3908/2016)
5. China: Tibetan education advocate detained: Tashi Wangchuk (ASA 17/3793/2016)
6. China: Authorities' revelations on detained Hong Kong booksellers "smoke and mirrors" (Press release, 5 February)

COLOMBIA

Republic of Colombia
Head of state and government: Juan Manuel Santos Calderón

A peace deal reached between the government and the guerrilla group the Revolutionary Armed Forces of Colombia (FARC) was ratified by Congress in November. This marked the official end of the five-decade armed conflict between the two sides after more than four years of talks. However, there was an increase in killings of human rights defenders, including Indigenous, Afro-descendant and peasant farmer leaders. The peace process with the second largest guerrilla group, the National Liberation Army (ELN) had not begun by the end of the year. Doubts remained over whether the peace agreement with the FARC would ensure that all those suspected of criminal responsibility for crimes against humanity and war crimes would be held accountable in line with international law.

PEACE PROCESS

In June, the government and the FARC signed a bilateral ceasefire and cessation of hostilities agreement.[1] This came into force on 29 August, although a de facto ceasefire had been in place since 2015. On 24 August, the two sides reached agreement on a peace deal,[2] which was signed on 26 September in Cartagena.[3] However, on 2 October, the peace deal was rejected in a referendum, in part because of concerns over the agreement's lax justice provisions.

On 12 November, the two sides announced a revised peace deal, which was signed on 24 November. The agreement was ratified by Congress on 30 November, after which the FARC was due to begin a six-month process of demobilization and disarmament, to be monitored and verified in part by a mission of unarmed UN observers. By the end of the year, FARC combatants had yet to congregate in the concentration zones from where they were due to start the demobilization process, because of delays in making these areas habitable.

On 28 December, Congress approved a law to provide amnesties or pardons to FARC combatants and the waiving of criminal prosecutions for security force personnel not under investigation for or convicted of crimes under international law. Those who had served at least five years in prison for crimes under international law will, under certain circumstances, be conditionally released. Ambiguities in the law could result in many human rights abusers evading justice.

The modifications made to the peace agreement did not significantly strengthen victims' rights. However, a provision requiring the FARC to provide an inventory of the assets it acquired in the conflict, which would be used to provide reparation to victims, would, if effectively implemented, be a positive development.

The peace agreement established a Special Jurisdiction for Peace – to come into force once approved by Congress – to investigate and punish those responsible for crimes under international law, a truth commission and a mechanism to locate and identify those missing as a result of the conflict.

Despite some positive features, however, it fell short of international law and standards on victims' rights, including punishments that appeared to be inconsistent with the gravity of certain crimes and a definition of command responsibility that could make it difficult to hold to account FARC and security force commanders for crimes committed by their subordinates.

On 30 March, the government and the ELN announced that they would begin peace talks. However, the process had not started by the end of the year because of the ELN's failure to release one of its high-profile hostages.

President Santos was awarded the Nobel Peace Prize on 7 October for his role in securing the peace deal.[4]

INTERNAL ARMED CONFLICT

By 1 December 2016, the state's Victims' Unit had registered almost 8 million victims of the conflict since 1985, including some 268,000 killings, most of them of civilians; more than 7 million victims of forced displacement; around 46,000 victims of enforced disappearances; at least 30,000 cases of hostage taking; more than 10,000 victims of torture; and some 10,800 victims of anti-personnel mines and unexploded ordnance. The security forces, paramilitaries and guerrilla groups were responsible for these crimes.

The de-escalation of hostilities between the security forces and the FARC during the year led to a sharp reduction in combat-related violence affecting civilians. But Indigenous, Afro-descendant and peasant farmer communities, especially those living in areas of interest to agro-industrial, mining and infrastructure concerns, continued to face human rights violations and abuses.

In August, four members of the Awá Indigenous people were shot dead by unidentified gunmen in three separate attacks in Nariño Department. Among the victims was Camilo Roberto Taicús Bisbicús, leader of the Awá Indigenous reservation (*resguardo*) of Hojal La Turbia, in Tumaco Municipality.

In March, more than 6,000 people, mainly from Indigenous and Afro-descendant communities, were forcibly displaced from three river areas in Chocó Department as a result of fighting between armed groups.

SECURITY FORCES

There were continued reports of unlawful killings by the security forces, as well as claims of excessive use of force, especially by the ESMAD anti-riot police, during protests.[5]

On 29 February, soldiers killed peasant farmer Gilberto de Jesús Quintero in the hamlet of Tesorito, Tarazá Municipality, Antioquia Department. The army initially claimed he was an ELN guerrilla killed in combat. However, witnesses stated they saw soldiers attempting to dress the corpse in military fatigues and the army subsequently claimed that the killing had been a military error.

Criminal investigations into extrajudicial executions implicating members of the security forces made slow progress. A report from the Office of the Prosecutor of the International Criminal Court, published in November, stated that by July the Office of the Attorney General was investigating 4,190 extrajudicial executions. By February, there had been a total of 961 convictions of which only a few involved high-ranking officers. According to a March report by the Office of the UN High Commissioner for Human Rights, by the end of 2015, 7,773 members of the security forces were under investigation for extrajudicial executions. In November a judge convicted more than a dozen members of the army for the unlawful killing of five young men from Soacha, Cundinamarca Department, in 2008.

ABUSES BY ARMED GROUPS

Guerrilla groups

The ELN and the FARC continued to commit human rights abuses, although cases attributable to the FARC fell as the peace process advanced.

Indigenous leaders and journalists were the targets of death threats. For example, in June, a man claiming to be from the ELN telephoned María Beatriz Vivas Yacuechime, a leader of the Huila Indigenous Regional Council, and threatened to kill her and her family. In July, journalist Diego D'Pablos and cameraman Carlos Melo received text death threats from someone claiming to be from the ELN. Both men and fellow journalist Salud Hernández-Mora had been taken hostage earlier in the year by the ELN in the northern region of Catatumbo.[6]

On 24 March, two men claiming to be FARC members called at the home of Indigenous leader Andrés Almendras in the hamlet of Laguna-Siberia, Caldono Municipality, Cauca Department. Andrés Almendras was not at home so the men asked his daughter where the "snitch" was as they wanted him to leave the area.

Paramilitaries

Paramilitary groups continued to operate despite their supposed demobilization a decade earlier. Acting either alone or in collusion with state actors, they were responsible for numerous human rights violations, including killings and death threats.[7]

In April, local NGOs reported that an armed group of around 150 paramilitaries from the Gaitanista Self-Defence Forces of Colombia (AGC) had entered the Afro-descendant community of Teguerré, part of the collective territory of Cacarica, Chocó Department. There were reports of other AGC incursions in the Cacarica area throughout the year. Some community leaders were threatened by the AGC, which declared them "military targets".

There were increasing reports of paramilitary incursions into the Peace Community of San José de Apartadó, Antioquia Department, some of whose members were threatened.[8]

By 30 September, only 180 of the more than 30,000 paramilitaries who supposedly laid down their arms in a government-sponsored demobilization process had been convicted for human rights-related crimes under the 2005 Justice and Peace Law; most appealed against their convictions. Most paramilitaries did not submit themselves to the Justice and Peace process and received de facto amnesties.

IMPUNITY

Very few of those suspected of responsibility for conflict-related crimes under international law were brought to justice. However, as part of the peace process, the government and the FARC formally apologized for their role in several emblematic human rights cases.

On 30 September, in La Chinita, Apartadó Municipality, Antioquia Department, the FARC apologized for killing 35 people from the village on 23 January 1994.

On 15 September, President Santos formally apologized for the state's role in the killing in the 1980s and 1990s of some 3,000 members of the Patriotic Union party, set up by the Colombian Communist Party and the FARC as part of the failed peace process with the government of Belisario Betancur.

In February the Constitutional Court ruled that a 2015 reform (Legislative Act No. 1) giving military courts jurisdiction over cases related to military service and over crimes committed on active service was constitutional. The reform also stipulated that international humanitarian law, rather than international human rights law, would apply when investigating armed forces personnel for conflict-related crimes, even though many such crimes were not committed during combat and the victims were overwhelmingly civilians. However, the Court ruled that international human rights law should also apply during investigations. Nevertheless, there were concerns that the Court's ruling would do little to overcome impunity given the military justice system's woeful record in bringing to justice members of the armed forces implicated in human rights violations.

HUMAN RIGHTS DEFENDERS

Threats against and killings of human rights defenders, especially community leaders, land rights and environmental activists and peace and justice campaigners, continued to be reported in significant numbers. Most of the threats were attributed to paramilitaries, but in most cases it was difficult to identify which groups were responsible for the killings. According to the NGO Somos Defensores (We are Defenders), at least 75 defenders had been killed by 8 December 2016, compared with 63 during the whole of 2015. In general, these attacks did not occur in the context of combat between the warring parties, but were targeted killings. Several human rights organizations also had sensitive information stolen from their offices. By 20 December the NGO National Trade Union School had recorded 17 killings of trade union members.

On 29 August, three leaders of the NGO Integration Committee of the Colombian Massif (CIMA), Joel Meneses, Nereo Meneses Guzmán and Ariel Sotelo, were shot dead by a group of armed men in Almaguer Municipality, Cauca Department.

In August, Ingrid Vergara, a spokesperson for the National Movement of Victims of State Crimes (Movice) received a threatening phone call after attending a public hearing on human rights in Congress in the capital, Bogotá. Over the years, Ingrid Vergara and other members of Movice have been repeatedly threatened and harassed because of their human rights work.

LAND RIGHTS

The land restitution process, implemented since 2012, continued to make only slow progress in returning land misappropriated during the conflict to its rightful occupants. According to the state's Land Restitution Unit, by 5 December, land judges had adjudicated on cases involving some 62,093 hectares claimed by peasant farmers and 131,657 hectares claimed by one Afro-descendant and four Indigenous communities.

Land rights activists continued to be threatened and killed.[9] On 11 September, Néstor Iván Martínez, an Afro-descendant leader, was shot dead by unidentified assailants in Chiriguaná Municipality, Cesar Department. Néstor Iván Martínez was active in environmental and land rights campaigns and had campaigned against mining activities.

On 29 January, Congress approved Law 1776, which would create large agro-industrial projects known as Zones of Rural Development, Economic and Social Interest (ZIDRES). Critics argued these could undermine the land rights of rural communities.

In February, the Constitutional Court ruled that legislation stipulating that land restitution claims would not be permitted in areas denominated Projects of National and Strategic Interest (PINES) was unconstitutional. It ruled that such lands could be expropriated by the state, but that land claimants would have the right to a formal expropriation hearing and to compensation set by the courts.

On 9 June, the Constitutional Court made public its December 2015 ruling annulling three resolutions by the National Mining Agency and Ministry of Mines and Energy declaring over 20 million hectares of land, including Indigenous and Afro-descendant territories, as Strategic Mining Areas (SMAs). The Court stated that delimitation of any SMAs was dependent on seeking the prior consent of Indigenous and Afro-descendant communities living in these areas.

VIOLENCE AGAINST WOMEN AND GIRLS

Allegations of crimes of sexual violence continued to be levelled against all parties to the conflict. By 1 December, the Victims' Unit had registered more than 17,500 victims of conflict-related crimes against sexual integrity since 1985.

In March, the NGO Follow-up Working Group on the Constitutional Court's Judicial Decrees (Autos) 092 of 2008 and 009 of 2015 issued a report on the state's implementation of the two Decrees. The Decrees highlighted the prevalence of conflict-related sexual violence against women and ordered the state to combat these crimes and bring to justice those suspected of criminal responsibility. The report concluded that although the state had made some progress in investigating these crimes, it had failed to take effective action to ensure the right of survivors to truth, justice and reparation. The vast majority of those suspected of criminal responsibility for these

crimes had yet to be brought to justice by the end of the year.

In August, the government issued Decree 1314 creating a commission to develop a Comprehensive Programme of Guarantees for Women Leaders and Human Rights Defenders, which would include prevention and protection mechanisms.

In June, the Office of the Attorney General issued a Resolution adopting a protocol for the investigation of crimes of sexual violence.

INTERNATIONAL SCRUTINY

In March the UN High Commissioner for Human Rights issued a report which congratulated the government and the FARC on the progress made to reach a peace agreement. However, the High Commissioner warned that paramilitary groups (referred to as "post-demobilization groups" in the report) "constantly undermine human rights and citizen security, the administration of justice and peacebuilding, including land restitution. Dismantling the groups that control stolen land through the use or threat of violence represents a permanent challenge to peace".

In its concluding observations on Colombia, published in October, the UN Committee on Enforced Disappearances acknowledged the efforts made by the Colombian authorities and noted the reduction in cases of enforced disappearance in recent years. However, it expressed concern about Colombia's continued failure to recognize the competence of the Committee on Enforced Disappearances to receive and consider communications from or on behalf of victims as well as the failure to make meaningful progress in investigating such crimes.

In November, the UN Human Rights Council noted the significant reduction in the conflict's impact on civilians. However, it expressed concern about ongoing violations, including arbitrary deprivations of life, enforced disappearances, torture, and the persistence of impunity. It also expressed concern about abuses by "illegal armed groups that emerged after the demobilization of paramilitary organizations" and allegations that state actors colluded with some of these groups.

---

1. Colombia: Agreement on a bilateral ceasefire and cessation of hostilities is an historic step forward (AMR 23/4311/2016)
2. Colombia: End of negotiations over conflict brings hopes of peace (News story, 25 August)
3. Colombia: Historic peace deal must ensure justice and an end to human rights abuses (News story, 26 September)
4. Colombia: Nobel Peace Prize shows Colombia must not close the door on hopes of peace with justice (News story, 7 October)
5. Colombia: Security forces must refrain from excessive use of force during rural protests (AMR 23/4204/2016)
6. Colombia: ELN must release journalists (AMR 23/4134/2016)
7. Colombia: Death threats to defenders and trade unionists (AMR 23/3837/2016)
8. Colombia: Paramilitary activity threatens Peace Community (AMR 23/4998/2016)
9. Colombia: Death threats to Afro-descendant leaders (AMR 23/3938/2016)

CONGO (REPUBLIC OF THE)

Republic of the Congo
Head of state and government: **Denis Sassou Nguesso**

Presidential elections were held amid violence and controversy. Political opponents were detained for peaceful criticism of the elections. Security forces used excessive force and sometimes torture to curb dissent. A new law further restricting the space for civil society organizations was passed.

BACKGROUND

On 20 March, presidential elections were held under a total communications blackout, with telephone and internet connections cut. Denis Sassou Nguesso was re-elected president.

Amnesty International was denied entry to the country to monitor the human rights situation before the presidential elections.

FREEDOMS OF EXPRESSION AND ASSEMBLY

Following the results of presidential elections, which were contested by the opposition, the authorities arrested several leading opposition figures, including senior campaign officials of presidential candidates Jean-Marie Michel Mokoko and André Okombi Salissa, accusing them of compromising national security. Those arrested and still in detention included Jean Ngouabi, Anatole Limbongo-Ngoka, Marcel Mpika, Jacques Banangazala and Ngambou Roland.

Between 4 April and 14 June, Jean-Marie Michel Mokoko was kept under de facto house arrest, with security forces surrounding his compound without a judicial warrant. He was arrested on 14 June, charged with jeopardizing state security and unlawful possession of weapons and munitions of war, and was detained at the main prison in the capital, Brazzaville. He was later also charged with incitement to disturb public order. André Okombi Salissa was believed to have fled the country in June, following a raid by security forces on his home.

A number of leading political figures, including Paulin Makaya, leader of the opposition Unis Pour le Congo, and Okouya Rigobert of the political group Convention d'action pour la démocratie et le développement (CADD) remained in detention, following their arrest in November 2015 for protesting against changes to the Constitution. On 25 July, Paulin Makaya was sentenced to two years' imprisonment and a fine of €3,800 for taking part in an unauthorized protest. An appeal he filed on the same day was considered on 6 December, more than four months later, even though the timeline defined by law had expired and a reminder had been sent to the relevant authorities. His appeal was adjourned twice and a decision had not been taken at the end of the year. He remained a prisoner of conscience.

The opposition platform "Initiative pour la démocratie au Congo - Front républicain pour le respect de l'ordre constitutionnel et

authorities did not have the capacity to register all of the minors, and some were allegedly turned away on the grounds of presumed age without undergoing a thorough assessment. On 2 November the UN Committee on the Rights of the Child raised concerns over minors in Calais who were left without adequate shelter, food and medical services during the eviction operation. As of mid-November, about 330 minors had been transferred to the UK.

Due to the lack of reception capacity and resources to register asylum applications in the Paris region, more than 3,800 asylum-seekers lived in degrading conditions and slept rough for months in the 19th district of Paris until the authorities transferred them to reception centres on 3 November.

On 29 November, authorities rejected the asylum application of a man from the war-torn region of South Kordofan and forcibly returned him to Sudan despite the risk of being persecuted. On 20 November, authorities released another Sudanese man from Darfur who was at risk of being forcibly returned.

The government pledged to accept 6,000 refugees under the EU-Turkey migration control deal and to resettle 3,000 refugees from Lebanon.

On 9 December the Council of State, the highest administrative court, rejected the decree signed by the Prime Minister in September 2015 that authorized the extradition of Moukhtar Abliazov, a Kazakh citizen, to Russia for financial offences as the extradition request had been motivated by political reasons.

FREEDOM OF ASSEMBLY

Frequent demonstrations took place between March and September to protest against the government-backed proposal to reform the Labour Code, which was adopted in July. A minority of demonstrators engaged in violent acts and clashed with police.

Since the fourth renewal of the state of emergency in July, the authorities were expressly permitted to ban public demonstrations by claiming that they were unable to ensure public order. Dozens of demonstrations were banned and hundreds of individuals were subjected to administrative measures, restricting their freedom of movement and preventing them from attending demonstrations.

On several occasions, police used excessive force against protesters, including by using tear gas grenades, charging at them violently and using rubber bullets and sting ball grenades that left hundreds injured.

DISCRIMINATION

Roma people continued to be forcibly evicted from informal settlements without being genuinely consulted or offered alternative housing. According to civil society organizations, 4,615 individuals were forcibly evicted in the first six months of the year. On 13 July, the UN Committee on Economic, Social and Cultural Rights called on the authorities to provide adequate notice and information as well as rehousing options to all those affected by an eviction.

In October, Parliament adopted a law on legal gender recognition for transgender people. The law established a procedure which allows transgender people to seek legal recognition of their gender without fulfilling any medical requirements. However, it still imposes on transgender people some requirements including a name change or a physical appearance in line with gender identity.

Several mayors adopted measures to restrict the wearing of beachwear deemed incompatible with hygiene and with the principles of secularism and maintenance of public order. In particular, authorities sought to ban the wearing of full-covering beachwear also known as the "burkini". On 26 August, the Council of State suspended the measure in Villeneuve-Loubet in southern France, deeming it not necessary to ensure public order.

CORPORATE ACCOUNTABILITY

On 29 November the National Assembly adopted a bill imposing a duty on certain large French companies to implement a "vigilance plan" to prevent serious human rights abuses and environmental damage in relation to their own activities and those of subsidiaries and other established business relations, and subjecting them to fines for non-compliance. In addition, any inadequacy in the plan which leads to human rights abuses could be used by victims to claim damages against the company before a French court. At the end of the year, the bill was pending before the Senate.

ARMS TRADE

In June a Palestinian family lodged a complaint against French company Exxelia Technologies for complicity in manslaughter and war crimes in Gaza. In 2014, three of the family's sons were killed by a missile fired at their house in Gaza City by Israeli forces. According to subsequent investigations, a component of the missile had been manufactured by Exxelia Technologies. France remained the fourth largest arms exporter in the world, selling to countries including Saudi Arabia and Egypt.

---

1. Upturned lives: The disproportionate impact of France's state of emergency (EUR 21/3364/2016)

GAMBIA

Islamic Republic of the Gambia
Head of state and government: **Yahya Jammeh**

Restrictive laws continued to curb the right to freedom of expression. Peaceful protests were violently repressed, and arrested demonstrators were subjected to torture and other ill-treatment. At least three government critics died in custody, including one tortured to death shortly after arrest. At least five men arrested in 2015 remained subject to enforced disappearance.

BACKGROUND

Adama Barrow, the opposition coalition candidate, won presidential elections held on 1 December. President Jammeh rejected the election results on 9 December. On 13 December, security forces evicted the Independent Electoral Commission chairman and his staff from their headquarters. On the same day, President Jammeh's party, the Alliance for Patriotic Reorientation and Construction (APRC), filed a challenge to the election results in the Supreme Court. Hearing the case would have required President Jammeh to appoint new judges; therefore the Gambian Bar Association described the appeal as "fundamentally tainted". His refusal to accept the election results was widely condemned internationally, including by the UN Security Council, the AU and ECOWAS.

FREEDOM OF EXPRESSION

Restrictive laws continued to curb the right to freedom of expression. They included laws banning criticism of officials, laws prohibiting the publication of false news and colonial-era laws on sedition. Journalists operated in a climate of self-censorship following past crackdowns on media workers and human rights defenders.

In December 2015 the UN Working Group on Arbitrary Detention stated that journalist Alagie Abdoulie Ceesay, Managing Director of the independent radio station Teranga FM, had been arbitrarily deprived of liberty since his arrest in July 2015 on charges of sedition. The Working Group called for his immediate release, compensation and an investigation by the UN Special Rapporteur on torture. In April, Alagie Abdoulie Ceesay escaped from custody.

On 8 November, Momodou Sabally, Director of the Gambia Radio and Television Services, and reporter Bakary Fatty, were arrested by agents from the National Intelligence Agency (NIA). Bakary Fatty remained in detention without charge and with no access to his family or a lawyer. Momodou Sabally was recharged for various economic offences which had previously been dropped in 2015. The two men appeared to have been arrested after airing footage of an opposition candidate's nomination.

On 10 November, Alhagie Manka, an independent photojournalist, and Yunus Salieu, a journalist at the *Observer*, were both arrested after filming supporters of the President. Yunus Salieu was released without charge the following day, and Alhagie Manka was released without charge on 16 November.

In October, the ECOWAS Community Court of Justice heard a case brought by the Federation of African Journalists and four exiled Gambian journalists, challenging the draconian press laws and claiming that the measures adopted in enforcing these laws violated the rights of journalists, including the right to freedom from torture.

FREEDOM OF ASSEMBLY

Peaceful protests were violently repressed and protesters arrested.

On 14 April, members of the opposition United Democratic Party (UDP) and youth groups demonstrated peacefully in Serrekunda in favour of electoral reform. Police dispersed the protest violently and arrested several people. Some of those arrested were seriously injured and one man – Solo Sandeng, UDP Organizing Secretary – died in custody shortly after his arrest.

Twenty-five of those arrested were eventually charged and detained in Mile 2 Prison in the capital Banjul. Thirteen were later released and 12 were moved to Janjanbureh Prison. On 21 July, 11 people were convicted of participating in an unauthorized protest and related offences and sentenced to three years' imprisonment. They were released on bail pending appeal on 8 December.

On 16 April, UDP members gathered peacefully in Banjul outside the house of UDP leader Ousainou Darboe, calling for justice for Solo Sandeng's death and the release of arrested UDP members. Police fired tear gas at the demonstrators and beat them with batons. Several UDP executive members, including Ousainou Darboe, were arrested along with other protesters and bystanders. On 20 July, 19 people, including Ousainou Darboe, were sentenced to three years' imprisonment for participating in an unauthorized protest and related offences. They were released on bail pending appeal on 5 December.

On 9 May, around 40 protesters were arrested as they made their way towards Westfield, a suburb of Banjul, after the court hearing of Ousainou Darboe and others. Protesters were stopped by the Police Intervention Unit (PIU) who beat them. Some protesters threw stones in reaction and several people, including a PIU officer, were injured. Fourteen people were on trial at the end of the year following this protest. Two women were granted bail in May and the remaining twelve men were granted bail on 6 December.

Campaign rallies were permitted during the official two-week election campaign period before 30 November, with thousands of Gambians taking part peacefully.

TORTURE AND OTHER ILL-TREATMENT

Those arrested during the April protests were subjected to torture and other ill-treatment. Among them was businesswoman Nogoi Njie, who stated in an affidavit filed at the High Court that she had been beaten with hosepipes and batons by men wearing black hoods and gloves while water was poured over her at the headquarters of the National Intelligence Agency (NIA) in Banjul. She also stated that she had seen Solo Sandeng there; his beaten body was swollen and bleeding and she feared he was dead.

On 13 June, the authorities admitted in their response to a habeas corpus application that Solo Sandeng had died during his arrest and detention and that an inquiry had been launched. No further information had been made publicly available by the end of the year.

DEATHS IN CUSTODY

On 21 February, trade union leader Sheriff Dibba, Secretary-General of the Gambian National Transport Control Association

(GNTCA), died at a medical facility in Banjul. He had fallen ill in police custody, but had not received prompt medical attention. According to the International Transport Workers' Federation (ITF), Sheriff Dibba and eight other GNTCA leaders had been arrested after the union called on the authorities to reduce the price of fuel. The ITF filed a case against the Gambian government at the International Labour Organization (ILO) concerning Sheriff Dibba's death and the "punitive measures" taken against the GNTCA, whose activities were suspended by presidential order. Sheriff Dibba's family had not been given his autopsy results and no investigation into his death had been initiated by the end of the year.

On 21 August, Ebrima Solo Krummah, a senior UDP member arrested on 9 May and detained at Mile 2 Prison, died after surgery in hospital. There were allegations that he had been refused medical care in detention. No information as to the cause of death was made public and no inquiry into the death was announced by the end of the year.

ENFORCED DISAPPEARANCES, ARBITRARY DETENTIONS AND INCOMMUNICADO DETENTION

Three Imams arrested in 2015 remained subject to enforced disappearance. Alhagi Ousman Sawaneh, Imam of Kanifing South, was arrested on 18 October 2015 by men in plain clothes. He was reportedly detained because he had petitioned the President for the release of Haruna Gassama, President of the Rice Farmers' Cooperative Society, who had at the time been in NIA custody for six months without charge. Two other Imams – Sheikh Omar Colley and Imam Gassama – were arrested in October and November 2015, allegedly for the same reason.

The three Imams were believed to be held incommunicado in Janjanbureh Prison, but despite repeated requests from their families the authorities did not confirm their whereabouts. On 21 March 2016 the High Court in Banjul ordered the release of Imam Sawaneh following a habeas corpus application, but the court order was ignored.

Ousman Jammeh, former Deputy Minister of Agriculture, also continued to be subject to enforced disappearance. He was removed from his post and arrested in October 2015, and reportedly detained at the NIA headquarters for several days before being transferred to Mile 2 Prison. However, neither his family nor his lawyer had any contact with him and the authorities provided no information about his whereabouts or the reason for his arrest.

Omar Malleh Jabang, a businessman and opposition supporter, was taken away by men in plain clothes on 10 November and had not been seen since, despite requests made to the authorities.

On 1 September Sarjo Jallow was dismissed as Deputy Minister of Foreign Affairs. From 2 September his family and lawyers were unable to contact him, although they were told unofficially that he was detained at the NIA headquarters. His wife was a vocal supporter of the UDP. On 10 October lawyers filed an application for his release from NIA custody; he was not released by the end of the year.

CHILDREN'S RIGHTS

In July, Gambia passed a law banning child marriage (a marriage of anyone under 18 years old). The offence is punishable by up to 20 years' imprisonment for any adult involved in arranging a child marriage, including the child's husband and parents. According to the UN, 40% of women aged 20 to 49 in Gambia were married before the age of 18, while 16% married before they turned 15.

GEORGIA

Georgia
Head of state: **Giorgi Margvelashvili**
Head of government: **Giorgi Kvirikashvili**

Concerns persisted about the lack of judicial independence and about political interference following a series of favourable rulings for the government in high-profile cases. New cases of torture and other ill-

treatment by police were reported. Continuing border fencing along the administrative boundary lines of the breakaway regions of Abkhazia and South Ossetia had further negative impact on economic and social rights of local residents.

BACKGROUND

Parliamentary elections on 8 October resulted in the ruling party – the Georgian Dream – increasing its majority to 115 seats. The main opposition party – United National Movement (UNM) – gained 27 seats and the right-wing conservative party – Patriot's Alliance – six.

Secretly recorded private conversations and intimate activities by opposition figures and journalists were leaked ahead of elections. Five people, including a former security official, were arrested on suspicion of being responsible for illegally obtaining the recordings. The investigation was ongoing at the end of 2016.

De facto authorities and Russian forces in the breakaway regions of Abkhazia and South Ossetia continued to restrict movement across the administrative boundary line, detaining dozens of people: several detainees complained of torture and other ill-treatment, including beatings, during the prolonged arbitrary detentions. On 19 May, a man was killed by a Russian soldier while trying to cross into Abkhazia. An investigation into his death by the de facto authorities was ongoing at the end of the year.

The increased fencing along the administrative boundary lines negatively impacted the rights to work, food and adequate standard of living of local residents, after they lost access, partly or completely, to their orchards, pasture and arable land.

JUSTICE SYSTEM

Concerns over the lack of judicial independence and selective justice were raised, by both local and international observers.

On 12 January, the Council of Europe Commissioner for Human Rights reported that courts were more likely to approve detention or give custodial sentences to members of the UNM compared with bail and fines issued to pro-government activists in comparable cases.

On 16 May, five former senior Ministry of Defence officials (appointed by former Minister of Defence Irakli Alasania, who had since become a key political opposition figure), were convicted of "misusing" GEL 4.1 million (US$2.1 million) by the Tbilisi City Court and sentenced to seven years' imprisonment each. They were found guilty despite the prosecution's failure to provide sufficient evidence of "malicious intent", a necessary element of the crime they were charged with.

On 10 June, the Tbilisi Court of Appeals upheld the 2015 ruling of the lower court, which transferred the ownership of the pro-opposition broadcaster, Rustavi 2, to its former owner. He had claimed that he sold the company more than a decade earlier under pressure from the then UNM government. The litigation took place after the statute of limitations had expired, and was widely believed to have been supported by the current government with a view to depriving the UNM of its main mouthpiece ahead of the parliamentary elections.

On 14 June, the European Court of Human Rights ruled in *Merabishvili v Georgia* that the repeated extension of the applicant's pre-trial detention on corruption charges "lacked reasonableness" and was used "as an additional opportunity to obtain leverage over the unrelated investigation" into the death of former Prime Minister Zurab Zhvania and financial activities of former President Mikheil Saakashvili.

On 21 July, the Chairman of the Constitutional Court stated that some judges of the Court were pressured by the authorities to delay verdicts or rule in their favour in several high-profile cases. Prosecutors opened an investigation into his allegations on 1 August.

FREEDOM OF ASSEMBLY

The right to freedom of peaceful assembly remained largely unrestricted, bar some incidents of politically motivated violence against rivals by Georgian Dream party loyalists, but also on occasion by UNM supporters.

On 22 May, around a dozen unidentified men assaulted a group of prominent UNM members at a polling station in Kortskheli village. Eyewitnesses said the attack appeared to be organized. Footage shows UNM members being punched, knocked to the ground and beaten with wooden batons. Several police officers at the scene failed to prevent the assault and allowed the attackers to leave the scene. On 1 June, six men were charged with hooliganism in connection with the attack and released on bail.

FREEDOM OF EXPRESSION

On 15 February, Parliament dropped a bill that sought to make "insulting religious feelings" an administrative offence. The bill had been approved by the parliamentary Human Rights Committee and sought, among other things, to penalize criticism of religious leaders.

RIGHTS OF LESBIAN, GAY, BISEXUAL, TRANSGENDER AND INTERSEX PEOPLE

On 9 August, President Margvelashvili refused to call a referendum on a constitutional amendment to restrict the definition of marriage in the Constitution from "the voluntary union based on equality between the spouses" to "a union between a man and a woman". The bill originally calling for the constitutional amendment had been endorsed by the parliamentary Human Rights Committee in May.

On 23 November, a transgender woman, attacked and beaten by two men, died of her injuries in hospital. A local women's rights NGO reported registering at least 35 attacks on LGBTI women during the year. The Public Defender Office joined local rights groups in raising concerns regarding the lack of effective investigation and accountability over crimes targeting LGBTI people.

TORTURE AND OTHER ILL-TREATMENT

Amid concerns about torture and other ill-treatment, and other abuses, by law enforcement officers, the government failed to bring forward legislation creating an independent investigation mechanism for human rights violations committed by law enforcement bodies.

On 7 August, a local police inspector summoned Demur Sturua, a 22-year-old resident of Dapnari, Western Georgia, for questioning about someone growing cannabis in the village. The following day, Demur Sturua committed suicide. His suicide note blamed the police inspector and mentioned beating and threats. His family's lawyer said that a postmortem examination found physical injuries. The investigation into the case was ongoing at the end of the year.

There were subsequent media reports that residents in remote villages, who may have suffered similar treatment at the hands of police officials, were not willing to present a complaint for fear of reprisals and lack of trust in the authorities.

GERMANY

Federal Republic of Germany
Head of state: **Joachim Gauck**
Head of government: **Angela Merkel**

The authorities made considerable efforts to house and process the large number of asylum-seekers who arrived in 2015. However, the government also adopted several laws to restrict the rights of asylum-seekers and refugees, including on family reunification. The number of racist and xenophobic attacks on asylum shelters remained high and the authorities failed to adopt effective strategies to prevent them.

REFUGEES AND ASYLUM-SEEKERS

The number of new asylum-seekers decreased considerably compared to 2015. The government registered approximately

304,900 arrivals between January and November compared with 890,000 in 2015.

The authorities improved their capacity to process asylum applications throughout the year. Between January and November, approximately 702,490 individuals, many of whom had arrived in Germany the previous year, claimed asylum. The authorities made a decision in about 615,520 cases. The rate at which Syrians, Iraqis and Afghans received full refugee status decreased compared with the previous year; more individuals were granted subsidiary protection and fewer received full refugee status. The former status granted fewer rights, including with respect to family reunification. Between January and November, 59% of Syrian applicants obtained full refugee status compared with 99.6% in the same period of 2015.

In March, new amendments to asylum laws entered into force. The right to family reunification for individuals with subsidiary protection status was suspended until March 2018. A new fast-track procedure for assessing asylum applications from a variety of categories of applicants, including asylum-seekers from countries deemed to be "safe", was introduced without providing for sufficient guarantees to ensure access to a fair asylum procedure. At the end of the year, a law defining Algeria, Morocco and Tunisia as "safe" countries of origin was pending before the Federal Council. The new fast-track procedure had not been implemented by the end of the year.

In May, Parliament passed the first ever law on integration for refugees and asylum-seekers. The law aimed at creating employment and educational opportunities for refugees and imposed on them the obligation to follow integration courses. It also allowed authorities of the federal states to impose restrictions on where refugees could reside, tightened conditions for issuing residence permits and introduced new benefit cuts for those not complying with the new rules.

Until 19 December, Germany relocated 640 refugees from Greece and 455 from Italy. As part of the EU-Turkey Deal, Germany accepted the transfer of 1,060 Syrian refugees from Turkey. Despite the worsening security situation in Afghanistan, authorities forcibly returned more than 60 Afghan nationals whose asylum applications had been rejected. In 2015, fewer than 10 unsuccessful Afghan asylum-seekers were forcibly returned.

TORTURE AND OTHER ILL-TREATMENT

The authorities continued to fail to effectively investigate allegations of ill-treatment by the police and did not establish any independent complaints mechanism to investigate those allegations.

At the end of the year, the governments of North-Rheine Westphalia and Sachsen Anhalt were planning to introduce the obligation for police officers to wear identity badges while on duty.

The Joint Commission of the National Agency for the Prevention of Torture – Germany's preventive mechanism under the Optional Protocol to the UN Convention against Torture – remained understaffed and underfinanced.

In April, the Hannover Prosecution Office closed the investigation into allegations of ill-treatment by a federal police officer against two Afghan and Moroccan refugees in the holding cells of the federal police at Hannover's main train station in 2014. In September, the Celle Upper Regional Court rejected the request introduced by one of the victims to reopen the investigation.

DISCRIMINATION

The second Committee of Inquiry, established by Parliament in October 2015, pursued its investigation into some of the authorities' failures to investigate the racist and xenophobic crimes perpetrated against members of ethnic minorities by the far-right group National Socialist Underground between 2000 and 2007. No official inquiry was launched into the potential role of institutional racism behind those failures, despite the 2015 recommendations of the UN Committee on the Elimination of Racial

Discrimination and the Council of Europe Commissioner for Human Rights.

Dozens of anti-refugee and anti-Muslim demonstrations were staged throughout the country. In the first nine months of the year, authorities registered 813 crimes against asylum shelters. In the same period, 1,803 crimes against asylum-seekers were registered by the authorities, 254 of them resulted in bodily injuries. The authorities failed to put in place an adequate national strategy to prevent attacks on asylum shelters.

Civil society organizations continued to report discriminatory identity checks by police on members of ethnic and religious minorities.

In June, the Federal Court of Justice rejected the request of an intersex person to be legally registered according to a third gender option. The applicant's appeal was pending before the Federal Constitutional Court at the end of the year.

COUNTER-TERROR AND SECURITY

In October, Parliament passed a new law on surveillance that granted the Federal Intelligence Service broad powers to subject non-EU citizens to surveillance without effective judicial oversight and for a wide range of purposes, including national security. In August, several UN special procedures, including the Special Rapporteur on freedom of expression, expressed concern regarding the negative impact of the law on freedom of expression and the lack of judicial oversight.

In April, the Federal Constitutional Court ruled that some of the surveillance powers of the Federal Criminal Police Office, which had been introduced in 2009 to counteract terrorism and crimes more generally, were unconstitutional. In particular, some of the measures did not ensure the respect of the right to privacy. Those provisions remained in force pending their amendment.

ARMS TRADE

In March, the government put in place the necessary legal framework for selective post-shipment controls to improve the monitoring of German exports of war weapons and specific types of firearms to ensure compliance with end-use certificates and that they were not used to commit human rights violations. Under these controls, the whereabouts of exported war weapons would be checked post-shipment in the recipient countries. Governments receiving German military equipment would have to declare in an end-use statement that they agree to on-the-spot controls. Such end-use statements were signed for at least four licensed small arms exports. The government was implementing the first pilot phase of the new mechanism at the end of the year.

CORPORATE ACCOUNTABILITY

In August, the Regional Court of Dortmund accepted to exercise jurisdiction over a legal claim brought in 2015 by four Pakistani victims against the German clothing retailer KiK and granted them legal aid. In September 2012, 260 workers died and 32 were seriously injured in a fire that destroyed one of the main textile factories in Pakistan supplying KiK.

In December, the government adopted a National Action Plan to implement the UN Guiding Principles on Business and Human Rights. However, the Plan did not include adequate measures to comply with all standards set out in the Principles and did not ensure that German business enterprises exercise due diligence to respect human rights.

GHANA

Republic of Ghana
Head of state and government: **John Dramani Mahama**

Concerns were raised about the rights of women and children, discrimination against people with disabilities, and legal shortcomings in relation to human rights protection. Lesbian, gay, bisexual, transgender and intersex (LGBTI) people continued to face discrimination, violence and police harassment. Death sentences were handed down.

BACKGROUND

In June, Ghana's human rights record was reviewed for the first time by the UN Human Rights Committee to assess compliance with its obligations under the ICCPR.

In September, Ghana ratified the Optional Protocol to the UN Convention against Torture, which establishes a system of regular visits to places of detention as a measure to protect detainees and prisoners from torture or other ill-treatment. General elections took place in December; Nana Akufo-Addo of the New Patriotic Party was elected President.

FREEDOM OF EXPRESSION

In February, the Interception of Postal Packets and Telecommunication Messages Bill (2015) was put before Parliament. It proposes the interception of all communications for the undefined purposes of "protecting national security" and "fighting crime generally". Civil society raised concerns that the lack of clear definition would give authorities wide discretion to intercept communications, and said that the bill lacked sufficient safeguards.

The Human Rights Committee stated that Ghana should expedite the enactment of the Right to Information Bill and ensure that its provisions conform to the ICCPR.

WOMEN'S RIGHTS

The Human Rights Committee raised concerns about legislative provisions that discriminate against women in relation to property ownership, access to formal credit and inheritance. It noted delays in the adoption of the Property Rights of Spouses Bill, which was put forward in 2013. It made recommendations concerning domestic violence, including further legislation to enhance implementation of the Domestic Violence Act 2007, increased social services and shelters for survivors of domestic violence, and improved investigation and prosecution of cases.

CHILDREN'S RIGHTS

The Human Rights Committee and civil society organizations remained concerned at the persistence of child labour. The Committee called for investigations into the worst forms of child labour and better public sensitization campaigns on the issue.

EXCESSIVE USE OF FORCE

The Human Rights Committee recommended that Ghana establish an independent mechanism to investigate alleged misconduct by police officers, as well as measures to ensure that its law and practice comply with the Basic Principles on the Use of Force and Firearms by Law Enforcement Officials.

RIGHT TO HEALTH

The Human Rights Committee raised concern at the stigmatization and discrimination faced by people with disabilities, which it cited as major contributing factors to the inadequate treatment of patients with mental health illness and the poor conditions at public psychiatric institutions. It also expressed concern at the hundreds of unregistered private "prayer camps" to deal with illness, particularly mental illness, which operated with little oversight and no state regulation. It noted reports regarding the use of torture and other ill-treatment in such camps, including shackling and forced fasting.

RIGHTS OF LESBIAN, GAY, BISEXUAL, TRANSGENDER AND INTERSEX PEOPLE

Consensual same-sex relations between men remained a criminal offence. Local organizations reported that LGBTI people continued to face police harassment as well as discrimination, violence and instances of blackmail in the wider community.

DEATH PENALTY

Courts continued to hand down death sentences, although the last execution was in 1993. Ghana retains the mandatory death penalty for some offences despite the Human Rights Committee's condemnation of mandatory death sentences. The main death row facility for men remained overcrowded and inmates continued to be denied access to activities such as sport and education.

Proposals made by the Constitutional Review Implementation Committee to abolish the death penalty continued to be stalled as a result of delays in the constitutional review process.

GREECE

Hellenic Republic
Head of state: **Prokopis Pavlopoulos**
Head of government: **Alexis Tsipras**

Greece faced considerable challenges in providing adequate reception conditions and access to asylum procedures for refugees, asylum-seekers and migrants following the announcement of the EU-Turkey migration deal. There was evidence that at least eight Syrian refugees were forcibly returned to Turkey. The closure of the Balkans route left thousands of refugees, asylum-seekers and migrants stranded in mainland Greece in poor conditions. Allegations of torture and other ill-treatment by members of the security forces during arrest and/or detention continued. In December, new legislation established a national police complaints mechanism.

BACKGROUND
Parliament adopted further austerity measures including tax rises, pension cuts and the transfer of state assets to a privatization fund. In February, the UN Independent Expert on the effects of foreign debt concluded that austerity measures implemented since 2010 contributed significantly to the widespread erosion of social and economic rights and pervasive poverty in Greece.

REFUGEES' AND MIGRANTS' RIGHTS
By the end of the year, 173,450 refugees, asylum-seekers and migrants had arrived by

sea in Greece. More than 434 people died or were reported missing while trying to cross the Aegean Sea. There were around 47,400 refugees, asylum-seekers and migrants on the mainland and 15,384 on the islands.

The EU-Turkey migration deal
On 18 March 2016, the EU and Turkey agreed to a far-reaching migration control deal under which Turkey agreed to take back all "irregular migrants" arriving on the Greek islands after 20 March, in exchange for €6 billion of targeted assistance. While people were formally guaranteed access to an asylum determination process, the deal allowed for those arriving on the Greek islands via Turkey to be returned to Turkey without a substantive examination of their claims. This was based on the premise that Turkey was a "safe third country". Research during the year established that Turkey was not a safe country for asylum-seekers and refugees. The numbers arriving dropped sharply after 20 March, and by the end of the year, an average of 50 people were arriving daily.

Between May and June, dozens of asylum applications lodged by refugees from Syria which were refused on "safe third country" grounds, were upheld on appeal. In June, Parliament adopted an amendment that changed the composition of the Asylum Appeals Committees (Appeals Committees) panel to include two judges and a person nominated by UNHCR, the UN refugee agency, or the National Commission of Human Rights.

During the same month, two Syrians who had arrived in Greece via Turkey were the first to be at imminent risk of forcible return to Turkey after the Appeals Committees rejected their appeals on "safe third country" grounds. In October, a third Syrian refugee was threatened with forcible return to Turkey after he was detained when his asylum appeal was dismissed by an Appeals Committee, on the same grounds. In November, the Council of State heard a petition which challenged the rejection of his asylum appeal on safe third-country grounds;

and the constitutionality of the composition of the Appeals Committees. It had not ruled on the case by the end of the year.

There was evidence that at least eight Syrian refugees were forcibly returned to Turkey. They had registered their intention to claim asylum but were returned from Kos on 20 October before they could lodge their applications.

Reception conditions for refugees, asylum-seekers and migrants stranded on the islands were overcrowded and insanitary; they provided inadequate security and people faced uncertainty about their future. This fuelled tension that occasionally erupted into violence, including riots in the Lesvos, Chios and Leros "hotspots".

Detention of asylum-seekers and migrants

In April, thousands of people who arrived on the islands after the implementation of the EU-Turkey migration deal, were detained arbitrarily. Although the most vulnerable were soon released and the vast majority of asylum-seekers were gradually allowed to move freely in and out of the "hotspots", a large number of people were not permitted to leave the island of arrival until their asylum applications were examined.

The closure of the Balkan route

In March, the closure of the Greek border with Macedonia resulted in thousands of refugees, asylum-seekers and migrants left stranded on mainland Greece (see Macedonia entry). Thousands stayed in the large informal camps in Idomeni and Piraeus in dire conditions. Others found shelter in official refugee camps that were being set up across the country. Between May and July, the Greek authorities evacuated the camps of Polykastro, Idomeni and Piraeus ports.

Conditions in the majority of official refugee camps around mainland Greece were inadequate for hosting individuals even for a few days. The camps, hosting around 20,000 at the end of the year, were either tented or established in abandoned warehouses and some were in remote areas far from hospitals and other services. By the end of the year, 23,047 relocation applicants, particularly vulnerable asylum-seekers and unaccompanied children, were provided with accommodation through a project run by UNHCR, the UN refugee agency.

By the end of the year, only 7,286 asylum-seekers had been relocated from Greece to other European countries, while the total number of places pledged was 66,400.

Access to asylum

Those seeking access to asylum procedures met with serious obstacles including being unable to lodge their asylum requests through Skype or only after repeated attempts. In June, the Greek Asylum Service carried out a large scale pre-registration programme of applications for international protection in mainland Greece. In July, the authorities announced that they had pre-registered 27,592 people, including 3,481 belonging to vulnerable groups.

Right to education

In August, Parliament adopted a legislative provision for the creation of special classes for school-age children. In October, around 580 school-age refugees, asylum-seekers and migrants began classes in the capital Athens and Thessaloniki. There were reports of xenophobic incidents including parents refusing to accept the children in schools in Oreokastro and Lesvos.

CONSCIENTIOUS OBJECTORS

In September, Greece was found in breach of Article 9 of the European Convention on Human Rights (in the *Papavasilakis v Greece* case) for failing to ensure that conscientious objectors' interviews with the Special Board met procedural efficiency and equal representation standards. The Special Board examines requests for alternative civilian service.

The same month, the Greek government rejected recommendations by the UN Human Rights Council to establish an alternative to military service which was not punitive or discriminatory and to ensure that conscientious objectors do not face harassment or prosecution.

TORTURE AND OTHER ILL-TREATMENT

Allegations of torture or other ill-treatment of individuals, including refugees, asylum-seekers and migrants during arrest or in immigration detention, persisted.

On 27 September, five Syrian boys, aged between 12 and 16, were stopped by the police in central Athens while they were carrying toy guns as props on their way to perform in a play. The children said that they were beaten and forced to strip naked during their detention in the Omonoia police station. A criminal and a disciplinary investigation were ordered into the incident.

The national NGO Greek Helsinki Monitor (GHM) reported that three Roma men were beaten by the police during their arrest and detention at a western Athens police station in October. One of the men suffered a heart attack and was hospitalized with serious injuries. Despite requests by the victims and GHM, a forensic examination was refused. GHM filed a complaint of torture and breach of duty with the Athens Prosecutor tasked with investigating hate crimes.

During the same month, a court in Thessaloniki found 12 prison guards guilty of torturing and causing serious bodily harm to Ilia Karelli, an Albanian national found dead in his cell in Nigrita prison in March 2014. They were given prison sentences ranging between five and seven years.

In December, Parliament adopted a law designating the Greek Ombudsperson as a national police complaints mechanism. The mechanism has the power to conduct its own investigations but its recommendations to the disciplinary bodies of law enforcement agencies are non-binding.

PRISON CONDITIONS

Prison conditions remained a cause of serious concern. Greece was found to be in breach of the European Convention on Human Rights on account of poor prison conditions and/or lack of effective remedies to challenge such conditions in nine cases

concerning prisoners in Larissa, Thessaloniki, Trikala and Komotini.

DISCRIMINATION - ROMA

In August, the UN Committee on the Elimination of Racial Discrimination expressed concern about the situation of Roma in Greece including the obstacles they faced in accessing basic services such as education and housing; and being subjected to frequent identity checks and police harassment.

RACISM

Hate-motivated attacks continued to be documented against people belonging to vulnerable groups including refugees, asylum-seekers and migrants.

In July, a squat providing shelter for refugees in Athens was targeted in an arson attack by members of a far-right group. The perpetrators had not been identified by the end of the year.

In November, suspected far-right extremists attacked refugees in Souda camp on Chios Island, injuring at least two. Two activists who tried to assist the refugees were also attacked and subsequently hospitalized. A criminal investigation into the incidents began.

At the end of November, a court in Piraeus upheld on appeal a first-instance decision which found four men guilty of abducting, robbing and causing serious bodily harm to Egyptian migrant worker Walid Taleb in 2012.

The trial of leaders and members of the Golden Dawn, a far-right political party, who were charged with the murder of Pavlos Fyssas in 2013 and the founding of a criminal organization, continued at the end of the year.

RIGHTS OF LESBIAN, GAY, BISEXUAL, TRANSGENDER AND INTERSEX PEOPLE

In May, the Ministry of Justice established a preparatory committee to draft a bill allowing for the legal recognition of the gender identity of transgender people through an administrative process without the requirement to undergo gender reassignment surgery. In June, the Athens Magistrates' Court allowed a transgender man to change his gender marker in his identification documents without gender reassignment surgery.

GUATEMALA

Republic of Guatemala
Head of state and government: **Jimmy Morales Cabrera** (replaced Alejandro Maldonado Aguirre in January)

Smear campaigns and the misuse of the criminal justice system to harass and intimidate human rights defenders continued. Defenders working on land, territorial and environmental issues were at particular risk. People continued to flee the country to escape high levels of inequality and violence. There was a landmark decision by the High-Risk Court A in a case concerning sexual violence and the domestic slavery of 11 Indigenous women during the internal armed conflict. Other high-profile cases against former members of the military continued to suffer setbacks and undue delays. The Congressional Human Rights Commission presented a bill to abolish the death penalty.

TRANSITIONAL JUSTICE

In January, the trial of José Efraín Ríos Montt, former President and Commander-in-Chief, and José Mauricio Rodríguez Sánchez, former Military Intelligence Director, on charges of genocide and crimes against humanity was postponed.[1] In March, the trial began before a High-Risk Court and, in May, a Court of Appeals found in favour of the plaintiffs' request to be tried separately. The Rios Montt trial had to take place behind closed doors in light of the special provisions adopted after it was determined that he was mentally unfit to stand trial. Both trials remained stalled at the end of the year.

Five former members of the military, including Benedicto Lucas García, former head of the High Command of the Guatemalan Army, were charged in relation to the illegal detention, torture and sexual violence committed against Emma Guadalupe Molina Theissen, and the enforced disappearance of Marco Antonio Molina Theissen. According to local NGOs, several hearings were suspended and the judiciary imposed restrictions and requirements on the victim's family and the general public. Members of the Molina Theissen family were subjected to harassment, including online. Women family members faced particular forms of gender-based violence, including harassment and vilification.

In a landmark decision by the High-Risk Court A in February, two former military officials were found guilty of crimes against humanity for the sexual and domestic enslavement of and the sexual violence against 11 Indigenous Maya Q'eqchi' women. The crimes took place in the military base located in the community of Sepur Zarco during the internal armed conflict.[2]

In June, High-Risk Court A ruled that eight former members of the military should face trial on charges related to cases of enforced disappearances and unlawful killings carried out in a military base now known as Creompaz in the northern Alta Verapaz region.[3] Relatives of the victims were the targets of online harassment, intimidation inside and outside the courtroom, surveillance and threats.

Civil society organizations continued to push for the approval of Law 3590, which would create a National Commission for the Search for Victims of Enforced Disappearance and Other Forms of Disappearance. The law, which was first presented before Congress in 2006, had not been discussed by the end of 2016.

HUMAN RIGHTS DEFENDERS

Human rights defenders faced continuing threats, stigmatization, intimidation and attacks. According to the NGO UDEFEGUA, 14 human rights defenders were killed. The environmental human rights defenders were the group who faced the highest number of attacks. Defenders of the land, territory and the environment faced vilification and attempts to cast them as criminals, both by officials in their public statements and by private individuals, as well as through baseless criminal proceedings.[4]

The prosecution of human rights defender Daniel Pascual on criminal charges of slander, libel and defamation continued during the year. The charges were linked to public statements he had made in 2013. The judge ignored the defendant's petition that the case be dealt with under the Constitutional Law on the Expression of Thought and not through ordinary criminal proceedings. On 7 June, the Constitutional Court granted an interim injunction that temporarily suspended proceedings against Daniel Pascual.

In early 2016, a well-known human rights defender received death threats against herself and her children. Threats against the defender coincided with the publication in a newspaper of a paid advertisement on 6 April in which the president of a private company alleged that the purpose of human rights NGOs was to stop economic development, calling them enemies of the country.

On 22 July, High-Risk Court A in Guatemala City acquitted seven defenders of the rights of the Indigenous Maya Q'anjobal People. They had been accused of illegal detention, threats and incitement to commit a crime. By the time they were released, they had spent more than a year in pre-trial detention.

REFUGEES' AND MIGRANTS' RIGHTS

For decades, Guatemalans have migrated to the USA via Mexico in an effort to escape the high levels of inequality and violence affecting marginalized groups, including Indigenous Peoples, in the country. Over the past five years, large numbers have been forcibly returned to Guatemala. However, no comprehensive mechanism or protocol had been put in place to address the needs of returnees. According to UNHCR, the UN refugee agency, between January and August, 11,536 Guatemalans sought asylum in other countries. In September, the

Congress approved a new Migration Code to replace the existing outdated migration law.[5]

LAND DISPUTES

In February, the Supreme Court temporarily suspended the operating licence for El Tambor mine in a judgment concerning the failure to carry out prior consultation. The Ministry of Energy and Mines stated that the licence had already been granted and so could not be suspended. As a result, from March onwards the community held sit-ins at the headquarters of the Ministry of Energy and Mines calling for the interim relief granted by the Supreme Court to be enforced. At the end of June, the Supreme Court upheld its previous decision in a definitive manner.

---

1. Guatemala: Shameful decision to postpone Ríos Montt trial a new stain on Guatemala's justice system (News story, 11 January)

2. Guatemala: Conviction of military in sexual abuse case, a historic victory for justice (Press release, 26 February)

3. Guatemala: Decision to take Creompaz case to trial an advance for justice (AMR 34/4218/2016)

4. Americas: "We are defending the land with our blood": Defenders of the land, territory and environment in Honduras and Guatemala (AMR 01/4562/2016)

5. Americas: Home sweet home? Honduras, Guatemala and El Salvador's role in a deepening refugee crisis (AMR 01/4865/2016)

GUINEA

Republic of Guinea
Head of state: **Alpha Condé**
Head of government: **Mamady Youla**

The security forces used excessive force against peaceful demonstrators and harassed people expressing dissent. Torture and other ill-treatment were reported. The security forces continued to enjoy impunity for human rights violations. The death penalty was abolished for ordinary crimes. Early and enforced marriage was criminalized.

BACKGROUND

Local elections were postponed to February 2017, maintaining a tense political and social environment. The last local elections were held in 2005.

EXCESSIVE USE OF FORCE

On 17 June, soldiers publicly ill-treated a lorry driver, sparking spontaneous protests in the northern town of Mali. The army used excessive force to disperse demonstrators, including using firearms and batons. Over two days, at least 14 people were wounded, including four shot with live ammunition. On 16 November, 11 soldiers were charged, including with assault and battery, pillage and arson.

On 16 August, police shot dead Thierno Hamidou Diallo as he was standing on his balcony in the capital Conakry during a mass, peaceful march of 500,000 to 700,000 opposition supporters. The Security Minister announced that a policeman had been arrested in relation to the killing.[1]

FREEDOM OF EXPRESSION

Security forces harassed and arbitrarily arrested people expressing dissent.

On 24 March, Jean Dougou Guilavogui and four other trade unionists were sentenced to six months in prison and ordered to pay damages for defamation and "contempt of the President". Jean Dougou Guilavogui was released for time served on 25 March and his colleagues on 8 April.[2]

On 22 June, the Tribunal of Kankan fined journalist Malick Bouya Kébé 1 million Guinean francs (approximately €100) for complicity in "contempt of the President" because he did not interrupt a listener who was criticizing the President during a phone-in programme. His guest, also a journalist, was sentenced in his absence to one year in prison and a fine of 1.5 million Guinean francs (approximately €150) for "contempt of the President". They were tried without a lawyer.

On 25 June, journalist Malick Diallo was covering a meeting of the ruling party attended by President Condé in Conakry. A presidential guard asked him to hand over his camera. When he refused, he was pushed inside a car and taken to the office of the presidential guards where he was beaten and threatened. The guards took his camera and deleted some of the pictures before releasing him. The police refused to record his complaint.

The revised Criminal Code, adopted on 4 July, criminalized contempt, defamation and insult, including of public figures, with penalties of up to five years' imprisonment and a fine. Vaguely worded provisions could allow the prosecution of people who express dissent or expose human rights violations, including journalists and human rights defenders.

The law on cyber-security and personal data protection, passed on 2 June, criminalized cyber-insults, the dissemination and communication of "false information" as well as the production, distribution or transfer to third parties of data "likely to disturb law and order or public security or jeopardize human dignity". The law likened the disclosure of data "that should be kept confidential" for national security reasons to the crimes of treason or espionage, making it punishable by life imprisonment. This provision could be used against whistleblowers.[3]

TORTURE AND OTHER ILL-TREATMENT

Torture and other ill-treatment were reported.

On 4 March, Ibrahima Diogo Sow was arrested and taken to the Anti-Crime Brigade in Kipé, a neighbourhood of Conakry. The security forces suspended him by his hands and feet from a wooden bar and hit him with rifle butts and wooden sticks over three days. Ibrahima Diogo Sow filed a complaint, but no action was taken and he remained in detention at the end of the year.

On 26 June, three gendarmes arrested Oumar Sylla in Conakry and took him to a building where they were posted. They tied his feet and hands behind his back. One of the gendarmes stabbed him in his left side and poured boiling water on his chest. They asked him to confess to stealing a motorbike, which he refused to do. He was taken to the gendarmerie base ECO III the next day and beaten with belts. Fearing for his life, Oumar Sylla confessed and signed a statement he said he did not understand.

The revised Criminal Code criminalized torture and made it punishable by up to 20 years' imprisonment. However, some acts defined as torture under international law, including rape, electric shocks, burns, holding in stress positions, sensory deprivation, mock executions and simulated drowning, were classified as "inhuman and cruel" treatment, for which no penalties were specified.

DEATH PENALTY

The revised Criminal Code abolished the death penalty for ordinary crimes. The Military Code of Justice still provided for capital punishment for exceptional crimes, including treason and revolt at time of war or state of emergency. A bill seeking to remove these provisions was pending in the National Assembly.

IMPUNITY

There was little progress in the trial relating to the massacre in the Grand Stade de Conakry in 2009, when security forces killed more than 100 peaceful demonstrators and injured at least 1,500 others. Dozens of women were raped.

None of the members of the security forces suspected of using excessive force against peaceful opposition demonstrators, leading to death and injuries between 2011 and 2016, have been brought to justice.[4]

There was still no investigation of members of the security forces involved in rape and other forms of torture, systematic pillage and contamination of water in Womey village, Nzérékoré region, in September 2014.

No progress was made in the trial of four members of the security forces charged with killing six people during a strike at a mine in Zogota in 2012.

The revised Criminal Code contained vague language relating to actions justifiable as "self-defence" as well as a new provision called "state of necessity" that could shield members of the security forces who caused death or injury by using excessive force.

WOMEN'S RIGHTS

The revised Criminal Code criminalizes early and enforced marriage, raising the legal age for marriage to 18. However, ambiguity remains as the Code refers to "marriage according to custom" for children aged 16. Guinea has one of the highest rates of child marriage in the world, with three in five girls married before the age of 18, according to the latest study by the UN Population Fund (UNFPA).

1. Guinée: Consternation face à la mort d'un homme par balle (News story, 17 August)

2. Guinée: La condamnation de cinq syndicalistes est une violation du droit à la liberté d'expression (News story, 25 March)

3. Guinea: New criminal code drops death penalty but fails to tackle impunity and keeps repressive provisions (News story, 5 July)

4. Guinea: One year on, no justice for election violence (News story, 10 October)

GUINEA-BISSAU

Republic of Guinea-Bissau
Head of state: **José Mário Vaz**
Head of government: **Umaro Sissoco Embaló (replaced Baciro Djá in November, who replaced Carlos Correia in May)**

The continuing political crisis delayed implementation of recommendations of the UN Universal Periodic Review (UPR) of 2015, and hindered economic and social reforms. No progress was made in improving prison conditions. The judiciary did not always follow due process, and was criticized for incompetence and corruption.

BACKGROUND

In February, the UN Security Council extended the mandate of the UN Integrated Peace Building Office in Guinea-Bissau (UNIOGBIS) for another year.

Tension between President Vaz, the government and parliament, as well as within the ruling African Party for the Independence of Guinea and Cape Verde (PAIGC), escalated, paralysing parliamentary proceedings.

In January the National Assembly's Permanent Commission expelled 15 parliamentarians for refusing to support the government's programme. Political tension was exacerbated when Prime Minister Correia was dismissed in mid-May. The appointment two weeks later of Baciro Djá as Prime Minister triggered violent protest in which police used force, including tear gas, to disperse demonstrators who were throwing stones and burning tyres outside the presidential palace.

In September, Guinea-Bissau acceded to the UN Convention relating to the Status of Stateless Persons and the UN Convention on the Reduction of Statelessness.

JUSTICE SYSTEM

The criminal justice system remained weak and failed to guarantee due process. In June, the UN Special Rapporteur on the independence of judges and lawyers reported on her 2015 visit to Guinea-Bissau, describing the justice system as "sad" and "terrible". She highlighted lack of resources, incompetence, corruption, impunity and limited access to justice as the main obstacles to judicial independence.

In July, the Supreme Court took over 20 days, instead of the 10 days allowed by law, to respond to the writs of habeas corpus challenging the detention of parliamentarian Gabriel So. His arrest was ordered by the Bissau Regional Court despite his parliamentary immunity.

In August, the Public Prosecutor's Office ordered the arrest and detention of João Bernardo Vieira for allegedly violating bail. In contravention of the law, he was not brought before a judge within 48 hours from his arrest; he was released after one week.

Accountability

Investigations into past human rights violations, including political killings between 2009 and 2012 made no progress. However, in May the Bissorã Regional Court, in the Oio region, convicted four police officers of beating Tchutcho Mendonça to death in July 2015 in police custody. Three officers were sentenced to seven years and three months' imprisonment and one to five years' imprisonment.

PRISON CONDITIONS

The authorities took no action to improve prison conditions. Inadequate sanitation, lack of health care and food provision, and severe overcrowding in prisons and detention centres persisted. Detainees and prisoners had to rely on their families for food and medicine or on the goodwill of other inmates.

Conditions in detention centres in the capital, Bissau, amounted to cruel, inhuman or degrading treatment. The Criminal Investigation Police cells, with capacity for 35 people, regularly held over 90. Detainees were not separated according to sex, age or type of crime, and uncharged detainees were routinely held for longer than the 48 hours prescribed by law.

HAITI

Republic of Haiti
Head of state: **Jocelerme Privert (replaced Michel Joseph Martelly in February as acting President)**
Head of government: **Enex Jean-Charles (replaced Evans Paul in February as acting Prime Minister)**

Elections were postponed several times. A hurricane hit Haiti in October causing a major humanitarian crisis. Thousands of people returned or were deported from the Dominican Republic, including stateless people, creating humanitarian concerns. Little progress was made on the situation of people displaced by the 2010 earthquake.

BACKGROUND

In January presidential and legislative elections scheduled for 17 January and later for 24 January were postponed by the Provisional Electoral Council (CEP) following violent protests, where police were alleged to have used force, in response to allegations of electoral fraud during the first rounds of elections in 2015.

On 5 February a national agreement establishing a transitional government was reached to find a solution to the political crisis. President Martelly ended his mandate on 7 February. Jocelerme Privert was elected interim President and Enex Jean-Charles was appointed as interim Prime Minister. Elections scheduled for April were once again postponed as the Independent Electoral Verification Commission, which was established in April, confirmed that there was widespread fraud during the October 2015 balloting and recommended new elections take place. The CEP issued a new electoral calendar for elections in October and January 2017.

In October, Hurricane Matthew caused the country's largest humanitarian emergency since the 2010 earthquake, particularly in the southern provinces. More than 500 people were killed and almost as many injured. Extensive flooding and mudslides damaged infrastructure and buildings and caused water shortages. Livelihoods in some areas were almost entirely destroyed while 1.4 million people needed urgent humanitarian assistance. It caused an increase in internal migration from rural areas to overcrowded cities where access to adequate housing was already limited. In this context elections were again postponed and took place on 20 November. Jovenel Moïse was elected as President and was due to be sworn in on 7 February 2017. Although President Privert's term expired on 14 June, he remained as interim President at the end of the year. The political crisis severely affected the country's capacity to adopt essential legislation and policies to improve the protection and promotion of human rights.

The mandate of the UN Stabilization Mission in Haiti (MINUSTAH) was renewed for six months in October.

In November, Haiti's human rights record was examined under the UN Universal Periodic Review (UPR) process. Haiti accepted various recommendations, including to accede to the UN Conventions on Statelessness, to strengthen its legal framework against gender-based violence and to enhance protection of human rights defenders. It rejected recommendations to protect lesbian, gay, bisexual, transgender and intersex (LGBTI) people or to join the ICC.[1]

INTERNALLY DISPLACED PEOPLE

Hurricane Matthew affected 2.1 million people across the country, including nearly 900,000 children. One hundred and seventy five thousand people were left homeless. The situation was compounded by the fact that 55,107 were still homeless from the 2010 earthquake and, by November, were living in 31 camps, a number which had hardly decreased since June 2015.

REFUGEES' AND MIGRANTS' RIGHTS

People of Haitian origin continued to arrive spontaneously in Haiti from the Dominican Republic, while others had been deported by the Dominican authorities. About 2,220 of them settled in makeshift camps at the southern border region of Anse-à-Pitre where they lived in dismal conditions with restricted access to water, sanitation, health care and education.[2] Despite a relocation programme in operation up until June, dozens of families remained in the camps at the end of the year.

RIGHT TO HEALTH – CHOLERA EPIDEMIC

Between January and July, 21,661 suspected cholera cases and 200 related deaths were registered, with nearly 9,000 cases reported after Hurricane Matthew. In August, the UN acknowledged, for the first time, its role in the initial outbreak for which the UN Secretary-General apologized publicly in December. He also announced a new plan to deal with the outbreak. The UN continued to deny all attempts by victims to gain access to legal remedies.

RIGHTS OF LESBIAN, GAY, BISEXUAL, TRANSGENDER AND INTERSEX PEOPLE

In September, public threats, including by several parliamentarians, were made against individuals and NGOs who were planning an LGBTI Film Festival event. In September, the Public Prosecutor of Port-au-Prince ordered its cancellation for security reasons. In the following days, there was a marked increase in reports of homophobic attacks.

IMPUNITY

No progress was made in the investigation into alleged crimes against humanity committed by former President Jean-Claude Duvalier and his collaborators.[3]

---

1. Haiti: Internal displacement, forced evictions, statelessness – the catalogue to violations continue (AMR 36/4658/2016)

2. "Where are we going to live?": Migration and statelessness in Dominican Republic and Haiti (AMR 36/4105/2016)

3. Haiti: Move ahead with ex-dictator case (AMR 36/3478/2016)

HONDURAS

Republic of Honduras
Head of state and government: **Juan Orlando Hernández Alvarado**

A general climate of violence forced thousands of Hondurans to flee the country. Women, migrants, internally displaced people, human rights defenders – especially lesbian, gay, bisexual, transgender and intersex (LGBTI) people as well as environmental and land activists – were particularly targeted with violence. A weak criminal justice system contributed to a climate of impunity.

BACKGROUND

The government assigned several public security tasks to units made up of officers with military training in an attempt to tackle violence, corruption and organized crime. The Inter-American Commission on Human Rights (IACHR) raised concerns about the military carrying out public security operations, including use of excessive force. The presence of military corps on Indigenous territories contributed to social unrest. Over 100 high-ranking police officers were dismissed in a move to purge security forces accused of being infiltrated by organized crime.

REFUGEES' AND MIGRANTS' RIGHTS

Widespread violence across the country forced many to flee – mostly women, children, youth and LGBTI people. People perceived by criminal gangs to have refused to comply with their authority or who had witnessed a crime were routinely harassed, attacked and extorted; young people in particular were forced to join criminal gangs.

Deportees forcibly returned from Mexico and the USA continued to face the same life-threatening situations which initially pushed them to leave. In July, an asylum-seeker who had been forcibly returned from Mexico after the rejection of his asylum application was murdered less than three weeks after his return.[1]

HUMAN RIGHTS DEFENDERS

Honduras remained one of the most dangerous countries in Latin America for human rights defenders, especially for environmental and land activists. According to the NGO Global Witness, Honduras had the highest number per capita of killings of environmental and land activists in the world.[2] Berta Cáceres, leader and co-founder of the Civil Council of Popular and Indigenous Organizations of Honduras (COPINH), was shot dead in her home on 2 March. The Inter-American Commission on Human Rights had granted her precautionary measures since 2009, but the authorities failed to implement effective measures to protect her. Along with other COPINH members who protested against the construction of the Agua Zarca dam in the community of Río Blanco, she suffered continued harassment, threats and attacks by state and non-state actors before her death.

On 18 October, José Ángel Flores and Silmer Dionisio George of the Unified Campesino Movement of the Aguán were murdered. Both human rights defenders were shot dead after attending a meeting with several *campesino* (peasant farmer) people in the Bajo Aguán region, northeastern Honduras. In November, Bertha Oliva, co-ordinator of the Committee of Relatives of the Disappeared in Honduras (COFADEH) was subjected to a smear campaign, aimed at linking her with drug cartels and discrediting her human rights work. COFADEH has a long history of promoting human rights of *campesino* people in the Bajo Aguan region.

According to the NGO ACI-PARTICIPA, more than 90% of all killings and abuses against human rights defenders remained unpunished.

LGBTI human rights defenders were also particularly targeted with threats and attacks. René Martínez, president of the Sampedrana Gay Community in the city of San Pedro Sula, was found dead on 3 June with his body bearing signs of torture. The Worldwide Movement for Human Rights reported that members of the LGBTI rights group Asociación Arcoiris were victims of 36 security incidents between July 2015 and January 2016, including killings, threats, surveillance and harassment. The military was accused of infiltrating social movements and attacking human rights defenders.

The Law to Protect Human Rights Defenders, Journalists, Social Commentators and Justice Officials had yet to be properly implemented.

INDIGENOUS PEOPLES' RIGHTS

A lack of resources for institutions responsible for supporting Indigenous Peoples continued to be a concern. Several Indigenous Peoples claimed their rights to consultation and to free, prior and informed consent had been violated in the context of projects to explore and exploit natural resources in their territories. A lack of access to justice for Indigenous Peoples in cases of aggression, including killings, remained a challenge. In addition to Berta Cáceres, one Tolupán Indigenous leader was killed on 21 February; he had been granted precautionary measures by the Inter-American Commission on Human Rights in December 2015. The perpetrators had yet to be brought to justice.

WOMEN'S RIGHTS

Women were routinely subjected to violence. Between January and June, 227 women were murdered. During the same period, 1,498 attacks and 1,375 incidents of sexual violence against women were recorded. Attacks against women remained widely underreported. The country continued to lack specific mechanisms for collection and disaggregation of data related to the killings of women. Abortion remained a crime in all cases, including when the life and health of a woman were at risk, or when the pregnancy was a result of sexual violence. Emergency contraception continued to be banned.

JUSTICE SYSTEM

In February, the National Congress elected 15 new members of the Supreme Court of Justice for the next seven years. Several civil society organizations raised concerns about the selection process, which they said failed to comply with international standards of impartiality, independence and transparency.

Honduras had not yet complied with the resolution of October 2015 of the Inter-American Court of Human Rights in which it found that the rights of four judges dismissed for opposing a coup in 2009 were violated. The judges had yet to be reinstated, and other measures of reparation were still pending.

---

1. Home sweet home? Honduras, Guatemala and El Salvador's role in a deepening refugee crisis (AMR 01/4865/2016)

2. We are defending the land with our blood: Defenders of the land, territory and environment in Honduras and Guatemala (AMR 01/4562/2016)

HUNGARY

Hungary
Head of state: János Áder
Head of government: Viktor Orbán

An amendment to the Constitution allowed the government to declare a state of emergency under broad and vaguely worded conditions, with little democratic oversight. Roma continued to face discrimination and to be victims of hate crimes. Hungary continued its systematic crackdown on the rights of refugees and migrants despite growing international criticism.

COUNTER-TERROR AND SECURITY

The government continued to extend the use of anti-terror legislation. In January, the European Court of Human Rights found in *Szabó and Vissy v Hungary* that the Law on Police violated the applicants' right to respect for private and family life as it enabled the executive to intercept any communications without supporting evidence and for extended periods of time. The Court found that Hungary failed to ensure adequate judicial oversight and effective remedies against unlawful surveillance.

In June, Parliament adopted a "Sixth Amendment" to Hungary's Fundamental Law (Constitution) introducing a broadly worded definition of a state of emergency on the grounds of a "terror threat situation" that did not meet the tests required under international human rights law. The package would allow the government to introduce wide-ranging powers, including: restricting freedom of movement within the country; freezing assets of states, individuals, organizations and legal entities; banning or restricting events and public assemblies; and applying undefined special measures to prevent terrorism, without judicial or full parliamentary oversight. Those powers could be increased after 15 days if approved by Parliament. Such a state of emergency would also grant wide powers for the security forces to use firearms in circumstances which went

well beyond what was permitted under international law and standards.

In late November, a Syrian national was sentenced to ten years' imprisonment for "acts of terror" for his involvement in clashes with Hungarian border guards at a Serbia-Hungary border crossing in September 2015. Both parties appealed the first-instance decision.

FREEDOM OF ASSOCIATION

In October, the supposedly independent Government Control Office (*Kormányzati Ellenőrzési Hivatal*, known as KEHI) was compelled by court order to disclose the paper trail of its 2014 ad hoc audit of several NGOs critical of government policies, revealing that it was ordered personally by the Prime Minister. The audit involved police raids, confiscation of computers and servers and lengthy investigations, but ended without finding any criminal wrongdoing. Government representatives continued to threaten several NGOs involved with further investigations, which contributed to a chilling effect on civil society.

FREEDOM OF EXPRESSION – JOURNALISTS

Népszabadság – a newspaper critical of the government – abruptly suspended publication in October 2016 and all the journalists were discharged. The shutdown was carried out days before the company was sold to an entrepreneur close to the government.

JUSTICE SYSTEM

In June, the Grand Chamber of the European Court of Human Rights found in *Baka v Hungary* that terminating the mandate of the President of the Hungarian Supreme Court on account of his criticisms of legislative reforms was contrary to the European Convention on Human Rights. It found a violation of Article 6 paragraph 1 (right of access to a court) and of Article 10 (freedom of expression).

DISCRIMINATION – ROMA

In January, a court in the capital Budapest instructed the municipality of Miskolc to develop an action plan for the mostly Roma residents who were evicted or facing eviction from the Numbered Streets neighbourhood of the city. However, the housing action plan envisaged only 30 housing units for the approximately 100 families affected, and did not allocate additional funding for housing or compensation.

In March, a court in Eger issued a first-instance verdict that Roma children in Heves County were unlawfully segregated in schools and classes providing education designed for children with special needs. In June, the European Commission initiated infringement proceedings against Hungary for discrimination of Roma in education.

Hate crimes

The investigation and prosecution of hate crimes continued to lack consistency. In January, the Curia (Supreme Court) finally issued its verdict in the case of the serial killing of Roma people in 2008 and 2009, targeted on the ground of their ethnicity. Six people were killed including a five-year-old boy, and several others were injured. Three defendants were sentenced to life imprisonment without parole (in contravention of European human rights law), and the fourth to 13 years in prison.

In April, an appeals court in Debrecen reversed a first instance verdict which had found that police discriminated against Roma in the town of Gyöngyöspata when they failed to protect local Roma residents from far-right groups in 2011. The Hungarian Civil Liberties Union appealed against the decision to the Curia.

REFUGEES AND MIGRANTS

Hungary continued to severely restrict access to the country for refugees and asylum-seekers, criminalizing thousands of people for irregular entry across the border fences put up at its southern border. The government repeatedly extended a "state of emergency due to mass immigration" and, despite plummeting numbers of new arrivals to the country, deployed over 10,000 police and military personnel along the border. Nearly 3,000 people were taken to court and expelled for entering the country irregularly, without a proper examination of their protection needs, by the end of the year. A number of legal amendments enabled the immediate return of all non-citizens caught in an irregular situation at the border or up to 8km inside Hungarian territory, and over 16,000 people were denied entry or were returned forcibly, sometimes violently, to Serbia.

On 31 March, the government's list of "safe countries of origin" and "safe third countries" was expanded to include Turkey. In May, the national assembly passed a set of amendments significantly cutting access to housing, health care and integration programmes for people with protection status.

Hungary suspended co-operation with other EU countries and refused to accept asylum-seekers from states participating in the Dublin system. It attempted to return at least 2,500 asylum-seekers already in Hungary to Greece, despite the presumption against returns to Greece in light of systemic shortcomings in the Greek asylum system confirmed by the European Court of Human Rights.

Conditions in the Hungarian asylum system prompted a number of other European countries to rule against returning people to Hungary, in some cases recommending the suspension of Dublin transfers altogether.

The detention of asylum-seekers in-country continued to be implemented without the necessary safeguards to ensure that it was lawful, necessary and proportional. In June, the European Court of Human Rights found in *O.M. v Hungary*, that the asylum detention of a gay asylum-seeker was in violation of his right to liberty and safety. The Court ruled that Hungary failed to make an individualized assessment justifying the applicant's detention and to take into account the applicant's vulnerability in the detention facility based on his sexual orientation.

The government spent over €20 million on communication campaigns labelling refugees and migrants as criminals and threats to national security. In October, it held a national referendum on its opposition to the relocation of asylum-seekers to Hungary within an EU-wide scheme. The referendum was invalid due to insufficient turnout. Together with Slovakia, the government challenged the legality of the European Council decision on relocation quotas at the Court of Justice of the European Union. The case was pending at the end of the year.

In November, the European Committee for the Prevention of Torture issued a report on immigration and asylum detention centres in the country. It found that a considerable number of foreign nationals, including unaccompanied minors, reported that they had been subjected to physical ill-treatment by police officers. The government denied the allegations.

INDIA

Republic of India
Head of state: **Pranab Mukherjee**
Head of government: **Narendra Modi**

The authorities used repressive laws to curb freedom of expression and silence critics. Human rights defenders and organizations continued to face harassment and intimidation, and vigilante cow protection groups carried out several attacks. Thousands protested against discrimination and violence faced by Dalit communities. Millions of people opposed changes to labour laws. Marginalized communities continued to be frequently ignored in the government's push for faster economic growth. Tensions between India and Pakistan intensified following an attack by gunmen on an army base in Uri, Jammu and Kashmir. Jammu and Kashmir state witnessed months of curfew and a range of human rights violations by authorities. A ban on India's largest currency bills, intended as a crackdown on the country's black market, severely affected the livelihoods of millions.

ABUSES BY ARMED GROUPS

Armed groups in central India, northeastern states and Jammu and Kashmir committed a range of human rights abuses. The Communist Party of India (Maoist) armed group was suspected of extortion, abductions and unlawful killings, including of local government officials and suspected police "informers", in states such as Chhattisgarh, Jharkhand, Odisha, Maharashtra, Bihar and Andhra Pradesh. The group was reported to have used a lottery system to conscript children in Jharkhand. It also targeted mobile towers and vehicles used in road construction and mining.

Armed groups in northeastern states including Assam, Manipur and Meghalaya were accused of extortion, abduction and unlawful killings. In August, 14 people were killed in an attack allegedly carried out by the National Democratic Front of Bodoland (Songbijit faction) armed group in Kokrajhar, Assam.

Armed groups were also suspected of killing people in Jammu and Kashmir. In January, suspected members of the Jaish-E-Mohammed armed group attacked an air force base in Pathankot, Punjab state, killing one civilian and seven security force personnel.

CASTE-BASED DISCRIMINATION AND VIOLENCE

Dalits and Adivasis continued to face widespread abuses. According to official statistics released in August, more than 45,000 crimes against members of Scheduled Castes and almost 11,000 crimes against Scheduled Tribes were reported in 2015. Dalits in several states were denied entry into public and social spaces, and faced discrimination in accessing public services.

In January, the suicide of Dalit student Rohith Vemula led to nationwide protests and debates on the discrimination and violence faced by Dalits in universities. In March, the police arrested students and faculty peacefully protesting at the University of Hyderabad, where Rohith Vemula had studied. In July, widespread protests broke out in Una, Gujarat state, following the public flogging of four Dalit men by a vigilante cow protection group for skinning a dead cow – a traditional occupation for certain Dalits.

In April, the central government passed the Scheduled Castes and Scheduled Tribes (Prevention of Atrocities) Amendment Rules, which specified relief mechanisms available to victims of caste-based violence.

CHILDREN'S RIGHTS

According to statistics released in August, reports of crimes against children in 2015 rose by 5% compared with the previous year. Under new laws that came into force in January, juvenile justice authorities ordered that children aged 16 to 18 be treated as adults in cases of serious crimes. In June, a juvenile justice board ordered that a 17-year-old in Delhi be tried as an adult in an alleged hit-and-run driving case. In August, another 17-year-old in Delhi was ordered to be prosecuted as an adult in a case of alleged rape.

In July, Parliament amended a child labour law to prohibit the employment of children under 14, but made an exception for children working in family enterprises. The amendments also allowed children aged 14 to 18 to work in occupations that were not "hazardous". Many child rights activists opposed the amendments, which they said would encourage child labour and disproportionately affect children from marginalized groups and girls.

In August, the central government released a draft national education policy, which made no mention of human rights education.

COMMUNAL AND ETHNIC VIOLENCE

Vigilante cow protection groups harassed and attacked people in states including Gujarat, Haryana, Madhya Pradesh and Karnataka in the name of upholding laws prohibiting the killing of cows.

In March, the bodies of two Muslim cattle traders were found hanging from a tree in Jharkhand. In June, members of a cow protection group in Haryana forced two Muslim men, who they suspected were beef transporters, to eat cow dung. In August, a woman in Haryana said that she and her 14-year-old cousin were gang-raped by men who accused them of eating beef.

In May, the High Court of Bombay, hearing a case on a beef ban law, ruled that preventing people from consuming a particular type of food could violate their right to privacy.

A team formed to reinvestigate closed cases related to the 1984 Sikh massacre identified 77 cases for further investigation and invited people to testify. The functioning of the team continued to lack transparency.

Black people faced racist harassment, discrimination and violence in various cities. In February, a Tanzanian woman was stripped and beaten by a mob in Bengaluru, Karnataka state. In May, a man from the Democratic Republic of the Congo was beaten to death by a group of men in New Delhi.

CORPORATE ACCOUNTABILITY

In February, the Ministry of Environment approved the expansion of a coal mine in Kusmunda, Chhattisgarh state, operated by the state-owned company South Eastern Coalfields, despite authorities not having obtained the free, prior and informed consent of affected Adivasi communities. The central government continued to acquire land using the Coal Bearing Areas Act, which allows for the acquisition of Adivasi land without consent.

In April, the Gujarat government amended a central land acquisition law to exempt a range of projects from seeking the consent of affected families and conducting social impact assessments. The same month, the UN Special Rapporteur on adequate housing stated that most forced evictions occurred with impunity in India. In May, the Supreme

Court rejected a petition challenging the decision of 12 village assemblies in 2013 to refuse permission for a bauxite mine operated by a subsidiary of Vedanta Resources and a state-owned company.

In July, the US-based Dow Chemical Company and its subsidiary Union Carbide Corporation failed, for the fourth time, to appear before a Bhopal court to face criminal charges related to the 1984 gas leak disaster. In Jharkhand, police shot dead three men demonstrating against a power plant in August, and four villagers were killed by the police following a protest against a state-owned coal mine in October.

EXTRAJUDICIAL EXECUTIONS

In April, a former Manipur state policeman told journalists that he had been involved in more than 100 extrajudicial executions in the state between 2002 and 2009. In July, the Supreme Court, hearing a case related to over 1,500 extrajudicial executions in Manipur, ruled that armed forces personnel should not enjoy "blanket immunity" from trials in civilian courts, and that the allegations needed to be looked into.

In April, a Central Bureau of Investigation court convicted 47 police personnel of extrajudicially executing 10 men in Pilibhit, Uttar Pradesh, in 1991. Security forces were accused of carrying out several extrajudicial executions in Chhattisgarh through the year.

In February, an Adivasi man was killed by Chhattisgarh police in Bastar, Chhattisgarh, in an alleged extrajudicial execution. The same month, an Adivasi man was killed in an alleged extrajudicial execution in Rayagada, Odisha. In both cases, the police claimed that the victims were Maoists.

In July, five people, including an infant, were shot dead by security forces in Kandhamal, Odisha. The security forces claimed that the deaths had occurred during crossfire in an encounter with Maoist groups. In November, eight pre-trial detainees were shot dead by the Madhya Pradesh police near Bhopal after they escaped from prison.

FREEDOM OF ASSOCIATION

The central authorities continued to use the Foreign Contribution (Regulation) Act (FCRA) – which restricts civil society organizations from receiving foreign funding – to harass NGOs. The authorities suspended the FCRA registration of Lawyers Collective in June and cancelled it in December.

In October the government refused to renew the FCRA licences of 25 NGOs without offering valid reasons. In December, it cancelled the licences of seven other NGOs, including Greenpeace India, Navsarjan, Anhad, and two NGOs run by human rights defenders Teesta Setalvad and Javed Anand. Media reports quoted government sources as saying that the NGOs had acted against "national interest".

In April, the UN Special Rapporteur on the rights to freedom of peaceful assembly and of association said that the FCRA restrictions were not in conformity with international law, principles and standards. In June, the UN Special Rapporteurs on human rights defenders, freedom of expression, and freedom of association called on the Indian government to repeal the FCRA.

FREEDOM OF EXPRESSION

Regressive laws continued to be used to persecute people who legitimately exercised their right to freedom of expression. In February, three students at the Jawaharlal Nehru University were arrested by police in Delhi for sedition after they allegedly raised "anti-national" slogans. The same month, Delhi police also arrested an academic for sedition for allegedly raising "anti-India" slogans at a closed-door event. The sedition law was also used to arrest people for writing "anti-national" Facebook posts in Kerala, for printing a map in Madhya Pradesh which did not show all of Kashmir within Indian borders, and for organizing a protest for better working conditions for police personnel in Karnataka.

In August, police in Karnataka registered a sedition case against unnamed representatives of Amnesty International

India for allegedly conducting an "anti-national" event on human rights violations in Jammu and Kashmir. A complaint of sedition was filed the same month in a Karnataka court against an actress for refuting a statement by a central government minister that "visiting Pakistan was like going to hell".

India's information technology law was used to persecute people. In March, two men were arrested in Madhya Pradesh for allegedly sharing a satirical image of a Hindu nationalist group.

HUMAN RIGHTS DEFENDERS

Journalists, lawyers and human rights defenders were harassed and attacked with impunity.

In February, journalist Karun Mishra was shot dead by gunmen in Sultanpur, Uttar Pradesh. The state police said he had been targeted for his reports on illegal soil mining. In May, Rajdeo Ranjan, a journalist in Siwan, Bihar, who had faced threats from political leaders for his writing, was shot dead.

In February, journalist Malini Subramaniam was forced to leave Bastar following an attack on her home and pressure from police on her landlord. Another journalist, Prabhat Singh, was arrested for sharing a message online that mocked a senior police official in Bastar. Bela Bhatia, a researcher and activist, faced intimidation and harassment from vigilante groups in Bastar. Adivasi activist Soni Sori had a chemical substance thrown at her face by unidentified assailants. A group of human rights lawyers who provided free legal aid to Adivasi pre-trial detainees were also forced to leave their home in Jagdalpur, Chhattisgarh state, following police pressure on their landlord.

Journalist Santosh Yadav, who was arrested in 2015 on politically motivated charges, remained in detention at the end of the year.

In June, police in Tamil Nadu state arrested Dalit author Durai Guna and activist Boopathy Karthikeyan on false charges of assault. In July, the police arrested environmental activists Eesan Karthik, Muthu Selvan and Piyush Sethia for protesting against the construction of a railway bridge.

Irom Sharmila ended her 16-year hunger strike in protest against the Armed Forces (Special Powers) Act in August. She was released from detention and a local court dismissed charges of attempted suicide against her. Irom Sharmila was a prisoner of conscience.

In October, members of the police and security forces in Chhattisgarh burned effigies of human rights defenders, after some officers were charged with attacking and burning Adivasi homes in Tadmetla, Chhattisgarh in 2011.

JAMMU AND KASHMIR

The killing of a leader of the Hizbul Mujahideen armed group in July sparked widespread protests. More than 80 people, mostly protesters, were killed in clashes and thousands injured. At least 14 people were killed and hundreds blinded by security forces' use of pellet-firing shotguns, which are inherently inaccurate and indiscriminate. Security forces used arbitrary or excessive force against demonstrators on several occasions. In August, Shabir Ahmad Monga, a lecturer, was beaten to death by army soldiers.

The Jammu and Kashmir government imposed a curfew which lasted over two months. Private landline, mobile and internet service providers suspended their services for weeks on orders from state authorities. The communications shutdown undermined a range of human rights. Residents reported being unable to reach medical assistance in cases of emergencies.

In July, the state government prevented the publication of local newspapers in Kashmir for three days. In September, Khurram Parvez, a Kashmiri human rights defender, was arrested and detained for over two months on spurious grounds, a day after he was prevented from travelling to a UN Human Rights Council session in Geneva, Switzerland. In October, the government ordered a Srinagar-based newspaper to cease printing and publication on vague grounds. Hundreds of people, including children, were placed in administrative detention. Dozens of schools were set on fire by unidentified people.

RIGHTS OF LESBIAN, GAY, BISEXUAL, TRANSGENDER AND INTERSEX PEOPLE

In February, the Supreme Court referred to a larger bench a petition challenging Section 377 of the Indian Penal Code, which criminalizes consensual same-sex relations. In June, five people who identified themselves as members of the LGBTI community filed another petition in the Supreme Court asking for Section 377 to be struck down.

In July, the cabinet approved a flawed bill on transgender people's rights. Activists criticized the bill for its problematic definition of transgender people, and for its provisions on anti-discrimination which were not aligned with a 2014 Supreme Court judgment.

VIOLENCE AGAINST WOMEN AND GIRLS

Reported crimes against women and girls continued to rise. According to statistics released in August, over 327,000 crimes against women were registered in 2015. Women from marginalized communities continued to face systemic discrimination, making it harder for them to report sexual or other forms of violence.

In January, two groups of Adivasi women reported that they were raped and sexually assaulted by security force personnel during search operations in their villages in Chhattisgarh. Little progress was made in both investigations. In April, women garment workers protesting in Bengaluru, Karnataka, faced arbitrary and abusive actions by police. In May, a Dalit law student from Kerala was found raped and murdered at her home. The police had failed to investigate previous complaints of caste-based discrimination by the family.

In July, the government released a flawed draft law on trafficking without adequate consultation. Indian law continued to criminalize soliciting in public places, leaving sex workers vulnerable to a range of human rights abuses.

INDONESIA

Republic of Indonesia
Head of state and government: Joko Widodo

Broad and vaguely worded laws were used to arbitrarily restrict the rights to freedom of expression, of peaceful assembly and of association. Despite the authorities' commitments to resolve past cases of human rights violations, millions of victims and their families were still denied truth, justice and reparation. There were reports of human rights violations by security forces, including unlawful killings and the use of excessive or unnecessary force. At least 38 prisoners of conscience remained in detention. Four people were executed.

BACKGROUND

In January, the armed group Islamic State (IS) claimed responsibility for a series of attacks in the capital, Jakarta, in which four attackers and four civilians were killed. In response, the government proposed changes to the Anti-Terrorism Bill, which could undermine safeguards against torture and arbitrary detention and expand the scope of the application of the death penalty. In July, retired General Wiranto was appointed as Co-ordinating Minister for Political, Law and Security Affairs. He had been indicted for crimes against humanity by a UN-sponsored tribunal in Timor-Leste. He was named as a suspect in the inquiry initiated in 1999 by the National Commission on Human Rights (Komnas HAM), for gross violations of human rights in East Timor surrounding the 1999 referendum. No charges had been brought against him by the end of the year.

FREEDOM OF EXPRESSION

Broad and vaguely worded laws continued to arbitrarily restrict the rights to freedom of expression, of peaceful assembly and of association, and of religion or belief. In July, Yanto Awerkion and Sem Ukago, Papuan political activists in Timika, were charged with "rebellion" under Article 106 of the Criminal Code. In November, prisoner of conscience Steven Itlay, leader of the Timika branch of the West Papuan National Committee was sentenced to one year in prison for "incitement" under Article 160 (see below). Another activist from Ternate, North Maluku, was charged with "rebellion" for posting online a photo of a T-shirt with a caricature of the communist hammer and sickle symbol. In May, Ahmad Mushaddeq, Andry Cahya and Mahful Muis Tumanurung, former leaders of the disbanded religious group, Gafatar, were arrested and later charged with blasphemy under Article 156a of the Criminal Code, and with "rebellion" under Articles 107 and 110 of the Code. They were penalized for peacefully practising their beliefs.

Vague language in the 2008 Electronic Information and Transaction (ITE) Law allowed for the wide interpretation of definitions of defamation and blasphemy, and the criminalization of expression. Haris Azhar, Executive Coordinator of the human rights NGO KontraS, was threatened by the police, the military and the National Anti-Narcotics Agency with defamation charges under the Law. This followed an article he published on social media linking security and law enforcement officials to drug trafficking and corruption. The charges were suspended.[1] In August, Pospera, a pro-ruling party organization, filed a criminal defamation complaint under the ITE Law against I Wayan Suardana, a human rights defender from Bali. The complaint was made in response to I Wayan Suardana's using Twitter to mock supporters of a large-scale land reclamation project by a commercial developer in Benoa Bay, southern Bali.[2] The police were still investigating the complaint at the end of the year. At least 11 other activists were reported to the police by state or non-state actors for criminal defamation under the ITE Law after the activists criticized government policies.

Between April and September, at least 2,200 Papuan activists were arrested after participating in peaceful demonstrations in Jayapura, Merauke, Fakfak, Sorong and Wamena in Papua and West Papua Provinces, in Semarang in Central Java Province, in Makassar in South Sulawesi Province and in Yogyakarta Province. Most were released without charge after one day. The arbitrary arrests highlighted the ongoing repressive environment for political activists in the Papua region.[3]

RIGHTS OF LESBIAN, GAY, BISEXUAL, TRANSGENDER AND INTERSEX PEOPLE

Discrimination increased against LGBTI people after officials made inflammatory, grossly inaccurate or misleading statements in January on the grounds of "defending the country's public morality and public security". In February, police disbanded a workshop organized by a leading LGBTI NGO in Jakarta and prevented a pro-LGBTI rally from taking place in Yogyakarta.[4] In the same month, the Indonesian Broadcasting Commission issued a letter calling for a ban on any television or radio broadcasts promoting LGBTI activities, to "protect the children".

Also in February, amid increasing anti-LGBTI rhetoric, the Islamic school for transgender people, Al Fatah in Yogyakarta, was forced to close following intimidation and threats by the Islamic Jihadist Front. In June, the government voted against a resolution by the UN Human Rights Council, and again at the UN General Assembly in November, to appoint an independent expert on violence and discrimination based on sexual orientation and gender identity.

FREEDOM OF RELIGION AND BELIEF

Discriminatory legislation continued to be used to restrict the activities of members of minority religious groups who faced harassment, intimidation and attacks. In January, a mob set alight nine houses belonging to members of the Gafatar movement in Menpawah District, West Kalimantan. After the attacks, at least 2,000 people were forcibly moved by local security forces to temporary shelters in Kubu Raya

District and Pontianak City, West Kalimantan Province, and later transferred to locations on Java without prior consultation.

In February, a Joint Ministerial decree (No. 93/2016) was issued by the Minister of Religious Affairs, the Attorney General and the Minister of Home Affairs proscribing the Millah Abraham religious belief, adhered to by former members of Gafatar.[5]

Members of the Ahmadiyya community, whose teachings are viewed as "deviant" by the government, were intimidated and threatened in various locations.[6] In February, at least 12 members were forced to leave their homes in Bangka Island, off the east coast of Sumatra, after being intimidated by a group of at least 100 local residents. Members of the Ahmadiyya community had been under threat of expulsion since January when the Bangka District government issued an order that they convert to mainstream Sunni Islam or leave the district. Local authorities allowed them to return after three weeks following national and international pressure.

IMPUNITY

In April, the government organized a symposium on the 1965-66 mass human rights violations that brought together survivors, scholars, activists and artists, as well as military and other government officials. In October, the government announced that it would redress the violations using non-judicial measures to ensure "national harmony and unity". Victims and NGOs raised concerns that this process may prioritize reconciliation while abandoning the quest for truth and justice. Authorities continued to silence and disband activities relating to 1965-66, including a film screening and a cultural festival.[7]

The authorities took limited steps to address serious human rights violations. In March, the National Human Rights Commission completed its investigations into the 2003 human rights violations by security forces in Jambo Keupok village, South Aceh. The Commission found that there was sufficient evidence to conclude that crimes

against humanity occurred, as defined in Law No.26/2000 on Human Rights Courts. The Commission made similar findings in June in connection with security force violations in 1999 in Simpang KKA, Dewantara sub-district, North Aceh. No criminal investigations or prosecutions had been initiated by the end of the year.

In July the local Aceh provincial parliament selected seven commissioners to the Aceh Truth and Reconciliation Commission, which was expected to operate between 2016 and 2020. The Commission was established to examine the circumstances which led to past abuses during the Aceh conflict between the Indonesian security forces and the Free Aceh Movement, in particular between 1989 and 2004.

In September, President Widodo made a public pledge to resolve the case of human rights defender Munir Said Thalib. In October, the Public Information Commission ruled that the 2005 report into his killing, which reportedly implicated senior intelligence officers, should be made public. The government appealed against the ruling.

POLICE AND SECURITY FORCES

Reports continued of unnecessary or excessive use of force, including the use of firearms, by police and military, and of the lack of independent, effective and impartial mechanisms to investigate violations by security forces. Criminal investigations into human rights violations by police were rare, and attempts to hold alleged perpetrators to account, mostly through internal disciplinary mechanisms, left many victims without access to justice and reparation. There was no progress towards holding to account those involved in the killing of four men in December 2014 after police and military personnel opened fire on a crowd of protesters in Paniai regency, Papua Province. An inquiry in March by Komnas HAM made no progress.

In April, the then chief of the Indonesia National Police confirmed that an alleged terrorism suspect had died after being assaulted and kicked by members of the

Detachment-88 counter-terrorism unit. In May, two members of Detachment 88 received administrative sanctions after an internal police hearing.

In August, officers of the Mobile Brigade (Brimob) shot dead a Papuan teenager in Sugapa, Intan Jaya regency, Papua Province. Otianus Sondegau and four others created a road block to ask for money and cigarettes from passing traffic. Police attempted to disperse the blockade violently and fired shots at the five teenagers at which point they threw stones at the police. Five officers were found guilty of "misusing firearms" after internal disciplinary hearings; four served 21-day prison sentences and another was sentenced to a year in prison related to the shooting.

In October, members of the Madiun Infantry 501 Raider Battalion attacked a journalist from NET TV who was covering a brawl between members of a military unit and a martial arts group in Madiun, East Java Province. They beat him, destroyed his camera's memory card and threatened him if he reported the incident. Despite promises by the Armed Forces chief to investigate the attack, no one had been held to account at the end of the year.

PRISONERS OF CONSCIENCE

At least 38 prisoners of conscience remained in detention, many for their peaceful political activism in Papua and Maluku. Prison authorities delayed access to adequate and free medical treatment to Johan Teterissa and Ruben Saiya who were suffering long-term health conditions. The two men were among at least nine prisoners of conscience from Maluku held in Java, more than 2,500km from family and friends. Steven Itlay, imprisoned in Timika, Papua, suffered ill health as a result of poor conditions and was granted only limited access to his family and lawyer.[8]

In May, three leaders of the Millah Abraham religious group were arrested and detained by the Indonesian National Police and were charged with "blasphemy" under

Article 156a of the Criminal Code and "rebellion" under Articles 107 and 110.

TORTURE AND OTHER ILL-TREATMENT

Reports of torture and other ill-treatment continued. In September, Asep Sunandar died in police custody in Cianjur, West Java Province. He had been arrested, with two others, without a warrant, by three officers of the Cianjur Resort police. He was taken to an undisclosed location and later reported dead. His family said that when they visited the hospital, they saw multiple gunshot wounds to his body and his hands still tied behind his back. No investigation into the death is known to have been carried out.

Cruel, inhuman or degrading punishment

Caning was used as a punishment under Shari'a law in Aceh for a range of criminal offences including selling alcohol, consensual relations, and being alone with someone of the opposite sex who was not a marriage partner or relative. At least 100 people were caned during the year. The law was applied to non-Muslims for the first time in April when a Christian woman received 28 strokes of the cane for selling alcohol.[9]

In October, the House of Representatives ratified Government Regulation in Lieu of Law (Perppu) No.1/2016, which amended Article 81 of Law No.23/2002 on the Protection of Children. The revised law imposed forced chemical castration as an additional punishment for those convicted of sexual violence against a child under 18. According to the revised law, chemical castration would be carried out for up to two years after the expiry of the offender's prison term. The Indonesian Doctors' Association stated that it would refuse to administer the procedure.

DEATH PENALTY

In July, one Indonesian national and three foreign nationals were executed, three of them while their appeals were pending. Ten other prisoners who had been moved to Nusa Kambangan Island, where the executions took place, were given last-minute stays of execution to allow for a review of their cases.

1. Indonesia: Defamation investigation suspended (ASA 21/4734/2016)

2. Indonesia: Defender under investigation for defamation (ASA 21/4833/2016)

3. Indonesia: End mass arrests and crackdowns on peaceful protests (ASA 21/3948/2016)

4. Indonesia: Stop inflammatory and discriminatory statements that put the LGBTI community at risk (ASA 21/3648/2016)

5. Indonesia: Authorities must repeal joint ministerial decree (ASA 21/3787/2016)

6. Indonesia: Religious minority members forcibly evicted (ASA 21/3409/2016)

7. Indonesia: President must not undermine efforts to seek truth, justice and reparation (ASA 21/3671/2016)

8. Indonesia: Poor prison conditions for Papuan activist (ASA 21/4085/2016)

9. Indonesia: End caning as a punishment in Aceh (ASA 21/3853/2016)

IRAN

Islamic Republic of Iran
Head of state: **Ayatollah Sayed Ali Khamenei (Supreme Leader of the Islamic Republic of Iran)**
Head of government: **Hassan Rouhani (President)**

The authorities heavily suppressed the rights to freedom of expression, association, peaceful assembly and religious belief, arresting and imprisoning peaceful critics and others after grossly unfair trials before Revolutionary Courts. Torture and other ill-treatment of detainees remained common and widespread, and were committed with impunity. Floggings, amputations and other cruel punishments continued to be applied. Members of religious and ethnic minorities faced discrimination and persecution. Women and girls faced pervasive violence and discrimination. The authorities made extensive use of the death penalty, carrying out hundreds of executions, some in public. At least two juvenile offenders were executed.

BACKGROUND

In March, the UN Human Rights Council renewed the mandate of the UN Special Rapporteur on the situation of human rights in Iran. The government continued to deny the Special Rapporteur entry to Iran and to prevent access by other UN human rights experts.

The government and the EU discussed initiating a renewed bilateral human rights dialogue.

INTERNATIONAL SCRUTINY

The UN Committee on the Rights of the Child conducted its third and fourth periodic review of Iran and criticized continued executions of juvenile offenders, and the impact of public executions on the mental health of children who witnessed them. The Committee also criticized continued discrimination against girls; children of religious and ethnic minorities; lesbian, gay, bisexual, transgender and intersex (LGBTI) children; and the low age at which girls in particular become criminally liable.

FREEDOMS OF EXPRESSION, ASSOCIATION AND ASSEMBLY

The authorities cracked down further on the rights to freedom of expression, association and peaceful assembly, arbitrarily arresting and imprisoning peaceful critics on vague national security charges. Those targeted included human rights defenders, journalists, lawyers, bloggers, students, trade union activists, film makers, musicians, poets, women's rights activists, ethnic and religious minority rights activists, and environmental and anti-death penalty campaigners.

As the year closed, many prisoners of conscience undertook hunger strikes to protest against their unjust imprisonment, exposing the abusive nature of Iran's criminal justice system.

The authorities intensified their repression of human rights defenders, sentencing them to long prison terms for their peaceful activities. Courts increasingly cited criticism of Iran's human rights record on social media and communicating with international human rights mechanisms, particularly the UN Special Rapporteur on Iran and human rights organizations based abroad including Amnesty International as evidence of "criminal" activism deemed threatening to national security.

The authorities also cracked down on musical expression, disrupting and forcibly cancelling performances, including some licensed by the Ministry of Culture and Islamic Guidance; and repressed activities such as private mixed-gender parties that they deemed "socially perverse" or "un-Islamic", arresting hundreds and sentencing many to flogging.

Opposition leaders Mehdi Karroubi and Mir Hossein Mousavi and the latter's wife, Zahra Rahnavard, remained under house arrest without charge since 2011. They were subject to frequent extreme intrusions on their privacy and inadequate access to medical care.

The authorities continued to censor all media, jamming foreign satellite TV broadcasts, closing or suspending newspapers including *Bahar* and *Ghanoun* and forcing the women's rights magazine *Zanan-e Emrooz* to suspend publication.

In February, a judicial order added WhatsApp, Line and Tango to the list of blocked social media sites, which already included Facebook and Twitter. The Cyber Crime Unit of the Revolutionary Guards blocked or closed down hundreds of Telegram and Instagram accounts and arrested or summoned for interrogation the administrators of more than 450 groups and channels in Telegram, WhatsApp and Instagram, including several hundred fashion designers and employees of fashion boutiques, as part of a massive crackdown on social media activities deemed "threatening to moral security".

The suspended Association of Iranian Journalists addressed an open letter to President Rouhani urging him, unsuccessfully, to honour his 2013 election campaign pledge to lift its suspension, while 92 student groups urged the President to release universities from the grip of fear and repression. The authorities did not permit the Teachers' Trade Association of Iran to renew its licence, and sentenced several of its members to long prison terms on charges that included "membership of an illegal group".

The authorities continued to suppress peaceful protests and subject protesters to beatings and arbitrary detention. Numerous individuals remained convicted of "gathering and colluding against national security" for attending peaceful protests.

A new Law on Political Crimes, which was adopted in January and took effect in June, criminalized all expression deemed to be "against the management of the country and its political institutions and domestic and foreign policies" and made "with intent to reform the affairs of the country without intending to harm the basis of the establishment".

TORTURE AND OTHER ILL-TREATMENT

Torture and other ill-treatment of detainees remained common, especially during interrogation, and was used primarily to force "confessions". Detainees held by the Ministry of Intelligence and the Revolutionary Guards were routinely subjected to prolonged solitary confinement amounting to torture.

The authorities systematically failed to investigate allegations of torture and other ill-treatment, sometimes threatening to subject complainants to further torture and harsh sentences. Judges continued to admit "confessions" obtained under torture as evidence against the defendant, although such confessions were inadmissible under the 2015 Code of Criminal Procedure. The Code failed to set out the procedure that judges and prosecutors must follow to investigate allegations of torture and ensure that confessions were made voluntarily. Other provisions of the Code, such as the provision guaranteeing the detainee's right to access a lawyer from the time of arrest and during the investigation stage, were frequently ignored in practice, facilitating torture.

Judicial authorities, particularly the Office of the Prosecutor, and prison authorities frequently denied access to adequate medical care for political prisoners, including prisoners of conscience. This was often done to punish prisoners or to coerce "confessions".

In June, detainee Nader Dastanpour died in custody as a result of injuries that his family said were inflicted during torture at a Tehran police station. No independent investigation was reported.

Cruel, inhuman or degrading punishment
Judicial authorities continued to impose and carry out cruel, inhuman or degrading punishments that amounted to torture, including floggings, blindings and amputations. These were sometimes carried out in public.

In April, the Public Prosecutor of Golpayegan, Esfahan Province, announced that a man and woman convicted of "having an illegitimate relationship" had been sentenced to 100 lashes each.

In May, the Public Prosecutor of Qazvin Province announced that the authorities had arrested 35 young women and men "dancing and mingling at a graduation party... while half-naked and consuming alcohol" and convicted them within 24 hours of engaging in acts "incompatible with chastity which disturbed the public opinion". The authorities carried out the 99-lash floggings to which they were sentenced at a special court hearing the same day.

In West Azerbaijan Province, authorities carried out flogging sentences of between 30 and 100 lashes against 17 miners who had engaged in a protest against employment conditions and dismissals at the Agh Darreh gold mine in 2014. In June, a criminal court in Yazd Province sentenced nine miners to floggings ranging from 30 to 50 lashes.

In July, an appeal court sentenced journalist and blogger Mohammad Reza Fathi to 459 lashes on charges of "publishing lies" and "creating unease in the public mind" through his writings.

In November, a man was forcibly blinded in both eyes in Tehran, in retribution for blinding a four-year-old girl in June 2009. Several other prisoners including Mojtaba Yasaveli and Hossein Zareyian remained at risk of being forcibly blinded. Doctors associated with the official Legal Medicine Organization of Iran provided the Supreme Court with "expert" advice on how the implementation of blinding sentences was medically feasible, an act that breached medical ethics.

In April, judicial authorities at Mashhad Central Prison amputated four fingers from the right hand and the toes from the left foot of a man convicted of armed robbery. The same authorities amputated the fingers of another man convicted of robbery in May. In August, a judicial official in Tehran announced that several men had appealed after they were sentenced to amputation of four fingers from one hand. In December, judicial authorities at Urumieh Central Prison amputated four fingers from the right hands of two brothers convicted of armed robbery.

UNFAIR TRIALS
Trials, including those resulting in death sentences, were generally unfair. The judiciary was not independent. The Special Court for the Clergy and the Revolutionary Courts remained particularly susceptible to pressure from security and intelligence forces to convict defendants and impose harsh sentences.

Officials exercising judicial powers, including from the Ministry of Intelligence and Revolutionary Guards, consistently flouted due process provisions of the 2015 Code of Criminal Procedure. These included provisions protecting the right to access a lawyer from the time of arrest and during investigations and the right to remain silent. Defence lawyers were frequently denied full access to case files and prevented from meeting defendants until shortly before trial. Pre-trial detainees were frequently held in prolonged solitary confinement, with little or no access to their families and lawyers. "Confessions" extracted under torture were used as evidence at trial. Judges often failed to deliver reasoned judgments and the judiciary did not make court judgments publicly available.

The Office of the Prosecutor used Article 48 of the Code of Criminal Procedure to prevent detainees accessing lawyers of their own choosing, telling them that they were not on the list of lawyers approved by the Head of the Judiciary, even though no official list had been issued.

Several foreign nationals and Iranians with dual nationality were detained in Tehran's Evin Prison with little or no access to their families, lawyers and consular officials. These prisoners were sentenced to long prison terms on vague charges such as "collaborating with a hostile government" after grossly unfair trials before Revolutionary Courts. The authorities accused the prisoners of being involved in a foreign-orchestrated "infiltration project" pursuing the "soft overthrow" of Iran. In reality, the convictions appeared to stem from their peaceful exercise of the rights to freedom of expression and association.

FREEDOM OF RELIGION AND BELIEF

Members of religious minorities, including Baha'is, Sufis, Yaresan (Ahl-e Haq), Christian converts and Sunni Muslims, faced discrimination in law and practice, including in education, employment and inheritance, and were persecuted for practising their faith.

The authorities engaged in hate speech and allowed hate crimes to be committed with impunity against Baha'is, and imprisoned scores of Baha'is on trumped-up national security charges imposed for peacefully practising their religious beliefs. Allegations of torture of 24 Baha'is in Golestan Province were not investigated. The authorities forcibly closed down dozens of Baha'i-owned businesses and detained Baha'i students who publicly criticized the authorities for denying them access to higher education.

The authorities detained tens of Christian converts after raiding house churches where they peacefully gathered to worship. Sites considered sacred by Baha'is, Sunni Muslims and Yaresan, including cemeteries and places of worship, were destroyed by men believed to be affiliated with security forces.

Spiritual teacher Mohammad Ali Taheri remained in solitary confinement in Section 2A of Evin Prison despite completing, in February, a five-year sentence for "insulting Islamic sanctities" for establishing the Erfan-e Halgheh spiritual doctrine and group. His followers continued to be arbitrarily arrested and detained.

DISCRIMINATION – ETHNIC MINORITIES

Iran's disadvantaged ethnic minorities, including Ahwazi Arabs, Azerbaijani Turks, Baluchis, Kurds and Turkmen, remained subject to entrenched discrimination, curtailing their access to employment, adequate housing, political office, and their exercise of cultural, civil and political rights. Continued economic neglect of minority-populated regions by state authorities further entrenched poverty and the marginalization of ethnic minorities.

Members of minorities who spoke out against violations of their political, cultural and linguistic rights faced arbitrary arrest, torture and other ill-treatment, grossly unfair trials, imprisonment, and in some cases the death penalty.

Dozens of Kurds were reportedly arrested without warrant for their real or perceived affiliations with the Kurdish Democratic Party of Iran after it renewed armed opposition to the Iranian authorities in March. Scores of Kurds served prison sentences or remained under sentence of death for membership of or sympathy with banned Kurdish opposition groups.

Ahwazi Arabs were imprisoned and subjected to torture and other human rights violations. They complained that the authorities repressed expressions of Arabic culture, including dress and poetry.

Security forces continued to repress protests by ethnic minorities. In July and August, they detained several members of the Azerbaijani Turkish ethnic group after largely peaceful demonstrations in several cities sparked by a report in the newspaper *Tarheh No* which Azerbaijani Turks deemed offensive. Police also beat protesters.

The authorities continued to prohibit ethnic minority groups from using their own language in primary education. In June the government announced that optional Turkish and Kurdish language courses would be offered in schools in two provinces, Kurdistan and West Azerbaijan, although implementation remained unclear. Members of the Turkmen minority publicly appealed to President Rouhani for a similar dispensation.

WOMEN'S RIGHTS

The authorities renewed their crackdown on women human rights defenders and increasingly likened any collective initiative relating to feminism and women's rights to criminal activity. Women's rights activists who had campaigned for greater representation of women in the February parliamentary elections were subjected by the Revolutionary Guards to lengthy, oppressive interrogations, and threats of imprisonment on national security charges.

Women remained subject to pervasive discrimination in law and practice, including in access to divorce, employment, equal inheritance and political office and in the area of criminal law.

Several draft laws that would further erode women's right to sexual and reproductive health remained pending. Women continued to have reduced access to affordable modern contraception as the authorities failed to restore the budget of the state family planning programme cut in 2012.

In September, Supreme Leader Ali Khamenei issued national family policies promoting early marriage, repeated childbearing, fewer divorces and greater compliance to "traditional" roles of women as housewives and men as breadwinners. The policies raised concern that women victims of domestic violence may face further marginalization and increased pressure to "reconcile" with abusers and remain in abusive marital relationships.

Women and girls remained inadequately protected against sexual and other gender-based violence, including early and forced marriage. The authorities failed to adopt laws criminalizing these and other abuses, including marital rape and domestic violence, although the Vice-President on Women and Family Affairs pushed a draft bill that had been pending since 2012.

Compulsory "veiling" (*hijab*) laws, which violated women's rights to equality, privacy, and freedoms of expression, belief and religion, continued to empower police and paramilitary forces to target women for harassment, violence, and imprisonment.

DEATH PENALTY

The authorities continued to use the death penalty extensively, including against juvenile offenders. Hundreds of executions were carried out after unfair trials. Some executions were conducted in public.

Those executed were mostly sentenced for drugs offences that did not meet the threshold of "most serious crimes" under international human rights law. The Supreme Court ruled that those sentenced for drugs offences prior to the adoption of the 2015 Code of Criminal Procedure had the right to appeal, but many death row prisoners remained unaware of this development. Others were sentenced for murder, or on vague offences such as "enmity against God".

Following the mass execution of 25 Sunni men in August, the authorities broadcast forced "confession" videos, apparently to demonize the men and divert attention from the deeply flawed trials that led to their death sentences. At least two men convicted of "insulting the Prophet" received death sentences, in violation of their rights to life and freedoms of belief, religion and expression.

At least 78 juvenile offenders remained on death row. They included 15 juvenile offenders who were sentenced to death for the first time under the revised juvenile sentencing guidelines of the 2013 Islamic Penal Code as well as several who again received death sentences after they were retried.

Amnesty International was able to confirm the execution of two juvenile offenders during the year, among them Hassan Afshar, although the total number could be much higher.

The Islamic Penal Code continued to provide for stoning as a method of execution; at least one woman, Fariba Khaleghi, remained under a sentence of death by stoning.

Some consensual same-sex sexual conduct remained punishable by death.

IRAQ

Republic of Iraq
Head of state: **Fuad Masum**
Head of government: **Haider al-Abadi**

Government forces, paramilitary militias and the armed group Islamic State (IS) committed war crimes, other violations of international humanitarian law and gross human rights abuses in the internal armed conflict. IS fighters carried out execution-style killings targeting opponents and civilians fleeing IS-held territory, raped and otherwise tortured captives, used civilians as human shields and used child soldiers. Militias extrajudicially executed, forcibly disappeared and tortured civilians fleeing conflict, and destroyed homes and other civilian property. Thousands remained detained without trial on suspicion of links to IS. Torture in detention remained rife. Courts sentenced terrorism suspects to death, frequently after unfair trials. Executions continued at a high rate.

BACKGROUND

Armed conflict continued between IS and an array of Iraqi government forces, paramilitary militias and Peshmerga (Kurdish armed forces), supported by US-led international coalition air strikes. IS held areas of northwestern and western Iraq, but lost significant territory during the year, including Falluja in June, al-Qayyara in August and Sharqat in September. Military operations to recapture Mosul, the largest remaining IS stronghold, were continuing at the end of the year.

The armed conflict, car bombings and other violence led to 6,878 fatalities and 12,388 injuries among civilians during the year, according to the UN.

Prime Minister al-Abadi issued Order 91 in February and Parliament passed a law in November designating the Popular Mobilization Units (PMU), established in June 2014 and comprising mostly Shi'a paramilitary militias, as a "military formation and part of the Iraqi armed forces".

In August, Parliament passed the General Amnesty Law. It did not cover certain types of crimes, such as terrorist acts that resulted in death or permanent injury; but it provided a right of judicial review for those convicted under the Anti-Terrorism Law and other laws in cases where court verdicts were based on "confessions" extracted under "duress".

Anti-government protesters calling for institutional reform and an end to corruption twice breached the heavily fortified Green Zone, where the government is based, in the capital Baghdad. On the second occasion, 20 May, government forces fired tear gas, rubber bullets and stun grenades to disperse protesters, leading to four deaths. The authorities announced an investigation but disclosed no information about its outcome or any prosecutions. A proposed law restricting the right to freedom of peaceful assembly was tabled for discussion by Parliament in July, but withdrawn following a public outcry.

The remaining Iranian political exiles, who were residents of Camp Liberty in Baghdad, were resettled outside Iraq by late September. On 4 July, the camp had come under rocket attack leading to injuries and material damage.

ARMED CONFLICT – VIOLATIONS BY MILITIAS AND GOVERNMENT FORCES

Paramilitary militias and government forces committed war crimes and other violations of international humanitarian law and human rights law, mostly against members of the Sunni Arab community. They carried out extrajudicial executions, other unlawful killings and torture, forcibly disappeared hundreds of men and boys, and deliberately destroyed homes and property.

Following a suicide bombing that killed 27 men and injured 41 others in Muqdadiya on 11 January, militias carried out revenge attacks against the Sunni community, abducting and killing dozens of men and burning and destroying Sunni mosques, shops and other property.

On 3 June, PMU militias abducted an estimated 1,300 men and boys fleeing Saqlawiya, north of Falluja. Three days later, 605 men reappeared bearing marks of torture, while the fate of 643 remained unknown. An investigative committee established by the Governor of Anbar found that 49 had been killed by being shot, tortured or burned to death. On 30 May, at least 12 men and four boys who were fleeing al-Sijir, north of Falluja, were extrajudicially executed. Prime Minister al-Abadi established a committee to investigate abuses, but the authorities did not disclose any outcome or report any criminal process against the perpetrators.

The PMU and Tribal Mobilization militias, composed of Sunni fighters, were reported to have recruited children and used them in fighting against IS.

The authorities took no steps to clarify the whereabouts and fate of thousands of Sunni Arab men and boys who remained forcibly disappeared after being seized from their homes, at checkpoints, and from camps for internally displaced persons (IDPs) by militias and government forces in previous years.

ABUSES BY ARMED GROUPS

IS killed and injured civilians throughout Iraq in suicide bombings and other deadly attacks that were indiscriminate or deliberately targeted civilians in crowded markets, Shi'a religious shrines and other public spaces. IS particularly targeted locations within Baghdad.

A series of attacks in May across Baghdad, mainly in predominantly Shi'a neighbourhoods, killed 150 people and injured 214, mostly civilians, according to officials and media reports.

In areas under its control, IS fighters carried out execution-style killings of perceived opponents and those suspected of collaborating with government forces. IS fighters carried out abductions, including of civilians, and systematically tortured captives. IS imposed a draconian code of conduct and severely punished infractions. Its self-declared "courts" ordered stoning for "adultery" and floggings and other corporal punishments against inhabitants for smoking, failing to adhere to the IS-imposed dress code or other IS rules. IS imposed severe restrictions on the use of telephones and the internet and on women's freedom of movement. IS prevented civilians from fleeing areas it controlled, and used civilians as human shields. Fighters shot at those attempting to escape, destroyed their property and carried out revenge attacks against relatives left behind. The group indoctrinated and recruited boys, including Yazidi captives, using them in battles and suicide attacks. In October, IS used chemical weapons to attack the town of al-Qayyara after it had been recaptured by Iraqi forces, leading to burns and other injuries among civilians.

VIOLENCE AGAINST WOMEN AND GIRLS

Women and girls faced discrimination in law and practice, and were inadequately protected from sexual and other gender-based violence. An estimated 3,500 Yazidis captured in Iraq remained in IS captivity in Iraq and Syria and were subjected to rape and other torture, assault and enslavement. Those who managed to escape or were freed after their relatives paid ransoms received inadequate psychological and material support; several committed or attempted suicide.

ARBITRARY ARRESTS AND DETENTIONS

All males considered to be of fighting age (roughly 15 to 65) fleeing territories controlled by IS underwent security screenings by security forces at makeshift detention facilities or temporary reception sites, where they were held for days or months in often dire conditions. Those suspected of terrorism were transferred into the custody of security agencies such as the Anti-Crime Directorate or Anti-Terrorism Directorate, or the General Intelligence branch of the Ministry of the Interior, where they were at risk of torture and other ill-treatment and frequently denied contact with families and lawyers.

Security forces and militias arrested alleged terrorism suspects without judicial warrant from their homes, checkpoints and IDP camps, failing to inform those taken or their relatives of any charges. Many were held in prolonged incommunicado detention, in some cases in conditions amounting to enforced disappearance, in facilities controlled by the Ministries of the Interior and Defence or secret detention centres, where they were interrogated by security officers without lawyers present. Thousands remained in detention without appearing before judicial authorities or being referred for trial.

TORTURE AND OTHER ILL-TREATMENT

Torture and other ill-treatment remained rife in prisons, detention centres controlled by the Ministries of the Interior and Defence, and militia-controlled facilities. The most frequently reported methods of torture used against detainees were beatings on the head and body with metal rods and cables, suspension in stress positions by the arms or legs, electric shocks and threats of rape of female relatives. Torture appeared to be carried out to extract "confessions", obtain information and punish detainees. Several detainees died in custody as a result of torture.

In October, Tribal Mobilization fighters subjected villagers from south of Mosul, suspected of links to IS, to beatings with metal cables, public humiliation and use of electric-shock weapons.

UNFAIR TRIALS

The criminal justice system remained deeply flawed and trials were systematically unfair. Defendants, in particular terrorism suspects, were routinely denied the rights to adequate defence, to not incriminate oneself or confess guilt and to cross-examine prosecution witnesses. Courts continued to admit into evidence torture-tainted "confessions" without ordering investigations into defendants' claims or referring them for forensic examination. Some of those convicted after unfair trials were sentenced to death.

REFUGEES AND INTERNALLY DISPLACED PEOPLE

More than 3.1 million people remained internally displaced across Iraq, sheltering with host communities or in IDP camps, informal settlements, and buildings under construction. Many were destitute and lived in dire conditions, while humanitarian agencies reported significant shortfalls in international funding. Thousands fled across the border to Syria.

The Iraqi authorities and those of the semi-autonomous Kurdistan Regional Government (KRG) imposed arbitrary and discriminatory restrictions on the freedom of movement of Sunni Arab IDPs. Tens of thousands remained confined to camps with no access to the job market or essential services because they were without local sponsors and therefore unable to obtain the official permits required to enter cities.

Tens of thousands of IDPs were able to return home to areas that government and allied forces recaptured from IS, including the cities of Ramadi and Falluja, after completing onerous security checks. However, tens of thousands of Sunni Arab IDPs from areas recaptured from IS in Babil, Diyala and Salah al-Din governorates were prevented from returning home through a mix of onerous bureaucratic procedures, and intimidation tactics by militias, including abductions, arbitrary detention and extrajudicial executions. Relatives of suspected IS fighters were barred from returning and some had their homes deliberately destroyed or appropriated. Peshmerga and other Kurdish security forces also prevented tens of thousands of Arab residents of KRG-controlled areas, displaced by the conflict, from returning home.

FREEDOM OF EXPRESSION – MEDIA WORKERS

Journalists worked in a dangerous and at times deadly environment, and reported physical assaults, abduction, intimidation, harassment and death threats for covering topics deemed sensitive, including corruption and militia abuses.

Media workers Saif Talal and Hassan al-Anbaki from the al-Sharkia TV channel were shot dead on 12 January in northwestern Diyala while returning from covering a suicide bombing in Muqdadiya and revenge attacks by militias targeting Sunni Arabs. The channel accused unidentified militiamen, but the authorities failed to adequately investigate the killing of the media workers.

In April, the Iraqi Communications and Media Commission shut down al-Jazeera's Baghdad bureau, accusing the channel of "incit[ing] sectarianism and violence". In March, the authorities closed the Baghdadia TV Channel's offices in Iraq purportedly for operating illegally without a licence. The channel had published articles on government corruption and pro-reform protests, and had been subjected to several closures in recent years.

KURDISTAN REGION OF IRAQ

Media workers, activists and politicians critical of the ruling Kurdistan Democratic Party (KDP) faced harassment and threats and some were expelled from Erbil governorate. No progress was made in conducting investigations into the killings in previous years of journalists and other perceived critics and opponents of the Kurdish authorities.

On 13 August, relatives collected the body of Wedad Hussein Ali, a journalist who worked for a publication seen as supporting the Kurdish Workers' Party (PKK). The body bore injuries indicating that he had been tortured, including deep lacerations to the head. Witnesses told his family that he had been found alive earlier that day in a village west of Dohuk after unidentified men seized him from the street at gunpoint. His family

and co-workers reported that he was previously questioned by the Asayish (security forces) in Dohuk and had received death threats. The authorities announced an investigation two days after his killing but had disclosed no outcome by the end of the year.

Asayish and other Kurdish security forces detained thousands of terrorism suspects, mainly Sunni Arab men and boys, amid severe delays in referring them to the judiciary, denial of family visits for prolonged periods of time, and other breaches of due process. In October, the KRG authorities said that the Asayish Ghishti (General Security Agency) and the Asayish branch in Erbil had arrested 2,801 terrorism suspects since the beginning of the year.

Bassema Darwish, a Yazidi survivor of IS captivity, remained detained without trial in Erbil since her arrest in October 2014 in the town of Zummar when it was recaptured by Peshmerga forces from IS. The authorities accused her of complicity in the killing of three Peshmerga officials, but denied her the right to a lawyer of her own choosing and failed to conduct an independent investigation into allegations that General Security Directorate officials in Dohuk tortured her after her arrest.

Courts in the Kurdistan Region of Iraq continued to pass death sentences for terrorism-related offences; no executions were carried out.

DEATH PENALTY

Courts sentenced dozens to death by hanging; scores of executions were carried out. Public and political pressure on the authorities to execute "terrorists" mounted following a suicide bombing in the Karrada neighbourhood of Baghdad on 2 July that killed nearly 300 people, mostly civilians. A militia leader threatened to kill death row inmates at Nasriya Prison if the government failed to act. On 12 July, President Masum ratified a law amending the Code of Criminal Procedures to limit the possibility of retrials, aimed at speeding up the execution process.

On 21 August, the government announced the execution of 36 men convicted of participating in the massacre by IS fighters of up to 1,700 Shi'a cadets at the Speicher military training camp in June 2014, after President Masum ratified their death sentences. They were convicted after a trial of only a few hours' duration marred by breaches of the right to a fair trial, including the court's failure to adequately investigate the defendants' allegations that their pre-trial "confessions" were extracted under torture.

IRELAND

Republic of Ireland
Head of state: **Michael D. Higgins**
Head of government: **Enda Kenny**

Access to and information about abortion remained severely restricted and criminalized. Travellers' rights to adequate housing were violated. Concerns remained about "direct provision" accommodation provided to asylum-seekers.

SEXUAL AND REPRODUCTIVE RIGHTS

In February, the UN Committee on the Rights of the Child expressed concern that legislation allowed abortion only where a girl's life is at "real and substantial risk", and prevented doctors from providing services in accordance with objective medical practice. The Committee called on Ireland to decriminalize abortion in all circumstances and review its legislation to ensure children's access to safe abortion and post-abortion care. It also found a "severe lack of access to sexual and reproductive health education and emergency contraception for adolescents".

In June, the UN Human Rights Committee decided in *Mellet v Ireland* that Ireland's abortion laws violated a woman's right to be free from inhuman or degrading treatment, and to enjoy privacy and non-discrimination. The complainant had to travel to the UK for an abortion, despite a diagnosis of a fatal fetal impairment causing her "intense physical and mental suffering". The Committee found that the suffering was

exacerbated by the stigma caused by the criminalization of abortion. On 30 November, the government agreed to provide the complainant, Amanda Mellet, with compensation and counselling.

A Citizens' Assembly, comprising 99 randomly selected members of the public and established by the government to make recommendations on constitutional reform, including on abortion, held its first meetings in October and November.

HOUSING RIGHTS

In January, the government referred the right to housing to a parliamentary committee, responding partially to the 2014 recommendation of the government-established Constitutional Convention. However, it chose not to task the same committee with examining the full recommendation that the Constitution be amended to incorporate economic, social and cultural rights. This was despite the fact that as recently as 2015 the UN Committee on Economic, Social and Cultural Rights reiterated its recommendation that the government take all appropriate measures to ensure the direct applicability of provisions in the International Covenant on Economic, Social and Cultural Rights, including through incorporation of the Covenant in its domestic legal order.

The shortage of state housing and private rental accommodation contributed to homelessness. The Committee on the Rights of the Child expressed deep concern at reports that homeless families experienced significant delays in accessing social housing, frequently living long-term in inappropriate, temporary or emergency accommodation.

DISCRIMINATION
Travellers and Roma

In May, the European Committee of Social Rights ruled, in *European Roma Rights Centre v Ireland*, that Travellers faced a violation of their right to social, legal and economic protection on the grounds of insufficient provision of accommodation, poor conditions of many sites and inadequate safeguards when threatened with and during evictions.

The UN Committee on the Rights of the Child raised concerns over structural discrimination against Traveller and Roma children, including in their access to education, health and an adequate standard of living.

Sex workers

A government bill which proposed to criminalize the purchase of sex, fails to take adequate account of sex workers' needs and views or international evidence that criminalization increases their isolation and marginalization, and violates their safety and human rights. The bill did not fully decriminalize sex workers but maintained and even increased penalties for brothel-keeping and loitering offences that are frequently used against sex workers.

REFUGEES' AND ASYLUM-SEEKERS' RIGHTS

Provisions in 2015 legislation which established a single procedure for dealing with both claims for refugee status and other forms of protection came into force on 31 December.

Concerns remained about the poor living conditions in "direct provision" accommodation centres for asylum-seekers and the slow implementation of recommendations for improvement set out in a government-established working group's 2015 report. Concerns highlighted by the UN Committee on the Rights of the Child, included inadequate child protection services, access to education, and inappropriate clothing and food.

Resettlement and relocation

The Department of Justice and Equality confirmed that by the end of the year, only 240 of the 2,622 asylum-seekers agreed for relocation from the EU in 2015 had arrived in Ireland; 519 of 520 Syrian refugees agreed for resettlement from the Middle East, however, had arrived. In July, Ireland

undertook to resettle another 260 refugees from Lebanon.

National security deportation

In July, the authorities deported a man to Jordan, deeming him a national security threat for allegedly organizing and facilitating travel of people to join the armed group Islamic State (IS). He faced the risk of torture and other ill-treatment in Jordan. His applications to the Irish courts and the European Court of Human Rights to prevent his deportation were unsuccessful.[1]

---

1. Ireland: Deportation to Jordan would risk backsliding on absolute ban on torture (News story, 6 July)

ISRAEL AND THE OCCUPIED PALESTINIAN TERRITORIES

State of Israel
Head of state: **Reuven Rivlin**
Head of government: **Benjamin Netanyahu**

Israeli forces unlawfully killed Palestinian civilians, including children, in both Israel and the Occupied Palestinian Territories (OPT), and detained thousands of Palestinians from the OPT who opposed Israel's continuing military occupation, holding hundreds in administrative detention. Torture and other ill-treatment of detainees remained rife and was committed with impunity. The authorities continued to promote illegal settlements in the West Bank, including by attempting to retroactively "legalize" settlements built on private Palestinian land, and severely restricted Palestinians' freedom of movement, closing some areas after attacks by Palestinians on Israelis. Israeli forces continued to blockade the Gaza Strip, subjecting its population of 1.9 million to collective punishment, and to demolish homes of Palestinians in the West Bank and of Bedouin villagers in Israel's Negev/Naqab region, forcibly evicting residents. The authorities imprisoned conscientious objectors to military service and detained and deported thousands of asylum-seekers from Africa.

BACKGROUND

Israeli-Palestinian relations remained tense. International efforts to revive negotiations failed, with Israel continuing to develop illegal settlements on territory it occupied. In December the UN Security Council passed a resolution calling on Israel to cease all settlement activities in the West Bank.

In June the government announced a reconciliation agreement between Israel and Turkey which saw the two countries restore diplomatic relations. Israel agreed to pay compensation to the families of Turkish citizens killed by Israeli forces when they intercepted the humanitarian aid ship *Mavi Marmara* in 2010.

In September the government of the USA agreed to increase its military aid to Israel to $3.8 billion annually for 10 years from 2019.

The year saw stabbing, car-ramming, shooting and other attacks by Palestinians on Israelis in the West Bank and in Israel. The attacks, mostly carried out by Palestinians unaffiliated to armed groups, killed 16 Israelis and one foreign national, mostly civilians. Israeli forces killed 110 Palestinians and two foreign nationals during the year. Some were killed unlawfully while posing no threat to life.

Palestinian armed groups in Gaza periodically fired indiscriminate rockets and mortars into Israel, without causing deaths or serious injuries. Israeli forces responded with air strikes and artillery fire, killing three Palestinian civilians, including two children, in Gaza.

FREEDOM OF MOVEMENT – GAZA BLOCKADE AND WEST BANK RESTRICTIONS

Israel's military blockade of the Gaza Strip entered its 10th year, continuing the collective punishment of Gaza's entire population. Israeli controls on the movement of people and goods into and from Gaza, combined with Egypt's almost total closure of the Rafah border crossing and funding shortages, damaged Gaza's economy and hindered post-conflict reconstruction. Some 51,000 people were still displaced from the 2014 war, and unexploded ordnance from that conflict continued to cause civilian deaths and injuries. The number of Palestinians leaving Gaza via the Erez Crossing declined during the year, as the Israeli authorities denied, delayed or revoked permits for businesspeople, staff of international organizations, and medical patients and their companions.

Israeli forces maintained a "buffer zone" inside Gaza's border with Israel and used live fire and other weapons against Palestinians who entered or approached it, killing four and wounding others. Israeli forces also fired at Palestinian fishermen in or near the "exclusion zone" that they maintained along Gaza's coastline.

In the West Bank, the Israeli authorities severely restricted the movement of Palestinians on a discriminatory basis, particularly around illegal Israeli settlements and near the fence/wall. In response to Palestinian attacks on Israelis, the military authorities imposed collective punishment, revoking permits of attackers' family members to work in Israel and closing off entire areas and villages.

ARBITRARY ARRESTS AND DETENTIONS

The authorities detained or continued to imprison thousands of Palestinians from the OPT, holding most of them in prisons in Israel, in violation of international law. Many prisoners' families, particularly those in Gaza, were not permitted entry to Israel to visit their relatives in prison. The Israeli authorities continued to arrest hundreds of Palestinian children in the West Bank including East Jerusalem. Many were subjected to abuse by Israeli forces including beatings and threats.

The authorities held hundreds of Palestinians, including children, under renewable administrative detention orders based on information that they withheld from the detainees and their lawyers. The numbers held under such orders since October 2015 were the highest since 2007; more than 694 were held at the end of April 2016 (the last month for which reliable data was available). Some detainees undertook lengthy protest hunger strikes; Palestinian detainee Bilal Kayed remained on hunger strike for 71 days. He was released without charge in December. Anas Shadid and Ahmad Abu Farah ended their hunger strike on 22 December after 90 days without food.

Three Israeli Jews held as administrative detainees were released.

The authorities gave circus performer Mohammed Faisal Abu Sakha two additional six-month administrative detention orders in June and December, based on secret evidence. His first six-month detention order had been issued in December 2015.

Palestinians from the West Bank who were charged with protest-related and other offences faced unfair military trials, while Israeli civilian courts trying Palestinians from the Gaza Strip issued harsh sentences, even for minor offences.

Mohammed al-Halabi, a Gaza-based humanitarian worker, was denied access to his lawyer and interrogated intensively for three weeks after his arrest in June. He was charged in August with embezzling money from the charity World Vision and passing it to Hamas, the de facto administration in Gaza. World Vision said it had not seen any substantive evidence to support the charge.

TORTURE AND OTHER ILL-TREATMENT

Israeli soldiers, police and Israel Security Agency (ISA) officers subjected Palestinian detainees, including children, to torture and other ill-treatment with impunity, particularly on arrest and during interrogation. Reported methods included beatings, slapping, painful shackling, sleep deprivation, use of stress positions and threats. Although complaints alleging torture by ISA officers have been handled by the Ministry of Justice since 2014, and more than 1,000 had been filed since 2001, no criminal investigations were opened. Complaints that the Israeli police used torture or other ill-treatment against asylum-seekers and members of the Ethiopian community in Israel were also common.

The UN Committee against Torture conducted its fifth periodic review of Israel, criticizing continued reports of torture and other ill-treatment, impunity, and the authorities' failure to proscribe torture as a crime under the law. Israeli officials noted that legislation criminalizing torture was being drafted by the Ministry of Justice, but it was not put before the Knesset (parliament).

In September the High Court upheld a 2015 law allowing the authorities to force-feed hunger-striking detainees; the law was not used in 2016.

UNLAWFUL KILLINGS

Israeli soldiers, police and security guards killed at least 98 Palestinians from the OPT in the West Bank, including East Jerusalem; eight in the Gaza Strip; and three in Israel. In addition, one Palestinian citizen of Israel, responsible for killing three Israelis in Tel Aviv on 1 January, was killed by Israeli police inside Israel. Most of those killed were shot while attacking Israelis or suspected of intending an attack. Some, including children, were shot when they were posing no immediate threat to others' lives and appeared to be victims of unlawful killings.

Extrajudicial executions

Some of those killed appeared to have been victims of extrajudicial executions. They included 16-year-old Mahmoud Shaalan, shot dead by Israeli soldiers at a Ramallah checkpoint in February; Mohammed Abu Khalaf, killed in February by Israeli border police in East Jerusalem; and Maram Abu Ismail and her 16-year-old brother Ibrahim, who were shot dead at Qalandia checkpoint in April by private contractors employed by the Israeli Ministry of Defence.

EXCESSIVE USE OF FORCE

Israeli forces used excessive, sometimes lethal, force against Palestinian protesters in the West Bank and Gaza Strip, killing 22 and injuring thousands with rubber-coated metal bullets and live ammunition. Many protesters threw rocks or other projectiles but were posing no threat to the lives of well-protected Israeli soldiers when they were shot.

FREEDOMS OF EXPRESSION, ASSOCIATION AND ASSEMBLY

The authorities used a range of measures to target human rights defenders, in both Israel and the OPT, who criticized Israel's continuing occupation of the Palestinian territories.

On 11 July the Knesset passed the so-called Transparency Law, which imposed new reporting requirements on organizations that receive more than 50% of their funding from foreign governments, almost all of which were human rights groups or other NGOs critical of the Israeli government.

Using military orders prohibiting unauthorized demonstrations in the West Bank, the authorities suppressed protests by Palestinians and arrested and prosecuted protesters and human rights defenders. Following the annual "Open Shuhada Street" protest in Hebron on 26 February, the authorities prosecuted Palestinian human rights defenders Issa Amro and Farid al-Atrash on charges that included participating in a march without a permit and entering a closed military zone. They were apparently prosecuted on account of their peaceful exercise of the rights to freedom of expression and peaceful assembly. Issa Amro also faced charges arising from his peaceful activism in previous years.

For months after he filmed the extrajudicial execution of Abed al-Fatah al-Sharif by an Israeli soldier on 24 March in Hebron, B'Tselem volunteer Imad Abu Shamsiyeh received death threats from Israelis in nearby illegal settlements. Police turned him away and threatened to arrest him when he sought to lodge a complaint in August.

Palestinians and foreign nationals assisting human rights NGOs such as Al-Haq with their work in connection with the ICC received death threats.

A number of prominent Israeli human rights organizations and their staff, including Breaking the Silence, B'Tselem and Amnesty International Israel, were targeted by a government campaign to undermine their work.

In May the authorities charged former nuclear whistle-blower and prisoner of conscience Mordechai Vanunu with breaching the severe and arbitrary restrictions the authorities have imposed on his rights to freedom of movement and expression. The case was still pending at the end of the year.

HOUSING RIGHTS – FORCED EVICTIONS AND DEMOLITIONS

In the West Bank, including East Jerusalem, the Israeli authorities demolished 1,089 homes and other structures built without Israeli permits, an unprecedentedly high number of demolitions, forcibly evicting more than 1,593 people. Permits remained virtually impossible for Palestinians to obtain. Many of the demolitions were in Bedouin and herding communities which the Israeli authorities planned to transfer against the residents' wishes. The authorities also collectively punished the families of Palestinians who carried out attacks on Israelis by demolishing or making uninhabitable 25 family homes, thereby forcibly evicting their inhabitants.

The authorities also demolished hundreds of Palestinian homes and other structures inside Israel that they said were built without permits, mostly in Bedouin villages in the Negev/Naqab region. Many of the villages were officially "unrecognized".

IMPUNITY

More than two years after the end of the 2014 Gaza-Israel conflict, in which some

1,460 Palestinian civilians were killed, many in evidently unlawful attacks including war crimes, the Israeli authorities had indicted only three soldiers for looting and obstructing an investigation. In August the Military Advocate General announced the closure of investigations into 12 incidents, despite evidence that some should be investigated as war crimes. Israel's military investigations were not independent or impartial, and failed to deliver justice.

In a rare move, the Israeli military investigated, indicted and tried Elor Azaria, a soldier whose extrajudicial execution by shooting of a wounded Palestinian in Hebron was captured on film. The verdict in his case was expected to be delivered in January 2017. Most members of the Israeli forces who committed unlawful killings of Palestinians faced no repercussions. The Israeli army, Ministry of Justice and police also did not investigate, failed to investigate adequately, or closed investigations into cases of alleged unlawful killings of Palestinians by Israeli forces in both Israel and the OPT.

The authorities prosecuted several Jewish settlers for carrying out lethal attacks on Palestinians. In January, they charged two Israelis with committing an arson attack in July 2015 that killed three members of the Dawabsheh family, including a child aged 18 months. In May, a Jerusalem court sentenced Yosef Ben David to life imprisonment plus 20 years after convicting him of the abduction and murder of 16-year-old Palestinian Mohammed Abu Khdeir in July 2014.

The prosecutor of the ICC continued her preliminary examination of allegations of crimes under international law carried out by Israeli forces and Palestinian armed groups since 13 June 2014. The Israeli government allowed an ICC delegation to visit Israel and the West Bank in October.

VIOLENCE AGAINST WOMEN AND GIRLS

There were new reports of violence against women, particularly within Palestinian communities in Israel. Activists reported that at least 21 women were killed by partners or family members during the year. Some women were reportedly killed by abusive partners after police failed to afford them adequate protection.

REFUGEES AND ASYLUM-SEEKERS

The authorities continued to deny asylum-seekers, more than 90% of whom were from Eritrea or Sudan, access to a fair and prompt refugee status determination process. More than 3,250 asylum-seekers were held at the Holot detention facility and at Saharonim Prison in the Negev/Naqab desert at the end of the year.

According to figures provided by the Ministry of Interior, there were more than 37,000 Eritrean and Sudanese asylum-seekers in Israel as of October 2016. More than 18,900 asylum claims were still pending as of October 2016.

In February the Knesset passed the fourth version of an amendment to the Prevention of Infiltration Law, allowing the authorities to detain asylum-seekers for up to one year without charge. Conditions in detention centres were reported to be severely deficient due to inadequate food and medical care, poor sanitation and overcrowding.

In September, a custody appeals tribunal in Jerusalem declared the government's policy of automatically rejecting the asylum requests of Eritrean army deserters invalid, although thousands had been rejected on that basis.

The authorities granted asylum to a Sudanese national for the first time in June but continued to press thousands of Sudanese and Eritrean asylum-seekers, including those detained at Holot, to leave Israel "voluntarily". More than 2,500 were reported to have agreed to depart "voluntarily" by the end of the year. The government refused to disclose details of its reported agreements with Rwandan and Ugandan authorities, as to whether they included guarantees that asylum-seekers who left Israel voluntarily would not be at real risk of serious human rights violations, thus violating the prohibition of *refoulement*.

CONSCIENTIOUS OBJECTORS

At least five conscientious objectors to military service were imprisoned. They included Tair Kaminer, who was held for almost six months, longer than any woman conscientious objector previously.

ITALY

Italian Republic
Head of state: **Sergio Mattarella**
Head of government: **Paolo Gentiloni (replaced Matteo Renzi in December)**

Over 4,500 refugees and migrants died or disappeared in the central Mediterranean trying to reach Italy, the highest number of victims on record, while over 181,000 reached Italy. The implementation by Italian authorities of the EU "hotspot approach" to identify and separate refugees from alleged irregular migrants resulted in cases of excessive use of force, arbitrary detention, and collective expulsions. Roma continued to suffer discrimination in access to housing, with thousands living in segregated camps and hundreds subjected to forced evictions. Parliament passed legislation establishing civil unions for same-sex couples. Italy continued to fail to introduce the crime of torture in its criminal code.

REFUGEES' AND MIGRANTS' RIGHTS

Over 4,500 people were estimated to have died in the central Mediterranean while attempting to reach Italy on overcrowded and unseaworthy vessels, the worst figure on record.

Over 181,000 refugees and migrants reached Italy from North Africa – a slight increase on previous years. The vast majority departed from Libya and were rescued at sea by the Italian Coastguard and Navy, other countries' and merchant vessels and, to an increasing extent, NGOs' vessels. Of these, over 25,700 were children travelling alone, more than twice the number of 2015. The

authorities struggled to ensure they were looked after according to international standards.

The Italian Navy continued to lead the EU military operation in the southern Central Mediterranean (EUNAVFOR MED Operation Sophia). In October, the operation started training the Libyan Coastguard, notwithstanding reports that it was involved in shooting incidents against vessels carrying refugees and migrants, and that people rescued and returned to Libya were exposed to arbitrary detention and torture.

The "hotspot approach", agreed by the EU in 2015 to achieve the swift identification and screening of refugees and migrants on the point of arrival, continued to be implemented in Italy. Under pressure from the EU to fingerprint all those arriving by sea, Italian authorities used arbitrary detention and excessive force against individuals refusing to co-operate. Several cases of ill-treatment were also reported.

Traumatized people, exhausted from their journey, were hastily interviewed and were not provided with adequate information on their rights and the legal consequences of their statements, by police officials not trained to assess the status of those in need of protection. Thousands deemed not to be in need of protection, and therefore irregularly present on the territory, were issued with expulsion orders or deferred rejection orders requiring them to leave the country autonomously. Those issued with such orders, effectively unable to leave Italy for lack of funds and documents to cross borders, were left vulnerable to abuse and exploitation.

Nationals of countries with which Italy negotiated repatriation agreements continued to be forcibly returned to their countries of origin, often within a few days from disembarkation, raising concern that they were not given adequate access to an asylum procedure and that they were expelled without an assessment of each individual's potential risks upon return, in breach of the prohibition of collective expulsions.

In August, Italian and Sudanese police authorities signed a Memorandum of Understanding to strengthen co-operation in "migration management", including through swift repatriation procedures. While individuals seeking asylum in Italy cannot be returned to Sudan on the basis of this agreement, the identification process provided is so superficial that it could result in returning to Sudan people who could face human rights violations there, in violation of the principle of *non-refoulement*.

On 24 August, a group of 40 people identified on the basis of the agreement as Sudanese nationals were repatriated from Italy to Sudan. The group, including people who had fled violence in Darfur before reaching Italy, were interrogated upon arrival by the Sudanese National Intelligence and Security Service, an agency implicated in serious human rights violations in Sudan.

The reception system was hosting over 176,500 people by the end of the year, mostly in emergency centres. The redistribution of asylum-seekers across the country continued to encounter opposition from some local authorities and residents. Protests took place in several towns, often organized or endorsed by far-right groups and the Lega Nord party.

As of mid-December about 120,000 people sought asylum in Italy, up from 83,000 in 2015. Nigerian and Pakistani nationals were the largest groups. Throughout the year about 40% of applicants received some form of protection in the first instance.

The relocation scheme of asylum-seekers from Italy and Greece to other EU countries, adopted by the EU in September 2015, failed to materialize. Of the 40,000 asylum-seekers who should have been relocated from Italy, only 2,654 moved to other countries. No unaccompanied children were relocated.

Italy also granted humanitarian access to about 500 people transferred through a scheme funded by faith-based NGOs S. Egidio and Federation of Evangelical Churches in Italy.

The government failed to adopt the decrees required to abolish the crime of "illegal entry and stay", despite being instructed to do so by Parliament in April 2014.

In December, in the case of Khlaifia and others against Italy, the European Court of Human Rights held that some Tunisian migrants who had reached Italy in 2011 had been arbitrarily detained and that they had been deprived of a remedy to challenge their detention before being returned to Tunisia.

In November, prosecutors in Perugia, Umbria, charged seven police officials, a magistrate and three Kazakhstani diplomats with offences related to the abduction and illegal expulsion to Kazakhstan in May 2013 of Alma Shalabayeva and Alua Ablyazova, wife and six-year-old daughter of Mukhtar Ablyazov, a Kazakhstani opposition politician. In July 2013, the Italian government retroactively rescinded the expulsion order, acknowledging that their forced return to Almaty violated Italian law.

DISCRIMINATION – ROMA

Thousands of Roma families continued to live in segregated camps. Roma-only camps were frequently located in remote areas, away from essential services. Living conditions in many camps remained sub-standard and often breached national housing regulations as well as international standards. Hundreds of Roma families were subjected to forced evictions in violation of international law.

The government's failure to effectively implement the National Strategy for Roma Inclusion with respect to housing continued. Five years after its adoption, there were no national plans to combat segregation in camps. Instead, authorities continued to plan and construct new camps.

In February, in Giugliano, near Naples, €1.3 million was designated by the municipal and regional authorities, with the Prefecture of Naples and the Ministry of Interior, to build a new segregated camp for the Roma then living in the Masseria del Pozzo camp. The Masseria del Pozzo camp was set up near landfills stocking toxic waste in 2013 to house Roma families who had already suffered forced evictions. In June, following a court order that the families be removed from Masseria del Pozzo, local authorities forcibly evicted the approximately 300 people living there including dozens of small children. No alternative was given except the transfer to an isolated site, in a former fireworks factory with no working toilets, no electricity and extremely limited access to water. As of December the community was still living at the site in inadequate conditions.

In December, the CERD Committee expressed concern that Roma continued to face forced evictions and segregation in camps and that they were still discriminated against when trying to access social housing and other housing benefits.

RIGHTS OF LESBIAN, GAY, BISEXUAL, TRANSGENDER AND INTERSEX PEOPLE

In May, Parliament passed Law no.76/2016, establishing civil unions for same-sex couples and rules governing the cohabiting of different-sex couples, extending to them most of the rights of married couples. However, second-parent adoption was not addressed in the law.

TORTURE AND OTHER ILL-TREATMENT

In March, the national ombudsperson started his role, with a mandate to monitor conditions of detention and prevent torture and other ill-treatment. His remit included monitoring repatriation flights of irregular migrants.

Parliament's failure to introduce the crime of torture into the criminal code, as required by the UN Convention against Torture, and overdue since Italy's ratification in 1989, continued.

Parliament and government also failed to agree on measures for the identification of law enforcement officers, such as tags on uniforms, which would facilitate accountability for abuses.

DEATHS IN CUSTODY

In July, five doctors charged with the manslaughter of Stefano Cucchi, who died a week after his arrest in the prison wing of a Rome hospital in 2009, were acquitted in a second appeal trial ordered by the Supreme Court. A second investigation against the police officers involved in his arrest was looking at allegations that he may have died as a result of beatings while in custody.

JAMAICA

Jamaica
Head of state: Queen Elizabeth II, represented by Patrick Linton Allen
Head of government: Andrew Michael Holness (replaced Portia Simpson Miller in March)

Unlawful killings and extrajudicial executions continued. Violence against women and discrimination against lesbian, gay, bisexual, transgender and intersex (LGBTI) people persisted. Children continued to be detained in violation of international standards.

BACKGROUND

In February, the Jamaica Labour Party won the general election and Andrew Holness became Prime Minister.

Despite committing to the establishment of a national human rights institution, Jamaica had not established the mechanism by the end of the year.

Jamaica continued to have one of the highest homicide rates in the Americas.

POLICE AND SECURITY FORCES

In June, a Commission of Enquiry published its much-anticipated report into the events that took place in Western Kingston during the state of emergency, declared on 23 May 2010, which left at least 69 people dead. Almost 900 pages long, the report identified a number of cases of possible extrajudicial execution and produced a number of important recommendations for police reform.[1]

In an official response, the Jamaica Constabulary Force accepted a number of recommendations, such as committing to hold administrative reviews into the conduct of officers named in the Commissioners' report. However, the police continued to refuse to accept any responsibility for human rights violations or extrajudicial executions during the state of emergency. By the end of the year, the government had still not officially indicated how it would implement the recommendations of the Commissioners.

While the number of killings by police have significantly reduced in recent years, 111 people were killed by law enforcement officials in 2016, compared with 101 in 2015. Women whose relatives were killed by police, and their families, experienced pervasive police harassment and intimidation, and faced multiple barriers to accessing justice, truth and reparation.

VIOLENCE AGAINST WOMEN AND GIRLS

According to local NGOs, national legislation to address violence against women remained inadequate. For example, the Sexual Offences Act continued to narrowly define rape as non-consensual penile penetration of a woman's vagina by a man, and to protect against marital rape in certain circumstances only. By December, over 470 women and girls had reported rape during the year, according to the police.

Criminalization of women engaged in sex work continued to place them at risk of discrimination, arbitrary arrest and violence by the police.[2]

CHILDREN'S RIGHTS

The NGO Jamaicans for Justice reported that children were still being detained in police lockups for being "uncontrollable", often for illegal periods and in inhumane conditions.

RIGHTS OF LESBIAN, GAY, BISEXUAL, TRANSGENDER AND INTERSEX PEOPLE

There remained no legal protection against discrimination based on real or perceived sexual orientation or gender identity. Young LGBTI people continued to face bullying and harassment in the absence of legal protection. Consensual sex between men remained criminalized.

Between January and June, 23 people reported to the LGBTI rights NGO J-FLAG that they had been physically assaulted or attacked because of their real or perceived sexual orientation or gender identity.

A survey published by J-FLAG found deeply homophobic attitudes. For example, only 36% of Jamaicans surveyed said they would allow their gay child to continue to live at home. Almost 60% of respondents said they would harm an LGBTI person who approached them.

In June, the Attorney General used social media to criticize the US Embassy for flying a Pride flag after the killings of LGBTI people in a nightclub in Orlando, USA.

In August, for the second year in a row, J-FLAG held activities to celebrate Pride Week.

INTERNATIONAL JUSTICE

Jamaica again failed to ratify the Rome Statute of the International Criminal Court, signed in September 2000, nor had it adhered to the UN Convention against Torture or the International Convention for the Protection of All Persons from Enforced Disappearance.

---

1. Jamaica: State of Emergency 2010 – ten things the government must learn, and ten things it must do (AMR 38/4337/2016)

2. "I feel scared all the time": A Jamaican sex worker tells her story (News story 27 May 2016)

JAPAN

Japan
Head of government: **Shinzo Abe**

Progress towards a revision of the Constitution by the governing Liberal Democratic Party gained momentum after the party and its coalition members secured a two thirds majority in both houses of the parliament following upper house elections. There were fears that the revision could curtail human rights guarantees. Several municipalities and large corporations took measures to acknowledge same-sex unions

in a context of pervasive discrimination against lesbian, gay, bisexual, transgender and intersex (LGBTI) people. Executions of prisoners on death row continued.

RIGHTS OF LESBIAN, GAY, BISEXUAL, TRANSGENDER AND INTERSEX PEOPLE

More municipalities adopted written instruments to recognize same-sex unions. A growing number of mostly multinational corporations amended their internal rules to extend benefits to employees in same-sex unions. The major political parties pledged to campaign for LGBTI rights ahead of upper house elections in July.

Discrimination against LGBTI people continued, particularly in rural areas. A transgender woman filed a lawsuit against the state after she was refused hormone injections while imprisoned. Parents of a gay student at Hitotsubashi University in the capital, Tokyo, filed a lawsuit against the university and another student for accountability and compensation; their son had committed suicide after being "outed" and bullied.

DISCRIMINATION – ETHNIC MINORITIES

In May the parliament passed the first national law to condemn the advocacy of hatred ("hate speech") towards residents of overseas origin and their descendants. The legislation followed an increase in demonstrations promoting discrimination. Its effectiveness was questioned by civil society organizations and lawyers due to its narrow focus and the fact that it failed to legally ban "hate speech" or to set penalties. Later that month in Kanagawa prefecture, a court issued the first-ever provisional injunction preventing an anti-Korean activist from organizing a rally within a radius of 500m of the premises of an organization supporting ethnic Koreans.

Also in May, the Supreme Court dismissed a case brought against the police practice of blanket surveillance of Japan's Muslim community, including people perceived as Muslim. In 2010, 114 internal Tokyo Metropolitan Police Department documents

had been leaked online which included personal and financial information about Muslims labelled as suspected "terrorists" in Japan. The Court confirmed that there was a breach of the right to privacy, but left this type of intelligence gathering unchallenged.

VIOLENCE AGAINST WOMEN AND GIRLS

Following the bilateral agreement with the Republic of Korea (South Korea) in late 2015 on the military sexual slavery system before and during World War II, in July the South Korean government launched the Japanese-government-funded "Reconciliation and Healing Foundation". The Japanese government emphasized that the funds were not for reparations, in line with its stance that all such claims were settled during post-war negotiations. Civil society in South Korea continued to call for the 2015 agreement to be revoked, deeming it unconstitutional and invalid because survivors were not represented during the negotiations. While the Imperial Army had forced women from throughout the Asia-Pacific region into sexual slavery, by the end of the year Japan had not started negotiations with any other countries.

REFUGEES AND ASYLUM-SEEKERS

Authorities continued to reject a majority of asylum applications. The government reported that in 2015, of the 7,586 asylum applications filed (a 52% increase over the previous year), only 27 were granted. An asylum-seeker from Sri Lanka prepared to sue the state claiming deprivation of his right to seek asylum because he was deported the day after his claim was denied by the Ministry of Justice.

JUSTICE SYSTEM

The parliament amended a series of laws relating to criminal justice. For the first time the electronic recording of both police and prosecutor interrogations was required, although in a limited number of cases. The existing wiretap law was expanded and a plea bargaining system was introduced. The expansion of the use of wiretapping risked violating the right to freedom of expression.

In June, the Kumamoto District Court granted Koki Miyata a retrial due to doubts concerning the credibility of his "confessions". Koki Miyata had served a 13-year prison term for murder after being convicted in 1985.

FREEDOM OF ASSEMBLY

There were renewed protests in Okinawa after construction resumed at the US military base in Takae, marked by scuffles between riot police and protesters. Some protesters were injured during the dispersal.

JORDAN

Hashemite Kingdom of Jordan
Head of state: King Abdullah II bin al-Hussein
Head of government: Hani Mulki (replaced Abdullah Ensour in May)

The authorities continued to restrict the rights to freedom of expression, association and assembly, and detained and prosecuted critics and opponents under criminal defamation, blasphemy and anti-terrorism laws. Torture and other ill-treatment continued in detention centres. Trials before the State Security Court were unfair. Women faced discrimination in law and in practice and were inadequately protected against sexual and other violence. Migrant domestic workers were exploited and abused. Jordan hosted more than 655,000 refugees from Syria but sealed its borders to new arrivals in June. Courts continued to pass death sentences; there were no executions.

BACKGROUND

Jordan remained part of the Saudi Arabia-led international coalition engaged in armed conflict in Yemen (see Yemen entry).

In March, the government submitted a national human rights plan to the King, intended to phase in human rights improvements over a 10-year period.

In May, Parliament approved constitutional amendments empowering the King to directly appoint senior judicial, army, gendarmerie and General Intelligence Department (GID) officials. Parliamentary elections held in September used a proportional representation system for the first time.

There was continued insecurity along the border with Syria. In June, a bomb attack killed several Jordanian soldiers near an inter-border area in which some 70,000 Syrian refugees remained stranded in extreme hardship. Following the attack, the government sealed border crossing points, denying entry to refugees fleeing the conflict in Syria. In December, an attack by armed men near Karak killed 10 people, including three civilians; the armed group Islamic State (IS) claimed responsibility.

TORTURE AND OTHER ILL-TREATMENT

The government's 10-year national human rights plan listed objectives that included strengthening legal protections against torture and increasing prosecutions of and "sanctions" against perpetrators of torture, but it was not clear that any such reforms were made in 2016. Cases of police officers accused of torturing detainees continued to be handled by special police courts whose proceedings were neither independent nor transparent.

DEATHS IN CUSTODY

In January the Adaleh Centre for Human Rights Studies, an NGO based in the capital, Amman, reported that at least eight deaths in detention resulting from torture had occurred in the previous two months. In April the government's human rights co-ordinator said journalists and human rights activists would be permitted to attend some police court trials, including the trial of three officers accused of beating to death Omar al-Naser while he was in Criminal Investigation Department custody in September 2015. The trial was subject to lengthy adjournments without explanation and was not resolved by the end of 2016. Meanwhile, no information was made public about plans to prosecute police officers charged in connection with the beating to death in police custody of Abdullah Zu'bi in Irbid in 2015.

UNFAIR TRIALS

The authorities continued to prosecute alleged supporters of IS and other armed groups, as well as journalists and opposition political activists, under anti-terrorism and other laws before the State Security Court (SSC), a quasi-military court whose procedures failed to meet international fair trial standards.

Those tried included Adam al-Natour, a Polish Jordanian who received a four-year prison sentence after the SSC convicted him of "joining an armed group and terrorist organization" on the basis of a "confession" that he said he was forced to make under torture by GID interrogators who beat and electrocuted him during three weeks of incommunicado detention. Following this detention, he was brought before the SSC Prosecutor and made to sign a statement in Arabic, a language he could not read or understand.

ADMINISTRATIVE DETENTION

The authorities held tens of thousands of individuals under the 1954 Crime Prevention Law, which allows detentions for up to one year without charge or trial or any means of legal remedy.

FREEDOMS OF EXPRESSION, ASSOCIATION AND ASSEMBLY

The authorities restricted freedoms of expression, association and peaceful assembly and detained or prosecuted tens of journalists and critics under criminal defamation provisions of the Penal Code and anti-terrorism law provisions that criminalize criticism of foreign leaders or states. In July, the official National Centre for Human Rights reported an increase in arrests and SSC referrals of peaceful critics and protesters under these laws.

In May, the authorities released Dr Eyad Qunaibi, a university professor who had been sentenced to two years' imprisonment in December 2015 after the SSC convicted him of "undermining the political regime… or inciting opposition to it" for criticizing Jordan's relations with Israel in a Facebook post.

On 25 September, a gunman shot dead journalist Nahed Hattar outside the court in Amman where he was being tried for posting a satirical cartoon on Facebook that the authorities deemed offensive to Islam. He had been held for almost a month in pre-trial detention before a court allowed his release on bail. Jordan's official news agency said the alleged perpetrator was arrested at the scene of the killing; the case was later referred to the SSC on charges including murder.

Draft amendments to the Societies Law proposed in March, if implemented, would increase government powers to prevent the legal registration of NGOs or their operations on national security or public order grounds, and would deny them access to international funding without any justification. The amendments had not been enacted by the end of the year.

WOMEN'S RIGHTS

Women continued to face discrimination in law and practice, and were inadequately protected against so-called honour crimes and other forms of gender-based violence.

In April, a parliamentary legal committee endorsed proposed amendments to Article 308 of the Penal Code that would end the provision allowing rapists to avoid prosecution if they marry their victims. However, it would keep the provision when the victim is aged between 15 and 18. At the end of the year, the amendments had still to be enacted.

In July the CEDAW Committee requested information from the government ahead of its scheduled 2017 review of Jordan. Among other things, they requested details of any government plans to amend the Citizenship Law to allow Jordanian women married to foreign spouses to pass their nationality to their children and husbands on the same basis as Jordanian men, and to allow their families increased access to medical care, education and other services. The Committee also requested information on government plans to amend Article 308 and other Penal Code provisions that allow rapists to escape prosecution and mitigate penalties for perpetrators of so-called honour crimes.

MIGRANT WORKERS' RIGHTS

Migrant domestic workers continued to face exploitation and abuse. In February the Amman-based NGO Tamkeen reported that 80,000 women migrant domestic workers were excluded from the protection of labour laws and exposed to violence and other abuse by employers. The UN Special Rapporteur on trafficking in persons reported during a visit to Jordan that migrant women employed as domestic workers who fled abusive employers were at risk of trafficking for sexual exploitation. The Special Rapporteur also reported that refugee women and girls from Syria were trafficked for sexual exploitation.

REFUGEES AND ASYLUM-SEEKERS

Jordan hosted more than 655,000 refugees from Syria, including 16,000 Palestinians, as well as almost 60,000 refugees from other countries including Iraq, Yemen and Somalia, and 2.1 million long-term Palestinian refugees.

By the end of the year, there were 75,000 Syrian refugees stranded in harsh conditions in the "berm" desert area between the Rukban and Hadalat border crossings with Syria. The government denied most of them entry into Jordan on security grounds but allowed around 12,000 to enter Jordan in May, confining them to Village 5, a fenced-off area of Azraq refugee camp. On 21 June the authorities sealed Jordan's border with Syria after a suicide bomb attack, thereby cutting off regular humanitarian access to refugees in the berm. Jordan has tightened border controls since 2012. The authorities also deported several refugees on alleged security grounds.

By July, Jordan had received only 45% of the funding it required from the international community, according to the UN, to meet the needs of refugees from Syria. Around 86% of Syrians in urban areas of Jordan were

reported to be living below the poverty line with limited access to services.

DEATH PENALTY

Courts imposed death sentences; there were no executions. In February, a government spokesperson denied media reports that the authorities planned to execute 13 prisoners.

KAZAKHSTAN

Republic of Kazakhstan
Head of state: **Nursultan Nazarbayev**
Head of government: **Bakytzhan Sagintayev (replaced Karim Massimov in September)**

The rights to freedom of expression, of peaceful assembly and of association remained restricted. The authorities used administrative detention to stop people from participating in unauthorized protests and criminal prosecution to target social media users and independent journalists. Harsher penalties for NGO leaders – who were a separate category of offenders in the Administrative Offences and Criminal Codes – were used for the first time. New cases of torture and other ill-treatment against suspects and prisoners were reported. The large number of migrant workers in the country faced exploitation and restricted access to health care and education. One person was sentenced to death.

FREEDOM OF ASSEMBLY

Organizing or participating in a peaceful public assembly without prior authorization from the authorities was a violation under both the Administrative Offences Code and the Criminal Code, punishable by heavy fines or up to 75 days' detention. Providing "assistance" to "illegal" assemblies, including by "means of communication", including social media, constituted a criminal offence.

In April and May, "unsanctioned" demonstrations took place across Kazakhstan as people protested peacefully against proposed changes to the Land Code to allow unused agricultural land to be leased to foreign citizens for up to 25 years. Authorities responded by blocking access to main squares and thoroughfares, and by using administrative detention to stop would-be protesters from participating.

Further Land Code protests were planned for 21 May in the capital Astana, Almaty, the largest city, and in other towns. Between 17 and 20 May, at least 34 people were arrested and charged as "organizers" of the protests after they had announced on social media their intention to participate or provided information about the demonstrations. Most were sentenced to 10-15 days' detention under the Administrative Code.

On 21 May, in Almaty, Astana and other towns, police blocked access to the areas where the demonstrations were supposed to take place. Police detained up to 500 people in Almaty, and smaller numbers elsewhere. At police stations, the detainees had to sign statements that they had participated in an unsanctioned public meeting and give their fingerprints. They were released after a few hours. On 21 May, at least 48 journalists were detained while attempting to cover the protests, according to freedom of expression NGO Adil Soz. All were released within a few hours.

FREEDOM OF EXPRESSION
Social media
Prosecutors used the Criminal Code to target activists for posts on social media.

In January, Yermek Narymbaev and Serikzhan Mambetalin were sentenced to prison terms for posting on Facebook extracts of an unpublished book which was considered offensive to ethnic Kazakhs. Their sentences were suspended on appeal. Also in January, blogger Igor Sychev's five-year prison sentence for posting a survey on another social media site on whether his town should become part of Russia was upheld on appeal.

On 28 November, prisoners of conscience Maks Bokaev and Talgat Ayan were convicted on criminal charges of "inciting social, national, clan, racial, class, or religious discord", "dissemination of information

known to be false" and organizing unsanctioned meetings and demonstrations. Maks Bokaev and Talgat Ayan were both sentenced to five years' imprisonment. Their posts on Facebook and other social media platforms in April and May about the proposed changes to the Land Code and the ongoing protests formed part of the charges against them. In July, folk singer Zhanat Esentaev was convicted under the Criminal Code for posts on Facebook in relation to the Land Code protests and sentenced to two and a half years' probation.

Criminal prosecution of journalists
In May, Guzyal Baidalinova, journalist and owner of the Nakanune.kz independent news portal, was convicted of "dissemination of information known to be false" and sentenced to one and a half years' imprisonment which was converted to a suspended sentence in July. The outlet had published articles on the activities of a leading commercial bank. Nakanune.kz had been critical of the authorities.

In October, Seitkazy Mataev and his son Aset Mataev were sentenced to six and five years' imprisonment respectively on charges of embezzlement and tax evasion. Seitkazy Mataev was the chair of the Union of Journalists of Kazakhstan and the chair of the National Press Club; Aset Mataev was the General Director of KazTAG news agency. The Union of Journalists had provided support to independent journalism.

Internet
In January, changes to the Law on Communications came into force. They required internet users to download and install a "national security certificate". The certificate allowed authorities to scan communications sent over the HTTPS protocol and to block access to individual webpages with content which the authorities judged to be illegal.

FREEDOM OF ASSOCIATION
NGOs
Leading or participating in an unregistered organization was an offence under articles in the Criminal and Administrative Offences Codes. "Leaders" of associations were treated as a separate category of offenders, providing for harsher penalties. The definition of "leader" was broad, potentially including any active member of an NGO or other civic association. These clauses were used for the first time in 2016, including in the criminal cases against Maks Bokaev and Talgat Ayan.

Legislative changes introduced at the end of 2015 mandated the creation of a central state database of NGOs. Failure to regularly supply accurate information for the database could lead to fines or a temporary ban on activities. In February, the NGO International Legal Initiative in Almaty challenged the provision in a civil court, but lost the case. Soon afterwards, the NGO faced a lengthy tax inspection. Civil society activists were concerned that this new law placed overly broad requirements on NGOs and constrained their activities.

Religious groups
By law, religious groups were required to register with the Ministry of Justice. Membership of an unregistered religious group was an offence under the Administrative Offences Code. There were restrictions on where religious groups could hold services, with steep fines for meeting or distributing religious literature in unsanctioned premises. According to the NGO Forum 18, which promotes religious freedom, groups were fined for meeting to worship in each other's homes. Seven Baptists in East Kazakhstan Region were fined in August.

TORTURE AND OTHER ILL-TREATMENT
The practice of torture and other ill-treatment continued. The Coalition of NGOs of Kazakhstan against Torture registered 163 new cases of torture and other ill-treatment between January and November 2016.

Article 419 of the Criminal Code ("false reporting of a crime") was invoked by prosecutors against those whose allegations of torture or other ill-treatment were investigated and deemed to be unfounded.

In September, a former prison officer was convicted of the rape and torture of a woman prisoner in Almaty Region and sentenced to nine years' imprisonment. The woman had reported being gang-raped and beaten by four prison officers; she gave birth as a result of the rape. The prosecution of the other three prison officers was dropped due to lack of evidence. The one conviction secured was based on a paternity test that showed that the former prison officer had fathered the child. The case drew attention to the wider issue of sexual violence against women prisoners in places of detention.

MIGRANT WORKERS' RIGHTS
Labour migration to Kazakhstan, mainly from neighbouring Kyrgyzstan, Tajikistan and Uzbekistan, was predominantly irregular. Officials estimated that there were between 300,000 and 1.5 million migrant workers in the country, and that the number of people arriving for work in 2016 was much higher than in 2015. Most migrant workers worked without written contracts and were vulnerable to exploitation, including having to work long hours with little or no rest time, low and irregularly paid wages, and dangerous working conditions, particularly in the agriculture and construction sectors. Many depended on their employers for housing, which was often overcrowded and of poor quality. Some employers also confiscated migrant workers' passports, leaving them in circumstances that amounted to forced labour. Migrant workers without permanent residency were unable to access free health care and faced problems enrolling their children in schools.

Kazakhstan had not ratified the International Convention on the Protection of the Rights of All Migrant Workers and Members of Their Families.

DEATH PENALTY

Kazakhstan was abolitionist for ordinary crimes, but retained the death penalty for 17 crimes that constituted terrorism-related offences or war crimes. In November, Ruslan Kulekbaev was convicted on terrorism-related charges of killing 10 people in Almaty in July and sentenced to death. He was the sixth person to be sentenced to death since President Nazarbayev signed a moratorium on executions in 2003. Since then all death sentences have been commuted to life imprisonment.

KENYA

Republic of Kenya
Head of state and government: **Uhuru Muigai Kenyatta**

Security forces carried out enforced disappearances, extrajudicial executions and torture with impunity, killing at least 122 people by October. Some abuses were committed by security agencies in the context of counter-terror operations, others by unaccountable police officers and other security agencies. Police used excessive and lethal force to disperse demonstrators calling for fair election practices. Political opposition, anti-corruption groups and other civil society activists, as well as journalists and bloggers, were harassed. Families in informal settlements and marginalized communities were forcibly evicted from their homes.

BACKGROUND

Corruption remained rife. President Kenyatta asked almost a quarter of his cabinet secretaries to resign after the state's Ethics and Anti-Corruption Commission (EACC) accused them of corruption. Some faced trial for corruption, others appeared before oversight institutions to answer allegations of corruption. According to the EACC, at least 30% of GDP – equivalent to about US$6 billion – is being lost annually to corruption.

Local governments were also accused of corruption, largely by inflating costs in procurement processes. The Ministries of Health and of Devolution and Planning were under investigation for alleged misappropriation of funds, among other things.

In May, civil society organizations launched Kura Yangu, Sauti Yangu, a movement to ensure legitimate, fair and well-organized elections due in August 2017. Soon after, the opposition Coalition for Reform and Democracy (CORD) organized weekly demonstrations over what it considered the bias of the Independent Electoral and Boundaries Commission (IEBC). On 3 August, IEBC commissioners resigned, ending months of protests over the election process. On 14 September, the Election Laws (Amendment) Bill came into force, inaugurating the process of recruiting new IEBC commissioners. However, the recruitment of new commissioners was delayed after the recruiting panel postponed indefinitely the recruitment of the Chairperson after five interviewed candidates failed to meet the requirements. The delay will negatively impact the electoral preparations timeline.

ABUSES BY ARMED GROUPS

Al-Shabaab, the Somali-based armed group, continued to carry out attacks in Kenya.

On 25 October, for example, in the northeastern town of Mandera, at least 12 people were killed in an attack by al-Shabaab on a guesthouse hosting members of a theatre group.

COUNTER-TERROR AND SECURITY

In the context of counter-terrorism operations targeting al-Shabaab, security agencies were implicated in human rights violations, including extrajudicial executions, enforced disappearances and torture. Despite an increase in reported cases of these violations, meaningful investigations were not carried out with a view to ensuring accountability.

EXTRAJUDICIAL EXECUTIONS

Police and other security agencies carried out extrajudicial executions as well as enforced disappearances, and torture.[1]

Willie Kimani, a lawyer with a legal aid charity, his client Josphat Mwendwa and their taxi driver Joseph Muiruri, were abducted on 23 June at an unknown location. On 1 July, their bodies were found dumped in a river in Machakos County, eastern Kenya; post mortems showed they had been tortured. Josphat Mwendwa, a motorcycle taxi driver, had accused a member of the Administration Police (AP) of attempted murder after the officer shot him in the arm during a routine traffic check. The officer then charged him with a traffic offence to intimidate him into dropping the complaint. The abduction happened after Willie Kimani and Josphat Mwendwa left Mavoko law courts in Machakos County after attending a hearing in the traffic offence case. On 21 September, four AP officers – Fredrick ole Leliman, Stephen Cheburet Morogo, Sylvia Wanjiku Wanjohi and Leonard Maina Mwangi – were found guilty of murdering the three men. The officers were remanded in custody awaiting sentencing at the end of the year.

The killings of the three men triggered protests and mobilized human rights organizations, the media and legal and other professional organizations across the country to demand action against enforced disappearance and extrajudicial executions.

Job Omariba, a nurse in the eastern town of Meru was reported to have gone missing in Nairobi on 21 August. His body was discovered at Machakos mortuary on 30 August. Later that day, the Special Crime Prevention Unit arrested three police officers on suspicion of his abduction and murder.

On 29 August, two policemen walked into Mwingi Level 4 Hospital and shot dead Ngandi Malia Musyemi, a hawker, after he reported to police that he had been carjacked. His sister witnessed the killing. Officers from Nairobi, Machakos and Embu were assigned to investigate the killing.

Kenya does not have an official database of police killings or enforced disappearances. According to Haki Africa, a human rights group, there were 78 extrajudicial executions and enforced disappearances in Mombasa County in the first eight months of 2016. The *Daily Nation* newspaper documented 21 cases of police killings during the same period.

FREEDOM OF ASSEMBLY

The police used excessive and lethal force to disperse protesters in Nairobi and other towns during demonstrations against the IEBC.

On 16 May, a male protester in Nairobi was shot and injured in a confrontation with police as residents from the informal settlement of Kibera tried to march to the electoral commission's offices.

On 23 May, police used batons, tear gas, water cannons and, in some cases, live ammunition to disperse protesters marching towards the electoral commission's office. A video showed three policemen kicking and beating a protester after he fell down.[2] The same day, at least two people were killed and 53 injured during a demonstration in the western city of Kisumu.

FREEDOM OF EXPRESSION

The authorities continued to curtail freedom of expression by intimidating and harassing journalists, bloggers and other members of civil society, particularly by using the ambiguity of the Kenya Information and Communication Act. At least 13 people were prosecuted under Section 29 of the law, which includes vague terms such as "grossly offensive" and "indecent". On 19 April, the High Court found that Section 29 was in breach of the Constitution's provisions on the right to freedom of expression.

Mbuvi Kasina, a journalist, continued to face six counts of misuse of a licensed telecommunication system for questioning the expenditure of Kitui South Constituency Development Funds.

On 27 September, police harassed, attacked and destroyed the camera of

Duncan Wanga, a K24 TV journalist and cameraman, while he was covering a demonstration in the western city of Eldoret.

On 1 October, the Deputy President threatened to sue activist Boniface Mwangi after he posted a tweet linking the Deputy President to the murder in May of businessman Jacob Juma. The Deputy President's lawyers demanded that the activist offer an apology, retraction and clarification within seven days. Boniface Mwangi's lawyers welcomed the suit, citing ICC cases and allegations made by a Member of Parliament about Jacob Juma's killing to show that the Deputy President's reputation had not been injured by the tweet.

REFUGEES AND ASYLUM-SEEKERS

In May, shortly after it revoked the assumed refugee status of Somalis who had fled to Kenya, the government announced it would close Dadaab refugee camp on 30 November. To justify the move, it cited national security concerns and the need for the international community to share the responsibility of hosting the refugees. Dadaab is home to over 280,000 refugees, of whom 260,000 are from Somalia. The short timeframe, government statements about the repatriation process and the lack of security in Somalia raised concerns that the repatriation of Somalis would be forced, in violation of international law, and put at risk the lives of tens of thousands of people.[3] According to UNHCR, the UN refugee agency, by mid-October, 27,000 Somali refugees had returned to Somalia from Dadaab in 2016, nominally voluntarily. On 16 November, the authorities stated they would extend the deadline for the closure of Dadaab by six months.

In May, the government disbanded the Department of Refugee Affairs (DPA), created in accordance with the 2006 Refugee Act, and established instead the Refugee Affairs Secretariat. The Secretariat is not established by law and functions at the behest of the Ministry of Interior and National Government Co-ordination.

RIGHTS OF LESBIAN, GAY, BISEXUAL, TRANSGENDER AND INTERSEX PEOPLE

On 16 June, the High Court in Mombasa upheld the legality of anal examinations of men suspected of engaging in same-sex sexual activity. Two men had petitioned the Court to declare unconstitutional anal examinations as well as HIV and Hepatitis B tests they had been forced to undergo in February 2015. The Court ruled that there had been no violation of rights or breach of the law. Forced anal examinations and forced HIV testing violate the right to privacy and the prohibition of torture and other ill-treatment under international law. The High Court's ruling breached several human rights treaties ratified by Kenya.

HOUSING RIGHTS – FORCED EVICTIONS

Families living in informal settlements and marginalized communities continued to be forcibly evicted in the context of large infrastructure development projects.

In Deep Sea informal settlement in Nairobi, 349 families were forcibly evicted on 8 July to allow construction of the road linking Thika Super Highway to Westlands Ring Road. The eviction took place without notice and while consultation was taking place between the community and the Kenya Urban Roads Authority (KURA). Residents were attacked during the evictions by armed youth ferried in by government construction and private vehicles. Armed police officers were present and threatened to shoot residents if they resisted eviction. KURA and the EU, which is funding the road, had assured Deep Sea residents they would not be forcibly evicted.

KURA took responsibility for the violations of the rights of residents during a meeting with Deep Sea community leaders. In a letter to the community, it agreed to urgently put in place corrective measures, including to restore the sanitation facilities, facilitate reconstruction of people's houses, and provide humanitarian assistance such as cooking facilities and blankets for those who had lost everything. KURA and Deep Sea residents agreed that permanent residents would each receive 20,000 Kenya shillings (around US$200) and that this would not be recognized as covering losses incurred in the forced eviction.

Representatives of the Sengwer Indigenous People reported that Kenya Forest Service repeatedly burned houses in Embobut forest. Local courts heard cases concerning Sengwer people who had been arrested for being in the forest, despite a pending court case brought by Sengwer to challenge their eviction and a 2013 injunction issued by the High Court of Eldoret to stop arrests and evictions while the legal challenge was being considered.

1. Kenya: Set up judicial inquiry into hundreds of enforced disappearances and killings (News story, 30 August)

2. Kenya: Investigate police crackdown against protesters (News story, 17 May)

3. Kenya: Government officials coercing refugees back to war-torn Somalia (News story, 15 November)

KOREA (DEMOCRATIC PEOPLE'S REPUBLIC OF)

Democratic People's Republic of Korea
Head of state: **Kim Jong-un**
Head of government: Pak Pong-ju

Citizens of the Democratic People's Republic of Korea (North Korea) continued to suffer violations of most aspects of their human rights. North Koreans and foreign nationals were arbitrarily detained and sentenced after unfair trials for criminal "offences" that were not internationally recognized. Severe restrictions on the right to freedom of expression continued. Thousands of North Koreans were sent by the authorities to work abroad, often under harsh conditions. The number of North Koreans fleeing their country and arriving in the Republic of Korea (South Korea) increased.

BACKGROUND

The government tested nuclear weapons twice, once in January and again in September, increasing tension between North Korea and the international community. The UN increased its economic sanctions on North Korea as a result, leading to fears from inside the country and from foreign experts of heightened food shortages and a further deterioration in living standards. Experts considered the possible economic impact to be a motivation for more people leaving the country, but the risk of political purges in the form of imprisonment and reported executions among the ruling elite was seen as a key contributing factor.

The Korean Workers' Party held its congress in May for the first time in 36 years. Journalists from international media were invited to the country for the occasion, but operated under strict restrictions and were not allowed to cover congress meetings.

Severe floods in August killed at least 138 people and displaced 69,000 others, according to the World Food Programme. The government asked for humanitarian assistance including food, shelter, water and sanitation but international response was minimal due to concerns expressed by potential donors about the country's nuclear programme.

FREEDOM OF MOVEMENT

A total of 1,414 people left North Korea and arrived in South Korea. The figure increased by 11% from 2015, and rose for the first time since 2011 when Kim Jong-un came to power.

Along with reports of ordinary North Koreans leaving, media in South Korea and Japan reported several high profile government officials deserting their posts and seeking asylum. The South Korean government confirmed in August the arrival of Thae Young-ho, North Korea's deputy ambassador to the UK and his family.

Thirteen restaurant workers, sent by the government to work in Ningbo, China, flew directly from China to South Korea in April (see Korea (Republic of) entry). On their arrival in South Korea, the North Korean authorities claimed that the 12 women in the group were abducted from China and taken to South Korea. According to a media interview with their former colleagues arranged in Pyongyang by the North Korean government, the workers had their passports taken away from them while in China, which would have restricted their ability to travel freely.[1]

Interviews with North Koreans who left the country as well as media reports said that the government had increased its surveillance efforts to prevent people from leaving via the Chinese-Korean border. Those who successfully left continued to be at risk of detention, imprisonment, forced labour, and torture and other ill-treatment if arrested and returned from China.

MIGRANT WORKERS' RIGHTS

The government continued to dispatch through state-owned enterprises at least 50,000 people to work in some 40 countries including Angola, China, Kuwait, Qatar and Russia in various sectors including medicine, construction, forestry and catering. Workers did not receive wages directly from employers, but through the North Korean government after significant deductions. Most workers were deprived of information about international or domestic labour laws, and often lacked access in the host countries to any government agencies and other organizations monitoring compliance with or offering assistance in claiming labour rights.

These workers were frequently subjected to excessive working hours and were vulnerable to occupational accidents and diseases. Poland announced in June that it was no longer allowing workers from North Korea to enter the country following media reports of a fatal shipyard accident involving a North Korean worker in 2014. Malta made a similar announcement in July, and denied visa extensions to existing North Korean workers.

ARBITRARY ARRESTS AND DETENTIONS

The authorities sentenced people, including foreign nationals, to long prison terms after unfair trials. Frederick Otto Warmbier, a US student, was convicted of "subversion"; he only admitted stealing a propaganda banner. He was sentenced to 15 years' hard labour in March; he was not given consular access for at least six months. Kim Dong-chul, a 62-year-old US citizen born in South Korea, was sentenced to 10 years' hard labour in April for "spying"; the authorities failed to provide details about the alleged spying activities. The sentences were imposed as new UN sanctions on North Korea were authorized earlier in the year, and before the Korean Workers' Party Congress in May when there was increased international attention on North Korea.[2] Up to 120,000 people remained in detention in the four known political prison camps, where they were subjected to systematic, widespread and gross human rights violations such as forced labour, and torture and other ill-treatment – some amounting to crimes against humanity. Many of those held in these camps had not been convicted of any internationally recognized criminal offence but were detained for "guilt-by-association", simply for being related to individuals deemed threatening to the state.

FREEDOM OF EXPRESSION

The authorities continued to impose severe restrictions on the right to freedom of expression, including the right to seek, receive and impart information regardless of national borders. The government persisted in restricting access to outside sources of information; there were no national independent newspapers, media or civil society organizations.

The professional activities of the very few international journalists allowed into the country remained severely restricted. BBC journalists visiting North Korea ahead of the Korean Workers' Party Congress in May were briefly detained incommunicado, interrogated and expelled from the country because the government found the stories they produced highlighting aspects of everyday life in Pyongyang to be 'disrespectful'. Agence France-Presse became one of the very few foreign media companies to operate in North Korea when it opened a Pyongyang office in September.

Almost everyone was denied internet and international mobile phone services. North Koreans who lived close to the Chinese border took significant risks in using smuggled mobile phones connected to Chinese networks in order to make contact with individuals abroad. People who did not own such phones had to pay exorbitant fees to brokers in order to make international calls. The use of smuggled mobile phones to connect to Chinese mobile networks exposed everyone involved to increased surveillance, as well as the risk of arrest and detention on various charges, including espionage.[3]

The existing computer network remained available to a very limited number of people, providing access to domestic websites and email services only. In September, the misconfiguration of a server in North Korea revealed to the world that the network contained only 28 websites, all controlled by official bodies or state-owned enterprises.

ENFORCED DISAPPEARANCES

In February, the authorities stopped all investigations into abductions of Japanese citizens, reversing the 2014 bilateral agreement to investigate cases. Media reports said that the decision followed Japan's reinstating previously eased sanctions after North Korea's nuclear weapons tests in January. North Korea had previously admitted that its security agents abducted 12 Japanese nationals during the 1970s and 1980s.

---

1. South Korea: End secrecy surrounding North Korean restaurant workers (ASA 25/4413/2016)

2. North Korea: U.S. citizen hard labour sentence shrouded in secrecy (News story, 29 April)

3. Connection denied: Restrictions on mobile phones and outside information in North Korea (ASA 24/3373/2016)

KOREA (REPUBLIC OF)

Republic of Korea
Head of state and government: **Park Geun-hye**

Restrictions on the rights to freedom of peaceful assembly and expression persisted. Asylum-seekers were detained and conscientious objectors were imprisoned for exercising their human rights. The detention in a state facility of 13 restaurant workers originally from the Democratic People's Republic of Korea (North Korea) called into question the legality of the existing settlement support process for North Koreans arriving in the country.
The government failed to prevent private companies from hindering lawful trade union activity, and only belatedly followed up on deaths and adverse health effects resulting from the use of harmful products. The decision of the government to proceed with the deployment of the US-built Terminal High Altitude Area Defence (THAAD) anti-missile system triggered strong opposition from domestic groups, as well as condemnation from China and North Korea.
Lawmakers voted to impeach President Park Geun-hye on 9 December, which must be confirmed through a decision by the Constitutional Court.

FREEDOM OF ASSEMBLY

Authorities continued to restrict people from exercising their right to freedom of peaceful assembly, often under the pretext of protecting public order. By the end of the year, the authorities had not completed an investigation into the excessive use of force by police against largely peaceful protesters during the anti-government "People's Rally" in November 2015, nor held accountable any officers or commanding authorities responsible. On 25 September, Baek Nam-gi, a veteran rural activist critically injured after he was hit by a water cannon during the demonstrations, died after spending 10 months in a coma.[1]

The delay in investigating Baek Nam-gi's injuries was in sharp contrast to the conviction of Han Sang-gyun, president of the Korean Confederation of Trade Unions, and co-organizer of several demonstrations, including union participation in the People's Rally. Han Sang-gyun was sentenced to five years in prison on 4 July on charges including inciting illegal acts among a small number of protesters during the largely peaceful demonstrations. The sentence was reduced to three years on 13 December on appeal.[2]

In another instance of what critics of the government saw as an attempt to limit freedom of assembly, the Korean Navy filed a civil lawsuit against 116 individuals and five groups protesting against the construction of a naval base on Jeju island. In March, the Navy sought 3.4 billion KRW (US$2.9 million) as compensation for losses incurred from construction delays allegedly caused by protests that had been ongoing for eight years.

FREEDOM OF EXPRESSION

The National Assembly passed an anti-terrorism law in March after the opposition staged a nine-day filibuster due to concerns over what they saw as its potential for abuse. The law greatly expanded the power of the state to conduct surveillance of communications and to collect personal information on people suspected of links with terrorism.

The authorities undercut press freedom through increasingly heavy interference with news reporting, especially by television broadcasters. In July, the National Union of Media Workers denounced an array of tactics used by the government to influence news coverage, including nominating individuals close to the government to the boards of influential, publicly owned media corporations and launching disciplinary actions against individual journalists as a warning to others. These tactics were evident during the reporting of the Sewol Ferry disaster in 2014 and the discussions on the THAAD system.

The authorities continued to use the vaguely worded National Security Law to intimidate and imprison people exercising their right to freedom of expression. Individuals arrested for alleged violations of the law included members of the Corean Alliance for an Independent Reunification and Democracy (CAIRD), which was forced to disband as a direct result of repeated repressions. Kim Hye-young, a CAIRD activist suffering from thyroid cancer, was sentenced to two years' imprisonment in January after being arrested in July 2015 during a peaceful protest.[3] Yang Ko-eun, another CAIRD representative, was prohibited from travelling overseas in June to speak about the conditions of her fellow members, and was arrested in September.

CORPORATE ACCOUNTABILITY

In May, the UK company Reckitt Benckiser accepted full responsibility for the deaths of at least 95 people, as well as for adverse health effects suffered by hundreds and potentially thousands more. These were linked to a humidifier sterilizer product sold by its Korean subsidiary over a period of many years. Following a country visit the previous year, the UN Special Rapporteur on human rights and hazardous substances concluded in an August report that this and other companies had failed to conduct a reasonable degree of human rights due diligence with respect to the safety of the chemicals they sold to consumers. He recommended that Reckitt Benckiser ensure that all victims be identified and receive compensation.

WORKERS' RIGHTS

Businesses, particularly those in the construction sector, continued to hinder union activities among employees and workers employed by subcontractors without being sanctioned by the government. According to a June report by the UN Working Group on the issue of human rights and transnational corporations and other business enterprises, some companies had set up so-called "yellow unions" that were not independent and did not meet standards for collective bargaining. Other companies hired legal consultants to design "union-busting" measures, or private security firms to harass union members.

REFUGEES AND ASYLUM-SEEKERS

The National Immigration Service detained more than 100 asylum-seekers for months at Incheon International Airport, including 28 men from Syria whom the Incheon District Court ruled in June should be released and allowed to apply for asylum. Dozens of asylum-seekers from other countries such as Egypt remained detained at the airport under inhumane conditions and without basic necessities and services, including beds, adequate showers and sanitation facilities, food acceptable for religious beliefs, or the opportunity to exercise outdoors.

ARBITRARY ARRESTS AND DETENTIONS

Thirteen North Korean restaurant workers who had been working in Ningbo, China, were detained for four months in a facility run by the National Intelligence Service after their arrival from China in April (see Korea (Democratic People's Republic of) entry). Relatives said in media interviews facilitated by the North Korean government that the workers had been involuntarily taken to South Korea. The individuals were not allowed to contact their families or lawyers of their choosing, nor to talk to anybody outside the facility about their reasons for travelling to South Korea. This undermined a review of the lawfulness of their detention by an independent and impartial judicial power and raised questions about the government's enforced settlement support process for arrivals from North Korea.[4]

CONSCIENTIOUS OBJECTORS

Approximately 400 conscientious objectors to military service remained in prison solely for exercising their right to freedom of thought, conscience and religion, which also constituted a case of arbitrary detention under international law. Those who had completed their jail terms for refusing to perform military service in the absence of any alternatives continued to face economic and social disadvantages due to these criminal records. Following legal amendments which came into force in 2015, on 20 December the government published the names and personal information of 237 conscientious objectors on the website of the Military Manpower Administration.

The Constitutional Court was still examining the legality of conscientious objections in cases brought between 2012 and 2015. District courts ruled in favour of four men refusing military duty, adding to the six men receiving acquittals in 2015. Appeals by the prosecution, however, resulted in the overturning of two of the acquittals. In October, an appeals court acquitted two other men who had appealed against the guilty verdicts handed down by the court of first instance.

1. Urgent action: Protester seriously injured by water cannon (ASA 25/4503/2016)

2. South Korea: Five year sentence against union leader a chilling blow to peaceful protest (News story, 4 July)

3. South Korea: Woman denied medical help on hunger strike (ASA 25/4150/2016)

4. South Korea: End secrecy surrounding North Korean restaurant workers (ASA 25/4413/2016)

KUWAIT

State of Kuwait
Head of state: **Sheikh Sabah al-Ahmad al-Jaber al-Sabah**
Head of government: **Sheikh Jaber al-Mubarak al-Hamad al-Sabah**

The authorities further curtailed freedom of expression and prosecuted and imprisoned government critics under criminal defamation laws; some were prisoners of conscience. Members of the Bidun minority continued to face discrimination and were denied citizenship rights. Migrant workers remained inadequately protected against exploitation and abuse. Courts handed down new death sentences; no executions were reported.

BACKGROUND

Parliament approved a new law lowering the age of minors from 18 to 16 years on 31 December 2015. When enacted in January 2017, anyone arrested at the age of 16 or 17 would be tried as an adult, and in some cases could face the death penalty.

The UN Committee against Torture considered Kuwait's third periodic report in July.[1] The Committee subsequently expressed concern about proposed amendments to the Code of Criminal Procedures that would double to four days the period for which police can hold detained suspects without bringing them before a judge and increase pre-trial detention on remand from 10 days to a maximum of 21 days.

In July, after reviewing Kuwait's third report on its application of the ICCPR, the UN Human Rights Committee presented recommendations to the government, including on reform of criminal blasphemy and insult laws; criminalization of domestic violence, including marital rape; and action to address Bidun statelessness.[2]

Kuwait remained part of the Saudi Arabia-led international coalition engaged in armed conflict in Yemen (see Yemen entry).

FREEDOMS OF EXPRESSION AND ASSEMBLY

The authorities tightened restrictions on freedom of expression. A new cybercrime law that took effect in January further restricted online expression, penalizing peaceful criticism of the government, the judiciary and others with up to 10 years' imprisonment.

Also in January, Parliament approved an electronic media law regulating all online publications, including electronic news services, online newspapers, television, social media and blogs, placing them under a legal obligation to obtain a government licence to operate. The authorities began implementing the new law in July. In February, the Law on Print and Publications was amended to cover online publications. In June, a new law came into force prohibiting anyone with a confirmed conviction on charges of insulting God, the prophets or the Emir, from running for Parliament, in effect barring some government critics from being elected.

Abdulhamid Dashti, a Shi'a opposition MP, was stripped of his parliamentary immunity in March. He then went abroad but faced prosecution and separate trials on an array of charges – including some arising from his peaceful criticism of the governments of Bahrain and Saudi Arabia in social and other media – and possible prison sentences totalling over 40 years. In December, an appeal court overturned his acquittal in one case and imposed a 10-year sentence. He was unable to lodge an appeal while he remains outside Kuwait.

Musallam al-Barrak, a former MP and leading government critic, continued to serve a two-year prison term for criticizing the government in a speech and faced separate trials on other charges. In November the Appeal Court upheld the suspended prison sentences of 13 people for publicizing or reciting extracts from Musallam al-Barrak's speech.

In February, the Appeal Court confirmed the one-year prison sentence followed by expulsion from Kuwait imposed on Bidun rights activist Abdulhakim al-Fadhli in 2015 for participating in a peaceful "illegal gathering". He was arrested in April to serve his sentence, which was confirmed in May by the Cassation Court. In June, on appeal, the Misdemeanours Cassation Court ordered his release pending review, and in September it upheld the initial verdict. The authorities released Abdulhakim al-Fadhli in August after he completed a three-month prison term in a separate case but he handed himself to the authorities in September following the Misdemeanours Cassation Court's verdict.

COUNTER-TERROR AND SECURITY

The number of terrorism-related arrests and trials increased. Courts sentenced at least two defendants to death and others to prison terms. A 2015 law requiring all citizens and residents of Kuwait to provide the authorities with samples of their DNA came into force in July, despite local and international calls for its amendment due to it being disproportionate and a violation of the right to privacy. Under the law, anyone who does not comply or has no valid excuse for failing to provide a sample faces up to one year in prison and/or a fine of up to 10,000 Kuwaiti dinars (US$33,150).

In May, the Court of Cassation confirmed the death sentence of one man convicted of perpetrating the July 2015 bombing of the Imam Sadiq Mosque in Kuwait City, but reduced the sentence of his co-accused to 15 years' imprisonment. The Court failed to exclude statements that were alleged to have been extracted under torture and other ill-treatment as evidence in the proceedings.

In January, the Criminal Court sentenced two men to death and 20 others to prison terms ranging from five years to life on charges that included "spying for Iran and Hizbullah". Some of the 26 defendants in the case alleged that security officials tortured them in pre-trial detention to coerce "confessions". The Court failed to investigate their allegations of torture. In July, an appeal court confirmed one death sentence in the case, while reducing other sentences and acquitting nine defendants. The authorities then referred 17 of the defendants for trial on new terrorism-related charges.

DEPRIVATION OF NATIONALITY

In April, the Administrative Cassation Court rejected a ruling of the Administrative Appeal Court that a case brought by former MP Abdullah Hashr al-Barghash against a government decision to strip him of his Kuwaiti nationality was outside its jurisdiction. In December the Cassation Court rejected his appeal.

DISCRIMINATION – BIDUN

The authorities continued to withhold citizenship from more than 100,000 Bidun residents of Kuwait, who remained stateless. In May, Parliament approved a draft law that would grant Kuwaiti citizenship to up to 4,000 Bidun and referred it to the government; it had not been enacted by the end of 2016. The government of the island state of Comoros said in May that it would consider granting "economic citizenship" to Bidun if it received an official request from the Kuwaiti authorities.

WOMEN'S RIGHTS

Women continued to face discrimination in law and in practice. In May, the Committee for Legislative and Legal Affairs approved a proposed amendment to the citizenship law that would allow Kuwaiti women to pass their nationality on to their children, regardless of the father's nationality. The amendment had not been enacted by the end of the year.

MIGRANT WORKERS' RIGHTS

Migrant workers, including those in the domestic, construction and other sectors, continued to face exploitation and abuse under the official *kafala* sponsorship system, which ties workers to their employers and prevents them from changing jobs or leaving the country without the employer's permission. In July, the authorities issued a decree setting minimum wages for domestic workers, most of whom are women.

DEATH PENALTY

Courts handed down death sentences for offences including murder and drug-related charges. No executions were reported.

1. Kuwait: Amnesty International submission to the UN Committee against Torture (MDE 17/4395/2016)

2. Kuwait: Amnesty International submission to the UN Human Rights Committee (MDE 17/4145/2016)

KYRGYZSTAN

Kyrgyz Republic
Head of state: **Almazbek Atambaev**
Head of government: **Sooronbai Jeenbekov (replaced Temir Sariev in April)**

Prisoner of conscience Azimjan Askarov remained in prison, despite a recommendation by the UN Human Rights Committee that he be immediately released. A "foreign agents" law that would have negatively affected NGOs was rejected, but a draft law on propaganda of "non-traditional sexual relations" remained under discussion. Constitutional amendments threatened human rights protection. Perpetrators of torture and of violence against women enjoyed impunity, and police carried out discriminatory raids against sex workers. The authorities continued to make no genuine effort to effectively investigate the June 2010 violence in Osh and Jalal-Abad.

PRISONER OF CONSCIENCE

On 31 March, the UN Human Rights Committee urged Kyrgyzstan to immediately release prisoner of conscience Azimjan Askarov, an ethnic Uzbek human rights defender, who was sentenced in 2010 to life in prison for purportedly participating in the 2010 ethnic violence and the murder of a police officer. The Committee considered that he had been arbitrarily detained, tortured and denied his right to a fair trial. In response, the Supreme Court reviewed the case on 11 and 12 July, but did not follow the Committee's conclusions that Azimjan Askarov should be released, and ordered a retrial which opened at Chui Regional Court on 4 October. It continued through to 20 December with a verdict expected in January 2017. Azimjan Askarov participated in all 10 hearings, seated in a metal cage.

FREEDOM OF ASSOCIATION

The Parliament rejected the proposed "foreign agents" law, originally proposed in 2014, on its third reading in May. It would have forced NGOs receiving foreign aid and engaging in any form of vaguely defined "political activities" to adopt and publicly use the stigmatizing label of "foreign agent".

RIGHTS OF LESBIAN, GAY, BISEXUAL, TRANSGENDER AND INTERSEX PEOPLE

In May, the Parliamentary Committee on Law, Order and Fighting Crime withdrew draft legislation to criminalize "fostering a positive attitude" towards "non-traditional sexual relations" for further review before the final parliamentary vote. LGBTI rights activists said that even though the law had not yet been passed, it was already "hanging over them" and limiting their activities.

LEGAL, CONSTITUTIONAL OR INSTITUTIONAL DEVELOPMENTS

In a referendum held on 11 December, voters accepted constitutional amendments that undermine human rights protection. These amendments introduce clauses on "supreme state values" and weaken the supremacy of international law over domestic law stipulated in the current Constitution. An amendment to the article on marriage and the family states that the family is formed on the basis of a union between a woman and a man; the current Constitution does not include this wording.

DISCRIMINATION – SEX WORKERS

In June and July, police in the capital, Bishkek, the surrounding Chui region, and in the southern city of Osh carried out co-ordinated and targeted operations in areas where sex workers were known to congregate, and detained and penalized women they found there. Sex work is not criminalized in Kyrgyzstan, but some of the women received administrative fines for "petty hooliganism" or for failing to produce identity documents. High-ranking police officials made discriminatory and stigmatizing statements about women engaged in sex work in June, referring to the need to "cleanse" the streets and encouraged "community patrols" to photograph people they believed to be sex workers and pass the photographs to the police. This risked increased intimidation and violence towards sex workers from nationalist groups and other non-state actors that had targeted sex workers in the past.

NGOs working with sex workers found that women engaged in sex work faced barriers in accessing health care, including reproductive and sexual health services. Sex work is highly stigmatized in Kyrgyzstan. Health care providers discriminated against sex workers by denying them treatment or offering low quality treatment, and by not respecting confidentiality. Many sex workers did not have identity documents, which are difficult to replace without registration at a permanent address. Lack of identity documents also limited sex workers' access to health care and other essential services.

IMPUNITY

Torture and other cruel, inhuman or degrading treatment, and lack of accountability for these human rights violations, remained commonplace. Court cases involving accusations of torture often dragged on for months or years.

The authorities failed to make a genuine effort to effectively investigate the June 2010 inter-ethnic violence in southern Kyrgyzstan. While violence was used by members of both ethnic Kyrgyz and Uzbek communities, and while the latter sustained most deaths, injuries and damage, prosecutions were disproportionately aimed at members of the ethnic Uzbek community.

No one was held responsible for the death of Usmanzhan Khalmirzaev, an ethnic Uzbek with Russian citizenship who died of his injuries in August 2011 after being detained and beaten by police. On 22 July, a judge at Chui Regional Court upheld the October 2015 acquittal of the four police officers suspected of being implicated in his death, on grounds of lack of evidence.

VIOLENCE AGAINST WOMEN AND GIRLS

Domestic violence, forced marriage, and other forms of violence against women and girls remained pervasive. In most cases, women who survived violence did not go to the police, due to social stigma and discriminatory attitudes, and because they had little faith in the police and justice system. Lack of economic opportunities made it difficult for women to leave abusive relationships and live independently, particularly if they wanted to take their children with them.

According to the National Statistics Committee, 4,960 cases of domestic violence were registered in the period between January and October of which 158 cases proceeded to criminal prosecution.

A law that will help protect adolescent girls from early and forced marriages passed its final parliamentary reading in October and was signed into law by the President on 18 November. The law introduces criminal sanctions of up to five years' imprisonment for anyone involved in organizing or officiating at a religious marriage ceremony where one or both of the spouses is under the age of 18. This will include religious leaders, as well as parents of the would-be spouses.

LAOS

Lao People's Democratic Republic
Head of state: **Bounnhang Vorachith (replaced Choummaly Sayasone in April)**
Head of government: **Thongloun Sisoulith (replaced Thongsing Thammavong in April)**

The rights to freedom of expression, association and peaceful assembly remained severely restricted. State control of media and civil society was tightened as Laos hosted international meetings. Repression of human rights defenders continued. Two prisoners of conscience were released in March after being held for almost 17 years.
There was no progress in the investigation into the enforced disappearance in 2012 of a civil society member. The death penalty remained mandatory for serious drug offences.

BACKGROUND

The ruling Lao People's Revolutionary Party appointed a new General Secretary and Politburo in its internal leadership ballot in January. National Assembly elections in March were followed by the appointment of a President and Prime Minister. Laos remained a one-party state.

UN Special Procedures expressed serious concerns about the potential impact of the Don Sahong Dam on the livelihood of millions of people in Laos and downstream countries, including the threat to rights to adequate food, housing, information and participation and the rights of Indigenous People.

Laos also held the Chair of the Association of Southeast Asian Nations (ASEAN) in 2016.

ENFORCED DISAPPEARANCES

The fate of Sombath Somphone, a prominent civil society member, remained unclarified since his abduction in 2012 outside a police post in the capital, Vientiane. CCTV cameras captured his being stopped by police and driven away.

Authorities failed to provide information on the whereabouts of Kha Yang, a Lao ethnic Hmong, arrested after his second forced return from Thailand in 2011. He was also forcibly returned in 2009, although he had been granted refugee status by the UNHCR, the UN refugee agency, and fled back to Thailand in 2011.

FREEDOM OF EXPRESSION

Civil society organizations continued to be under stringent state control.

In January, a decree restricted the press activities of international media and other bodies. Provisions included a requirement to submit materials for state approval before publishing. In November the 2008 Media Law was amended to ensure that the media strictly adhered to and promoted government policies.

In line with Decree 327 which prohibits online criticism of the state, the authorities continued to monitor internet activity. In August a Public Security Ministry official stated that police were monitoring Facebook for anyone connected to three detained activists – Lodkham Thammavong, Somphone Phimmasone and Soukan Chaithad.

Laos cancelled its hosting of the ASEAN Civil Society Conference/ASEAN People's Forum, citing insufficient funds and the risk of foreign civil society actors using the event to criticize ASEAN-member governments.

HUMAN RIGHTS DEFENDERS

Lodkham Thammavong, Somphone Phimmasone and Soukan Chaithad were arrested in March after returning from Thailand. Reports indicated they were detained incommunicado for at least six months and denied legal representation.[1] They were accused of threatening national security in relation to online criticism of the Lao government while in Thailand. They had also participated in a peaceful demonstration outside the Lao Embassy in Bangkok in 2015. In May, state television showed them apologizing for their actions and confessing to protesting against government policies. Somphone Phimmasone's family visited him briefly in jail in September. All three individuals remained in detention at the end of the year.

LAND DISPUTES

Reports of land disputes between the state and individuals continued. Mechanisms for resolving land complaints were inadequate.

---

1. Laos: Three Lao activists held incommunicado (ASA 26/4603/2016)

LATVIA

Republic of Latvia
Head of state: **Raimonds Vējonis**
Head of government: **Māris Kučinskis (replaced Laimdota Straujuma in February)**

The Council of Europe and the UN raised serious concerns about the situation of children with disabilities. Over 247,000

people remained stateless. Individuals continued to be at risk of *refoulement*.

DISCRIMINATION
Stateless persons
The number of stateless persons continued to be high – over 247,000 as of July, the latest published government data. Stateless people, the vast majority ethnic Russians, were excluded from enjoying political rights.

Rights of people with disabilities
Following a five-day visit to Latvia in September, the Council of Europe Commissioner for Human Rights raised concerns about the situation of persons with disabilities in institutions, in particular that of children with intellectual and psychosocial disabilities. His comments echoed the concerns of the UN Committee on the Rights of the Child which, in March, called for the government to set up comprehensive measures to ensure that inclusive education is given priority over the placement of children with disabilities in specialized institutions.

REFUGEES AND ASYLUM-SEEKERS
The number of asylum applications remained low, with about 350 received during the year.

The European Commission criticized the government for rejecting relocation requests of asylum-seekers from other European countries without providing substantiated reasons or for rejecting requests on unjustified grounds. By the end of the year, Latvia had relocated 148 asylum-seekers under the EU relocation and resettlement scheme. Concerns remained about the non-suspensive effect of appeals against negative decisions under the accelerated asylum procedure. The procedure increases the risk of individuals being returned to countries where they could face serious human rights violations.

In March, the UN Committee on the Rights of the Child raised concerns about the detention of asylum-seeking children during the asylum-seeking procedure and called on the government to end the practice.

LEBANON

Lebanese Republic
Head of state: Michel Aoun (assumed office in October)
Head of government: Saad Hariri (replaced Tammam Salam in December)

The human rights situation continued to be affected by the armed conflict in Syria. Lebanon hosted more than 1 million refugees from Syria, but the authorities severely restricted their right to asylum and maintained restrictions that effectively closed Lebanon's borders to those fleeing Syria. Most refugees faced severe economic hardship. Women were discriminated against in law and practice and were inadequately protected against sexual and other violence. Migrant workers faced exploitation and abuse. The authorities took no steps to investigate the fate of thousands of people who disappeared or went missing during the conflict of 1975 to 1990. Long-resident Palestinian refugees continued to face discrimination. Parliament approved a new law to establish a National Human Rights Institute. Courts continued to impose death sentences; there were no executions.

BACKGROUND
Tensions between the main political parties caused continued political impasse. However, in October, the Parliament elected a new president; the presidency had been vacant since May 2014. Public protests against the government's continued failure to implement sustainable solutions to the country's waste collection and disposal problems diminished compared with 2015.

Security conditions deteriorated; there were bomb attacks in the capital Beirut and in Beqaa governorate. Suicide bombers killed five people and wounded 28 others, mostly civilians, on 27 June in the predominantly Christian village of Qaa in the Beqaa Valley. The army detained dozens of refugees following the attacks in Qaa, accusing them of having irregular status in Lebanon.

Lebanese border areas continued to come under fire from Syria, where the armed group Islamic State (IS) continued to hold Lebanese soldiers and security officials that its forces abducted from Lebanon in 2014.

In September, judicial authorities indicted two Syrian government intelligence officers. They were accused of committing simultaneous bomb attacks in 2013 at two mosques in the northern city of Tripoli, in which 42 people were killed and some 600 injured, mostly civilians. Neither of those indicted had been apprehended by the end of 2016.

TORTURE AND OTHER ILL-TREATMENT

In October the Parliament approved a new law to establish a National Human Rights Institute, including a committee to investigate the use of torture and other ill-treatment in all places of detention, including prisons, police stations and immigrant detention sites.

REFUGEES AND ASYLUM-SEEKERS

Lebanon hosted more than 1 million refugees from Syria in addition to some 280,000 long-term Palestinian refugees and more than 20,000 refugees from Iraq, Sudan, Ethiopia and other countries.

Lebanon again failed to become party to the 1951 UN Refugee Convention and its 1967 Protocol. Refugees from Syria continued to face serious restrictions on their right to seek asylum, as the Lebanese authorities did not formally recognize them as refugees. The authorities also maintained strict criteria introduced in January 2015 and denied entry to all refugees from Syria who did not meet the criteria, effectively closing Lebanon's borders to people fleeing the armed conflict and persecution in Syria. A government decision from May 2015 continued to bar UNHCR, the UN refugee agency, from registering newly arrived refugees. Within Lebanon, Syrian refugees faced financial and administrative difficulties in obtaining or renewing residency permits, exposing them to a constant risk of arbitrary arrest, detention and forcible return to Syria. They also faced severe economic hardship.

According to the UN, 70% of Syrian refugee households lived below the poverty line and more than half lived in substandard conditions in overcrowded buildings and densely populated neighbourhoods.

The UN humanitarian appeal for Syrian refugees in Lebanon was only 52% funded by the end of the year and resettlement places in other countries remained inadequate. Cuts in funding led the UN to reduce both the amount of its support to Syrian refugees in Lebanon and the number in receipt of UN support.

On 8 January, security officials at Beirut Airport forcibly returned more than 100 Syrians to Syria, in violation of the principle of *non-refoulement*. The returned refugees had been seeking to travel to Turkey via Lebanon.

Palestinian refugees, including many long-resident in Lebanon, remained subject to discriminatory laws that deny them the right to own or inherit property and access public education and health services, and that prevent them from working in at least 35 professions. At least 3,000 Palestinian refugees who did not hold official identity documents faced further restrictions denying them the right to register births, marriages and deaths.

WOMEN'S RIGHTS

Women remained subject to personal status laws that retained discriminatory provisions pertaining to marriage, divorce, child custody and inheritance. The nationality law continued to prevent Lebanese women married to foreign nationals from passing on their nationality to their children. The same law did not apply to Lebanese men.

Women remained unprotected from marital rape, which the 2013 Law on Protection of Women and Family Members from Domestic Violence failed to criminalize. This law was used in 2016 to charge the husbands of Roula Yaacoub and Manal Assi for beating their wives to death in 2013 and 2014 respectively; the latter was sentenced to death, which was reduced in July to five years in prison.

Syrian and Palestinian refugee women from Syria faced serious human rights abuses, including gender-based violence, exploitation and sexual harassment, particularly in public places. Refugee women heads of households were especially at risk of harassment by men if they had no adult male relatives residing with them. Many refugee women from Syria lacked valid residence permits and, as a result, feared reporting sexual harassment or other abuse to the Lebanese authorities.

MIGRANT WORKERS' RIGHTS

Migrant workers were excluded from the protections provided to other workers under the Labour Law, exposing them to labour exploitation and physical, sexual and psychological abuse by their employers. Migrant domestic workers, mostly women, remained especially vulnerable under the *kafala* sponsorship system that ties workers to their employer.

INTERNATIONAL JUSTICE
Special Tribunal for Lebanon

The Netherlands-based Special Tribunal for Lebanon (STL) continued to try in their absence four men accused of complicity in the killing of former Lebanese Prime Minister Rafic Hariri and others in a 2005 car bombing in Beirut. The four continued to evade arrest. A fifth accused died in Syria.

On 8 March, the STL Appeals Panel acquitted Lebanese journalist Karma Khayat and her employer Al Jadeed TV of contempt of court. On 15 July, the STL charged *al-Akhbar* newspaper and its editor-in-chief, Ibrahim al-Amine, with contempt of court for failing to comply with a court order requiring them to remove information concerning confidential witnesses and obstruction of justice. On 29 August the court sentenced Ibrahim al-Amine to a fine of €20,000 and *al-Akhbar* newspaper to a fine of €6,000.

IMPUNITY

The government again failed to establish an independent national body to investigate the fate of thousands of people who were forcibly disappeared or went missing during the civil war of 1975 to 1990 and who may have been unlawfully killed. This failure perpetuated the suffering of the families of the disappeared, who continued to face administrative, legal, social and economic hurdles resulting from the enforced disappearance of their relatives.

DEATH PENALTY

Courts imposed at least 107 death sentences for terrorism-related crimes. No executions have been carried out since 2004.

LESOTHO

Kingdom of Lesotho
Head of state: **King Letsie III**
Head of government: Pakalitha Mosisili

Political instability persisted following an attempted coup in 2014 and the killing of a former army chief in 2015. Several opposition party members remained in exile. The right to freedom of expression remained severely limited. Journalists faced intimidation, physical attacks and politically motivated criminal charges in relation to their work, prompting several to flee the country. The rights to health and an adequate standard of living were undermined.

POLITICAL INSTABILITY

The report of the Southern Africa Development Community (SADC) Commission of Inquiry into instability in Lesotho was made public in February. Among other things, the inquiry looked into the killing by soldiers of Lieutenant-General Maaparankoe Mahao in June 2015 following his dismissal from the Lesotho Defence Force (LDF) and replacement by Lieutenant-General Tlali Kamoli. The soldiers said that Maaparankoe Mahao fired on them when they attempted to arrest him on suspicion of plotting a mutiny in the army. The SADC report found no evidence that Maaparankoe Mahao had planned a mutiny and concluded that he was deliberately killed. It recommended criminal investigations into the killing and the dismissal of Tlali Kamoli. The government announced Tlali Kamoli's retirement effective from 1 December.

Prime Minister Mosisili commissioned a joint task force, comprising members of the police and army, to investigate the circumstances of the killing. Maaparankoe Mahao's family dismissed it as lacking impartiality.

The SADC summit in June urged opposition leaders who had fled Lesotho after receiving death threats in 2015 to return by August to participate in constitutional and security reforms recommended by the SADC. In November, the government introduced an Amnesty Bill which if passed would enable impunity for serious human rights violations.

UNFAIR TRIALS

Fifteen LDF members charged with sedition and mutiny in May 2015 remained held at Maseru Maximum Security Prison, even though the SADC inquiry found no conclusive evidence of a mutiny and recommended that the soldiers be released.[1] In October 2015 the High Court had ordered the release of all the soldiers on "open arrest" – a form of military bail – but only seven were released. Tlali Kamoli was charged with contempt of court after failing to comply with the court order. On 29 April, the Appeals Court rejected a request by the remaining soldiers to be placed under "open arrest", thereby overruling the High Court order. The court martial of the detained soldiers was repeatedly postponed.

All five lawyers representing the soldiers faced death threats.[2] One of the lawyers was arrested and charged with perjury allegedly committed while representing the detained soldiers. Additional charges of fraud, contempt of court and obstruction of justice were added to his indictment.

TORTURE AND OTHER ILL-TREATMENT

The imprisoned LDF soldiers continued to face cruel, inhuman and degrading treatment.[3] After a march organized by the detainees' children on 16 June, some of the soldiers were held in solitary confinement and denied food. One was denied specialized medical treatment and some were shackled. Makoae Taoana, a medical doctor who examined the soldiers after their arrest and torture, died in an unexplained accident in July. Police announced they were investigating the circumstances of his death.

FREEDOM OF EXPRESSION

Journalists working in broadcast, print and social media continued to face physical attacks and harassment. On 23 June, after publishing an article that alleged that Tlali Kamoli was to receive an exit package of R50 million (US$3.5 million), Lesotho Times reporter Keiso Mohloboli was interrogated at Maseru police headquarters and asked to disclose her sources. The following day she was arrested and interrogated along with the newspaper's editor, Lloyd Mutungamiri. On 5 July, Lloyd Mutungamiri and Lesotho Times publisher Basildon Peta were interrogated. Basildon Peta was charged with criminal defamation and a related offence. The charges arose from a column that satirized Tlali Kamoli. On 9 July, unidentified gunmen attacked and injured Lloyd Mutungamiri in his driveway. There was no known investigation into the incident. Lloyd Mutungamiri had been charged with criminal defamation in September 2014 for reporting on police corruption; no further action was known to have been taken. Keiso Mohloboli fled Lesotho, fearing for her life.

RIGHT TO HEALTH

The public health care system faced a deepening crisis, largely due to debts owed to South Africa and the World Bank relating to the provision of health care. Patients unable to afford new hospital charges imposed because of debt repayments were told to access free health care in neighbouring South Africa, but without help for travel costs.

RIGHT TO AN ADEQUATE STANDARD OF LIVING

Villagers, livestock and ancestral graves were resettled in Mokhotlong town during the ongoing construction of Polihali Dam, a major project in Lesotho designed to supply water to South Africa. The limited space offered in Mokhotlong meant that villagers lost their livelihoods, which were based on livestock and subsistence farming. People living near the dam continued to have no access to piped clean water and electricity.

---

1. Lesotho: Call for immediate release of detained soldiers following the report of SADC Commission of Inquiry on Lesotho (AFR 33/3444/2016)

2. Lesotho: Trial of 23 soldiers postponed again (AFR 33/3481/2016)

3. Lesotho: Continued ill-treatment of detained soldiers (AFR 33/4411/2016)

LIBYA

State of Libya
Head of state: **Disputed**
Head of government: **Fayez Serraj**

Rival government forces and other armed groups and militias committed serious violations of international law and abuses of human rights with impunity. All sides to the conflict carried out indiscriminate attacks and direct attacks on civilians, forcing thousands to become internally displaced and causing a humanitarian crisis. Thousands of people continued to be detained without trial in the absence of a functioning justice system, and torture and other ill-treatment were rife. Armed groups including Islamic State (IS) abducted, detained and killed civilians and severely curtailed the rights to freedom of expression and assembly. Women faced discrimination and were subjected to sexual and other violence, particularly by IS. Refugees, asylum-seekers and migrants faced serious abuses, including indefinite detention and torture and other ill-treatment by the authorities, armed groups and people smugglers. The death penalty remained in force; no executions were reported.

BACKGROUND

Libya remained deeply divided as rival governments continued to vie for political legitimacy and assert control against a background of economic collapse and widespread lawlessness in which armed groups and militias abducted people for ransom and committed unlawful killings with impunity.

The Presidency Council of a UN-backed Government of National Accord (GNA) entered the capital, Tripoli, in March and seized power from the National Salvation Government (NSG) with support from armed groups from western cities and towns who previously backed the NSG. The NSG continued to claim legitimacy and unsuccessfully sought to reclaim power by force in October. The GNA failed to consolidate power amid continued sporadic clashes between armed groups, including in areas it controlled, while its legitimacy remained contested by Libya's recognized parliament, the House of Representatives (HOR) based in Tobruk.

The HOR-affiliated Libyan National Army (LNA), an armed group composed of former army units and tribal militias, commanded by retired army General Khalifa Haftar, consolidated its power and made significant territorial gains in the east. The LNA replaced some elected municipal council heads with military-appointed governors in areas they controlled, while their forces captured vital oil terminals from a GNA-allied armed group in September. The LNA continued to participate in fighting against the Shura Council of Benghazi Revolutionaries (SCBR) armed group in Benghazi, and conducted air strikes in Derna.

IS controlled parts of the coastal city of Sirte and contested other areas. In February, a US air strike on an alleged IS training camp in the western city of Sabratha reportedly killed up to 50 people, including two Serbian nationals held hostage by IS. In May, GNA forces composed mostly of armed groups from Misrata began an offensive against IS positions in Sirte, supported by US air strikes in August, and gained control of the city in early December.

In April the Constitution Drafting Assembly issued a revised draft constitution to be approved by national referendum, but no date for the referendum had been set by the end of the year.

The UN Security Council extended the mandate of the United Nations Support Mission in Libya (UNSMIL) until 15 September 2017.

INTERNAL ARMED CONFLICT
Indiscriminate shelling and direct attacks on civilians

Armed groups on all sides of the conflict committed war crimes, including direct attacks on civilians and indiscriminate attacks using imprecise weapons such as mortars and artillery shells, killing and injuring scores of people. IS carried out indiscriminate attacks using improvised explosive devices and suicide bombings against pro-GNA forces.

In Benghazi, the LNA shelled and launched air strikes in the suburb of Ganfouda and other civilian areas under SCBR control and the SCBR shelled other densely populated civilian areas. A LNA air strike on 1 July killed two civilians in Ganfouda. On 4 October, indiscriminate shelling apparently by SCBR forces killed three civilians in Sidi Hussein, central Benghazi.

Some attacks by armed groups and militias in Benghazi targeted hospitals and other civilian buildings. They included a car bomb attack on 24 June at al-Jalaa hospital that killed five and wounded 13, mostly civilians.

LNA air strikes killed civilians in the eastern city of Derna while targeting al-Qa'ida-linked armed groups in the city. In June, LNA air strikes killed six civilians, including children, according to UNSMIL.

Fighting between rival armed groups in Tripoli, al-Zawiya and other cities in western Libya, as well as tribal fighting in southern Libya, also caused deaths and injuries among civilians. On 16 October, indiscriminate shelling between GNA forces and pro-NSG armed groups hit a camp for internally displaced people in Tripoli, killing one civilian and injuring others.

Humanitarian impact

The conflict had a devastating impact on civilians, cutting or severely curtailing their access to food, health care, education, electricity, fuel and water supplies, and causing many to be displaced from their homes. Economic collapse left many struggling to support their families.

The World Health Organization reported in April that Libya's health care system had virtually collapsed and in June estimated that almost 60% of public hospitals in areas of conflict had shut down or become inaccessible.

Hundreds of civilians remained trapped without access to clean water, food, power or medical care in Benghazi's Ganfouda area due to fighting.

In October, the UN Office for the Coordination of Humanitarian Affairs estimated that 1.3 million people across Libya were in need of humanitarian assistance.

Abductions and hostage-taking

Armed groups, including some operating under Libya's rival governments, abducted and detained civilians on account of their origin, opinions and perceived political or tribal affiliations. Rising criminality in the absence of a functioning justice system also saw armed groups and gangs abducting civilians for ransom in Tripoli and other cities.

Those abducted included political, human rights and other activists, journalists, and judicial and other public officials. Some foreign nationals were targeted based on their religion, race or nationality. Some were released after payment of ransoms or local mediation.

Some armed groups continued to hold civilians abducted in 2014 as hostages for use in prisoner exchanges. In September, a Zintan-based armed group released Suleiman al-Zubi, a former member of Libya's

General National Congress abducted in 2014, reportedly in exchange for Zintani prisoners held in Misrata.

IS abducted and detained members of opposing armed groups and civilians, including foreign nationals employed in the oil industry, migrant workers and refugees.

Other armed groups also targeted foreign nationals for abduction for ransoms. Victims included two Italians and a Canadian abducted on 19 September while working in Ghat, southwest Libya. They were freed in early November.

Unlawful killings

Armed groups, including some affiliated to the rival governments, committed unlawful killings of captured opposition fighters and civilians they perceived as opponents.

In February, IS forces reportedly beheaded 11 members of a local security force whom they had captured in Sabratha.

In June, 12 men detained in connection with alleged offences during Mu'ammar al-Gaddafi's rule were reportedly shot dead shortly after their release from Tripoli's al-Baraka Prison, run by the Ministry of Justice. They appeared to be victims of extrajudicial execution.

In July the bodies of 14 men were found dumped in al-Laithi, an area of Benghazi that the LNA had recaptured from the SCBR. The men's hands and legs had been tied and they had been shot dead by unidentified perpetrators.

Libya's rival governments failed to conduct independent or effective investigations into such killings or hold those responsible to account.

IMPUNITY

Impunity continued to prevail, although in January Libya's Public Prosecutor informed the International Criminal Court (ICC) that arrest warrants had been issued against three officials accused of torturing As-Saadi al-Gaddafi in detention. It remained unclear whether those accused were arrested and prosecuted. The head of al-Hadba Prison, who was suspended after the torture of As-

Saadi al-Gaddafi, was reportedly restored to his position.

In November the ICC committed to prioritize its investigations in 2017 into ongoing crimes in Libya, including those committed by IS and other armed groups, and issue new arrest warrants. However, the ICC initiated no new investigations in 2016, citing security concerns and insufficient resources.

Saif al-Islam al-Gaddafi, against whom the ICC issued a Warrant of Arrest in relation to alleged crimes against humanity committed during the 2011 conflict, continued to be detained by a militia in Zintan.

None of the parties to the conflict implemented any human rights provisions of the UN-brokered Libya Political Agreement of December 2015, including those obliging them to release detainees held without legal basis.

INTERNALLY DISPLACED PEOPLE

By August the number of internally displaced people in Libya had risen to almost 350,000, according to the International Organization for Migration (IOM). This included an estimated 40,000 former residents of Tawargha who had been forced from their homes five years earlier. In August, a reconciliation agreement between Misrata and Tawargha representatives aimed to facilitate their return to the town.

Most of Sirte's civilian inhabitants fled the city at the time of the GNA offensive against IS in May. The fighting caused extensive damage but some residents were able to return. Conflict in Benghazi and tribal fighting in southern Libya also caused population displacement.

FREEDOMS OF EXPRESSION, ASSOCIATION AND ASSEMBLY

Armed groups and militias continued to harass, abduct, torture and kill human rights defenders, political and other activists and journalists.

In March, unidentified assailants killed human rights activist Abdul Basit Abu-Dahab in a car bombing in Derna. The same month, members of an armed group ransacked the offices of Tripoli's al-Nabaa TV station and assaulted journalists, and in al-Marj, eastern Libya, armed men abducted blogger and journalist Ali al-Asbali, releasing him four months later.

In August, members of an armed group briefly abducted al-Ahrar TV station journalist Aboubaker Al-Bizanti in Tripoli after he criticized the presence of armed groups and militias in the capital.

People who attended public gatherings and demonstrations faced attack. In May, unidentified assailants fired mortars at protesters demonstrating in al-Kish Square, Benghazi, killing six civilians.

JUSTICE SYSTEM

The justice system remained in a state of collapse, with courts unable to process thousands of untried detainees' cases, some dating from 2011. Thousands of detainees continued to be held without trial in official prisons and detention facilities and in unofficial prisons run by armed groups. Some detainees were freed in amnesties, including 17 men held in Misrata who were released in March.

The trial of As-Saadi al-Gaddafi continued to be postponed while he remained detained at al-Hadba Prison, Tripoli. In April, the UN Working Group on Arbitrary Detention declared that his detention and that of 11 other former al-Gaddafi-era officials was arbitrary and without legal basis.

At the end of the year, the Supreme Court had still to review the death sentences imposed on Saif al-Islam al-Gaddafi, Abdallah al-Senussi and seven other former officials in 2015.

Torture and other ill-treatment

Torture and other ill-treatment remained common and widespread and was committed with impunity, especially upon arrest or abduction and during detention in official and unofficial prisons.

Conditions deteriorated in official prisons including al-Hadba, al-Baraka and others, where those held included former high-level al-Gaddafi-era officials. Inadequate health care and food led to a decline in many inmates' health, while torture was reportedly used to punish inmates.

REFUGEES' AND MIGRANTS' RIGHTS

Refugees and migrants were subjected to serious abuses by armed groups, people smugglers and traffickers, and guards in government-run detention centres.

The IOM said in October that it had identified 276,957 migrants in Libya but estimated the true number to be between 700,000 and 1 million. UNHCR, the UN refugee agency, had registered 38,241 refugees by the end of the year.

Libyan law continued to criminalize foreign nationals who irregularly enter, leave or remain in the country. Many actual and suspected irregular migrants and asylum-seekers were seized at checkpoints and in house raids or reported to the authorities by their employers. Thousands were held in indefinite detention pending deportation in facilities of the Department for Combating Irregular Migration (DCIM). Although they formally reported to the Ministry of the Interior, DCIM detention facilities were often run by armed groups outside the effective control of the GNA. Those detained were held in squalid conditions and were subject to torture and other ill-treatment by guards, including beatings, shootings, exploitation and sexual violence. UNHCR reported that there were 24 migrant detention centres across Libya.

On 1 April, guards shot dead at least four people seeking to escape from al-Nasr migrant detention centre in al-Zawiya.

Thousands of refugees, asylum-seekers and migrants sought to flee Libya and cross the Mediterranean Sea to Europe in unseaworthy craft provided by people smugglers. The UN estimated that 5,022 people had died while trying to cross the Mediterranean from North Africa by the end of the year, mostly departing from Libya.

The EU renewed its anti-smuggling naval mission "Operation Sophia" in June, extending its mandate to include training for

Libya's coastguard service, which began in October. The Libyan coastguard intercepted thousands of those seeking to cross the Mediterranean, returning them to Libya and indefinite detention in the DCIM-run facilities. At times the coastguard committed abuses, including shooting at and abandoning boats at sea, and beating migrants and refugees aboard their vessels and on shore. By 18 December, the Libyan coastguard had intercepted and/or rescued more than 14,038 people, according to UNHCR.

Refugees, asylum-seekers and migrants were subjected to serious human rights abuses by criminal gangs, including abduction, extortion, sexual violence and killing. IS also abducted refugees and migrants, forcing some to convert to Islam, and sexually abused migrant and refugee women reportedly subjecting some to forced marriage. In October the IOM reported that 71% of migrants who took the central Mediterranean route from Africa to Europe said they had experienced practices amounting to human trafficking, with 49% having faced abduction and extortion in Libya.

WOMEN'S RIGHTS

Women continued to face discrimination in law and practice and were marginalized socially, politically and economically. The draft constitution published in April proposed to guarantee women 25% of HOR and local council seats for 12 years.

In Sirte and other areas that they controlled, IS and other armed groups imposed strict interpretations of Shari'a law that restricted women's movement and dress, and reportedly sanctioned the practice of child marriage.

Armed groups also threatened and harassed women who engaged in public activism.

DEATH PENALTY

The death penalty remained in force for a wide range of crimes; no executions were reported.

LITHUANIA

Republic of Lithuania
Head of state: Dalia Grybauskaitė
Head of government: Saulius Skvernelis (replaced Algirdas Butkevičius in November)

The 2016 Baltic Pride March for Equality in Vilnius took place without serious incidents. A Saudi Arabian national who alleged he was tortured and held in secret CIA detention in Lithuania was denied victim status, putting an end to his domestic appeal process.

COUNTER-TERROR AND SECURITY

In June, the European Court of Human Rights (ECtHR) held a hearing in a case against Lithuania for complicity in the US-led rendition and secret detention programmes, which the CIA operated globally in the aftermath of the 11 September 2001 attacks in the USA.[1] Abu Zubaydah, a stateless Palestinian born in Saudi Arabia and detained at the US detention centre at Guantánamo Bay, Cuba, lodged an application against Lithuania in 2011. He alleged he had been forcibly disappeared and tortured at a secret CIA detention centre in Antaviliai between 2005 and 2006, and that Lithuania had failed to effectively investigate his secret detention. A judgment in the case remained pending at the end of 2016.

In June, the Vilnius Regional Court ruled that Mustafa al-Hawsawi, a Saudi Arabian national detained at Guantánamo Bay, would not be granted victim status in a domestic investigation into Lithuanian complicity in the same CIA programmes. Mustafa al-Hawsawi claimed he had been held at the secret CIA detention site at Antaviliai, subjected to enforced disappearance and tortured between 2004 and 2006. In December, he lodged an application at the ECtHR against Lithuania.

RIGHTS OF LESBIAN, GAY, BISEXUAL, TRANSGENDER AND INTERSEX PEOPLE

On 18 June, 3,000 people joined the March for Equality in Vilnius to celebrate Baltic Pride 2016. The march took place without serious incidents and with adequate police protection.

On 28 June, the Lithuanian Parliament voted in favour of a proposal to amend the Constitution to restrict the definition of "family" under Article 38 to exclude same-sex couples. The process would require two votes in Parliament before the amendment could be officially adopted.

DISCRIMINATION – PEOPLE WITH DISABILITIES

In May, the Committee on the Rights of Persons with Disabilities issued several recommendations and raised a range of concerns, including around access to education and systemic barriers to access to health services.

1. CIA rendition victims challenge Romania and Lithuania at Europe's Human Rights Court (News story, 29 June)

MACEDONIA

The former Yugoslav Republic of Macedonia
Head of state: Gjorge Ivanov
Head of government: Emil Dimitriev (replaced Nikola Gruevski in January)

Prosecutions following the 2015 revelations of high-level corruption were slowed down by political infighting while witness protection was limited. Roma faced discrimination in accessing basic rights and services. Refugees and migrants were routinely pushed back at the border with Greece or faced detention in poor facilities in Macedonia.

BACKGROUND

The political crisis prompted by the publication in 2015 of audio recordings revealing government corruption and widespread illegal surveillance continued. A transitional technical government composed of majority and opposition MPs was formed after a political agreement was brokered with EU and US assistance.

In April, the President announced a pardon for 56 high-level political figures under investigation for their involvement in the wire-tapping scandal. The pardons were revoked by the President in June following a wave of protests dubbed the "colourful revolution".

Parliamentary elections eventually took place in December after being called and postponed several times. The previous ruling party (Internal Macedonian Revolutionary Organization – Democratic Party for Macedonian National Unity) returned to power. The main opposition party, narrowly failing to acquire the majority of votes, disputed the end result.

JUSTICE SYSTEM

The Special Public Prosecutor appointed by Parliament in September 2015 to investigate officials involved in the wire-tapping scandal and crimes by political figures continued to face pressure in carrying out her work. In October, the transitional Parliament rejected a proposal to extend the Prosecutor's June 2017 deadline for concluding all investigations and to improve access to witness protection services for witnesses involved in her office's investigations.

DISCRIMINATION – ROMA

In September, the European Court of Human Rights (ECtHR) communicated to Macedonia a complaint in relation to 53 Roma individuals who challenged their forced eviction from the "Polygon" settlement in Skopje in August which left them in tents and makeshift shelters on the outskirts of the capital.

About 600 refugees, mainly Roma, who had fled Kosovo in 1999-2000, remained at risk of losing their access to livelihoods and other rights as the authorities continued to revoke their right to stay in the country on dubious grounds related to national security. By the end of the year, over 80 of them (including 30 children) had their protection status withdrawn after failing routine security checks carried out as part of the annual renewal of their temporary protection status. The substance of the security assessments was not shared with applicants and could not be challenged in courts. A Roma woman whose protection status was not renewed subsequently lodged an appeal at the ECtHR.

REFUGEES' AND MIGRANTS' RIGHTS

In early March, the Ministry of Interior announced the closure of the country's southern border with Greece, thereby preventing the arrival of refugees and migrants to the country (see Greece entry). Until their eviction in May, thousands were stranded in the Idomeni makeshift camp on the Greek side of the border. Throughout the year, the authorities continued to return refugees and migrants summarily to Greece, sometimes violently. UNHCR, the UN refugee agency, did not register official new arrivals following the March border closure, as refugees and migrants barred from entering the country were pushed back or continued their journeys into Macedonia clandestinely.

In September, eight complainants from Syria, Iraq and Afghanistan submitted an application to the ECtHR to challenge their summary expulsion in March from Macedonia to Greece.

Also in September, the UN High Commissioner for Human Rights criticized the authorities for leaving hundreds of refugees and migrants – who had arrived before the border closure – stranded in inadequate transit centres at the southern and northern land borders and in the Gazi Baba detention centre for foreigners in Skopje. The de facto detention of irregular migrants and asylum-seekers continued to be implemented without lawful grounds and without detainees being able to challenge the legality of their detention.

MADAGASCAR

Republic of Madagascar
Head of state: **Hery Rajaonarimampianina**
Head of government: **Olivier Mahafaly Solonandrasana (replaced Jean Ravelonarivo in April)**

Poverty was widespread, with extensive malnutrition and deteriorating primary health care. Children's rights were routinely flouted. Human rights violations by police were committed with impunity and corrupt officials were involved in trafficking activities. Discrimination against women in law and practice continued. The right to freedom of expression was restricted. Prison conditions remained dire.

BACKGROUND

Madagascar struggled to overcome the instability resulting from its five-year political crisis. In April, following weeks of political conflict, Olivier Mahafaly Solonandrasana replaced Jean Ravelonarivo as Prime Minister.

Extreme levels of poverty were widespread, with approximately 91% of the population living on less than US$2 per day. A drought in the south aggravated an already dire humanitarian situation. According to UN agencies, 1.2 million people (around 80% of the population) living in the south were food insecure, of whom 600,000 were severely food insecure.

RIGHT TO HEALTH

Neonatal and maternal mortality remained very high, and the deterioration of the primary health care system was a major barrier to accessing even basic health services. Limited access to clean water and poor sanitation and hygiene practices were of particular concern, particularly given the level of chronic malnutrition.

CHILDREN'S RIGHTS

In Madagascar, 47% of all children suffer from stunting, and nearly 10% from acute malnutrition.

As families sought to cope with the impact of the drought, there were reports of alarming increases in economic exploitation, with children working in mines and leading cattle, and instances of sexual exploitation and child marriage. Drop out rates in primary schools reached 40% in some communities, according to UNICEF.

Child sex trafficking continued, often with the involvement of family members, and was most prevalent in tourist destinations and near mining sites.

IMPUNITY

The government failed to ensure respect for the rule of law, allowing human rights violations to be committed with impunity. Deadly clashes involving police, villagers and armed cattle rustlers (*dahalos*) continued in the southern region, leading to civilian casualties.

Civil society organizations denounced the lack of free and fair access to justice, the corruption of government officials, and their involvement in trafficking activities.

Madagascar continued to be a source country for forced labour and sex trafficking. Despite recent efforts, the government failed to prevent trafficking, protect victims, and prosecute suspected traffickers, including complicit officials.

WOMEN'S RIGHTS

The Nationality Law denied women the right to transmit nationality to their children on an equal basis with men, resulting in a large number of stateless persons.

The predominance of customary laws favoured harmful traditional practices including arranged, forced and early marriages. Women and girls continued to suffer sexual or other physical violence, but reporting rates were low and prosecutions rare. Efforts to prevent gender-based violence and to provide care and treatment for victims remained inadequate.

FREEDOM OF EXPRESSION

After months of protest from journalists and international media organizations, in August the High Constitutional Court approved a draft law on a new Code of Media Communication. The contentious Code punished with heavy fines offences such as contempt, defamation or insult against a government official.

Environmental activists reported threats and harassment for publicizing issues such as trafficking in rosewood and endangered species. They denounced a lack of protection by the government.

PRISON CONDITIONS

Prison conditions continued to be dire, with severe overcrowding and inadequate infrastructure. Almost half of all prisoners suffered moderate to severe malnutrition.

About half of prison inmates had not yet been tried, with pre-trial detention often exceeding the maximum potential sentence.

MALAWI

Republic of Malawi
Head of state and government: Arthur Peter Mutharika

Attacks against people with albinism continued; at least seven people were killed and their bodies mutilated. People with albinism also continued to suffer social isolation. Student protests over fee increases were violently repressed. Political opponents of the government were arrested and charged with treason.

DISCRIMINATION – PEOPLE WITH ALBINISM

People with albinism continued to be subjected to violent attacks and mutilations.[1] Although senior government officials, including the President, publicly condemned the attacks, victims and their relatives continued to be denied justice and reparations.

In March, a Special Legal Counsel was appointed to assist the prosecution of crimes related to people with albinism. In July, Parliament passed revisions to the Anatomy

Act and Penal Code that increased the penalties for the sale of body tissue and possession of a dead body or human tissue. They were signed into law in September.

At least seven people with albinism were killed during 2016 and many more suffered attacks. Among those killed by criminal gangs were 23-month-old baby Whitney Chilumpha and nine-year-old Harry Mokoshoni.

In May, unidentified men killed and mutilated Fletcher Masina, a man with albinism, while he was working in his garden.

In July, Lucia Kainga was attacked and had her right hand chopped off by unidentified men in Mweneipenza 5 village, bordering Tanzania. Her husband was tricked into opening the door by an attacker pretending to be in need of help.

On 19 August, a village headman was arrested after attempting to sell a seven-year-old boy with albinism in Phalombe district. He was remanded in custody pending trial.

Societal ignorance and stigmatization also contributed to people with albinism suffering widespread denial of their economic, social and cultural rights. This included: exclusion from government poverty alleviation programmes; lack of support in schools to address bullying and learning difficulties; failure to address their specific medical needs; and lack of economic opportunities.

REPRESSION OF DISSENT

In February, three parliamentarians of the Malawi Congress Party were arrested: Congress spokesperson Jessie Kabwila. Ulemu Msungama and Peter Chankwantha. They were charged with treason in connection with social media messages and released on bail. Their arrest contravened procedures protecting parliamentarians from arrest.

In July, students from the University of Malawi protested against a three fold rise in tuition fees imposed by the government. At Chancellor College in Zomba, police stormed hostels and fired tear gas at students who sought refuge in their rooms. A video showed police slapping two women students. On 26

July, 14 students from Malawi Polytechnic near Blantyre were arrested and charged with conduct likely to breach the peace. They were later released on bail. Eleven students from Kamuzu College of Nursing were also arrested and charged with "proposing violence". They were later released on bail.

---

1. Malawi: "We are not animals to be hunted or sold" — violence and discrimination against people with albinism in Malawi (AFR 36/4126/2016)

MALAYSIA

Malaysia
Head of state: **King Muhammad V (replaced King Abdul Halim Mu'adzam Shah in October)**
Head of government: **Najib Tun Razak**

The crackdown on the rights to freedom of expression, of peaceful assembly and of association persisted. Police were not held accountable for human rights violations. Former opposition leader and prisoner of conscience Anwar Ibrahim, convicted on trumped-up charges of "sodomy", remained in prison serving a five-year sentence. Refugees and asylum-seekers fleeing persecution faced prolonged detention in poor conditions.

FREEDOM OF EXPRESSION

Restrictive laws such as the Sedition Act and the Communications and Multimedia Act continued to be used to silence government critics, who were harassed, intimidated and often detained.

In March, the independent news portal, The Malaysian Insider, was shut down for commercial reasons after being blocked by the government. This was following critical coverage of a corruption scandal linked to the Prime Minister and the misappropriation of hundreds of millions of US dollars from the state-owned investment company 1Malaysia Development Berhad (1MDB).[1]

Prosecutions of political activists and government critics persisted. In May, political activist Hishamuddin Rais was found guilty by the Court of Appeal of sedition and fined MYR5,000 (US$1,140) for calling for electoral reform.[2] Student activist Adam Adli received the same fine for the same charge. Youth activist Mohd Fakhrulrazi was sentenced to eight months' imprisonment for sedition after calling for Anwar Ibrahim's release from prison.

The Communications and Multimedia Act was increasingly used to target government critics and dissidents. In June, activist Fahmi Reza was charged twice under the Act for depicting the Prime Minister as a clown in a caricature. Muhammad Amirul Zakwan pleaded guilty to making insulting comments about the Prince of Johor on Facebook and was sentenced to two years in reform school. At least three others were either charged, detained or investigated for social media posts criticizing the Prince.

Arbitrary travel bans were imposed on three government critics, including cartoonist and political activist Zunar.

FREEDOMS OF ASSEMBLY AND ASSOCIATION

Human rights activists and opposition parliamentarians were tried for participating in peaceful protests.[3] In October, protesters travelling the country in a convoy to advocate for electoral reform and raise awareness of the Bersih 5 demonstration were subjected to physical attacks and intimidation, as well as death threats against their leaders.[4]

ARBITRARY ARRESTS AND DETENTIONS

Preventive detention laws continued to be used to detain people alleged to have committed security crimes. Wording in the Prevention of Terrorism Act was overly broad and open to abuse; it failed to define what is meant by those "engaged in the commission or support of terrorist acts". It allowed the authorities to arrest individuals without providing grounds for detention, for up to 60 days without charge or trial. The Security Offences Measures Act (SOSMA) allowed for detention for up to 28 days without charge or trial.

In January and February, the human rights NGO Suara Rakyat Malaysia (SUARAM) reported that at least 13 people were tortured or otherwise ill-treated while detained under SOSMA, including being beaten and stepped on, and being forced to strip and perform sexual acts in the presence of the authorities. Investigations were ongoing by the National Human Rights Commission at the end of the year.

The National Security Council Act, which came into force in August, provided the executive with extensive powers including arrest, search and seizure without warrant, curfews, and authority to circumvent accountability measures such as inquests into deaths in security areas.[5]

In November, the chairperson of Bersih, Maria Chin Abdullah, was arrested in connection with the organization of the Bersih demonstration (see above). She was held under SOSMA for attempting to carry out activities detrimental to parliamentary democracy. She was placed in solitary confinement for 11 days and held without charge or access to a judge in deplorable conditions, in an unknown location.

POLICE AND SECURITY FORCES

Impunity for deaths in custody and excessive use of force persisted. In April, the Enforcement Agency Integrity Commission found that police officers in charge of interrogating N. Dharmendran, who died in police custody in 2013, were responsible for his death by physical force and that the police later fabricated evidence to cover up his treatment during interrogation. Despite this, in June, the Kuala Lumpur Criminal High Court acquitted the four policemen charged with his murder. His widow filed a civil suit against the police and government.[6]

REFUGEES AND ASYLUM-SEEKERS

In May 2015, amid intense international pressure, Malaysia agreed to accept 1,100 people stranded off its coastline. The group, including over 400 Rohingya, faced prolonged detention for over a year in harsh conditions. In June, the majority of the

Rohingya were released and some were resettled.[7] Immigration detention centres in Malaysia were overcrowded and conditions remained harsh.

A lack of transparency by the authorities regarding investigations into mass graves found on the Thai-Malaysian border in 2015, as well as identification of the remains, led to renewed calls on the authorities to take adequate action to investigate the deaths.

DEATH PENALTY

The death penalty continued to be retained as the mandatory punishment for offences including drug trafficking, murder and discharge of firearms with intent to kill or harm in certain circumstances. Reforms to the death penalty announced by the government in 2015 had not yet materialized. While executions and new death sentences continued to be recorded, no established procedure remained for notification to families of scheduled executions.[8]

---

1. Malaysia: Drop investigations against members of the Malaysia Bar (ASA 28/3758/2016)

2. Malaysia: Prison sentence overturned, fine upheld (ASA 28/4051/2016)

3. Malaysia: End crackdown on Bersih Activists (News story, 18 November)

4. Malaysia: Death threats against Bersih organizers (ASA 28/5014/2016)

5. Malaysia: National Security Council Act gives authorities unchecked and abusive powers (News story, 1 August)

6. Malaysia: Police must be held accountable for death in custody (News story, 29 June)

7. Malaysia: One year on, no justice for the "boat crisis" survivors (News story, 28 May)

8. Malaysia: Stop execution of prisoners due to be hanged (News story, 23 March)

MALDIVES

Republic of Maldives
Head of state and government: **Abdulla Yameen Abdul Gayoom**

The government intensified its crackdown on the rights to freedom of expression and of peaceful assembly. Authorities used new laws and criminal cases to silence political opponents, as well as human rights defenders, journalists and civil society. Lack of independence of the judiciary remained a concern. The government took steps to reintroduce executions after more than 60 years.

BACKGROUND

The ruling coalition enacted new legislation to curtail peaceful protests and expression. An opposition coalition, the Maldives United Opposition, was set up. It was headed by former Vice-President Mohamed Jameel and advised by former President Mohamed Nasheed who was granted political asylum in the UK. There were growing signs of splits in the ruling coalition between factions loyal to the current President and those loyal to former President Maumoon Abdul Gayoom.

UNFAIR TRIALS

The authorities increasingly ignored constitutional safeguards on the right to a fair trial, as evidenced by a string of criminal cases against political opponents. On 10 June, former Vice-President Adeeb received a 15-year jail sentence; he was convicted in connection with a plot to assassinate the President, amid serious concerns about the fairness of his trial. In February, Sheikh Imran Abdulla leader of the Adhaalath Party, was sentenced to 12 years' imprisonment for terrorism after a trial which was widely criticized as unfair and politically motivated. The Supreme Court upheld lengthy jail sentences for former President Nasheed and former Defence Minister Mohamed Nazim; both had been sentenced in trials criticized as grossly unfair.

JUSTICE SYSTEM

The judicial system continued to be deeply politicized. In July, a civil court threatened to hold the Attorney General in contempt after his office said it would appeal against a judgment that barred former staff of *Haveeru* newspaper from working for any other media organization for two years. The government failed to strengthen the Judicial Services Commission to ensure impartiality.

FREEDOM OF EXPRESSION

A new defamation law criminalizing "defamatory" speech, remarks and other actions was passed by Parliament and ratified by the President in August. The law is vaguely worded and broad in its application, giving the authorities wide discretion to target and silence peaceful critics.[1]

Free and independent media faced harassment in the form of lawsuits and bans. News outlets *Haveeru*, DhiTV, AdduLIVE and Channel News Maldives were on occasion blocked or forced to shut down. Four journalists from the pro-opposition Raajje TV were charged with obstructing law enforcement officers after covering a protest; their sentences were expected in early 2017.

Social media activist "Lucas" Jaleel was arrested for "inciting hatred" in July after he alleged excessive use of force by police in a series of tweets.

In April, police confirmed that reporter Ahmed Rilwan had been abducted outside his home in 2014, having previously denied there was evidence of an abduction. In May, the government denied involvement in his disappearance to the UN Working Group on Enforced and Involuntary Disappearances.

In September, police raided the premises of the newspaper *Maldives Independent*, on the basis that it was suspected of involvement in a coup plot. The raid took place hours after the premiere of an Al Jazeera documentary alleging large-scale corruption by the President and senior ministers, in which the newspaper's editor was interviewed.

FREEDOM OF ASSEMBLY

Arbitrary restrictions on peaceful protesters and human rights defenders continued. In February, police banned an anti-corruption rally in the capital, Malé. In April, 16 journalists were arrested after staging a peaceful protest against the defamation law outside the President's office,[2] and in August journalists were stopped from protesting

against the same law. In July, the Maldives United Opposition was refused permission by the government to hold a rally. A law was enacted in August requiring written permission from the police to hold a protest in Malé.

CRUEL, INHUMAN OR DEGRADING PUNISHMENT

Courts continued to sentence people, the vast majority of them women, to flogging. This was most commonly imposed for "fornication". Despite flogging constituting torture or cruel, inhuman or degrading punishment, the government continued to insist that it would not remove the punishment from Maldivian law.

DEATH PENALTY

Senior officials repeatedly pledged to resume executions and end a moratorium on the use of the death penalty that has been in effect for more than 60 years. The government declared that it would carry out executions within 30 days of the Supreme Court upholding death sentences and changed the method of execution from lethal injection to death by hanging. Death sentences against three people were upheld by the Supreme Court in June and July, despite well-documented fair trial concerns in at least one case.[3] No executions took place, as negotiations with the victims' families over possible pardons under Islamic law were ongoing. Of the 17 prisoners on death row, at least five were sentenced to death for crimes committed when they were below 18 years of age.

---

1. Maldives: Proposed defamation law is an attack on freedom of expression (ASA 29/4573/2016)

2. Maldives: Arrest of 16 journalists threatens freedom of the press (ASA 33/3773/2016)

3. Maldives: Halt plans to carry out first execution in more than six decades (ASA 29/4364/2016)

MALI

Republic of Mali
Head of state: Ibrahim Boubacar Keïta
Head of government: Modibo Keïta

Internal armed conflict and instability
increased. Armed groups committed
abuses, including killing peacekeepers.
Security forces and UN peacekeepers used
excessive and lethal force, including against
protesters.

BACKGROUND

Instability spread from the north to the centre
of the country, with a growing number of
armed groups carrying out attacks. In July,
for example, armed groups killed 17 soldiers
and wounded 35 others during an attack on
an army base in central Mali. Armed groups
retained control of the northern town of Kidal.
The proliferation of armed groups hampered
implementation of the 2015 Algiers peace
agreement. In July, following several attacks,
including in the north and the capital,
Bamako, the state of emergency was
extended until March 2017.

In June, the UN Security Council extended
the mandate of the UN Multidimensional
Integrated Stabilization Mission in Mali
(MINUSMA) to June 2017. More than
10,000 peacekeepers were stationed in the
country.

More than 135,000 Malians remained as
refugees in neighbouring countries because
of the conflict.

ABUSES BY ARMED GROUPS

Attacks by armed groups against MINUSMA
increased sharply. More than 62 attacks were
committed during the year, killing 25
peacekeepers and six civilian contractors
working for the UN. Landmines used by
armed groups killed and maimed civilians,
peacekeepers and members of the security
forces.

In January, Beatrice Stockly, a Swiss
missionary, was abducted in Timbuktu by al-
Qa'ida in the Islamic Maghreb (AQIM). She

had been captured and held by the same
group for nine days in 2012. In December,
Sophie Petronin, a French national working
for a humanitarian organization, was
kidnapped in Gao by AQIM.

In mid-May, the armed group Ansar
Eddine killed five Chadian peacekeepers and
wounded three in an ambush about 15km
north of Aguelhok in the eastern Kidal region.
Later that month, an attack on a MINUSMA
camp in the northeastern city of Gao, claimed
by AQIM, killed one Chinese peacekeeper
and injured others.

EXCESSIVE USE OF FORCE

Security forces and UN peacekeepers used
excessive force and were accused of
extrajudicial executions. The UN reported a
total of 24 instances of killings, summary
executions and enforced disappearances in
both March and May. In May, it reported that
of 103 people arrested by Malian and
international forces for terrorism-related
charges so far in 2016, three had been
summarily executed and 12 had been
tortured by Malian forces.

In April, two demonstrators were shot dead
and four others were wounded at Kidal
Airport during a protest against arrests by
international forces. MINUSMA established
an inquiry.

In July, Malian forces fired live ammunition
during a march in Gao organized by the Civil
Resistance Movement, killing Mahamane
Housseini, Seydou Douka Maiga and
Abdoulaye Idrissa, and wounding more than
40 others.

IMPUNITY

Despite some progress, measures taken to
ensure truth, justice and reparation for
victims of the conflict were limited. The UN
Independent Expert on Mali highlighted the
lack of progress, particularly regarding
meaningful access to justice for women who
had experienced violence. Insecurity and
lack of logistical support for magistrates were
cited as among the major impediments.

In May, 12 people charged with terrorism-
related offences were sentenced to prison

terms. Some of them had been released under the peace agreement.

In November, the trial began of General Haya Amadou Sanogo on charges linked to the abduction and murder in 2012 of soldiers accused of supporting the ousted President, Amadou Toumani Touré.[1]

The Truth, Justice and Reconciliation Commission, established in 2014 to investigate serious human rights violations between 1960 and 2013, was still not operational at the end of 2016.

INTERNATIONAL JUSTICE

In September, the International Criminal Court sentenced Ahmad Al Faqi Al Mahdi to nine years in prison for directing attacks against religious buildings and historic monuments. A member of Ansar Eddine, he was charged for his role in destroying nine mausoleums and a mosque in the northern town of Timbuktu in 2012. He pleaded guilty.

FREEDOM OF EXPRESSION

In August, Mohamed Youssouf Bathily (known as Rath Bath), a journalist working for Maliba FM radio, was arrested and charged with undermining decency and demotivating the army. He had called for the army's Chief of Staff to resign and criticized the army. He was released after two days under judicial supervision; his radio programme was banned.

RIGHT TO EDUCATION

According to the UN, 296 out of 2,380 schools were closed in the regions of Gao, Kidal, Ségou and Timbuktu because of insecurity, with no alternatives provided. The CEDAW Committee noted the poor quality of education owing to the high pupil-teacher ratio and the lack of textbooks and qualified teachers. The Committee also noted rural-urban disparities in enrolment. Seven armed groups continued to occupy schools.

RIGHT TO AN ADEQUATE STANDARD OF LIVING

More than 33,000 Malians remained internally displaced because of the conflict,

and some 3 million people faced food insecurity, including more than 423,000 at severe levels. Hijackings by armed groups in Gao and Ménaka regions hampered access to humanitarian assistance, including health care. In June, a warehouse in Kidal stocked with food for more than 10,000 people was looted.

WOMEN'S RIGHTS

In July, the CEDAW Committee voiced concern about the low level of representation of women on the Truth, Justice and Reconciliation Commission and at decision-making levels following the peace agreement. It also expressed concern at the extremely low completion rate for girls in secondary education owing to factors including early and child marriage, early pregnancy, indirect school costs, child labour and a preference for sending boys to school. The Committee urged Mali to reform legislation to eliminate discrimination against women, and to finalize the bill to prohibit female genital mutilation.

---

1. Mali: Trial of former junta leader must bring justice for abductions, torture and murder (News story, 28 November)

MALTA

Republic of Malta
Head of state : Marie-Louise Coleiro Preca
Head of government: Joseph Muscat

Implementation of a new reception regime for asylum-seekers and migrants started, which moved away from automatic and mandatory detention of people entering Malta irregularly. However, there were concerns that safeguards against arbitrary and unlawful detention remained insufficient. Abortion remained prohibited in all circumstances.

REFUGEES' AND MIGRANTS' RIGHTS

In January and February, UNHCR, the UN refugee agency, and national NGOs welcomed elements of the new legal and policy framework relating to the reception of asylum-seekers and migrants in Malta. It had been approved at the end of 2015 and introduced through amendments to the Immigration and the Refugee Acts, regulations and a new policy document of the Ministry for Home Affairs and National Security.

The new framework ended the problematic regime of long-term automatic and mandatory detention of asylum-seekers and migrants irregularly entering Malta. However, a period of detention upon arrival was maintained at the newly created Initial Reception Centres of around 70 hours, where asylum-seekers and migrants are medically screened, identified and assessed for release or further detention. While such initial detention should ordinarily be for no more than seven days, it could be longer for health-related concerns. The new framework also introduced legal grounds for detention, free legal assistance, the possibility to challenge detention orders and an automatic review of detention orders.

Concerns remained as to the interpretation of the legal grounds for detention, a lack of clarity on when alternatives to detention might apply, and the lack of safeguards to ensure the proportionate use of detention. In particular, UNHCR noted that some of the new guidelines for immigration authorities were not fully consistent with international law and standards, and could lead to arbitrary detention.

There were no irregular boat arrivals of refugees and migrants directly from North Africa, as most people were rescued at sea and disembarked in Italy. However, 29 people in need of urgent medical assistance during their rescue on the high seas were taken to Malta. The Armed Forces of Malta continued to participate in the rescue of refugees and migrants crossing the central Mediterranean on overcrowded and unseaworthy vessels, as part of Frontex Operation Triton and of EUNAVFOR MED Operation Sophia. By the end of November over 1,600 people had reached Malta by plane or ferry to seek asylum. Over a third were Libyans.

Those accepted under the EU relocation programme (80 people by the end of November) were held for medical screening for around 70 hours in the newly created Initial Reception Centres, although this was criticized by UNHCR.

In January, the European Court of Human Rights (ECtHR) found Malta in breach of Article 5, paragraph 4 of the European Convention on Human Rights, on the right to have lawfulness of detention assessed speedily by a court. The applicants were two Somali women who had been detained from August 2012 to August 2013, because of their irregular entry into Malta under the previous reception regime, and who had no adequate remedy to challenge the lawfulness of their detention.

In June, the UN Working Group on Arbitrary Detention released a report on Malta, following a visit to the country the previous year. The Working Group acknowledged the legislative reform to the automatic nature of detention. It also noted that programmes for the integration of migrants, asylum-seekers and refugees into Maltese society remained inadequate.

In November, the Ministry for Home Affairs and National Security announced a review of Temporary Humanitarian Protection – New (THPN) certificates, which are held by people whose asylum requests have failed. NGOs expressed concern that the decision could hamper the ability of those concerned to access basic services, including health and education. UNHCR recommended caution in implementing repatriations as a result of the review, as it was aware of cases of people who should have been granted international protection but were instead granted THPN.

SEXUAL AND REPRODUCTIVE RIGHTS

Abortion remained prohibited in all circumstances, with women being denied access to it even when their life was at risk.

LEGAL, CONSTITUTIONAL OR INSTITUTIONAL DEVELOPMENTS

In January, the ECtHR found Malta in breach of Article 6 of the European Convention on

Human Rights, which among other things, guarantees access to a lawyer at the initial stages of police interrogation. A convicted offender had complained that he had been denied legal assistance during questioning in police custody at the pre-trial stage.

MAURITANIA

Islamic Republic of Mauritania
Head of state: **Mohamed Ould Abdel Aziz**
Head of government: **Yahya Ould Hademine**

Human rights defenders and opponents of the government faced politically motivated prosecutions, with anti-slavery organizations particularly persecuted. The rights to freedom of expression, association and peaceful assembly were restricted. Torture and other ill-treatment in custody were common. Groups making up two thirds of the population faced systematic discrimination, and extreme poverty was widespread. The practice of slavery continued.

HUMAN RIGHTS DEFENDERS

Laws – including those covering public disorder, resisting arrest and belonging to an unauthorized organization – were used in politically motivated prosecutions against human rights defenders and government opponents, particularly anti-slavery activists.

In May, the Supreme Court ordered the release of two anti-slavery activists, Biram Ould Dah Abeid and Brahim Bilal, after reducing their prison sentences. The two prisoners of conscience, members of Initiative for the Resurgence of the Abolitionist Movement (IRA), were arrested in November 2014 after taking part in a peaceful protest. They had been sentenced to two years' imprisonment on charges of belonging to an unrecognized organization, taking part in an unauthorized assembly, failing to comply with police orders and resisting arrest. Another member of the IRA who received the same sentence, Djiby Sow,

was released on medical grounds in June 2015.

In June and July, 13 other members of the IRA were arrested after a protest against forced eviction by communities in the slum area of Bouamatou, in the capital Nouakchott. Although none of the IRA members had attended the protest, in August they were convicted on charges including rebellion and use of violence. The court refused to examine allegations of torture made by the accused.[1] In October a group of UN experts expressed serious concern that these activists had been targeted by the government for their anti-slavery advocacy, stating that the government was hostile to civil society groups that criticized its policies, especially groups such as the IRA, whose members are drawn from the Haratine minority and advocate for an end to slavery. In November, the Appeals Court of Nouadhibou acquitted three of the 13 IRA members and reduced the sentences of seven others who were released the same month. Three remaining IRA members were sentenced to six months and three years in prison.

FREEDOMS OF EXPRESSION, ASSOCIATION AND ASSEMBLY

The space for the exercise of the rights to freedom of expression, association and peaceful assembly shrank as journalists, human rights defenders and government critics were arrested and prosecuted by a politicized judiciary.[2]

In April, the Appeals Court in Nouakchott upheld the death sentence of Mohamed Mkhaïtir for apostasy in the first case of its kind in Mauritania. Mohamed Mkhaïtir was originally sentenced to death in December 2014 in Nouadhibou after a year in pre-trial detention for writing a blog critical of those who use Islam to foster discrimination against *Moulamines* (blacksmiths) and the descendants of slaves and griots. The Appeals Court referred the case to the Supreme Court.

In July, Cheikh Baye, manager of the Meyadine news website, was sentenced to three years' imprisonment for using violence against a public official. He had accused a government spokesperson of lying and threw his shoe at him during a press briefing. Five people who criticized the verdict were also convicted of the same charges in August. Three were sentenced to two years' imprisonment and two received suspended sentences.

The authorities continued to bar the legal registration of several NGOs and human rights organizations. For example, the Association des Veuves de la Mauritanie, an organization calling for the truth about summary executions and disappearances in the 1990s, has been waiting for recognition since 1993; it renewed its request in 2010.

TORTURE AND OTHER ILL-TREATMENT

Following a visit in February, the UN Special Rapporteur on torture welcomed legislative developments, including the introduction of a new law against torture, and the establishment of a National Preventive Mechanism (NPM). He stressed that the judiciary should step up efforts to implement these safeguards and highlighted the lack of investigations into allegations of torture. He also drew attention to the use of unofficial detention facilities and the denial of access to a lawyer for up to 45 days in terrorism-related cases.

Prisoners, male and female, reported in mid-2016 that they had been tortured and otherwise ill-treated in police custody and by prison guards. One prisoner charged with a terrorism-related offence said that following his arrest in March, he was beaten to make him "confess" with his hands and feet tied together behind his back.

The IRA members arrested in June and July were held separately in undisclosed places of detention and denied access to their families and lawyers. They were interrogated at night, deprived of sleep and denied access to toilets. At least four had their feet and hands bound in painful positions for hours and were suspended by ropes from the ceiling. Others were stripped, insulted and threatened with death. Despite

the new NPM programme to monitor places of detention, an NPM member was denied access to IRA members who were being held in incommunicado detention.

DISCRIMINATION – HARATINES AND AFRO-MAURITANIANS

The UN Special Rapporteur on extreme poverty and human rights, who visited Mauritania in April, highlighted a systematic absence of Haratines and Afro-Mauritanians from almost all positions of power and their exclusion from many aspects of economic and social life, including their inability to obtain a national identity card. The two groups make up two thirds of the population. He stressed that, although economic, social and cultural rights are mentioned in the preamble of the Constitution, there were no provisions dealing with them. He pointed out that in some rural areas only 10% of children attended secondary school and that the maternal mortality rate remained one of the highest in the world. In 2015, according to the World Bank, 602 mothers died for every 100,000 live births.

SLAVERY

Although slavery was abolished officially in 1981 and is recognized as a crime in domestic law, human rights organizations including SOS Esclaves and IRA regularly criticized the continuation of this practice.[3]

In May, the Special Tribunal against Slavery opened in Nema, and in the same month two former slave owners were handed a one-year prison sentence and a four-year suspended sentence and ordered to pay compensation to two women victims. Yet in the same month, in the same town, President Abdel Aziz denied that slavery existed and called on the Haratines, the former slave population, to have fewer children in order to address the legacy of slavery and poverty.

---

1. Mauritania: Drop all charges and release anti-slavery activists (News story, 1 August)

2. Mauritania: New law compromises right to freedom of association (News story, 2 June)

MEXICO

United Mexican States
Head of state and government: Enrique Peña Nieto

Ten years since the start of the so-called "war on drugs and organized crime", the use of military personnel in public security operations continued and violence throughout the country remained widespread. There continued to be reports of torture and other ill-treatment, enforced disappearances, extrajudicial executions and arbitrary detentions. Impunity persisted for human rights violations and crimes under international law. Mexico received its highest-ever number of asylum claims, mostly from people fleeing violence in El Salvador, Honduras and Guatemala. Human rights defenders and independent observers were subjected to intense smear campaigns; journalists continued to be killed and threatened for their work. Violence against women remained a major concern and "gender alerts" were issued in the states of Jalisco and Michoacán. Congress rejected one of the two bills presented to allow same-sex couples to marry and adopt children.

BACKGROUND

The ruling Institutional Revolutionary Party lost a number of governorships in various states in June elections. A prolonged social conflict between the government and teachers' unions led to mass protests and blockaded highways throughout the country, with unions calling for the government to revoke its 2013 educational reform.

Mexico completed its transition from a written, inquisitorial criminal justice system to one based on oral trials, after an eight-year preparatory period came to a close. Many challenges of the prior system remained – including a failure to respect the presumption of innocence – despite the implementation of the reform.

A 10-point security plan announced by President Peña Nieto in November 2014 had yet to be fully implemented, with promises to pass laws against torture and enforced disappearances as well as disappearances by non-state actors yet to be fulfilled. A package of anti-corruption laws was passed by Congress. The new legislation was widely criticized as falling short of earlier drafts.

Official records noted that the number of soldiers and marines employed in security operations throughout the country increased. In October the Minister of Defence admitted that the war on drugs had taken its toll on the exhausted armed forces and called for further legal clarity regarding their role in public security tasks. Legislators vowed to discuss reforms regarding the armed forces in security operations.

POLICE AND SECURITY FORCES

There was a marked increase in violence, with 36,056 homicides registered by the authorities up until the end of November – the highest number since the start of President Peña Nieto's term in 2012 – compared to 33,017 in 2015.

In response to widespread protests from teachers' movements, the authorities carried out a number of police operations, some of which resulted in civilians being killed and injured. Several leaders of the movements were arrested and detained in federal prisons. Many of them were subsequently released pending further investigation.

EXTRAJUDICIAL EXECUTIONS

Perpetrators of extrajudicial executions continued to enjoy impunity; the crimes were not properly investigated. The armed forces continued to contribute to investigations in cases involving military personnel, contrary to the 2014 reform of the Code of Military Justice. For the third consecutive year, the authorities failed to publish the number of people killed or wounded in clashes with the police and military forces.

Dozens of mass graves were uncovered throughout the country, often on the initiative of family groups rather than authorities or official forensic experts. Local authorities illegally disposed of over 100 unidentified bodies in at least one grave in the municipality of Tetelcingo, Morelos state. The perpetrators of the killings remained unidentified.

On 19 June, at least eight people were killed and dozens injured in Nochixtlán town, Oaxaca state, during a police operation following a roadblock as part of a demonstration against the government's education reform. Footage published by media outlets contradicted the authorities' original assertion that the policemen were unarmed.

In August, the National Human Rights Commission found that federal police members had tortured at least two people in the municipality of Tanhuato, Michoacán state, in May 2015 as part of a security operation; that at least 22 of the 43 people killed during the operation were victims of arbitrary execution; and that the police had tampered with evidence including by planting firearms on the victims.

Investigations into the killings by soldiers of 22 people in 2014 in Tlatlaya, Mexico state, had yet to produce concrete results. The authorities failed to take responsibility for the order "to take down criminals" (meant as "to kill" in this context) that was the basis for military operations in the area in 2014, or to investigate any officers with command responsibility.

No one was known to have been prosecuted for the killings in 2015 of 16 people by federal police officers and other security forces in Apatzingán, Michoacán state; the authorities failed to adequately investigate the killings or to look into the responsibility of those in command.

TORTURE AND OTHER ILL-TREATMENT

Impunity for torture and other ill-treatment remained almost absolute, with numerous reports of beatings, near asphyxiation with plastic bags, electric shocks, rape and other sexual assault taking place during police and military operations. Sexual violence used as a form of torture was commonplace during arrests of women.[1] For the first time in two years, the Federal Attorney General's Office announced charges of torture against five federal officials in April, in response to a leaked video showing police officers and soldiers torturing a woman. Also in April, in a rare case a federal judge sentenced an army general to 52 years' imprisonment for having ordered an operation which involved torture and homicide as well as destruction of a body in Chihuahua state in 2008.

In April, the Senate approved a bill for a General Law on Torture which complied with international standards. The bill was amended and remained pending a general vote in the Chamber of Deputies at the end of the year.

The Special Unit on Torture of the Federal Attorney General's Office reported 4,715 torture investigation files under revision at federal level.

As in previous years, the special medical examination procedure of the Federal Attorney General's Office for cases of alleged torture was not applied in most cases, with a backlog of over 3,000 requests on file. In many cases, investigations into torture and other ill-treatment failed to advance without an official examination.

In September, the Inter-American Commission on Human Rights (IACHR) referred the case of 11 women who were subjected to sexual violence as a form of torture in San Salvador Atenco in 2006 to the Inter-American Court of Human Rights, given Mexico's failure to fulfil the Commission's recommendations on the case.

REFUGEES' AND MIGRANTS' RIGHTS

A record number of asylum claims were registered, with 6,898 lodged as of October – 93% of whom were nationals of El Salvador, Honduras and Guatemala. Refugee status was granted to 2,162 people, despite estimates that more than 400,000 irregular migrants crossed Mexico's southern border each year, half of whom could qualify for asylum status, according to international organizations and academics. In the majority of cases, the authorities failed to adequately inform migrants of their right to seek asylum in Mexico.

In August, a constitutional reform to recognize the right to asylum entered into force.

The implementation of the Southern Border Plan again led to a surge in security operations on the Mexican border with Guatemala and Belize, with frequent reports of extortions, mass deportations, kidnappings and other human rights abuses against migrants. As of November, 174,526 irregular migrants had been apprehended and detained, and 136,420 returned to their country. Of those deported, 97% were from Central America. Data from the US Congress in February showed that the US government plans to allocate US$75 million to "security and migration enforcement" on Mexico's southern border, through the Mérida Initiative.

The Federal Attorney General's Office established a new Unit for the Investigation of Crimes against Migrants. Civil society organizations participated in the design of a Mexican Mechanism for Foreign Support in Search and Investigation to co-ordinate Mexican and Central American authorities' efforts to ensure justice for migrant victims of disappearances by non-state actors and other crimes in Mexico.

In September, President Peña Nieto announced a plan on refugees at a UN summit and officially acknowledged the refugee crisis in Mexico and Central America. The plan promised to increase funding of Mexico's refugee agency by 80%, to ensure that no child migrant under 11 years of age be detained, and to strengthen the inclusion and integration of refugees in the country. In May, a special report by the National Human Rights Commission identified at least 35,433 victims of internal displacement in Mexico, despite the fact that credible estimates based on official data were at least four times higher. In October, the Commission published a report highlighting the poor living conditions

in migration detention centres, especially for unaccompanied children.

ENFORCED DISAPPEARANCES

Enforced disappearances with the involvement of the state and disappearances committed by non-state actors continued to be widespread and those responsible continued to enjoy almost absolute impunity. The investigations into the cases of missing people continued to be flawed and unduly delayed. The authorities generally failed to immediately search for victims.

By the end of the year, 29,917 people (22,414 men and 7,503 women) were reported as missing by the government. The figures by the National Register of Missing and Disappeared Persons did not include federal cases that occurred prior to 2014 nor cases classified as other criminal offences such as hostage-taking or human trafficking.

Enforced disappearances and disappearances by non-state actors inflicted serious harm on victims' relatives, which constituted a form of torture and other cruel, inhuman or degrading treatment or punishment. Available data suggested that a majority of victims were men; women made up the majority of relatives seeking truth, justice and reparations. Some relatives of disappeared people who were searching for their family members received death threats.

The Senate held public hearings with relatives of disappeared people on the General Law on Disappearances that had been presented to Congress by President Peña Nieto in December 2015. The bill remained before Congress.

In March, criminal charges were presented against five marines for the enforced disappearance of Armando Humberto del Bosque Villarreal, who had been found dead weeks after his arbitrary arrest in 2013 in Nuevo León state.

In April, the Interdisciplinary Group of Independent Experts (GIEI) appointed by the IACHR published its second report on the 43 students from a teacher training college in Ayotzinapa, Guerrero state, who were victims of enforced disappearance in September

2014. The GIEI confirmed that the authorities' assertion that the students had been killed and burned in a local rubbish dump was scientifically impossible. The GIEI also revealed that in October 2014, officials had irregularly visited a scene later linked to the crime and handled important evidence without proper permission or documentation. A man held in custody in relation to the case was forced by the authorities to participate in the visit without his lawyer present or any oversight from a judge. The visit took place a day before the government discovered a small piece of bone in the same place, later identified as belonging to student Alexander Mora Venancio. The leading official involved in these investigations resigned from his post within the Federal Attorney General's Office, even though an investigation into his actions was ongoing. He was immediately appointed by President Peña Nieto to another senior federal position. In November, the IACHR presented its work plan for a follow-up mechanism on the Ayotzinapa case after the GIEI recommendations and the 2014 precautionary measure issued by the IAHCR ordering Mexico to determine the status and whereabouts of the 43 missing students.

HUMAN RIGHTS DEFENDERS AND JOURNALISTS

Human rights defenders and journalists continued to be threatened, harassed, intimidated, attacked or killed. At least 11 journalists were killed during the year. The federal Mechanism for the Protection of Human Rights Defenders and Journalists left human rights defenders and journalists inadequately protected. In February, international human rights organizations denounced the smear campaign against the GIEI and local NGOs involved in the Ayotzinapa case – a campaign that appeared to be tolerated by the authorities. The number of requests for protection under the Mechanism remained steady in relation to the previous year.

In July, Humberto Moreira Valdés, former governor of the state of Coahuila and former president of the Institutional Revolutionary

Party, sued prominent journalist Sergio Aguayo for US$ 550,000 in a civil lawsuit for alleged moral damage to his reputation due to an opinion piece published by Sergio Aguayo. The excessive amount demanded could constitute a form of punishment and intimidation, potentially affecting freedom of expression in public debate.

In August, prisoner of conscience and community environmental defender Ildefonso Zamora was released after nine months' imprisonment on fabricated charges.

FREEDOM OF ASSEMBLY

The Supreme Court continued to analyze a legal challenge to Mexico City's 2014 Law on Mobility. It ruled in August that the law should not be interpreted as imposing a prior authorization regime for demonstrations, but only as a rule allowing people to notify authorities in advance of any planned demonstration. The Court considered that the lack of provisions on spontaneous demonstrations did not mean that such acts were forbidden in any way. Finally, it voted in favour of a rule banning protests in the city's main avenues.

RIGHTS OF LESBIAN, GAY, BISEXUAL, TRANSGENDER AND INTERSEX PEOPLE

In May, President Peña Nieto presented two draft bills to Congress to reform the Constitution and the Federal Civil Code. The proposed constitutional reform to expressly guarantee the right to marry without discrimination was rejected by Congress in November.

The second proposed reform to the Civil Code would prohibit discrimination on grounds of sexual orientation and gender identity in allowing couples to marry and people to adopt children; the reform also included the right of transgender people to have their gender identity recognized by Mexico. The bill had yet to be discussed in Congress.

In September, Supreme Court jurisprudence upholding same-sex couples' rights to marry and adopt children without being discriminated against on the basis of sexual orientation and gender identity became binding on all judges in the country.

VIOLENCE AGAINST WOMEN AND GIRLS

Violence against women and girls remained endemic. In April, dozens of thousands of people demonstrated around the country, demanding an end to violence against women, including sexual harassment. The "Gender Alert" mechanism was activated in the states of Jalisco and Michoacán after it had already been activated in the states of Morelos and Mexico in the previous year. A lack of accurate, up-to-date and disaggregated data about gender-based violence constituted a major obstacle to tackling the problem.

INDIGENOUS PEOPLES' RIGHTS

Due to last-minute information from the Ministry of Economy regarding the cancellation of two mining concessions by companies in the community of San Miguel Progreso, Guerrero state, the Supreme Court declined to consider the effect that the Mining Law of 1991 had on Indigenous Peoples' rights. A legal framework on Indigenous Peoples' right to free, prior and informed consent remained largely absent from the legislative debate, despite the fact that a bill had been discussed in public forums and the National Human Rights Commission issued a recommendation in October to the Congress that it legislate on this matter. In September, the Indigenous municipality of Guevea de Humboldt, Oaxaca state, allowed women in the community to exercise their right to vote for the first time in local elections.

---

1. Surviving death: Police and military torture of women in Mexico (AMR 41/4237/2016)

MOLDOVA

Republic of Moldova
Head of state: **Igor Dodon (replaced Nicolae Timofti in December)**
Head of government: **Pavel Filip (replaced Gheorghe Brega in January)**

Police occasionally used unnecessary or excessive force during street protests. A number of high-profile cases of criminal prosecution prompted concern about unfair trials, including selective justice. The media remained largely free albeit less pluralistic than in previous years. No progress was made to address structural causes of impunity for torture and other ill-treatment. Overcrowding and poor conditions prevailed in some penitentiary institutions. Laws allowed forced detention and non-consensual administration of treatment to people with disabilities in psychiatric institutions.

BACKGROUND

A sense of impotence in the face of corruption and deteriorating living standards continued to define the political climate, prompting popular discontent and sporadic protests. Rumours of political meddling by a prominent oligarch, following the sudden arrest of former Prime Minister Vladimir Filat in October 2015, prompted some of the large street protests. Relative political stability was achieved in January, through opaque backstage party deals, leading to the appointment of the new Prime Minister. The Constitutional Court ruled on 3 March that the country's President should be elected by direct popular vote, leading to the first direct presidential election since 1996, on 30 October (with a second round on 13 November).

FREEDOM OF ASSEMBLY

Demonstrations in the capital Chişinău and elsewhere remained peaceful, except for some minor clashes between protesters and police. The police response, although generally restrained, occasionally involved unnecessary or excessive use of force, including tear gas and batons.

The trial continued of the seven "Petrenco group" protesters (for trying to force their way into the Prosecutor's Office during a demonstration on 6 September 2015), with six of them spending over six months in detention and all charged with "attempting to organize mass disturbances". Following much criticism in Moldova and internationally, the six detained defendants were placed under house arrest on 22 February and released one month later under travel restrictions.

UNFAIR TRIALS

The case against the "Petrenco group" and a number of other criminal prosecutions prompted concerns about political bias.

Following eight months of detention, on 27 June Vladimir Filat was found guilty of "passive corruption" and "benefiting from [his] influence" in relation to fraud in 2014 that cost the National Bank over a third of its reserves, and sentenced to nine years' imprisonment. His closed trial left more questions than answers, including over the lack of investigation against any other politicians. His defence appealed against the verdict and claimed that there were procedural violations and lack of equality of arms between the parties. The latter was officially denied, but because of the closed proceedings, neither claim could be independently verified. During the hearing, Vladimir Filat reportedly went on hunger strike for 20 days and once lost consciousness in the courtroom.

FREEDOM OF EXPRESSION – MEDIA

While media freedom was generally respected, concerns over independence persisted in light of the concentration of ownership in the hands of a few individuals. At least two prominent critical journalists complained of anonymous threats. In August, a bullet was fired into the window of Constantin Cheianu's daughter's flat. The journalist had received text messages warning that he "will be stopped" if he carried on writing about the oligarchic system. TV presenter Natalia Morari reported receiving similar warnings from a source which she described as credible. Both journalists filed official complaints with the authorities.

TORTURE AND OTHER ILL-TREATMENT

No progress was made to address structural causes of impunity for torture and other ill-treatment, while the prosecution of alleged perpetrators remained extremely rare. Between January and June, 331 people complained to the Prosecutor's Office about torture and other ill-treatment. Out of 19 torture-related cases in which courts gave decisions, 15 resulted in convictions but only two out of the 18 defendants convicted received custodial sentences.

Vladimir Filat's family and lawyer repeatedly alleged that he was ill-treated, including by being placed in solitary confinement where they said conditions amounted to torture. This once again shone a light on Penitentiary Institution no. 13 in Chişinău, which had been criticized by independent monitors in previous years. All requests for an independent visit to Filat, including by Amnesty International, were refused, even after his conviction. However, Amnesty International visited the institution and confirmed that while conditions had visibly improved in some cells (improvements usually sponsored by inmates' families), overcrowding and poor sanitary and hygiene conditions prevailed in others.

In June, the European Committee for the Prevention of Torture reported on its September 2015 visit to Moldova. It noted progress since 2011, but there were still concerns about excessive force by police during arrest, ill-treatment of detainees during "preliminary questioning", and overcrowding of "disturbing proportions" in some prisons.

LEGAL, CONSTITUTIONAL OR INSTITUTIONAL DEVELOPMENTS

Changes to the Criminal Procedure Code came into force on 26 May, introducing stronger safeguards against arbitrary use of pre-trial detention and requiring non-custodial alternatives wherever possible.

RIGHTS OF LESBIAN, GAY, BISEXUAL, TRANSGENDER AND INTERSEX PEOPLE

The biggest-ever Pride march took place on 22 May in Chişinău, involving around 300 participants. Some counter-demonstrators attempted to assault LGBTI rights activists. The police provided an effective cordon but decided to evacuate the participants by bus just before the march reached its final destination.

DISCRIMINATION – PEOPLE WITH DISABILITIES

The UN Special Rapporteur on the rights of persons with disabilities asked the government to urgently end the institutionalization of people with disabilities in psychiatric and psycho-neurological residential institutions. Various laws allow the forced detention and non-consensual administration of psychiatric treatment for people with disabilities as well as the non-consensual termination of pregnancies on the grounds of psychosocial or intellectual impairment.

MONGOLIA

Mongolia
Head of state: **Tsakhia Elbegdorj**
Head of government: **Jargaltulga Erdenebat (replaced Chimediin Saikhanbileg in July)**

The main opposition party Mongolia's People's Party obtained the majority of seats in the June parliamentary elections. The new government postponed the implementation of five laws passed by the previous government, including a new Criminal Code which would have abolished the death penalty. The government failed to protect human rights defenders from threats and attacks by state agencies and non-state actors. Torture and other ill-treatment remained pervasive, particularly in custody. Residents of the capital, Ulaanbaatar, remained at risk of forced eviction and violations of their right to adequate housing because legislation did not conform to international human rights law and standards.

HOUSING RIGHTS

Despite the advanced stage of urban redevelopment in Ulaanbaatar, relevant laws and policies continued to lag behind practice at both national and local levels. Large-scale redevelopment in the *ger* areas – areas without adequate access to essential services – in Ulaanbaatar were initiated 10 years earlier to manage the city's unplanned population growth and increased pollution levels.[1] In the absence of adequate government regulation and effective consultation and monitoring, individuals affected by redevelopment were vulnerable to human rights violations, particularly the right to adequate housing.

In one case, redevelopment plans had a devastating impact on residents. People in a dilapidated building in the Sukhbaatar district of Ulaanbaatar, including people with disabilities and families with young children, remained in apartments without heating during the winter temperatures of -30°C in 2015-2016. The authorities relocated them to temporary accommodation in October. Those who were relocated remained at risk of a wide range of human rights violations and abuses without effective safeguards and mechanisms for redress.[2]

HUMAN RIGHTS DEFENDERS

Human rights defenders continued to be subjected to physical and psychological threats and attacks by both state and non-state actors. An investigation continued into the suspicious death in late 2015 of Lkhagvasumberel Tomorsukh, an environmental activist from the Snow Leopard

Conservation Foundation. The National Human Rights Commission of Mongolia reported that the law on NGOs and other domestic laws did not fully protect the rights of human rights defenders.

TORTURE AND OTHER ILL-TREATMENT

Torture and other ill-treatment in detention centres continued to be widespread. The authorities frequently transferred detainees between detention centres or placed them in centres far from their homes in order to intimidate them and make their access to legal counsel and family visits difficult.

1. Mongolia: Falling short – the right to adequate housing in Ulaanbaatar (ASA 30/4933/2016)

2. Mongolia: 200 people face imminent risk of homelessness (ASA 30/3743/2016) and Further information (ASA 30/4793/2016)

MONTENEGRO

Montenegro
Head of state: Filip Vujanović
Head of government: Duško Marković (replaced Milo Đukanović in November)

Parliamentary elections in October cemented the rule of the governing coalition led by Milo Đukanović; independent election monitors reported irregularities in dozens of polling stations.

COUNTER-TERROR AND SECURITY

In January and June, Montenegro resettled two former detainees from the US detention centre at Guantánamo Bay, Cuba.

In September, the government signed the Additional Protocol to the Council of Europe Convention on the Prevention of Terrorism, to tackle the issue of "foreign terrorist fighters".

DISCRIMINATION – LESBIAN, GAY, BISEXUAL, TRANSGENDER AND INTERSEX PEOPLE

In May, two LGBTI organizations brought a case before an administrative court against the Ministry of Interior for failing to guarantee the right to freedom of peaceful assembly by allowing the police authorities to ban an LGBTI Pride march in Nikšić, the second largest town, three times consecutively. The organizations' initial complaint had been rejected by the Ministry. In June, the court rejected the applicants' claims; the organizations have turned to the Constitutional Court to request a constitutional review.

ENFORCED DISAPPEARANCES

By the end of the year, the authorities had not acted on the recommendations of the UN Committee on Enforced Disappearances to include disappearance as a separate criminal offence in the Criminal Code. The authorities also failed to enable access to justice and reparation for victims. Additionally, Montenegro failed to ensure that the continuous nature of enforced disappearance was recognized in its system of criminal law. The fate and whereabouts of the 61 individuals still reported missing following the 1991-1999 armed conflicts in the former Yugoslavia were not investigated.

FREEDOM OF EXPRESSION – JOURNALISTS

Journalists continued to receive threats and media offices were occasionally vandalized. The Minister of Interior announced in June that amendments to the Criminal Code would be introduced to address the prevalent impunity for attacks on journalists. A draft had not been submitted by end of year.

The trial of Jovo Martinović, an investigative journalist detained since October 2015, opened in late October. He was accused of being involved in the criminal network he was investigating. Human rights groups and journalist associations expressed concern that the charges were motivated by his investigative work.

REFUGEES AND INTERNALLY DISPLACED PEOPLE

Over 1,600 refugees who fled to Montenegro during the conflict in former Yugoslavia remained without durable solutions. They still lived in substandard conditions in camps without access to comprehensive integration programmes. The refugees, the majority of them Roma from Serbia/Kosovo, had not received adequate support to acquire formal international protection status, citizenship or permanent residency rights. This prevented them from accessing essential services, including health care and employment opportunities.

MOROCCO/ WESTERN SAHARA

Kingdom of Morocco
Head of state: **King Mohamed VI**
Head of government: **Abdelilah Benkirane**

The authorities restricted rights to freedom of expression, association and assembly, prosecuting journalists and forcibly dispersing protests. Women faced discrimination in law and in practice. Consensual same-sex sexual relations remained criminalized. Courts imposed death sentences; there were no executions.

BACKGROUND

In March, the government forced the UN to close a Military Liaison Office of the UN Mission for the Referendum in Western Sahara (MINURSO) and withdraw civilian staff after UN Secretary-General Ban Ki-moon referred to Morocco's "occupation" of Western Sahara. In April, the UN Security Council extended MINURSO's mandate for another year without including any human rights monitoring component. MINURSO had not returned to its previous capacity by the end of the year.[1]

In September, Morocco submitted a request to join the African Union (AU).

October saw protests against social and economic grievances erupt in different parts of the country. Residents clashed with police when the authorities began demolishing informal settlements in the town of Sidi Bibi, near Agadir. Thousands of people took to the streets in major cities including the capital, Rabat, and Marrakech after Mouhcine Fikri, a fish vendor, died trying to retrieve fish that officials had confiscated from him in Al Hoceima, in the Rif region. Al Hoceima also witnessed large demonstrations. The protests subsided after four days when the authorities charged 11 people in connection with Mouhcine Fikri's death.

The UN Human Rights Committee reviewed Morocco's human rights record in October.[2]

JUSTICE SYSTEM

The authorities pursued their efforts to reform the justice system. In February, Parliament passed laws on the Higher Judicial Council and the Statute for Judges but these failed to establish judicial independence. In June, the Council of Government approved draft legislation to amend and complete the Penal Code; it contained some progressive provisions but failed to address the significant deficiencies of the existing Code including the death penalty and undue restrictions on freedoms of expression and religion, among others. The draft legislation had yet to be enacted at the end of the year. A draft bill to amend the Code of Criminal Procedure remained under consideration.

FREEDOM OF EXPRESSION

The authorities continued to prosecute journalists and critics for exercising their right to freedom of peaceful expression. They included Ali Anouzla, a leading independent journalist charged in January with advocating, supporting and inciting terrorism in an article published on the website Lakome.com in 2013. If convicted, he would face up to 20 years in prison. Seven journalists and activists faced charges that included "undermining state security" and "failing to report foreign funding" for participating in a foreign-funded project to train people in citizen journalism. If convicted, they would face prison sentences of up to five years.[3]

In February, the Higher Judicial Council dismissed Judge Mohamed El-Haini from office after the Minister of Justice and Liberties accused him of violating the duty of discretion and expressing opinions of a political nature by criticizing the draft laws on the Higher Judicial Council and the Statute for Judges on social and other media.

A new Press Code adopted in August removed imprisonment as a penalty for exercising press freedom, one month after the authorities amended the Penal Code to criminalize certain forms of peaceful expression.

FREEDOMS OF ASSOCIATION AND ASSEMBLY

The authorities continued to block the legal registration of several human rights organizations, including branches of the Moroccan Association of Human Rights, Freedom Now and the Maghreb Co-ordination of Human Rights Organizations.

They also prevented human rights groups and other associations from holding public and other meetings and assemblies, and continued to expel or deny entry to foreign journalists, activists and human rights defenders. In June, the International Institute for Nonviolent Action (NOVACT), a Spanish NGO, closed its Morocco office after the authorities denied entry to two of its staff. Amnesty International remained in dialogue with the authorities to lift remaining restrictions on its own fact-finding activities in Morocco and Western Sahara.

The authorities continued to restrict the right to freedom of peaceful assembly. In January, police forcibly dispersed peaceful protests by trainee teachers in Inezgane and other cities, beating protesters with batons and shields and injuring more than 150, according to witnesses.

In August, a court sentenced eight activists after an unfair trial to prison terms ranging from four months to one year for participating in a peaceful protest in Sidi Ifni, in southern Morocco.[4] Convictions were upheld on appeal in October, with one four-month prison sentence reduced to three months.

REPRESSION OF DISSENT – SAHRAWI ACTIVISTS

The authorities continued to stifle peaceful dissent in Western Sahara, dispersing peaceful protests and prosecuting and restricting Sahrawi activists who advocated self-determination or reported human rights violations. The authorities interrogated some human rights defenders when they returned from foreign travel, and continued to block the legal registration of the Collective of Sahrawi Human Rights Defenders (CODESA) and other Sahrawi rights groups.

In July the Court of Cassation ruled that 23 Sahrawi protesters and activists imprisoned following deadly clashes in 2010 in Gdeim Izik should be re-tried before a civilian court. Most had been sentenced in 2013 to long prison terms after an unfair trial before a military court based on "confessions" that they alleged were obtained through torture. The new civilian trial opened in late December but was adjourned until January 2017. Twenty-one of the 23 remained in prison at the end of the year.[5]

The authorities continued to expel from or bar entry to Western Sahara for foreign journalists and activists as well as human rights activists. In April, they expelled Spanish, Belgian and French jurists and a Spanish judge who had travelled to Rabat to make representations on behalf of the Gdeim Izik prisoners.

TORTURE AND OTHER ILL-TREATMENT

In April, security forces arrested Brahim Saika, an activist of the Co-ordination of Unemployed Sahrawis group in Guelmim, as he left home to join a peaceful protest in support of greater employment. He was charged with insulting and assaulting public officials and insulting a public institution, and began a hunger strike after accusing the police of ill-treating him in custody. Soon afterwards he died in hospital while under police custody. According to media reports, an official autopsy concluded that his death was caused by a virus but the authorities failed to conduct an independent inquiry into his death, as his family requested, and buried his remains against his family's wishes.

Dual Belgian-Moroccan national Ali Aarrass remained in prison more than three years after the UN Working Group on Arbitrary Detention concluded that he had been convicted after an unfair trial based on a torture-tainted "confession". In June, he alleged in an open letter that he and other detainees had been subjected to ill-treatment. He was transferred to Tiflet II Local Prison in October and detained in solitary confinement where he remained at the end of the year. The Court of Cassation had yet to rule on his case, more than four years after hearing an appeal against his conviction.[6]

Detainees protested against harsh prison conditions, including poor hygiene, inadequate nutrition and health care, and severe overcrowding. A National Preventive Mechanism had yet to be established, more than two years after Morocco acceded to the Optional Protocol to the UN Convention against Torture, which requires such mechanisms to be set up.

IMPUNITY

The authorities failed to implement key recommendations from the Equity and Reconciliation Commission, 10 years after the Commission published its report examining human rights violations between 1956 and 1999.

WOMEN'S RIGHTS

In July, the lower house of Parliament adopted a long-awaited draft law on combating violence against women, but the draft remained under consideration before the upper house at the end of the year.[7] It contained some positive elements, including measures to protect survivors of violence during and after judicial proceedings, but without significant strengthening it would not afford women effective protection against violence and discrimination.

The Penal Code continued to criminalize abortion. The authorities proposed amendments that would allow exceptions in cases of incest and rape and on certain medical grounds. However, the amendments would include requirements for third party notification and approval that could delay access to legal abortions, putting pregnant women's health at risk. The amendments had not been enacted by the end of the year.

In July, Parliament adopted a law regulating employment of domestic workers, predominantly women and girls. It established 18 as the minimum age for domestic workers but provided a five-year transition period during which children aged 16 and 17 may continue to be employed as domestic workers.

RIGHTS OF LESBIAN, GAY, BISEXUAL, TRANSGENDER AND INTERSEX PEOPLE

The authorities continued to prosecute and imprison LGBTI people under Article 489 of the Penal Code, which criminalizes consensual same-sex sexual relations. In March, they prosecuted two men who were victims of a homophobic attack by youths in the city of Beni Mellal. Film of the attack sparked wide condemnation when it was circulated on the internet. One of the attack victims received a four-month prison term under Article 489, suspended on appeal, and a fine; the other received a three-month suspended prison sentence. According to news reports, two of their attackers were sentenced to prison terms on appeal of four months and six months respectively.

REFUGEES' AND MIGRANTS' RIGHTS

The authorities continued to prevent people from sub-Saharan Africa from irregularly entering the Spanish enclaves of Ceuta and Melilla in northern Morocco, with some people alleging excessive use of force by the Moroccan and Spanish authorities. The authorities repeatedly destroyed makeshift camps around the northeastern city of Nador and displaced dozens of people to cities in the south, according to human rights groups.

In July, lawmakers adopted legislation approving Morocco's ratification of ILO Convention 143 on Migrant Workers. In August the government promulgated a new law to combat human trafficking. In December, King Mohammed VI announced a new wave of regularization of undocumented migrants.

The authorities again failed to establish a national asylum system but allowed refugees access to basic rights and services, including education. They issued Syrians registered by UNHCR, the UN refugee agency, with documents protecting them against *refoulement* without taking a decision on their definitive status.

POLISARIO CAMPS

The Polisario Front again failed to hold to account those responsible for committing human rights abuses in camps under its control during the 1970s and 1980s. Brahim Ghali became Secretary General of the Polisario Front following the death of Mohamed Abdelaziz in May.

DEATH PENALTY

Courts continued to hand down death sentences; there have been no executions since 1993. In July, the authorities commuted the death sentences of 23 people to life imprisonment.

1. UN must monitor human rights in Western Sahara and Sahrawi refugee camps (News story, 26 April)

2. Morocco: The authorities must swiftly implement the recommendations of the UN Human Rights Committee (MDE 29/5158/2016)

3. Morocco ramps up crackdown on press freedom with trial over citizen journalism (News story, 26 January)

4. Morocco: Sidi Ifni protesters must be given fair appeal trial and released unless assault charges are proved (MDE 29/4763/2016)

5. Morocco/Western Sahara: Further information – Sahrawi defendants granted civilian re-trial (MDE 29/4615/2016)

6. Morocco: Torture survivor still detained despite UN calls for his immediate release (MDE 29/4119/2016)

7. Morocco: Violence against women bill needs stronger safeguards (MDE 29/4007/2016)

MOZAMBIQUE

Republic of Mozambique
Head of state and government: **Filipe Jacinto Nyusi**

The security forces and opposition members and supporters committed human rights abuses with impunity, including killings, torture and other ill-treatment. Thousands of refugees fled to Malawi and Zimbabwe. People expressing dissent or criticizing human rights violations, political and military instability or the country's hidden debts faced attacks and intimidation.

BACKGROUND

Violent clashes continued between the ruling party, the Mozambique Liberation Front (FRELIMO), and the main opposition party, the Mozambique National Resistance (RENAMO), in the centre of Mozambique.

On 5 March, President Nyusi invited Afonso Dhlakama, leader of RENAMO, to talks on "restoring peace in the country". Talks between FRELIMO and RENAMO teams started. On 10 June, the teams agreed to invite international mediators to facilitate talks around four points: RENAMO governing the six provinces where it claims it won elections in 2014; the cessation of armed activity; the formation of joint armed forces, police and intelligence services; and the disarmament and reintegration of RENAMO armed members.

In August, the mediators presented a proposed agreement. However, the parties disagreed over the condition that the government should withdraw its armed forces from the Gorongosa region, where Afonso Dhlakama is based, and no agreement was reached. Talks were continuing at the end of the year.

In April, the existence of hidden borrowing of more than US$1 billion for security and defence spending came to light. The disclosure led to the International Monetary Fund (IMF) and other international donors suspending financial aid to Mozambique pending an independent international audit.

In August, a parliamentary inquiry commission was established to investigate, but it had a majority of FRELIMO members and was boycotted by RENAMO. The commission's findings were discussed in Parliament on 9 December in a closed session. The report had not been made public by the end of the year.

Mozambique's human rights record was examined under the UN Universal Periodic Review (UPR) process in June; Mozambique accepted 180 and rejected 30 recommendations. Recommendations on the ratification of the International Convention against enforced disappearance and the Rome Statute of the ICC, and on freedom of expression and corporate accountability were among those rejected.[1]

LACK OF ACCOUNTABILITY

Members of the armed forces, police officials and secret service agents reportedly committed human rights violations against a number of people they suspected to be members or supporters of RENAMO. The violations included extrajudicial executions, torture and other ill-treatment, arbitrary detentions and destruction of property. There was continued impunity for such crimes under international law and human rights violations.

On 10 May, Benedito Sabão, a subsistence farmer from the town of Catandica, Manica province, was arbitrarily arrested, ill-treated and shot at by suspected secret service agents, allegedly for supporting RENAMO. He survived the attack but continued to receive threats.[2] Those suspected of criminal responsibility for the attack had not been identified, let alone brought to justice, by the end of the year.

In June, a group of Mozambican subsistence farmers in a refugee camp in Malawi said that their village in Tete province in Mozambique had been invaded by four vehicles with about 60 civilians armed with guns and machetes; the village had been labelled a RENAMO stronghold. The attackers set the village ablaze and torched crops that the farmers lived off. The refugees

believed that these men were members of the armed forces.

RENAMO members and supporters reportedly looted health facilities and carried out attacks on highways and police stations, resulting in a number of casualties among the general population, as well as attacking the police and armed forces. The government failed to investigate and prosecute crimes against the general population committed by . members and supporters of RENAMO.

In May, local and international media and civil society organizations reported the discovery of unidentified bodies and a mass grave near the Gorongosa region. An investigation was launched in June, but neither the bodies nor those suspected of responsibility had been identified at the end of the year.

On 8 October, Jeremias Pondeca, a senior RENAMO member and part of the mediation team to end the conflict between RENAMO and the government, was shot dead in the capital Maputo by unidentified men believed to be members of a death squad composed of security officers. Those suspected of criminal responsibility for the attack had not been identified at the end of the year.

REFUGEES AND ASYLUM-SEEKERS

According to UNHCR, the UN refugee agency, nearly 10,000 Mozambicans sought refuge in Malawi and Zimbabwe during the year. The Mozambican government did not recognize them as refugees, but considered them as economic migrants.

FREEDOM OF EXPRESSION

Intimidation and attacks against people expressing dissenting or critical views, including journalists and human rights defenders, occurred throughout the year.

On 23 May, political commentator and university professor José Jaime Macuane was abducted outside his home in Maputo by unidentified men believed to be members of a death squad composed of security officers. The men shot him in the legs and dumped him by the roadside in Marracuene district, 30km north of Maputo. The kidnappers told him that they had been ordered to leave him lame. José Jaime Macuane had publicly addressed issues of political governance, the ongoing clashes between FRELIMO and RENAMO, the hidden debts and violations of the right to freedom of expression. Those responsible for the abduction and shooting had not been identified at the end of the year.

FREEDOM OF ASSEMBLY

After the disclosure of hidden debts in April, a demonstration was called anonymously via text messages and social media. On 25 April, the police announced that any unauthorized demonstration would be repressed. On 28 and 29 April, the police reinforced their presence in the streets of Maputo but no demonstration took place.

In May, political parties without parliamentary representation and civil society organizations called for a peaceful demonstration to protest against the country's hidden debts and political and military instability. However, Maputo City Council refused to allow the protest to take place.

João Massango, a leading member of the Ecology Party, was one of the organizers of this protest. On 20 May, he was the victim of an attempted abduction and was beaten by unidentified armed men believed to be members of a death squad composed of security officers in Maputo. Those responsible for the attack had not been identified at the end of the year.

---

1. Mozambique: Amnesty International welcomes commitment to investigate extrajudicial executions, torture and other ill-treatment (AFR 41/4449/2016)

2. Mozambique: Accused of being opposition member, shot at: Benedito Sabão (AFR 41/4099/2016)

MYANMAR

Republic of the Union of Myanmar
Head of state and government: Htin Kyaw (replaced Thein Sein in March)

The formation of a new civilian-led government did not lead to significant improvements in the human rights situation. The persecuted Rohingya minority faced increased violence and discrimination. Religious intolerance and anti-Muslim sentiment intensified. Fighting between the army and ethnic armed groups escalated in northern Myanmar. The government increased restrictions on access for UN and other humanitarian agencies to displaced communities. Although scores of prisoners of conscience were released, restrictions on freedoms of expression, of association and of peaceful assembly remained. Impunity persisted for past and ongoing human rights violations.

BACKGROUND

Parliament convened for the first time on 1 February following the November 2015 elections in which the National League for Democracy won a landslide victory. In March, Htin Kyaw was elected as President and the formal transfer of power took place the same month. Aung San Suu Kyi remained constitutionally barred from holding the presidency but in April was appointed State Counsellor, a role created especially for her, which made her the de facto leader of the civilian government. Despite this, the military retained significant political power, with an allocated 25% of seats in Parliament which gave it a veto over constitutional changes, and control over key ministries. The military remained independent of civilian oversight.

DISCRIMINATION
The Rohingya minority

The situation of the Rohingya deteriorated significantly after attacks on border police outposts in northern Rakhine State in October by suspected Rohingya militants. Nine police officers were killed. Security forces responded with a major security operation, conducting "clearance operations" and sealing the area, effectively barring humanitarian organizations, media and independent human rights monitors from entering. Security forces were responsible for unlawful killings, random firing on civilians, rape and arbitrary arrests.[1] Tens of thousands of people were displaced after their homes were destroyed, and at least 27,000 fled to Bangladesh. The response collectively punished the entire Rohingya community in northern Rakhine State and the conduct of the security forces may have amounted to crimes against humanity. The government issued blanket denials that security forces had carried out human rights violations. An investigation commission established by the government in December lacked credibility as it was headed by a former army general and its members included the Chief of Police.

Elsewhere in Rakhine State, the situation remained serious, with Rohingya and other Muslim people facing severe restrictions to their freedom of movement. They were confined to their villages or displacement camps and segregated from other communities. Access to their livelihoods, to health care including life-saving treatment, food security and education were greatly restricted.

Most Rohingya people remained deprived of a nationality. Government efforts to restart a citizenship verification process stalled, with many Rohingya rejecting it because it was based on the discriminatory 1982 Citizenship Law.

The government established two committees in an attempt to resolve the situation: the Central Committee on Implementation of Peace, Stability and Development of Rakhine State in May, chaired by Aung San Suu Kyi; and in August, the Advisory Commission on Rakhine State, chaired by former UN Secretary-General Kofi Annan.

FREEDOM OF RELIGION AND BELIEF

Discrimination, religious intolerance and anti-Muslim sentiment intensified, particularly following the October attacks in Rakhine State. The authorities failed to take effective action to counter advocacy of religious hatred, or to bring the perpetrators of attacks against religious minorities to justice.

A mob attack in Bago Region in June left one man injured and a mosque and other Muslim-owned buildings destroyed. The Region's Chief Minister told the media that no action would be taken against the suspected perpetrators.[2] In July, a mob attacked a Muslim prayer hall in Hpakant Township, Kachin State, for which five people were arrested but no one was brought to justice by the end of the year.

INTERNAL ARMED CONFLICT

In August, the new government held the "Union Peace Conference-21st Century Panglong", which aimed to move the nationwide peace process forward. It was expected to convene every six months. The Conference was attended by the military, representatives of most ethnic armed groups and the UN Secretary-General.

Despite these efforts, fighting continued in some parts of the country. Between April and September conflict between the Kachin Independence Army and the Myanmar Army escalated with the latter resorting to air strikes and shelling, killing and injuring civilians. During September, fighting erupted in Kayin State when the Border Guard Force and the Myanmar Army clashed with a splinter group from the Democratic Karen Benevolent Army. Further fighting broke out between the Myanmar Army and the Arakan Army in Rakhine State. In November, the Brotherhood of the Northern Alliance, a new coalition of four armed ethnic groups in northern Myanmar, launched co-ordinated attacks on security outposts in Kachin and northern Shan states. The groups said the attacks were in response to ongoing offensives by the Myanmar Army.

Reports of violations of international human rights and humanitarian law in areas of armed conflict persisted. Violations included rape and other crimes of sexual violence, forced labour, arbitrary arrests, torture and other ill-treatment, the use of landmines and recruitment of child soldiers.

The Myanmar Army had discharged 101 children and young adults from its forces by the end of the year.

LACK OF HUMANITARIAN ACCESS

From April, the government increased restrictions on access for UN and other humanitarian agencies and actors to displaced communities in areas not under its control in northern Myanmar.[3] It considered requiring displaced people in these areas to cross internal front lines to receive aid, a move which if implemented would violate international humanitarian law.

In Rakhine State, international humanitarian agencies were required to undergo cumbersome procedures to obtain travel authorization to provide services to vulnerable communities. Following the October attacks in northern Rakhine State, all pre-existing humanitarian services were suspended, affecting over 150,000 people. While services resumed in some areas, an estimated 30,000 internally displaced people (IDPs) had no access to sustained humanitarian aid because of security operations by the end of the year.

REFUGEES AND INTERNALLY DISPLACED PEOPLE

According to the UN Office for the Coordination of Humanitarian Affairs (OCHA), there were over 250,000 IDPs in Myanmar. They included over 100,000 people displaced by fighting in Kachin and northern Shan states and 150,000 people, mostly Rohingya, in Rakhine State.

Around 100,000 refugees continued to live in nine camps in Thailand. In October, the first pilot voluntary return of 71 people began, supported by the Myanmar and Thailand governments, and UNHCR, the UN refugee agency, and other agencies. Many other refugees remained in Thailand and continued to express fears about returning to Myanmar.

PRISONERS OF CONSCIENCE

On 8 April, one week after the new government assumed office, dozens of student protesters detained since March 2015 were released. On 17 April, 83 prisoners, including many prisoners of conscience, were released following a presidential pardon.[4]

Prisoners of conscience remained held, and politically motivated arrests and imprisonment continued. Dozens of people were investigated for "online defamation" under the 2013 Telecommunications Act, a vaguely worded law used increasingly to stifle peaceful criticism of the authorities. In October, Hla Phone was sentenced to two years' imprisonment for "online defamation" and "incitement" for criticizing the former government and the Myanmar Army on Facebook.

Former prisoners of conscience continued to face a range of problems arising from the effects of their prison conditions and their status as former prisoners including lack of medical and psychological care, access to education and employment opportunities. There were no government programmes providing support and rehabilitation to former prisoners or their families.

FREEDOMS OF EXPRESSION, ASSOCIATION AND ASSEMBLY

The new government initiated a review of certain repressive laws, and repealed the 1975 State Protection Act and the 1950 Emergency Provisions Act which had been used to imprison peaceful critics of former governments. However, other repressive laws remained, leaving human rights defenders at risk of arrest and imprisonment for their peaceful activities.[5] The legal reform process lacked transparency and Parliament failed to consult adequately with civil society and legal experts. Proposed amendments to the 2012 Peaceful Assembly and Peaceful Procession Act fell far short of requirements under international human rights law and standards.[6] A draft privacy and security bill contained multiple provisions which, if adopted, could arbitrarily restrict the right to freedom of expression, and other rights.

Human rights defenders, lawyers and journalists continued to face intimidation, harassment and surveillance by the authorities. They reported being followed; photographed when attending events and meetings; late-night inspections of their homes and offices; and harassment of family members. Women human rights defenders were particularly vulnerable to sexual harassment and intimidation.

CORPORATE ACCOUNTABILITY

In October, Parliament adopted a new Investment Law. However, there were no provisions protecting people against forced eviction or from the impact of pollution caused by business.

In May, protests resumed at the Letpadaung mine following an announcement that it had started producing copper. Two protest leaders were subsequently charged with criminal offences and faced a maximum of four years' imprisonment. The Letpadaung project had a long history of causing forced eviction and violent repression of protests against the mine although no one had been held to account.

In October, the Ministry of Industry renewed the operating licence of the Moe Gyo acid factory which processes copper for the Letpadaung and S&K mines. The licence was renewed despite serious concerns that the health of villagers living nearby was adversely affected; and despite a decision by the Salyingyi municipal authorities not to renew the factory's licence pending an assessment of its health and environmental impact.

DEATH PENALTY

No executions were carried out although courts continued to impose death sentences. In January, then President Thein Sein commuted the death sentences of 77 prisoners to life imprisonment. In October, Parliament repealed the 1950 Emergency Provisions Act which allowed for the death penalty. The death penalty remained under other laws.

LACK OF ACCOUNTABILITY

The institutional and legislative framework maintained obstacles to holding perpetrators of human rights violations to account, and delivering justice, truth and reparations to victims and their families. Most perpetrators of past and current human rights violations continued to evade justice.

In January, just days before it was dissolved, Parliament adopted the Former Presidents Security Law, which could grant immunity to former presidents for crimes committed while they were in office, including for crimes against humanity, war crimes and other crimes under international law.[7]

In July, the army made a rare public admission of wrongdoing when it announced that seven soldiers had killed five villagers in northern Shan State and that a court-martial was underway. They were sentenced to five years in prison with hard labour in September. While a step forward for military transparency, the case also highlighted the need for reform in the military and civilian justice systems. Under the 2008 Constitution, the military retains control over its own judicial processes, including when allegations of human rights violations are involved.

The Myanmar National Human Rights Commission remained ineffectual in responding to reports of human rights violations and lacked independence. In October, four Commissioners resigned after the media reported that they had negotiated a financial settlement in a case involving child forced labour and ill-treatment.

INTERNATIONAL SCRUTINY

For the first time in 25 years, the UN General Assembly did not adopt a resolution on Myanmar after the EU decided not to propose a draft text. None of the key human rights recommendations in previous resolutions had been fully implemented.[8]

The UN Special Rapporteur on the situation of human rights in Myanmar made two official visits to the country. While her access improved, she reported ongoing surveillance and harassment of civil society members she met. She also reported finding a recording device placed by a government official during a community meeting in Rakhine State.

In March, the UN Human Rights Council adopted the outcome of the UN Universal Periodic Review (UPR) process on Myanmar. Although Myanmar accepted over half of the recommendations, it rejected key recommendations on the rights to freedom of expression, of association and of peaceful assembly, and the situation of the Rohingya.[9] In July, the UN Committee on the Elimination of Discrimination against Women raised concerns about discriminatory laws, barriers to justice for women and girls, and their under-representation in the peace process.[10]

There was still no agreement to establish an Office of the UN High Commissioner for Human Rights in Myanmar.

1. "We are at breaking point": Rohingya – Persecuted in Myanmar, neglected in Bangladesh (ASA 15/5362/2016)

2. Myanmar: Investigate violent destruction of mosque buildings (News story, 24 June)

3. Myanmar: Lift restrictions immediately on humanitarian aid (News story, 24 October)

4. Myanmar: Continue efforts to release all remaining prisoners of conscience (ASA 16/3981/2016)

5. New expression meets old repression: Ending the cycle of political arrests and imprisonment in Myanmar (ASA 16/3430/2016)

6. Myanmar: Open letter on amending the Peaceful Assembly and Peaceful Procession Act (ASA 16/4024/2016)

7. Myanmar: Scrap or amend new law that could grant immunity to former president (News story, 28 January)

8. Myanmar: Why a UNGA resolution is still needed (ASA 16/4745/2016)

9. Myanmar: Amnesty International calls on Myanmar to protect the rights of Rohingya and to release all prisoners of conscience (ASA 16/3670/2016)

10. Myanmar: Briefing to the UN Committee on the Elimination of Discrimination against Women (ASA 16/4240/2016)

NAMIBIA

Republic of Namibia
Head of state and government: **Hage Gottfried Geingob**

Detainees acquitted after the long-running Caprivi treason trial lived in fear of being rearrested after the Prosecutor General decided to appeal against the court ruling. There was a high incidence of gender-based violence, including rape, against women **and girls. Violations of the right to freedom of expression continued.**

BACKGROUND

Despite calls for the introduction of a universal basic income grant after a successful pilot project, the government announced its intention to introduce food banks in urban and peri-urban areas, failing to address widespread extreme poverty in rural areas.

CAPRIVI DETAINEES

Forty-two released Caprivi detainees – accused of treason after their arrests in 1999 and acquitted between 2013 and 2015 – continued to live in fear after facing threats and intimidation. On 17 May, they were notified that the Prosecutor General would appeal against their acquittals.

The Vice Chairperson of the Caprivi Concerned Group (CCG), Retief Kangongo, went missing on 30 April following alleged threats by the Inspector General of the Namibian police. The CCG supported the acquitted detainees. Retief Kangongo reportedly sought asylum in Botswana.

In August, the Supreme Court ruled in favour of Boster Mubuyaeta Samuele, one of the Caprivi detainees. He had fled to Bostwana, and, in December 2002, he was abducted by Namibian security forces in Botswana and brought to Namibia to face trial. He then spent 13 years in prison. Boster Mubuyaeta Samuele successfully argued that the Namibian courts had no jurisdiction to prosecute him since Namibian officials had violated international law when he was abducted and arbitrarily detained.

FREEDOM OF EXPRESSION

On 15 April, two Japanese journalists employed by Japan's television group Asahi were briefly detained by Namibian security forces soon after interviewing the Deputy Prime Minister Netumbo Nandi-Ndaitwah at the Hosea Kutako International Airport. The journalists interviewed the Deputy Prime Minister in connection with a munitions factory being built by nationals of the

Democratic People's Republic of Korea (North Korea) in Namibia. Their cameras and laptops were confiscated by Namibian security forces.

VIOLENCE AGAINST WOMEN AND GIRLS

Gender-based violence, including rape, against women and girls continued at a high rate as the government failed to address the problem adequately.

For example, on 20 June, Janet Haoes was strangled with electric wire, stabbed several times and hit with a hammer by her partner in the Otjomuise suburb of the capital, Windhoek. On 26 August, the body of Rosina Gaoses, who was pregnant, was found in the riverbed in the Dolam suburb of Windhoek. The body showed signs that she had been raped before being murdered.

Although the Namibian police initiated some investigations into cases of gender-based violence, efforts to eradicate violence against women and girls remained inadequate.

NAURU

Republic of Nauru
Head of state and government: **Baron Waqa**

The Crimes Act 2016 contained provisions to protect human rights but was inadequately implemented. Concerns about the denial of the rights to freedom of expression and of peaceful assembly, freedom of movement and access to the country for foreign media persisted. Passports of several former MPs were suspended. Nauru continued to hold hundreds of refugees and asylum-seekers in a centre while others were placed in the community under its transfer agreement with Australia. The death penalty was repealed for all crimes in May.

SEXUAL AND REPRODUCTIVE RIGHTS

The Crimes Act 2016, which came into force in May, decriminalized same-sex relations,

abortions carried out by medical professionals and criminalized marital rape. The authorities took no steps to implement the law to protect women and girls from gender-based violence or to ensure their access to sexual and reproductive health information and services, particularly affecting those in remote locations and/or in marginalized communities.

The Act criminalized the buying and selling of sex, impeding sex workers' access to sexual and reproductive health information and services and making them vulnerable to exploitation, abuse, violence and other crimes. It also adversely impacted HIV treatment and prevention.

FREEDOM OF MOVEMENT

In September, new laws granted the Foreign Ministry powers to cancel passports without court review. Twenty Nauruans claimed that the Ministry cancelled their passports. They included opposition MPs who were suspended after being charged in 2015 in connection with a pro-democracy rally in 2014. In September, Sprent Dabwido, former MP, was prevented from leaving Nauru for medical care. The government later reversed the decision. Roland Kun, a former MP, had his passport confiscated in 2015 after he was charged in connection with speaking to foreign media and protests against the government. He was granted a New Zealand passport and fled Nauru in July.

REFUGEES AND ASYLUM-SEEKERS

There were around 1,200 refugees and asylum-seekers remaining in Nauru. As of 30 November, there were 383 in the Australian-run Regional Processing Centre (RPC), of whom 44 were children, 49 women and 290 men (see Australia entry). There were around 800 refugees living in the community.

There was evidence that children were assaulted by staff working for companies hired by the Australian government to run the RCP and by private individuals. Health care was inadequate and many children were not attending school. Reports of attempted suicide and self-harm were commonplace.

Omid Masoumali, an Iranian refugee, died after setting himself on fire in April. The authorities failed to protect refugees and asylum-seekers from continued physical and verbal attacks by the community, as well as arbitrary arrest and detention. The conditions amounted to torture and caused severe psychological harm.[1]

In August, the UK newspaper *The Guardian* published over 2,000 leaked incident reports (known as the "Nauru Files") which had been recorded by staff employed at the RPC. The files documented incidents including physical and sexual abuse of refugees and asylum-seekers, including children, in Nauru, as well as cases of hunger strikes, self-harm and medical emergencies.

In November, the Australian government announced that some of the refugees detained in Nauru and Papua New Guinea's Manus Island would be resettled in the USA (see Papua New Guinea entry).

1. Island of despair: Australia's "processing" of refugees on Nauru (ASA 12/4934/2016)

NEPAL

Federal Democratic Republic of Nepal
Head of state: **Bidhya Devi Bhandari**
Head of government: **Pushpa Kamal Dahal (replaced Khadga Prasad Sharma Oli in August)**

Tens of thousands of people continued to be denied the right to adequate housing and other human rights following the 2015 earthquake. Marginalized groups expressed dissatisfaction with constitutional amendments, on the grounds that they did not address discriminatory clauses. The use of torture and unnecessary or excessive force against protesters in the Tarai region were not effectively investigated. There was little progress on justice for the grave human rights violations committed during the armed conflict. Migrant workers were exploited by recruitment companies despite a new government policy regulating the sector. Discrimination on the basis of gender, caste, class, ethnic origin, sexual orientation, gender identity and religion persisted. Women and girls were not adequately protected against gender-based violence.

RIGHT TO ADEQUATE HOUSING

Hundreds of thousands of people affected by the April 2015 earthquake continued to live in temporary shelters. The National Reconstruction Authority began work in January and reconstruction officially started in April. By December, detailed housing damage assessments were completed for 11 of the 14 worst affected districts. Grant distributions to enable people to reconstruct their houses were delayed and people affected expected to endure another cold season lacking basic shelter and other essential services. In September, Prime Minister Dahal announced a grant increase from around US$1,850 to 2,800 which was approved by the cabinet in late December.

In July the UN Committee on the Rights of the Child expressed concern about the earthquake's impact on children's rights and the number of displaced children living in camps for internally displaced people or informal settlements, without adequate access to food, safe drinking water, sanitation, health care or education.

EXCESSIVE USE OF FORCE

The use of torture and unnecessary or excessive force against protesters in the Tarai region were not effectively investigated. Madhesi and other marginalized groups in the Tarai continued to protest against the 2015 Constitution and its January amendments which, they claimed, discriminated against them and denied them fair political representation. Protesters blocked border crossings with India resulting in severe shortages of fuel, food, medicine and construction materials.

In August, an official commission to investigate incidents of excessive force by security forces in the Tarai during these protests which resulted in the killing of 27 men, four women and six children, and other incidents, was established but made little progress.

MIGRANT WORKERS' RIGHTS

The recruitment industry continued to be poorly regulated and allowed for the widespread abuse of migrants' rights. Subjected to extortionate recruitment fees, Nepalese working abroad were exposed to debt bondage, labour trafficking and forced labour. The abuse of migrants in destination countries was facilitated by, on the one hand, restrictive labour migration laws and, on the other hand, poorly implemented laws. There were few investigations into or prosecutions of local agents and private agencies for such abuses.

Labour migration law and policy were ineffective, and there was little improvement in protection mechanisms for migrant workers. The government's no-fee recruitment system largely failed because it was inadequately implemented or monitored.

As a result of age restrictions placed on women migrant workers, women frequently turned to informal channels to undertake foreign employment which left them susceptible to human trafficking.

TORTURE AND OTHER ILL-TREATMENT

Torture in police custody continued, particularly during pre-trial detention to extract confessions and intimidate people.

In September, the Torture and Cruel, Inhuman or Degrading Treatment (Control) Bill was tabled before Parliament but had not been adopted by the end of the year. It contained provisions that did not meet international human rights standards, such as an overly narrow definition of torture and a 90-day time limit for registering complaints.

In February, Kumar Lama, a Nepal Army Colonel, was tried by a UK court under the universal jurisdiction principle on two charges of torture committed in Nepal. He was acquitted of one charge in July and released in September after the prosecuting authorities decided not to proceed to a retrial

on the second charge, as the jury had been unable to reach a verdict.

IMPUNITY

In May, the ruling Communist Party of Nepal Unified Marxist Leninist and the Communist Party of Nepal (Maoist Centre) agreed an amnesty for perpetrators of human rights abuses during the conflict. In July, the Communist Party of Nepal (Maoist Centre) and the Nepali Congress agreed to form a coalition government with an understanding that the Commission on Truth and Reconciliation (TRC) and the Commission on Investigation of Enforced Disappeared Persons (CIEDP) would focus on reconciliation and compensation, and not prioritize criminal prosecutions for past human rights violations.

The 2014 Truth and Reconciliation Commission Act retained language which allowed amnesties for serious crimes under international law, despite the Supreme Court's ruling against these provisions in 2015. The government did not amend the law. The TRC and the CIEDP began registering complaints in mid-April, 14 months after their establishment. Officials of both commissions raised concerns about government delays and non-co-operation, lack of resources and unrealistically short deadlines for filing cases.

FREEDOM OF EXPRESSION

In April, the office of Prime Minister Oli summoned commissioners of the National Human Rights Commission for questioning about a statement they made while Nepal was being examined under the UN Universal Periodic Review (UPR) process.

In May, Kanak Dixit, a journalist and activist, was arrested by the Commission for the Investigation of Abuse of Authority on corruption charges. Ten days after his arrest, the Supreme Court ruled that his detention was illegal and ordered his release. Kanak Dixit said his arrest was an attempt to silence his critical views. In the same month, Canadian national residing in Nepal, Robert Penner, was arrested and deported for sowing "social discord" in social media. During the year, Madhesi activist Chandra Kant Raut and several supporters faced multiple sedition charges for peacefully expressing political opinions.

DISCRIMINATION

Discrimination on the basis of gender, caste, class, ethnic origin, sexual orientation, gender identity and religion persisted. Constitutional amendments did not guarantee equal rights to citizenship for women, or provide protection from discrimination to marginalized communities, including Dalits and lesbian, gay, bisexual, transgender and intersex people.

The law criminalizing rape was amended so that the statute of limitations on reporting the crime was raised from 35 to 180 days rather than being abolished altogether as required by human rights standards. Gender-based discrimination continued to undermine women's and girls' rights to control their sexuality and make informed choices related to reproduction; challenge early and forced marriages; and enjoy adequate antenatal and maternal health care. Women continued to face domestic violence, including marital rape. Women from marginalized groups, including Dalits and Indigenous women, remained at greater risk of intersecting forms of discrimination.

NETHERLANDS

Kingdom of the Netherlands
Head of state: King Willem-Alexander
Head of government: Mark Rutte

Irregular migrants continued to be routinely deprived of their liberty and the government still did not adequately consider alternatives to detention. Ethnic profiling by the police continued to be a matter of serious concern.

REFUGEES' AND MIGRANTS' RIGHTS

Following a fire in a detention facility in Rotterdam on 25 May, several migrants were placed in solitary confinement as a punitive measure for "disturbing public order" during the evacuation.

In October, a draft law regulating immigration detention was tabled before Parliament. It offered minor improvements, but major concerns remained as irregular migrants could be deprived of their liberty for a wide range of reasons. The punitive character of the detention regime also remained in place. Furthermore, the draft law included powers to hold migrants in a cell for at least 16 hours a day.

RIGHT TO AN ADEQUATE STANDARD OF LIVING

The authorities remained unwilling to implement the recommendation by the European Committee of Social Rights that all people, including irregular migrants, should have unconditional access to shelter and other basic necessities.

DISCRIMINATION
Ethnic profiling by police

Ethnic profiling by the police continued to be a matter of serious concern. While the authorities acknowledged the damaging effects of ethnic profiling, they failed to formulate a comprehensive plan for the fair and effective use of stop-and-search powers. The police also continued to refuse to systematically monitor and record stop-and-search operations, making it difficult to assess whether measures to combat ethnic profiling, such as training, diversity management and dialogue with communities, were effective in reducing discrimination.

Partial ban on face-covering

A government proposal for a ban on face-covering attire in certain spaces, such as public transport and public educational and health care institutions, passed the House of Representatives in November but was still pending before the Senate. The ban would restrict the rights to freedom of religion and of expression, particularly of Muslim women.

COUNTER-TERROR AND SECURITY

In May, the House of Representatives passed two controversial administrative counter-terrorism bills, which were likely to be debated by the Senate in early 2017. If enacted, the laws would enable the Minister of Security and Justice to impose administrative control measures on individuals, including travel bans, based on indications that they may pose a future terrorist risk. It would also allow for the revocation of Dutch nationality of dual citizens who have travelled abroad to join a foreign terrorist group and are believed to pose a risk to national security. The procedures to appeal the imposition of the measures lacked effective safeguards.

In October, a draft law on the Intelligence and Security Services was presented to Parliament. If enacted, the law would legitimize sweeping surveillance powers for the intelligence and security services, potentially leading to violations of the right to privacy, the right to freedom of expression and the right to non-discrimination. The draft law provides insufficient safeguards against abuse of powers by the intelligence and security services, and there are serious concerns that communications could be shared with other countries where the information could be used for human rights violations.

HUMAN RIGHTS DEFENDERS

Since February, Nada Kiswanson, a human rights lawyer based in The Hague, representing the Palestinian NGO Al-Haq, has been the subject of ongoing threats in response to her work at the International Criminal Court. She has received several death threats and been subjected to interference of her communications, intimidation, harassment and defamation. However, only in April did the Dutch authorities take specific measures to protect her and launch an investigation.

NEW ZEALAND

New Zealand
Head of state: **Queen Elizabeth II, represented by Patricia Lee Reddy (replaced Jerry Mateparae in September)**
Head of government: **Bill English (replaced John Key in December)**

New Zealand received criticism from the UN Human Rights Committee and Committee on the Rights of the Child for its high rates of Indigenous Māori incarceration, child poverty and domestic violence. The state's refugee resettlement quota was marginally increased.

JUSTICE SYSTEM

Rates of Māori representation among those facing the criminal justice system remained disproportionately high. An Ombudsman investigation was launched into the circumstances in which an intellectually disabled man was held in a health facility for five years, often in isolation, in conditions amounting to cruel, inhuman or degrading treatment. The government announced that it was considering a formal extradition treaty with China, where criminal suspects could be at risk of serious human rights violations.

REFUGEES AND ASYLUM-SEEKERS

The government announced plans to increase the annual refugee resettlement quota from 750 to 1,000 by 2018. As of March, two refugees were held in detention facilities alongside remand detainees. The Human Rights Committee expressed concerns over disparities in the quality of services provided to refugees who arrived under the humanitarian quota system and other categories of refugees. In June, New Zealand publicly reiterated the agreement to annually resettle 150 refugees from Nauru and Manus. The agreement was made in 2013 with the Australian government but Australia has since refused to carry out the deal.

VIOLENCE AGAINST WOMEN AND GIRLS

Sexual and other physical violence against women and girls remained high, despite wide recognition of the problem and efforts to address it. The Human Rights Committee expressed concern about low rates of reporting and prosecution of perpetrators. An overhaul of domestic violence laws was announced. After years of insufficient funding, the government announced NZ$46 million (US$33 million) will be provided to support services for victims of sexual violence.

CHILDREN'S RIGHTS

The 2016 Technical Report on Child Poverty found that nearly one in three New Zealand children live below the poverty line. The Human Rights Committee expressed concern about the significant number of children suffering physical and psychological abuse and neglect. The government announced the creation of a Ministry for Vulnerable Children, to be implemented in 2017.

LEGAL, CONSTITUTIONAL OR INSTITUTIONAL DEVELOPMENTS

By the end of the year, the government had still not formally responded to recommendations by the 2013 Constitutional Advisory Panel to improve the Bill of Rights Act 1990. Economic, social and cultural rights continued to lack full protection in domestic legislation, as recommended by the Advisory Panel.

NICARAGUA

Republic of Nicaragua
Head of state and government: **Daniel Ortega Saavedra**

Conflict over land in the North Atlantic Autonomous Region sparked violent attacks against Miskitu Indigenous Peoples. Human rights defenders continued to experience threats and intimidation because of their work. Indigenous and Afro-descendant communities denounced violations of their rights to consultation and free, prior and informed consent in the context of the development of the Grand Interoceanic Canal. Communities and human rights organizations expressed concern at the potential negative impact of the Canal on their lives. A total abortion ban remained in place.

BACKGROUND

In November, Daniel Ortega of the Sandinista Front for National Liberation (FSLN) was re-elected President for a third consecutive term. Rosario Murillo, his wife, was elected Vice-President for the first time. According to media reports, the FSLN also increased their representation in the Congress.

WOMEN'S RIGHTS

Impunity for gender-based violence against women persisted. A local observatory run by women's rights organizations reported that between January and October there had been 44 gender-based killings of women, 30 of which remained unprosecuted.

Women living in poverty continued to be the main victims of maternal mortality, and Nicaragua had one of the highest teenage pregnancy rates in the Americas region. Abortion was banned in all circumstances, even when vital to save the woman's life.

GRAND INTEROCEANIC CANAL

The proposal to build the Grand Interoceanic Canal continued to generate controversy, with civil society organizations reporting a number of potential human rights violations linked to the project. According to local organizations, if built, the Canal would lead to the eviction of tens of thousands of people and would directly affect the livelihoods of peasant farmer communities, Indigenous Peoples and others.

In April, members of the National Council for the Defence of the Land, Lake and National Sovereignty presented the National Assembly's First Secretary a citizen-sponsored bill supported by nearly 7,000 signatories calling for the repeal of the law regulating the Canal. Also in April, the proposal was rejected on grounds of lack of competence.[1] The issue was referred to the Supreme Court and a decision was pending at the end of the year.[2]

In February, leaders from affected Indigenous and Afro-descendant Rama-Kriol communities brought their case before a national court. They stated that officials had pressured communities to give consent to the project. According to the appeal, 52% of the Canal's route would affect Indigenous and Afro-descendant Rama-Kriol communities.[3]

In May, authorities from the RamaKriol community brought an action before a Court of Appeal. The communal authorities alleged that the agreement of prior, free and informed consent for the implementation of the Grand Interoceanic Canal had been signed without an effective consultation process. In June, the Court of Appeal declared the petition inadmissible. In July, community leaders and authorities filed another appeal with the Supreme Court; a decision was pending at the end of the year.[4]

INDIGENOUS PEOPLES' RIGHTS

Violence flared in the North Atlantic Autonomous Region. Indigenous Miskitu Peoples were threatened, attacked, subjected to sexual violence, killed and forcibly displaced by non-Indigenous settlers.

Against this background of territorial conflict and a lack of effective protection measures from the state, the Inter-American Commission on Human Rights granted precautionary measures in favour of Miskitu Peoples. In addition, in September the Inter-American Court of Human Rights ordered the state to immediately adopt all necessary measures to end the current violence and guarantee respect of the right to life, personal and territorial integrity and cultural identity.

HUMAN RIGHTS DEFENDERS

In June, a shelter run by the Civil Foundation for Support to Women Victims of Violence was raided. There was no evidence of a serious attempt by the authorities to investigate the incident.

In June, six foreign environmental activists were detained and expelled from the country. In the same context, several community members, who had publicly expressed their concerns about the Grand Interoceanic Canal's impact on their livelihoods, were briefly detained.

In August, the Inter-American Commission on Human Rights granted precautionary measures in favour of human rights defenders at the Centre for Justice and Human Rights of the Atlantic Coast of Nicaragua. According to the Commission, the defenders had stated that they had received death threats because of their work on Indigenous rights.

In October, the Inter-American Court of Human Rights held a hearing in the case of *Acosta et al. v Nicaragua*. According to his family, Francisco García, who was killed in 2002, was targeted because of his wife's human rights work as director of the Centre for Legal Assistance for Indigenous Peoples. His relatives allege that the state failed to diligently investigate the attack.

In addition, the Co-ordinator of the National Council for the Defence of the Land, Lake and National Sovereignty, reported intimidation and harassment against her and her family. She had actively denounced the potential impact of the Grand Interoceanic Canal on Nicaraguan peasant farmer communities.

---

1. Nicaragua: The state must guarantee the security and integrity of communities peacefully demonstrating their concerns over construction of the Canal (AMR 43/3887/2016)
2. Nicaragua: Authorities must listen to those expressing concern over the Grand Interoceanic Canal (AMR 43/4744/2016)
3. Nicaragua side-lines local communities over multi-billion dollar canal (News story, 9 February 2016)
4. Nicaragua: El Estado nicaragüense no debe ignorar a las comunidades indígenas y afrodescendientes que demandan el respeto a sus derechos (AMR 43/4919/2016)

NIGER

Republic of Niger
Head of state: **Mahamadou Issoufou**
Head of government: **Brigi Rafini**

Armed conflict continued, particularly in
the southeastern region of Diffa where most
attacks were carried out by the armed group
Boko Haram. Over 300,000 people needed
humanitarian aid as a result of the conflict
and the continuing state of emergency in
the Diffa region. Over 1,400 suspected
Boko Haram members were in prison, most
held in lengthy pre-trial detention in poor
conditions and at risk of torture. The rights
of refugees and migrants travelling through
Niger were violated.

BACKGROUND

President Issoufou was re-elected in March
after an election that was boycotted by the
main opposition parties. His principal
opponent, Hama Amadou, was in detention
during the election charged with complicity in
kidnapping; he was released shortly after the
election.

Niger was examined under the UN
Universal Periodic Review (UPR) process
and accepted almost all of the
recommendations, including those relating to
abolition of the death penalty, protection of
human rights defenders, measures to
eradicate traditional harmful practices such
as early and forced marriage and female
genital mutilation, and guaranteeing the right
to food. Niger rejected one recommendation
on ensuring participation of Indigenous
Peoples in decision-making.

ABUSES BY ARMED GROUPS

Civilians, including refugees from Nigeria,
continued to be affected by armed conflict,
most of it concentrated in the Diffa region.
The exact number of civilian casualties could
not be determined; the UN estimated that at
least 177 civilians had been killed since
February 2015. Boko Haram carried out

more than 50 attacks in the Diffa region in
2016.

Other armed groups were active in western
areas bordering Mali. In October, an
unidentified group attacked the refugee
camp of Tazalit, Tahoua region; and a US aid
worker was abducted in Abalak, Tahoua
region. On 17 October, a group calling itself
Islamic State attacked the high-security
detention centre in Koutoukalé, near Niamey,
Tillabériregion.

INTERNALLY DISPLACED PEOPLE

More than 300,000 displaced people needed
humanitarian assistance in the Diffa region
by the end of the year, according to the UN
Office for the Coordination of Humanitarian
Affairs (OCHA). This included more than
184,000 internally displaced people from
Niger, 29,000 returning Niger nationals and
88,000 Nigerian refugees. Many lived in
harsh conditions in makeshift camps.
Insecurity impeded access to basic
commodities and services, including food,
water and education, and the continuing
state of emergency hampered economic
activity.

REFUGEES' AND MIGRANTS' RIGHTS

Niger hosted more than 60,000 refugees
from Mali in the Tillabériand Tahoua regions,
who also needed assistance.

The number of people transiting through
Niger trying to reach Europe continued to
grow, with Agadez the principal transit hub
for West Africans. In October, a survey by the
International Organization for Migration
reported that 70% of people arriving in Italy
by boat – many of whom had travelled
through Niger – had been a victim of
trafficking or exploitation, including
thousands of women and girls forced into
prostitution in Libya or Europe. Despite an
anti-trafficking law passed in 2015, there was
limited action to prevent trafficking in Niger.

An undetermined number of people died
during dangerous journeys through the
desert in Niger. In June, 14 adults and 20
children were found dead in the desert after

they left the town of Tahoua aiming to reach Algeria.

In October, the UN Committee on Migrant Workers highlighted several concerns, including forced labour of migrant workers, including children, particularly as domestic labour and in the mines.

COUNTER-TERROR AND SECURITY

More than 1,400 people accused of being members of Boko Haram remained in detention, many charged under Niger's anti-terror law. Most had been arrested in the Diffa region since 2013, although some had been detained since 2012. Among them were Nigerians, including refugees from areas affected by Boko Haram. The vast majority remained held in lengthy pre-trial detention. In June, the Prosecutor responsible for terrorism cases said that most arrests followed denunciations, and that insecurity and the state of emergency in Diffa region had prevented effective investigations.

In June, the authorities said that they planned to extradite to Nigeria all adult Nigerian detainees to reduce prison overcrowding and because Nigeria was better placed to investigate their nationals. The plan was formally announced in September. Torture and other ill-treatment remained widespread in Nigeria, particularly against people accused of supporting Boko Haram.

The authorities announced that the Code of Criminal Procedure was to be amended to extend pre-charge detention in police custody (garde à vue) from 5 to 15 days, renewable for a further 15 days.

PRISON CONDITIONS

Prison conditions remained poor despite steps taken to monitor them. The large number of people arrested for alleged links with Boko Haram aggravated the problem. During the year, Koutoukalé detention centre held more than twice its capacity of 250 detainees, including around 400 Boko Haram suspects.

ENFORCED DISAPPEARANCES

The fate of eight people arrested by security forces in May 2015 remained unclarified. El Hadj Kannaï Kouliyi, Malam Bandama, Ari Kannai, Abor Madou, Awa Malloumi, El Hadj Katchouloumi, Mouché Ali Kou Lawan Dalla and El Hadji Bara were arrested in N'Guigmi, Diffa region. The families' request for information about their relatives' whereabouts were left unanswered.

FREEDOM OF EXPRESSION

Some people were prosecuted for exercising their right to freedom of expression.

In June, Ousmane Moumouni, President of Action for Democracy and Human Rights in Niger, was given a six-month suspended prison sentence for "plotting to change the constitution" after posting a message on Facebook about Niger's security situation following a Boko Haram attack.

Also in June, journalists Ali Soumana and Moussa Dodo were handed a three-month suspended sentence for "putting pressure on the judiciary". They had published in Le Courrier newspaper a list of people accused of trying to influence a national exam. The list included influential people such as the President of the Constitutional Court. The journalists were prosecuted under the Penal Code, not the Press Law, which made the punishment harsher.

NIGERIA

Federal Republic of Nigeria
Head of state and government: **Muhammadu Buhari**

The conflict between the military and the armed group Boko Haram continued and generated a humanitarian crisis that affected more than 14 million people. The security forces continued to commit serious human rights violations including extrajudicial executions and enforced disappearances. The police and military continued to commit torture and other ill-

treatment. **Conditions in military detention were harsh. Communal violence occurred in many parts of the country. Thousands of people were forcibly evicted from their homes.**

ARMED CONFLICT
Boko Haram

Boko Haram continued to commit war crimes and crimes against humanity in the northeast, affecting 14.8 million people. The group continued to carry out attacks and small-scale raids throughout the year. The national and regional armed forces recaptured major towns from Boko Haram's control.

In its response to Boko Haram attacks, the military continued to carry out arbitrary arrests, detentions, ill-treatment and extrajudicial executions of people suspected of being Boko Haram fighters – acts which amounted to war crimes and possible crimes against humanity.

In May, 737 men detained as Boko Haram suspects by the army were transferred to the prison in Maiduguri, capital of Borno state. They were charged for being "incorrigible vagabonds", which carried up to two years' imprisonment and/or a fine.

In April, the Defence Ministry started Operation Safe Corridor to "rehabilitate repentant and surrendered Boko Haram fighters" in a camp.

On 13 October, 21 Chibok schoolgirls abducted in 2014 were released by Boko Haram fighters following negotiations. One more girl was found in November; about 195 Chibok schoolgirls remained missing at the end of the year.

INTERNALLY DISPLACED PEOPLE

There remained at least 2 million internally displaced persons (IDPs) in northern Nigeria; 80% of them lived in host communities, while the remainder lived in camps. The camps in Maiduguri remained overcrowded, with inadequate access to food, clean water and sanitation.

In the so-called inaccessible territories in Borno state, tens of thousands of IDPs were held in camps under armed guard by the Nigerian military and the Civilian Joint Task Force (CJTF), a state-sponsored civilian militia formed to fight Boko Haram. Most of the IDPs were not allowed to leave the camps and did not receive adequate food, water or medical care. Thousands of people have died in these camps due to severe malnutrition. In June, in a guarded camp in Bama, Borno state, the NGO Médecins Sans Frontières reported over 1,200 bodies had been buried within the past year.

Both the CJTF and the army were accused of sexually exploiting women in the IDP camps in exchange for money or food, or for allowing them to leave the camps.

ARBITRARY ARRESTS AND DETENTIONS

The military arbitrarily arrested thousands of young men, women and children who fled to the safety of recaptured towns, including Banki and Bama, Borno state. These arrests were largely based on random profiling of men, especially young men, rather than on reasonable suspicion of having committed a recognizably criminal offence. In most cases, the arrests were made without adequate investigation. Other people were arbitrarily arrested as they attempted to flee from Boko Haram. Those detained by the military had no access to their families or lawyers and were not brought before a court. More than 1,500 detainees were released throughout the year.

The mass arrests by the military of people fleeing Boko Haram led to overcrowding in military detention facilities. At the military detention facility at Giwa barracks, Maiduguri, cells were overcrowded. Diseases, dehydration and starvation was rife. At least 240 detainees died during the year. Bodies were secretly buried in Maiduguri's cemetery by the Borno state environmental protection agency staff. Among the dead were at least 29 children and babies, aged between newborn and five years.

At Giwa barracks, children under five were detained in three overcrowded and insanitary women's cells, alongside at least 250 women and teenage girls per cell. Some children were born in detention.

LACK OF ACCOUNTABILITY

There was continued lack of accountability for serious human rights violations committed by security officers. No independent and impartial investigations into crimes committed by the military had taken place despite the President's repeated promises in May. Moreover, senior military officials alleged to have committed crimes under international law remained uninvestigated; Major General Ahmadu Mohammed was reinstated into the army in January. He was in command of operations when the military executed more than 640 detainees following a Boko Haram attack on the detention centre in Giwa barracks on 14 March 2014.

In its November preliminary report, the Office of the Prosecutor of the International Criminal Court (ICC) announced that it will continue its analysis of any new allegations of crimes committed in Nigeria and its assessment of admissibility of the eight potential cases identified in 2015, in order to reach a decision on whether the criteria for opening an investigation are met.

CORPORATE ACCOUNTABILITY

In June, the government launched a programme to clean up the contamination caused by oil spills and restore the environment of the Ogoniland region in the Niger Delta. There were hundreds of spills during the year.

The government continued to fail to hold oil companies to account, including Shell. It did not provide the oversight needed to ensure that companies prevented spills, or responded to oil spills. The National Oil Spill Detection and Response Agency (NOSDRA) remained ineffective and certified areas as clean that remained contaminated.

In March, two Niger Delta communities affected by oil spills filed a new law suit against Shell in the UK courts.

Oil companies continued to blame their failure to prevent spills, or restore contaminated areas, on sabotage and theft.

Their claims were based on a flawed oil spill investigation led by the oil companies rather than NOSDRA.

Niger Delta

In January, the armed group Niger Delta Avengers began attacking and blowing up pipelines in the Niger Delta region. The government responded by significantly increasing military presence in the region. The activities of Niger Delta Avengers caused oil production to slow down.

DEATH PENALTY

Three men were secretly executed on 23 December in Benin prison in Edo state. One of them was sentenced to death by a military tribunal in 1998, which meant he did not have a right to appeal. Judges continued to impose death sentences throughout the year. On 4 May, the Senate resolved to enact a law prescribing the death penalty as the punishment for kidnapping, following the rise in abductions across the country. A number of states have either enacted or proposed similar laws.

FREEDOM OF EXPRESSION – JOURNALISTS

The government arrested and detained, some without trial, at least 10 journalists and bloggers.

In August, Abubakar Usman, a prominent blogger, was arrested in Abuja, the capital, by the anti-corruption agency Economic and Financial Crimes Commission and accused of contravening the Cyber Crimes Act. The Commission did not point out the specific provisions the blogger had contravened; he was released without being charged. In September, Jamil Mabai, was arrested and detained by the police for posting comments on Facebook and Twitter that were critical of the Katsina state government.

In early September, the publisher Emenike Iroegbu was arrested in Uyo, Akwa Ibom state, over alleged defamation.

On 5 September, Ahmed Salkida, a Nigerian journalist based in the United Arab Emirates, was declared wanted by the military and later arrested by the state security services on arrival in Nigeria. He was among three people arrested and briefly detained for alleged links to Boko Haram and for facilitating the release of a Boko Haram video on the abducted Chibok girls. He was later released; his passport remained confiscated.

FREEDOM OF ASSEMBLY

The security forces disrupted, in some cases violently and with excessive use of force, peaceful protests and assemblies. On 6 September, police stopped members of the Bring Back Our Girls movement. They had given notice of the protest and gathered peacefully outside the office and residence of the President in Abuja to demand the release of the abducted Chibok girls.

On 22 September in Abuja, police fired tear gas canisters to disperse a peaceful protest by the Islamic Movement in Nigeria, resulting in some minor injuries.

A number of supporters of Biafran independence were in detention – many of them since late January – for attempting to hold or participate in peaceful assemblies. On several occasions, security forces used excessive force against pro-Biafran activists across southeastern Nigeria.

UNLAWFUL KILLINGS

The military was deployed in 30 out of Nigeria's 36 states and in the Federal Capital Territory of Abuja where they performed routine policing functions including responding to non-violent demonstrations. The military deployment to police public gatherings contributed to the number of extrajudicial executions and unlawful killings. Since January, in response to the continued agitation by pro-Biafra campaigners, security forces arbitrarily arrested and killed at least 100 members and supporters of the group Indigenous People of Biafra (IPOB). Some of those arrested were subjected to enforced disappearance.

On 9 February, soldiers and police officers shot at about 200 IPOB members who had gathered for a prayer meeting at the National High School in Aba, in Abia state. Video footage showed soldiers shooting at peaceful and unarmed IPOB members; at least 17 people were killed and scores injured.

On 29 and 30 May, at least 60 people were killed in a joint security operation carried out by the army, police, Department of State Security (DSS) and navy. Pro-Biafra campaigners had gathered to celebrate Biafra Remembrance Day in Onitsha. No investigation into these killings had been initiated by the end of the year.

ENFORCED DISAPPEARANCES

On 3 April, Chijioke Mba was arrested and detained by the anti-kidnapping unit of the police force in Enugu for belonging to an unlawful society. His family and lawyer had not seen him since May.

On 16 August, Sunday Chucks Obasi was abducted from his home in Amuko Nnewi, Anambra state, by five armed men suspected to be Nigerian security agents in a vehicle with a government registration number plate. Witnesses said he was injured during the incident. His whereabouts remained unknown.

TORTURE AND OTHER ILL-TREATMENT

The police and military continued to commit torture and other ill-treatment during the interrogation of suspects or detainees to extract information and confessions. The Special Anti-Robbery Squad (SARS) of the police frequently committed torture and other ill-treatment during interrogations.

In September, the Inspector General of the police warned SARS against committing torture and encouraged them to follow due process of law.

On 18 May, Chibuike Edu died in police custody after he was arrested for burglary and detained for two weeks by the SARS in Enugu. The police authorities were investigating the incident; no one had been held accountable for his death at the end of the year.

The National Assembly was yet to pass into law the anti-torture bill which seeks to further prohibit and criminalize torture. In

June, it passed its first reading in the Senate. It had earlier been passed by the House of Representatives and was revised by the Nigeria Law Reform Commission. The revised version was to be debated at the Senate.

COMMUNAL VIOLENCE

Inter-communal violence occurred in many parts of the country. Many incidents were linked to lingering clashes between herdsmen and farming communities.

In February, at least 45 people were killed in Agatu, Benue state, after attacks by suspected herdsmen. In April, at least nine people were killed by suspected herdsmen in the Nimbo/Ukpabi community in Enugu state. The community said they had warned the authorities about the pending attack but the security agencies failed to prevent it. Five people detained by the police over the killings were yet to be tried.

In May, at least two people were killed in the Oke-Ako community, Ekiti state, by suspected herdsmen. In response, in August, the state government enacted a law banning cattle on undesignated land in the state.

FREEDOM OF ASSOCIATION

Ibrahim El-Zakzaky, leader of the Islamic Movement of Nigeria (IMN), remained in incommunicado detention without trial since his arrest in December 2015. Between 12 and 14 December 2015, soldiers killed more than 350 protesters and supporters of IMN at two sites in Zaria, Kaduna state.

Hundreds of IMN members were arrested and continued to be held in detention facilities in Kaduna, Bauchi, Plateau and Kano states.

On 11 April, the Kaduna state authorities admitted to a Judicial Commission of Inquiry that they had secretly buried 347 bodies in a mass grave two days after the December 2015 massacre.

On 15 July, the Commission presented its report to the state government indicting the Nigerian military for unlawful killings. In December, the Kaduna state government published its white paper on the report, which rejected most of the Commission's recommendations.

On 22 September, the National Human Rights Commission released a report indicting the IMN for provoking the clashes that led to the killings of IMN members and the military for the killings of IMN members. On the same day, police blocked IMN protesters and fired tear gas canisters at members of the IMN during a protest to demand the release of their leader. On 6 October, the Governor of Kaduna state declared the IMN an unlawful society. Following the declaration, members of the IMN were violently attacked in several states across the country, including Kaduna, Kano, Katsina and Plateau. Several IMN members were also arrested and detained by the military.

HOUSING RIGHTS

Forced evictions of thousands of people from their homes impacting on a range of their rights occurred in at least two states and in the Federal Capital Territory of Abuja.

In February, a Tribunal of Inquiry set up by the Lagos state government found that the government had failed to genuinely and adequately consult, compensate and provide promised resettlement to agricultural communities who were forcibly evicted from their homes and farmlands between 2006 and January 2016.

Between 2 and 5 July, the Rivers state government forcibly evicted over 1,600 residents in Eagle Island claiming that this was to tackle crime.

Following earlier forced evictions in March and September, on 9 October the Governor of Lagos state announced plans to commence the demolition of all settlements along the state's waterfronts. The justification was the need to respond to kidnapping incidents in the state. There were no plans announced to consult the communities prior to eviction.

On 15 October, hundreds of residents in Ilubirin waterfront community were forcibly evicted from their homes. Between 9 and 10 November, over 30,000 residents of Otodo Gbame, a waterfront community in Lagos state, were forcibly evicted when state authorities set fire to and demolished their homes with a bulldozer. On 11 November, hundreds of residents were forcibly evicted from another nearby waterfront community, Ebute Ikate, in Lagos state.

WOMEN'S RIGHTS

In September, the Gender and Equal Opportunities Bill to eliminate all forms of discrimination against women passed its second reading in the Senate. Although Nigeria ratified the CEDAW in 1985, it was yet to domesticate the Convention as part of the national law.

RIGHTS OF LESBIAN, GAY, BISEXUAL, TRANSGENDER AND INTERSEX PEOPLE

The law prohibiting samesex marriages remained in force. Police continued to arrest LGBTI people. Men perceived to be gay were attacked by mobs and were blackmailed and targeted for extortion.

CHILDREN'S RIGHTS

In May, Bayelsa state passed the Child Rights Law bringing to 23 the number of states that have enacted the law. In addition, the State House of Assembly in Enugu state passed the law in August; the Governor was yet to give his assent.

NORWAY

Kingdom of Norway
Head of state: King Harald V
Head of government: Erna Solberg

The Immigration Law was amended to introduce significant restrictions on access to asylum. A new law granting transgender people the right to legal gender recognition was passed. Serious concerns remained about rape and other violence against women.

REFUGEES AND ASYLUM-SEEKERS

In April, the government tabled 40 amendments to the Immigration Law to restrict access to asylum. This was in line with the Minister of Immigration and Integration's aim of ensuring that Norway had "the strictest refugee policy in Europe". The proposals included granting police at the border – rather than the Immigration Directorate and the Immigration Appeal Board – the power to assess whether a person is in need of international protection. They also included severe restrictions on the right to family reunification and the rights of asylum-seeking children. The most restrictive elements of the proposed legislation did not pass; but the package approved by Parliament in June, which began to be implemented in August, marked a significant retrogression on Norway's approach to international protection. The new provisions included a requirement for refugees applying for permanent residency to demonstrate economic self-sufficiency for 12 months and a "crisis mechanism" allowing expulsions at the border when faced with large numbers of arriving asylum-seekers. As of August, 84 children in families whose claims for asylum had been rejected were detained together with their adult family members at the Trandum police immigration detention centre near Oslo Airport Gardermoen, pending return to their country of origin.

In early December, 40 young male Afghan nationals, some of whom claimed to be under 18, were returned to Afghanistan as part of the government's policy to return Afghan asylum-seekers.

RIGHTS OF LESBIAN, GAY, BISEXUAL, TRANSGENDER AND INTERSEX PEOPLE

In June, Parliament adopted a new law on legal gender recognition, granting transgender people aged 16 or older the right to legal gender recognition on the basis of self-identification. Children aged between six and 16 can apply for legal gender recognition with the consent of their parents or guardians. Violence motivated by discriminatory attitudes towards transgender people was still not classified as a hate crime in the Penal Code.

DISCRIMINATION – SEX WORKERS

While selling sex was not illegal, sex workers remained subject to a high level of policing and penalization. Sex workers faced human rights abuses such as physical and sexual violence including rape, exploitation and harassment, and risked facing penalization if they engaged with police. The enforcement of sex work, public nuisance and immigration laws to disrupt and prohibit sex work led to sex workers being subjected to forced eviction, police surveillance, fines, discrimination, loss of livelihood and deportation.[1]

VIOLENCE AGAINST WOMEN AND GIRLS

Rape and other sexual violence against women and girls remains endemic. The legal definition of rape in the Penal Code was not consent-based. Serious concerns remained about attrition rates in rape investigations and prosecutions, and in the lack of gender sensitivity among lay judges in hearing rape cases. There was systemic failure to ensure women's rights to legal protection and equality before the law. The number of rapes reported to police increased by 12% from 2014 to 2015, according to police statistics published in May.

INTERNATIONAL JUSTICE

On 24 June the Ministry of Justice ruled that a 43-year-old Rwandan national accused of complicity in the 1994 genocide in Rwanda, whose appeal rights were exhausted, could be extradited to Rwanda. The extradition had not been carried out by the end of the year.

---

1. The human cost of 'crushing' the market: Criminalization of sex work in Norway (EUR 36/4034/2016)

OMAN

Sultanate of Oman
Head of state and government: **Sultan Qaboos bin Said Al Said**

The authorities continued to restrict freedoms of expression and association, arresting and detaining government critics and human rights activists. Most were released within days but some faced prosecution and imprisonment, creating an environment of self-censorship. Women remained subject to discrimination in law and in practice. Migrant workers were exposed to exploitation and abuse. The death penalty remained in force; no executions were reported.

BACKGROUND

Oman accepted a number of recommendations following the UN Universal Periodic Review (UPR) of Oman's human rights record in 2015, but it rejected others, including abolition of the death penalty and bringing freedoms of expression and assembly in line with international standards.

In March, the UN Committee on the Rights of the Child urged Oman to cease harassment of human right defenders engaged in children's rights and to allow Omani women to pass on their nationality to their children on an equal basis with Omani men.

In June, the UN CERD Committee expressed concern about government restrictions on NGOs, racial discrimination and migrant workers' rights.

The government enacted a new Penal Code in April as well as laws prohibiting money laundering and financing terrorism.

In January, the authorities accepted the transfer of 10 detainees, all Yemeni nationals, from the US detention centre at Guantánamo Bay, Cuba.

FREEDOMS OF EXPRESSION AND ASSOCIATION

The authorities restricted freedoms of expression and association. State Security personnel arrested and detained online and print journalists, bloggers and others. Most were interrogated and then released without charge after several days but at least eight individuals were sentenced to prison terms under vaguely worded public order, insult or national security provisions, for the peaceful expression of their opinions.

Those sentenced included Hassan al-Basham, a former diplomat, sentenced in February to three years' imprisonment for Facebook posts the authorities said insulted God and the Sultan; Naser al-Busaidi, whose one-year prison sentence for criticizing officials was confirmed by the Nizwa Court of Appeal in February; and Sayyid Abdullah al-Darouri, whose 18-month sentence on sedition and public order charges imposed in 2015 was reduced to six months in February.

In May the authorities released former parliamentarian Talib al-Ma'mari after the Sultan issued a pardon. He was serving a four-year prison sentence imposed after an unfair trial in 2014 in connection with a demonstration to protect the environment.

In August, the authorities released Saeed Jaddad, a blogger and prisoner of conscience imprisoned following his convictions in September and November 2015.[1]

In August, the authorities closed down *Azamn* newspaper and arrested and prosecuted the editor and two of its journalists after it published articles alleging corruption by the government and the judiciary. Ibrahim al-Ma'mari, *Azamn*'s editor, faced four charges, local news editor Zaher al-'Abri faced one charge and deputy editor Yousef al-Haj faced six charges. Internal Security Service officers arrested another journalist, Hamoud al-Shukaily, for Facebook posts criticizing the action taken against the *Azamn* journalists. In December an appeal court overturned the ban on the newspaper, acquitted Zaher al-'Abri, and reduced the sentences handed down to Ibrahim al-Ma'mari and Yousef al-Haj.

WOMEN'S RIGHTS

Women faced discrimination in law and in practice, being accorded lesser rights than men in both criminal law and in personal status or family law in relation to matters such as divorce, child custody, inheritance and passing their nationality on to their children.

MIGRANT WORKERS' RIGHTS

Migrant workers faced exploitation and abuse. Domestic workers, mainly women from Asia and Africa, complained that employers to whom they were tied under the official *kafala* sponsorship system confiscated their passports, forced them to work excessive hours without time off, and denied them their full wages and adequate food and living conditions. The *kafala* system does not provide domestic workers with the protections available under the Labour Law. They remained vulnerable to abuse in the confines of private homes.

DEATH PENALTY

The death penalty remained in force for a range of crimes. Amendments to the Penal Code confirmed the use of firing squad as the method of execution. No executions were reported.

---

1. Oman: Further information: Omani prisoner of conscience released: Saeed Jaddad (MDE 20/4758/2016)

PAKISTAN

Islamic Republic of Pakistan
Head of state: **Mamnoon Hussain**
Head of government: **Muhammad Nawaz Sharif**

Armed groups continued to carry out targeted attacks against civilians, including government employees, which resulted in hundreds of casualties. Security forces, particularly paramilitary Rangers in Karachi, committed human rights violations with almost total impunity. Executions continued, often after unfair trials. State and non-state actors discriminated against religious minorities. Despite a new law in Punjab to protect women from violence, so-called "honour" crimes continued to be reported. Human rights defenders and media workers experienced threats, harassment and abuse from security forces and armed groups. Minorities continued to

face discrimination across a range of economic and social rights. Access to quality health care, particularly for poor and rural women, remained limited.

BACKGROUND

Operation Zarb-e-Azb, the Pakistan military's offensive against non-state armed groups that started in June 2014, continued in North Waziristan and Khyber tribal agency. Significant levels of armed conflict and political violence continued, in particular in the provinces of Khyber Pakhtunkhwa, the Federally Administered Tribal Areas (FATA), Balochistan and Sindh.

The National Commission for Human Rights, set up in May 2015, continued to lack sufficient staff and other resources, despite its budget finally being approved by Parliament. Concerns remained about the Commission's limited mandate with regard to investigation of cases of human rights violations allegedly committed by state agencies.

In late September, cross-border tension between Pakistan and India increased, with both states accusing the other of human rights violations at the UN Human Rights Council. There were repeated violations by both sides of the 2003 ceasefire, with exchange of fire across the Line of Control. India claimed to have carried out "surgical strikes" on militants in Pakistani-administered Azad Kashmir, which Pakistan denied.

ABUSES BY ARMED GROUPS

Armed groups continued to carry out attacks, despite a government-mandated National Action Plan to counter terrorism. The Plan was implemented in the wake of a Taliban attack on an army school in Peshawar in December 2014 that killed at least 149 people, mostly children.

On 20 January, armed attackers killed at least 30 people, mostly students and teachers, in Bacha Khan University, Charsadda, northwest Pakistan. Responsibility was claimed by a Pakistani Taliban commander who allegedly planned the 2014 army school attack in Peshawar, but this claim was contested.[1] The army subsequently claimed to have apprehended five "facilitators" of the attack.

On 16 March, a bomb attack on a bus carrying government employees in Peshawar killed at least 15 people and severely injured 25.[2]

On 8 August, a suicide bomb attack killed at least 63 people, mostly lawyers, and wounded more than 50 others at the Civil Hospital in Quetta, south-west Pakistan. Mourners had gathered to accompany the body of Bilal Anwar Kasi, President of the Balochistan Bar Association, who had been killed by gunmen earlier that day.[3]

POLICE AND SECURITY FORCES

Security forces including the Rangers, a paramilitary force under the command of the Pakistan Army, perpetrated human rights violations such as arbitrary arrests, torture and other ill-treatment, and extrajudicial executions. Security laws and practices, and the absence of any independent mechanisms to investigate the security forces and hold them accountable, allowed government forces to commit such violations with near-total impunity. Victims included members of political parties, in particular the Muttahida Qaumi Movement (MQM), and human rights defenders.

On 1 May, plainclothes police arrested Aftab Ahmed, a senior MQM member. On 3 May, after he was moved to Rangers custody, news of his death emerged, alongside photographs apparently showing wounds sustained during torture.[4] The Director-General of the Rangers for Sindh publicly acknowledged that Aftab Ahmed had been tortured in custody, but denied that his forces were responsible for the death. According to media reports, five Rangers soldiers were suspended after an investigation ordered by the Chief of Army Staff, but no further information was made public.

By the end of the year little progress had been made in the case of Dr Asim Hussain, a senior member of the Pakistan People's Party and a former federal minister who was allegedly ill-treated and denied proper medical attention while in the custody of the Rangers in 2015. Asim Hussain had been arrested on charges including for "being involved in offences relating to misappropriation of funds and for enhancing, supporting terrorism activities, and other criminal links/activities by using authority punishable under the Anti-Terrorism Act 1997".

Security forces detained several political activists without trial during the year. Some of them continued to be at risk of torture and other ill-treatment.

According to information published in August by the Pakistan Commission of Inquiry on Enforced Disappearances, 1,401 out of more than 3,000 cases of disappearance had not yet been investigated by the Commission.

DEATH PENALTY

Since the December 2014 lifting of a six-year moratorium on executions, more than 400 have been carried out. Some of those executed were juveniles at the time of the offence or had a mental disability.

Both civil and military courts imposed death sentences, in many cases after unfair trials. Contrary to international law, the 28 offences carrying the death penalty included non-lethal crimes.

MILITARY COURTS

Military courts were given jurisdiction in 2015 to try all those accused of terrorism-related offences, including civilians. By January 2016, the government had constituted 11 military courts to hear such cases.

In August, the Supreme Court ruled for the first time on cases from these courts, upholding the verdicts and death sentences imposed on 16 civilians. The Court ruled that the appellants had not proved that the military violated their constitutional rights or failed to follow procedure. According to lawyers, the accused were denied access to legal counsel of their choice, and to military court records when preparing their appeals. Some of the accused were allegedly subjected to enforced disappearance, torture and other ill-treatment, and at least two were reportedly under 18 when arrested.

DISCRIMINATION – RELIGIOUS MINORITIES

State and non-state actors continued to discriminate against religious minorities, both Muslim and non-Muslim, in law and practice. Blasphemy laws remained in force and several new cases were registered, mostly in Punjab. The laws violated the rights to freedom of expression, thought, conscience and religion. Minorities, particularly Ahmadis, Hazaras and Dalits, continued to face restricted access to employment, health care, education and other basic services.

Mumtaz Qadri, a security guard convicted of killing the Governor of Punjab in 2011 because he had criticized the blasphemy laws, was executed in February. His funeral was attended by thousands of people and was followed by protests in the capital, Islamabad, Lahore and Karachi where protesters damaged public property, attacked media stations and clashed with the police.

Asia Noreen, a Christian woman sentenced to death for blasphemy in 2010, remained imprisoned in Sheikhupura. On 13 October, the Supreme Court was scheduled to hear her case in the ultimate stage of her appeal process but adjourned it indefinitely.

Armed groups attacked a park in Lahore on 27 March, killing at least 70 people, many of them children, and injuring many more. A faction of the Pakistani Taliban, Jamaat-ul-Ahrar, claimed responsibility for the attack, saying they had targeted Christians celebrating Easter.

VIOLENCE AGAINST WOMEN AND GIRLS

The Human Rights Commission of Pakistan recorded almost 3,000 cases of violence against women and girls, including murder, rape and gang rape, sodomy, domestic violence and kidnappings.

The Punjab Protection of Women against Violence Act was passed by the Punjab Provincial Assembly in February, despite opposition from Islamic parties.

An amendment to the law on so-called "honour-based" killings was introduced to end impunity for such crimes, but allowed for the death penalty as a possible punishment and for perpetrators to have their sentences lessened if they secure a pardon from the victim's family. It remained unclear how the authorities will distinguish between an "honour killing" and other murders, or what standards of evidence would apply, or what penalties would ensue. Human rights NGOs and activists were concerned that the penalty imposed should not depend on whether or not the victim's family had pardoned the crime. According to the Human Rights Commission of Pakistan, around 512 women and girls, and 156 men and boys, were killed in 2016 by relatives on so-called "honour" grounds. As many cases went unreported, or were falsely described as suicides or natural deaths, the actual number was almost certainly much higher. Qandeel Baloch, a social media celebrity, was drugged and killed by her brother in July. He confessed to murdering her for "dishonouring the Baloch name".

Child marriage remained a concern. In January a bill to raise the legal minimum age of marriage to 18 for girls was withdrawn following pressure from the Council of Islamic Ideology, who considered it "un-Islamic and blasphemous".

RIGHT TO HEALTH – WOMEN AND GIRLS

Access to quality health care, particularly for poor and rural women, remained limited due to information, distance and cost barriers, as well as to perceived norms concerning women's health and wellbeing.

FREEDOM OF EXPRESSION – JOURNALISTS

Media workers continued to be harassed, abducted and sometimes murdered. Those in FATA and Balochistan and those working on national security issues were particularly at risk.

According to the Pakistani Press Foundation, as of October, at least two media workers were killed, 16 were injured and one was abducted in connection with their work. The authorities generally failed to provide adequate protection to media workers from attacks by non-state armed groups, security forces, political activists and religious groups. Of the 49 media workers murdered since 2001, only four caseshad resulted in a conviction by the end of 2016. In March, a man convicted of murdering journalist Ayub Khattak in 2013 was sentenced to life imprisonment and a fine.

Zeenat Shahzadi, a journalist abducted by gunmen in August 2015 in Lahore, remained forcibly disappeared. The Human Rights Commission of Pakistan believed she had been abducted by security forces. In October Cyril Almeida, assistant editor of *Dawn* newspaper, was placed briefly on the Exit Control List, which prohibits certain people from leaving Pakistan. The Prime Minister's Office had objected to an article he wrote on tensions between the civilian government and the military. A few weeks later the authorities held the Minister for Information responsible for leaking the information that led to Cyril Almeida's news report.

The Pakistan Electronic Media Regulatory Authority, the federal regulator of the broadcast media, restricted media outputs by issuing fines, threatening to cancel broadcasting licences, and, in some cases, threatening prosecutions. Self-censorship was routine as a result of these measures and because of the fear of reprisals from the intelligence agencies and armed groups.

A new law on cybercrimes – the Prevention of Electronic Crimes Act – was passed in August, giving the authorities broad powers to surveil citizens and censor online expression. There were fears that it posed a risk to the right to freedom of expression, as well as the right to privacy and access to information.

HUMAN RIGHTS DEFENDERS

State and non-state actors continue to harass, threaten, detain and kill human rights defenders, especially in Balochistan, FATA and Karachi.

On 8 May, the Pakistani Taliban shot dead prominent human rights activist and website editor Khurram Zaki in Karachi. A spokesman for a faction of the Pakistani Taliban said it had killed him because of his campaign against Abdul Aziz, a cleric of the Red Mosque in Islamabad.

On 16 January, Rangers personnel arrested human rights defender Saeed Baloch, an advocate for fishing communities, in Karachi. Following national and international pressure, he was presented in court on 26 January and released on bail in August.

According to eyewitnesses, human rights defender Wahid Baloch was abducted on 26 July by masked men in plain clothes, believed to be representatives of security forces in Karachi.[5] He was released on 5 December.

A policy was implemented from early 2016 requiring international NGOs to obtain government consent to raise funds and operate. In an increasingly hostile climate for human rights work, security forces harassed and intimidated several NGO staff.

In September, the Home Ministry shut down Taangh Wasaib, an NGO working for women's rights and against religious intolerance, stating that it was involved in "dubious activities".

REFUGEES AND ASYLUM-SEEKERS

The legal status of the 1.4 million registered Afghan refugees became increasingly precarious as hostility towards them intensified and abuses, including physical attacks, escalated. The authorities estimated that an additional 1 million unregistered Afghan refugees were also living in the country.

Senior Pakistani officials threatened to expedite the forced return of all Afghan refugees. On 29 June, the authorities extended the right of registered refugees to remain in Pakistan legally, but only until March 2017.

Following the December 2014 attack on the army public school in Peshawar, police targeted Afghan settlements, demolished their homes, and subjected refugees to arbitrary detention and harassment.

WORKERS' RIGHTS

Despite the Bonded Labour System (Abolition) Act of 1992, bonded labour practices continued, particularly in the brick kiln and textile industries and among the scheduled castes (Dalits).

1. Pakistan: Armed attack on Bacha Khan University a potential war crime (News story, 20 January)

2. Pakistan: Government must deliver justice for victims of Peshawar bus bombing (News story, 16 March)

3. Pakistan: Attack on Quetta hospital abhorrent disregard for the sanctity of life (News story, 8 August)

4. Pakistan: Investigation crucial after Karachi political activist tortured and killed in custody (News story, 4 May)

5. Pakistan: Human rights defender at risk of torture (ASA 33/4580/2016)

PALESTINE (STATE OF)

State of Palestine
Head of state: **Mahmoud Abbas**
Head of government: **Rami Hamdallah**

The Palestinian authorities in the West Bank and the Hamas de facto administration in the Gaza Strip both continued to restrict freedom of expression, including by arresting and detaining critics and political opponents. They also restricted the right to peaceful assembly and used excessive force to disperse some protests. Torture and other ill-treatment of detainees remained rife in both Gaza and the West Bank. Unfair trials of civilians before military courts continued in Gaza; detainees were held without charge or trial in the West Bank. Women and girls faced discrimination and violence. Courts in Gaza continued to hand down death sentences and Hamas carried out executions; no death sentences were imposed or executions carried out in the West Bank.

BACKGROUND

Negotiations between Israel and the Palestine Liberation Organization, which was led by President Abbas, remained stalled despite international efforts to revive them. Continued tension between Fatah and Hamas undermined the Palestinian national consensus government formed in June 2014; the Hamas de facto administration continued to control Gaza.

Gaza remained under an Israeli air, sea and land blockade, in force since June 2007. The continuing restrictions on imports of construction materials under the blockade, and funding shortages, contributed to severe delays in reconstruction of homes and other infrastructure damaged or destroyed in recent armed conflicts. Continuing restrictions on exports crippled the economy and exacerbated widespread impoverishment among Gaza's 1.9 million inhabitants. The Egyptian authorities' almost total closure of the Rafah border crossing with Gaza completed its isolation and compounded the impact of the Israeli blockade.

In June, Prime Minister Hamdallah said new municipal elections would be held on 8 October. However, the Palestinian High Court ruled in September that the elections should be indefinitely suspended on the grounds that Israeli controls prevented the participation of Palestinians in East Jerusalem and due to the illegality of local courts in Gaza. Both Palestinian authorities harassed and detained opposition candidates in the period before the court's decision.

There was a marked rise in tension in Nablus, Jenin and other northern governorates of the West Bank where gunmen affiliated to Fatah clashed with the security forces resulting in some deaths.

LEGAL, CONSTITUTIONAL OR INSTITUTIONAL DEVELOPMENTS

In February, President Abbas signed the juvenile protection bill into law, paving the way for the establishment in March of the West Bank's first juvenile court in Ramallah.

In March President Abbas approved the National Insurance Law establishing for the first time a state social security system for private sector workers and their families. The new law covered issues such as pensions for the elderly and the disabled, and employment injury benefits for workers in the Palestinian private sector. Civil society organizations criticized the new law, arguing that it failed to provide minimum standards of protection and social justice and could cause further marginalization of the most vulnerable.

In April a presidential decree established a nine-judge Palestinian Supreme Constitutional Court with supremacy over other Palestinian courts, a move seen widely as an unprecedented example of executive interference in the judiciary. In October, the President of the High Judicial Council was removed from his position. He stated in a media interview that he had been forced to sign his resignation at the time of his inauguration.

In December, the President stripped five members of the Palestinian Legislative Council of their immunity, including his political opponents, after a judgment by the Supreme Constitutional Court allowing him to do so. The move was criticized by civil society organizations as undermining the rule of law and separation of powers.

Palestine ratified the Kampala amendments to the Rome Statute on the crime of aggression in June. Representatives of the Office of the Prosecutor of the International Criminal Court visited Israel and the West Bank but did not travel to Gaza.

ARBITRARY ARRESTS AND DETENTIONS

Security authorities in the West Bank, including Preventative Security and General Intelligence, and those in Gaza, particularly the Internal Security Service, arbitrarily arrested and detained critics and supporters of rival political organizations. In the West Bank, security forces used administrative detention by order of governors to hold detainees without charge or trial for periods of up to several months.

UNFAIR TRIALS

In both the West Bank and Gaza, authorities failed to ensure adherence to basic due process rights, such as prompt access to legal counsel and the right to be charged or released. Palestinian security forces in the West Bank held detainees for long periods without trial on the orders of regional governors, and delayed or failed to comply with court orders for the release of detainees in dozens of cases. In Gaza, Hamas military courts continued to convict defendants, including civilians, in unfair trials, sentencing some to death.

TORTURE AND OTHER ILL-TREATMENT

Torture and other ill-treatment of detainees remained common and was committed with impunity by Palestinian police and other security forces in the West Bank, and Hamas police and other security forces in Gaza. In both areas, the victims included children. The Independent Commission for Human Rights, Palestine's national human rights institution, reported receiving a total of 398 allegations of torture and other ill-treatment of detainees between January and November; 163 from the West Bank and 235 from Gaza. The majority of complaints in both areas were against police. Neither the Palestine national consensus government nor the Hamas de facto administration in Gaza independently investigated torture allegations or held perpetrators to account.

Basel al-Araj, Ali Dar al-Sheikh and three other men alleged that General Intelligence officers held them incommunicado and tortured and otherwise ill-treated them for almost three weeks following their arrest on 9 April. They said officers beat them, forced them to remain in stress positions, and deprived them of sleep, leading them to launch a hunger strike protest on 28 August. Officers then subjected them to solitary confinement for the duration of their hunger strikes. They were released on bail and appeared before the Ramallah Magistrates' Court on 8 September on charges that included illegal possession of arms. Their trial was ongoing at the end of the year.

Ahmad Izzat Halaweh died in Jeneid prison in Nablus on 23 August shortly after being arrested. A national consensus government spokesperson said security officials had severely beaten Ahmad Halaweh prior to his death. The authorities began an investigation headed by the Minister of Justice. The investigation was continuing at the end of the year.

FREEDOMS OF EXPRESSION, ASSOCIATION AND ASSEMBLY

The authorities in both the West Bank and Gaza severely curtailed rights to freedom of expression, association and peaceful assembly, harassing, arresting and detaining critics and supporters of their political rivals and forcibly dispersing protests, assaulting journalists and others.

In the West Bank, police arrested university professor Abd al-Sattar Qassem in February after he criticized the Palestinian authorities on al-Quds TV, a Hamas-affiliated broadcaster. He was charged with incitement and released on bail after five days in custody.

In Gaza, Internal Security Service officers briefly detained journalist Mohamed Ahmed Othman in September. He reported being subjected to torture and other ill-treatment in an attempt to force him to reveal the source for a government document he had published. He was released the next day without charge. He was summoned again twice in the two days following his release.

In February, a two-day walkout by West Bank teachers complaining about low pay escalated into several weeks of mass strikes and protests following heavy-handed intervention by Palestinian security forces, who set up roadblocks around Ramallah to prevent teachers joining demonstrations and arrested 22 teachers. Those arrested were subsequently released without charge. Harassment of teachers continued at the end of the year, targeting those organizing a new union.

UNLAWFUL KILLINGS

Security forces in the West Bank killed at least three men and injured others while carrying out law enforcement activities.

On 7 June, Adel Nasser Jaradat was killed by gunfire from West Bank security forces in Silet al-Harethiya, a village northwest of Jenin. The authorities failed to hold those responsible to account.

On 19 August, security forces killed Fares Halawa and Khaled al-Aghbar in Nablus in unclear circumstances. Though the local authorities maintained they were killed in clashes, witnesses said they were alive and unarmed when the security forces seized them. An investigation was continuing at the end of the year.

In Gaza, the military wing of Hamas, the 'Izz al-Din al-Qassam Brigades, summarily executed one of their members, Mahmoud Rushdi Ishteiwi, on 7 February after the group said its "Military and Shari'a Judiciaries" had sentenced him for "behavioural and moral excesses". The victim's family said he had been detained incommunicado by the Brigades since 21 January 2015. The Hamas de facto administration in Gaza took no steps to investigate or bring the perpetrators of the killing to justice.

WOMEN'S AND GIRLS' RIGHTS

Women and girls continued to face discrimination in law and in practice, and were inadequately protected against sexual and other violence, including so-called "honour" killings. Women and girls were reported to have been killed by male relatives in "honour" killings.

In February the Attorney General issued a decision establishing a specialized prosecution unit to investigate and prosecute cases of family violence and violence against women.

DEATH PENALTY

The death penalty remained in force for murder and other crimes. Courts in the West Bank did not hand down any death sentences during the year.

In May, members of the Change and Reform Bloc, the Hamas parliamentary group in Gaza, paved the way for the Gaza authorities to execute prisoners whose sentences have not been ratified by the Palestinian President, contrary to the Palestinian Basic Law of 2003 and the 2001 Penal Procedure Law.

PAPUA NEW GUINEA

Independent State of Papua New Guinea
Head of state: Queen Elizabeth II, represented by Michael Ogio
Head of government: Peter Charles Paire O'Neill

The authorities failed to prevent widespread violence against children, women, sex workers, asylum-seekers and refugees. Cases of violence were rarely prosecuted. Cultural practices, including polygamy, continued to undermine women's rights. There was insufficient protection against torture or other ill-treatment. The police continued to use excessive force against protesters. Poverty remained endemic, particularly in rural areas, despite economic wealth generated by the mining industry. The death penalty was retained; no executions had been carried out since 1954.

FREEDOMS OF EXPRESSION AND PEACEFUL ASSEMBLY

Weeks of peaceful protests by students at the University of Papua New Guinea against alleged government corruption ended in violence on 8 June, when police fired shots and assaulted peaceful protesters. Thirty-eight people were injured and received medical treatment, including two who suffered gunshot wounds. Although separate investigations were initiated by the police, the Ombudsman and a parliamentary committee, the outcomes were not known at the end of the year.

VIOLENCE AGAINST WOMEN AND GIRLS

The government failed to address widespread sexual and gender-based violence in legislation or in practice. Cultural practices were allowed to persist, including the custom whereby wives are forced to repay a "bride price" to their husbands if they wish to separate from him, placing women in abusive marriages at greater risk. Women accused of "sorcery" were subjected to violence from the community.

There was also limited psychosocial support, women's shelters or other services to protect women from domestic violence.

DISCRIMINATION – SEX WORKERS

There were high levels of violence by state and non-state actors against sex workers on grounds of their gender identity, sexual orientation or status as sex workers and as a result of legislation criminalizing sex work.[1] Systemic gender inequality and discrimination in education, employment and in the community generally, forced many women, including transgender women, and gay men into selling sex for a living. Police officers were responsible for violations against sex workers, such as rape, physical assault, arbitrary arrest and detention and other ill-treatment. The criminalization of same-sex sexual relations as well as of sex work continued to drive and compound violence and discrimination against gay and transgender people. It also led to discrimination in the provision of health care and undermined the prevention and treatment of HIV.

REFUGEES AND ASYLUM-SEEKERS

As of 30 November, around 900 refugees and asylum-seekers, all men, remained in two Australian-run detention centres on Papua New Guinea's Manus Island (see Australia entry). In April, the Supreme Court held that their detention – for over three years – was illegal and unconstitutional. It ordered the Australian and Papua New

Guinean governments to close the camps immediately. Both camps remained open at the end of the year.

Refugees and asylum-seekers filed a civil court case seeking orders to force the camps' closure; for them to be returned to Australia; and for compensation for their unlawful detention.

A Sudanese refugee, Faysal Ishak Ahmed, died on 24 December, after being airlifted from one of the detention centres, to an Australian hospital, after a fall and a seizure. Refugees in the centre said his health had deteriorated over months but he was not given adequate health care.

There were continued reports of violence against refugees and asylum-seekers for which the perpetrators were rarely held to account. In April, two Papua New Guinean nationals employed in one of the detention centres were convicted of murdering asylum-seeker Reza Berat in 2014 although others allegedly involved were not prosecuted.

In November, the Australian government announced that some of the refugees detained on Nauru (see Nauru entry) and Manus Island would be resettled in the USA.

---

1. Outlawed and abused: Criminalizing sex work in Papua New Guinea (ASA 34/4030/2016)

PARAGUAY

Republic of Paraguay
Head of state and government: **Horacio Manuel Cartes Jara**

Figures on poverty reduction improved, although children and adolescents continued to be those principally affected. Indigenous Peoples continued to be denied their rights to land and to free, prior and informed consent on projects affecting them. Both Indigenous Peoples and Afro-Paraguayans faced racial discrimination. A bill to eliminate all forms of discrimination was pending approval at the end of the year. There were reports of violations of freedom

of expression and of the persecution of human rights defenders and journalists. Abortion remained criminalized and child and teenage pregnancies continued to be a concern.

BACKGROUND

In October a new Ombudsman was appointed after a gap of seven years.

INTERNATIONAL SCRUTINY

In January, Paraguay's human rights record was examined under the UN Universal Periodic Review (UPR) process. The Human Rights Council made a number of recommendations, including urging Paraguay to approve a bill to eliminate all forms of discrimination on the basis of sexual orientation and gender identity; to develop legal systems to prevent and punish violence against women and girls; to reinforce protection of the rights of Indigenous Peoples; to protect the free exercise of freedom of the press, expression and opinion; and to address impunity for human rights violations committed against human rights defenders and journalists. Paraguay accepted all the recommendations except those related to the decriminalization of abortion.

In October the UN CERD Committee issued its report and concluding observation based on Paraguay's fourth to sixth periodic reports. It made a number of recommendations, including urging Paraguay to take affirmative action to overcome systemic discrimination against Indigenous Peoples and Afro-Paraguayans. The Committee also highlighted weak state protection of rights to prior consultation and Indigenous Peoples' rights over their lands, territories and resources.

In November, the UN Special Rapporteur on the right to food visited Paraguay and met with public authorities and members of civil society. She was due to present her report on the visit in 2017.

INDIGENOUS PEOPLES' RIGHTS

In February, the Inter-American Commission on Human Rights granted precautionary measures to Ayoreo Totobiegosode communities living in voluntary isolation, calling on the Paraguayan government to protect the communities from third parties seeking to access their ancestral lands. In October, the CERD Committee called on Paraguay to fully abide by these precautionary measures.

In October, the Yakye Axa community remained without access to their lands despite a ruling from the Inter-American Court of Human Rights ordering the government to construct an access route. The CERD Committee called on Paraguay to intensify efforts to effectively comply with the Court's judgment.

The case regarding the ownership of land expropriated from the Sawhoyamaxa community was still pending at the end of the year despite the fact that in June 2015 the Supreme Court of Justice had rejected the appeal brought by a livestock company to stall the effects of a law passed to return the land to the community.

In October, the CERD Committee urged Paraguay to take effective measures to address problems related to access to food, drinking water, sanitation and child malnutrition among Indigenous Peoples and Afro-Paraguayans living in rural areas.

HOUSING RIGHTS – FORCED EVICTIONS

In September, members of the Senate filed a complaint with the Attorney General over the forced eviction of 200 families from the Guahory *campesino* (peasant farmer) community and the failure of the government to investigate the situation. In December, another eviction took place in this community during a dialogue process between Guahory members and representatives of the National Institute of Rural Development and Land, aimed at assessing information related to land tenure in the community.

In September, human rights organizations reported the forced eviction of the Avá

Guaraní de Sauce community in connection with the Itaipu hydroelectric installation.

JUSTICE SYSTEM

In July, the UN High Commissioner for Human Rights expressed concern over the conviction of 11 *campesinos* in connection with a massacre in Curuguaty in 2012 that left 17 dead. There were reports of irregularities during proceedings regarding the right to an adequate defence and due process.

In October, following a UPR recommendation, the Senate initiated proceedings to create an independent committee to investigate the massacre at Curuguaty in order to ensure access to justice for the victims and their relatives.

WOMEN'S AND GIRLS' RIGHTS

In December, the Chamber of Deputies issued Law 5.777 on comprehensive protection of women from all forms of violence. Femicide was recognized as a distinct criminal offence punishable by a minimum of 10 years' imprisonment. A ban on requiring conciliation between victims of violence and offenders was also approved. The law was due to enter into force after one year.

Pregnancies among girls and young teenagers were alarmingly high. In October, the Centre for Documentation and Research reported that there were on average between 500 and 700 pregnancies among girls aged between 10 and 14 each year. Similar concerns were raised in a UNFPA report, *Young Paraguay*, which indicated that pregnancy among this group had risen by over 62.6% in the last decade. The principal causes were given as violence against women, social exclusion and macho culture.

FREEDOM OF EXPRESSION

In November a draft bill was presented to establish protection mechanisms for journalists, media workers and human rights defenders. The failure to investigate and prosecute the killings of 17 journalists since 1991 was among the principal drivers behind the demand for increased protection.

HUMAN RIGHTS DEFENDERS

Lawyer and human rights defender Julia Cabello Alonso was warned that she would be disbarred from the Bar Association of Paraguay and prevented from exercising her professional functions because of alleged non-compliance with professional ethics when defending the restitution of Indigenous Peoples' lands.

In its October report, the CERD Committee recommended that Paraguay take steps to strengthen the protection of human rights defenders, including Indigenous leaders and those who defend Indigenous Peoples' rights, against intimidation, threats and arbitrary actions by governmental officials.

Similarly, the Human Rights Council recommended that Paraguay combats impunity for all violations against, including killings of, human rights defenders, as well as investigates allegations of abusive practices by security and law enforcement forces targeted at Indigenous People, and prosecutes those found responsible.

PERU

Republic of Peru
Head of state and government: Pedro Pablo Kuczynski Godard (replaced Ollanta Moisés Humala Tasso in July)

There was a notable increase in violence towards – and lack of protection of – marginalized groups, particularly women and girls, Indigenous Peoples as well as lesbian, gay, bisexual, transgender and intersex (LGBTI) people. The government ratified the Arms Trade Treaty.

BACKGROUND

In June, Pedro Pablo Kuczynski Godard was elected President in the second round of elections.

Over 200 cases of social protest were registered, around 70% of which were related to disputes between communities, extractive companies and the government over the ownership, use and enjoyment of natural resources as well as the protection of the environment.

HUMAN RIGHTS DEFENDERS

Human rights defenders continued to be harassed, threatened and attacked in the context of social protests – especially those related to land, territorial and environmental issues. The police used excessive and unnecessary force, including lethal weapons, to repress protests. In October, Quintino Cereceda died of a bullet wound to the head when the police dispersed a protest against the mining project in Las Bambas, Apurímac region.

On two occasions, Máxima Acuña and her family were attacked and intimidated by security personnel from the Yanacocha mining company, who destroyed their crops. The company claimed it was exercising its "possessory right to defence". Máxima Acuña, her family and another 48 activists and peasant farmers from Cajamarca region were beneficiaries of precautionary measures granted in 2014 by the Inter-American Commission on Human Rights to guarantee their safety.

INDIGENOUS PEOPLES' RIGHTS

The investigation into the deaths of four Ashaninka leaders from Ucayali region who had allegedly been killed in 2014 by illegal loggers had yet to be concluded by the end of the year. The leaders had previously denounced the continuous illegal logging on their territory.

Throughout the year there were 13 oil spills from the Northern Peruvian Pipeline, contaminating water and land belonging to Indigenous Peoples in the Amazon basin. Indigenous organizations in the affected areas went on strike from September, demanding that the government address issues like the population's health and reparations for damage to the environment. In December the Indigenous organizations and the government signed an agreement on the issue.

In September, the Bagua Criminal Court acquitted 53 accused Indigenous people, who had been charged with crimes including killing 12 police officers in clashes with security forces in 2009. At the end of the year no state officials had been prosecuted for their role in escalating the conflict.

IMPUNITY

Some progress was made in the investigation of human rights violations committed during the internal armed conflict (1980-2000).

In June, the Law on the Search of Disappeared Persons was enacted.

In July, the trial began of 11 military personnel accused of sexual violence against rural women between 1984 and 1995 in Manta and Vilca, Huancavelica region.

In August, 10 military personnel were found guilty of the extrajudicial execution of 69 people in Accomarca village in 1985. There were 23 children among the victims.

In September, three high-ranking officials were charged with having forcibly disappeared two students and a teacher in 1993 in basements of the Military Intelligence Service headquarters.

In October, the trial of 35 former marines began for the massacre in El Frontón prison in 1986, when 133 prisoners accused of terrorism were extrajudicially executed.

VIOLENCE AGAINST WOMEN AND GIRLS

Violence against women and girls continued; there were reports that 108 women had been killed by their partners as well as reports of 222 cases of attempted murder of women and girls. Most cases were not investigated or resulted in suspended prison sentences.

Trafficking for sexual exploitation

Women made up 80% of human trafficking victims; 56% of the victims were under 18 years of age, with the majority trafficked for sexual exploitation in mining areas.

In September, the Permanent Criminal Chamber of the Supreme Court of Justice ratified a judgment of acquittal in a human trafficking case involving a 15-year-old girl. The Chamber argued that working over 13 hours a day as an "escort" in a bar in an illegal mining operation did not constitute labour exploitation or sexual exploitation, as "the workload did not exhaust the worker".

SEXUAL AND REPRODUCTIVE RIGHTS

The rate of teenage pregnancy increased. In some regions of the Amazon it reached 32.8% of girls and women between 15 and 19 years of age; 60% of pregnancies among girls aged 12-16 resulted from rape.

Forty-three cases of "risk to personal safety" (cases of threats and intimidation) and eight murders of LGBTI people were registered by NGOs. However, a reform to the Criminal Code which would have criminalized discrimination and attacks on the grounds of sexual orientation and gender identity failed to pass due to the change of government and of Congress.

In December, a bill that would recognize the gender of transgender people was presented in Parliament.

In July, the Public Prosecutor's Office closed the investigation into the case of over 2,000 Indigenous men and women who were allegedly forcibly sterilized in the 1990s. Only five health personnel were investigated for their role in the forced sterilization.

The registration of victims of forced sterilization was initiated in five regions of the country, and by the end of the year more than 2,000 victims were registered.

In August, a court of first instance in Lima, the capital, ordered the Ministry of Health to distribute emergency oral contraceptives free of charge.

Abortion remained criminalized in almost all cases, leading to clandestine and unsafe abortions. In October, several members of Parliament presented draft legislation to Congress to decriminalize abortion in cases of sexual violence.

PHILIPPINES

Republic of the Philippines
Head of state and government: **Rodrigo Roa Duterte**
(replaced Benigno S. Aquino III in June)

The government launched a campaign to crackdown on drugs in which over 6,000 people were killed. Human rights defenders and journalists were also targeted and killed by unidentified gunmen and armed militia. The use of unnecessary and excessive force by police continued. In a landmark ruling the courts convicted a police officer for torture for the first time under the 2009 Anti-Torture Act.

BACKGROUND

In September, the Philippines accepted the Chair of ASEAN for 2017.

In November, street protests took place after the body of former President Ferdinand Marcos, during whose presidency widespread human rights violations were committed, was re-buried in the Heroes Cemetery, a move backed by the President. The Philippines was reviewed by the UN Committee against Torture, the UN Committee on Economic, Social and Cultural Rights (CESCR) and the UN Committee on the Elimination of Discrimination against Women (CEDAW).

UNLAWFUL KILLINGS

In June, the government launched a campaign to crackdown on drugs which led to a wave of unlawful killings across the country, many of which may have amounted to extrajudicial executions.[1] These killings followed the election of President Duterte, who repeatedly and publicly endorsed the arrest and killing of those suspected of using or selling drugs. No police officers or private individuals were known to have faced charges for over 6,000 deaths during the year. Witnesses and families of victims feared coming forward in case of reprisals.

The majority of victims were reported to be young men, some of whom were suspected of using or selling small amounts of methamphetamines. Victims included the Mayor of Albuera, Rolando Espinosa Senior, who was shot dead in his prison cell while being served a search warrant. President Duterte had publicly branded the Mayor a leading drug dealer. Despite an investigation by the National Bureau of Investigations, which recommended that charges be filed against the police officers allegedly responsible, the President promised to protect the police.

As a result of the so-called "war on drugs", at least 800,000 people reportedly "surrendered" to the authorities in fear they would be targeted on suspicion of drug-related offences. Consequently, prisons were severely overcrowded, exacerbating an already acute problem.

Journalists remained at risk, with at least three killed while carrying out their work. Alex Balcoba, a crime reporter for the *People's Brigada*, was killed when he was shot in the head in May by an unidentified gunman in Quiapo in the capital Manila, outside his family's shop. Families of victims marked the seventh anniversary of the Maguindanao massacre in which 32 journalists and another 26 people were killed. No one had been held to account for these crimes by the end of the year.

TORTURE AND OTHER ILL-TREATMENT

Reports of torture and other ill-treatment in police custody continued. In March, police officer Jerick Dee Jimenez was convicted of torturing bus driver Jerryme Corre, and sentenced to a maximum of two years and one month's imprisonment. It was the first conviction under the 2009 Anti-Torture Act. However, many other cases were still awaiting justice.[2] In July, a postmortem conducted by the Commission on Human Rights of the Philippines recorded torture marks on the bodies of father and son Renato and J.P. Bertes, who were shot dead in police custody.

A bill to establish a National Preventative Mechanism on torture stalled during the year. In May, the UN Committee against Torture

expressed concern about torture by police and urged the Philippines to close all places of secret detention where detainees, including children, were subjected to torture or other ill-treatment.

EXCESSIVE USE OF FORCE

The use of unnecessary and excessive force by police continued. In April, the police used force, including firearms, to disperse over 5,000 farmers who had blockaded a national highway in Kidapawan City during a demonstration demanding rice subsidies. At least two people died during the incident and dozens were injured.[3] In July, the Commission on Human Rights of the Philippines published a report which found that excessive and unjustified force had been used by the police during the incident but no police officers were prosecuted for related offences by the end of the year.

In October, the police brutally suppressed a rally organized by Indigenous Peoples' organizations in front of the US Embassy. The protest called for an end to militarization and encroachment onto ancestral lands.

HUMAN RIGHTS DEFENDERS

In July, environmentalist Gloria Capitan was killed by two gunmen in Mariveles, Bataan province. She was involved in opposing a coal mining project in her community. In October, the UN CESCR expressed concern at the continuing harassment, enforced disappearances and killings of human rights defenders, and the low level of investigations into, and prosecutions and convictions for these crimes.

DEATH PENALTY

In July, ruling party congressmen proposed bills to reintroduce the death penalty for a wide range of offences. If passed, the punishment, which was abolished in 2006, would apply to crimes including rape, arson, drug trafficking and possession of small amounts of drugs. The bills sparked an outcry from human rights organizations on the grounds that they would violate international human rights law, and would not deter crime.[4] Bills were also filed proposing to lower to nine years old the age of criminal responsibility.

ABUSES BY ARMED GROUPS

Abuses of international human rights and humanitarian law by armed militia continued. More than a year after the 2015 killing of three leaders of the Lumad community in Lianga, Surigao del Sur province, the suspected perpetrators had not been prosecuted and over 2,000 people remained displaced from their homes. In October, anti-mining activist, Jimmy P. Sayman died a day after being shot in an ambush by unidentified gunmen in Montevista town, Mindanao. Local human rights organizations alleged that paramilitaries were responsible.

RIGHT TO AN ADEQUATE STANDARD OF LIVING, EDUCATION AND JUSTICE

The UN CESCR condemned the failure to pay the minimum wage for all but 13% of the workforce, and the fact that several sectors were exempt from benefiting from the minimum wage.

1. Philippines: Duterte's 100 days of carnage (News story, 7 October)

2. Philippines: Historic ruling on police torture following Amnesty International campaign (News story, 1 April)

3. Philippines: Ensure accountability for police use of excessive force against demonstrators (ASA 35/3800/2016)

4. Philippines: Lawmakers must urgently oppose attempts to reintroduce death penalty (ASA 35/5222/2016)

POLAND

Republic of Poland
Head of state: **Andrzej Duda**
Head of government: **Beata Szydło**

The government undertook significant legal reforms, in particular concerning the Constitutional Tribunal. There were 214 legislative amendments and laws enacted since the Law and Justice party came to power in October 2015. The speed of the legal reforms and the lack of adequate consultation with civil society were widely criticized.

LEGAL, CONSTITUTIONAL OR INSTITUTIONAL DEVELOPMENTS

Several amendments to the Law on the Constitutional Tribunal deepened the constitutional crisis that started in 2015; they were considered wholly or partially unconstitutional, according to the Constitutional Tribunal's rulings in March and August.

In January, the European Commission initiated for the first time a structured dialogue with Poland under the Rule of Law Framework giving it until 27 October 2016 to outline steps taken to remedy the crisis. Poland responded that it would not implement the recommendations and that they were "based on incorrect assumptions".

The judges elected by the previous Parliament were not appointed and the Prime Minister refused to publish several of the Tribunal's judgments. A July amendment to the Law on the Constitutional Tribunal introduced a requirement to examine cases in sequence of registration, depriving the Tribunal of its case prioritization competence.

In November, the UN Human Rights Committee issued its concluding observations on Poland; the Committee recommended, among other issues, that Poland ensure respect for and protection of the integrity and independence of the Tribunal and its judges and that it ensure implementation and publication of all the Tribunal judgments.[1]

Following the adoption of three new laws regarding the Constitutional Tribunal and the appointment of a new Tribunal President, the European Commission raised new concerns and issued a complementary Recommendation in December, giving Poland two months to address the systemic threat to the rule of law in the country.

JUSTICE SYSTEM

Under the new Law on Prosecution enacted in January, the functions of Prosecutor General and Minister of Justice were merged and the Prosecutor General's powers broadened. These reforms had significant implications for the right to a fair trial and the independence of the judiciary.[2]

In June, President Duda refused to appoint nine judges nominated for promotion to higher instance courts and one judge nominated for office by the National Council of the Judiciary. No reason was given for the President's decision.

Counter-terror and security
In June, a new Counter-terrorism Law was enacted, following a fast-track legislative process. It consolidated extensive powers in the hands of the Internal Security Agency with no independent oversight mechanism to prevent abuse and ensure accountability.

Terrorism-related crimes and "incidents" were broadly defined in the law and the accompanying regulation. Foreign nationals were particularly targeted in the new law, which allowed for their covert surveillance, including through wire-tapping, monitoring of electronic communications, telecommunication networks, and devices without judicial oversight for three months, after which the surveillance may be extended by a court order. These measures could be employed if there was a "fear", rather than a reasonable suspicion, that the person may be involved in terrorism-related activities. The Counter-terrorism Law introduced several other provisions, such as admissibility of illegally obtained evidence, extension of pre-charge detention to 14 days, and the removal of certain safeguards around permissible use of lethal force in the context of counter-terrorism operations.

Under the amended Police Act, surveillance powers were expanded allowing courts to authorize secret surveillance for three months – to be extended to a maximum of 18 months – on the basis of a broad list of crimes and without a requirement to consider proportionality. The amendments also allowed for metadata to be accessed directly by the police without a court order. Confidentiality of information covered by professional privilege, for example, available to criminal defence solicitors, was also compromised as surveillance of lawyers' communications was not prohibited.[3]

The UN Human Rights Committee recommended, among other issues, that Poland ensured the Penal Code defined terrorism-related crimes in terms of purpose, narrowly defined their nature and that it provided a precise definition of "terrorist incidents".

The criminal investigation into Poland's co-operation with the CIA and the hosting of a secret detention site was still pending. The 2015 European Court of Human Rights (ECtHR) judgments in the cases of al-Nashiri and Abu Zubaydah were not fully implemented.

FREEDOM OF EXPRESSION – JOURNALISTS
In July, the National Media Council became operational; it appointed and recalled management and supervisory boards of public media organizations. Its composition and the rules of voting allowed the ruling party to control the Council's decisions.

The government's effective control over public media and the resulting restrictions on the freedom of the press resulted in Poland's drop in the 2016 World Press Freedom Index from place 18 down to 47, out of 180 countries. By the end of the year, 216 journalists and administrative staff in public media organizations were dismissed, forced to resign or transferred to less influential positions, according to the association Society of Journalists. In December, a proposal of the Marshal of the *Sejm* (lower house of the Parliament) to severely restrict journalists' access to the Parliament sparked mass protests and a parliamentary crisis, with opposition MPs "occupying" the podium.

FREEDOM OF ASSEMBLY
In December, the Parliament passed a restrictive amendment to the Law on Assemblies, despite negative opinions of the Polish Human Rights Commissioner and the Supreme Court and strong criticism from nearly 200 NGOs. The President did not sign

the amendment, referring it to the Constitutional Tribunal instead.

DISCRIMINATION

Serious gaps remained in the law regarding discrimination and hate crimes related to age, disability, gender, gender identity and expression, sexual orientation and social or economic status. In April, the Council for the Prevention of Racial Discrimination, Xenophobia and Related Intolerance was abolished.

REFUGEES' AND MIGRANTS' RIGHTS

Poland did not accept any refugees from other EU member states under the mandatory relocation quota. The authorities continued to use detention disproportionately for migrants and asylum-seekers.

Civil society organizations reported there were barriers to accessing the asylum procedure, including numerous cases where people were unable to apply for international protection at the Brest/Terespol border crossing between Belarus and Poland. In June, the ECtHR communicated the cases *A.B. v Poland* and *T.K. and S.B. v Poland* to the government. They concerned a family of three Russian citizens who tried unsuccessfully to enter Poland and lodge asylum claims at the Brest/Terespol border four times.

SEXUAL AND REPRODUCTIVE RIGHTS

Women continued to face systemic difficulties in accessing safe and legal abortion; a petition proposing to further restrict their access was considered before Parliament at the end of the year.

After mass protests and a general women's strike on 3 October, Parliament rejected a bill which proposed a near total ban on abortion and criminalization of women and girls who obtained an abortion and anyone assisting or encouraging them to have an abortion.[4]

---

1. Poland: Submission to the United Nations Human Rights Committee. 118th session, 17 October - 04 November 2016 (EUR 37/4849/2016)

2. Poland: Dismantling rule of law? Amnesty International submission for the UN Universal Periodic Review – 27th session of the UPR working group, April/May 2017 (EUR 37/5069/2016)

3. Poland: New surveillance law a major blow to human rights (EUR 37/3357/2016)

4. Poland: Women force historic U-turn on proposed abortion ban (News story, 6 October); A dangerous backward step for women and girls in Poland (News story, 19 September)

PORTUGAL

Portuguese Republic
Head of state: **Marcelo Rebelo de Sousa (replaced Aníbal António Cavaco Silva in March)**
Head of government: **António Costa**

Austerity measures restricted the rights of people with disabilities. There were reports of ill-treatment in prisons and of inadequate prison conditions. Discrimination against Roma continued unabated.

DISCRIMINATION

Portugal continued to fail to ensure that hate crimes were prohibited in law, and had not created a national data collection system for hate crimes.

People with disabilities

In April, the UN Committee on the Rights of Persons with Disabilities asked Portugal to review austerity measures that have reduced the availability of services for people with disabilities and forced many of them into poverty or extreme poverty. The Committee expressed concern about cuts to resources for inclusive education for children with disabilities and support for their families. These measures had particularly negative effects on women caregivers who in most cases cared for children with disabilities.

Roma

In June, the European Commission against Racism and Intolerance reported that Portugal had not fully implemented the measures it had recommended in 2013 to address racism and discrimination towards Roma communities, especially regarding data collection and the simplification of procedures to report cases of discrimination to the High Commissioner for Migration.

RIGHT TO HEALTH

In June, the Portuguese Observatory on the Health System reported continuing inequalities in accessing health care, in particular for the most marginalized people.

TORTURE AND OTHER ILL-TREATMENT

There were reports of unnecessary or excessive use of force by law enforcement officials throughout the year.

In October, according to a report by a Portuguese NGO, 13 prisoners were beaten by prison guards during the inspection of their cells at Carregueira Prison in the capital Lisbon. At least three of them required hospital treatment as a result.

PRISON CONDITIONS

Prison conditions remained inadequate; in some prisons they were degrading. There was a lack of hygiene, food quality, medical care and access to medicines.

RIGHTS OF LESBIAN, GAY, BISEXUAL, TRANSGENDER AND INTERSEX PEOPLE

In February, Parliament voted to override a presidential veto of a law granting same-sex couples the right to adopt children. The law was initially passed in November 2015; the new law entered into force in March.

REFUGEES' AND MIGRANTS' RIGHTS

Thirty-nine refugees previously selected for resettlement in Portugal between 2014 and 2016 had arrived in the country by the end of 2015. The government committed to resettle over 260 refugees in 2016/2017.

Only 781 asylum-seekers were transferred from Greece and Italy to Portugal under the EU relocation mechanism as of the end of the year, out of the 1,742 that Portugal had committed to receive.

In October, the municipal authorities of Amadora forcibly evicted at least four migrant families without meaningful prior consultation and the provision of adequate alternative accommodation.

SEXUAL AND REPRODUCTIVE RIGHTS

In February, the Parliament approved changes to legislation on access to sexual and reproductive health services. The new law removed mandatory psychological and social counselling as a condition for women's access to abortion.

In May, new legislation was adopted giving all women access to assisted reproductive technology (ART) – including in vitro fertilization and other methods – regardless of their marital status or sexual orientation. This put an end to former restrictions that limited ART to married women or women in a civil partnership with a man.

VIOLENCE AGAINST WOMEN AND GIRLS

In November, the government announced plans to exempt victims of sexual harassment, rape, female genital mutilation, slavery and human trafficking from the payment of judicial costs.

According to data provided by the NGO UMAR, as of November, 22 women had been killed, and there were 23 attempted murders.

PUERTO RICO

Commonwealth of Puerto Rico
Head of state: **Barack Obama**
Head of government: **Alejandro García Padilla**

There was progress towards achieving equality and justice in relation to the human rights of lesbian, gay, bisexual, transgender and intersex (LGBTI) people; however, they continued to face discrimination in terms of their health and wellbeing. The reform of the police continued to have limited impact and incidents of excessive use of force were reported. The new federal law Puerto Rico Oversight, Management, and Economic Stability Act (PROMESA) caused serious concern as to its possible repercussions on economic, social and cultural rights, in particular for the most vulnerable groups in society.

RIGHT TO AN ADEQUATE STANDARD OF LIVING

A report compiled by academic organizations and presented to the Inter-American Commission on Human Rights in April raised concerns about the impact of government fiscal austerity measures on the standard of living of Puerto Ricans. There were fears that these measures would trigger an increase in poverty among vulnerable groups and cause increased exclusion, inequality and discrimination.

RIGHTS OF LESBIAN, GAY, BISEXUAL, TRANSGENDER AND INTERSEX PEOPLE

Despite recent progress in ensuring the rights of LGBTI people, there were continued reports of violations of rights related to access to health services, particularly for transgender people. The policies of the Department of Health in relation to guaranteeing equal access to health services remained unchanged and, although the government allowed gender to be changed on state identity documents, there were continued reports of incidents of discrimination at the time of issue of identity documents.

Following the introduction of Charter 19, a new internal policy of the Puerto Rican Department of Education which sought to implement an educational curriculum with an integrated gender perspective in the country's public schools, cases of discrimination and harassment of LGBTI students or those perceived to be LGBTI came to light. There were reports of students being suspended for wearing a uniform or having a hairstyle which were "inconsistent with their biological sex".

In July, a US federal government directive was published which stipulated that transgender students must be allowed to use bathrooms which correspond to the gender they identify with. This directive had not been fully implemented.

POLICE AND SECURITY FORCES

In 2013, the government signed an agreement with the US Department of Justice aimed at bringing about an in-depth reform of the policies and practices of the Puerto Rican police. This led to the creation of important new policies on areas such as control of the use of force and interaction with members of the transgender community. However, civil society organizations expressed serious concern over the legitimacy of the reform due to the lack of transparency and genuine participation of civil society in the process. Internal accountability mechanisms for the police remained deficient and an external monitoring mechanism had still not been put in place, despite repeated calls from civil society for this to be implemented.

Civil society organizations continued to report excessive use of force by the police, death threats by police against citizens and excessive use of electric-shock weapons, including on people with mental health problems or people who did not comply with police orders.

DEATH PENALTY

Although the death penalty was abolished in Puerto Rico in 1929, it could still be imposed under US federal law. No death penalty cases were reported in 2016.

QATAR

State of Qatar
Head of state: Sheikh Tamim bin Hamad bin Khalifa Al Thani
Head of government: Sheikh Abdullah bin Nasser bin Khalifa Al Thani

The authorities unduly restricted the rights to freedom of expression, association and peaceful assembly. One prisoner of conscience was pardoned and released. Migrant workers faced exploitation and abuse. Discrimination against women remained entrenched in both law and practice. The courts imposed death sentences; no executions were reported.

BACKGROUND

Qatar remained part of the Saudi Arabia-led international coalition engaged in armed conflict in Yemen (see Yemen entry).

FREEDOMS OF EXPRESSION, ASSOCIATION AND ASSEMBLY

The authorities continued to unduly restrict the rights to freedom of expression, association and peaceful assembly. The authorities did not permit the existence of independent political parties, and worker associations were only permitted for Qatari citizens if they met strict criteria. Unauthorized public gatherings were not permitted and were dispersed, and laws criminalizing expression deemed offensive to the Emir were maintained.

The poet and prisoner of conscience Mohammed al-Ajami (also known as Ibn Dheeb) was released on 15 March under an unconditional pardon granted by the Emir. He had been serving a 15-year prison sentence imposed in 2012 for writing and reciting poems deemed offensive to the Emir and the state.

The independent online news outlet Doha News was blocked within Qatar for "licensing issues". Doha News' independent journalism had covered sensitive topics in Qatar, which is likely to have led to their blocking by the two local internet service providers.

TORTURE AND OTHER ILL-TREATMENT

On 2 May, the Court of Cassation in the capital, Doha, confirmed the conviction and 15-year prison sentence imposed on Filipino national Ronaldo Lopez Ulep on espionage charges. His conviction in 2014 was largely based on a "confession" in Arabic, a language that he cannot read, with no investigation into his allegation that security officers had forced him to sign the "confession" under torture and other ill-treatment. The Court of Appeal, which reduced his original life sentence to 15 years, and the Court of Cassation also failed to investigate his allegations of torture when upholding his conviction. While in prison, his right to access to his family continued to be violated.

MIGRANT WORKERS' RIGHTS

Migrant workers, who comprise a large majority of Qatar's population, continued to face exploitation and abuse. Law No.21 of 2015, which took effect on 13 December 2016, more than a year after its enactment, replaced the 2009 Sponsorship Law, introducing some minor improvements such as the removal of the two-year ban on migrant workers returning to Qatar after leaving. However, it retained key elements of the 2009 law that facilitate serious human rights abuses, including forced labour. Under the new law, migrant workers were still required to obtain an exit permit from their employer to leave Qatar, violating their right to freedom of movement. If workers were blocked from leaving, they could appeal; however, no official guidance on how appeals would be determined was published. The new law also allowed employers to prevent migrant workers from changing their jobs for up to five years, depending on the terms of their contracts, and allowed employers to retain migrant workers' passports with their written consent, enshrining into law the practice of passport retention which is used by exploitative employers to exert control over migrant workers.

The International Labour Organization (ILO) visited Qatar in March 2016. The high-level delegation assessed measures taken by the government to address issues raised in a complaint filed in relation to violation of the Forced Labour Convention and Labour Inspection Convention. The delegation's report acknowledged steps taken by the Qatari authorities to address migrant labour abuse but noted many remaining challenges. The ILO governing body deferred its decision on whether to appoint a commission of inquiry on Qatar until March 2017.

The Wage Protection System, which made payment of wages by electronic bank transfer mandatory, was implemented throughout 2016. According to government figures, by November some 1.8 million people were covered by the system. Some migrant workers employed on high-profile construction projects were relocated to the Labor City and Barwa Al Bahara complexes, built by the government to accommodate up to 150,000 low-income migrant workers with better conditions and facilities. A 2010 law effectively prohibiting migrant workers from living in urban residential districts continued to restrict the supply of available housing for migrant workers, thereby exacerbating overcrowding elsewhere and condemning most migrant workers to inadequate living conditions. In April, census data published by the Ministry of Development Planning and Statistics indicated that 1.4 million people were living in labour camps.

Domestic workers, mostly women, remained at particular risk of exploitation and abuse as they continued to be excluded from existing labour protections. A long-proposed law to protect domestic workers' rights continued to be delayed. In July, Qatar's National Human Rights Committee recommended the introduction of a law to protect the human rights of domestic migrant workers and provide them with access to justice for abuses.

In response to evidence that migrant workers had been subjected to abuse while refurbishing the Khalifa International Stadium and surrounding Aspire Zone sporting complex – a 2022 World Cup venue – the government announced in April that the Ministry of Administrative Development, Labour and Social Affairs would investigate the contractors involved in the abuses. The Supreme Committee for Delivery and Legacy, which is responsible for overseeing all 2022 World Cup projects, announced "rectification" programmes for contractors involved in abuses and placed restrictions on future bids for World Cup contracts from a main subcontractor. Some labour supply companies were banned from working on 2022 World Cup projects, including one found to be using forced labour. In November the Supreme Committee signed a year-long agreement with the international trade union Building and Wood Workers' International to carry out joint inspections of the working and housing conditions of certain migrant construction workers and to publish details of these inspections. The agreement was limited to World Cup projects and did not cover associated infrastructure projects such as highways, rail networks or hotels.

WOMEN'S RIGHTS

Women continued to face discrimination in law and practice and were inadequately protected against violence within the family. Personal status laws continued to discriminate against women in relation to marriage, divorce, inheritance, child custody, nationality and freedom of movement.

DEATH PENALTY

The courts imposed new death sentences and others were confirmed by the Appeals Court; no executions were reported.

ROMANIA

Republic of Romania
Head of state: **Klaus Iohannis**
Head of government: **Dacian Julien Cioloş**

Roma continued to experience systemic discrimination, forced evictions and other human rights violations. The Council of Europe Convention on preventing and combating violence against women and domestic violence entered into force in September. A public hearing was held in the European Court of Human Rights (ECtHR) case against Romania for complicity in the US-led rendition and secret detention programmes, but a ruling in the four-year-old case remained pending. Following parliamentary elections in December, Sorin Mihai Grindeanu was nominated as Prime Minister by the President and was to take office on 4 January 2017.

DISCRIMINATION – ROMA

In his April report, the UN Special Rapporteur on extreme poverty and human rights called on the authorities to acknowledge the severe discrimination against Roma, to implement the 2015-2020 Roma Inclusion Strategy and take targeted measures in education, health care and employment, including the introduction of legal safeguards against forced evictions and improved access to social housing. In June, the Council of Europe Commissioner for Human Rights raised similar concerns.

Housing rights – forced eviction

In March, the ECtHR issued interim measures urging the authorities to stop the eviction of 10 Roma families in the town of Eforie. This would have been the third forced eviction of the families who were among the 101 people, including 55 children, whose homes had been demolished in 2013. In June, the Constanța County Court ruled that the 2013 demolition was unlawful and the municipality should provide the families with adequate housing. At the end of year, their housing situation remained precarious.

The 300 Roma forcibly evicted from the centre of Cluj-Napoca in 2010 and relocated to Pata Rat area – known for its waste dump, chemical dump and two already existing Roma settlements – were still fighting for justice in domestic courts, assisted by the NGO European Roma Rights Centre (ERRC). Toxic smoke from several fires on newly established waste dumps caused inhabitants respiratory issues, according to residents and NGOs. The UN Special Rapporteur on extreme poverty and human rights visited the Pata Rat area and noted the "primitive conditions", including no electricity, as well as damp and overcrowded accommodation.

Right to education

In May, the NGOs ERRC and Romani CRISS urged the European Commission to launch an investigation into breaches by Romania of EU anti-discrimination legislation with respect to persistent patterns of segregation of Roma children in schools. The Centre for Advocacy and Human Rights in partnership with the Centre for Resources for Public Participation surveyed 112 municipalities in northeast Romania and found that 82 out of the 394 schools across the region displayed some form of segregation of Roma children. In November and December, the Ministry of Education held a public consultation on a draft framework which prohibited school segregation. The framework expanded the criteria for inclusion in education, set new legal obligations and sanctions for authorities and defined the role of a National Commission for Desegregation and Inclusion.

POLICE AND SECURITY FORCES

In January, the ECtHR ruled that Romania had violated the rights of four members of the Boaca family. It found that they were subjected to torture and other ill-treatment and discriminated against. In March 2006, police officers had physically assaulted them in the police station in Clejani in Giurgiu County. Ion Boaca, father of the other three Roma victims, required 19 days of hospitalization after being kicked in the ribs and punched.

In June, the Committee of Ministers of the Council of Europe closed the supervision of the implementation of a group of key ECtHR judgments – known as the Barbu Anghelescu group – concerning police brutality against Roma and ineffective investigations, including possible racist motives. ERRC, Romani CRISS and APADOR-Helsinki Committee warned against the decision arguing that the government had not taken adequate measures to execute the judgments and tackle, among other issues, widespread institutional racism.

DISCRIMINATION – PEOPLE WITH DISABILITIES

The monitoring mechanism required by the UN Convention on the Rights of Persons with Disabilities, ratified by Romania in 2011, was created but was not operational at the end of 2016.

RIGHTS OF LESBIAN, GAY, BISEXUAL, TRANSGENDER AND INTERSEX PEOPLE

According to the Civil Code, same-sex marriages and civil unions were prohibited and those contracted abroad not recognized. The case of a same-sex couple seeking recognition of their marriage officiated in Belgium remained under examination by the Constitutional Court. In November, the Constitutional Court sought preliminary ruling from the European Court of Justice on the harmonic interpretation of EU legislation on freedom of movement and residence for same-sex couples.

The Coalition for Family – a group of some 30 associations and foundations – ran a campaign until May to put forward a legislative proposal to restrict the constitutional definition of "family" from "marriage between spouses" to "marriage between a man and a woman". In July, the Constitutional Court allowed the proposal to be put to Parliament to decide on whether or not to hold a national referendum. The decision remained pending at the end of the year.

In April, the ECtHR found that authorities failed to carry out an effective investigation into the attack – including its potentially discriminatory motive – on Bucharest Pride march participants in 2006.

COUNTER-TERROR AND SECURITY

In June, the ECtHR held a public hearing in the case against Romania for complicity in the US-led rendition and secret detention programmes, which the CIA operated globally in the aftermath of the 11 September 2001 attacks in the USA.[1] Abd al-Rahim al-Nashiri, a Saudi Arabian national currently held in the US detention centre at Guantánamo Bay, Cuba, had lodged an application against Romania in 2012 alleging that he was forcibly disappeared and tortured at a secret CIA detention centre in Bucharest between 2004 and 2006, and that Romania had failed to effectively investigate his secret detention. The hearing came after the Council of Europe Secretary General summarily closed in February 2016 its Article 52 inquiry into European states' involvement in the CIA operations – a severe blow to accountability. The Romanian government denied the allegations and argued an investigation was

ongoing. A judgment in the case remained pending at the end of the year.

VIOLENCE AGAINST WOMEN AND GIRLS

According to General Police Inspectorate data, 8,926 cases of domestic violence were registered in the first six months of 2016 – 79% of the victims were women and 92.3% of the aggressors were men. National NGOs reported that the actual number of cases was much higher. In July, NGOs requested that the government expedite the adoption of measures to combat violence against women and domestic violence. The Council of Europe Convention on preventing and combating violence against women and domestic violence (Istanbul Convention) entered into force in September.

1. CIA rendition victims challenge Romania and Lithuania at Europe's human rights court (News story, 29 June)

RUSSIAN FEDERATION

Russian Federation
Head of state: **Vladimir Putin**
Head of government: **Dmitry Medvedev**

Restrictions on rights to freedom of expression, association and peaceful assembly increased. Prosecutions of those who had taken part in anti-government protests in Bolotnaya Square continued and gave rise to further concerns regarding the respect for fair trial standards. Human rights defenders faced fines or criminal prosecution because of their activities. The first criminal prosecution for failure to comply with the "foreign agents" law was initiated. A number of individuals were charged under anti-extremism legislation for criticizing state policy and publicly displaying or possessing materials alleged to be extremist. There were reports of torture and other ill-treatment in

penitentiary institutions, and prisoners' lives were at risk because of inadequate medical care in prisons. Serious human rights violations continued to be reported in the context of security operations in the North Caucasus. People criticizing the authorities in Chechnya faced physical attacks by non-state actors and prosecution, and human rights defenders reporting from the region faced harassment from non-state actors. Russia faced international criticism in relation to allegations of war crimes by its forces in Syria. The International Criminal Court (ICC) continued its preliminary examination of the situation in Ukraine, which included crimes committed in eastern Ukraine and Crimea. Russia failed to respect the rights of asylum-seekers and refugees.

LEGAL, CONSTITUTIONAL OR INSTITUTIONAL DEVELOPMENTS

On 7 July, amendments to anti-extremism legislation known as the "Yarovaya package" were passed. The amendments were largely inconsistent with Russia's international human rights obligations as they banned any form of missionary activity outside of specially designated religious institutions, obliged providers of information technology to store records of all conversations for six months and metadata for three years, increased the maximum punishment for extremism from four to eight years in prison, and increased the penalty for encouraging people to take part in mass disturbances from five to 10 years in prison.

FREEDOM OF ASSEMBLY

In March, the legislation governing public assemblies was extended to "unauthorized" motorcades. In August, this new provision was used to prosecute a group of farmers from Kuban in southern Russia who were travelling to the capital, Moscow, in tractors and private cars to protest against land grabbing by agricultural holding companies. Their leader, Aleksei Volchenko, was sentenced to 10 days' administrative detention for taking part in an

"unsanctioned" demonstration[1] after participating in a meeting between the farmers and the deputy regional Plenipotentiary of the President. Other participants of the meeting paid fines or served short periods of administrative detention.

Four people were still serving their sentences for taking part in the Bolotnaya Square demonstration in Moscow on 6 May 2012, and two more people were charged in connection with the events. On 5 January, the European Court of Human Rights (ECtHR) found that Yevgeniy Frumkin's right to freedom of peaceful assembly had been violated and that he had been arbitrarily detained for 15 days for "failing to obey police orders" following his participation in the Bolotnaya Square protest. The Court found that Yevgeniy Frumkin's arrest, detention and administrative punishment had been "grossly disproportionate" and designed to discourage him and others from participating in protest rallies or engaging in opposition politics.

On 12 October, Dmitry Buchenkov was charged with taking part in mass disorder and six counts of "non-lethal force" against police officers during the Bolotnaya Square demonstration. He claimed that he had been in Nizhny Novgorod at the time and had not participated in the demonstration. He remained in detention at the end of the year, having been detained since December 2015.

FREEDOM OF ASSOCIATION – HUMAN RIGHTS DEFENDERS

During the year, dozens of independent NGOs receiving foreign funding were added to the list of "foreign agents", including the International Historical and Human Rights Society of Memorial.

NGOs continued to face administrative fines for failing to comply with legislation on "foreign agents". On 24 June, Valentina Cherevatenko, the founder and Chair of the Women of the Don Union, was informed of criminal proceedings initiated against her for "systematic evasion of duties imposed by the law on non-profit organizations performing the functions of a foreign agent", charges punishable by up to two years in prison. This was the first time the relevant Criminal Code article had been invoked since its introduction in 2012. The criminal investigation against Valentina Cherevatenko was ongoing at the end of the year. Staff of the Women of the Don Union were frequently questioned by investigators who also monitored all the organization's publications.

Lyudmilla Kuzmina, a retired librarian and the co-ordinator of the Samara branch of the election watchdog Golos, was sued by the tax authorities for 2,222,521 roubles (€31,000). The tax authorities classified a grant given to Golos by the US funding organization USAID as profit following the declaration of the organization as "undesirable", and claimed that Lyudmilla Kuzmina had falsely declared the money a grant. On 14 March 2016, the tax authorities successfully appealed against a decision taken by the Samara District Court on 27 November 2015 which found that Lyudmilla Kuzmina had not defrauded the government of that amount, and had not used the money for her own gain. Following the successful appeal by the tax authorities, bailiffs confiscated her car and her pension payments were stopped.

FREEDOM OF EXPRESSION

Anti-extremism legislation continued to be used excessively in violation of the right to freedom of expression. According to the NGO SOVA Centre, 90% of all convictions under anti-extremism legislation were for statements and reposts on social media websites. On 3 November, following a request from SOVA Centre and other NGOs, the Plenum of the Supreme Court issued guidelines to judges on the use of anti-extremism legislation specifying that in order to qualify as incitement to hatred, statements need to include an element of violence such as calls for genocide, mass repression, deportation or calls for violence.

On 20 February, Yekaterina Vologzheninova, a shop assistant from Yekaterinburg in the Ural region, was found guilty of "inciting hatred and enmity on the grounds of ethnicity" under Article 282 of the Criminal Code following her online criticism of Russia's annexation of Crimea and Russia's military involvement in Donbass, eastern Ukraine, which consisted primarily of reposts of articles from Ukrainian media. Yekaterina Vologzheninova, a single mother and sole carer for her elderly mother, served 320 hours of unpaid "corrective labour". The judge also ruled that her computer must be destroyed as a "crime weapon".

The trial of Natalya Sharina, prisoner of conscience and director of the state-run Library of Ukrainian Literature in Moscow, began on 2 November. She was accused of "inciting hatred and enmity through misuse of office" under Article 282 of the Criminal Code and of fraudulent use of library funds, offences for which she could face up to 10 years' imprisonment. A number of books classified as "extremist" were purportedly found among uncatalogued literature in the library. She remained under house arrest which began on 30 October 2015.

NORTH CAUCASUS

Serious human rights violations, including enforced disappearances and alleged extrajudicial executions committed in the course of security operations continued to be reported from the North Caucasus. Human rights defenders were also at risk. On 9 March, two members of the human rights organization Joint Mobile Group (JMG), along with their driver and six journalists from Russian, Norwegian and Swedish media, were assaulted while travelling from North Ossetia to Chechnya. Their minibus was stopped by four cars near a security checkpoint at the administrative border between Ingushetia and Chechnya. Twenty masked men dragged them out of the vehicle and severely beat them before setting fire to the minibus. Two hours later, the JMG's office in Ingushetia was ransacked. On 16 March, the JMG's leader Igor Kalyapin was asked to leave a hotel in the Chechen capital Grozny by the manager because he "did not love" the Chechen leader Ramzan Kadyrov. Igor Kalyapin was then punched and pelted with eggs, cakes, flour and disinfectant by an angry mob.

On 5 September, Zhalaudi Geriev, an independent journalist known for his criticism of the leadership of Chechnya, was sentenced to three years' imprisonment by the Shali District Court of Chechnya for possessing 167g of marijuana. At his trial he withdrew his confession to the drugs charge, saying that three men in plain clothes had detained him on 16 April, forced him into a car and driven him to a forest outside Grozny, where he was tortured before being handed over to law enforcement officers who forced him to "confess".

The Chechen leadership continued to exercise direct pressure on the judiciary. On 5 May, Ramzan Kadyrov called a meeting of all judges and forced four of them to resign. There was no response from the federal authorities.

UNFAIR TRIALS

Ukrainian nationals Mykola Karpyuk and Stanislav Klykh were sentenced after an unfair trial at the Supreme Court in Chechnya to 22-and-a-half and 20 years' imprisonment respectively on 26 May. The sentence was confirmed on appeal at the Russian Supreme Court. They were convicted of leading and fighting in an armed group that allegedly killed 30 Russian soldiers during the conflict in Chechnya (1994 to 1996). Both men said that they were tortured following their arrests in March 2014 and August 2014 respectively. Their lawyers were denied access and basic information about their clients' whereabouts for several months after their arrest. Stanislav Klykh, who had no history of mental illness, appeared severely disturbed throughout the trial, which began in October 2015, possibly as a result of torture.[2] Mykola Karpyuk's lawyer alleged that vital evidence for the defence that supported his client's alibi was left out of the case file. The judge refused to allow witnesses to be interviewed in Ukraine.

TORTURE AND OTHER ILL-TREATMENT

Torture and other ill-treatment continued to be widespread and systematic during initial detention and in prison colonies.

On 30 August, Murad Ragimov and his father were beaten and tortured by officers from the Ministry of the Interior's Special Response Unit for two hours in the kitchen of their home in Moscow. The officers accused Murad Ragimov of killing a policeman in Dagestan, and of fighting for the armed group Islamic State in Syria. Murad Ragimov's cousin was handcuffed to the kitchen table while officers tortured Murad Ragimov using an electric-shock baton, and suffocating him with a plastic bag. Finally, the officers claimed to find drugs in his pockets. Murad Ragimov was taken to the police station and remained in detention at the end of the year facing trial on drugs charges.

Ildar Dadin said in a letter to his wife that he had been subjected to torture and other ill-treatment in the prison colony in Segezha in the Karelia region of Russia. He described how he was repeatedly beaten by groups of 10 to 12 prison guards, including on one occasion by the director of the prison colony. He described his head being pushed down a toilet and being hung by handcuffs and threatened with rape. Ildar Dadin was placed in a punishment cell seven times between his arrival in the prison colony in September and the end of the year. Following his allegations, the prison authorities carried out an inspection and asserted that there had been no ill-treatment. In 2015, Ildar Dadin was the first person to be convicted for participating in peaceful demonstrations under Article 212.1 of the Criminal Code, which criminalized violating the regulations for the conduct of public meetings. He was sentenced to three years' imprisonment, reduced to two-and-a-half years on appeal.

Failure to provide adequate medical care

During the course of the year the European Court of Human Rights found in 12 cases that prisoners in Russia had been subjected to torture or other ill-treatment because of failure to provide adequate medical care in prisons and pre-trial detention centres. On 27 April, in a report to the Federal Council, the Prosecutor General stated that lack of antiretroviral drugs in prisons was placing at risk the lives of prisoners living with HIV. According to a report by the NGO Zona Prava, released in November, prison health services were critically underfunded, resulting in shortages of antiretroviral drugs for treating HIV. The report also found that many conditions were only diagnosed at the critical stage, and medical staff who were employees of the Prison Service were not sufficiently independent. The law in principle allowed for early release on health grounds, but this was granted in only one in five cases where the prisoner requested early release.

Amur Khakulov died in a prison hospital in Kirov region, central Russia, of kidney failure in early October. On 15 June, a court had refused to release Amur Khakulov on medical grounds despite a medical panel's recommendation that he be released. Amur Khakulov had been in detention since October 2005; according to his family he developed chronic kidney disease while in detention.

ARMED CONFLICT – SYRIA

Together with the Syrian government, Russia carried out indiscriminate attacks and direct attacks on civilians and civilian objects in Syria, including civilian residential areas, medical facilities and aid convoys, causing thousands of civilian deaths and injuries.

INTERNATIONAL JUSTICE

On 14 November the Prosecutor of the ICC said that the situation within the territory of Crimea and Sevastopol amounted to an international armed conflict between Russia and Ukraine. The ICC Prosecutor was conducting an assessment as to whether the same was true for eastern Ukraine.

On 16 November, President Putin announced that Russia no longer intended to become a party to the Rome Statute of the ICC, which it signed in 2000 but did not ratify.

REFUGEES' AND MIGRANTS' RIGHTS

Russia continued to return asylum-seekers, refugees and migrant workers to Uzbekistan and other countries despite the real risk that they would be tortured and otherwise ill-treated.[3] In many cases the individuals were deported for overstaying their visa or not having the correct documents under the Administrative Code, which does not require the court to take into account the seriousness of the offence committed, the circumstances of the individual and any potential consequences for them if expelled from Russia, nor does it provide for the individual to receive free legal advice.

On 1 July, Uzbekistani asylum-seeker Olim Ochilov was forcibly returned from Russia to Uzbekistan in blatant disregard of interim measures issued by the ECtHR on 28 June to stop his forcible return to Uzbekistan, where he would be at real risk of torture.

1. Russian Federation: Farmers and truck drivers imprisoned for a peaceful protest against corruption (EUR 46/4760/2016)

2. Russian Federation: Urgent Action: Victim of unfair trial, health at risk (EUR 46/4398/2016)

3. Uzbekistan: Fast track to torture, abductions and forcible returns from Russia to Uzbekistan (EUR 62/3740/2016); Uzbekistan: Asylum-seeker returned from Russia to Uzbekistan in blatant violation of international law (EUR 62/4488/2016)

RWANDA

Republic of Rwanda
Head of state: **Paul Kagame**
Head of government: **Anastase Murekezi**

In the run-up to presidential elections in 2017, the environment for free debate and dissent continued to be hostile. High-ranking army officers were handed heavy sentences after a flawed trial.

BACKGROUND

President Paul Kagame announced a substantial cabinet reshuffle in October and the closure of the Ministry for Internal

Security, whose responsibilities were taken over by the Ministry of Justice.

Rwanda hosted the African Union Summit in July.

FREEDOMS OF ASSOCIATION AND ASSEMBLY

In March, the Democratic Green Party of Rwanda, a registered opposition political party, announced that it would not participate in the 2017 presidential elections if the government did not respond to its demands for political and electoral reforms. The Rwanda Governance Board rejected the requested reforms in September. The party nominated their president Dr Frank Habineza as their presidential candidate on 17 December.

The United Democratic Forces (FDU-Inkingi), an unregistered opposition political party, continued to face serious challenges. Party member Illuminée Iragena went missing on her way to work on 26 March. People close to her believe she was unlawfully detained and tortured, and may have died. Family members who requested a police investigation were not given an official response.

Another FDU-Inkingi member, Léonille Gasengayire, was arrested and detained for three days in March after visiting the party's president, Victoire Ingabire, in Kigali Central Prison. She was arrested again in August in Kivumu, Rutsiro district, and charged with inciting insurrection. She remained in custody awaiting trial.

FREEDOM OF EXPRESSION

The Rwanda Law Reform Commission began discussions with media practitioners in early 2016 on revising the 2013 Media Law. In its roadmap for implementing the recommendations accepted during Rwanda's examination in 2015 under the UN Universal Periodic Review (UPR), the government pledged to decriminalize "defamation".

Journalist John Ndabarasa was last seen in Kigali on 7 August. After his disappearance was reported to police by the Rwanda Media Commission, the police announced that they were opening an investigation. It was not clear whether the disappearance was related to John Ndabarasa's journalism or his family connections to Joel Mutabazi, President Kagame's former bodyguard serving a life sentence for treason.

HUMAN RIGHTS DEFENDERS

On 28 May, Congolese national Epimack Kwokwo, programme co-ordinator of the regional NGO Human Rights League of the Great Lakes Region (LDGL), was expelled from Rwanda when his work permit expired after long delays in renewing the NGO's registration. He attended an appointment at the immigration offices, was notified of his expulsion and then driven to the border with the Democratic Republic of the Congo without being allowed to return home to collect his belongings or inform his family. LDGL's re-registration was granted in November.

CRIMES UNDER INTERNATIONAL LAW

Individuals suspected of involvement in the 1994 genocide faced trial in Rwanda and Sweden.

In March, the Congolese authorities transferred Ladislas Ntaganzwa to Rwanda to stand trial on charges of genocide and crimes against humanity, in line with an arrest warrant issued by the UN Mechanism for International Criminal Tribunals – the body responsible for following up the work of the International Criminal Tribunal for Rwanda, which closed in December 2015.

In April, Rwanda's High Court sentenced to life imprisonment Léon Mugesera, extradited from Canada in 2012. He was convicted of incitement to commit genocide, inciting ethnic hatred and persecution as a crime against humanity. He was acquitted of preparing and planning the genocide and conspiracy to commit genocide.

In May, a court in Sweden convicted Claver Berinkindi of genocide and sentenced him to life in prison. Damages of US$3,900 to 13,000 were awarded to 15 people who had witnessed the loss of a relative or had survived the threat of being killed themselves.

In December, a French court confirmed the 25-year prison sentence of Rwandan former intelligence chief Pascal Simbikangwa for genocide and complicity in crimes against humanity.

Other action was taken against people suspected of genocide-related crimes.

In July, Enoch Ruhigira, who in 1994 was chief of staff of the then President, Juvénal Habyarimana, was arrested in Germany at the request of the Rwandan authorities, who are seeking his extradition on genocide charges.

On 28 September, university professor Léopold Munyakazi was deported from the USA to Rwanda. He was charged with committing genocide, complicity in genocide, conspiracy to commit genocide, extermination and genocide negation. He had been arrested after the genocide, but was released in 1999 due to a lack of evidence. Rwanda issued an international warrant for his arrest in 2006 a month after he gave a speech in which he described the massacres of 1994 as fratricide rather than genocide. In a hearing in October, Léopold Munyakazi pleaded not guilty.

On 12 November, genocide suspects Jean-Claude Iyamuremye and Jean-Baptiste Mugimba were extradited from the Netherlands and transferred to Kigali Central Prison. On 17 November, Henri Jean-Claude Seyoboka was deported from Canada, accused of involvement in the genocide. He had not disclosed his military background in his asylum application.

UNFAIR TRIALS

On 31 March, the Military High Court of Kanombe sentenced Colonel Tom Byabagamba and retired Brigadier General Frank Rusagara to 21 and 20 years in prison respectively. Both were found guilty of inciting insurrection and tarnishing the image of the government when in a leadership position. In violation of their right to freedom of expression, their conviction was based on accusations of sharing critical online articles by email and for comments made in social gatherings. Colonel Byabagamba was additionally convicted of concealing evidence and for contempt of the flag, and stripped of his military rank and decorations. Frank Rusagara was additionally convicted of illegal possession of weapons. His former driver, retired Sergeant François Kabayiza, was sentenced to five years' imprisonment for concealing evidence. An appeal was lodged against the verdict.

The judges failed to address adequately François Kabayiza's complaints in court that he had been tortured during interrogation and his request for the resulting testimony to be set aside. The court found that he had not provided evidence that he was tortured, in violation of the principle that the prosecution bears the burden of proving beyond reasonable doubt that evidence was obtained lawfully. Rwanda's law on evidence and its production prohibits the use of evidence obtained through torture in court proceedings.

As both Frank Rusagara and François Kabayiza were retired from the military, their lawyers argued that they should not be tried in a military tribunal and asked for the cases to be separated. This was refused. Despite repeated requests, Frank Rusagara was not permitted to call his wife in the UK before her death from terminal cancer in August.

REFUGEES AND ASYLUM-SEEKERS

Burundians continued to seek asylum in Rwanda, although at a slower rate than in 2015. At the end of 2016, Rwanda was hosting over 80,000 Burundian refugees. Following allegations of recruitment and military training of refugees from camps in Rwanda, the government announced in February that it planned to relocate Burundian refugees to third countries. It later clarified that it had no relocation plans and would continue to receive refugees from Burundi.

Reports continued of Eritrean and Sudanese asylum-seekers being sent from Israel to Rwanda (see Israel and the Occupied Palestinian Territories entry). In a joint press conference with President Kagame during his visit to Israel on 6 July,

Israeli Prime Minister Benjamin Netanyahu said that these were not asylum-seekers but "job seekers". President Kagame said the two countries were discussing the issue.

SAUDI ARABIA

Kingdom of Saudi Arabia
Head of state and government: **King Salman bin Abdul Aziz Al Saud**

The authorities severely curtailed the rights to freedom of expression, association and assembly, detaining and imprisoning critics, human rights defenders and minority rights activists on vaguely worded charges. Torture and other ill-treatment of detainees remained common, particularly during interrogation, and courts continued to accept torture-tainted "confessions" to convict defendants in unfair trials. Women faced discrimination in both law and practice and were inadequately protected against sexual and other violence. The authorities continued to arrest, detain and deport irregular migrants. Courts imposed many death sentences, including for non-violent crimes and against juvenile offenders; scores of executions were carried out. Coalition forces led by Saudi Arabia committed serious violations of international law, including war crimes, in Yemen.

BACKGROUND

Saudi Arabia faced growing economic problems due to the fall in world oil prices and the cost of its continued military intervention in the armed conflict in Yemen. This was reflected by reduced state spending on social welfare and on construction leading to the laying off of thousands of mostly south Asian migrant workers. In April, the authorities launched "Vision 2030", a plan to diversify the economy and end the country's dependence on income from fossil fuel extraction. In September, the Cabinet announced cuts to government ministers'

salaries and bonuses paid to state employees.

Relations between Saudi Arabia and Iran continued to deteriorate, exacerbated by their support for opposing sides in the region's conflicts. Following the government's execution of prominent Shi'a Muslim Sheikh Nimr al-Nimr and others on 2 January, protesters stormed the Saudi Arabian embassy in Iran's capital, Tehran, and set it alight, prompting Saudi Arabia to sever diplomatic relations with Iran and expel Iranian diplomats. The Tehran authorities prohibited Iranians from attending the annual Hajj pilgrimage to Mecca in Saudi Arabia.

On 4 July, suicide bombers carried out apparently co-ordinated attacks on one of Islam's holiest sites in Medina, the US Consulate in Jeddah, and a Shi'a mosque in Qatif, killing four people.

In September, the US Congress voted by a large majority to overturn US President Barack Obama's veto of the Justice Against Sponsors of Terrorism Act (JASTA), opening the way for families of those killed in the 11 September 2001 terrorist attacks in the USA to seek damages from the Saudi Arabian government.

In October, the UN Committee on the Rights of the Child urged the government to immediately halt the execution of death row prisoners sentenced for crimes allegedly committed when they were under 18; to immediately release all children sentenced to death after unfair trials and to commute the sentences of others; and to "unambiguously" prohibit by law the sentencing to death of offenders aged under 18 at the time of their alleged crime.

ARMED CONFLICT IN YEMEN

Throughout the year the Saudi Arabia-led military coalition supporting the internationally recognized government in Yemen continued to bomb areas controlled or contested by Huthi forces and their allies in Yemen, killing and injuring thousands of civilians. Some attacks were indiscriminate, disproportionate or directed against civilians and civilian objects including schools, hospitals, markets and mosques. Some coalition attacks amounted to war crimes. The coalition used armaments supplied by the US and UK governments, including internationally banned cluster bombs that are inherently indiscriminate and pose a continuing risk to civilians because of their frequent failure to detonate on initial impact. In December the coalition admitted that its forces had used UK-manufactured cluster munitions in 2015 and stated that it would not do so in the future. The US and UK governments continued to assist the coalition with arms, training, intelligence and logistical support, despite the serious violations of international law committed by its forces in Yemen.

In June the UN Secretary-General removed Saudi Arabia from a list of states and armed groups responsible for serious violations of children's rights during conflict after the government threatened to cut its funding support for key UN programmes.

Huthi forces and their allies repeatedly carried out indiscriminate cross-border attacks, shelling civilian populated areas such as Najran and Jazan in southern Saudi Arabia, killing and injuring civilians and damaging civilian objects.

FREEDOMS OF EXPRESSION, ASSOCIATION AND ASSEMBLY

The authorities maintained tight restrictions on freedom of expression and repressed dissent. They harassed, arrested and prosecuted critics, including writers and online commentators, political and women's rights activists, members of the Shi'a minority, and human rights defenders, imprisoning some after courts sentenced them to prison terms on vague charges.

In March, the Specialized Criminal Court (SCC) in the capital, Riyadh, sentenced journalist Alaa Brinji to five years in prison and a fine, followed by an eight-year travel ban, for comments he posted on Twitter.

Also in March, the SCC sentenced writer and Islamic scholar Mohanna Abdulaziz al-Hubail to six years' imprisonment followed by a six-year travel ban after convicting him in

his absence on charges that included "insulting the state and its rulers", inciting and participating in demonstrations, and "being in solidarity with the detained members" of the Saudi Civil and Political Rights Association (ACPRA) held as prisoners of conscience. The SCC also ordered the closure of his Twitter account.

The authorities did not permit the existence of political parties, trade unions or independent human rights groups, and continued to arrest, prosecute and imprison those who set up or participated in unlicensed organizations.

All public gatherings, including peaceful demonstrations, remained prohibited under an order issued by the Ministry of the Interior in 2011. Some who previously defied the ban were arrested and imprisoned. Strikes remained extremely rare but in September foreign and Saudi Arabian nationals employed at a private hospital in Khobar took strike action to protest against months of unpaid wages.

HUMAN RIGHTS DEFENDERS

The authorities continued to arrest, detain and prosecute human rights defenders on vague and overly broad charges using anti-terrorism legislation and laws designed to stifle peaceful criticism. Those detained, on trial or serving prison sentences included several members of ACPRA, an independent human rights organization formed in 2009, which the authorities closed down in 2013.

In May the SCC sentenced Abdulaziz al-Shubaily, one of ACPRA's founders, to eight years in prison followed by an eight-year travel ban and a ban on communicating through social media. He was convicted of defaming and insulting senior judges under the anti-cybercrime law. Other charges against him included "communicating with foreign organizations" and providing information on human rights violations to Amnesty International.

In October, Mohammad al-Otaibi and Abdullah al-Attawi, both co-founders of the Union for Human Rights, were brought to trial before the SCC. Both men were presented with a list of charges related to their human rights work including, among other things, "participating in setting up an organization and announcing it before getting an authorization" and "dividing national unity, spreading chaos and inciting public opinion".

Scores of other activists and human rights defenders continued to serve lengthy prison sentences on similar charges based on their peaceful exercise of their human rights.

In January, security officials briefly detained human rights defender Samar Badawi in connection with her activities in campaigning for the release of her former husband, the imprisoned human rights lawyer Waleed Abu al-Khair.

COUNTER-TERROR AND SECURITY

The authorities said that the security forces had rounded up and detained hundreds of people they suspected of terrorism-related offences, including alleged supporters and affiliates of the armed groups Islamic State and al-Qa'ida, but provided few details. Some detainees were held in the Mohammed bin Naif Counselling and Care Centre, a centre designated for "terrorists" and those "following deviant thought".

The US authorities transferred nine detainees – all Yemeni nationals – from their Guantánamo Bay detention facility in Cuba to Saudi Arabia in April.

Human rights defenders and those who expressed political dissent continued to be equated to "terrorists". After being released from al-Ha'ir prison in Riyadh where he served a four-year term, Mohammed al-Bajadi, a human rights defender and ACPRA founder was held for a further four months in the Mohammed bin Naif Counselling and Care Centre where he received weekly religious and psychological "counselling sessions".

In February the SCC began trying 32 defendants, including 30 members of the Shi'a minority, on charges of spying for, and passing military intelligence to Iran and supporting protests in Qatif in the Eastern Province, where Shi'a form a majority of the population. The prosecution sought the death penalty against 25 of the defendants. In December, the SCC sentenced 15 of the defendants to death following an unfair trial. Another 15 received prison terms ranging from six months to 25 years, and two were acquitted.

In November, 13 women were put on trial at the SCC on charges relating to their participation in protests in the city of Buraydah.

ARBITRARY ARRESTS AND DETENTIONS

In April, the Council of Ministers issued new regulations reducing the powers of the Committee for the Promotion of Virtue and Prevention of Vice, Saudi Arabia's religious police. In particular, the regulations barred the religious police from making arrests and from following suspects and requiring the suspects to produce identification.

The authorities continued to carry out numerous arbitrary arrests and held detainees for prolonged periods without referring them to a competent court, although the Law of Criminal Procedures requires that all detainees be referred to a court within six months. Detainees were frequently held incommunicado during interrogation and denied access to lawyers, undermining their right to fair trial and putting them at increased risk of torture and other ill-treatment.

In September, security authorities arbitrarily arrested human rights activist Salim al-Maliki after he published video footage on Twitter of border guards evicting tribal residents of the Jazan region, close to Saudi Arabia's border with Yemen. He was held incommunicado for the first six weeks and remained in detention at the end of the year.

TORTURE AND OTHER ILL-TREATMENT

Security officials continued to torture and otherwise ill-treat detainees with impunity, particularly to extract "confessions" for use as evidence against them at trial. Courts frequently convicted defendants on the basis of contested pre-trial "confessions".

The lawyer representing most of the 32 defendants accused of spying for Iran said that they were forced to "confess". After arrest, they were detained incommunicado and denied access to their families and lawyers for three months; some were subjected to prolonged solitary confinement.

Cruel, inhuman or degrading punishment

The authorities continued to impose and administer corporal punishments that violate the prohibition of torture and other ill-treatment, particularly floggings. In February, the General Court in Abha sentenced Palestinian poet and artist Ashraf Fayadh to 800 lashes and eight years' imprisonment when commuting his death sentence for apostasy on account of his writing in 2015.

DISCRIMINATION – SHI'A MINORITY

Saudi Arabia's Shi'a Muslim minority continued to face entrenched discrimination that severely limited their access to government services and state employment and their freedom of religious expression. The authorities continued to arrest, detain and sentence Shi'a activists to prison terms or death after unfair trials before the SCC.

In June, the SCC sentenced 14 members of the Shi'a minority to death after convicting them on charges that included shooting at security officials, inciting chaos and participating in demonstrations and riots. Nine others received prison terms and one was found not guilty.

WOMEN'S RIGHTS

Women and girls continued to face discrimination in law and in practice, and were inadequately protected against sexual and other forms of violence. Women remained legally subordinate and inferior in status to men in relation to marriage, divorce, child custody and inheritance, and could not access higher education, take paid employment or travel abroad without the approval of their male guardian. Women also remained banned from driving.

The government's "Vision 2030" economic reform plan included goals to increase the participation of women in Saudi Arabia's workforce from 22% to 30% and "invest" in their productive capabilities so as "to strengthen their future and contribute to the development of our society and economy". No legal reforms or other measures needed to achieve these aims appeared to have been initiated by the end of the year, although the Minister of Justice ruled in May that women must be given a copy of their marriage certificate, which is required in case of legal disputes between spouses. The Shura Council debated a proposed law that, if enacted, would allow women to obtain a passport without the approval of a male guardian.

In August, an online Twitter campaign entitled "Saudi women demand the end of guardianship" prompted tens of thousands of women to express opposition to the system of male guardianship. Activists reported that by September an estimated 14,000 Saudi Arabian women had signed an online petition calling on King Salman to abolish the system.

On 11 December, Malak al-Shehri was detained and interrogated after she posted a picture of herself on social media without an *abaya* (full-length garment). She was released on 16 December, but her legal status remained unclear.

MIGRANT WORKERS' RIGHTS

The authorities maintained their crackdown on irregular migrants, arresting, detaining and deporting hundreds of thousands of migrant workers.

Tens of thousands of migrant workers were laid off without having been paid for months, after the government cut spending on contracts with construction and other companies. Indian, Pakistani, Filipino and other foreign nationals were left stranded without food, water or exit visas; some took to the streets to block roads in protest.

DEATH PENALTY

Courts continued to impose death sentences for a range of crimes, including non-violent drugs offences which, under international law, should not incur the death penalty. Many defendants were sentenced to death after unfair trials by courts that convicted them without adequately investigating their allegations that their "confessions" were coerced, including with torture.

On 2 January the authorities carried out 47 executions, reportedly 43 by beheading and four by shooting, in 12 locations around the country.

Those facing execution included juvenile offenders, including four Shi'a men sentenced to death for participating in protests in 2012 when they were under 18.

SENEGAL

Republic of Senegal
Head of state: **Macky Sall**
Head of government: **Mohammed Dionne**

The authorities continued to restrict the rights to freedom of peaceful assembly and expression. Prisons remained overcrowded. Although several police officers were convicted of unlawful killings, impunity remained a concern. Men and women faced arrest because of their real or perceived sexual orientation. Despite efforts to reduce the number of children begging on the streets, impunity for child exploitation and child abuse persisted.

BACKGROUND

In May the capital, Dakar, hosted the Extraordinary African Chambers which sentenced former Chadian President Hissène Habré to life imprisonment after he was found guilty of crimes against humanity, war crimes and torture committed in Chad between 1982 and 1990.

Amendments to the Constitution were adopted following a referendum in March, including one which reduced the presidential mandate to five years.

FREEDOM OF ASSEMBLY

The authorities banned peaceful demonstrations and arrested demonstrators.

In October, the security forces fired tear gas to disperse a peaceful demonstration organized by the opposition. The Prefect of Dakar had justified a decision to impose an alternative route on the march on the basis of a 2011 decree banning all assemblies in parts of the city centre.

FREEDOM OF EXPRESSION

Journalists and artists who expressed dissent, including through their choice of clothing, were subjected to intimidation, harassment and arbitrary detention.

In February, Mamadou Mouth Bane, journalist and President of the social movement Jubanti, was detained for more than 12 hours at the Police Department of Criminal Investigation for comments deemed "seditious" made on television in the run-up to a constitutional referendum. He was later released without charge.

In June, rapper Ramatoulaye Diallo, also known as Déesse Major, was detained for three days and charged with "indecency" and "offending moral principles" for her choice of clothing in videos posted on social media. All charges were dropped and she was released.

At least two people were detained in Dakar for insulting religion.

COUNTER-TERROR AND SECURITY

The National Assembly adopted amendments to the Criminal Code and the Code of Criminal Procedure which could be used to stifle dissent. The amendments provide vague and broad definitions of terrorism-related offences, criminalize the production and dissemination of "immoral material" online and empower the authorities to restrict access to "illicit content" online.

Amendments to the Code of Criminal Procedure violated the right to personal liberty by extending to 12 days the period that people can be detained before appearing before a judge in terrorism-related cases. The amendments also undermined the right to fair trial by failing to provide that people should have access to a lawyer as soon as they are deprived of their liberty.

At least 30 people were in detention for terrorism-related offences. Several detainees raised concerns about the conditions of their arrest and detention. For example, Imam Ndao, who remained in pre-trial detention throughout the year on various charges including "acts of terrorism" and "glorifying terrorism", was only allowed out of his cell for 30 minutes a day.

PRISON CONDITIONS AND DEATHS IN CUSTODY

Prisons remained overcrowded. Some 2,090 people were held in Rebeuss Prison in Dakar, which has a maximum capacity of 1,600.

At least six people died in custody in 2016, including a detainee who was shot during a mutiny at Rebeuss Prison in September. Forty-one others were wounded, including 14 prison guards.

IMPUNITY

After protracted legal proceedings, there were breakthroughs in four cases of unlawful killings by the security forces. However, no commanding officers were held to account for failing to prevent excessive use of force and no one was brought to justice for the dozens of other cases of torture, unlawful killings and deaths in custody since 2007.

In January, the driver of the police vehicle that killed student Mamadou Diop during a peaceful pre-election demonstration in 2012 was sentenced to two years' imprisonment and fined for "assault causing death" and "intentional assault and battery." The co-driver was sentenced to three months' imprisonment for "failure to prevent a crime against physical integrity". The court also ordered the two policemen to pay damages to Mamadou Diop's relatives.

In June, a policeman who shot Bassirou Faye during a peaceful demonstration at the University Cheikh Anta Diop in Dakar in August 2014 was found guilty of murder and sentenced to 20 years' hard labour and ordered to pay damages to Bassirou Faye's family.

In June, a policeman was sentenced to two years' imprisonment in connection with the killing of Ndiaga Ndiaye, also known as Matar Ndiaye, who died after being shot in the leg during a police operation in 2015.

In July, four policemen were convicted of the killing of Ibrahima Samb in 2013 and sentenced to 10 years' hard labour. Ibrahima Samb suffocated after the officers locked him in the trunk of a car for over 16 hours.

DISCRIMINATION – SEXUAL ORIENTATION

At least seven men and one woman were detained in relation to their perceived sexual orientation.

In January, the Dakar Court of Appeal acquitted seven men of "acts against nature." They had been arrested in July 2015 and sentenced in August 2015 to 18 months' imprisonment with 12 months suspended.

CHILDREN'S RIGHTS

In July, the government launched an operation to remove children from the streets. However, the authorities continued to fail to fully implement laws criminalizing child exploitation and abuse, with few cases investigated or prosecuted.

SERBIA

Republic of Serbia, including Kosovo
Head of state: **Tomislav Nikolić**
Head of government: **Aleksandar Vučić**

Pro-government media continued to smear independent journalists and human rights defenders, as well as the Ombudsperson's Office. Prosecutions of crimes under international law committed during the armed conflict in the 1990s remained stalled. Several forced evictions took place in Belgrade. Refugees and migrants stranded in Serbia on their way to the EU lacked access to protection and essential services.

BACKGROUND

Early elections in April increased the majority of the Serbian Progressive Party led by Prime

Minister Aleksandar Vučić, who retained his position as head of government.

CRIMES UNDER INTERNATIONAL LAW

Prosecutions of war crimes and crimes against humanity continued to stall as the position of chief war crimes prosecutor remained vacant throughout the year. In March, the Prosecutor's Office confirmed the indictment of eight former members of the Special Brigade of the Ministry of the Interior of Republika Srpska, the ethnic Serb party to the war in Bosnia, for war crimes committed against civilians in Srebrenica in 1995.

Also in March, the International Criminal Tribunal for the former Yugoslavia acquitted Vojislav Šešelj, President of the Serbian Radical Party. He had been indicted on three counts of crimes against humanity (persecution, deportation and inhumane acts of forcible transfer) and six counts of war crimes (murder, torture and cruel treatment, wanton destruction, destruction or wilful damage done to institutions dedicated to religion or education and plunder of public or private property). The prosecution lodged an appeal which was pending at the end of the year. Following the April elections, Vojislav Šešelj returned to the National Assembly.

FREEDOM OF EXPRESSION

Proceedings against Radomir Marković, former head of state security, and three former security service officers for the murder in April 1999 of journalist Slavko Ćuruvija were stalled as a key witness failed to appear at court.

Independent journalist associations registered dozens of incidents targeting journalists, including physical assaults and death threats.

HOUSING RIGHTS

More than 200 families had been evicted in central Belgrade since the beginning of works in 2015 making way for the construction of the Belgrade Waterfront site. In April, a forced eviction was carried out at night by 30 masked men, who violently destroyed residents' homes. Local police were alerted

but refused to intervene. The Ombudsperson and activist groups condemned these acts; several protests were held calling for the municipal and state authorities to be held accountable. The Minister of the Interior subsequently sued a newspaper for defamation for alleging that he and the Ministry were responsible for failing to act during the demolitions. In late November, the court upheld the allegations and ordered the newspaper to pay the minister compensation of RSD 300,000 (€2,400).

Following her mission to Serbia the UN Special Rapporteur on the right to adequate housing highlighted the deplorable situation of people, in particular Roma, living in informal settlements without access to essential services. As well as calling for a housing law to prohibit forced evictions and an end to discrimination, the Special Rapporteur stressed the need to prioritize addressing insecure tenure and the lack of access to public services for those without a registered residence.

A draft law regulating evictions and resettlement was passed at the end of the year.

REFUGEES' AND MIGRANTS' RIGHTS

Over 120,000 refugees and migrants travelled through Serbia on their way to the EU. This significant decrease compared to 2015 was in part due to the closure of borders to irregular migrants in the south and north. Serbia's refusal to provide beds to accommodate more than 6,000 people on the move at any one time resulted in thousands being stranded in informal makeshift camps in appalling conditions at the border with Hungary, in derelict buildings and parks in Belgrade and other locations across the country. Infections and serious diseases among refugees and migrants were reported by volunteer groups and medical organizations.

In November, the Ministry of Labour and Employment, which is responsible for organizing accommodation and care for refugees and migrants, informed groups providing support that they should cease all activity outside the formal reception centres, which were overcrowded and mostly unsuitable for long-term accommodation. Many refugees and migrants were subsequently evicted and returned to the south, where they remained at risk of unlawful and summary return to the former Yugoslav Republic of Macedonia and to Bulgaria.

Serbia failed to provide access to a fair and individualized asylum process for the vast majority of registered asylum-seekers, including refugee status determination procedures, and considered itself to be a country of transit towards the EU. Serbian asylum authorities allowed most asylum-seekers to remain in accommodation centres while waiting to enter Hungary on the basis of an informal waiting list co-ordinated between the asylum-seekers and the Serbian and Hungarian authorities respectively. Some of the nominally open accommodation centres restricted the free movement of asylum-seekers and were effectively places where people were being arbitrarily detained.

International border police patrols operated at the borders with Macedonia and Bulgaria from 22 July onwards. This dramatically reduced the number of refugees and migrants arriving in Serbia. According to the Ministry of Defence, by the end of November, over 16,000 people had been prevented from entering the country. The authorities failed to deploy adequately trained civilian personnel along with border guards in a systematic way to ensure that the intention to claim asylum could be declared at the border, as required by Serbian and international law.

The Serbian authorities upheld the suspension of a re-admission agreement with its northern neighbour, Hungary. Thousands returned by the Hungarian authorities despite the suspension remained stranded in Serbia without legal status or access to basic services.

Over 12,000 asylum applications were submitted between January and the end of the year, but only 74 decisions were issued by the end of October: 17 applicants were granted refugee status and 17 were given subsidiary protection while 40 asylum applications were rejected. Almost half of all asylum applications were filed by children.

KOSOVO

A Stabilization and Association Agreement between the EU and Kosovo entered into force in April. In November, the first Council between the two parties was held, paving the way for Kosovo's future accession to the EU. The de facto administration of Kosovo continued to be implemented by the Kosovo authorities jointly with the EU Rule of Law Mission (EULEX). Progress in the EU-facilitated dialogue between Serbia and Kosovo remained limited.

Access to justice

In June, the Human Rights Advisory Panel (HRAP) of the UN Mission in Kosovo (UNMIK) issued a scathing final report, condemning the UN mission for its overall failure to ensure accountability for human rights violations committed under UNMIK's mandate and for failing to follow any of its recommendations.

Crimes under international law

The mandate of EULEX was extended until June 2018. However, the EU Rule of Law Mission announced it would not launch new investigations into cases of crimes under international law. At the end of the year, hundreds of pending cases were due to be transferred to the Kosovo authorities despite the European Commission declaring the Kosovo judiciary "slow" and "vulnerable to undue political influence".

The Kosovo Special Prosecution Office remained understaffed and struggled to recruit adequately trained and experienced prosecutors to investigate and prosecute crimes under international law and to launch new investigations.

The Kosovo Specialist Chambers, a relocated special court to prosecute former members of the Kosovo Liberation Army (KLA), was set up in The Hague. At the end of the year, the first indictments by the

Specialist Prosecutor had yet to be issued. The Council of the EU allocated €29 million to support the setting up and functioning of the relocated judicial proceedings between April 2016 and June 2017.

In January, Oliver Ivanović, leader of a Kosovo Serb political party, was sentenced by a panel of international judges at the Basic Court of Mitrovicë/Mitrovica to nine years' imprisonment for ordering the murder of ethnic Albanians in the town in April 1999. He remained under house arrest at the end of the year while his appeal against his conviction was pending before the Court of Appeals in Pristinë/Pristina.

Enforced disappearances

Over 1,600 people remained missing in the aftermath of the armed conflict. No further grave sites were identified in Serbia or Kosovo despite exhumations at potential mass graves. Co-operation agreements between the two parties remained unimplemented.

Discrimination – Roma, Ashkali and Egyptians

Roma, Ashkali and Egyptian communities continued to suffer institutional discrimination, in particular in accessing sustainable solutions for housing and employment, as internally displaced persons (IDPs). These communities continued to live in overcrowded conditions in informal settlements without adequate access to water and other essential services.

In February, the HRAP issued its opinion on a complaint brought to it by Roma, Ashkali and Egyptian families who had suffered lead poisoning in a UN-run camp for IDPs in the northern town of Mitrovicë/Mitrovica. The HRAP found that the UN Mission had subjected the families to inhuman and degrading treatment, failed to respect their rights to respect for private and family life and to health and discriminated against them on the grounds of their ethnic background. The HRAP found the UN action to have been particularly detrimental for women and children who were exposed to multiple discrimination. It called on UNMIK to publicly acknowledge the failure to comply with human rights standards and, among other measures, to pay adequate compensation to the families. By the end of the year, UNMIK had not implemented the HRAP's recommendations.

SIERRA LEONE

Republic of Sierra Leone
Head of state and government: **Ernest Bai Koroma**

Sierra Leone agreed to ratify several international human rights treaties, but did not accept a number of recommendations made during the UN Universal Periodic Review (UPR) process. Unwarranted restrictions on the freedoms of expression, peaceful assembly and association continued to be imposed. Violence against women and girls was widespread and pregnant girls were excluded from school, including exams. Disputes over land use caused growing tensions.

INTERNATIONAL SCRUTINY

After undergoing its second UPR in April, Sierra Leone accepted 177 of 208 recommendations.[1] These included ratifying international human rights treaties, such as Optional Protocols to the ICCPR, the ICESCR, the Convention against Torture and CEDAW. Sierra Leone agreed to repeal or revise laws used to restrict freedom of expression and association, but refused to prohibit by law female genital mutilation (FGM), to allow pregnant girls to attend school or to guarantee the human rights of lesbian, gay, bisexual, transgender and intersex people.[2] In September, Sierra Leone was reviewed by the Committee on the Rights of the Child, which made various recommendations regarding addressing sexual exploitation and FGM.

FREEDOMS OF EXPRESSION, ASSEMBLY AND ASSOCIATION

Unwarranted restrictions on freedom of expression, assembly and association continued to be imposed.

On 27 April, Independence Day, 29 people were arrested and detained for over a week following a parade organized by the opposition Sierra Leone People's Party (SLPP). Police said the parade was unauthorized and used tear gas to stop it. Several people were injured, including the women's leader Lulu Sheriff. In August, six of the 29 were sentenced to six months' imprisonment, and one to nine months' imprisonment, on charges including unlawful procession and riotous conduct. They appealed against their conviction. The trial of the others continued.

The trial of 15 members of the SLPP and a senior officer from the Human Rights Commission arrested in the town of Kenema on Independence Day in 2015 following a protest had not concluded by the end of 2016.

In July, police refused permission for women's groups to assemble outside a conference centre in the capital, Freetown, during the Constitutional Review process to request greater protection of gender rights in the draft Constitution.

On 24 July, journalist Sam Lahai was detained for two days by police after raising questions on social media about the role of the Deputy Internal Affairs Minister. He was released on police bail after intervention by the Sierra Leone Association of Journalists, which had been calling for reform of restrictive criminal libel laws for many years.

In August, two people were shot dead and several injured by police in Kabala during a protest against the loss of a planned youth training centre. A curfew was imposed after several buildings were burned down. Seventeen people were sent to trial for offences such as arson and riotous conduct. The recently formed Independent Police Complaints Board launched an investigation into allegations that police used excessive force. Its recommendations to the Director of Public Prosecutions and the Inspector General of Police were not made public.

NGO Policy Regulations were proposed containing provisions which human rights defenders said would restrict their activities.

WOMEN'S RIGHTS

The incidence of violence against women and girls remained high. Specialist organizations providing support to women and girls risked closure due to funding constraints.

In March, President Koroma refused to sign a bill legalizing abortion in certain situations, despite the fact that it had been adopted by Parliament twice.[3]

Sierra Leone had a very high rate of FGM. During the Ebola crisis, FGM was banned and this ban was not officially lifted during 2016. However, FGM of young girls and women remained common.

In September, a woman in her late 20s was subjected to FGM and locked in a house for four days in Kenema. She was rescued by the police and went into hiding. The woman accused of cutting her was detained by police but released after several cutters mounted a protest outside the police station.

RIGHT TO EDUCATION

Pregnant girls were banned from attending mainstream school and sitting exams, in violation of their rights to education and non-discrimination. Pregnant girls could only participate in a part-time "temporary alternative education scheme" offering a reduced curriculum. This temporary scheme ended in August but was expected to continue under a new scheme. Many girls who had given birth were unable to pay school fees to return to school.[4]

In September, the UN Committee on the Rights of the Child urged Sierra Leone to immediately lift the discriminatory ban on pregnant girls attending mainstream schools and sitting exams, and ensure that they and adolescent mothers are supported to continue their education in mainstream schools.[5]

LAND DISPUTES

There were growing tensions over land-related issues. In February, six people were sentenced to six months' imprisonment or fines for destroying palm oil trees during protests in the Pujehun District in 2013 against a palm oil project operated by Socfin. Landowners claimed that they had not given consent to the acquisition of their land.

In February, the High Court ordered a Chinese company, Orient Agriculture Limited, to restore 1,486 acres of land to about 70 families in Nimiyama Chiefdom, Kono District. The company had signed a deal in 2013 with the Paramount Chief and local leaders to purchase land cheaply without the knowledge of the landowners.

---

1. Sierra Leone: Amnesty International Submission to the UN Universal Periodic Review (AFR 51/2905/2015)
2. Sierra Leone must protect and promote women's and girls' human rights, including to education and physical integrity (AFR 51/4353/2016)
3. Sierra Leone: Sign bill allowing safe abortions (News story, 4 February)
4. Sierra Leone: Continued pregnancy ban in schools and failure to protect rights is threatening teenage girls' futures (News story, 8 November)
5. Sierra Leone: Submission to the Committee on the Rights of the Child (AFR 51/4583/2016)

SINGAPORE

Republic of Singapore
Head of state: **Tony Tan Keng Yam**
Head of government: **Lee Hsien Loong**

The authorities continued to harass and prosecute bloggers and dissidents. Media remained heavily regulated through the Newspaper and Printing Presses Act. Judicial caning and the death penalty continued to be applied.

FREEDOMS OF EXPRESSION AND ASSEMBLY

Political activists, bloggers and government critics faced prosecution and other reprisals for the peaceful exercise of their rights to freedom of expression and of peaceful assembly.

There were concerns that the Administration of Justice (Protection) Act, passed in August, could target human rights defenders for criticizing the courts or the administration of justice. Punishments for contempt of court offences included up to three years' imprisonment and fines of up to SG$100,000 (US$70,000).

In June, blogger and political activist Han Hui was convicted of illegal assembly and "causing a public nuisance"; this prevented her from running in parliamentary elections. She was fined SG$3,100 (US$2,281), for leading a peaceful protest in 2014 in Hong Lim Park, the only space where people were permitted to demonstrate without a police permit. She appealed the decision.[1]

Also in June, political activists Roy Ngerng and Teo Soh Lung were subjected to hours of investigation for Facebook postings on a by-election "cooling off" day, which prohibits campaigning on the eve of elections.[2]

In September, Amos Yee, a teenage blogger, was sentenced to six weeks' imprisonment for uploading videos in which he allegedly "wounded the religious feelings of others".[3]

There were concerns that a decision by the Court of Appeal to prohibit human rights lawyer M. Ravi from practising law for a further two years, may have been politically motivated.

DEATH PENALTY

Death sentences continued to be imposed and carried out. In June, Kho Jabing, a Malaysian national convicted of murder, was executed hours after his final appeal was rejected. The mandatory death penalty remained applicable for a range of offences, some of which did not meet the threshold of "most serious crimes" under international law.

COUNTER-TERROR AND SECURITY

Concerns remained about the Internal Security Act (ISA) which allows the detention of suspects without trial for indefinitely renewable two-year periods. Fifty-eight people were said to have been detained under the ISA since January 2015.

RIGHTS OF LESBIAN, GAY, BISEXUAL, TRANSGENDER AND INTERSEX PEOPLE

Section 377A of the Penal Code, which criminalizes consensual sexual relations between men, remained. In June, the Home Affairs Ministry called on corporate sponsors to rescind sponsorship of the Pink Dot festival, an annual LGBTI gathering.

1. Singapore: End harassment of peaceful protesters (ASA 36/4342/2016)

2. Singapore: Government critics, bloggers and human rights defenders penalized for speaking out (ASA 36/4216/2016)

3. Singapore: Blogger faces up to three years in prison (ASA 36/4685/2016)

SLOVAKIA

Slovak Republic
Head of state: **Andrej Kiska**
Head of government: **Robert Fico**

Discrimination against Roma continued and little progress was made towards realizing Roma pupils' right to education. Slovakia continued to be the subject of a race equality infringement procedure by the European Commission.

BACKGROUND

In March, Prime Minister Fico's party, Direction-Social Democracy, won the parliamentary elections, while losing its overall majority, and formed a four-party coalition government. The far-right party, People's Party – Our Slovakia, entered Parliament for the first time with 14 seats. On 1 July, Slovakia assumed the rotating six-month Presidency of the Council of the EU.

DISCRIMINATION – ROMA

Police and security forces

There was concern over the continued lack of effective investigation and lengthy proceedings in several cases of excessive use of force by police against Roma. In July, the European Court of Human Rights (ECtHR) found that Slovakia had failed to adequately investigate allegations of police ill-treatment of a Roma man in detention in 2010.

In August, the government announced that the Law on Police would be amended to move the Department of Control and Inspection Service (SKIS) under the Prosecutor General's office – rather than it being under the Ministry of Interior – in order to increase SKIS' independence. However, a fully independent and transparent police accountability mechanism was not in place at the end of the year.

Several investigations into police ill-treatment of Roma were pending at the end of the year. In November, the investigation by the SKIS into the alleged excessive use of force by police during an operation in the Roma settlement of Vrbnica in April 2015 resulted in criminal charges being brought against the police officer who led the raid. However, the SKIS found that there was insufficient evidence to charge other police officers involved; the decision was appealed by the Roma families in December.

SKIS' investigation into police officers' conduct during an operation in the Roma settlement at Moldava nad Bodvou in June 2013 was discontinued in March 2016. The victims, supported by the European Roma Rights Centre and the Centre for Civil and Human Rights, appealed against this decision; the case was pending before the Constitutional Court at the end of the year.

Following the Public Prosecutor's appeal, the acquittal of 10 police officers accused of ill-treatment of six Roma boys at a police station in Košice in 2009 was quashed in April and the case sent back to the District Court.

Right to education

An amendment to the Schools Act prohibiting the placement of children from socially disadvantaged backgrounds in "special" schools solely based on their socioeconomic background came into force in January.

However, Roma children continued to be over-represented in "special" schools and classes for children with "mild mental disabilities" and were placed in ethnically segregated mainstream schools and classes. Despite ongoing infringement proceedings, initiated by the European Commission in 2015 against Slovakia for breaching the prohibition of discrimination set out in the EU Racial Equality Directive in relation to the access to education of Roma, there was no evidence of the government taking any effective measures to prevent or tackle the issue. This was highlighted by the European Commission in its annual assessment of Roma integration plans, as well as by the UN Committee on the Rights of the Child.

A public interest case, initiated in 2015 by the Centre for Civil and Human Rights against the Ministry of Education and the municipality of Stará Ľubovňa for the segregation of Roma children at a primary school, was dismissed by the District Court in Bratislava on 6 October 2016. The Centre appealed against the decision; the case was pending at the end of the year.

Forced sterilization

In February, the Košice II District Court ruled that the Louis Pasteur University Hospital in Košice unlawfully subjected a Roma woman to a forced sterilization in 1999. The woman had been subjected to the procedure without her informed consent after giving birth through a caesarean section. It took Slovak courts over 10 years to conclude the case and award the victim €17,000 in compensation. An appeal by the hospital was pending at the end of the year.

COUNTER-TERROR AND SECURITY

Anti-terrorism provisions introduced into the Constitution, the Criminal Code and the Criminal Procedure Code, as well as several other laws, came into force in January. They include the extension of the maximum period of pre-charge detention to 96 hours for individuals suspected of terrorism-related offences.

REFUGEES AND ASYLUM-SEEKERS

Despite placing "sustainable migration" high on its agenda during its EU presidency, Slovakia continued to oppose mandatory relocation quotas for refugees from other EU member states but expressed a willingness to accept 100 refugees from Greece and Italy by the end of 2017 on a voluntary basis. Only three families were relocated from Greece by the end of the year.

DISCRIMINATION

In August, the Slovak National Centre for Human Rights and the State Trade Inspectorate concluded that the owners of a guesthouse in Bratislava discriminated against three Turkish students. The owners had rejected their booking request based on a policy of "not accepting people from Turkey or Arab countries due to security reasons".

Prime Minister Fico continued to publicly associate Muslims and refugees with terrorism and used anti-migrant rhetoric. The People's Party – Our Slovakia organized anti-Roma and anti-immigration marches in January, March, June, July and October.

SLOVENIA

Republic of Slovenia
Head of state: **Borut Pahor**
Head of government: **Miro Cerar**

Asylum procedures were slow. The International Protection Act was amended to introduce expedited border procedures. Discrimination against Roma continued.

REFUGEES AND ASYLUM-SEEKERS

Before the closure of the Western Balkans route in March, 99,187 refugees and migrants entered Slovenia; the vast majority of them passed through on their way to Austria. 1,308 people – most of them Syrian, Afghan and Iraqi nationals – applied for asylum. After the closure of the Western

Balkans route, those who entered Slovenia and did not apply for asylum, including minors, were detained in the Centre for Foreigners in Postojna. In July, the authorities offered alternative accommodation for unaccompanied minors.

The asylum procedures were slow, partly as a result of the authorities' limited capacity to process applications. Throughout the year, more than 100 asylum-seekers, including unaccompanied minors, waited for first instance decisions for more than six months.

In March, the National Assembly amended the International Protection Act, introducing expedited asylum procedures for those who expressed the intention to apply for asylum at Slovenia's border or in transit areas at airports or ports. The law also removed the right to financial assistance of €288 in the first month after international protection has been granted.

Slovenia received 124 asylum-seekers relocated from Greece and Italy under the EU relocation scheme by the end of the year, out of a total of 567 asylum-seekers it had committed to accept by the end of 2017.

DISCRIMINATION

In April, the National Assembly passed the Protection against Discrimination Act, harmonizing legislation with EU anti-discrimination law. The law represented a milestone in combating discrimination based on gender identity, gender expression, social status or health, among other things. The law strengthened the mandate and autonomy of the Advocate of the Principle of Equality – a special post designed to prevent and eliminate discrimination including by hearing cases and offering assistance to victims of discrimination – as an independent anti-discrimination body.

The "erased"

Long-standing human rights violations against the "erased" – former permanent residents of Slovenia originating from other former Yugoslav republics – persisted. No new options were offered to the remaining "erased" to restore their legal status and related rights since the expiry of the Legal Status Act in 2013.

In November, the European Court of Human Rights (ECtHR) dismissed the complaint against Slovenia of some of the "erased" whose legal status had already been regulated. However, additional human rights issues of the "erased" remained pending before the ECtHR at the end of the year.

Roma

Discrimination against and social exclusion of the majority of Roma continued. Many were living in segregated settlements in inadequate housing, lacking security of tenure and access to water, electricity, sanitation and public transport. After the expiry of the National Action Programme for Roma inclusion in 2015, the government started a process of adopting a new set of measures. The government had yet to adopt a comprehensive national Roma Strategy as recommended by the parliamentary commission for human rights.

RIGHTS OF LESBIAN, GAY, BISEXUAL, TRANSGENDER AND INTERSEX PEOPLE

In April, Parliament adopted the Law on Partnerships. The new law offers same-sex couples the same rights as those originating from marriage, but fails to guarantee the right to adopt and to access assisted reproductive services procedures.

LEGAL, CONSTITUTIONAL OR INSTITUTIONAL DEVELOPMENTS

In November, the Constitution was amended to include the right to drinking water. According to the amendment, water resources are to be used primarily to supply the population with drinking water and households with water. The Constitution stated that those water resources could not be transformed from a public good into a tradeable commodity.

SOMALIA

Federal Republic of Somalia
Head of state: **Hassan Sheikh Mohamud**
Head of government: **Omar Abdirashid Ali Sharmarke**
Head of Somaliland Republic: **Ahmed Mohamed Mahamoud Silyano**

Armed conflict continued in central and southern Somalia between Somali Federal Government (SFG) forces, African Union Mission in Somalia (AMISOM) peacekeepers, and the armed group al-Shabaab. The areas controlled by SFG and AMISOM forces in the south-central regions remained in their hands. More than 50,000 civilians were killed, injured or displaced as a result of the armed conflict and generalized violence. All parties to the conflict were responsible for violations of human rights and international humanitarian law, some amounting to war crimes. There was no accountability for these violations. Armed groups continued to conscript children, and abduct, torture and unlawfully kill civilians. Rape and other crimes of sexual violence were widespread. The continuing conflict, insecurity and restrictions imposed by the warring parties hampered aid agencies' access to some regions. About 4.7 million people needed humanitarian assistance; 950,000 suffered from food insecurity. Tens of thousands of people were forcibly evicted from their homes. Freedom of expression was curtailed: two journalists were killed and others were attacked, harassed or fined.

BACKGROUND

The SFG and AMISOM remained in control of the capital, Mogadishu. They also retained areas taken from al-Shabaab in 2015 and consolidated their control through the federal administrations in Galmudug, Jubbaland and South-West states. AMISOM and the Somali National Armed Forces (SNAF) fought intermittent battles with al-Shabaab but control of territory did not change. By the end of 2016, al-Shabaab still controlled many rural areas, especially in Bay, Gedo, Lower Shabelle and Middle Juba regions. The fighting displaced more people. Inter-clan clashes and al-Shabaab attacks against civilians continued, particularly in districts where control repeatedly shifted between AMISOM and al-Shabaab. Civilians were killed and wounded in crossfire and targeted attacks, and as a result of grenades, improvised explosive devices (IEDs), suicide attacks and complex assaults. All parties to the conflict committed war crimes.

UN Security Council Resolution 2275, passed in March, extended the mandate of the UN Assistance Mission in Somalia (UNSOM) until 31 March 2017, while Resolution 2297, passed in July, extended the mandate of AMISOM until 31 May 2017. International support for government security forces, allied militias and AMISOM continued. As a result of pressure for accountability, nine Ugandan soldiers serving under AMISOM were sentenced to imprisonment for violating the rules and regulations of peacekeeping.

An acute humanitarian situation persisted and it was feared that the return of Somalis from neighbouring countries would exacerbate the crisis. At least 4.7 million people (40% of the population) needed support; most vulnerable were the more than 1.1 million internally displaced persons (IDPs).

A political crisis emerged over the electoral colleges for parliamentary and presidential elections due in September and October respectively. A forum set up by political leaders eventually agreed that 275 electoral colleges, each comprising 51 delegates selected by clan elders, would each elect an MP. Elections were scheduled for the lower and upper houses of Parliament in September and October respectively, but were twice postponed. Meanwhile, al-Shabaab rejected all forms of election, intensified attacks and called on followers to attack polling venues and kill clan elders, government officials and MPs taking part in the elections.

ABUSES BY ARMED GROUPS
Indiscriminate attacks
Al-Shabaab carried out indiscriminate and lethal attacks in heavily guarded areas of Mogadishu and other towns, killing or injuring hundreds of civilians. High-profile targets remained vulnerable to such attacks. It was difficult to establish the total number of civilians killed because there was no reliable casualty tracking system.

An al-Shabaab attack on Beach View Hotel and Lido Seafood restaurant at Lido beach in Mogadishu on 21 January killed at least 20 people. A suicide car bomb attack at a police station in Mogadishu on 9 March killed at least three people. A suicide bomb attack on a restaurant near a local government building in Mogadishu on 9 April killed at least four people and wounded seven. A suicide car bomb attack at Mogadishu's traffic police headquarters on 9 May killed at least five people. An al-Shabaab attack on Nasa Hablod Hotel in Mogadishu on 26 June killed at least 15 people and injured more than 20. Clashes between al-Shabaab fighters and SNAF in Bay region on 18 July killed 14 civilians caught in the crossfire. Two car explosions on 26 July outside a UN office in Mogadishu killed at least 10 people, both civilians and security officers. Two suicide attacks on the local government headquarters in Galkayo in Puntland (a semi-autonomous region in the northeast) on 21 August killed at least 20 civilians. An al-Shabaab attack on Banadir Beach Restaurant at Lido beach in Mogadishu on 26 August killed at least 10 civilians. A truck explosion outside SYL Hotel in Mogadishu near the presidential palace on 30 August killed at least 15 people and injured 45.

Targeting of civilians
Civilians were also directly targeted in attacks, especially by al-Shabaab fighters and clan militias. On 15 June, al-Shabaab fighters fired mortars into densely populated areas of Mogadishu; five loud explosions were heard but no deaths were reported. On 6 August, al-Shabaab fired mortar shells into a neighbourhood near the general hospital in Baidoa, killing one man and injuring six others.

In addition, al-Shabaab continued to torture and extrajudicially kill people they accused of spying or not conforming to its interpretation of Islamic law. The group killed people in public, including by beheading and stoning, and carried out amputations and floggings, especially in areas from which AMISOM had withdrawn. On 19 January, al-Shabaab killed a man in Kurtuway district after accusing him of witchcraft. On 20 May, al-Shabaab beheaded three men in Buur Hakaba district in Bay region after accusing them of spying for the federal government. On 17 August, al-Shabaab publicly killed a man by firing squad in Biyoley settlement, near Baidoa, after accusing him of spying for the federal government.

Clan and government-aligned militias continued to carry out extrajudicial killings, extortion, arbitrary arrests and rape. On 7 August, a clan militia in Qansax Dheere district in Bay region fired mortar shells at civilians, killing three. In August, several civilians were killed during clan clashes in Bay region.

CHILD SOLDIERS
Children continued to suffer grave abuses by all parties to the armed conflict. Somalia is a party to the UN Convention on the Rights of the Child but the federal government had yet to implement the two action plans it signed in 2012 to end the recruitment and use of child soldiers, as well as the killing and maiming of children.

In June, UNICEF stated that it believed there were up to 5,000 child soldiers in Somalia, mostly recruited by al-Shabaab and clan militias.

INTERNALLY DISPLACED PEOPLE, REFUGEES AND ASYLUM-SEEKERS
More than 1.1 million Somalis remained internally displaced. Most continued to settle along the Afgooye corridor between Mogadishu and Afgooye town. Intermittent clashes between SNAF and its AMISOM allies

and al-Shabaab disrupted trade in various regions. While SNAF and AMISOM forces controlled major towns, al-Shabaab blocked supply routes and taxed the civilian population in districts that it controlled. Continued conflict threatened to exacerbate the dire humanitarian situation.

In January, the federal parliament passed a law to protect and rehabilitate IDPs and Somali refugees, but implementation of it was slow. Over 1.1 million Somali refugees remained in neighbouring countries and the wider diaspora. As violence intensified in Yemen, Somalis who had fled there continued to return to Somalia. By the end of the year, over 30,500 Somalis had done so. Meanwhile, other host states, including Denmark and the Netherlands, put pressure on Somali asylum-seekers and refugees to return to Somalia on the grounds that security had improved in the country.

HOUSING RIGHTS – FORCED EVICTION

Forced evictions of IDPs and the urban poor remained a major problem, especially in Mogadishu. The government and private landowners forcibly evicted nearly 31,000 people in Deynile, Dharkeinly, Hamar Weyne, Heliwa, Hodan, Kaxda and Wardhigley districts of Mogadishu in the first half of the year. Over 14,000 people were forcibly evicted in January alone. The majority of those evicted moved to insecure and isolated locations on the outskirts of the capital, where social services were limited or non-existent and living conditions were deplorable.

FREEDOM OF EXPRESSION

Journalists and media workers continued to be intimidated, harassed and attacked. Two journalists were killed. On 4 June, unidentified gunmen shot dead Sagal Salad Osman, a journalist for state-run radio and television. On 27 September in Mogadishu, two assailants shot dead Abdiasis Mohamed Ali of Radio Shabelle. Several media houses were closed. On 9 July, police raided the premises of City FM, shut down the radio station and arrested the editor-in-chief,

Abdishakur Abdullahi Ahmed, and deputy editor-in-chief, Abdirahman Hussein Omar Wadani. They also confiscated radio equipment. On 13 August, police in Beledweyn region detained a freelance journalist, Ali Dahir Herow. Al-Shabaab continued to suppress the media and retained a ban on the internet in areas under its control.

In Somaliland, which lacks a functioning media law to protect journalists, media freedom was also restricted. The government curtailed freedom of expression of those who criticized its policies. By October, nine journalists had been arrested in relation to their work, seven of whom faced criminal cases in courts. On 25 May, Ahmed Mouse Sakaaro, a journalist based in Burao, was arrested and charged with inciting violence. In June, police officers arrested the publisher of the independent *Foore* newspaper, Abdirashid Abdiwahaab Ibraahim, and the editor-in-chief, Mohamed Mahamoud Yousuf, for covering an agreement on the management of Berbera port between the Somaliland government and a private company based abroad. Also in May, two journalists – Cabdirashid Nuur Wacays and Siciid Khadar, publisher and editor-in-chief of *Hubsad* newspaper respectively – were arrested and the newspaper was closed down. In addition, the government suspended publication of *Haartif* newspaper, a court revoked its licence and the police occupied its premises.

DEATH PENALTY

Somalia continued to use the death penalty despite its support for the UN General Assembly resolution on a moratorium on the death penalty. Few executions were reported, but the Military Court did sentence people to death in proceedings that fell short of international fair trial standards. Among those sentenced to death was a former journalist accused of helping al-Shabaab to kill five fellow reporters. On 14 August, a military court in Puntland ordered the execution of an army officer by firing squad in Garowe city. It was not known whether the execution was carried out.

In Somaliland, six prisoners at the Mandera maximum security complex were executed in January. On 25 July, a civilian court in Berbera sentenced eight men to death. Civilian courts continued to impose death sentences and at least 50 people were on death row at the end of the year.

SOUTH AFRICA

Republic of South Africa
Head of state and government: Jacob G. Zuma

Police used excessive force against protesters. Torture, including rape, and other ill-treatment of people in police custody continued to be reported. Xenophobia and violence against refugees, asylum-seekers and migrants resulted in deaths, injuries and displacement. Women and girls, particularly those in marginalized communities, continued to face gender inequality and discrimination. Lesbian, gay, bisexual, transgender and intersex (LGBTI) people were subjected to discrimination and hate crimes, including killings. Human rights defenders were attacked.

BACKGROUND

Political violence erupted in KwaZulu-Natal Province in the run-up to local elections held on 3 August. Between January and July, 25 violent incidents were reported, including 14 murders of local councillors, election candidates or members of political parties. The Police Minister set up a task force to investigate and prosecute incidents of politically motivated crime in the province.

From July, widespread and often violent student protests demanded free tertiary education. The protests followed the government's announcement of fee increases of up to 8% for the 2017 academic year.

Courts affirmed the independence of state oversight institutions. On 31 March, the Constitutional Court backed the findings of

the Office of the Public Protector's inquiry into non-security upgrades at the President's personal residence, requiring him to pay back the public funds used. On 6 September, the Constitutional Court ruled that the Police Minister's decision to suspend Robert McBride, Executive Director of the Independent Police Investigative Directorate (IPID), under the IPID Act was unconstitutional. In November, charges of fraud against Robert McBride were withdrawn.

EXCESSIVE USE OF FORCE

In response to the student protests, police sometimes used excessive force, including firing rubber bullets at close range at students and supporters when the use of force was neither necessary nor proportionate.

On 11 December, President Zuma announced steps taken by departments to implement the recommendations of the Farlam Commission of Inquiry into the police killings of striking miners in Marikana in 2012. These included revising the protocols governing the use of force, the launch on 15 April of a ministerial task force to ensure the psychological and physical fitness of police officers, and the setting up on 29 April of a panel of experts to revise public order policing processes. The Board of Inquiry into the fitness of national Police Commissioner Riah Phiyega to hold office concluded and was due to submit its final report to the President.

POLICE

The IPID reported 366 deaths as a result of police action and 216 deaths in police custody in 2015/2016, both figures lower than for the previous year. It also reported 145 cases of torture, including 51 cases of rape, by police officers on duty, and 3,509 cases of assault by police. Legal proceedings relating to unlawful killings by police remained slow.

In Durban High Court, the trial of 27 police officers, most of them members of the now disbanded Cato Manor Organized Crime Unit, on charges including 28 counts of murder, was further delayed until 31 January 2017.

In October, the Public Protector issued a report into violence at Durban's Glebelands hostel complex between March 2014 and November 2016 during which over 60 people died in targeted killings. The report found that the conflict was a result of the municipality's failure to assume responsibility for rental accommodation at the hostel. The report highlighted the detention and torture by police of at least three Glebelands residents in 2014, with no action taken against those suspected of criminal responsibility. The IPID investigation into the March 2014 death in custody of Zinakile Fica, a Glebelands resident, was not completed.

The Public Protector's report also found that the police failed in its duty to prevent and investigate crime and to protect hostel residents, highlighting the low ratio of arrests and lack of successful prosecution of murder suspects. The Public Protector promised to monitor investigations of allegations of police torture and killings of Glebelands residents.

In April, Glebelands residents submitted an urgent appeal to the UN High Commissioner for Human Rights, calling for the UN Human Rights Council to intervene regarding the targeted killings. On 7 November, a Glebelands peace committee leader was shot dead after leaving Umlazi Magistrate's Court. No arrests have been made.

INTERNATIONAL JUSTICE

In October, the government submitted an instrument of withdrawal from the Rome Statute of the International Criminal Court (ICC) without consulting Parliament.[1] The withdrawal takes effect after one year. The move followed non-co-operation procedures by the ICC against South Africa after the authorities failed to execute warrants of arrest for genocide, crimes against humanity and war crimes against Sudanese President Omar al-Bashir when he visited South Africa in June 2015 to attend the African Union (AU) summit. The move also followed the

dismissal by South Africa's Supreme Court of Appeal on 15 March of an appeal against the 2015 North Gauteng High Court judgment that the failure to arrest President al-Bashir violated South Africa's Constitution. State authorities had allowed President al-Bashir to leave South Africa in contravention of an interim order by North Gauteng High Court that he must remain.

CORPORATE ACCOUNTABILITY

New research concluded that the failure of mining company Lonmin to address housing conditions at Marikana contributed to the events of August 2012, when police shot dead 34 striking mineworkers.[2] Under its legally binding 2006 Social and Labour Plan, Lonmin had promised to construct 5,500 houses for mineworkers by 2011. It had built only three by 2012. In August 2016, Lonmin said that approximately 13,500 of its 20,000 permanent employees still needed formal accommodation. Many mineworkers continued to live in informal settlements such as Nkaneng within Lonmin's mine lease area. The shacks in Nkaneng do not meet the most basic international requirements for adequate housing. As a result, Lonmin's operations were inconsistent with the right to an adequate standard of living, including adequate housing.

REFUGEES' AND MIGRANTS' RIGHTS

Xenophobia and violence against refugees, asylum-seekers and migrants continued, resulting in deaths, injuries and displacement. Many incidents involved the targeted looting of foreign-owned small businesses in townships.

In June, shops in Pretoria townships were looted and at least 12 refugees and migrants were seriously injured and hundreds displaced. Earlier in the year, residents of Dunoon in the Western Cape looted foreign-owned businesses.

In April, findings were released of an inquiry into the 2015 violence against refugees, migrants and asylum-seekers in KwaZulu-Natal Province. The inquiry found the tensions were due to competition for scarce employment opportunities in the context of poverty and socioeconomic inequality. Its recommendations included educating civil servants on the rights and documentation of foreign nationals; strengthening the capacities of institutions managing migrants, refugees and asylum-seekers; ensuring leaders make responsible public statements; and education campaigns in schools to promote cohesion.

The previous closure of three of six refugee reception offices continued to put severe pressure on refugees who must consequently travel long distances to renew asylum permits.

Draft legislation on international immigration put forward in June includes a security-based approach to asylum-seekers, restricting their rights. It proposes asylum processing and administrative detention centres at South Africa's borders. These would house asylum-seekers while their applications are processed and limit their rights to work and movement while awaiting a decision on their application.

WOMEN'S RIGHTS

Gender inequality and discrimination continued to exacerbate the detrimental impact of racial, social and economic inequalities, especially for marginalized groups of women and girls.

Nearly a third of pregnant women were living with HIV, but improved access to free anti-retroviral treatment for pregnant women continued to reduce maternal mortality. Department of Health figures showed that the maternal mortality ratio continued to fall, from 197 for every 100,000 live births in 2011 to 155 in 2016. Problems persisted in rural communities relating to the availability and cost of transport for pregnant women and girls needing to access health services. The lives of pregnant women and girls continued to be put at unnecessary risk due to barriers to abortion services.

In June, the government launched a campaign, She Conquers, to address the disproportionately high rates of HIV infection among girls and young women and to reduce high levels of adolescent pregnancy. Although focused on improving access to health, education and employment opportunities for girls, campaign messaging was criticized for perpetuating negative stereotypes of girls' sexuality.

Also in June, the Commission for Gender Equality found the requirement that girls undergo virginity testing (*ukuhlolwa*) to access tertiary education bursaries, as imposed by a municipality in KwaZulu-Natal Province, violated constitutional rights to equality, dignity and privacy and would perpetuate patriarchy and inequality in South Africa. The *ukuhlolwa* requirement was removed.

A report by the UN Special Rapporteur on violence against women, its causes and consequences issued in June called on South Africa to implement a co-ordinated approach to end the pandemic of gender-based violence and discrimination, and recommended the decriminalization of sex work.

In March, the South African National AIDS Council (SANAC) launched a plan to address high rates of HIV among sex workers, including access to pre-exposure prophylaxis and anti-retroviral medicine. SANAC and sex worker activists warned that South Africa's laws relating to "prostitution" risked undermining the plan.

RIGHTS OF LESBIAN, GAY, BISEXUAL, TRANSGENDER AND INTERSEX PEOPLE

Hate crimes, hate speech and discrimination against LGBTI people, including killings and assaults, continued. Such attacks were believed to be grossly under-reported to police.

In March, Lucia Naido was stabbed to death in Katlehong, Ekurhuleni. Katlehong police opened a murder investigation, which was ongoing.

In April, a young, openly gay man, Tshifhiwa Ramurunzi, was attacked and seriously injured in Thohoyandou, Limpopo Province. His attacker was charged with attempted murder.

On 6 August, the body of Lesley Makousaan, an openly gay 17-year-old student, was found in Potchefstroom, North West Province; he had been strangled. A suspect was arrested shortly afterwards and was awaiting trial.

The body of Noluvo Swelindawo, an openly lesbian woman, was found in Khayelitsha, Western Cape Province, on 4 December, the day after she was kidnapped. A suspect was arrested on charges including housebreaking, kidnapping and murder, and appeared in court on 7 December. On 21 December, the suspect withdrew his bail application.

HUMAN RIGHTS DEFENDERS

Human rights defenders were attacked for carrying out their work, and justice for such crimes was slow.

In March, land rights activist Sikhosiphi "Bazooka" Rhadebe was shot dead at his home in Lurholweni, Eastern Cape Province, by two men claiming to be police officers.[3] He was Chairperson of the community-led Amadiba Crisis Committee and opposed the opencast mining of titanium and other heavy minerals on communal land in Xolobeni by a local subsidiary of Australia-based Mineral Commodities Limited.

The trial of a police officer charged with the October 2013 shooting and killing of 17-year-old housing rights activist Nqobile Nzuza during a protest in Cato Crest informal settlement in Durban was scheduled to begin in February 2017.

On 20 May, Durban High Court found two councillors representing the ruling African National Congress (ANC) and a co-accused hit man guilty of murdering housing rights activist Thulisile Ndlovu in September 2014. The three were sentenced to life imprisonment.

In a landmark judgment on 17 November, Bloemfontein High Court upheld the appeal by 94 community health workers and Treatment Action Campaign activists who had successfully challenged the constitutionality of the use of apartheid-era legislation, the 1993 Regulation of Gatherings Act. The Act criminalizes the gathering of more than 15 people in a public space without notifying the police in advance. The judgment affirmed that participating in a gathering without prior notice is not an offence.

FREEDOM OF EXPRESSION

In June, three senior journalists of the South African Broadcasting Corporation (SABC) were summarily suspended, allegedly for disagreeing with the decision not to cover a peaceful protest against censorship and abuse of power by the SABC, organized by the advocacy organization Right2Know. When five other SABC journalists objected to the suspensions they were accused of misconduct. All eight SABC employees were then fired. The group filed a case with the Constitutional Court in July, arguing that their right to freedom of expression had been violated; the case was pending. Four of the journalists won a case at the Labour Court in July that SABC had violated labour procedures. The eight subsequently returned to work but continued to face threats. On 12 December, four of the eight testified on behalf of the group at Parliament's inquiry into the fitness of the SABC board. Right2Know testified on 14 December.

DISCRIMINATION
People with albinism

Attacks against and the abduction of people with albinism were reported.

Four-year-old Maneliswa Ntombel was abducted by two men near his home on 21 June in KwaZulu-Natal Province. He remained missing at the end of the year.

In February, Mtubatuba Regional Court sentenced a 17-year-old youth to 18 years' imprisonment for the murder of Thandazile Mpunzi, who was killed in August 2015 in KwaZulu-Natal Province. Her remains were discovered in a shallow grave. Parts of her body had been sold to traditional healers. Two other men who pleaded guilty to the murder had each been sentenced in September 2015 to 20 years' imprisonment.

Hate crime legislation

In October, the draft Hate Crimes Bill was introduced. It aims to address racism, racial discrimination, xenophobia and discrimination based on gender, sex, sexual orientation and other issues, by providing an offence of hate crime. It includes controversial provisions that criminalize hate speech in ways that could be used to impermissibly restrict the right to freedom of expression.

RIGHT TO EDUCATION
Children with disabilities

Children with disabilities continued to face multiple challenges of discrimination, exclusion and marginalization which, among other things, denied them equal access to education despite legal and policy frameworks guaranteeing inclusive education. On 27 October, the UN Committee on the Rights of the Child recommended a review of Education White Paper No.6 to develop a framework for inclusive education that would see expansion of full-service schools and the inclusion of children with disabilities in mainstream education.

1. South Africa: Decision to leave International Criminal Court a "deep betrayal of millions of victims worldwide" (News story, 21 October)

2. South Africa: Smoke and mirrors – Lonmin's failure to address housing conditions at Marikana (AFR 53/4552/2016)

3. South Africa: Human rights defenders under threat (AFR 53/4058/2016)

SOUTH SUDAN

Republic of South Sudan
Head of state and government: **Salva Kiir Mayardit**

Despite the Agreement on the Resolution of the Conflict in the Republic of South Sudan (ARCSS), fighting continued between government and opposition forces, along with violations and abuses of international human rights and humanitarian law. A Transitional Government of National Unity (TGoNU) was formed in April, but it fell apart following heavy fighting between government and opposition forces in Juba in July. The reconstituted government in Juba was accepted by the international community but rejected by opposition leader Riek Machar and his allies. The ongoing fighting continued with devastating humanitarian consequences for civilian populations. Government security services actively suppressed independent and critical voices from the opposition, media and human rights defenders.

BACKGROUND

Implementation of the ARCSS, the peace agreement, was slow and faced numerous hurdles including disagreement over the number of states, the cantonment of opposition fighters and security arrangements in the capital Juba.

On 26 April, opposition leader Riek Machar returned to Juba to be sworn in as First Vice-President of the TGoNU, as provided for in the ARCSS. Ministers of the TGoNU were sworn in the following week.

In early July, a series of violent clashes between government and opposition forces in Juba heightened tensions and led to a deadly shoot-out on 8 July between bodyguards of President Salva Kiir and then First Vice-President Riek Machar outside the Presidential Palace, where the two were meeting. On 10 and 11 July, there were heavy clashes between government and opposition forces in Juba.

The fighting in Juba forced Riek Machar and opposition forces to flee southward, where they evaded active pursuit by government forces over the next month. Meanwhile President Salva Kiir dismissed Riek Machar as First Vice-President and replaced him on 25 July with opposition politician Taban Deng Gai. Riek Machar rejected and denounced the dismissal which resulted in a split in the Sudan People's Liberation Army/Movement in Opposition (SPLM/A-IO). The international community eventually accepted the new government and urged it to resume implementation of the ARCSS.

Relative calm was restored in Juba following the flight of Riek Machar and opposition forces but the fighting in Juba triggered a surge of violence in the southern Equatoria region, resulting in killings of civilians, looting, and arbitrary detentions. Lainya, Yei, Kajokeji, Morobo and Maridi counties were particularly affected. Between July and December, more than 394,500 South Sudanese arrived in northern Uganda as refugees as a result of the insecurity.

In September, the UN Security Council (UNSC) adopted resolution 2304 authorizing the establishment of a 4,000-member Regional Protection Force (RPF), as an addition to the existing 12,000 members of the UN Mission in South Sudan (UNMISS) peacekeeping force. The RPF mandate would be to facilitate safe movement in and out of Juba; protect the airport and key facilities in Juba; and engage any actor preparing for or engaging in attacks against civilians, humanitarian actors, or UN personnel and premises. However, the RPF was not in place by the end of the year.

The same resolution provided that the UNSC would consider the imposition of an arms embargo should South Sudan create political or operational impediments to operationalizing the RPF or obstruct UNMISS in the performance of its mandate. Despite reports of attacks on and obstruction of UNMISS staff and the government's averseness to the RPF's mandate and establishment, in December the UN Security Council failed to approve a resolution that would have imposed an arms embargo.

INTERNAL ARMED CONFLICT

Despite the ARCSS, there was fighting in many areas of the country throughout the year. The fighting was continuously accompanied by violations and abuses of international human rights and humanitarian law by parties to the conflict, including killings, looting and destruction of civilian property, abductions and sexual violence.

On 17 and 18 February, fighting took place in the UN Protection of Civilians site in Malakal, which housed around 45,000 people. Government soldiers entered the site and participated in the fighting. Around one third of the camp was burned to the ground, and at least 29 internally displaced people were killed.

In Western Bahr el Ghazal in early 2016, government soldiers carried out attacks against civilians: killings, torture including rape, looting and burning down of civilian homes. Clashes between government and opposition allied forces in Wau town on 24-25 June displaced an estimated 70,000 people and killed dozens.

During the July fighting in Juba, armed actors, particularly government soldiers, committed violations and abuses of international human rights and humanitarian law, including killings, sexual violence, and looting of civilian property and humanitarian assets. Government soldiers also fired indiscriminately near Protection of Civilians sites and, in some cases, deliberately targeted them. Fifty-four displaced people were killed in the sites during the fighting, according to the UN.

In September, the number of refugees who had arrived in neighbouring countries since the start of the conflict in December 2013, reached 1 million. The number of internally displaced people seeking protection in Protection of Civilians sites rose over the course of the year to 204,918 in October. A total of 1.83 million people continued to be displaced within the country and 4.8 million people were affected by food insecurity.

ARBITRARY DETENTIONS AND TORTURE AND OTHER ILL-TREATMENT

South Sudan's National Security Service (NSS) and the national army's Military Intelligence Directorate continued to conduct arbitrary arrests, prolonged and – in some cases – incommunicado detentions, and enforced disappearances of perceived government opponents. Detainees were subjected to torture and other ill-treatment in multiple detention facilities.

Over 30 men were detained by the NSS at a two-storey detention facility within its headquarters in the Jebel neighbourhood of Juba. They were detained on accusations of supporting the SPLM/A-IO, but were not charged or presented in court. None of them had had access to legal counsel by the end of the year. The NSS restricted access to family members and failed to provide adequate medical care. Some were subjected to beatings and other forms of physical assault, especially during interrogation or as punishment for breaking internal detention rules. Some had been in detention for over two years.

The NSS continued to arbitrarily detain George Livio, a journalist with the UN's Radio Miraya, without charge or trial, in Juba. The NSS arrested George Livio in Wau on 22 August 2014. The NSS has denied requests from his lawyer to meet him and has restricted his access to family members.

Loreom Joseph Logie, who had been arbitrarily detained by the NSS since September 2014, died on 17 July. Prior to his death he had suffered from a tapeworm infection that was untreated and caused liver damage.

A detention facility at a military base in Gorom, about 20km south of Juba, was used, at least between November 2015 and May 2016, to detain soldiers and civilians allegedly affiliated with the opposition. Detainees were held without charge or trial. They were held in poorly ventilated metal shipping containers, fed only once or twice a week and given insufficient drinking water. Many detainees died at this facility due to harsh conditions; others were victims of extrajudicial executions.

The Giyada military barracks in Juba remained a site where arbitrary and incommunicado detentions, torture and disappearances continued to be carried out. Conditions were particularly harsh in an underground military intelligence cell, where detainees were held without access to natural light or sanitary facilities.

Elias Waya Nyipouch, former Governor of Wau state, was arrested at his home on 26 June. He was detained in Juba at the Giyada military barracks and moved on 21 October to the Bilpam barracks, also in Juba. He was held without charge or trial at the end of the year.

LACK OF ACCOUNTABILITY

There were no credible investigations and prosecutions of violations and abuses of international human rights and humanitarian law conducted in fair trials by civilian courts. Some crimes committed against civilians by government soldiers were reportedly prosecuted before military courts, despite the provision under South Sudan's SPLA Act providing that if military personnel commit an offence against a civilian, the civil court should assume jurisdiction over the offence.

Although the ARCSS provided for the establishment of a Hybrid Court for South Sudan by the African Union Commission, little progress was made towards its establishment. There was also little progress towards the establishment of a Commission on Truth Reconciliation and Healing or a Compensation and Reparations Authority. These two bodies were also provided for in the ARCSS.

FREEDOM OF EXPRESSION

The space for journalists and human rights defenders to work freely continued to shrink, as it had since the start of the conflict. The authorities, especially the NSS, continued to harass and intimidate journalists, summoning them for questioning and arbitrarily arresting and detaining them. Numerous journalists and human rights defenders have fled South Sudan due to perceived security risks.

Joseph Afandi, a journalist in Juba with the daily El Tabeer, was arrested by the NSS on 23 December 2015 for criticizing in an article the human rights record of the Sudan People's Liberation Movement (SPLM). He was held in incommunicado detention at the NSS headquarters in Juba until his release in February. While in detention, he was subjected to torture and other ill-treatment.

Alfred Taban, a journalist and chief editor of the daily Juba Monitor, published an opinion piece on 15 July in which he said that both Machar and Kiir had "completely failed" and "should not remain in their seats". Alfred Taban was arrested the following day by NSS agents and detained at their headquarters in Juba for one week. He was then transferred to police custody and charged with "publishing or communicating false statements prejudicial to South Sudan" and with "undermining the authority of or insulting the president." He was released on bail on 29 July. No court date had been set for a trial by the end of the year.

On 12 September, staff of the newspaper *Nation Mirror* were summoned by the NSS and shown a letter ordering the paper to "close down because they had indulged in activities incompatible with their status." The order followed the publication of an opinion article condemning corruption within the armed forces and an article about corruption allegations against government officials.

FREEDOM OF ASSOCIATION

In February, two laws regulating NGOs activities' were enacted. The laws restricted the right to freedom of association by mandating that all NGOs needed to register; non-registered NGOs were prohibited from operating. The Relief and Rehabilitation Commission held sweeping powers to register and monitor NGOs and to revoke registration of NGOs that were judged not to be in conformity with the NGO Act. The acceptable "objectives of NGOs" listed in the Act did not include human rights work or policy advocacy.

RIGHT TO HEALTH – MENTAL HEALTH

Although levels of post-traumatic stress disorder and depression among the population remained high, the availability and accessibility of mental health and psychosocial support services remained limited. Juba Teaching Hospital – the only public medical facility that provided psychiatric care – still only had 12 beds in its psychiatric ward. The availability of psychotropic drugs was inconsistent and limited. There were only two practising

psychiatrists in the country, both of whom were in Juba. Neither of them saw patients on a full-time basis. Due to the lack of appropriate services and facilities, people with mental health conditions continued to be routinely housed in prisons, even if they had not committed any crime. In prison, mental health patients continued to receive insufficient medical care and were sometimes chained or held in solitary confinement for long periods.

LEGAL, CONSTITUTIONAL OR INSTITUTIONAL DEVELOPMENTS

In May, South Sudan completed ratification of the African Charter on Human and Peoples' Rights and of the Organization of African Unity Convention Governing the Specific Aspects of Refugee Problems in Africa.

SPAIN

Kingdom of Spain
Head of state: King Felipe VI de Borbón
Head of government: Mariano Rajoy

The offence of "glorifying terrorism" continued to be used to prosecute people peacefully exercising their right to freedom of expression. New cases of torture and other ill-treatment, excessive use of force and collective expulsions by police officials were reported, including against individuals who attempted to enter irregularly from Morocco into the Spanish enclaves of Ceuta and Melilla. Investigations into allegations of torture and other ill-treatment were sometimes not effectively conducted. Authorities accepted the resettlement and relocation of only a few hundred refugees, far below the commitments undertaken. Spanish authorities continued to refuse to co-operate with the Argentine judiciary to investigate crimes committed during the Civil War and by the Franco regime.

FREEDOMS OF EXPRESSION AND ASSEMBLY

Throughout the year, unwarranted restrictions on the rights to freedom of expression, information and assembly were imposed, on the basis of the 2015 legislative amendments to the Law on Public Security and the Criminal Code.

On 5 February, Alfonso Lázaro de la Fuente and Raúl García Pérez, professional puppeteers, were imprisoned for five days after performing a play which included scenes in which a nun was stabbed, a judge hanged and police and pregnant women were subjected to beatings. During the show, one of the puppets displayed a banner bearing the sign "Gora ALKA-ETA" ("Up with ALKA-ETA"). The puppeteers were charged with glorifying terrorism and incitement to hatred. Their arrest took place after several individuals said they were offended by the play. In September, the National Court dismissed charges of glorifying terrorism. However, at the end of the year, the prosecution continued on charges of incitement to hatred.

In April, the Minister of Interior urged the General Council of the Judiciary to take measures against José Ricardo de Prada, a National High Court judge. He had participated in a round table organized by the City Council of Tolosa, Guipúzcoa, where he expressed agreement with the concerns of international human rights organizations regarding the barriers to effective investigations of cases of torture in Spain. In addition, the Prosecutor's Office supported a request by the Association of Victims of Terrorism that he should be removed as member of a court in two criminal trials because of his alleged bias. In June, the National High Court dismissed both requests to take action against the judge.

During the year, the National High Court delivered 22 guilty verdicts against 25 people for glorifying terrorism offences. Most rulings came as a result of "Operation Spider", involving the interception of messages published on social media. Between April 2014 and April 2016, 69 individuals were arrested as part of the operation.

TORTURE AND OTHER ILL-TREATMENT

New cases of torture and other ill-treatment, including excessive use of force by law enforcement officers, were reported throughout the year. Investigations into allegations of torture and other ill-treatment were sometimes not effectively and thoroughly conducted.

In January, the judge investigating the death in Cadiz on 4 April 2015 of Juan Antonio Martínez González, as a result of the injuries sustained while he was being restrained by law enforcement officers, made his ruling. He found that there was no evidence to support charges that the officers used banned methods of restraint or that they exceeded their powers in their intervention. At the end of the year, an appeal against the ruling before the Provincial Court of Cádiz was upheld.

In May, in the case of *Beortegui Martinez v Spain* the European Court of Human Rights once again found that Spain violated the prohibition of torture and other ill-treatment by failing to conduct an effective and thorough investigation into allegations of torture of individuals under incommunicado detention. This was the seventh ruling of this kind against Spain.

In May, the Audiencia Provincial of Barcelona heard the trial against two officers regarding the case of Ester Quintana, who lost an eye in November 2012 as a result of being hit by a rubber bullet shot by the Mossos d'Esquadra during a protest in Barcelona. The trial ended with the acquittal of both officers, as the court was unable to establish which officer had fired the bullet.

In July, the Supreme Court partially annulled the conviction by the High Court of Saioa Sánchez for an act of terrorism in December 2015.

The High Court had convicted Saioa Sánchez and two others of terrorism-related offences. Her appeal to the Supreme Court claimed that the High Court refused to investigate whether the statement of one of the defendants, Iñigo Zapirain, implicating her in the offence, had been made under duress. The Supreme Court ordered a new hearing, asking that the Manual on the Effective Investigation and Documentation of Torture and Other Cruel, Inhuman or Degrading Treatment or Punishment (Istanbul Protocol) be followed to assess the veracity of the statement of Iñigo Zapirain. The ruling took account of the concerns expressed by international human rights bodies about impunity and lack of thorough and effective investigations, as well as about shortcomings in the quality and accuracy of forensic investigations.

REFUGEES' AND MIGRANTS' RIGHTS

The number of irregular arrivals of refugees and migrants, crossing from Morocco into the Spanish enclaves of Ceuta and Melilla through the fence separating the two countries, decreased on the previous year. However, the overall number of arrivals including those passing through regular border crossings increased. There continued to be collective expulsions by Spanish law enforcement officers in Ceuta and Melilla towards Morocco. The Spanish reception system for asylum-seekers remained inadequate, with too few places in official reception centres and too little assistance for those housed outside them. Spain failed to implement European Directives on stateless persons, asylum procedures and reception conditions. There continued to be no implementation of the Asylum Act, six years after its entry into force. As a result, asylum-seekers across the country experienced uneven access to the assistance they are entitled to. Between January and October, 12,525 asylum applications were submitted in Spain, according to Eurostat data, compared with 4,513 in 2013. By August, the growing backlog of unprocessed asylum applications had reached 29,845 cases.

On 9 September, at least 60 people from sub-Saharan Africa who had gained access to Spanish territory by climbing the fences separating Ceuta from Morocco were collectively expelled. Before being expelled some of them were beaten by Moroccan officers who entered the area between the fences, which is Spanish territory. Some of those returned to Morocco were injured while scaling the fences and as a result of the beatings.

Although Spain agreed to receive 1,449 people from the Middle East and North Africa under resettlement schemes, only 289 people, all Syrian nationals, had reached Spanish territory by December. Likewise, in contrast to the commitment made to receive 15,888 people in need of international protection from Italy and Greece under the EU internal relocation programme, only 609 were relocated to Spain by December.

IMPUNITY

Spanish authorities continued to refuse to co-operate with the Argentine judiciary to investigate crimes under international law committed during the Civil War and by the Franco regime. Spanish authorities obstructed Argentine prosecuting authorities in the class action known as "Querella Argentina" from taking statements from some of the victims and the 19 defendants. By means of a circular dated 30 September, the Spanish Prosecutor's Office instructed territorial prosecutor offices to refuse to conduct any of the judicial inquiries requested by the Argentine prosecuting authorities, arguing that it would not be possible to investigate the crimes reported, such as enforced disappearances and torture, under the Amnesty Act (among other acts) and because of the statute of limitations.

DISCRIMINATION – MIGRANTS' HEALTH

Austerity measures continued to have a detrimental effect on human rights, especially with regard to access to health and social protection for some of the most vulnerable groups. The Constitutional Court declared that legislation approved in 2012, restricting access to free health care for undocumented migrants including primary health care, was constitutional. This reform has taken away the health care cards from 748,835 migrants, removing or seriously limiting their access to the health system and in some situations putting their lives at risk. There has been a particular impact on women, in terms of barriers to information on, and services related to, sexual and reproductive health.

RIGHT TO HOUSING

Public spending on housing was cut by over 50% between 2008 and 2015, while mortgage foreclosures continued unabated. According to statistics from the General Council of the Judiciary, up to September 2016 there were 19,714 forced mortgage evictions and 25,688 evictions for non-payment of rent. However, there were no official figures showing the number of people affected by foreclosures in Spain, nor disaggregated data by sex or age, which prevented the adoption of measures to protect the most vulnerable. Householders facing repossession claims continued to lack adequate legal remedies to enforce the protection of their right to housing before courts.

VIOLENCE AGAINST WOMEN

According to figures from the Ministry of Health, Social Services and Equality, 44 women were killed by their partners or ex-partners as of December. The Act on Comprehensive Protection Measures Against Gender-Based Violence and the establishment of Courts on Violence Against Women came into force in 2004. However, there has not been a participatory and transparent review of the impact of the law since then, despite concerns about the effectiveness of prosecutions and the adequacy of victim protection measures.

SRI LANKA

Democratic Socialist Republic of Sri Lanka
Head of state and government: **Maithripala Sirisena**

Sri Lanka continued to pursue commitments to deliver accountability for alleged crimes under international law, although the process was slow. Many human rights challenges remained, including the authorities' reliance on the Prevention of Terrorism Act (PTA) to arrest and detain suspects; torture and other ill-treatment in police custody, and impunity for enforced disappearance and other violations. Victims of violations during the armed conflict faced challenges in rebuilding lives and livelihoods as coherent relief and reparation plans had yet to be implemented.

BACKGROUND

Sri Lanka initiated a constitutional reform process, began to design truth, justice and reparation mechanisms, and began to institute legal and procedural reforms to address, and ensure, non-repetition of the serious human rights violations and abuses that plagued the country for decades. It initiated public consultations on these mechanisms, but failed to adequately support implementation of the process.

ARBITRARY ARRESTS AND DETENTIONS

Tamils suspected of links to the Liberation Tigers of Tamil Eelam (LTTE) continued to be detained under the PTA, which permits extended administrative detention and shifts the burden of proof onto the detainee alleging torture or other ill-treatment. In 2015 the government pledged to repeal the PTA and replace it with legislation that complied with international standards, but had not implemented this commitment by the end of 2016. A draft policy and legal framework for replacement legislation submitted for cabinet approval in October retained many of the PTA's most problematic elements although it did introduce safeguards against torture.

In June, President Sirisena instructed the police and armed forces to abide by Human Rights Commission of Sri Lanka directives, that were designed to protect those arrested under the PTA and other emergency measures and to end practices that can lead to abuse. Such abuses include the failure of arresting officials to identify themselves, the transport of suspects in unmarked vehicles, and the use of unofficial places of detention. The directives also guaranteed detainees' access to a lawyer, including during interrogation, but these were not fully respected.

In late August, human rights lawyer Lakshan Dias petitioned the Supreme Court accusing the Terrorist Investigation Division of the police of violating the directives by refusing to allow him to meet with his client. An amendment to the Code of Criminal Procedure that would have deprived those arrested of access to legal counsel until the police recorded their statements was withdrawn in October after lawyers protested.

TORTURE AND OTHER ILL-TREATMENT

The UN Special Rapporteur on torture visited Sri Lanka in May. He found that severe forms of torture by police continued, although probably at lower levels than during the armed conflict, and that impunity persisted for both old and new cases. He noted that procedural norms such as prolonged arbitrary detention without trial under the PTA "almost invite torture and ill-treatment as a routine method of work." In August, Sri Lanka made a declaration under the UN Convention against Torture recognizing the competence of the UN Committee against Torture to receive and consider communications from individuals alleging violations of their rights under the Convention.

EXCESSIVE USE OF FORCE

Reports continued of excessive use of force in the context of policing. Impunity continued to persist for past incidents. The killings by the army of unarmed demonstrators demanding clean water in August 2013 had yet to be prosecuted. In October a magistrate ruled that the killings were crimes, and ordered further hearings in 2017 to determine whether there was sufficient evidence to refer the case for prosecution.

ENFORCED DISAPPEARANCES

In May, Sri Lanka ratified the International Convention against Enforced Disappearance, but by the end of the year had not passed legislation criminalizing enforced disappearance in domestic law. The Presidential Commission to Investigate into Complaints Regarding Missing Persons concluded in July, having received over 19,000 civilian complaints. However, little progress was made in clarifying the fate of the missing or bringing perpetrators of enforced disappearance to justice. In August, Parliament bypassed public consultation when it adopted an Act establishing the Office on Missing Persons to assist families to trace missing relatives and take on the case load left by the Commission.

IMPUNITY

Impunity persisted for alleged crimes under international law committed during the armed conflict. Impunity also remained for many other human rights violations. These included the January 2006 extrajudicial executions of five students in Trincomalee by security personnel and the killing of 17 aid workers with the NGO Action Against Hunger in Muttur in August 2006.

In May, the former Media Minister, testifying in a habeas corpus case into the December 2011 disappearances of political activists Lalith Weeraraj and Kugan Muruganandan, stated that his claim at the time that the two activists were in government custody and that their whereabouts could not be revealed was based on information from the Defence Ministry. The investigation into the involvement of army intelligence officers in the 2010 disappearance of dissident cartoonist Prageeth Eknaligoda was ongoing. In August a court in the capital, Colombo, ordered a new autopsy of the remains of newspaper editor Lasantha Wickrematunge, who was murdered in 2009.

HUMAN RIGHTS DEFENDERS

In August, Balendran Jeyakumari, an activist against enforced disappearances, who had previously been detained without charge for a year under the PTA, was once again summoned for questioning. Human rights defender Ruki Fernando remained barred by court order from speaking about an ongoing police investigation into his advocacy on her case; his confiscated electronic equipment was not returned.

Sandhya Eknaligoda, the wife of disappeared dissident cartoonist Prageeth Eknaligoda, faced repeated threats and acts of intimidation. These included protests outside the court where her husband's habeas corpus case was being heard, and a poster campaign that accused her of supporting the LTTE after the police identified seven army intelligence officers suspected of involvement in his disappearance.

FREEDOMS OF EXPRESSION, ASSEMBLY AND ASSOCIATION

In June, journalist Freddy Gamage was beaten by men he identified as supporters of a politician in the town of Negombo. Freddy Gamage had been threatened previously over articles he wrote exposing the politician's alleged corruption and links to organized crime. He was further threatened by one of his attackers when they met in court after he pointed him out in an identification parade. Impunity persisted for past attacks on media workers; according to media NGOs, attacks included some 44 killings since 2004.

People engaged in activism in the north and east continued to report harassment and surveillance by security forces.

LEGAL, CONSTITUTIONAL OR INSTITUTIONAL DEVELOPMENTS

Sri Lanka initiated a Constitutional reform process aimed at ensuring checks on executive power and more equitable ethnic power sharing. The results of public consultations on the content of a new Constitution were published in May. Parliament was expected to debate a proposed draft Constitution in early 2017.

In July, Sri Lanka passed the Right to Information Act. In August, the cabinet approved a National Policy on Durable Solutions for Conflict-Affected Displacement. This aimed to protect human rights by guiding the return of private lands seized by the military, creation of livelihood and income generating opportunities for the displaced, and assistance for returning refugees. The policy emphasized non-discrimination, access to justice and reparations. Implementation was expected to begin in February 2017.

DISCRIMINATION

Tamils continued to complain of ethnic profiling, surveillance and harassment by police who suspected them of LTTE links. In August, the UN Committee on the Elimination of Racial Discrimination found that the PTA was disproportionately used against Tamils and was discriminatory in effect.

Christians and Muslims reported incidents of harassment, threats and physical violence by members of the public and supporters of hardline Sinhala Buddhist political groups. Police failed to take action against attackers or in some cases blamed religious minorities for inciting opponents. In June, a group calling itself Sinha Le (Lion's Blood) was linked to protests against a mosque construction in the city of Kandy. In June, its supporters waged a social media campaign of threats and intimidation against Equal Ground, an organization seeking human and political rights for the lesbian, gay, bisexual, transgender, intersex and questioning (LGBTIQ) community of Sri Lanka.

In June, the Health Ministry noted that "transgender people are often socially, economically, politically and legally marginalized... and vulnerable to harassment violence and sexual assault and discrimination in access to public spaces." It ordered health services for transgender individuals, including physician-certified Gender Recognition Certificates to assist in the amendment of birth certificates to accurately reflect the sex with which the individual identified.

VIOLENCE AGAINST WOMEN AND GIRLS

Impunity persisted for violence against women and girls, including rape by military personnel and civilians, and also in situations of domestic violence such as marital rape. Women human rights defenders supporting constitutional reforms advocated repeal of Article 16(1), which upheld laws existing prior to the current Constitution, even when they were inconsistent with the Constitution. This included tenets of Muslim personal law that permitted child marriage and failed to recognize marital rape.

DEATH PENALTY

Death sentences continued to be imposed; no executions were carried out. In September, a former MP was sentenced to death for the murder of a political rival.

SUDAN

Republic of the Sudan
Head of state and government: **Omar Hassan Ahmed al-Bashir**

The authorities refused to execute arrest warrants issued by the International Criminal Court (ICC). The security and humanitarian situation in Darfur, Blue Nile and South Kordofan states remained dire, with widespread violations of international humanitarian and human rights law. Evidence pointed to the use of chemical weapons by government forces in Darfur. The rights to freedom of expression, association and peaceful assembly were arbitrarily restricted and critics and suspected opponents of the government were subjected to arbitrary arrest, detention and other violations. Excessive use of force by the authorities in dispersing gatherings led to numerous casualties.

BACKGROUND

Armed conflicts persisted in Darfur, Blue Nile and South Kordofan, leading to civilian casualties and widespread disruption and hardship.

In March, the African Union High-Level Implementation Panel (AUHIP) proposed a Roadmap Agreement for peace and dialogue to end the conflicts. The Agreement commits parties to end conflicts in Darfur, Blue Nile and South Kordofan and ensure humanitarian access to all populations in these areas. It also commits parties to engage in an inclusive national dialogue process. The government signed the Agreement in March but opposition groups refused at first to sign.

On 8 August, the agreement was signed by four opposition groups: the National Umma Party; the Sudan People's Liberation Movement-North (SPLM-N); the Justice and Equality Movement (JEM); and the Sudan Liberation Movement (SLM-MM) led by Minni Minnawi. The following day, negotiations resumed in Addis Ababa, Ethiopia, along two tracks: between the SPLM-N and the government; and on Darfur around cessation of hostilities and humanitarian access. However, on 14 August, the talks collapsed between the government and the armed opposition groups, the SPLM-N, JEM and SLM-MM. The AUHIP announced an indefinite suspension of the peace talks. Both sides blamed each other for the collapse of the talks.

When Sudan's human rights record was examined under the UN Universal Periodic Review (UPR) process in May, Sudan accepted a number of recommendations including ratification of the UN Convention against Torture and efforts to prevent torture and inhuman treatment. However, Sudan rejected recommendations to remove impunity provisions from the National Security Act 2010 and ensure independent investigation and prosecution of crimes under international law and human rights violations committed by the National Intelligence and Security Service (NISS), the armed forces and the police.[1]

In January, Parliament passed an amendment that increased the maximum penalty for rioting from two to five years' imprisonment.

INTERNATIONAL CRIMINAL COURT

The authorities continued to refuse to execute five arrest warrants issued by the ICC for Sudanese nationals, including two warrants for President al-Bashir on charges of genocide, crimes against humanity and war crimes allegedly committed in Darfur.

ARMED CONFLICT

Darfur

The security and humanitarian situation in Darfur remained dire, as the armed conflict entered its thirteenth year in 2016.

In January, government forces launched a large-scale military campaign in the Jebel Marra area of Darfur. Co-ordinated ground and air attacks targeted locations throughout Jebel Marra until May. After that, the seasonal rains intensified, making ground attacks impractical throughout most of the area; air operations continued, however, through to mid-September.

A large number of crimes under international law and human rights violations committed by Sudanese government forces were documented, including the bombing of civilians and civilian property, the unlawful killing of men, women and children, the abduction and rape of women, the forced displacement of civilians and the looting and destruction of civilian property, including the destruction of entire villages.

Evidence was also documented that suggested the Sudanese government forces repeatedly used chemical weapons during attacks in Jebel Marra.[2] Satellite imagery, more than 200 in-depth interviews with survivors and expert analysis of dozens of images of injuries indicated that at least 30 probable chemical attacks took place in Jebel Marra between January and September 2016. An estimated 200 to 250 people may have died as a result of exposure to chemical weapons agents, with many – or most – being children. Most survivors of the suspected chemical weapons attacks had no access to adequate medical care.

South Kordofan and Blue Nile

On 24 April, the Sudan Revolutionary Front, a coalition of four armed opposition groups, announced a unilateral ceasefire of six months, extending a previous ceasefire announced in October 2015. On 17 June, President al-Bashir declared a four-month unilateral cessation of hostilities in Blue Nile and South Kordofan. In October, he extended the cessation of hostilities in these areas to the end of year.

Despite the declared cessation of hostilities, government forces and the SPLM-N engaged in sporadic military attacks in Sudan People's Liberation Army-North (SPLA-N) controlled areas. The armed conflict was characterized by aerial and ground attacks by government forces, many directed at civilian objects – that is, objects which are not military objectives – as well as denial of humanitarian access to civilians.[3]

FREEDOM OF ASSOCIATION

Civil society activists were subjected to arbitrary arrests and arbitrary restrictions on their activities.

On 28 January, the NISS stopped a seminar organized at Al Mahas Club in the capital Khartoum by a committee opposed to the building of the Kajbar and Dal dams in Northern Sudan state. The committee claimed the dams would have a damaging social and environmental impact. The NISS detained 12 people before releasing them later that day.

The NISS raided the office of the NGO TRACKS (Khartoum Centre for Training and Human Development) on 29 February and confiscated mobile phones and laptops, as well as documents, the passports of those present and two vehicles. They detained the Director of TRACKS, Khalafalla Mukhtar, for six hours, along with another TRACKS employee and Mustafa Adam, a visitor and Director of Al Zarqaa, another civil society organization.[4] On 22 May, the NISS arrested eight TRACKS employees and affiliates. Five were released on bail in June, but three were detained without charge for nearly three months by the Office of the Prosecutor for State Security before being transferred to Al Huda Prison to await trial.[5] In August, a total of six TRACKS employees and affiliates were charged with various offences including crimes against the state that carry the death penalty. The trial had not concluded by the end of the year.[6]

Between 23 and 28 March, four civil society representatives were intercepted by security officials at Khartoum International Airport while on their way to a high-level meeting with diplomats in Geneva, Switzerland, in preparation for Sudan's examination under the UPR process.[7]

The authorities continued to prevent opposition political parties from organizing peaceful public activities. The NISS prevented the Republican Party from marking the anniversary of the execution of its founder, Mahmoud Mohamed Taha, on 18 January. In February, NISS agents prevented two opposition political parties – the Sudanese Communist Party and Sudanese Congress Party – from holding a public event in Khartoum.

FREEDOM OF EXPRESSION

Arbitrary restrictions on freedom of expression continued. The authorities regularly confiscated newspaper print runs. During 2016, 12 newspapers had their issues confiscated on 44 different occasions. Dozens of journalists were arrested and interrogated by the NISS Media Office and the Press and the Publications Prosecution Office in Khartoum.

In April, the NISS confiscated the daily newspapers *Akhir Lahzah*, *Al Sihaa* and *Al-Tagheer*, without giving reasons. In May, *Alwan*, *Al-Mustagilla* and *Al-Jareeda* newspapers were confiscated by the NISS from the printers. In October, *Al Sihaa* and *Al-Jareeda* newspapers were confiscated.

On 14 August, the National Council for Press and Publications suspended indefinitely the publication of four newspapers: *Elaf*, *Al-Mustagilla*, *Al Watan* and *Awal Al Nahar*. The Council said it had suspended the newspapers because of their continued violation of the regulations in the Press and Publications Act.

ARBITRARY ARRESTS AND DETENTIONS

Across Sudan, NISS officials and members of other security forces targeted opposition political party members, human rights defenders, students and political activists for arbitrary arrest, detention and other violations.

On 1 February, NISS officials arrested four students from Darfur in Khartoum after a protest organized by the United Popular Front, affiliated with the Sudan Liberation Movement-Abdul Wahid Al Nour, against the conflict in Jebel Marra.

In April, violent confrontations between students and security agents went on for three weeks at the University of Khartoum. The protests erupted because of reports that the government was planning to sell some of the university's buildings. Dozens of students were arrested during these protests, including five who were detained without charge in Khartoum.[8] They were released in late April, but some were rearrested in May.

NISS agents raided the office of a prominent human rights lawyer, Nabil Adib, in Khartoum on 5 May and arrested 11 people, including eight students who had been expelled or suspended from the University of Khartoum. All were released by late June.

In Central Darfur state, on 31 July, NISS agents arrested 10 people who had attended a meeting with the US Special Envoy for Sudan and South Sudan during his visit to the region. Of the 10, seven were internally displaced persons. They were all released in September.[9]

EXCESSIVE USE OF FORCE

The authorities arbitrarily restricted freedom of assembly and, on many occasions, used excessive force to disperse gatherings, resulting in several deaths and numerous injuries. No investigations were conducted into the deaths.

In February, NISS officials and students affiliated to the ruling National Congress Party violently disrupted a public seminar organized by a political opposition party at the University of El Geneina. A number of students were seriously injured, and one, Salah al Din Qamar Ibrahim, died as a result of his injuries.

On 19 April, Abubakar Hassan Mohamed Taha, an 18-year-old student at the University of Kordofan, was shot in the head by NISS agents in Al Obied, capital of North Kordofan state. The students had been marching peacefully when heavily armed NISS agents intercepted them, reportedly shooting into the crowd, in an attempt to prevent them from taking part in student union elections. Another 27 students were injured, five of them seriously. The killing of Abubakar Hassan Mohamed Taha provoked nationwide student protests.[10]

On 27 April, 20-year-old Mohamad Al Sadiq Yoyo, a second-year student at the Omdurman Al Ahlia University in Khartoum state, was shot dead by NISS agents.

On 8 May, police forces in Kosti city in White Nile state violently dispersed a peaceful sit-in organized by the Faculty of Engineering Students' Association of the University of Al-Imam Al-Mahdi. The police reportedly used tear gas and batons, injuring about seven students, four of them seriously.

---

1. Sudan: Amnesty International public statement at the 33rd session of the UN Human Rights Council (AFR 54/4875/2016)

2. Sudan: Scorched earth, poisoned air – Sudanese government forces ravage Jebel Marra, Darfur (AFR 54/4877/2016)

3. Sudan: Five years and counting – Intensified aerial bombardment, ground offensive and humanitarian crisis in South Kordofan state (AFR 54/4913/2016)

4. Sudan: Ten civil society activists harassed by NISS (AFR 54/3634/2016)

5. Sudan: Further Information – three human rights defenders still detained (AFR 54/4267/2016)

6. Sudan: Drop all charges and release activists detained for exercising their rights (News story, 29 August)

7. Sudan blocks civil society participation in UN-led human rights review (AFR 54/4310/2016)

8. Sudan: Student activists detained without charge (AFR 54/3861/2016)

9. Sudan: Eight arrested, whereabouts unknown (AFR 54/4617/2016)

10. Sudan: Government must investigate brutal killing of 18-year-old university student by intelligence agents (News story, 20 April)

SWAZILAND

Kingdom of Swaziland
Head of state: **King Mswati III**
Head of government: **Barnabas Sibusiso Dlamini**

Legislation continued to be used to repress dissent. The High Court ruled that security legislation violated the rights to freedom of expression, of association and of assembly, which were protected under the Constitution. The findings of an inquest into a death in police custody were not disclosed. There was insufficient protection against torture and other ill-treatment. Legislation gave the police wide-ranging powers to use lethal force, contrary to international human rights law and standards.

BACKGROUND

Two thirds of the population continued to live below the poverty line. In October, the Afrobarometer research network reported that around half the population said they often went without food and water, and over a third said that medical care was inadequate.

LEGAL DEVELOPMENTS

In May, the King appointed seven senior lawyers to act as Supreme Court judges. The appointments were made in contravention of Article 153 of the Constitution, which stipulates that judges be appointed in an open, transparent and competitive process. As a result, the Law Society of Swaziland boycotted the November Supreme Court session and demanded the appointment of permanent judges in line with the Constitution.

In September, the High Court ruled that sections of the 1938 Sedition and Subversive Activities Act (SSA) and the 2008 Suppression of Terrorism Act (STA) were invalid as they infringed on constitutionally protected rights to freedom of expression, association and assembly. The judgment came after provisions in the laws were challenged in the applications filed in 2009 by human rights lawyer Thulani Maseko. Thulani Maseko was charged under the SSA in 2009. Another application was filed in 2014 by Mario Masuku and Maxwell Dlamini, leaders of the banned opposition People's United Democratic Movement (PUDEMO), who were charged under both Acts in 2014; and by Mlungisi Makhanya and seven others, who were also charged under the Acts in 2014. The government appealed against the High Court's decision in September. The appeal was due to be heard in early 2017.

FREEDOMS OF ASSEMBLY AND ASSOCIATION

The Public Order Bill, if passed, would undermine rights to freedom of peaceful assembly and of association. Among other things, it would criminalize the act of organizing a public gathering without prior notification to the authorities. The bill, which was expected to be passed by the Senate, before being ratified by the King, remained in draft form at the end of the year.

FREEDOM OF EXPRESSION

In June 2016, *The Nation Magazine* published an article by Thulani Maseko in which he questioned the independence of the judiciary. Following this, he and the magazine's editor, Bheki Makhubu, were served with summonses for defamation by an acting judge of the Supreme Court who had been appointed in May.

William Mkhaliphi, an elderly sugar cane farmer from Vuvulane, in northeastern Swaziland, was arrested by police in August after he voiced concerns about alleged royal investments and land grabbing. He had raised concerns at the traditional *Sibaya* meeting convened by the King in Ludzidzini Royal Village where the community were invited to give their views on national issues. William Mkhaliphi was charged following spurious allegations of theft and released on bail by the Magistrates' Court in Simunye the

same month. He was awaiting trial at the end of the year.

DEATHS IN CUSTODY

The authorities had still not made public any findings of an inquest into the death in police custody of Luciano Reginaldo Zavale, a Mozambican national, in June 2015. Independent forensic evidence indicated that he did not die of natural causes and the inquest began in August 2015. According to reports, it reached a conclusion the same year. Luciano Reginaldo Zavale died on the day he was arrested on allegations that he was in possession of a stolen laptop.

TORTURE AND OTHER ILL-TREATMENT

The authorities failed to address inadequate legislative protection against torture and other ill-treatment. Swaziland took no steps to enact national legislation to give effect to its obligations under the UN Convention against Torture to which it acceded in 2004, nor to ratify the Optional Protocol to the UN Convention against Torture.

The Constitution (under Section 15(4)) allowed for the use of lethal force by police in a range of circumstances, including to defend property; to make a lawful arrest or to prevent the escape of a lawfully detained person; to suppress a riot; or to prevent the commission of a serious criminal offence. These grounds remained inconsistent with international human rights law and standards.

There was no independent mechanism for investigating abuses committed by the police. By the end of the year, no investigations had been undertaken into an incident in February when Ayanda Mkhabela, a student at the University of Swaziland (UNISWA), was run over by an armoured police vehicle during a student protest, and left paralysed.

WOMEN'S RIGHTS

Despite high levels of gender-based violence, the Sexual Offences and Domestic Violence Bill, introduced in Parliament in 2009, had not been enacted. Women and girls experiencing gender-based violence had few remedies available to them under domestic law. Nor were they sufficiently protected in law from forced or early marriages.

RIGHT TO AN ADEQUATE STANDARD OF LIVING

In May, Swaziland's human rights record was examined under the UN Universal Periodic (UPR) review process during which a number of concerns were raised. They included the need to address barriers in access to primary education; the reintegration of girls into the education system after giving birth; non-discriminatory access to health and education services irrespective of perceived or actual sexual orientation or gender identity; and the need for measures to be taken to combat and eradicate forced labour.

DEATH PENALTY

No death sentences were imposed during the year. Despite recommendations for a moratorium on the death penalty during the UPR, the death penalty was maintained by Swaziland.

SWEDEN

Kingdom of Sweden
Head of state: King Carl XVI Gustaf
Head of government: Stefan Löfven

New restrictions on residence permits and family reunification for refugees and others granted protection came into force. Roma and Sami peoples faced ongoing discrimination. A parliamentary committee published recommendations to reform inadequate laws on rape.

REFUGEES AND ASYLUM-SEEKERS

In June, Parliament passed a temporary law affecting people entitled to international protection that would apply for three years after coming into force in July. The law limits the length of the residence permits given to persons granted protection, from permanent residence permits to temporary permits of three years for persons granted refugee status and of 13 months for persons granted subsidiary protection. The law also withdrew the possibility of family reunification for those granted subsidiary protection.

DISCRIMINATION – ROMA AND SAMI PEOPLES

Two UN Committees expressed serious concerns about Sweden's treatment of Roma citizens of other European countries. In April, the UN Human Rights Committee called on Sweden to ensure that Roma had equal access to opportunities and services, citing concerns about their limited access to education, employment, housing and health care. In July, the UN ICESCR Committee raised similar concerns, including the resulting vulnerability to forced eviction of many Roma living in informal settlements. Romani people remained at risk of hate crimes based on their ethnicity.

In July, the District Court of Stockholm found that the Skåne police database of nearly 5,000 Swedish-Roma people constituted ethnic discrimination and breached Swedish law. The Court awarded compensation to the complainants for the harm suffered; an appeal by the state was pending at the end of the year.

The UN Human Rights Committee and the ICESCR Committee, in April and July respectively, raised continuing concerns about the ability of Sami people to enjoy the rights of Indigenous Peoples, notably their land rights.

RIGHTS OF LESBIAN, GAY, BISEXUAL, TRANSGENDER AND INTERSEX PEOPLE

In April, the government announced a scheme to provide financial compensation to transgender people who had been required to undergo forced sterilization to legally change their gender.

VIOLENCE AGAINST WOMEN AND GIRLS

In October, the 2014 Sexual Offences Committee inquiry into sexual offences presented its proposals to the government. They included the introduction of a consent-based definition of rape, and liability for negligence for sexual offences.[1]

ARMS TRADE

The Inspectorate of Strategic Products (ISP) – the national authority charged with the control and compliance of defence material and dual-use products – cleared the sale by the Saab Group of the advanced air radar system GlobalEye to the United Arab Emirates. Concerns raised by journalists alleging a lack of due diligence prior to the 2010 sale of the Saab 2000 airborne early warning and Erieye control system to Saudi Arabia, were left unanswered as the ISP's records remained classified. Concerns remained regarding the possible use of these technologies by the Saudi Arabia-led coalition in the conflict in Yemen to commit or facilitate serious violations of international human rights and humanitarian law.

---

1. Sweden: Submission to the UN Committee on the Elimination of Discrimination against Women (EUR 42/3305/2016)

SWITZERLAND

Swiss Confederation
Head of state and government: Johann Schneider-Ammann (replaced Simonetta Sommaruga in January)

A new law on asylum introduced free legal counselling for asylum-seekers. However, concerns remained regarding the respect of the rights of refugees and migrants. Authorities pushed back thousands of asylum-seekers to Italy. In September, the new surveillance law was accepted in a referendum.

REFUGEES' AND MIGRANTS' RIGHTS

In June, a new law on asylum, which had been adopted in September 2015, was accepted by referendum and partly entered into force. The law introduced some positive measures, including free legal counselling for asylum-seekers as of 2019, and the legal duty to take into account the needs of vulnerable asylum-seekers.

In the second half of the year, civil society organizations reported that authorities had pushed back to Italy several thousand asylum-seekers, including several hundred unaccompanied minors; some of them had close family members living in Switzerland.

In July, the Federal Administrative Court concluded that the State Secretariat for Migration had not effectively investigated the case of an asylum-seeking Nigerian woman who was allegedly trafficked into Switzerland.

Asylum-seeking children in reception centres continued to be denied access to education. On 1 October, a new law imposing a duty on cantonal authorities to ensure their right to education entered into force. Concerns remained regarding the restrictions imposed on the right of freedom of movement of asylum-seekers in most federal reception centres.

POLICE AND SECURITY FORCES

In July, the National Commission for the Prevention of Torture raised concerns about police using disproportionate force in some cantons during operations to deport migrants.

Concerns remained regarding the attempted deportations of asylum-seekers with severe mental illnesses. In June, authorities in Neuchâtel unsuccessfully tried to deport a Kurdish asylum-seeker to Bulgaria despite his earlier attempt to commit suicide. In September, two Syrian women asylum-seekers, who had been admitted to a psychiatric hospital in Schaffhausen, attempted suicide shortly after police had removed them from the hospital to deport them. The Zurich Public Prosecutor Office opened an investigation into the events shortly after.

DISCRIMINATION

In May, the Lower Chamber of the Federal Parliament (National Council) voted in favour of a bill allowing second-parent adoption for same-sex couples.

In July, the prohibition of full-face veils entered into force in the Ticino canton. In

September, the Lower Chamber of the Federal Parliament (National Council) adopted a bill to ban full-face veils at the national level. The bill was pending before the Upper Chamber (Council of States) at the end of the year.

In November, the Zurich District Court rejected the appeal introduced by Mohamed Wa Baile, a Swiss citizen of Kenyan origin, who in February 2015 alleged that the police identity check that he was subjected to at the Zurich train station was based on racial discrimination.

On 2 December, the government submitted to Parliament the bill authorizing the ratification of the Council of Europe Convention on preventing and combating violence against women and domestic violence (Istanbul Convention).

COUNTER-TERROR AND SECURITY

In May, the Secretary of State for Migration launched a procedure to strip a 19-year-old bi-national of his Swiss nationality for having allegedly joined the armed group Islamic State without him being charged with any criminal offence.

In September, the surveillance law, which had been adopted in September 2015, was accepted in a referendum. The law grants far-reaching powers to the Federal Intelligence Service to access personal information from a variety of sources and for vaguely defined aims, including counteracting terrorist threats.

SYRIA

Syrian Arab Republic
Head of state: **Bashar al-Assad**
Head of government: **Imad Khamis (replaced Wael Nader al-Halqi in June)**

Parties to the armed conflicts in Syria committed war crimes, other serious violations of international humanitarian law and gross human rights abuses with impunity. Government and allied Russian forces carried out indiscriminate attacks and direct attacks on civilians and civilian objects using aerial bombing and artillery, causing thousands of civilian casualties. There were reports that government forces also used chemical agents. Government forces maintained lengthy sieges that trapped civilians and cut their access to essential goods and services. The authorities arbitrarily arrested and detained thousands, subjecting many to enforced disappearance, prolonged detention and unfair trials, and continued to systematically torture and otherwise ill-treat detainees causing deaths in detention. They also committed unlawful killings, including extrajudicial executions. The armed group Islamic State (IS) besieged civilians, carried out direct attacks on civilians and indiscriminate attacks, sometimes reportedly using chemical agents, perpetrated numerous unlawful killings, and subjected thousands of women and girls to sexual slavery and other abuses. Other non-state armed groups indiscriminately shelled and besieged predominantly civilian areas. US-led forces carried out air strikes on IS and other targets, in which hundreds of civilians were killed. By the end of the year, the conflict had caused the deaths of more than 300,000 people, displaced 6.6 million people within Syria and forced 4.8 million people to seek refuge abroad.

BACKGROUND

The armed conflicts in Syria continued throughout the year with ongoing international participation. Syrian government and allied forces, including Lebanese Hizbullah and other non-Syrian armed groups and militias, controlled much of western Syria and made advances in other contested areas. They were supported by Russian armed forces, which carried out large-scale aerial attacks across Syria, killing and injuring thousands of civilians according to human rights organizations. Some Russian air strikes appeared to be indiscriminate or to amount to direct attacks on civilians and civilian objects, which would constitute war crimes.

Non-state armed groups primarily fighting government forces controlled northwestern and other areas, while forces of the Autonomous Administration controlled most of the predominantly Kurdish northern border regions. IS held parts of eastern and central Syria but lost ground during the year.

The UN Security Council remained divided on Syria and unable to secure a path to peace. Efforts made by the UN Special Envoy for Syria to promote peace talks were largely unsuccessful. In February, a Security Council resolution endorsed a cessation of hostilities agreed by Russia and the USA, but it was short-lived. In October, Russia vetoed a draft Security Council resolution calling for an end to aerial attacks on Aleppo city and for unimpeded humanitarian access. After government forces gained control of Aleppo in December, however, Russian President Vladimir Putin announced that a ceasefire backed by both Russia and Turkey had been agreed between the government and some opposition forces, to be followed by new peace negotiations that would commence in January 2017. On 31 December, the UN Security Council unanimously adopted a resolution welcoming the new peace effort while also calling for the "rapid, safe and unhindered" delivery of humanitarian aid across Syria.

The Independent International Commission of Inquiry on the Syrian Arab Republic, established by the UN Human Rights Council in 2011, monitored and reported on violations of international law committed in Syria although the Syrian government continued to deny it entry to the country.

In December, the UN General Assembly agreed to establish an independent international mechanism to ensure accountability for war crimes and crimes against humanity committed in Syria since March 2011.

ARMED CONFLICT – VIOLATIONS BY SYRIAN GOVERNMENT FORCES AND ALLIES, INCLUDING RUSSIA

Indiscriminate attacks and direct attacks on civilians

Government and allied forces continued to commit war crimes and other serious violations of international law, including direct attacks on civilians and indiscriminate attacks. Government forces repeatedly attacked areas controlled or contested by armed opposition groups, killing and injuring civilians and damaging civilian objects in unlawful attacks. They regularly bombarded civilian areas using explosive weapons with wide-area effects, including artillery shelling and unguided, high-explosive barrel bombs dropped from helicopters. The attacks caused numerous civilian deaths and injuries, including of children.

Government and allied Russian aircraft carried out several apparently deliberate attacks on hospitals, medical centres and clinics and aid convoys, killing and injuring civilians, including medical workers.

As the year progressed, government forces with Russian support increased attacks on eastern Aleppo, hitting residential homes, medical facilities, schools, markets and mosques, killing hundreds of civilians. Russian-made cluster munitions were also scattered across the area, with unexploded munitions posing an ongoing risk to civilians.

Two barrel bombs allegedly containing chlorine gas were dropped by suspected government aircraft on 1 August on two residential neighbourhoods controlled by non-state armed groups in Saraqeb city, Idleb province, reportedly injuring at least 28 civilians.

On 26 October, suspected government or Russian aircraft bombed a school compound in Haas, Idleb governorate, killing at least 35 civilians including 22 children and six teachers.

Sieges and denial of humanitarian access

Government forces maintained prolonged sieges of predominantly civilian areas controlled or contested by armed groups, including in Eastern Ghouta, Mouadhamiyah al-Sham, Madaya, Daraya and, from September, eastern Aleppo. The government sieges exposed civilian residents to starvation and deprived them of access to medical care and other basic services, while subjecting them to repeated air strikes, artillery shelling and other attacks.

The sieges prevented civilians leaving the area to seek medical care. For example, on 19 March a three-year-old boy reportedly died in al-Waer, in Homs city, after government forces prevented him from leaving the area to receive medical care for a head injury.

On 12 May, government forces prevented a UN humanitarian aid delivery, due to be the first since 2012, from entering Daraya. Government forces fired mortars into a residential area of the town, killing two civilians. In June, government forces allowed two limited convoys to enter Daraya but simultaneously intensified their indiscriminate attacks using barrel bombs, a napalm-like incendiary substance and other munitions, forcing the town's remaining inhabitants to submit to being evacuated in late August.

From July, government forces trapped some 275,000 people in eastern Aleppo, subjecting them to intensified air strikes, including bombing by Russian forces. Suspected government and Russian aircraft bombed a UN/Syrian Arab Red Crescent aid convoy destined for eastern Aleppo on 19 September at Urum al-Kubra, killing at least 18 civilians including aid workers, and destroying aid lorries.

Attacks on medical facilities and workers
Government forces continued to target health facilities and medical workers in areas controlled by armed opposition groups. They repeatedly bombed hospitals and other medical facilities, barred or restricted the inclusion of medical supplies in humanitarian aid deliveries to besieged and hard-to-reach areas, and disrupted or prevented health care provision in these areas by detaining medical workers and volunteers. In June, the NGO Physicians for Human Rights accused government forces and their allies of responsibility for more than 90% of 400 attacks against medical facilities and 768 deaths of medical personnel since March 2011.

The UN reported that 44 health facilities were attacked in July alone. Four hospitals and a blood bank in eastern Aleppo city were struck in aerial attacks on 23 and 24 July. One, a children's hospital, was hit twice in less than 12 hours.

ARMED CONFLICT – ABUSES BY ARMED GROUPS
Non-state armed groups committed war crimes, other violations of international humanitarian law and serious human rights abuses.

Indiscriminate attacks and direct attacks on civilians
IS forces carried out direct attacks on civilians as well as indiscriminate attacks in which there were civilian casualties. IS claimed responsibility for a series of suicide and other bomb attacks in the Sayida Zaynab district of southern Damascus, including one on 21 February in which 83 civilians were killed.

IS forces also carried out suspected chemical weapons attacks, including in August and September in northern Syria. Munitions fired by IS at Um Hawsh, near Marea, Aleppo governorate, on 16 September caused blistering and other symptoms common with exposure to mustard agent. Some of those affected were civilians.

The Fatah Halab (Aleppo Conquest) coalition of opposition armed groups repeatedly carried out indiscriminate artillery, rocket and mortar attacks on the Sheikh Maqsoud district of Aleppo city, controlled by Kurdish People's Protection Units known as the YPG, killing at least 83 civilians and injuring more than 700 civilians between February and April. In May, at least four civilians in the area required medical treatment for symptoms that suggested they had been exposed to a chlorine attack.

Armed opposition groups fired imprecise mortars and missiles into government-held western Aleppo, killing at least 14 civilians on 3 November, according to the independent monitoring group Syrian Network for Human Rights.

Unlawful killings

IS forces committed war crimes by summarily killing civilians as well as members of rival armed groups and government forces whom they held prisoner. In areas of al-Raqqa, Deyr al-Zur and eastern Aleppo that it controlled, IS carried out frequent public execution-style killings, including of people they accused of spying, smuggling, adultery and blasphemy.

On 28 July, IS members were reported to have summarily killed at least 25 civilian women, men and children, at Buwayr village near Manbij.

On 19 July, a video published on the internet showed members of the Nour al-Dine al-Zinki Movement ill-treating and then beheading a young male.

Sieges and denial of humanitarian assistance

IS forces besieged and at times indiscriminately shelled government-held neighbourhoods of Deyr al-Zur city. UN agencies and Russian forces repeatedly air-dropped aid into the besieged areas; however, local human rights activists reported that government forces within the besieged areas seized much of the aid intended for civilians.

Abductions

Both IS and other non-state armed groups abducted civilians and held them hostage.

In January, Jabhat al-Nusra abducted at least 11 civilians from their homes in the city of Idleb. Their fate and whereabouts remained undisclosed at the end of the year.

The fate and whereabouts of human rights defender Razan Zaitouneh, her husband Wa'el Hamada, and Nazem Hamadi and Samira Khalil also remained undisclosed following their abduction on 9 December 2013 by unidentified armed men in Duma,

an area controlled by Jaysh al-Islam and other armed groups.

There was no news of the fate or whereabouts of human rights defender Abdullah al-Khalil since his abduction by suspected IS members in al-Raqqa city on the night of 18 May 2013.

ARMED CONFLICT – AIR STRIKES BY US-LED FORCES

The US-led international coalition continued its campaign of air strikes begun in September 2014, predominantly against IS but also certain other armed groups in northern and eastern Syria, including Jabhat Fatah al-Sham (previously known as Jabhat al-Nusra). The air strikes, some of which appeared to be indiscriminate and others disproportionate, killed and injured hundreds of civilians. They included suspected coalition air strikes near Manbij that killed at least 73 civilians at al-Tukhar on 19 July, and up to 28 civilians at al-Ghandoura on 28 July. On 1 December, the US-led coalition was reported to have admitted causing the deaths of 24 civilians near Manbij in July while asserting that its attack had "complied with the law of armed conflict".

ARMED CONFLICT – ATTACKS BY TURKISH FORCES

Turkish forces also carried out air and ground attacks in northern Syria targeting IS and Kurdish armed groups. A Turkish air strike reportedly killed 24 civilians near Suraysat, a village south of Jarablus, on 28 August.

ARMED CONFLICT – ABUSES BY THE PYD-LED AUTONOMOUS ADMINISTRATION

Forces of the Autonomous Administration, which was led by the Democratic Union Party (PYD), controlled most of the predominantly Kurdish northern border regions. In February, YPG forces demolished the houses of dozens of Arab civilians in Tal Tamer, al-Hassakeh governorate, accusing the owners of being IS supporters, according to the UN Office of the High Commissioner for Human Rights. The High Commissioner also reported the forced recruitment of 12 children by the Asayish, Kurdish security forces and the YPG.

According to the Syrian Network for Human Rights, YPG shelling and sniper attacks killed at least 23 civilians in opposition-held areas of Aleppo city between February and April.

REFUGEES AND INTERNALLY DISPLACED PEOPLE

Millions of people continued to be displaced by the conflicts. Some 4.8 million people fled Syria between 2011 and the end of 2016, including 200,000 who became refugees during 2016, according to UNHCR, the UN refugee agency. In the same six-year period, around 6.6 million others were internally displaced within Syria, half of them children, according to the UN Office for the Coordination of Humanitarian Affairs. The authorities in the neighbouring states of Turkey, Lebanon and Jordan, which hosted nearly all of the refugees (including Palestinians displaced from Syria), restricted the entry of new refugees, exposing them to further attacks and deprivation in Syria. More than 75,000 refugees from Syria crossed by sea or land to Europe; many European and other states failed to accept a fair share of refugees from Syria through resettlement or other safe and legal routes.

ENFORCED DISAPPEARANCES

Government forces held thousands of detainees without trial, often in conditions that amounted to enforced disappearance, adding to the tens of thousands whose fate and whereabouts remained undisclosed following their enforced disappearance by government forces since 2011. They included peaceful critics and opponents of the government as well as family members detained in place of relatives whom the authorities sought.

Those who remained forcibly disappeared included human rights lawyer Khalil Ma'touq and his friend Mohamed Thatha, missing since October 2012. Released detainees said they had seen Khalil Ma'touq in government detention but the authorities denied holding

the men. Thousands of people, mostly Islamists, remained disappeared since they were detained by Syrian government forces in the late 1970s and early 1980s.

TORTURE AND OTHER ILL-TREATMENT

Torture and other ill-treatment of detainees by government security and intelligence agencies and in state prisons remained systematic and widespread. Torture and other ill-treatment continued to result in a high incidence of detainee deaths, adding to the thousands of deaths in custody since 2011.[1]

In August the Human Rights Data Analysis Group, an NGO that uses scientific approaches to analyze human rights violations, estimated that there were at least 17,723 deaths in government custody between March 2011 and December 2015, resulting from torture and other ill-treatment.

UNFAIR TRIALS

The authorities prosecuted some perceived opponents before the Anti-Terrorism Court and the Military Field Court, both of whose proceedings were flagrantly unfair. Judges failed to order investigations into allegations by defendants that they had been tortured or otherwise ill-treated or coerced into making "confessions" that were used as evidence against them at trial.

UNLAWFUL KILLINGS

Government and allied forces committed unlawful killings, including extrajudicial executions. On 13 December, the UN High Commissioner for Human Rights said that government and allied forces had entered civilian homes and committed summary killings as they advanced through east Aleppo and that, according to "multiple sources", they had killed at least 82 civilians, including 13 children, on 12 December.

WOMEN'S RIGHTS

On 15 June the independent Commission of Inquiry determined that thousands of Yazidi women and girls were forcibly transferred by IS forces into Syria from Sinjar, Iraq, sold in markets and held in slavery, including sexual slavery. Many women and girls were subjected to sexual violence, rape and other torture. Women and girls caught trying to escape were gang-raped or otherwise tortured or harshly punished; one woman said that the fighter who had bought her killed several of her children and repeatedly raped her after she had tried to flee.

DEATH PENALTY

The death penalty remained in force for many offences. The authorities disclosed little information about death sentences and no information on executions.

1. "It breaks the human": Torture, disease and death in Syria's prisons (MDE 24/4508/2016)

TAIWAN

Taiwan
Head of state: Tsai Ing-wen (replaced Ma Ying-jeou in May)
Head of government: Lin Chuan (replaced Mao Chi-kuo in May)

Elections in January resulted in Tsai Ing-wen of the Democratic Progressive Party (DPP) becoming the country's first woman President. There were some positive developments in three longstanding death penalty cases but several violent incidents sparked public calls for retaining the punishment. The new government decided to drop charges against more than 100 protesters from the 2014 "Sunflower Movement". The same-sex couple relationship register was extended to 10 municipalities and counties. The Legislative Yuan's judicial committee passed amendments to the Civil Code proposed by two DPP legislators, a step towards legalizing same-sex marriage.

FREEDOM OF ASSEMBLY

On 23 May, Prime Minister Lin Chuan announced that the new cabinet was dropping criminal charges against 126 protesters. He stated that the previous government's decision to charge the protesters was a "political reaction" to the demonstration instead of merely a "legal case". In March 2014, student-led protests against the Cross-Strait Services Trade Agreement between Taiwan and China, referred to as the "Sunflower Movement", had led to 24 days of demonstrations, the occupation of the Legislative Yuan (Taiwan's parliament), and a 10-hour occupation of the Executive Yuan, the government offices.

DEATH PENALTY

Two weeks before the previous government ended its term in May, the Taichung Branch of the Taiwan High Court released Cheng Hsing-tse on bail pending a retrial. He had served 14 years in prison after he was convicted of the murder of a police officer during an exchange of gunfire at a karaoke parlour in Taichung in 2002. The Prosecutor-General's office applied for a retrial in March, citing new evidence which raised doubts about his conviction. This was the first retrial sought in a case where the final Supreme Court's ruling upheld the death sentence.

In July 2016, the Prosecutor-General applied for an extraordinary appeal for Chiou Ho-shun. He had been imprisoned since 1989, the longest-serving death row inmate in modern Taiwan history. The application cited the failure of previous courts to omit evidence from a coerced "confession". Chiou Ho-shun was tortured in custody and forced to "confess" before being found guilty of robbery, kidnapping and murder.

On 13 October, the Supreme Court upheld the High Court's decision to acquit Hsu Tzi-chiang, who had repeatedly appealed against his convictions for kidnapping, extortion and murder in 1995.

REFUGEES AND ASYLUM-SEEKERS

The Legislative Yuan's Internal Administration Committee passed a second reading of a refugee bill on 14 July. It would be the first such law in Taiwan if passed, and may allow asylum-seekers from mainland China to apply for political asylum in Taiwan.

TAJIKISTAN

Republic of Tajikistan
Head of state: **Emomali Rahmon**
Head of government: **Qokhir Rasulzoda**

The space for peaceful dissent continued to shrink drastically. The authorities invoked national security concerns and the fight against terrorism to justify increasingly harsh restrictions on freedoms of expression and association. Members of the banned opposition Islamic Renaissance Party of Tajikistan (IRPT) were sentenced to life and long-term imprisonment on terrorism charges in blatantly unfair secret trials. Allegations that they were tortured to obtain confessions were not effectively and impartially investigated. Lawyers representing IRPT members faced harassment, arbitrary detention, prosecution and long prison terms on politically motivated charges.

BACKGROUND

In May a national referendum approved wide-ranging amendments to the Constitution. These included removing the limit on presidential terms in office, effectively enabling President Rahmon to retain the presidency beyond the next elections, and banning religion- and nationality-based political parties. In November "insulting the leader of the nation" was made a criminal offence.

At least 170 individuals were prosecuted, convicted and sentenced to prison for their alleged involvement in the armed clashes between government forces and armed groups in the capital, Dushanbe, in September 2015, which the authorities described as an attempt to seize power by a former deputy defence minister, Abdukhalim Nazarzoda. Due to the authorities' near-total control of news reporting there was little independent public scrutiny of the official account which, in turn, cast doubt on the prosecutions.

Exiled members of the banned opposition party, Islamic Renaissance Party of Tajikistan (IRPT) and opposition "Group 24" activists attended and picketed the annual Human Dimension Implementation Meeting of the OSCE in Warsaw, Poland, in September. Some reported that police and security services threatened, arbitrarily detained, questioned and in some cases physically assaulted their family members in Tajikistan in retaliation for their peaceful protest in Warsaw. The government delegation left the event early in protest against a "terrorist organisation banned in Tajikistan" being admitted among other civil society participants.

UNFAIR TRIALS

The authorities continued to emphatically reject allegations of the politically motivated criminal prosecution, unfair trial and torture and other ill-treatment of 14 IRPT leaders for their alleged role in the September 2015 clashes. The trial at the Supreme Court began in February and was conducted in secrecy, inside the pre-trial detention centre of the State Committee for National Security. In June, all the defendants were convicted. Two deputy IRPT leaders, Umarali Khisainov (also known as Saidumur Khusaini) and Makhmadali Khaitov (Mukhammadalii Hait), were given life sentences. Zarafo Khujaeva (Rakhmoni) was sentenced to two years in prison; she was released on 5 September under a presidential pardon. Other sentences ranged from 14 to 28 years.

The sparse initial official information relating to the prosecution of the IRPT leaders, including the charges they faced, had already been removed from official sources (including the Prosecutor General's Office website and the official news agency Khovar) in 2015, and any further information suppressed. The defence lawyers were compelled to sign non-disclosure agreements regarding all details of the case and the legal proceedings. The verdict and official records of the court proceedings were not officially released. In August, a leaked copy of the verdict was published online. The Prosecutor

General's Office refused to comment on its authenticity but its suspected source was nevertheless prosecuted (see below).

In March the UN Special Rapporteur on freedom of expression expressed concern that "the drastic measures taken against IRPT represent a serious setback for an open political environment. The government accuses the IRPT and its members of serious crimes but it has refused to give public access to the trial and evidence".[1]

Persecution of defence lawyers

Lawyers who worked on the case of the 14 IRPT leaders faced harassment, intimidation and, in some cases, arbitrary detention and prosecution. In October, the Dushanbe City Court sentenced Buzurgmekhr Yorov and Nuriddin Makhkamov, two lawyers representing several co-defendants in the IRPT case, to 23 and 21 years in prison respectively following an unfair trial. Apart from the first court hearing in May, all sessions were closed to the media and the public. Both lawyers were found guilty of "arousing national, racial, local or religious hostility", fraud, "public calls for violent change of the constitutional order of the Republic of Tajikistan", and "public calls for undertaking extremist activities". Buzurgmekhr Yorov was also found guilty of forgery. Both denied any wrongdoing and an appeal was pending at the end of the year. Neither will be able to practise law upon release unless their convictions are fully overturned.[2]

On 22 August, Jamshed Yorov, also a defence lawyer in the IRPT case and the brother of Buzurgmekhr Yorov, was detained on charges of "divulging state secrets". He was accused of leaking the text of the Supreme Court's decision in the IRPT case. He was released on 30 September.

A second trial against Buzurgmekhr Yorov opened on 12 December at pre-trial detention centre number 1 in Dushanbe. He was accused of disrespecting the court and insulting government officials in his final statement to Dushanbe City Court.

TORTURE AND OTHER ILL-TREATMENT

In May, legal safeguards against torture and other ill-treatment of detainees were strengthened. These included: reducing the maximum length of time a person can be held in detention without charge to three days; defining detention as starting from the moment of de facto deprivation of liberty; giving detainees the right to confidential access to a lawyer from the moment of deprivation of liberty; and making medical examinations of suspects obligatory prior to placing them in temporary detention.

There were still no independent mechanisms for the investigation of torture or other ill-treatment. The NGO Coalition against Torture registered 60 complaints of torture but believed the real figure to be much higher.

In September, the UN Human Rights Council adopted the outcomes of the Universal Periodic Review (UPR) of Tajikistan. The government rejected recommendations to ratify the Optional Protocol to the Convention against Torture and set up a National Preventive Mechanism. It did, however, accept recommendations to ratify the Second Optional Protocol to the ICCPR and to fully abolish the death penalty.

FREEDOM OF ASSOCIATION

The Ministry of Justice provided draft regulations for the implementation of the amended Law on Public Associations. However, it failed to specify time limits for decisions on the compulsory registration of foreign funding for NGOs, or to clarify whether a grant could be used before the official registration. The draft regulations limited inspections of NGOs to once every two years, but left this rule and the grounds for inspections open to wide interpretation.

In January a district court dismissed the Tax Committee's liquidation proceedings against the established human rights and democracy think tank, Nota Bene.

FREEDOM OF EXPRESSION

The authorities continued to impose further restrictions on the media and reduced access to independent information. In August the government issued a five-year decree giving it the right to "regulate and control" the content of all television and radio networks through the State Broadcasting Committee.

Independent media outlets and individual journalists faced intimidation and harassment by police and the security services for covering the IRPT case and other politically sensitive issues. Some were forced to leave the country. In November, independent newspaper *Nigoh* and independent website Tojnews announced their closure because "conditions no longer exist for independent media and free journalism". *Nigoh* had reported on the trial of lawyer Buzurgmekhr Yorov.

The authorities continued to order internet service providers to block access to certain news or social media sites, but without acknowledging this publicly. Individuals and groups affected by the measures were not able to effectively challenge them in court. A government decree also required internet providers and telecommunications operators to channel their services through a new single communications centre under the state-owned company Tajiktelecom. In March, the UN Special Rapporteur on freedom of expression expressed concern that "the widespread blocking of websites and networks, including mobile services… was disproportionate and incompatible with international standards".

RIGHTS TO WATER AND SANITATION

In July the UN Special Rapporteur on the human right to safe drinking water and sanitation published his report on Tajikistan. The report found that approximately 40% of the population, and nearly half of the rural population, relied on water supply sources which were often insufficient or did not meet water quality standards. This put a significant burden on women and children, some of whom spent on average four to six hours each day fetching water. The Special Rapporteur noted that the lack of water and sanitation in public institutions in particular had a direct negative impact on other rights, such as the rights to health, education, work and life. He urged the government to eliminate disparities in access to water and sanitation and to address the needs of the most vulnerable groups, including women and girls in rural areas, resettled people, refugees, asylum-seekers and stateless persons.

The government accepted recommendations from the UPR process to improve access to safe drinking water but rejected recommendations to ratify the Optional Protocol to the ICESCR.

1. Tajikistan: A year of secrecy, growing fears and deepening injustice (EUR 60/4855/2016)

2. Tajikistan: A year of secrecy, growing fears and deepening injustice (EUR 60/4855/2016)

TANZANIA

United Republic of Tanzania
Head of state: **John Magufuli**
Head of government: **Kassim Majaliwa**
Head of Zanzibar government: **Ali Mohamed Shein**

The rights to freedom of expression and of peaceful assembly were restricted. The authorities failed to address discrimination on grounds of gender identity and sexual orientation.

FREEDOM OF ASSEMBLY

The months leading up to elections in Zanzibar in March were marked by violence. At least 200 people were injured, 12 women sexually assaulted and one woman was raped. More than 100 members of the opposition Civic United Front (CUF), including the Director of Publicity, were arrested for protesting against the election re-run, after the 2015 general elections were nullified following claims of irregularities. There were reports of excessive use of force against CUF supporters by the police, and an unidentified armed group of masked men using government registered vehicles. Despite many complaints to the authorities, no prosecutions were brought against the police.

In June, all political rallies were banned by the President until 2020. In response, opposition parties called for peaceful protests under the banner UKUTA (Alliance against Dictatorship in Tanzania), which resulted in the police extending the ban to include internal party meetings. Two opposition leaders and 35 supporters from both the mainland and Zanzibar were arrested and charged with various offences including incitement to protest.

FREEDOM OF EXPRESSION – JOURNALISTS

Four media houses were closed and journalists arrested and charged with various offences under the Penal Code, the Cybercrimes Act and the Newspapers Act. The weekly *Mawio* was permanently closed and three journalists were charged with sedition for reporting on the elections in Zanzibar and the ensuing political crisis. The weekly *Mseto* was banned for three years for breach of the Newspapers Act after it published an article implicating a senior government official in corruption. Radio stations Radio Five and Magic FM were also closed for allegedly airing seditious material.

Two women and six men were charged under the Cybercrimes Act for posting information about the elections and the President on Facebook.

WOMEN'S RIGHTS

Tanzania failed to implement the recommendations of the UN Committee on the Elimination of Discrimination against Women (CEDAW Committee) in the 2015 case *E.S. and S.C. v the United Republic of Tanzania*. The case, submitted before the Committee in 2012, concerned two Tanzanian widows who, under Tanzania's customary inheritance law, were denied the right to inherit or administer the estates of their late husbands. In 2016, the Committee

recommended reform of the Local Customary Law (Declaration No.4) which discriminated against women in relation to property administration and inheritance rights.

A landmark court decision in September declared unconstitutional Sections 13 and 17 of the Law of Marriage Act, which allowed child marriage of girls aged under 18. Tanzania has one of the highest child marriage rates in the world, with 37% of girls under 18 already married. The Attorney General appealed against the ruling.

RIGHTS OF LESBIAN, GAY, BISEXUAL, TRANSGENDER AND INTERSEX PEOPLE

The authorities began a crackdown on LGBTI people, threatening to suspend organizations that supported them. Staff were arrested and documents confiscated during a raid of the offices of the Community Health Education Services and Advocacy in August.

Police arrested 20 LGBTI people in Dar es Salaam in August. Most were held for more than 48 hours before being released without charge. In November, the authorities suspended community-based HIV/AIDS prevention programmes for gay men.

THAILAND

Kingdom of Thailand
Head of State: **King Maha Vajiralongkorn Bodindradebayavarangkun (replaced King Bhumibol Adulyadej in December)**
Head of Government: **Prayut Chan-o-Cha**

The military authorities further restricted human rights. Peaceful political dissent, whether through speech or protests, and acts perceived as critical of the monarchy were punished or banned. Politicians, activists and human rights defenders faced criminal investigations and prosecutions for, among other things, campaigning against a proposed Constitution and reporting on state abuses. Many civilians were tried in military courts. Torture and other ill-treatment was widespread. Community land rights activists faced arrest, prosecution

and violence for opposing development projects and advocating for the rights of communities.

BACKGROUND

Thailand remained under the authority of the National Council for Peace and Order (NCPO), a group of military authorities which have held power since a 2014 coup. The August referendum approved a draft Constitution that would allow the army to retain considerable power. Elections were set to follow in late 2017 at the earliest.

The prosecution of former Prime Minister Yingluck Shinawatra for alleged criminal negligence in the management of a government rice subsidy scheme continued. In October, the government ordered her to pay a 35.7 billion baht (US$1 billion) fine over the government losses from the scheme.

The EU remained unsatisfied with the authorities' progress to end illegal and unregulated fishing and abusive labour practices.

JUSTICE SYSTEM

The Head of the NCPO continued to use extraordinary powers under Article 44 of the interim Constitution to issue orders, some of which arbitrarily restricted the exercise of human rights, including peaceful political activities. In March he issued an order expanding the law enforcement powers of military officers, which allowed officers to detain individuals without court approval for a broad range of criminal activities.[1]

Civilians were tried before military courts for violations of NCPO orders, crimes against national security and insulting the monarchy. In September, the Head of the NCPO issued an order rescinding the military courts' jurisdiction over cases involving civilians, which was not retroactive. Trials continued in military courts.

FREEDOMS OF EXPRESSION, ASSOCIATION AND ASSEMBLY

Peaceful critics were penalized for exercising their rights to freedom of expression, of peaceful assembly and of association.

Individuals perceived as supporting government critics – including relatives, members of the public, lawyers and journalists – also faced harassment and prosecution.

The Constitutional Referendum Act, which governed the August referendum, provided for up to 10 years' imprisonment for activities and statements "causing confusion to affect orderliness of voting", including by using "offensive" or "rude" language to influence votes. The law was used to target those who opposed the draft Constitution. More than 100 people were reportedly charged with offences related to the referendum.[2]

Amendments to the Computer Crimes Act allowed for continued surveillance without prior judicial authorization and failed to bring the law in line with international law and standards on the rights to privacy and freedom of expression. The authorities also considered increased online surveillance and greater control of internet traffic.

Individuals were charged with or convicted of offences under Article 112 of the Penal Code for criticizing the monarchy. The Article carried a prison sentence of up to 15 years. Military courts interpreted the provisions broadly and imposed sentences of up to 60 years' imprisonment for convictions on multiple counts of the offence, including against people with mental illnesses. Bail was routinely denied to those arrested under Article 112.

Individuals were charged or convicted under a ban on political gatherings of five or more people imposed by a 2015 order from the NCPO Head. It was used especially against opposition political groups and pro-democracy activists. In June, the authorities initiated criminal proceedings against 19 members of the United Front for Democracy against Dictatorship for holding a press conference to celebrate the opening of a centre to monitor the constitutional referendum. Pro-democracy student activists faced charges in multiple criminal cases for peaceful protests and other public activities opposing military rule and Thailand's draft Constitution.

The authorities sought to silence those raising concerns about torture and other ill-treatment. In September, Amnesty International was forced to cancel a press conference in the capital Bangkok to launch a report on torture, after officials threatened to arrest the scheduled speakers.[3]

Somchai Homla-or, Anchana Heemmina and Pornpen Khongkachonkiet were charged with criminal defamation and violations of the Computer Crime Act for reporting on torture by soldiers in southern Thailand.[4] A 25-year-old woman faced similar charges after campaigning to hold accountable military officers responsible for the torture and killing of her uncle, a military trainee.

Authorities cancelled many events involving discussions about human rights or political events. In October, immigration officials detained and forcibly returned to Hong Kong pro-democracy activist Joshua Wong, who was invited to speak at a commemoration of the 1976 massacre of student protesters by Thai authorities.[5]

ARBITRARY ARRESTS AND DETENTION

The authorities continued to use Head of NCPO Order 3/2015 to arbitrarily detain individuals incommunicado for up to seven days without charge for what became known as "attitude adjustment" sessions.[6]

Journalist Pravit Rojanaphruk, like many others previously arbitrarily detained, remained bound by restrictive conditions of release. He was prevented from travelling to Helsinki for a UNESCO World Press Freedom Day event.

HUMAN RIGHTS DEFENDERS

Human rights defenders faced prosecution, imprisonment, harassment and physical violence for their peaceful work. Sirikan Charoensiri, a leading human rights lawyer, was charged with multiple offences, including sedition, for her legal work. She faced up to 15 years' imprisonment.

Economic, social and cultural rights activists were subject to prosecutions and lawsuits initiated by private corporations, often for alleged defamation or violations of the Computer Crimes Act. A gold mining company had initiated criminal and civil proceedings against at least 33 people who opposed its operations. Andy Hall, a migrants' rights activist, was convicted in September for his contribution to a report on labour rights violations by a fruit company.[7]

Human rights defenders, especially those working on land issues or with community-based organizations, faced harassment, threats and physical violence. In April, unidentified assailants shot and injured Supoj Kansong, a land rights activist from the Khlong Sai Pattana community in southern Thailand. Four activists from that community had previously been killed; by the end of the year no one had been held accountable for the killings.[8] In October, the Department of Special Investigations informed human rights lawyer Somchai Neelapaijit's family that it was closing its investigation into his enforced disappearance in 2004, due to lack of evidence.

ARMED CONFLICT

There was little progress in government negotiations to resolve a decades-long conflict with ethnic-Malay separatists in southern Thailand. Insurgents carried out numerous attacks on military and civilian targets in the region and both sides of the conflict were accused of grave human rights abuses. Insurgent groups targeted civilians with bombings and, in March, attacked a hospital in Narathiwat province.

TORTURE AND OTHER ILL-TREATMENT

Members of the military continued to torture individuals suspected of links to insurgents in the south and political and security detainees elsewhere, facilitated by laws and orders allowing soldiers to detain individuals in unofficial places of detention without judicial oversight for up to seven days.[9] Two military recruits reportedly died after alleged torture in military camps. Torture and other ill-treatment by the security forces in the context of routine law enforcement operations were also reported. Police officers and soldiers were also responsible for human rights violations against members of vulnerable communities, including migrant workers, ethnic minorities, and suspected drug users at police stations, roadblocks, and various unofficial places of detention.

Thailand considered new legislation criminalizing torture and enforced disappearances.

REFUGEES AND ASYLUM-SEEKERS

The legal system did not provide formal recognition for refugees and asylum-seekers, leaving many vulnerable to abuse. Asylum-seekers, including children, faced months or years of indefinite detention in crowded immigration detention centres. Scores of Rohingya people had remained in these centres since they arrived by boat during a regional migration crisis in 2015. The authorities did not adequately address their protection needs as asylum-seekers and potential victims of human trafficking.

1. Thailand: Human rights groups condemn NCPO Order 13/2016 and urge for it to be revoked immediately (ASA 39/3783/2016)

2. Thailand: Open letter on human rights concerns in the run-up to the constitutional referendum (ASA 39/4548/2016)

3. Thailand: Torture victims must be heard (News story, 28 September)

4. Amnesty International Thailand's Chair and other activists face jail for exposing torture (News story, 25 July)

5. Thailand: Denial of entry to Hong Kong student activist a new blow to freedom of expression (News story, 5 October)

6. Thailand: Prisoner of conscience must be released: Watana Muangsook (ASA 39/3866/2016)

7. Thailand: Another human rights activist is unjustly targeted (News story, 20 September)

8. Thailand: Authorities must protect human rights defenders in the line of fire (ASA 39/3805/2016)

9. "Make him speak by tomorrow": Torture and other ill-treatment in Thailand (ASA 39/4747/2016)

TIMOR-LESTE

Democratic Republic of Timor-Leste
Head of state: **Taur Matan Ruak**
Head of government: **Rui Maria de Araújo**

Victims of serious human rights violations committed during the Indonesian occupation (1975-1999) continued to demand justice and reparations. Security forces were accused of unlawful killings, torture and other ill-treatment, arbitrary arrests, and arbitrarily restricting the rights to freedom of expression and of peaceful assembly.

BACKGROUND

In August, hundreds of civil society activists gathered in the capital, Dili, at a parallel conference to an ASEAN summit to discuss human rights and other regional issues. In November, Timor-Leste's human rights record was examined under the UN Universal Periodic Review (UPR) process.

IMPUNITY

A working group was established by the Prime Minister in May to advise the government on implementation of the recommendations of the Commission for Reception, Truth and Reconciliation (CAVR), issued in 2005. Many recommendations related to impunity had not been implemented by the end of 2016. The expulsion of non-Timorese judges in 2014 continued to hamper the trials of individuals indicted for serious crimes.

POLICE AND SECURITY FORCES

Concerns remained about allegations of unnecessary or excessive use of force, torture and other ill-treatment by security forces, and a lack of accountability. In August a member of the Border Control Unit shot and killed a man with mental illness in Suai. In the same month a police officer hit a journalist in Dili. By the end of the year, no one had been held to account for the torture and other ill-treatment of dozens of individuals detained during joint security operations in Baucau district in 2015. These were launched in response to attacks allegedly carried out by Mauk Moruk (Paulino Gama) and his banned Maubere Revolutionary Council against police in Laga and Baguia subdistricts.[1]

FREEDOM OF EXPRESSION

In January, security forces ordered an activist from the NGO Yayasan HAK to remove his T-shirt saying "Free West Papua". They also threatened to arrest other human rights activists for their role in organizing a peaceful protest during a visit by the Indonesian President and signing a joint statement calling for accountability for crimes against humanity during the Indonesian occupation.[2]

On 11 April, two journalists were charged in relation to a defamation lawsuit.

VIOLENCE AGAINST WOMEN AND GIRLS

Gender-based violence remained a significant issue. A survey revealed that three in five women between the ages of 15 and 49, who had ever been in a relationship, had suffered sexual or other physical violence by a husband or male partner in their lifetime. In April, Timor-Leste became the third southeast Asian state to adopt a National Action Plan for Women, Peace and Security for 2016-2020.

---

1. Timor-Leste: Still no justice – submission to the UN Universal Periodic Review, November 2016 (ASA 57/4531/2016)

2. Timor-Leste: Harassed for organizing peaceful rally (ASA 57/3334/2016)

TOGO

Togolese Republic
Head of state: **Faure Gnassingbé**
Head of government: **Komi Sélom Klassou**

Security forces continued to use excessive force against demonstrators. Arbitrary arrests and detentions, torture and other ill-treatment, and impunity for human rights violations persisted. A law revising the Criminal Code was adopted to make torture not subject to prescription under Togolese law. Other legislative developments undermined the independence of the National Human Rights Commission and the right to freedom of association.

BACKGROUND

In September, Togo ratified the Second Optional Protocol to the International Covenant on Civil and Political Rights, aiming at the abolition of the death penalty.

Togo was examined under the UN Universal Periodic Review (UPR) process in October.[1] Concerns by UN member states included impunity and restrictions on freedom of expression and freedom of peaceful assembly. States also raised concerns about the failure of the authorities to guarantee free birth registration, which can undermine children's access to education, health care and other social services.

EXCESSIVE USE OF FORCE

In January, police and gendarmerie officers threw tear gas canisters at the University of Lomé during a protest in which five students and three members of the security forces were injured.

In August, the security forces injured at least 10 people during a protest in Abobo-Zéglé. People were protesting against evictions from their land to make room for phosphate extraction. During the protest, security forces charged them with tear gas, batons and live ammunition. The community considered they had not received adequate compensation for their eviction.

TORTURE AND OTHER ILL-TREATMENT

In October, the National Assembly adopted a revision of the Criminal Code which defined torture in line with the UN Convention against Torture and made it an imprescriptible crime.

Cases of torture and other ill-treatment continued to be reported throughout the year.

In June, three police officers arrested Ibrahim Agriga at his home in Guerin Kouka. He was taken to a police station and beaten with batons on his buttocks and the soles of his feet to make him "confess" to a motorbike theft. He was released without charge after three days and filed a complaint with the tribunal of Guerin Kouka. No investigation was known to have been initiated at the end of the year.

ARBITRARY ARRESTS AND DETENTIONS

The authorities continued to subject people to arbitrary detention, in particular those who expressed dissent.

On 1 April, Adamou Moussa and Zékeria Namoro were arbitrarily detained in Dapaong after they had called for justice for people killed during protests in Mango in November 2015; seven civilians and one police officer were killed. During their interrogation, the gendarmes accused Zékeria Namoro of sharing information on the human rights situation in Mango with journalists, diaspora groups and human rights organizations. The men were charged with "incitement to commit a crime" and released on bail on 6 September.

Five men remained in detention without trial in relation to the November 2015 demonstrations in Mango. There were concerns that they may be held solely because they were the organizers of the protest.

Seven out of 10 men convicted in September 2011 for participating in a 2009 coup plot, including Kpatcha Gnassingbé, half-brother of the President, remained in detention at the end of 2016.

FREEDOM OF ASSOCIATION

In April, the Council of Ministers adopted a bill on freedom of association which failed to meet international standards. It stated that "foreign or international associations" required prior authorization to operate in Togo. The law also provided that associations must respect national laws and morals. This could be used to discriminate against lesbian, gay, bisexual, transgender and intersex people, as sexual relations between consenting adults of the same sex remained a crime. The bill also provided that associations may be dissolved on the basis of a decision of the Council of Ministers or the Minister of Territorial Administration in the case of "foreign and international associations". Finally, it granted tax incentives to associations which accepted increased government control over their objectives and activities.

IMPUNITY

The climate of impunity for human rights violations persisted.

In March, a law was adopted on freedom to access to information and public documentation to facilitate greater transparency and accountability. However, in April, the National Assembly adopted a new Code of Military Justice which will fuel impunity as it gives military courts the power to investigate and judge ordinary criminal offences committed by military personnel, including rape and torture. The courts' jurisdiction extended to civilians.

In March, the National Human Rights Commission published its report on the November 2015 demonstrations in Mango. Despite its conclusion that "a lack of professionalism of certain elements of the security and law enforcement forces and the insufficiency of the elements deployed" led to "an excessive use of force", no member of the security forces had been brought to trial and none of the victims had received compensation at the end of 2016.

More than 11 years have passed since the deaths of nearly 500 people during the violence surrounding the presidential election of 24 April 2005, the authorities have taken no steps to identify those responsible for the deaths. Of the 72 complaints filed by the victims' families with the Atakpamé, Amlamé and Lomé courts, none are known to have been fully investigated.

LEGAL, CONSTITUTIONAL OR INSTITUTIONAL DEVELOPMENTS

In March, the National Assembly adopted a law enabling the President to appoint members of the National Human Rights Commission without parliamentary oversight. The law also established the National Preventive Mechanism – aimed at preventing and investigating cases of torture – within the National Human Rights Commission, raising concerns about its ability to function independently.

1. Togo: The participating states to the UPR review must call for the protection of the rights to freedom of association, peaceful assembly and expression in Togo (AFR 03/5064/2016)

TUNISIA

Republic of Tunisia
Head of state: Beji Caid Essebsi
Head of government: Youssef Chahed (replaced Habib Essid in August)

The authorities continued to restrict the rights to freedom of expression and of assembly, and used emergency powers and anti-terrorism laws to impose arbitrary restrictions on liberty and freedom of movement. There were new reports of torture and other ill-treatment of detainees. Women remained subject to discrimination in law and practice and were inadequately protected against gender-based violence. Same-sex sexual relations remained criminalized, and lesbian, gay, bisexual, transgender and intersex (LGBTI) people faced arrest and imprisonment. Courts continued to impose death sentences; there were no executions.

BACKGROUND

The authorities renewed the nationwide state of emergency in force since November 2015 and announced in February that they had completed the construction of a security wall along Tunisia's border with Libya. Despite this, armed clashes between government forces and Libya-based members of the armed group Islamic State (IS) continued in border areas. On 7 March, at least 68 people were killed, including seven civilians, in clashes that ensued when government forces repulsed an IS attack on military bases and a police station in Ben Guerdane, a southern border town. Clashes between armed groups and the security forces continued on the border with Algeria with fatalities on both sides.

New members of the Supreme Judicial Council, which is responsible for the selection, appointment, transfer, removal, discipline and training of judges and prosecutors, were announced in October. The establishment of the Supreme Judicial Council finally allowed for the creation of the Constitutional Court, as it is responsible for appointing a third of the Court's members.

Parliament approved a proposed law criminalizing racial and other discrimination; it had still to be enacted at the end of the year.

The UN Committee against Torture and the UN Committee on Economic, Social and Cultural Rights reviewed Tunisia's human rights record in May and September respectively. The UN Subcommittee on Prevention of Torture visited Tunisia in April.

TRANSITIONAL JUSTICE

The Truth and Dignity Commission, created to address political, social and economic crimes and investigate human rights violations committed between 1 July 1955 and December 2013, reported in June that it had received more than 62,000 complaints concerning a wide range of human rights violations, including arbitrary detentions, torture, unfair trials, sexual violence and religious and ethnic discrimination. The Commission's first public hearings were held on 17 November.

Parliament resumed consideration of a controversial draft law in June that would offer immunity for some financial crimes. Discussion of the proposed law, first proposed by President Essebsi, was suspended in 2015 following protests led by the popular movement Manich Msameh ("I will not forgive"). If adopted, the proposed law would offer officials and business executives accused of corruption and embezzlement under the administration of former President Zine El 'Abidine Ben 'Ali an amnesty and immunity from further prosecution if they return the proceeds of their crimes. Its immunity provisions would also undermine investigations under the transitional justice process. The draft law had not been enacted at the end of the year.

ARBITRARY ARRESTS AND DETENTIONS, AND FREEDOM OF MOVEMENT

The authorities used their powers under the state of emergency to conduct thousands of arrests and house searches, in many cases without judicial warrants. The authorities subjected hundreds of people to administrative house arrest, assigned places of residence, travel bans or restrictions on movement – measures that curtailed their social and economic rights, including the right to work.

COUNTER-TERROR AND SECURITY

Security officials harassed and intimidated many families of people they suspected of joining or supporting armed groups, repeatedly raiding and searching their homes, threatening and interrogating them, harassing them at their places of work and restricting their freedom of movement. Security officials also harassed and intimidated dozens of former prisoners sentenced under repressive laws during the former Ben 'Ali administration and other people on account of their appearance, including men with beards and men and women dressed in what officials deemed to be religious clothing.

TORTURE AND OTHER ILL-TREATMENT

There were new reports of torture and other ill-treatment of detainees, mostly during arrest and in pre-charge detention. Several of those detained following the attack in Ben Guerdane in March alleged that police and counter-terrorism officers tortured them during interrogation in both Ben Guerdane and the capital, Tunis. They said officers subjected them to the "roast chicken" method of torture – rotating them on a pole inserted between their handcuffed wrists and feet – as well as beatings, sexual assault and prolonged solitary confinement. While some were released, others remained in detention at the end of the year.

Parliament approved changes to the Code of Criminal Procedures in February, strengthening safeguards against torture and other ill-treatment, which took effect in June. The reforms cut the maximum period that a detainee can be held without charge from six to four days and gave those detained the rights of immediate access to a lawyer and their family and to have their lawyer present at their interrogation. The new provisions also required that detentions be authorized by prosecutors and that prosecutors and judicial police must allow detainees access to medical care and doctors if they or their lawyers or families request it. The reforms did not, however, affect the authorities' powers to detain without charge suspects arrested for terrorism-related offences for up to 15 days, and allowed authorities to deny them access to a lawyer for 48 hours and interrogate them without the presence of their lawyer. In March, the government appointed the 16 members of the National Body for the Prevention of Torture, which was created under a 2013 law and was a requirement for Tunisia as a party to the Optional Protocol to the UN Convention against Torture. A lack of clarity regarding its function and financing hampered its ability to operate fully.

FREEDOMS OF EXPRESSION AND ASSEMBLY

The authorities used their powers under the state of emergency to ban strikes and demonstrations, forcibly disperse gatherings deemed to threaten public order, and control and censor print, broadcast and other media and publications. Despite this, there were new protests against unemployment, underdevelopment particularly in Tunisia's interior regions, and poor living conditions. The police dispersed such protests, reportedly using excessive force in some cases.

In January, protests against unemployment erupted in Kasserine after an unemployed graduate was electrocuted while climbing a utility pole in protest at being rejected for a government job. The protests quickly spread to other cities. The authorities arrested hundreds of protesters and bystanders, some of whom were prosecuted and sentenced to prison terms. They included 37 men who were arrested in Gabès on 22 January and sentenced to prison terms of between one and three years on charges of "breaking the curfew".

In April, demonstrators in El Kef protesting against unemployment said the police used excessive force to disperse them.

The authorities continued to restrict freedom of expression under criminal defamation laws enacted by the Ben 'Ali administration. In August, police arrested blogger Salwa Ayyari, her husband and four of her children outside the Presidential Palace in Tunis. They were held without food or water and denied access to a lawyer for several hours during which police officers insulted and ill-treated Salwa Ayyari, beating her and fracturing her arm. They were then moved to another police station where she was accused of attacking the officer who fractured her arm. Salwa Ayyari and her family were released after 13 hours' detention, but she was charged with insulting the President, which carries a penalty of imprisonment for up to two years, and assaulting a police officer. In December, she was acquitted of insulting the President and fined 200 Tunisian Dinar (US$86) for the charge of assaulting an officer.

WOMEN'S RIGHTS

Women continued to face discrimination in law and in practice and were inadequately protected against sexual and gender-based violence. The Penal Code failed to explicitly criminalize marital rape and allowed men who raped women aged 15 to 20, or who abducted girls under the age of 18, to escape prosecution if their victim consented to marry them.

Existing social and health services for survivors of sexual and gender-based violence were limited and inadequate. Among other necessary aspects of care, survivors of rape faced particular difficulties in accessing pregnancy prevention and psychological support. In addition, lack of protection mechanisms, including shelters for women and girl survivors of violence, left survivors vulnerable to further abuse.

In July the Council of Ministers approved a draft law to combat violence against women and girls, and submitted it for parliamentary consideration. The draft law focused on addressing shortcomings in existing law and practice and improving access to protection and services for survivors. It had not been enacted at the end of the year.

RIGHTS OF LESBIAN, GAY, BISEXUAL, TRANSGENDER AND INTERSEX PEOPLE

LGBTI people continued to face arrest under Article 230 of the Penal Code, which criminalized consensual same-sex sexual relations. They also faced violence, exploitation and sexual and other abuse by police. Transgender people faced arrest and prosecution under laws that criminalize "indecency" and acts deemed offensive to public morals.

The authorities subjected men accused of same-sex sexual relations to forced anal examinations, in violation of the prohibition of torture.

In March, the Sousse Court of Appeal confirmed the guilty verdict of six men on sodomy charges under Article 230 but reduced their three-year prison sentence to time already served and overturned their five-year banishment order from Kairouan. The men had been arrested and sentenced in December 2015 by the Kairouan Court of First Instance. In April, a court in Tunis acquitted eight men who were arrested in March and charged under Article 230. They were acquitted due to lack of evidence as they had not been subjected to forced anal examinations.

LGBTI rights activists also faced harassment and abuse. In January, the Court of First Instance in Tunis ordered the suspension of the LGBTI rights group Shams for 30 days in response to a government allegation that Shams had breached the law on associations by stating that it aimed to "defend homosexuals". Shams won an appeal against the Court's ruling in February.

In April, a televised verbal attack against LGBTI people by a leading Tunisian actor sparked an outbreak of homophobia that saw restaurants, internet cafés, grocery stores and taxis display posters barring LGBTI people. In May, the UN Committee against Torture criticized the criminalization of consensual same-sex sexual relations, urged the authorities to repeal Article 230 of the Penal Code, and condemned forced anal examinations.

DEATH PENALTY

Courts continued to hand down death sentences; no executions have been carried out since 1991.

TURKEY

Republic of Turkey
Head of state: Recep Tayyip Erdoğan
Head of government: Binali Yildirim (replaced Ahmet Davutoğlu in May)

An attempted coup prompted a massive government crackdown on civil servants and civil society. Those accused of links to the Fethullah Gülen movement were the main target. Over 40,000 people were remanded in pre-trial detention during six months of emergency rule. There was evidence of torture of detainees in the wake of the coup attempt. Nearly 90,000 civil servants were dismissed; hundreds of media outlets and NGOs were closed down and journalists, activists and MPs were detained. Violations of human rights by security forces continued with impunity, especially in the predominantly Kurdish southeast of the country, where urban populations were held under 24-hour curfew. Up to half a million people were displaced in the country. The EU and Turkey agreed a "migration deal" to prevent irregular migration to the EU; this led to the return of hundreds of refugees and asylum-seekers and less criticism by EU bodies of Turkey's human rights record.

BACKGROUND

President Erdoğan consolidated power throughout the year. Constitutional amendments aimed at granting the President executive powers were submitted to the Parliament in December.

Armed clashes between the Kurdistan Workers' Party (PKK) and state forces continued, mainly in the majority Kurdish east and southeast of the country. The government replaced elected mayors from 53 municipalities with government trustees; 49 mayors were from the Kurdish, opposition Democratic Regions Party (DBP). Along with many elected local officials, nine MPs from the Kurdish-rooted left-wing Peoples' Democracy Party (HDP) were remanded in pre-trial detention in November.[1] A UN fact-finding mission to the south-east was blocked by the authorities who also obstructed national and international NGOs, including Amnesty International, from documenting human rights abuses in the region.

In March, the EU and Turkey agreed a "migration deal" aimed at preventing irregular migration from Turkey to the EU. It also resulted in muting EU criticism of human rights abuses in Turkey.

On 15 July, factions within the armed forces launched a violent coup attempt. It was quickly suppressed in part by ordinary people taking to the streets to face down tanks. The authorities announced the death toll to be 237 people including 34 coup plotters and 2,191 people injured, during a night of violence that saw the Parliament bombed and other state and civilian infrastructure attacked.

Following the coup attempt the government announced a three-month state of emergency, extended for a further three months in October, derogating from a list of articles in the International Covenant on Civil and Political Rights and the European Convention on Human Rights. The government passed a series of executive decrees that failed to uphold even these reduced standards. Nearly 90,000 civil servants including teachers, police and military officials, doctors, judges and prosecutors were dismissed from their positions on the grounds of links to a terrorist organization or threat to national security. Most were presumed to be based on allegations of links to Fethullah Gülen, a former government ally whom the government accused of masterminding the coup. There was no clear route in law to appeal these decisions. At least 40,000 people were remanded in pre-trial detention accused of links to the coup or the Gülen movement, classified by the authorities as the Fethullah Gülen Terrorist Organisation (FETÖ).

In August, Turkey launched a military intervention in northern Syria, targeting the armed group Islamic State (IS) and the Peoples' Defence Forces, the PKK-affiliated Kurdish armed group. In October Parliament extended a mandate for Turkey to conduct military interventions in Iraq and Syria for another year.

FREEDOM OF EXPRESSION

Freedom of expression deteriorated sharply during the year. After the declaration of a state of emergency, 118 journalists were remanded in pre-trial detention and 184 media outlets were arbitrarily and permanently closed down under executive decrees, leaving opposition media severely restricted.[2] People expressing dissent, especially in relation to the Kurdish issue, were subjected to threats of violence and criminal prosecution. Internet censorship increased. At least 375 NGOs, including women's rights groups, lawyers' associations and humanitarian organizations, were shut by executive decree in November.

In March, a court in the capital Ankara appointed a trustee to the opposition Zaman media group in relation to an ongoing terrorism-related investigation. After police stormed Zaman offices, a pro-government editorial was imposed on the group's newspapers and television channels. In July, Zaman group media outlets were permanently closed down along with other Gülen-linked media. New titles, set up after the government take over of the Zaman group, were also shut down.

In May, Cumhuriyet editor-in-chief Can Dündar and the daily's Ankara representative Erdem Gül were convicted of "revealing state secrets" and sentenced to five years and ten months' imprisonment and five years' imprisonment respectively, for publishing articles alleging that Turkey's authorities had attempted to covertly ship weapons to armed opposition groups in Syria. The government claimed the trucks were sending humanitarian supplies to Turkmens. The case remained pending on appeal at the end of the year. In October, a further 10 journalists were remanded in pre-trial detention for committing crimes on behalf of both FETÖ and the PKK.

In August, police closed the offices of the main Kurdish daily Özgür Gündem on the basis of a court order for its closure due to ongoing terrorism investigations, a sanction not provided for in law. Two editors and two journalists were detained pending trial and prosecuted for terrorism offences. Three were released in December while editor İnan Kızıkaya remained in detention.[3] In October under an executive decree, Özgür Gündem was permanently closed down along with all the major Kurdish-orientated national media.

Signatories to a January petition by Academics for Peace calling for a return to peace negotiations and recognition of the demands of the Kurdish political movement were subjected to threats of violence, administrative investigation and criminal prosecution. Four signatories were detained until a court hearing in April; they were released but not acquitted.[4] By the end of the year, 490 of the academics were under administrative investigation and 142 had been dismissed. Since the coup, more than 1,100 of the signatories were formally under criminal investigation.

Internet censorship increased, with the authorities issuing orders rubber-stamped by the judiciary to withdraw or block content including websites and social media accounts, to which there was no effective appeal. In October, the authorities cut internet services across southeast Turkey and engaged in throttling of various social media services.

FREEDOM OF ASSEMBLY

The authorities banned the annual May Day marches in Istanbul for the fourth year running, and the annual Pride march in Istanbul for a second year running, on spurious grounds. Police used excessive force against people peacefully attempting to go ahead with these marches. After July, the authorities used state of emergency laws to issue blanket bans preventing demonstrations in cities across Turkey. And again, the police used excessive force against people attempting to exercise the right to freedom of peaceful assembly regardless of the bans.

TORTURE AND OTHER ILL-TREATMENT

There was an increase in cases of torture and other ill-treatment reported in police detention, from curfew areas in southeast Turkey and then more markedly in Ankara and Istanbul in the immediate aftermath of the coup attempt. Investigations into abuses were ineffective.

The state of emergency removed protections for detainees and allowed previously banned practices, which helped facilitate torture and other ill-treatment: the maximum pre-charge detention period was increased from four to 30 days; and facilities to block detainees' access to lawyers in pre-charge detention for five days, and to record conversations between client and lawyer in pre-trial detention and pass them to prosecutors were introduced. Detainees' access to lawyers and the right to consult with their choice of lawyers – rather than state-provided lawyers – was further restricted. Medical examinations were carried out in the presence of police officers and the reports arbitrarily denied to detainees' lawyers.

No national mechanism for the independent monitoring of places of detention existed following the abolition of the Human Rights Institution in April, and the non-functioning of its successor body. The Council of Europe Committee for the Prevention of Torture visited detention facilities in August and reported to the Turkish authorities in November. However, the government did not publish the report by the end of the year. The UN Special Rapporteur on torture visited in November, after his visit was delayed on the request of the Turkish authorities.

The authorities professed their adherence to "zero tolerance for torture" policies but on occasion, spokespeople summarily dismissed reports against them, stating that coup plotters deserved abuse and that allegations would not be investigated. The authorities accused Amnesty International and Human Rights Watch of being tools for the "FETÖ terrorist organization" following the NGOs' joint publication on torture and ill-treatment.[5] Three lawyers' associations that worked on police violence and torture were shut down in November under an executive decree.

Lawyers said that 42 people, detained in Nusaybin in May after clashes between PKK-affiliated individuals and state forces were beaten and subjected to other ill-treatment in police detention. They said that the group, which included adults and children, were hooded, beaten during police interrogation and not able to access appropriate medical care for their injuries.

Widespread torture and other ill-treatment of suspects accused of taking part in the coup attempt was reported in its immediate aftermath. In July, severe beatings, sexual assault, threats of rape and cases of rape were reported, as thousands were detained in official and unofficial police detention. Military officers appeared to be targeted for the worst physical abuse but holding detainees in stress positions and keeping them handcuffed behind their backs, and denying them adequate food and water or toilet breaks were reported to have taken place on a far wider scale. Lawyers and detainees' relatives were often not informed that individuals had been detained until they were brought for charge.

EXCESSIVE USE OF FORCE

Until June, the security forces conducted security operations against armed individuals affiliated to the PKK, who had dug trenches and erected barricades in urban areas in the southeast of Turkey. The authorities' use of extended round-the-clock curfews, a total ban on people leaving their homes, combined with the presence of heavy weaponry including tanks in populated areas, was a disproportionate and abusive response to a serious security concern and may have amounted to collective punishment.[6] Evidence suggests that the security forces' operated a shoot-to-kill policy against armed individuals that also caused deaths and injuries to unarmed residents and widespread forced displacement.

In January, IMC TV journalist Refik Tekin was shot while bringing injured people to receive medical treatment in Cizre, a city under curfew. He continued recording after being shot, apparently from an armoured police vehicle. He was later detained and investigated under terrorism laws.

IMPUNITY

The entrenched culture of impunity for abuses committed by the security forces remained. The authorities failed to investigate allegations of widespread human rights violations in the southeast, where few or none of the basic steps were taken to process cases, including deaths, and in some instances witnesses were subjected to threats. In June, legislative amendments required the investigation of military officials for conduct during security operations to be subject to government permission and for any resulting trial to take place in military courts, which have proved especially weak in prosecuting officials for human rights abuses.

Government statements dismissing allegations of torture and ill-treatment in police detention after the coup attempt were a worrying departure.

Despite the ratification of the Council of Europe Convention on preventing and combating violence against women (Istanbul Convention), the authorities made little or no progress in halting pervasive domestic violence against women nor did they adopt procedures to investigate the hate motive in

cases of people perceived to have been killed due to their sexual orientation or gender identity.

No progress was made in investigations into the deaths of some 130 people who died while sheltering from clashes in three basements during the curfew in Cizre in February. The authorities alleged that access for ambulances was blocked by the PKK when local sources reported that people in the basements were injured and needed emergency medical care, and died of their injuries or were killed when security forces stormed the buildings.

The Governor of Ağrı province in eastern Turkey denied permission for an investigation against police officers to proceed into the deaths of two youths, aged 16 and 19 in Diyadin. The authorities claimed that police shot the youths in self-defence but a ballistics report showed that a gun found at the scene had not been fired and did not have either of the youths' fingerprints on it.

The authorities failed to make progress in investigation of the November 2015 killing of Tahir Elci, Head of the Diyarbakir Bar Association and a prominent human rights defender. It was hampered by an incomplete crime scene investigation and missing CCTV footage.

More than three years on, investigations into use of force by police at Gezi Park protests had failed and resulted in only a handful of unsatisfactory prosecutions. The court issued a 10,100 liras (€3,000) fine to the police officer in his retrial for the fatal shooting of Ankara protester Ethem Sarisülük. A court reduced the compensation awarded to Dilan Dursun by 75% – she had been left with permanent injuries after being hit in the head by a tear gas canister fired by police during protests in Ankara on the day of Ethem Sarisülük's funeral. The court ruled that she had culpability given that it was an "illegal demonstration".

ABUSES BY ARMED GROUPS

There was a sharp increase in indiscriminate attacks and attacks directly targeting civilians, showing contempt for the right to life and the principle of humanity. IS, PKK, its offshoot Kurdistan Freedom Falcons (TAK) and Revolutionary People's Liberation Party-Front were blamed or claimed responsibility for the attacks.

REFUGEES AND ASYLUM-SEEKERS

Turkey was the world's biggest host of refugees and asylum-seekers with an estimated 3 million refugees and asylum-seekers residing in the country with significant populations of Afghans and Iraqis alongside 2.75 million registered Syrians, who were provided with temporary protection status. The EU concluded a migration deal with Turkey in March aimed at preventing irregular migration to the EU. It provided for the return of refugees and asylum-seekers to Turkey, ignoring many gaps in protection there.[7] Turkey's border with Syria remained effectively closed. Despite improvements, the majority of Syrian refugee children had no access to education and most adult Syrian refugees had no access to lawful employment. Many refugee families, without adequate subsistence, lived in destitution.

There were mass forced returns of Syrians by the Turkish security forces in the early months of the year, as well as instances of unlawful push-backs to Syria and cases of fatal and non-fatal shootings of people in need of protection by Turkish border guards.

INTERNALLY DISPLACED PEOPLE

Hundreds of thousands of people were displaced from the areas under curfew in the southeast of Turkey. The imposition of curfews with only hours' warning forced people to leave with few, if any, possessions. In many cases, displaced people were not able to access their social and economic rights such as adequate housing and education. They were offered inadequate compensation for loss of possessions and livelihoods. Their right to return was severely compromised by the high levels of destruction and the announcement of redevelopment projects likely to exclude former residents.[8]

1. Turkey: HDP deputies detained amid growing onslaught on Kurdish opposition voices (News story, 4 November)
2. Turkey: Massive crackdown on media in Turkey (EUR 44/5112/2016)
3. Turkey: End pre-trial detention of Özgür Gündem guest editors (EUR 44/4303/2016)
4. Turkey: Further information – academics targeted for peace appeal, released (EUR 44/3902/2016)
5. Joint Statement: Turkey – state of emergency provisions violate human rights and should be revoked (EUR 44/5012/2016)
6. Turkey: Security operations in southeast Turkey risk return to widespread human rights violations seen in the 1990s (EUR 44/4366/2016)
7. Turkey: No safe refuge – asylum-seekers and refugees denied effective protection in Turkey (EUR 44/3825/2016)
8. Turkey: Displaced and dispossessed – Sur residents' right to return home (EUR 44/5213/2016)

TURKMENISTAN

Turkmenistan
Head of state and government:
Gurbanguly Berdymukhamedov

Human rights did not improve, despite a National Human Rights Action Plan for 2016-2020 launched in April. Independent civil society organizations could not operate freely. Turkmenistan remained closed to independent human rights monitors. Freedoms of expression, association and religion were heavily restricted and limits on freedom of movement were retained. Sex between men remained a criminal offence.

FREEDOM OF EXPRESSION

Media remained subject to state control and no independent media outlets were able to operate. The authorities continued to harass and intimidate journalists, including those based outside Turkmenistan.

Freelance journalist Saparmamed Nepeskuliev remained in prison. He had reported on corruption and was convicted in August 2015 on drug-related offences.

Access to the internet was monitored and restricted; social networking sites were frequently blocked.

FORCED LABOUR

The government continued to use forced labour in the cotton-picking industry, one of the largest in the world. To harvest the cotton, local authorities compel public sector workers, including teachers, medical staff and civil servants, to pick and to meet individual government-set quotas or risk losing their jobs. Children often help their parents meeting the quotas. The ILO Committee of Experts on the Application of Conventions and Recommendations urged Turkmenistan to end practices that give rise to forced labour in the cotton industry.

LEGAL, CONSTITUTIONAL OR INSTITUTIONAL DEVELOPMENTS

A law to establish a Human Rights Commissioner (Ombudsman) was still under development.

A new Constitution was adopted on 16 September. It extended the presidential tenure to seven years and removed a previous presidential age limit.

ENFORCED DISAPPEARANCES

The whereabouts of prisoners who were subjected to enforced disappearance after an alleged assassination attempt on then President Saparmurat Niyazov in 2002 remained unknown.

FREEDOM OF RELIGION AND BELIEF

In the town of Dashoguz, bearded men under 50 years were detained and questioned about their religious beliefs and practices, and some were forcibly shaved, according to the Alternative Turkmenistan News service.

The new Law on Freedom of Conscience and Religious Organizations was signed into law in March. It retained an earlier ban on exercising freedom of religion and belief with others without state permission. Under the new law, religious groups need to have 50 founding members to register, rather than five, as stipulated in the previous law.

Conscientious objectors faced criminal prosecution. Forum 18, a human rights organization promoting religious freedom, reported that a young Jehovah's Witness was sentenced to corrective labour for refusing to perform his military service.

TORTURE AND OTHER ILL-TREATMENT

Former prisoners told Alternative Turkmenistan News about poor prison conditions and treatment in detention amounting to torture and other ill-treatment. According to these accounts, prison officers beat prisoners and forced them to stand outside for long periods in high temperatures. Prison officers also practised extortion. Prisons were overcrowded and prisoners not provided with adequate food. Some prisoners had to sleep on the floor or in the prison yard. Tuberculosis rates were high and infected prisoners did not always receive appropriate treatment.

Reports continued to be received on the use of torture or ill-treatment by law enforcement officers to force detainees to "confess" and incriminate others. Activist Mansur Mingelov remained in prison. He was convicted in 2012 after an unfair trial for drug offences after publicizing information on torture and other ill-treatment of Baloch ethnic community members in Mary province.

INTERNATIONAL SCRUTINY

Turkmenistan remained closed to international scrutiny and rejected or failed to respond to requests from the UN Special Rapporteurs to visit the country.

FREEDOM OF MOVEMENT

Citizens have not needed "exit visas" to leave the country since 2006. But arbitrary restrictions on the right to travel abroad remained in practice: they targeted, among others, relatives of people accused of involvement in the alleged attempt to assassinate President Niyazov in 2002, relatives of members of the opposition resident abroad, as well as civil society activists, students, journalists and former migrant workers.

UGANDA

Republic of Uganda
Head of state and government: **Yoweri Kaguta Museveni**

The rights to freedom of expression, association and assembly were severely restricted in the context of general elections marred by irregularities. Human rights defenders faced new restrictions on their activities and some organizations were harassed. The rights of lesbian, gay, bisexual, transgender and intersex (LGBTI) people continued to be violated.

BACKGROUND

Uganda held its fifth presidential and parliamentary elections on 18 February. The Commonwealth election observation mission said the election fell short of key democratic benchmarks. The EU's election observation mission said the election took place in an "intimidating atmosphere", with the police using excessive force against opposition politicians, media workers and the general public. President Museveni was declared the winner on 20 February. He had already been in power for 30 years.

On 1 March, Amama Mbabazi, an opposition presidential candidate, filed a petition in the Supreme Court contesting the election result on the grounds that the incumbent party bribed voters, used public servants and state resources in political activities, and interfered with opposition activities. On 9 March, when affidavits were due to be submitted in court, files and computers were stolen from the offices of two of his lawyers. On 31 March, the Supreme Court ruled that there was not enough evidence of irregularities that would have affected the election result.

FREEDOMS OF ASSOCIATION AND ASSEMBLY

Police severely restricted the rights of political opposition parties to freedom of association and peaceful assembly before, during and after the elections.

Three days before the elections, Kizza Besigye, presidential candidate for the opposition Forum for Democratic Change (FDC), was arrested as he headed towards a campaign rally. The police subsequently barricaded the road leading to his house, effectively placing him under house arrest, on the grounds that they had intelligence that he intended to cause unrest. On 20 February he was arrested again when he tried to leave his house to obtain detailed copies of the results from the Electoral Commission in order to contest them.[1] On 12 May, the day before Yoweri Museveni was to be sworn in as President, a video appeared online showing Kizza Besigye being sworn in, claiming to be the people's President. The police immediately arrested him and charged him with treason. The case was continuing at the end of the year.

FREEDOM OF EXPRESSION

In the run-up to the elections, security officials attacked media outlets they deemed critical of government policies and actions.

On 20 January, Endigyito FM, a privately owned radio station, was closed down after opposition candidate Amama Mbabazi was a guest on a show.

On 13 February, police entered Radio North FM in Lira, northern Uganda, and arrested journalist Richard Mungu and a guest. The police accused Richard Mungu of defacing President Museveni's election posters and charged him with malicious damage to property. The charges were later amended to aiding and abetting a crime, an apparent reference to the damaged posters. He was released on bail on 17 February.

On election day, the official Uganda Communications Commission (UCC) blocked access to Facebook, Twitter and WhatsApp between 6am and 9.30am, citing an unspecified threat to national security. The Mobile Telecommunications Network (MTN), a leading provider of mobile phone and internet services in Uganda, said on its Twitter handle that the UCC had ordered it to disable all social media and mobile money-transferring services "due to a threat to public order and safety". Such actions violated the right to seek and receive information.

The Deputy Chief Justice stopped a peaceful demonstration organized by the FDC and Kizza Besigye planned for 5 May. His order followed an application by the Deputy Attorney General for interim orders to prevent FDC's "defiance campaign". The FDC's campaign sought, among other things, an international audit to review the presidential election results. However, the Court of Appeal ruled on 30 April that the campaign breached several articles of the Constitution.

On 14 September, 25 women were arrested and detained for four hours, before being released without charge, shortly before they were to present a petition to Parliament. The petition opposed proposed amendments to mandatory retirement ages for judicial officers and electoral commissioners set out in the Constitution. The Speaker of the Parliament rejected the bill and asked the government to table comprehensive constitutional amendments instead.

UNLAWFUL KILLINGS

On 28 November, at least 100 people were killed and 139 others arrested in clashes between security agencies and palace guards in the western town of Kasese, according to police.[2] In some cases, security forces summarily shot people dead and then dumped the bodies on river banks and in bushes. The clashes followed attacks by the local king's guards on several police stations on 26 November, during which at least 14 police officers were killed. Charles Wesley Mumbere, King of the Rwenzururu kingdom, was arrested and transferred to the capital, Kampala, where he was charged with murder.

HUMAN RIGHTS DEFENDERS

On 14 March, the Non-Governmental Organisations Act (NGO Act) came into force. Some of its provisions were vaguely worded and could be used to clampdown on civil society organizations. For example, it restricted organizations from engaging in activities that are "prejudicial to the security, interests or dignity of the people of Uganda", without defining these terms.

Between April and May, offices of the Forum for African Women Educationalists (FAWE), the Human Rights Awareness and Promotion Forum (HRAPF), and the Human Rights Network for Journalists-Uganda (HRNJ-Uganda) were broken into by unidentified people and items stolen. At FAWE, the intruders stole an internet server, computers, cameras and projectors. At HRNJ-Uganda, CCTV footage shows a visitor giving security guards food apparently containing sedatives, allowing four intruders to search the premises as the guards slept. The Inspector General of Police formed a committee in July to investigate the break-ins, but the affected organizations were concerned that investigations were not carried out. No one was arrested, charged or prosecuted in connection with the break-ins.[3]

RIGHTS OF LESBIAN, GAY, BISEXUAL, TRANSGENDER AND INTERSEX PEOPLE

On 4 August, police broke up an LGBTI beauty pageant in Kampala, part of Uganda Pride. They arrested 16 people – most of them Ugandan LGBTI rights activists – who were released after about an hour. A man was seriously injured after he jumped from a sixth-floor window fearing police abuse.

On 24 September, the police prevented more than 100 people from joining a Pride parade on a beach in Entebbe. They ordered people back onto minibuses and told them to leave the area. The participants tried to go to another beach, but police prevented them from holding the parade there too.

The HRAPF and the Civil Society Coalition on Human Rights and Constitutional Law (CSCHRCL), a coalition of 50 organizations, filed a petition in the East African Court of Justice, arguing that Uganda's Anti-Homosexuality Act was contrary to the rule of law and the good governance principles of the East African Community Treaty. On 27

September, the Court refused to consider the petition on the basis that the Anti-Homosexuality Act had been declared null and void by Uganda's Constitutional Court in August 2014.

CRIMES UNDER INTERNATIONAL LAW

The pre-trial hearing of former Lord's Resistance Army (LRA) commander Colonel Thomas Kwoyelo, charged with war crimes and crimes against humanity in northern Uganda, began on 15 August in the International Crime Division of Uganda's High Court. The hearing was adjourned because Thomas Kwoyelo's lawyers were not notified in time. The prosecution also introduced new charges relating to sexual and gender-based violence. In September, a court in Gulu, northern Uganda, ruled that victims could participate in the proceedings in line with their right to participate before the International Criminal Court (ICC). Thomas Kwoyelo, who was captured by the Ugandan army in 2008, remained in detention.

On 23 March, the ICC Pre-Trial Chamber confirmed 70 charges against Dominic Ongwen, a former LRA commander who had been abducted as a child and forcibly recruited into the LRA. The charges included crimes against humanity and war crimes, sexual and gender-based crimes, and conscription and use of child soldiers in northern Uganda.

COUNTER-TERROR AND SECURITY

On 26 May, the High Court convicted seven of 13 people charged in relation to the 2010 World Cup bombing in Kampala. The Somali-based armed group al-Shabaab claimed responsibility for the attack, which killed 76 people. The Court said the prosecution had failed to link five of the defendants to the bombing. The five were immediately rearrested and charged with new offences of creating documents and materials while in Luzira Prison connected with "preparations to facilitate, assist or engage co-conspirators to undertake terrorist acts in Uganda".

1. Uganda: Violations against opposition party impeding its efforts to contest election outcome (News story, 26 February)

2. Uganda: Denounce unlawful killings and ensure accountability in aftermath of deadly clashes (News story, 28 November)

3. Uganda: Investigate break-ins at groups' offices (News story, 13 June)

UKRAINE

Ukraine
Head of state: **Petro Poroshenko**
Head of government: **Volodymyr Hroysman (replaced Arseniy Yatsenyuk in April)**

Sporadic low-scale fighting continued in eastern Ukraine with both sides violating the ceasefire agreement. Both the Ukrainian and pro-Russian separatist forces continued to enjoy impunity for violations of international humanitarian law, including war crimes, such as torture. Authorities in Ukraine and the self-styled People's Republics of Donetsk and Luhansk conducted unlawful detention of individuals perceived to support the other side, including for use in prisoner exchanges. The long-awaited State Investigation Bureau, intended to investigate violations by the military and law enforcement officials, was formally established but not operational by the end of the year. Independent media and activists were not allowed to work freely in the People's Republics of Donetsk and Luhansk. Media perceived as pro-Russian faced harassment in government-controlled territories. The largest-ever Pride march for lesbian, gay, bisexual, transgender and intersex (LGBTI) people in the capital, Kyiv, was supported by the city authorities and effectively protected by the police. In Crimea, the de facto authorities continued their campaign to eliminate pro-Ukrainian dissent. It increasingly relied on Russian anti-extremism and anti-terrorism legislation and criminal prosecution of dozens of people perceived to be disloyal.

BACKGROUND

Following a two-month political crisis, after several reform-oriented politicians resigned from top government positions alleging widespread corruption, Parliament accepted Arseniy Yatsenyuk's resignation on 12 April. He was replaced by Volodymyr Hroysman.

Sporadic fighting and exchange of fire between government and Russia-backed separatist forces continued. Gunfire, shelling and unexploded ordnance continued to cause civilian deaths and injuries. The UN Human Rights Monitoring Mission estimated that there were more than 9,700 conflict-related deaths, of which around 2,000 were civilians, and at least 22,500 conflict-related injuries since the beginning of the conflict in 2014.

The International Criminal Court (ICC) published its preliminary examination of Ukraine on 14 November. It concluded that the "situation within the territory of Crimea and Sevastopol amounts to an international armed conflict between Ukraine and the Russian Federation" and that "information… would suggest the existence of an international armed conflict in the context of armed hostilities in eastern Ukraine". An amendment to the Constitution was passed in June, postponing the ratification of the Rome Statute of the ICC for an "interim period" of three years.

The Ukrainian authorities continued to heavily restrict the movement of residents of the separatist-controlled Donetsk and Luhansk regions to government-controlled territory.

The Russian authorities held parliamentary elections in Crimea, which were not internationally recognized.

The conflict-affected economy started to grow slowly: GDP increased by 1%. Prices of basic commodities and services such as heating and water continued to rise, adding to the declining living standards of the majority of the population. Living standards in the separatist-controlled areas continued to deteriorate.

TORTURE AND OTHER ILL-TREATMENT

Little progress was made in bringing to justice law enforcement officials responsible for the abusive use of force during EuroMaydan protests in Kyiv in 2013-2014. The investigation was marred by bureaucratic hurdles. On 24 October, the Prosecutor General reduced the staff and the powers of the special department responsible for the EuroMaydan abuses investigations, and created a new unit to investigate only former President Vyktor Yanukovych and his close confidants.

The new State Investigation Bureau was formally created in February to investigate crimes committed by law enforcement officials and the military, but the selection of its head, on an open competition basis, was not completed by the end of the year.[1]

The UN Subcommittee on Prevention of Torture (SPT) suspended its visit to Ukraine on 25 May after the Security Service of Ukraine (SBU) denied it access to some of its facilities in eastern Ukraine where secret prisoners were reportedly held as well as tortured and otherwise ill-treated. The SPT resumed and completed its visit in September and produced a report which the Ukrainian authorities did not give their consent to publish.

ENFORCED DISAPPEARANCE

Lawyer Yuriy Grabovsky went missing on 6 March and was found murdered on 25 March. Before his disappearance, Yuriy Grabovsky complained of intimidation and harassment by the Ukrainian authorities in an attempt to make him withdraw from the case of one of two alleged Russian servicemen who were captured in eastern Ukraine by government forces. During a press conference on 29 March, the Chief Military Prosecutor of Ukraine announced that two suspects had been detained in connection with Yuriy Grabovsky's murder. At the end of the year, they remained in pre-trial detention and the investigation was ongoing.[2]

ARBITRARY ARRESTS AND DETENTIONS

Both the Ukrainian authorities and separatist forces in eastern Ukraine engaged in unlawful detentions in the territory under their respective control. Civilians they suspected of sympathizing with the other side were used as currency for prisoner exchanges.[3] Those unwanted by the other side remained in detention, often unacknowledged, for months with no legal remedies nor prospect of release.

Kostyantyn Beskorovaynyi returned home on 25 February after his abduction and indirect official acknowledgement of his secret arrest became the subject of international campaigning.[4] In July, Ukraine's Chief Military Prosecutor promised an effective investigation into his allegations of enforced disappearance, torture and 15-months' secret detention by the SBU, but no tangible outcomes of the investigation were reported by the end of the year.

Dozens more individuals were held secretly on SBU premises in Mariupol, Pokrovsk, Kramatorsk, Izyum and Kharkiv, and possibly elsewhere. Some were eventually exchanged for prisoners held by the separatists. Amnesty International and Human Rights Watch received the names of 16 individuals from three separate sources, all independently confirming them as secret prisoners held by the SBU in Kharkiv since 2014 or 2015, and shared the list with the Ukrainian authorities. At least 18 people, including the 16 independently confirmed prisoners, were subsequently secretly released; their detention was never officially acknowledged. Of them, Vyktor Ashykhmyn, Mykola Vakaruk and Dmytro Koroliov decided to speak out and submit official complaints.[5]

In the self-proclaimed People's Republics of Donetsk and Luhansk, local "Ministries of State Security" used their powers under local "decrees" to detain individuals arbitrarily for up to 30 days and repeatedly extend this. Igor Kozlovsky (arrested on 27 January), and Volodymyr Fomychev (arrested on 4 January), were both accused of possessing illegal weapons, which they denied, and of

"supporting" the "Ukrainian side". A court in Donetsk sentenced Volodymyr Fomychev to two years in jail on 16 August. Igor Kozlovsky remained in pre-trial detention at the end of the year.

INTERNALLY DISPLACED PEOPLE

The CERD Committee highlighted a number of concerns about difficulties faced by internally displaced people (IDPs) in its 2016 review of Ukraine. These included the linking of social benefits, including pensions, to the status of IDPs and residence in government-controlled areas.

FREEDOM OF EXPRESSION – JOURNALISTS

Media outlets perceived as espousing pro-Russian or pro-separatist views, and those particularly critical of the authorities, faced harassment including threats of closure or physical violence. The TV channel Inter was threatened with closure repeatedly by the Interior Minister, and on 4 September around 15 masked men attempted forcefully but unsuccessfully to enter Inter's premises, accusing it of pro-Russian news coverage. They then threw petrol bombs into the building, starting a fire.

Popular TV presenter Savik Shuster (who holds Italian and Canadian nationality) had his work permit annulled by the Ukrainian Migration Service, in violation of the existing procedure. The Kyiv Appeals Court reinstated the permit on 12 July. Subsequently, criminal proceedings were launched against Savik Shuster's TV channel 3STV by the tax authorities. On 1 December, Savik Shuster decided to close the channel due to the pressure and lack of funds.

Ruslan Kotsaba, a freelance journalist and blogger from Ivano-Frankivsk, was sentenced to three-and-a-half years in jail on 12 May, for "obstructing legitimate activities of the Ukrainian Armed Forces in a special period". He had been arrested in 2015 after posting a video on YouTube in which he demanded an immediate end to fighting in Donbass and called on Ukrainian men to resist conscription. He was fully acquitted on appeal on 12 July and immediately released.

On 20 July, journalist Pavel Sheremet was killed by a bomb planted in his car in the capital Kyiv. No perpetrators had been identified by the end of the year. The investigation into the killing of journalist Oles Buzina, shot dead by two masked gunmen in 2015, had likewise yielded no results.

Journalists with pro-Ukrainian views or reporting for Ukrainian media outlets were not able to operate openly in separatist-controlled areas and Crimea. A Russian crew from the independent Russian Dozhd TV channel was arrested in Donetsk and deported to Russia by the Ministry of State Security after recording an interview with a former separatist commander.

In Crimea, independent journalists were unable to work openly. Journalists from mainland Ukraine were denied access and turned back at the de facto border. Local journalists and bloggers critical of the Russian occupation and illegal annexation of Crimea risked prosecution, and few dared to express their views. Mykola Semena, a veteran journalist, was investigated under "extremism" charges (facing up to seven years' imprisonment if convicted) and placed under travel restrictions. He had published an article online under a pseudonym in which he supported the "blockade" of Crimea by pro-Ukrainian activists as a necessary measure for the peninsula to be "returned back" to Ukraine. He was officially designated as a "supporter of extremism", and his bank account was frozen. At the end of the year, the investigation into his case was ongoing.

RIGHTS OF LESBIAN, GAY, BISEXUAL, TRANSGENDER AND INTERSEX PEOPLE

On 19 March, a court in Lviv, western Ukraine, banned the holding of the LGBTI Festival of Equality in the street due to public safety concerns. The organizers moved the event indoors, but on 20 March the venue was attacked by a group of masked right-wing activists. No injuries were reported but the organizers were forced to cancel the event.

An LGBTI Pride march, supported by the Kyiv authorities and heavily protected by police, was held in central Kyiv on 12 June. With around 2,000 participants, it became the largest-ever event of its kind in Ukraine.[6]

CRIMEA

None of the enforced disappearances that followed the Russian occupation were effectively investigated. Ervin Ibragimov, member of the World Congress of Crimean Tatars, was forcibly disappeared near his home in Bakhchisaray, central Crimea, on 24 May. Available video footage from a security camera shows uniformed men forcing Ervin Ibragimov into a minivan and driving him away. An investigation was opened, but no progress had been made at the end of the year.[7]

Freedoms of expression, association and peaceful assembly, already heavily restricted, were further reduced. Some of the independent media that had been forced to relocate to mainland Ukraine in earlier years had access to their websites blocked by the de facto authorities in Crimea. On 7 March, the mayor of Crimean capital Simferopol banned all public assemblies except those organized by the authorities.

Ethnic Crimean Tatars continued to bear the brunt of the de facto authorities' campaign to eliminate all remaining vestiges of pro-Ukrainian dissent.[8] The Mejlis of the Crimean Tatar People, a body elected at an informal assembly, Kurultai, to represent the community, was suspended on 18 April and banned by a court as "extremist" on 26 April. Its banning was upheld by the Supreme Court of the Russian Federation on 29 September.[9]

The trial continued of the Mejlis' deputy leader, Ahtem Chiygoz, on trumped-up charges of organizing "mass disturbances" on 26 February 2014 in Simferopol (a predominantly peaceful rally on the eve of the Russian occupation, marked by some clashes between pro-Russian and pro-Ukrainian demonstrators). Held in a pre-trial detention centre in the vicinity of the court building, he was only allowed to attend his court hearings via a video link, purportedly because of the "danger" he would pose. Ahtem Chiygoz remained one of several prisoners of conscience in Crimea. Ali Asanov and Mustafa Degermendzhi also continued to be held in pre-trial detention for allegedly participating in the same "mass disturbances" on 26 February 2014.

The Russian authorities used allegations of possession of "extremist literature" and of membership of the Islamist organization Hizb ut-Tahrir as a pretext for house searches of ethnic Crimean Tatars (predominantly Muslims) and arrests. At least 19 men were arrested as alleged members of Hizb ut-Tahrir. Of them, four men from Sevastopol were put on trial in a military court in Russia, in violation of international humanitarian law governing occupied territories, and sentenced to between five and seven years in prison. During the trial, nearly all prosecution witnesses tried to retract their earlier statements, claiming that these had been forcibly extracted under threat of criminal prosecution by members of the Russian security service.

1. Ukraine: Two years after Euromaydan – The prospect for justice is threatened (EUR 50/3516/2016)

2. Ukraine: Further information – Body of missing lawyer has been found (EUR 50/3734/2016)

3. "You don't exist": Arbitrary detentions, enforced disappearances, and torture in eastern Ukraine (EUR 50/4455/2016)

4. Ukraine: Authorities must disclose missing man's fate: Kostyantyn Beskorovaynyi (EUR 50/3275/2016)

5. Five men in secret detention in Ukraine (EUR 50/4728/2016)

6. Ukraine: Kyiv Pride – A genuine celebration of human rights (EUR 50/4258/2016)

7. Ukraine: Crimean Tatar activist forcibly disappeared – Ervin Ibragimov (EUR 50/4121/2016)

8. Ukraine: Crimea in the Dark – The silencing of dissent (EUR 50/5330/2016)

9. Ukraine: Crimea – Proposed closure of the Mejlis marks culmination of repressive measures against the Crimean Tatar community (EUR 50/3655/2016)

UNITED ARAB EMIRATES

United Arab Emirates
Head of state: **Sheikh Khalifa bin Zayed Al Nahyan**
Head of government: **Sheikh Mohammed bin Rashed Al Maktoum**

The authorities continued to arbitrarily restrict the rights to freedom of expression and association, detaining and prosecuting government critics, opponents and foreign nationals under criminal defamation and anti-terrorism laws. Enforced disappearances, unfair trials and torture and other ill-treatment of detainees remained common. Scores of people sentenced after unfair trials in previous years remained in prison; they included prisoners of conscience. Women continued to be discriminated against in law and in practice. Migrant workers faced exploitation and abuse. The courts continued to impose death sentences; no executions were reported.

BACKGROUND

The United Arab Emirates (UAE) remained part of the Saudi Arabia-led international coalition engaged in armed conflict in Yemen (see Yemen entry) and participated in international military action in Syria and Iraq against the armed group Islamic State (IS).

In August, the authorities agreed to the transfer of 15 detainees from the US detention centre at Guantánamo Bay, Cuba, to the UAE.

The government failed to respond to requests to visit the UAE made by the Special Rapporteur on torture and other UN human rights experts.

FREEDOMS OF EXPRESSION AND ASSOCIATION

The authorities tightened the law relating to electronic information and restricted online expression and association, enacting legislation to ban the use of virtual private networks. They also arrested and prosecuted peaceful critics and others, including foreign nationals, under criminal defamation provisions of the Penal Code, the 2012 cybercrime law and the 2014 anti-terrorism law in unfair trials before the State Security Chamber (SSC) of the Federal Supreme Court. The SSC's proceedings fell far short of international fair trial standards.

In May, the SSC acquitted Moza 'Abdouli of "insulting" UAE leaders and political institutions and "spreading false information". She had been arrested in November 2015 together with her sister, Amina 'Abdouli, and brother, Mos'ab 'Abdouli. Another brother, Waleed 'Abdouli, arrested in November 2015 for criticizing his siblings' detention at Friday prayers, was released without charge in March.

Tayseer al-Najjar, a Jordanian journalist arrested in December 2015, remained in detention at the end of the year awaiting trial before the SSC, apparently in connection with Facebook posts criticizing the UAE and alleged links to Egypt's banned Muslim Brotherhood organization. In October, he told his wife that his eyesight was deteriorating in detention.

In August, the government appeared to be behind an attempt to remotely hack into the iPhone of human rights defender Ahmed Mansoor. If successful, it would have allowed remote access to all information on the phone, and remote control of his phone's applications, microphone and camera. The sophisticated spyware used to carry out this operation is sold by NSO Group, an Israel-based, US-owned company which claimed to sell their product exclusively to governments.

Human rights defender and prisoner of conscience Dr Mohammed al-Roken remained in prison, serving a 10-year sentence imposed after the unfair "UAE 94" mass trial in 2013.

ENFORCED DISAPPEARANCES

The authorities subjected scores of detainees, including foreign nationals, to enforced disappearance, holding them for months in secret and unacknowledged detention for interrogation. Upon release, many reported that they had been tortured and otherwise ill-treated.

'Abdulrahman Bin Sobeih was subjected to enforced disappearance for three months by UAE authorities after he was forcibly returned to the UAE by Indonesia in December 2015. He had been sentenced in his absence in 2013 to a 15-year prison term after the unfair UAE 94 trial. Following a retrial, in November he was sentenced to 10 years' imprisonment, followed by three years' surveillance.

Prisoner of conscience Dr Nasser Bin Ghaith, an academic and economist arrested in August 2015, was subjected to enforced disappearance until April when he was brought before the SSC. He faced charges relating solely to the peaceful exercise of his rights to freedom of expression and association. He told the court that officials had tortured and otherwise ill-treated him, but the judge failed to order an investigation. In December his case was transferred to an appeal court.

TORTURE AND OTHER ILL-TREATMENT

Torture and other ill-treatment of detainees, particularly those subjected to enforced disappearance, remained common and were committed with impunity. Neither the government nor the SSC conducted independent investigations into detainees' allegations of torture.

Between March and June the authorities released six of at least 12 men of Libyan origin whom they had arrested in 2014 and 2015. They were released after the SSC acquitted them of providing support for Libyan armed groups. During 2015, State Security officials had subjected at least 10 of the men to months of incommunicado detention and torture, including beatings, electric shocks and sleep deprivation, before they were brought to trial. The fate of two of the men remained undisclosed, while those freed in 2016 included Salim al-Aradi, a Canadian-Libyan national, and Kamal Eldarat and his son, Mohammed Eldarat, both US-Libyan nationals.

UNFAIR TRIALS

Scores of people, including foreign nationals, were prosecuted before the SSC, often on vaguely worded charges relating to national security. The SSC denied defendants the right to an effective defence and accepted evidence obtained under torture to convict defendants. In December, the government enacted legislation providing for an appeal in state security cases.

In March, the SSC convicted 34 men on charges that included establishing Shabab al-Manara (Minaret Youth Group) to overthrow the government and create an "IS-style caliphate". They received prison sentences ranging from three years to life. Authorities detained them in 2013 and subjected them to enforced disappearance for 20 months. Some appeared to have been convicted based on "confessions" they said were extracted through torture.

In June, the SSC sentenced Egyptian national Mosaab Ahmed 'Abdel-'Aziz Ramadan to three years' imprisonment for running an "international group in the UAE affiliated to the Egyptian Muslim Brotherhood". Before trial, the authorities subjected him to several months of enforced disappearance during which he alleged that security officials forced him to "confess" under torture.

WOMEN'S RIGHTS

Women remained subject to discrimination in law and in practice, notably in matters of marriage and divorce, inheritance and child custody. They were inadequately protected against sexual violence and violence within the family.

MIGRANT WORKERS' RIGHTS

Migrant workers, who comprise around 90% of the private workforce, continued to face exploitation and abuse. They remained tied to employers under the *kafala* sponsorship system and were denied collective bargaining rights. Trade unions remained banned and migrant workers who engaged in strike action faced deportation and a one-year ban on returning to the UAE.

In January, Ministerial Decrees 764, 765 and 767 of 2015 came into effect, which the government said would address some abuses against migrant workers, including the longstanding practice of contract substitution whereby employers require migrant workers to sign new contracts with reduced wages when they arrive in the UAE.

The decrees did not apply to domestic workers, mostly women from Asia and Africa, who remained explicitly excluded from labour law protections and particularly vulnerable to exploitation and serious abuses, including forced labour and human trafficking.

DEATH PENALTY

Courts handed down death sentences; no executions were reported. Law 7/2016, relating to data protection and expression, expanded the applicability of the death penalty.

UNITED KINGDOM

United Kingdom of Great Britain and Northern Ireland
Head of state: **Queen Elizabeth II**
Head of government: **Theresa May (replaced David Cameron in July)**

Full accountability for torture allegations against UK intelligence agencies and armed forces remained unrealized. An extremely broad surveillance law was passed. Women in Northern Ireland faced significant restrictions on access to abortion. The government failed to establish a review into the impacts of cuts to civil legal aid. Hate crimes rose significantly following the UK's referendum vote to leave the EU.

LEGAL, CONSTITUTIONAL OR INSTITUTIONAL DEVELOPMENTS

In June, the majority of the electorate in the UK and Gibraltar voted in a referendum to leave the EU.

Although the new Justice Secretary announced in August that the government intended to continue with plans to replace the Human Rights Act (which incorporates the European Convention on Human Rights into domestic law) with a British Bill of Rights, by the end of the year the Attorney General suggested that concrete proposals would be deferred until after the EU referendum process had been completed.

JUSTICE SYSTEM

Calls intensified for a review of cuts to civil legal aid brought about by the Legal Aid, Sentencing and Punishment of Offenders Act 2012 (LASPO), based on their impact on vulnerable and marginalized people in various contexts, including inquests, immigration, welfare, family and housing law.[1] Official statistics published in June by the Legal Aid Agency showed that legal help in civil cases had dropped to one third of pre-LASPO levels. In July, the UN Committee on Economic, Social and Cultural Rights called on the government to reassess the impact of reforms to the legal aid system. The government failed to establish a review.

COUNTER-TERROR AND SECURITY

Counter-terrorism powers and related policy initiatives to counter "extremism" continued to raise concerns.

Definition of terrorism

Despite a Court of Appeal judgment in January which narrowed the definition of terrorism, and recurring criticism of the over-broad statutory definition by the Independent Reviewer of Terrorism Legislation, the Home Secretary confirmed, in October, that the government had no intention of changing it.

Administrative controls

In November, Parliament extended the Terrorism Prevention and Investigation Measures (TPIM) Act 2011 for five more years. TPIMs are government-imposed administrative restrictions on individuals suspected of involvement in terrorism-related activity.

The Independent Reviewer's annual report, published in November, documented that new powers to prevent suspected "foreign terrorist fighters" from travelling were applied 24 times during 2015, and pre-existing powers to withdraw passports from British citizens were exercised 23 times, but that a power available since 2015 to temporarily exclude returning "foreign terrorist fighters" had not been used.

"Counter-extremism" policy

Plans for a Counter-Extremism and Safeguarding Bill were announced in May, but no concrete legislative proposal had been tabled by end of year.

NGO research into the statutory "prevent duty" on certain public bodies, including schools, to "have due regard to the need to prevent people from being drawn into terrorism", found that the scheme created a serious risk of violating human rights, including peaceful exercise of freedom of expression, and that its application in educational and health care settings undermined trust.

In April, the UN Special Rapporteur on the rights to freedom of peaceful assembly and of association warned that the government's approach to "non-violent extremism" risked violating both freedoms. In July, the Parliamentary Joint Committee for Human Rights recommended the use of existing laws rather than drafting new, unclear legislation.

Drones

In May, the Joint Committee for Human Rights published its inquiry into the use of drones for targeted killing. The inquiry examined the drone strike by the Royal Air Force in 2015 in al-Raqqa, Syria, killing three people, including at least one British national, believed to be members of the armed group Islamic State (IS). The inquiry called on the government to clarify its policy of targeted killings in armed conflict and its role in targeted killing by other states outside armed conflict.

TORTURE AND OTHER ILL-TREATMENT
Internment in Northern Ireland
In December, the government responded to questions put to it by the European Court of Human Rights (ECtHR), following a 2014 request by the Irish government to review the 1978 judgment in *Ireland v UK*, on torture techniques used in internment in Northern Ireland in 1971-72.

Rendition
In June, the Crown Prosecution Service (CPS) decided not to bring any criminal charges relating to allegations by two Libyan families that they had been subject to rendition, torture and other ill-treatment in 2004 by the US and Libyan governments, with the knowledge and co-operation of UK officials. In November, the two families – Abdul-Hakim Belhaj and Fatima Boudchar, and Sami al-Saadi and his wife and children – began judicial review proceedings to challenge the CPS decision.

Armed forces
In September, it emerged that the Royal Military Police were investigating approximately 600 cases of alleged mistreatment and abuse in detention in Afghanistan between 2005 and 2013.

As of November, the Iraq Historic Allegations Team, the body investigating allegations of abuse of Iraqi civilians by UK armed forces personnel, had concluded or was about to conclude investigations into 2,356 of 3,389 allegations received.

The Iraq Fatality Investigations, a separate body established in 2013, reported in September on the death of 15-year-old Ahmad Jabbar Kareem Ali, finding that he drowned after being forced into the Shatt-al-Basra canal in southern Iraq in 2003 by UK soldiers. The Ministry of Defence apologized for the incident.

Allegations of war crimes committed by UK armed forces in Iraq between 2003 and 2008 remained under preliminary examination by the Office of the Prosecutor of the International Criminal Court.

SURVEILLANCE
In November, the Investigatory Powers Act (IPA), which overhauled the existing, piecemeal domestic legislation on surveillance, became law. The IPA granted increased powers to public authorities to interfere with private communication and information in the UK and abroad. It permitted a broad range of vaguely defined interception, interference and data retention practices, and imposed new requirements on private companies, facilitating government surveillance by creating "internet connection records". The new law lacked a requirement for clear prior judicial authorization.

In October, the Investigatory Powers Tribunal (IPT) ruled that the secret, bulk collection of domestic and foreign communications data and the collection of "bulk personal datasets" had violated the right to privacy previously, but were now lawful.

Proceedings were pending before the ECtHR regarding the legality of the pre-IPA mass surveillance regime and intelligence sharing practices. The Court of Justice of the EU ruled in December that the general, indiscriminate retention of communications data under the Data Retention and Investigatory Powers Act 2014 was not permitted.

NORTHERN IRELAND: LEGACY ISSUES
The former and current Secretaries of State for Northern Ireland both referred to those raising allegations of collusion or focusing on human rights violations by state agents as contributing to a "pernicious counter narrative". NGOs advocating for accountability for victims raised concerns that such language placed their work as human rights defenders at risk.

In November, the Special Rapporteur on the promotion of truth, justice, reparation and guarantees of non-recurrence urged the UK government to address structural or systemic patterns of violations and abuses, rather than focusing solely on existing "event-based" approaches. He suggested widening the focus of measures from cases of death to include torture, sexual abuse and unlawful detention, with a gender-sensitive approach. The Special Rapporteur also urged limiting national security arguments against claims for redress, and ensuring that reparations for all victims be tackled seriously and systematically.

The Lord Chief Justice of Northern Ireland set out a detailed five-year plan to address the backlog of "legacy" coroner's inquests, but failed to receive funding from the Northern Ireland Executive and central government.

The government continued to refuse to establish an independent public inquiry into the 1989 killing of Patrick Finucane, despite having acknowledged previously that there had been "collusion" in the case.

SEXUAL AND REPRODUCTIVE RIGHTS

Access to abortion in Northern Ireland remained limited to exceptional cases where the life or health of the woman or girl was at risk.[2] The abortion law in Northern Ireland was criticized by both the Committee on Economic, Social and Cultural Rights and the Committee on the Rights of the Child in July.

Women in Northern Ireland faced criminal prosecution for taking WHO-approved medication to induce abortions. A woman was given a three-month suspended sentence after pleading guilty to two offences under the 1861 law governing abortion in Northern Ireland.

Official statistics for the previous year showed that 833 women from Northern Ireland had travelled to England or Wales to access abortion, and that 16 lawful abortions had been performed in Northern Ireland.

In June, the Northern Ireland Court of Appeal heard appeals of a 2015 High Court, ruling that the region's abortion law was incompatible with domestic and international human rights law.

In November, Scotland's First Minister set out proposals to provide access to abortion services through the National Health Service in Scotland for women and girls from Northern Ireland.

DISCRIMINATION

The National Police Chiefs' Council's official statistics in June and September showed a 57% spike in reporting of hate crime in the week immediately following the EU membership referendum, followed by a decrease in reporting to a level 14% higher than the same period the previous year. The UN High Commissioner for Human Rights expressed his concern in June. Government statistics published in October showed an increase in hate crimes of 19% over the previous year, with 79% of the incidents recorded classified as "race hate crimes". In November, the CERD Committee called on the UK to take steps to address the increase in such hate crimes.

In the first inquiry of its kind, the UN Committee on the Rights of Persons with Disabilities reported on the cumulative impact of legislative changes on welfare, care and legal assistance. The government disagreed with the Committee's findings of "grave or systematic violations of the rights of persons with disabilities."

REFUGEES' AND MIGRANTS' RIGHTS

The Immigration Act became law in May. It extended sanctions against landlords whose tenants' immigration status disqualifies them from renting, while increasing landlords' eviction powers; extended powers to block limited appeal rights against removal from the UK until after the person has left the country; and introduced a scheme whereby separated children seeking asylum in the UK may be transferred between local authorities.

The government continued to resist calls to take more responsibility for hosting refugees. In April, the government announced it would resettle up to 3,000 people from the Middle East and North Africa by May 2020. In October, the government accepted a few dozen separated children from the "Jungle" camp in Calais, France, alongside a larger number of other children relocated to join family under provisions of the Dublin III regulations.

In January, an Independent Review into the welfare in detention of vulnerable persons made strong criticisms of the scale and longevity of immigration detention. In August, the Home Office responded with a new "adults at risk" policy. However, NGOs criticized the policy for further removing safeguards against harmful detention, including by adopting a narrow definition of "torture" when considering the risk posed by detention to a person's welfare. In November, the High Court permitted a challenge to the policy, ordering that the previous wider definition of torture be used for the time being.

VIOLENCE AGAINST WOMEN AND GIRLS

In December, the House of Commons voted to ratify the Council of Europe Convention on preventing and combating violence against women and domestic violence (Istanbul Convention), which the government had signed in 2012. In July, the UN Committee on the Rights of the Child recommended improved collection of information on violence against children, including domestic and gender-based violence.

Serious concerns remained about the reduced funding of specialist services for women who had experienced domestic violence or abuse. Research by the domestic women's rights organization Women's Aid showed that refuges were being forced to turn away two in three survivors due to lack of space or inability to meet their needs, and that the rate for ethnic minority women was four in five.

TRADE UNION RIGHTS

In May, the Trade Union Act, which placed more restrictions on unions organizing strike action, came into force. During the year, the UN Special Rapporteur on the rights to freedom of peaceful assembly and of association and the UN Committee on Economic, Social and Cultural Rights called on the government to review and revise the law.

1. United Kingdom: Cuts that hurt – the impact of legal aid cuts in England on access to justice (EUR 45/4936/2016)

2. United Kingdom: Submission to the UN Committee on Economic, Social and Cultural Rights (EUR 45/3990/2016)

UNITED STATES OF AMERICA

United States of America
Head of state and government: **Barack Obama**

Two years after a Senate committee reported on abuses in the secret detention programme operated by the CIA, there was still no accountability for crimes under international law committed under it. More detainees were transferred out of the US detention centre at Guantánamo Bay, Cuba, but others remained in indefinite detention there, while pre-trial military commission proceedings continued in a handful of cases. Concern about the treatment of refugees and migrants, the use of isolation in state and federal prisons and the use of force in policing continued. There were 20 executions during the year. In November, Donald Trump was elected as President; his inauguration was scheduled for 20 January 2017.

INTERNATIONAL SCRUTINY

In August, the UN Human Rights Committee expressed concern that the investigation into torture in the counter-terrorism context, which the USA was legally obliged to conduct, had not taken place. The Committee noted that the USA had provided no further information on the Senate Select Committee on Intelligence (SSCI) report into the secret detention programme operated by the CIA after the attacks of 11 September 2001 (9/11). The full 6,963-page report remained classified top secret and the SSCI had not released it by the end of the year.

On 16 August, the Committee noted that the USA had provided no further information on reports that Guantánamo Bay detainees had been denied access to judicial remedy for torture and other human rights violations incurred while in US custody.

IMPUNITY

No action was taken to end impunity for the systematic human rights violations, including torture and enforced disappearance, committed in the secret CIA detention programme after 9/11.

In May, the US Court of Appeals for the District of Columbia (DC) Circuit ruled that the SSCI report into the secret CIA detention programme remained a "congressional record" and was not subject to disclosure under the Freedom of Information Act. A petition seeking US Supreme Court review of the ruling was filed in November. Separately, in late December, a DC District Court judge ordered the administration to preserve the SSCI report, and to deposit an electronic or paper copy of it with the Court for secure storage. At the end of the year, it was not known if the government would appeal the order.

On 12 August, the DC Circuit Court of Appeals dismissed a lawsuit for damages brought on behalf of Afghan national Mohamed Jawad who had been held in US military custody from 2002 to 2009. During that time he was subjected to torture or other cruel, inhuman or degrading treatment. He was under 18 years old when taken into US custody in Afghanistan and transferred to detention in Guantánamo Bay.[1] The Court of Appeals upheld a lower court decision to dismiss the lawsuit on the grounds that the federal courts lacked jurisdiction under Section 7 of the Military Commission Act (MCA) of 2006.[2]

In October, the US Court of Appeals for the Fourth Circuit overturned a lower court's dismissal of a lawsuit brought by Iraqi nationals who claimed they were tortured by interrogators employed by CACI Premier Technology, Inc. at Abu Ghraib prison in Iraq in 2003 and 2004. The Court held that intentional conduct by contracted interrogators, which was unlawful at the time it was committed, could not be shielded from judicial review.

COUNTER-TERROR AND SECURITY

At the end of the year, nearly eight years after President Obama made the commitment to close the Guantánamo Bay detention facility by January 2010, 59 men were still held there, the majority of them without charge or trial. During 2016, 48 detainees were transferred to government authorities in Bosnia and Herzegovina, Cape Verde, Ghana, Italy, Kuwait, Mauritania, Montenegro, Oman, Saudi Arabia, Senegal, Serbia and the United Arab Emirates.

In August, the UN Committee against Torture said that its recommendation to end indefinite detention without charge or trial, which amounted per se to a violation of the UN Convention against Torture, had not been implemented.

Pre-trial military commission proceedings continued against five detainees accused of involvement in the 9/11 attacks and charged in 2012 for capital trial under the MCA of 2009. The five – Khalid Sheikh Mohammed, Walid bin Attash, Ramzi bin al-Shibh, Ammar al Baluchi and Mustafa al Hawsawi – were held incommunicado in secret US custody for up to four years prior to their transfer to Guantánamo Bay in 2006. Their trial had not begun by the end of 2016.

Pre-trial military commission proceedings also continued against 'Abd al-Rahim al-Nashiri. He was arraigned for capital trial in 2011 on charges relating to the attempted bombing of the USS The Sullivans in 2000, and the bombings of the USS Cole in 2000 and of the French supertanker Limburg in 2002, all in Yemen. He had been held in secret CIA custody for nearly four years prior to his transfer to Guantánamo Bay in 2006. In August 2016, the DC Circuit Court of Appeals ruled that a decision on his claim, that the offences with which he had been charged were not triable by military commission because they were not committed in the context of and associated with hostilities, had to await a final appeal in the case in what was still likely a decade away.

Omar Khadr who pleaded guilty in 2010 to charges under the MCA relating to conduct in 2002 in Afghanistan when he was aged 15, and was transferred to his native Canada in 2012, sought disqualification of one of the judges on the Court of Military Commission Review (CMCR) on grounds of lack of impartiality. The DC Circuit Court of Appeals rejected the challenge, again ruling that the claim would have to wait for a final appeal to be decided.

During the year, Omar Khadr's appeal to the CMCR against his conviction, including on grounds that he had pleaded guilty to offences that were not war crimes triable by military commission, was held in abeyance pending the Court of Appeals' decision on the case of Guantánamo Bay detainee Ali Hamza Suliman al Bahlul who is serving a life sentence imposed in 2008 under the MCA of 2006. In 2015, a three-judge panel of the Court had overturned Ali Hamza Suliman al Bahlul's conviction for conspiracy to commit war crimes on the grounds that the charge was not recognized under international law and could not be tried by a military tribunal. The government successfully sought reconsideration by the full court, which in October 2016 upheld the conspiracy conviction in a fractured vote involving five separate opinions and no resolution of the ultimate issue. Three of the nine judges dissented, arguing that Congress did not have the power to make conspiracy an offence triable by military commission, stressing that "whatever deference the judiciary may owe to the political branches in matters of national security and defense, it is not absolute". Two judges wrote separately to say that it was improper to decide the ultimate issue for procedural reasons unique to Ali Hamza Suliman al Bahlul's case.

EXCESSIVE USE OF FORCE

The authorities continued to fail to track the exact number of people killed by law enforcement officials during the year – documentation by media outlets put the numbers at nearly 1,000 individuals killed. The US Department of Justice (DOJ) announced plans to create a system to track these deaths under the Deaths in Custody Reporting Act, to be implemented in 2017. However, the programme is not compulsory for law enforcement agencies and the data compiled may not reflect the total numbers. According to the limited data that is available, black men are disproportionately victims of police killings.

At least 21 people across 17 states died after police used electric-shock weapons on them, bringing the total number of such deaths since 2001 to at least 700. Most of the victims were not armed and did not appear to pose a threat of death or serious injury when the electric-shock weapon was deployed.

FREEDOM OF ASSEMBLY

In July, the deaths of Philando Castile in Falcon Heights, Minnesota, and Alton Sterling in Baton Rouge, Louisiana, sparked protests against the police across the country. Similar protests against police use of force occurred in other cities such as Tulsa in Oklahoma and Charlotte in North Carolina. The use of heavy-duty riot gear and military-grade weapons and equipment to police these demonstrations raised several concerns in terms of the demonstrators' right to peaceful assembly.

Protests in and around Standing Rock, North Dakota, against the Dakota Access Pipeline to transport crude oil, despite being largely peaceful, drew a heavy police response from local and state law enforcement authorities. Local law enforcement agencies placed a police barricade on the road leading to the protest sites. Officers responded in riot gear and with assault weapons and used pepper spray, rubber bullets and electric-shock weapons against protesters. There were more than 400 arrests after August, mainly for acts of trespassing and non-violent resistance. Authorities targeted reporters and activists for low-level offences such as trespassing.

GUN VIOLENCE

Attempts by US Congress to pass legislation to prevent the sale of assault weapons or implement comprehensive background checks for weapon buyers, failed to pass. Congress continued to deny funding to the Center for Disease Control and Prevention to conduct or sponsor research into the causes of gun violence and ways to prevent it.

REFUGEES' AND MIGRANTS' RIGHTS

More than 42,000 unaccompanied children and 56,000 individuals who comprised family units were apprehended crossing the southern border irregularly during the year. Families were detained for months, some for more than a year, while pursuing claims to remain in the USA. Many were held in facilities without proper access to medical care and legal counsel. The UN High Commissioner for Refugees called the situation in the Northern Triangle a humanitarian and protection crisis.

The authorities resettled more than 12,000 Syrian refugees by the end of the year and said they would go from taking in 70,000 refugees per year to accepting 85,000 in fiscal year 2016 and 100,000 in the year 2017. Legislators introduced bills attempting to prevent lawfully admitted refugees from living in their state. In September, Texas announced its withdrawal from the federal Refugee Resettlement Program on the basis of alleged security concerns, despite refugees being required to undergo an exhaustive screening process before entering the USA. Kansas and New Jersey also withdrew from the Program.

WOMEN'S RIGHTS

Native American and Alaskan Native women remained more than 2.5 times more likely to be raped or sexually assaulted than non-Indigenous women. Gross inequalities remained for Indigenous women in accessing post-rape care, including access to examinations, rape kits – a package of items used by medical staff to gather forensic evidence – and other essential health care services.

Disparities in women's access to sexual and reproductive health care, including maternal care, continued. The maternal mortality ratio rose over the last six years; African-American women remained nearly four times more likely to die of pregnancy-related complications than white women.

The threat of criminal punishment for drug use during pregnancy continued to deter women from marginalized groups from accessing health care, including prenatal care. However, a harmful amendment to Tennessee's "fetal assault" law expired in July after successful advocacy ensured the law did not become permanent.[3]

RIGHTS OF LESBIAN, GAY, BISEXUAL, TRANSGENDER AND INTERSEX PEOPLE

Legal discrimination against LGBTI people persisted at the state and federal level. No federal protections existed banning discrimination on the grounds of sexual orientation and gender identity in the workplace, housing or health care. While some individual states and cities enacted non-discrimination laws that included protection on the grounds of sexual orientation and gender identity, the vast majority of states provided no legal protections for LGBTI people. Conversion therapy, criticized by the UN Committee against Torture as a form of torture, remained legal in most states and territories. Transgender people continued to be particularly marginalized. Murder rates of transgender women were high and discriminatory state laws, such as North Carolina's "bathroom bill" which bans cities from allowing transgender individuals to use public bathrooms in accordance with their gender identity, undermined their rights.

PRISON CONDITIONS

Over 80,000 prisoners at any given time were held in conditions of physical and social deprivation in federal and state prisons throughout the country. In January, the DOJ issued guiding principles and policy recommendations that would limit the use of solitary confinement and restrictive housing – prison or jail housing that had different rules than were in place for the general prison population – in federal prisons. The recommendations emphasized housing prisoners in the least restrictive environment possible, diverting persons with mental illness out of isolation, and drastically limiting the use of solitary confinement for juveniles.

DEATH PENALTY

Twenty men were executed in five states, bringing to 1,442 the total number of executions since the US Supreme Court approved new capital laws in 1976. This was the lowest annual total since 1991. Approximately 30 new death sentences were passed. Around 2,900 people remained on death row at the end of the year.

Texas carried out fewer than 10 executions for the first time since 1996. Oklahoma did not carry out any executions for the first time since 1994. Texas and Oklahoma combined accounted for 45% of executions in the USA between 1976 and 2016.

In the November elections, the Oklahoma electorate voted to amend the state constitution to prohibit Oklahoma's state courts from declaring the death penalty a "cruel or unusual" punishment. In California, the state with the largest death row population, voters opted not to repeal the death penalty; and in Nebraska the electorate voted to reject the legislature's 2015 repeal of the death penalty.

Execution moratoriums remained in force in Pennsylvania, Washington State and Oregon throughout the year.

Florida, where executions had been on the increase in recent years, saw them on hold all year after the US Supreme Court ruled in *Hurst v Florida* in January that Florida's capital sentencing statute was unconstitutional for giving juries only an advisory role in who was sentenced to death. Florida legislature passed a new statute, but in October the Florida Supreme Court ruled it unconstitutional because it did not require juror unanimity on death sentencing. In

December, the Florida Supreme Court ruled that the *Hurst* ruling applied to those death row inmates – just over 200 of nearly 400 – whose death sentences had not yet been finalized on mandatory appeal by 2002. They could be entitled to new sentencing hearings as a result.

In August, the Delaware Supreme Court struck down Delaware's capital sentencing statute in the wake of *Hurst v Florida*, because it gave judges the ultimate power to decide whether the prosecution had proved all facts necessary to impose the death penalty. Delaware's Attorney General announced that he would not appeal the ruling.

States continued to face difficulties with their lethal injection protocols and the acquisition of drugs. Louisiana will not carry out any executions throughout 2017 due to the litigation in federal court on its lethal injection protocol. Ohio continued to face problems sourcing lethal injection drugs and there were no executions for the second year running in Ohio. In March, Ohio Supreme Court ruled 4-3 that the state could try to execute Romell Broom for the second time. The first attempt in 2009 was abandoned after the lethal injection team failed to establish an intravenous line during two hours of trying. An execution date for Romell Broom had not been set by the end of the year.

The US Supreme Court intervened in a number of capital cases. In March, it granted Louisiana death row inmate Michael Wearry a new trial, 14 years after he was convicted. The Court found that prosecutorial misconduct, including the withholding of exculpatory evidence, had violated Michael Wearry's right to a fair trial. In May, it granted Georgia death row inmate Timothy Foster a new trial because of racial discrimination at jury selection. Timothy Foster, an African-American, was sentenced to death by an all-white jury after prosecutors had peremptorily removed every black prospective juror from the jury pool.

In August, the National Hispanic Caucus of State Legislators "overwhelmingly" approved a resolution calling for abolition of the death penalty across the USA. The resolution cited racial discrimination, ineffectiveness, cost and the risk of error.

In April, Gary Tyler was released after 42 years in prison in Louisiana. Gary Tyler, an African-American, had originally been sentenced to death for the fatal shooting of a 13-year-old white boy in 1974 during a riot over school integration. Gary Tyler, aged 16 at the time of the shooting, was convicted and sentenced to death by an all-white jury. His death sentence was overturned after the US Supreme Court ruled Louisiana's mandatory death penalty statute unconstitutional in 1976; and his life sentence was overturned after the Court in 2012 barred mandatory life without parole sentences for crimes committed by under-18-year-olds. The prosecution agreed to vacate the murder conviction, allowed him to plead guilty to manslaughter, and he received the maximum prison sentence of 21 years, less than half the time he had already served.[4]

---

1. USA: From ill-treatment to unfair trial – the case of Mohamed Jawad, child "enemy combatant" (AMR 51/091/2008)

2. USA: Chronicle of immunity foretold (AMR 51/003/2013)

3. USA: Tennessee "Fetal Assault" Law – a threat to women's health and human rights (AMR 51/3623/2016)

4. USA: The Case of Gary Tyler, Louisiana (AMR 51/089/1994); Louisiana: Unfair Trial – Gary Tyler (AMR 51/182/2007)

URUGUAY

Eastern Republic of Uruguay
Head of state and government: **Tabaré Vázquez**

Despite efforts by the Working Group for Truth and Justice, little progress was made in the few criminal prosecutions of crimes under international law and human rights violations committed during the period of civil-military government (1973-1985). Discrimination against people with disabilities persisted and lack of gender equality remained a concern. Uruguay hosted the Global LGBTI Human Rights Conference. The exercise of conscientious objection among medical practitioners continued to pose significant barriers to women's access to safe and legal abortion.

BACKGROUND

The Action Plan 2016-2019 "for a life free of gender violence", drafted by the National Advisory Council against Domestic Violence, came into effect.

In July, the UN CEDAW Committee urged Uruguay to increase action to reduce discrimination against Afro-descendant women and to improve their access to education, employment and health. The Committee also expressed concern about the lack of a specific mechanism to ensure reparations for women who had suffered sexual violence under the civil-military government, among other issues.

In August, the UN Committee on the Rights of Persons with Disabilities called for the creation of consultation mechanisms for people with disabilities to enable them to participate in the adoption of public and legislative policies and to ensure accessible methods for reporting discrimination on grounds of disability.

PRISON CONDITIONS

In June, the Parliamentary Commissioner for the Penitentiary System, with the support of other national institutions and the UN High Commissioner for Human Rights, facilitated workshops on human rights education for prison directors. These workshops aimed to improve public servants' understanding of human rights-based approaches in order to avoid internal conflicts and the excessive use of force.

IMPUNITY

The Truth and Justice Working Group, established in May 2015 to investigate crimes against humanity committed between 1968 and 1985, continued to collect testimonies, conduct exhumations, and locate the remains of missing persons. It also gained access to important documentation, including archives at the headquarters of

Naval Fusiliers and was due to make its findings public in 2017.

RIGHTS OF LESBIAN, GAY, BISEXUAL, TRANSGENDER AND INTERSEX PEOPLE

In July, Uruguay hosted the Global LGBTI Human Rights Conference. Uruguay chaired the thematic group discussion calling for LGBTI people to be included in the 2030 Agenda for Sustainable Development.

For the first time Uruguay carried out a census of transgender people to better understand their situation. The multiple discrimination suffered by transgender people remained a problem, despite efforts and policies to improve the situation.

Homophobia-free health centres were successfully developed; however, the lack of comprehensive health care for LGBTI people remained a challenge.

SEXUAL AND REPRODUCTIVE RIGHTS

The UN CEDAW Committee commended Uruguay for a drastic reduction in maternal mortality and the expansion of women's access to sexual and reproductive health services. However, it expressed concern that such access remained limited in rural areas. The Committee expressed further concern at the widespread use of conscientious objection among medical practitioners, which limited women's access to safe and legal abortion services. The Committee called on the government to assess the nationwide availability of sexual and reproductive health services in order to identify underserved areas and ensure appropriate funding; to take measures to ensure that women have access to legal abortion and post-abortion services; and to introduce more rigorous requirements to prevent blanket use of conscientious objection in cases of abortion.

UZBEKISTAN

Republic of Uzbekistan
Head of state: Shavkat Mirzioiev (replaced Islam Karimov in September)
Head of government: Abdulla Aripov (replaced Shavkat Mirzioiev in December)

Torture in detention centres and prisons continued to be pervasive. The authorities secured the return, including by secret rendition, of hundreds of people they suspected of criminal activity, of being in opposition to the government or of being a threat to national security; they were at risk of torture. Forced labour was widely used. The rights to freedom of expression and of association remained severely restricted. Human rights defenders continued to face routine harassment and violence.

BACKGROUND

President Karimov died on 2 September, after 27 years in power. The authorities controlled all information surrounding his death and launched sustained attacks on social media against independent news outlets and human rights activists who criticized the late President's human rights record.

Prime Minister Mirzioiev, appointed acting President in September, was elected President on 4 December.

TORTURE AND OTHER ILL-TREATMENT

The authorities continued to categorically deny reports of pervasive torture and other ill-treatment by law enforcement officials. In October, the Director of the National Centre for Human Rights said that torture allegations were based on fabricated evidence and "clearly designed as a means of disinformation… to put undue pressure" on Uzbekistan.[1]

Human rights defenders, former prisoners and relatives of prisoners continued to provide credible information that police and National Security Service (NSS) officers routinely used torture to coerce suspects, detainees and prisoners into confessing crimes or incriminating others.

Judges continued to ignore or dismiss as unfounded allegations of torture or other ill-treatment, even when presented with credible evidence.

In February, the Dzhizakh Regional Criminal Court convicted fish farmer Aramais Avakian and four co-defendants of plotting anti-constitutional activities and of membership of an "extremist organization". They were sentenced to between five and 12 years in prison.

Aramais Avakian consistently denied the charges and told the court that NSS officers had abducted him, held him incommunicado for a month, tortured and forced him to confess. They broke several of his ribs and gave him electric shocks. In court, several of the prosecution witnesses said that NSS officers had detained and tortured them in order to incriminate Aramais Avakian and his co-defendants. During the appeal hearing in March, his co-defendant Furkat Dzhuraev told the judge that he, too, had been tortured. The trial and appeal judges ignored all allegations of torture and admitted the defendants' forced "confessions" as evidence against them.

COUNTER-TERROR AND SECURITY

The authorities continued to secure the return – through extradition proceedings or otherwise – of numerous Uzbekistani nationals they suspected of criminal activity, or labelled as opponents or a threat to national security.

Forced returns

In October, the authorities said they had secured the return of 542 individuals between January 2015 and July 2016.

The government offered assurances to the authorities of the sending state saying that independent monitors and diplomats would have free and confidential access to extradited individuals and that they would receive a fair trial; in reality, access was limited. In some cases it took up to a year for diplomats to be granted permission to see a detainee or prisoner, and they were generally accompanied by officials, precluding confidential conversations.

NSS officers continued the practice of secret renditions (abducting wanted individuals) from abroad. In Russia, local security services were complicit in this practice in those rare instances when the Russian authorities refused to comply with extradition requests.

Those abducted or otherwise forcibly returned were subjected to incommunicado detention, often in undisclosed locations, and tortured or otherwise ill-treated to force them to confess or incriminate others. In many cases, security forces pressured relatives not to seek support from human rights organizations, and not to file complaints about alleged human rights violations.

On 4 March, Russian intelligence officers apprehended asylum-seeker Sarvar Mardiev as he was released from prison in Russia and drove him away. His whereabouts were undisclosed until October, when the Uzbekistan authorities confirmed that Sarvar Mardiev was detained in Kashkadaria the day after his release from prison in Russia. They said he was in pre-trial detention charged with crimes against the state. He was not granted access to a lawyer for a month.

Persecution of family members

The authorities increased pressure on relatives of those suspected or convicted of crimes against the state, including individuals working or seeking protection abroad.

The authorities used the threat of bringing charges of membership of a banned Islamist group against a detained relative to prevent families from exposing human rights violations and seeking help from human rights organizations at home and/or abroad.

Local *mahalla* (neighbourhood) committees continued to collaborate with security forces and local and national authorities in closely monitoring residents of their *mahallas* for any signs of behaviour or activities considered improper, suspect or illegal. *Mahalla* committees publicly exposed residents and their families and took punitive action against them.

In February, *mahalla* members informed the wife of Aramais Avakian that local residents had decided to expel her and her children from their neighbourhood because of the "actions of her terrorist husband" and because she had given interviews to foreign journalists, slandered local officials and brought Uzbekistan into disrepute.

FORCED LABOUR

Forced labour was used in the cotton industry. International organizations estimated that the authorities compelled over a million public sector employees to work in the cotton fields, in the preparation of the fields in spring and the harvest in the autumn. Uzbekistan was the world's second biggest user of modern-day slavery according to the 2016 Global Slavery Index.

FREEDOM OF EXPRESSION – HUMAN RIGHTS DEFENDERS

The rights to freedom of expression and association remained severely restricted.

Activists who attempted to document the use of forced labour in the cotton fields were repeatedly detained and searched.

On 8 October, police and NSS officers detained the head of the independent NGO Human Rights Defenders' Alliance of Uzbekistan, Elena Urlaeva, and independent photographer Timur Karpov as well as two French activists in Buk District of Tashkent Region. They were interviewing medical staff and teachers sent to work in the cotton fields. Elena Urlaeva reported that she was escorted to an interrogation room in Buk police station by a group of women, two of whom pulled her by her hair, punched and verbally insulted her. Police officers did not stop them but instead threatened Elena Urlaeva and refused to call medical assistance for her. They released her without charges after six hours. Timur Karpov was detained for 10 hours and threatened. Their recording equipment and documentation materials were confiscated.

1. Uzbekistan: Fast-track to torture – abductions and forcible returns from Russia to Uzbekistan (EUR 62/3740/2016)

VENEZUELA

Bolivarian Republic of Venezuela
Head of state and government: **Nicolás Maduro Moros**

The government declared a state of emergency which was renewed four times. Most of those suspected of responsibility for crimes under international law and for human rights violations during the 2014 protests had yet to be brought to justice. Prison overcrowding and violence continued. Survivors of gender-based violence faced significant obstacles in accessing justice. Human rights defenders and journalists frequently faced campaigns to discredit them, as well as attacks and intimidation. Political opponents and critics of the government continued to face imprisonment. There were reports of excessive use of force by the police and security forces.

BACKGROUND

On 15 January, President Maduro declared a state of general emergency and economic emergency which lasted the year. The declaration established provisions which could restrict the work of civil society and NGOs, including by allowing the authorities to audit signed agreements between national organizations and legal entities with companies or institutions based abroad.

The authorities failed to report on the results of the implementation of the National Human Rights Plan, which had been approved in 2015.

Most of the judgments and orders passed on Venezuela by the Inter-American Court of Human Rights had yet to be complied with by the end of the year.

Food and medicine shortages intensified dramatically, provoking protests throughout the country. In July, the executive announced a new mandatory temporary work regime under which employees in public and private companies could be transferred to state-run food production companies, which would amount to forced labour.

In October, the UN High Commissioner for Human Rights stated that several Special Rapporteurs had experienced difficulties in visiting the country because the government failed to grant them the relevant permits.

In November, Venezuela's human rights record was examined for the second time under the UN Universal Periodic Review (UPR) process.

There was concern that the temporary nature of the positions held by more than 60% of judges made them susceptible to political pressure. Contrary to international human rights standards, civilians were tried before military courts. Police forces refused to comply with release orders issued by courts.

The powers of the opposition-led National Assembly were severely limited by resolutions from the Supreme Court of Justice, which hindered the ability of MPs to represent Indigenous Peoples. The Court also annulled a parliamentary declaration on non-discrimination connected with sexual orientation and gender identity; and a declaration which called for compliance with the decisions issued by intergovernmental organizations.

IMPUNITY

The country's withdrawal from the jurisdiction of the Inter-American Court of Human Rights (in effect since 2013) continued to deny victims of human rights violations and their relatives access to justice, truth and reparation.

Although two officials were convicted in December of murdering Bassil Da Costa and Geraldine Moreno during the 2014 protests, progress was slow in bringing to justice those suspected of criminal responsibility for the killing of 41 other people – including security force personnel – as well as the torture and other ill-treatment of demonstrators during the protests. The suspects included members of the security forces. Information

provided by the Attorney General during the UPR process revealed that nine officials had been convicted of various crimes and that 18 others were under investigation, even though 298 investigations had been initiated the previous year. However, the only official data published by the Public Prosecutor's Office was about the conviction of one man for the 2014 murder of Adriana Urquiola in the city of Los Teques, Miranda State.

According to a report presented to Parliament by the Public Prosecutor's Office in January, over 11,000 reports of crimes under international law and human rights violations were received in 2015, while only 77 trials were initiated during that year. No one had been brought to justice for the killings of eight members of the Barrios family or the threats and intimidation against other family members in Aragua State since 1998. Alcedo Mora Márquez, an employee of the Government Secretariat in Merida State and a community leader in the area, went missing in February 2015. Before his disappearance, he submitted reports on the misconduct of local public officials.

In March, 28 miners disappeared in Bolivar State; in October, the Public Prosecutor's Office presented a report revealing that it had found the miners' corpses and determined who was responsible for their disappearance. Twelve people were charged with murder, robbery and "deprivation of liberty".[1]

EXCESSIVE USE OF FORCE

There were continued reports of excessive use of force by security forces, particularly in the repression of protests over the lack of food and medicine. In June, Jenny Ortiz Gómez died as a result of several gunshots to the head when police officers carried out public order operations. The suspected perpetrator was charged with intentional homicide and misuse of firearms.

According to the Venezuelan Observatory of Social Conflict, approximately 590 protests were registered each month during the year. The majority were related to demands for economic, social and cultural rights, in particular access to food, health and housing.

HUMAN RIGHTS DEFENDERS

Human rights defenders continued to be targeted with attacks and intimidation by state media and high-ranking government officials.

In April, Humberto Prado Sifontes, director of the Venezuelan Prisons Observatory (OVP), was once again the victim of threats and insults when his email and social media accounts were hacked following the publication of an interview where he reported on crisis and violence in the prison system.[2]

In May, Rigoberto Lobo Puentes, a member of the Human Rights Observatory of the University of The Andes, was shot in the head and back with a pellet gun by police officers in Merida State, when tending to injured victims during a protest. The officers continued to shoot at him after he got into his car.

In June, lawyers Raquel Sánchez and Oscar Alfredo Ríos, members of the NGO Venezuelan Penal Forum, were attacked by a group of hooded assailants who smashed the windscreen and side mirrors of their car when they were travelling through Tachira State. Raquel Sánchez was severely wounded when she was hit on the head as she got out of the car.[3]

PRISON CONDITIONS

Prisons remained seriously overcrowded, and despite the announcement concerning new detention centres, prisoners' living conditions – including their access to food and health – worsened. The presence of weapons held by prisoners remained a problem which the authorities failed to control. According to the OVP, the number of prisoners exceeded prison capacity by 190% in the first half of the year. Local NGOs also denounced the critical situation in pre-trial detention facilities.

In March, 57 people – including four inmates, a custodian and the prison director – were injured at the Fenix Penitentiary Centre in Lara State.

In August, seven people were killed and several others wounded by grenades during a riot at the Aragua Penitentiary Centre.

In October, several inmates were evicted from the General Penitentiary of Venezuela after weeks of confrontation with the Bolivarian National Guard, who allegedly used excessive force in the confrontation.

The Office of the Ombudsman announced a proposal to reduce overcrowding in pre-trial detention facilities. According to its annual report, presented to Parliament, 22,759 people remained in pre-trial detention in police facilities, resulting in overcrowding and the spread of diseases and violence.

ARBITRARY ARRESTS AND DETENTIONS

Lawyer Marcelo Crovato remained under house arrest at the end of the year. He had been detained without trial in April 2014 for defending residents whose houses had been raided by the authorities during protests, and was placed under house arrest in 2015.

Decisions of the UN Working Group on Arbitrary Detention had yet to be complied with by the end of the year. They included decisions on the cases of Daniel Ceballos and Antonio Ledezma, two prominent government critics.

In June, Francisco Márquez and Gabriel San Miguel, two activists supporting the opposition party Popular Will, were arrested while on their way from the capital, Caracas, to Portuguesa State to help organize electoral activities. In August, Gabriel San Miguel was freed following action taken by the Spanish government, while Francisco Márquez was freed in October.

Emilio Baduel Cafarelli and Alexander Tirado Lara were transferred on three occasions to detention centres known as dangerous, prompting concern for their lives and physical integrity. They had been convicted of incitement, intimidation using explosives and conspiracy to commit a crime during the 2014 protests.

Opposition members Coromoto Rodríguez, Yon Goicoechea, Alejandro Puglia and José Vicente García were arrested in May, August, September and October respectively, under circumstances which amounted to arbitrary detention. Coromoto Rodríguez and Alejandro Puglia were released in October.

In September, Andrés Moreno Febres-Cordero, Marco Trejo, James Mathison and César Cuellar were arrested and – despite being civilians – were brought before a military court for participating in the production of a video for the political party Justice First which had criticized the government.[4] Marco Trejo and Andrés Moreno Febres-Cordero were released in November.

PRISONERS OF CONSCIENCE

Political opponents of the government continued to face imprisonment. In July, an appeals court dismissed prisoner of conscience Leopoldo López's appeal against his prison sentence, without taking into account the absence of credible evidence to support the charges and public statements made before his conviction by the authorities, thus seriously undermining his right to a fair trial. He had been sentenced to 13 years and nine months in prison.

According to the Venezuelan Criminal Forum, more than 100 people remained in detention due to political reasons.

In November, the lesbian, gay, bisexual, transgender and intersex (LGBTI) activist and prisoner of conscience Rosmit Mantilla was released from jail. He had been imprisoned since 2014. The circumstances and conditions of his release remained unclear by the end of the year.

POLICE AND SECURITY FORCES

Recent official data on homicides remained unavailable. The Venezuelan Violence Observatory reported that the country had the second highest homicide rate in the Americas.

In January, the Public Prosecutor's Office reported that investigations had been initiated into 245 deaths which occurred in alleged armed clashes with officials during the government's Operation Liberation and Protection of the People (OLP), which had been implemented by security forces in July

2015 to tackle the high crime rate. The high number of civilian casualties suggested that security forces may have used excessive force or carried out extrajudicial executions.

On 15 October, 12 young people were arbitrarily detained in the region of Barlovento, in the state of Miranda, during an OLP security operation. On 28 November their bodies were found in two mass graves. According to the Public Prosecutor's Office, 18 members of the armed forces were detained for their presumed participation in the massacre.

The UN Human Rights Committee raised concerns over reports of abuses by military forces against Indigenous Peoples settled in la Guajira, Zulia State, on the border with Colombia.

FREEDOM OF EXPRESSION

The authorities continued to single out media outlets and journalists critical of the government.

In March, David Natera Febres, director of the regional newspaper *The Caroní Post,* was sentenced to four years in prison and fined for publishing reports on corruption. The sentence had yet to be implemented by the end of the year.

In June, 17 journalists and media workers who were covering protests in Caracas over the lack of food were attacked and their equipment stolen. The case was reported to the Public Prosecutor's Office to no avail.

VIOLENCE AGAINST WOMEN AND GIRLS

Implementation of the 2007 legislation criminalizing gender-based violence remained slow due to a lack of resources; by the end of the year there were still no shelters available to victims seeking refuge.

Statistics from the Public Prosecutor's Office indicated that 121,168 complaints of gender-based violence were received in 2015. Criminal proceedings were initiated in 19,816 cases and civil protection measures such as restraining orders were granted in less than 50% of cases. According to women's rights organizations, 96% of the cases that did reach the courts did not result in convictions.

RIGHTS OF LESBIAN, GAY, BISEXUAL, TRANSGENDER AND INTERSEX PEOPLE

In May, the National Assembly approved the declaration of 17 May as the "Day against Homophobia, Transphobia and Biphobia".

In August, the Ministry of Interior and Justice and the Public Prosecutor's Office agreed that transgender people could freely express their gender identity on the photograph on their identification documents. However, there were no advances in legislation to guarantee equal rights, including to provide for the possibility for an individual to adjust their name, gender and other details in official documentation to correspond to their gender identity, or to criminalize hate crimes based on sexual orientation, gender identity or expression.

SEXUAL AND REPRODUCTIVE RIGHTS

Access to contraceptives, including emergency contraception, was increasingly limited due to shortages of medicine. Abortion continued to be criminalized in all cases except when the life of the woman or girl was at risk.

According to a report by the UN Population Fund, the maternal mortality rate in the country was 95 per 100,000 live births, significantly higher than the regional average of 68 deaths per 100,000 live births. Contraceptive usage stood at 70% for traditional methods and 64% for modern methods, with regional averages at 73% and 67% respectively.

INDIGENOUS PEOPLES' RIGHTS

The legal provisions to guarantee and regulate consultation with Indigenous Peoples over matters affecting their livelihoods were not complied with. There were reports of criminalization of Indigenous and environmental rights defenders. Concern was raised over the impact on Indigenous land and environment of large-scale mining projects in the southern region of Venezuela known as the Mining Arc. Approval for the implementation of the projects was granted without consulting with and seeking the free, prior and informed consent of Indigenous communities in the area.

RIGHT TO HEALTH – LACK OF FOOD AND MEDICINE

The economic and social crisis in the country continued to worsen. In light of the lack of official statistics, private and independent agencies such as the Workers' Centre for Documentation and Analysis (CENDA) reported an inflation of 552% for food products from November 2015 to October 2016, which made it extremely difficult for the population to purchase food even when they were able to find it. According to the Venezuelan Health Observatory, 12.1% of the population ate only twice a day or less. The Bengoa Foundation for Food and Nutrition estimated that 25% of children were malnourished.

Studies on living conditions carried out by three major universities revealed that 73% of homes in the country suffered from income poverty in 2015, while official data from the National Institute of Statistics put that figure at 33.1%.

The government's refusal to allow international aid efforts to address the humanitarian crisis and provide medicine exacerbated the critical health situation. The poor state of public health services led to an increase in preventable and treatable diseases such as malaria and tuberculosis. NGOs such as the Coalition of Organizations for the Right to Life and Health and professional associations calculated that there was a shortage of 75% of high-cost drugs and 90% of essential drugs.

1. Venezuela: Establish the whereabouts of missing miners (AMR 53/3602/2016)

2. Venezuela: Human rights defender threatened: Humberto Prado Sifontes (AMR 53/3952/2016)

3. Venezuela: Human rights defenders assaulted (AMR 53/4223/2016)

4. Venezuela: Arrested and prosecuted by military tribunal (AMR 53/5029/2016)

VIET NAM

Socialist Republic of Viet Nam
Head of state: **Tran Dai Quang (replaced Truong Tan Sang in April)**
Head of government: **Nguyen Xuan Phuc (replaced Nguyen Tan Dung in April)**

Severe restrictions on the rights to freedom of expression, of association and of peaceful assembly continued. The media and the judiciary, as well as political and religious institutions, remained under state control. Prisoners of conscience were tortured and otherwise ill-treated, and subjected to unfair trials. Physical attacks against human rights defenders continued, and prominent activists were subjected to daily surveillance and harassment. Peaceful dissidents and government critics were arrested and convicted on national security charges. Demonstrations were repressed, with participants and organizers arrested and tortured. The death penalty was retained.

BACKGROUND

The five-yearly leadership change took place in January at the congress of the Communist Party of Viet Nam. In May, a general election for the 500 seats in the National Assembly was contested by 900 Communist Party members nominated by central or local authorities and 11 independent candidates. Over 100 non-party candidates who attempted to register, including prominent government critics such as Nguyễn Quang A, were disqualified on tenuous administrative grounds. Some were subject to harassment and intimidation.

The implementation of key new laws, scheduled for July, was postponed due to flaws in the amended Penal Code. They included the Criminal Procedure Code, the Law on the Organization of Criminal Investigation Agencies, the Law on the Implementation of Custody and Temporary Detention, and the amended Penal Code itself.

REPRESSION OF DISSENT

Peaceful criticism of government policies continued to be silenced through judicial and extra-legal means. There was extensive surveillance and harassment of activists, including those who demonstrated against the Formosa ecological disaster which affected the lives of an estimated 270,000 people (see below). Attacks against human rights defenders were commonplace.[1]

The authorities continued to use vaguely worded legislation to convict peaceful activists under the national security section of the 1999 Penal Code, in particular: Article 258 "abusing democratic freedoms to infringe upon the interests of the state, the legitimate rights and interests of organizations and/or citizens"; Article 88 "spreading propaganda against the Socialist Republic of Viet Nam"; and Article 79 "carrying out activities aimed at overthrowing the people's administration".

In an eight-day period in March, seven activists and government critics were convicted and sentenced to imprisonment for the peaceful expression of their views. They included Nguyễn Hữu Vinh, founder of the popular blog site Anh Ba Sàm, and his assistant Nguyễn Thi Minh Thúy who were convicted under Article 258 and given five- and three-year prison sentences respectively.[2] They had spent nearly two years in pre-trial detention.

Prominent human rights lawyer Nguyễn Văn Đài and his assistant Lê Thu Hà remained in incommunicado detention following their arrest on charges under Article 88 in December 2015.[3]

In October, well-known activist Nguyễn Ngọc Như Quỳnh, known as blogger Mẹ Nấm (Mother Mushroom), was arrested on charges under Article 88 in connection with her blog postings criticizing the government.[4] The Article carries a three- to 20-year prison sentence.

Routine beatings of human rights defenders and their relatives continued. In April, Trần Thị Hồng, wife of prisoner of conscience Pastor Nguyễn Công Chính, was arrested and severely beaten in custody soon after she met with a US delegation visiting Viet Nam.[5]

FREEDOM OF ASSEMBLY

Large peaceful demonstrations over the Formosa disaster were frequent. Weekly demonstrations in urban centres around the country in April and May resulted in mass arrests and attacks against participants by police and individuals in plain clothes believed to be police or working under police orders. Many of those detained were tortured or otherwise ill-treated, including with beatings and the use of electric shocks.[6] Demonstrations continued throughout the year, with those in provinces affected by the Formosa disaster gathering momentum. There were reports that 30,000 people demonstrated in August in Vinh City, Nghệ An province.

LAND DISPUTES

In July, a demonstration of around 400 ethnic minority Ede villagers in Buôn Ma Thuột, Đắk Lắk province protesting against the sale of 100 hectares of the community's ancestral land to a private company was violently repressed by security forces; at least seven demonstrators were arrested and held in incommunicado detention.[7]

In August, land activist Cấn Thị Thêu was convicted under Article 245 of "causing public disorder" by a court in the capital Ha Noi and sentenced to 20 months' imprisonment.[8] She was accused of inciting protests against reclamation of land in Hà Đông district, Ha Noi, by posting photographs online.

TORTURE AND OTHER ILL-TREATMENT

Torture and other ill-treatment, including incommunicado detention, prolonged solitary confinement, beatings, withholding of medical treatment, and punitive transfers between facilities were practised on prisoners of conscience throughout the country.[9] At least 88 prisoners of conscience were held in harsh conditions after unfair trials, some of whom were subjected to beatings, prolonged solitary confinement, deprivation of medical treatment and electric shocks. They included bloggers, labour and land rights activists, political activists, religious followers, members of ethnic groups and advocates for human rights and social justice.

Land rights activist Bùi Thị Minh Hằng, and Hòa Hảo Buddhist Trần Thị Thúy continued to be denied adequate medical treatment since 2015; Catholic activist Đặng Xuân Diệu was held in solitary confinement for prolonged periods and tortured; and Trần Huỳnh Duy Thức had been transferred between several prisons since 2009, apparently as a punishment or to intimidate him.

REFUGEES AND ASYLUM-SEEKERS

In April and May, in two separate cases, eight asylum-seekers among groups intercepted en route to Australia and forcibly returned to Viet Nam were sentenced to between two and four years' imprisonment under Article 275 of the Penal Code for "organizing and/or coercing other persons to flee abroad or to stay abroad illegally".[10]

RIGHT TO AN ADEQUATE STANDARD OF LIVING

An ecological disaster in early April killed huge numbers of fish stocks along the coast of Nghệ An, Hà Tĩnh, Quảng Bình, Quảng Trị and Thừa Thiên-Huế provinces, affecting the livelihoods of 270,000 people. After a two-month investigation, the authorities confirmed allegations by the public that a steel plant owned by the Taiwanese Formosa Plastics Group had caused toxic waste discharges. At the end of June, Formosa publicly acknowledged responsibility and announced that it would provide compensation of US$500 million. In October, a court in Hà Tĩnh rejected 506 cases filed by those affected. The plaintiffs were calling for increased compensation in damages for the impact on their livelihoods.

DEATH PENALTY

Death sentences continued to be imposed, including for drug-related offences. Official statistics remained classified as a state secret. Death sentences were reported in the media. There was no available information about executions.

---

1. Viet Nam: Crackdown on human rights amidst Formosa related activism (ASA 41/5104/2016)

2. Viet Nam: Convictions of Nguyễn Hữu Vinh and Nguyễn Thị Minh Thúy are an outrageous contravention of freedom of expression (ASA 41/3702/2016)

3. Ending torture of prisoners of conscience in Viet Nam (News story, 12 July)

4. Viet Nam: Vietnamese human rights blogger arrested (ASA 41/4979/2016)

5. Viet Nam: Detained pastor on hunger strike since 8 August (ASA 41/4759/2016)

6. Viet Nam: Government cracks down on peaceful demonstrations with range of rights violations, including torture and other ill-treatment (ASA 41/4078/2016)

7. Viet Nam: Minority group's protest met with violence (ASA 41/4509/2016)

8. Viet Nam: Failing to uphold human rights as land rights activist sentenced to 20 months in prison (ASA 41/4866/2016)

9. Prisons within prisons: Torture and ill-treatment of prisoners of conscience in Viet Nam (ASA 41/4187/2016)

10. Viet Nam: Imprisonment of asylum-seeker forcibly returned by Australia would be unlawful and could be disastrous for her young children (ASA 41/4653/2016)

YEMEN

Republic of Yemen
Head of state: **Abd Rabbu Mansour Hadi**
Head of government: **Ahmed Obeid bin Daghr (replaced Khaled Bahah in April)**

All parties to the continuing armed conflict committed war crimes and other serious violations of international law with impunity. The Saudi Arabia-led coalition supporting the internationally recognized Yemeni government bombed hospitals and other civilian infrastructure and carried out indiscriminate attacks, killing and injuring civilians. The Huthi armed group and forces allied to it indiscriminately shelled civilian residential areas in Ta'iz city and fired artillery indiscriminately across the border into Saudi Arabia, killing and injuring civilians. Huthi and allied forces severely curtailed the rights to freedom of expression, association and peaceful assembly in areas they controlled, arbitrarily arresting critics and opponents, including journalists and human rights defenders, forcing NGOs to close. They subjected some detainees to enforced disappearance and to torture and other ill-treatment. Women and girls continued to face entrenched discrimination and other abuses, including forced marriage and domestic violence. The death penalty remained in force; no information was publicly available on death sentences or executions.

BACKGROUND

The armed conflict between the internationally recognized government of President Hadi, supported by a Saudi Arabia-led international coalition, and the Huthi armed group and allied forces, which included army units loyal to former President Ali Abdullah Saleh, continued to rage throughout the year. The Huthis and forces allied to former President Saleh continued to control the capital, Sana'a, and other areas. President Hadi's government controlled southern parts of Yemen including the governorates of Lahj and Aden.

The armed group al-Qa'ida in the Arabian Peninsula (AQAP) continued to control parts of southern Yemen and to carry out bomb attacks in Aden and in the port city of al-Mukallah, which government forces recaptured from AQAP in April. US forces continued to target AQAP forces with missile strikes. The armed group Islamic State (IS) also carried out bomb attacks in Aden and al-Mukallah, mostly targeting government officials and forces.

According to the Office of the UN High Commissioner for Human Rights, 4,125 civilians, including more than 1,200 children, had been killed and more than 7,000 civilians wounded since the conflict began in March 2015. The UN Office for the Coordination of Humanitarian Affairs (OCHA) reported that more than 3.27 million people had been forcibly displaced in the conflict by October and nearly 21.2 million people, 80%

of the population, relied on humanitarian assistance.

In April, UN-sponsored peace negotiations between the parties to the conflict began in Kuwait, accompanied by a brief lull in hostilities. Fighting intensified after the negotiations collapsed on 6 August. On 25 August, US Secretary of State John Kerry announced a "renewed approach to negotiations"; this had produced no clear outcome by the end of the year.

Huthi and allied forces appointed a 10-member Supreme Political Council to rule Yemen, which in turn appointed former Aden Governor Abdulaziz bin Habtoor to lead a government of "national salvation". In September, President Hadi ordered the Central Bank to move from Sana'a to Aden, deepening the fiscal crisis caused by the depletion of its reserves and the humanitarian crisis by curtailing the ability of the de facto Huthi administration in Sana'a to import essential food, fuel and medical supplies.

ARMED CONFLICT
Violations by armed groups

Huthi and allied forces, including army units loyal to former President Saleh, repeatedly carried out violations of international humanitarian law, including indiscriminate and disproportionate attacks. They endangered civilians in areas they controlled by launching attacks from the vicinity of schools, hospitals and homes, exposing residents to attacks by pro-government forces, including aerial bombing by the Saudi Arabia-led coalition. They also indiscriminately fired explosive munitions that affect a wide area, including mortars and artillery shells, into residential areas controlled or contested by opposing forces, particularly in Ta'iz city, killing and injuring civilians. By November, Huthi and allied forces had reportedly carried out at least 45 unlawful attacks in Ta'iz, killing and injuring scores of civilians. One attack on 4 October killed 10 civilians, including six children, and injured 17 others in a street near the Bir Basha market, the UN reported. The Huthis

and their allies also continued to lay internationally banned anti-personnel landmines that caused civilian casualties, and to recruit and deploy child soldiers. In June, the UN Secretary-General reported that the Huthis were responsible for 72% of 762 verified cases of recruitment of child soldiers during the conflict.

In Sana'a and other areas they controlled, the Huthis and their allies arbitrarily arrested and detained critics and opponents as well as journalists, human rights defenders and members of the Baha'i community, subjecting scores to enforced disappearance. Many arrests were carried out by armed men belonging to Ansarullah, the Huthi political wing, at homes, workplaces, checkpoints or public venues such as mosques. Such arrests were carried out without judicial warrant or stated reasons, and without disclosing where those arrested were being taken or would be held.

Many detainees were held in unofficial locations such as private homes without being told the reason for their imprisonment or allowed any means to challenge its legality, including access to lawyers and the courts. Some were subjected to enforced disappearance and held in secret locations; Huthi authorities refused to acknowledge their detention, disclose any information about them or allow them access to legal counsel and their families. Some detainees were subjected to torture or other ill-treatment. In February, one family reported seeing guards beat their relative at the Political Security Office detention facility in Sana'a.

Anti-Huthi forces and their allies led a campaign of harassment and intimidation against hospital staff, and endangered civilians by stationing fighters and military positions near medical facilities, particularly during fighting in the southern city of Ta'iz. At least three hospitals were shut down due to threats against their staff.

The Huthis and their allies also curtailed freedom of association in areas under their de facto administration.

Violations by the Saudi Arabia-led coalition

The international coalition supporting President Hadi's government continued to commit serious violations of international human rights and humanitarian law with impunity. The coalition's partial sea and air blockade further curtailed the import of food and other necessities, deepening the humanitarian crisis caused by the conflict, and prevented commercial flights to Sana'a.

Coalition aircraft carried out bomb attacks on areas controlled or contested by Huthi forces and their allies, particularly in the Sana'a, Hajjah, Hodeidah and Sa'da governorates, killing and injuring thousands of civilians. Many coalition attacks were directed at military targets, but others were indiscriminate, disproportionate or directed against civilians and civilian objects, including funeral gatherings, hospitals, schools, markets and factories. Some coalition attacks targeted key infrastructure, including bridges, water facilities and telecommunication towers. One attack in August destroyed the main road bridge between Sana'a and Hodeidah. Some coalition attacks amounted to war crimes.

In August, the humanitarian NGO Médecins Sans Frontières (MSF) said it had lost "confidence in the Coalition's ability to avoid such fatal attacks". MSF withdrew its staff from six hospitals in northern Yemen after coalition aircraft bombed an MSF-supported hospital for the fourth time in a year, killing 19 people and injuring 24. In early December, the Joint Incidents Assessment Team (JIAT) created by the Saudi Arabia-led coalition to investigate alleged violations by its forces concluded that the strike was an "unintentional error". The JIAT public statement contradicted MSF's own investigations which found that the incident was not the result of an error, but rather of hostilities conducted "with disregard for the protected nature of hospitals and civilian structures".

On 21 September a coalition air strike on a residential area of Hodeidah city killed 26 civilians, including seven children, and injured 24 others, according to the UN. On 8 October, a coalition air strike killed more than 100 people attending a funeral gathering in Sana'a and injured more than 500 others. The coalition initially denied responsibility for the 8 October attack but admitted liability after it was condemned internationally, and said the attack had been based on "incorrect information" and that those responsible would be disciplined.

Coalition forces also used imprecise munitions in some attacks, including large bombs made in the USA and the UK that have a wide impact radius and cause casualties and destruction beyond their immediate strike location. The coalition forces also continued to use cluster munitions made in the USA and the UK in attacks in Sa'da and Hajjah governorates although such munitions were widely prohibited internationally because of their inherently indiscriminate nature. Cluster munitions scattered explosive bomblets over a wide area and presented a continuing risk because of their frequent failure to detonate on initial impact. In December the coalition admitted that its forces had used UK-manufactured cluster munitions in 2015 and stated that it would not do so in the future.

IMPUNITY

All parties to the armed conflict committed serious violations of international law with impunity. The Huthis and their allies took no steps to investigate serious violations by their forces and hold those responsible to account.

The National Commission of Inquiry, established by President Hadi in September 2015, had its mandate extended for another year in August. It conducted some investigations but lacked independence and impartiality; it was unable to access large parts of the country, and focused almost entirely on violations by the Huthis and their allies.

The JIAT created by the Saudi Arabia-led coalition to investigate alleged violations by its forces was also seriously flawed. It did not disclose details of its mandate, methodology or powers, including how it determines which incidents to investigate, conducts investigations, or verifies information; nor what status its recommendations carry either with coalition commanders or member states.

LACK OF HUMANITARIAN ACCESS

All parties to the conflict exacerbated the suffering of civilians by restricting the provision of humanitarian assistance. Huthi forces and their allies continued to curtail the entry of food and vital medical supplies into Ta'iz, Yemen's third most populous city, throughout the year, exposing thousands of civilians to further suffering. Elsewhere, humanitarian workers accused Huthi security officials of imposing arbitrary and excessive restrictions on their movement of goods and staff, seeking to compromise the independence of aid operations, and forcibly closing some humanitarian aid programmes.

Humanitarian aid workers accused the Saudi Arabia-led coalition of hampering the delivery of humanitarian assistance by imposing excessively burdensome procedures that required them to inform the coalition of their planned operations in advance, in order to avoid possible attack.

INTERNALLY DISPLACED PEOPLE

The armed conflict caused massive civilian displacement, particularly in the Ta'iz, Hajjah and Sana'a governorates. In October, the UN Office for the Coordination of Humanitarian Affairs reported that some 3.27 million people, half of them children, were internally displaced within Yemen, an increase of more than 650,000 since December 2015.

INTERNATIONAL SCRUTINY

The UN Panel of Experts on Yemen released its final report on 26 January. The Panel concluded that all parties to the conflict had repeatedly attacked civilians and civilian objects, documenting "119 coalition sorties relating to violations of international humanitarian law", including many that "involved multiple air strikes on multiple civilian objects". A subsequent report to the UN Security Council by a new Panel of Experts, leaked in August, accused all parties

to the conflict of violating international human rights law and international humanitarian law.

In June, the UN Secretary-General removed the Saudi Arabia-led coalition from an annual list of states and armed groups that violate the rights of children in armed conflict after the Saudi Arabian government threatened to cease funding key UN programmes.

In August, the UN High Commissioner for Human Rights called for the establishment of an "international, independent body to carry out comprehensive investigations in Yemen". However, the UN Human Rights Council resolved in September that the High Commissioner would continue providing technical support to the National Commission established in 2015 and allocate additional international experts to their Yemen office.

WOMEN'S AND GIRLS' RIGHTS

Women and girls continued to face discrimination in law and in practice and were inadequately protected against sexual and other violence, including female genital mutilation, forced marriage and other abuses.

DEATH PENALTY

The death penalty remained in force for many crimes; no information was publicly available about death sentences or executions.

ZAMBIA

Republic of Zambia
Head of state and government: Edgar Chagwa Lungu

A contested presidential election was marked by increased political violence. The authorities used the Public Order Act to repress the rights to freedom of expression, assembly and association; the police used excessive force to disperse meetings of opposition parties. The authorities cracked down on independent media outlets and harassed journalists. In April, there was a

wave of xenophobic violence against foreign nationals.

BACKGROUND

Edgar Chagwa Lungu was returned as President in an election on 11 August which saw increased tension and violence, primarily between members of the ruling Patriotic Front and the opposition United Party for National Development (UPND). The election was held under a new Constitution promulgated on 5 January following a controversial process.

The UPND questioned the independence of the judiciary after a UPND petition was dismissed without being heard by three Constitutional Court judges who took the decision without involving two other Constitutional Court judges.

A constitutional referendum held on 11 August at the same time as the general election failed to gain the votes required to amend the country's bill of rights.

In April, there was a wave of xenophobic violence against foreign nationals in Zingalume and George Compounds following allegations of ritual killings. Shops belonging to Rwandan and Zimbabwean nationals were looted. Two Zambian nationals were burned to death in the xenophobic attacks. The alleged perpetrators were arrested and convicted of murder.

The Global Hunger Index of 2016 ranked Zambia as the third hungriest country in the world, with nearly half of the population undernourished.

FREEDOM OF ASSEMBLY

The authorities used the Public Order Act, enacted in 1955, selectively; they arbitrarily restricted the right to freedom of assembly for opposition political parties. Police used excessive force to disperse crowds. On 8 July, police used live ammunition to disperse protesters in Chawama Township in the capital Lusaka, killing Mapenzi Chibulo, a young woman UPND supporter.

On 5 October, UPND leaders Hakainde Hichilema and Geoffrey Mwamba were arrested and charged with unlawful assembly

and seditious practices following a brief meeting with party supporters at a village in Mpongwe District.[1] They were released on bail pending trial in October.

FREEDOM OF EXPRESSION

On 21 March, Eric Chanda, leader of the Fourth Revolution political party, was arrested and charged with defaming the President in 2015.

On 20 June, the printing presses of *The Post* newspaper were seized by the tax authorities and its operations shut down. On 27 June, police beat and arrested editor-in-chief Fred M'membe and his wife Mutinta Mazoka-M'membe, and deputy managing-editor Joseph Mwenda. The charges against them included breaking into *The Post* building.

On 22 August, the Zambian Independent Broadcasting Authority (IBA) suspended the licences of three independent broadcasters – Muvi TV, Komboni Radio and Radio Itezhi. Four Muvi TV media workers – John Nyendwa, Mubanga Katyeka, Joe Musakanya and William Mwenge – who had reported for work were arrested and charged with criminal trespass. The licences were subsequently reinstated.

Despite the reinstatement of Komboni Radio's licence, on 5 October the station's director, Lesa Kasoma Nyirenda, was beaten by six armed policemen who prevented her from accessing the premises. She was also charged with assaulting a police officer.

CHILDREN'S RIGHTS

In March the UN Committee on the Rights of the Child issued its concluding observations on Zambia. The Committee expressed concern that vulnerable children were being denied equal access to a range of services including health and education. Under-five and infant mortality rates remained high while adolescents lacked access to adequate reproductive health services and information. The Committee also highlighted the imposition of primary school fees and the high dropout rates for girls due to discriminatory traditional attitudes and the exclusion of pregnant girls.

---

1.   Zambia: Drop sedition charges against opposition leaders (Press release, 19 October)

ZIMBABWE

Republic of Zimbabwe
Head of state and government: **Robert Gabriel Mugabe**

Activists and human rights defenders mobilized to hold the government to account for increasing corruption, unemployment, poverty and inequality. In the face of increasing activism, the authorities intensified the crackdown on government critics, imposing blanket bans on protest in central Harare, the capital, and detaining journalists and activists, some of whom were tortured.

BACKGROUND

A report by the Zimbabwe Vulnerability Assessment Committee released in July stated that approximately 4.1 million people would experience food insecurity between January and March 2017 following a drought caused by El Niño.

Cash shortages left the government struggling to pay civil servants their monthly salaries, leading to government proposals to introduce bond notes. The fear of bond notes becoming a worthless currency and returning the country to the unpopular period of hyperinflation similar to 2008 sparked continuous protest up to December.

In June, the government introduced Statutory Instrument SI64 in a desperate bid to curb cheap imports and promote domestic manufacturing, sparking protests by those opposed to the measure.

Tensions in the ruling Zimbabwe African National Union – Patriotic Front (ZANU-PF) party continued to affect the functioning of government.

FREEDOM OF EXPRESSION

The government sought to stifle critical reporting in the privately owned media.

In January, the Permanent Secretary of the Ministry of Media, Information and Broadcasting Services (MIMBS), George Charamba, threatened the privately owned media with arrests if they reported on factional strife within ZANU-PF. His comments followed the arrest in January of three members of staff of *Newsday*: Nqaba Matshazi, deputy editor; Xolisani Ncube, a reporter; and Sifikile Thabete, the legal assistant. The two journalists were charged with publishing falsehoods. At the end of the year, their trial was pending a decision by the Constitutional Court on the validity of the law used to arrest them.

In February, while attending World Radio Day commemorations, Anywhere Mutambudzi, Director of Urban Communications within the MIMBS, threatened to clamp down on community radio initiatives, accusing them of operating illegally. The government has failed to license a single community radio station since the enactment of the Broadcasting Services Act (2001).

Journalists

Journalists faced harassment, arrest and assault while covering protests. The Media Institute of Southern Africa (MISA) recorded assaults on 32 journalists between January and September.

Paidamoyo Muzulu, a *Newsday* journalist, was arrested and detained in June together with 15 other activists who were holding a protest vigil in Africa Unity Square in Harare. He was charged with robbery and obstructing or defeating the course of justice. The activists were charged with robbery and resisting arrest. All were released on bail pending trial at the end of the year.

Five journalists were arrested while covering demonstrations against the Vice-President's lengthy stay in the five star Rainbow Towers Hotel. They were detained for six hours before being released without charge.

Freelancer Godwin Mangudya and three Alpha Media Holding (AMH) journalists – Elias Mambo, Tafadzwa Ufumeli and Richard Chidza – were briefly detained at the Marimba police station for covering protests in the suburb of Mufakose on 6 July. Police officers released them after ordering them to delete images of the protests.

Mugove Tafirenyika, a journalist with the *Daily News,* was assaulted at the ZANU-PF headquarters by party supporters on 27 July while covering a war veterans' meeting.

On 3 August, seven journalists – Lawrence Chimunhu and Haru Mutasa of Al Jazeera, and Tsvangirayi Mukwazhi, Christopher Mahove, Tendayi Musiya, Bridget Mananavire and Imelda Mhetu – were assaulted by police while covering demonstrations against government plans to introduce bond notes. All seven were released without charge.

On 24 August, freelance journalist Lucy Yasin was assaulted by riot police while covering a march by the opposition Movement for Democratic Change (MDC-T) and Tendai Mandimika, a freelance journalist, was arrested and charged with public violence.

On 31 August, Crispen Ndlovu, a Bulawayo-based freelance photojournalist, was arrested and assaulted by riot police for taking pictures of police as they assaulted Alfred Dzirutwe in Bulawayo. He was charged with criminal nuisance and beaten up in a truck and later admitted to a private hospital for treatment of the injuries sustained.

In August, security and intelligence officers dressed in military attire made several visits to Trevor Ncube, the publisher of Alpha Media Holdings (AMH), in a clear attempt to intimidate him.

Social media

The authorities attempted to stifle social media.

In April, President Mugabe threatened to introduce laws to restrict access to the internet.

In August, in response to the rising discontent expressed on social media, the authorities introduced a draft bill on Computer and Cyber Crimes to curb anti-government criticism. The bill had not become law by the end of the year.

During a national stay-away on 6 July in protest against corruption, fronted by the social media movement #ThisFlag, social media apps such as WhatsApp were shut down by the government.

REPRESSION OF DISSENT

Activists and human rights defenders were subjected to intimidation, harassment and arrests by the authorities and the youth wing of the ruling ZANU-PF party with impunity.

In July alone, 332 people were arrested in connection with anti-government protests. Hundreds were arrested across the country for participating in demonstrations organized by the National Electoral Reform Agenda (NERA), a coalition of 18 political parties campaigning for electoral reform. Organizers of the protests were assaulted the night before the demonstrations.

During celebrations of Independence Day in April, state security agents brutally assaulted and arrested Patson Dzamara for staging a one-man demonstration by raising a placard in front of President Mugabe. He was protesting the abduction and disappearance of his brother, Itai Dzamara, in March 2015. Patson Dzamara was later released without charge. However, in November, he was abducted by armed men shortly before an anti-government protest and severely beaten.

About 105 people were arrested and charged with public violence when workers on commuter omnibuses went on strike on 4 July in Bulawayo and Harare and barricaded roads with stones and burning tyres. They were later released on bail.

Evan Mawarire, leader of the #ThisFlag movement, was arrested by police on 12 July and charged with inciting public violence. While in court, the state changed the charges to "subverting a constitutionally elected government". He was released after the magistrate ruled the change of charges illegal and unconstitutional. However, Evan Mawarire left the country in July following continued state persecution.

In August, pictures emerged of a 62-year-old woman, Lillian Chinyerere Shumba, being brutally beaten by riot police outside the Harare Magistrates' Court. The authorities also arrested Sten Zvorwadza, Chairperson of the National Vendors Union of Zimbabwe (NAVUZ), and Promise Mkwananzi, spokesperson for the Tajamuka/Sesjikile ("We've had enough"), campaign, and charged them with inciting public violence.

The unprecedented clampdown on former allies of ZANU-PF intensified following the publication of a communiqué by the Zimbabwe National Liberation War Veterans Association renouncing President Mugabe's leadership and blaming him for the deteriorating economic situation. Police arrested five war veterans and charged them with undermining the authority of or insulting the President in contravention of section 33(2) of the Criminal Law Act. All five were released on bail and their trials were indefinitely postponed at the end of the year.

FREEDOM OF ASSOCIATION

President Mugabe launched an attack on the judiciary following significant judgments that upheld the right to protest. He criticized the country's judges, labelling them "reckless" and warning them not to be negligent.

In September, in response to an increasing number of demonstrations, police imposed a two-week ban on protests in Harare Central District under Statutory Instrument 101 A. However, a High Court judge lifted the ban, declaring it to be unconstitutional.[1]

On 16 September, police imposed a one-month ban on protests in central Harare under Government Notice No.239 A of 2016. An appeal to set aside this ban was dismissed by the courts.[2]

On 29 September, three students at the University of Zimbabwe – Tonderai Dombo, Andile Mqenqele and Zibusiso Tshuma – were arrested for raising placards in front of President Mugabe demanding jobs during the university's annual graduation ceremony.

They were charged with criminal nuisance and fined US$10.

TORTURE AND OTHER ILL-TREATMENT

Activists reported cases of attempted abductions by unidentified armed groups often linked to state security forces. These took place either during the night or just before a planned demonstration. Some of those abducted and taken to ZANU-PF headquarters were subjected to torture including sexual violence.

On 13 September, Silvanos Mudzvova, a well-known actor, director and activist and member of Tajamuka/Sesjikile, was abducted from his home at night by six armed men alleged to be state security agents. He was blindfolded and taken to an area near Lake Chivero where he was tortured. He was injected with an unknown substance and left for dead. He required hospital treatment for the serious injuries sustained, which included abdominal trauma, and was still recovering at the end of the year.

Unidentified men travelling in five vehicles abducted Kudakwashe Kambakunje, NAVUZ Chairperson for the Central Business District, on 27 September in Harare. He was later found 22km outside the city, badly wounded. He had been severely beaten and injected with an unknown substance.

In September, pictures emerged of serious lacerations sustained by Esther Mutsiru and Gladys Musingo while in police custody in Harare. The women had been detained and tortured after participating in a NERA demonstration.

Activist and public relations officer for the Rural Teachers' Union of Zimbabwe Ostallos Siziba was abducted on 26 August in the lead-up to the NERA demonstrations. He was taken to ZANU-PF headquarters where he was severely beaten. He stated that his abductors tried to force him to have sex with an elderly woman, but he refused. He was later handed over to Harare Central Police station, charged with public violence and released on bail.

CONSTITUTIONAL AND LEGAL DEVELOPMENTS

In January the Constitutional Court outlawed child marriage by setting a minimum age for marriage at 18 years.

In February, the Constitutional Court ruled the criminal defamation law to be invalid and unconstitutional.

DEATH PENALTY

In its report to the UN Universal Periodic Review (UPR), the government revealed that 10 death row inmates had been pardoned during the year after they requested clemency.

RIGHT TO HEALTH

In January, following its review of Zimbabwe's second periodic report, the UN Committee on the Rights of the Child noted the negative impact of the severe economic decline on the delivery of services to children. The Committee expressed serious concern about the high rates of maternal, neonatal and child mortality; malnutrition among children under the age of five; and the significant number of deaths of children under five owing to inadequate sanitation and the lack of clean drinking water.

In the context of continuing widespread food insecurity, particularly among poor households in the south of the country, the Zimbabwe Human Rights Commission criticized the government for partisan distribution of food aid and agricultural subsidies in five districts.

CHILDREN'S RIGHTS

The UN Committee on the Rights of the Child expressed extreme concern about the high rate of sexual violence experienced by adolescent girls as well as early pregnancy and child marriage and its correlation with the school dropout rate of adolescent girls.

HOUSING RIGHTS

On 21 January, Harare City Council demolished over 100 houses in Arlington Estate belonging to members of the Nyikavanhu Housing Cooperative without following due process, including consultation and adequate notice. The demolitions took place after President Mugabe ordered the relocation of the settlers.

---

1. Zimbabwe: Allow public demonstrations as per court ruling (News story, 7 September)

2. Zimbabwe: Court ruling upholding police ban on protests must be rescinded (News story, 5 October)

3305074